THE CONSCIENTIOUS

MARINE AQUARIST

Front Cover
Flame Angelfish (*Centropyge loriculus*); photograph by Scott W. Michael
Back Cover
Top: Queen Angelfish (*Holacanthus ciliaris*); photograph by Foster Bam
Middle: Orange Marble Starfish (*Fromia monilis*); photograph by Denise Nielsen Tackett
Bottom: Clown Triggerfish (*Balistoides conspicillum*); photograph by Foster Bam

T.F.H. Publications, Inc.
One T.F.H. Plaza
Third and Union Avenues
Neptune City, NJ 07753
www.t.f.h.com

THE CONSCIENTIOUS
MARINE AQUARIST

A Commonsense Handbook
for Successful Saltwater Hobbyists

ROBERT M. FENNER

With a Foreword by Christopher Turk

Principal Photographers:
Scott W. Michael, Foster Bam, and Paul Humann

MICROCOSM

t.f.h.

PROFESSIONAL
SERIES™

T.F.H. Publications
One T.F.H. Plaza
Third and Union Avenues
Neptune City, NJ 07753
www.t.f.h..com

First printing 1998. Revised and reprinted 1999, 2001.

ISBN 1-890087-03-3 (hardcover); ISBN 1-890087-02-5 (pbk.)

Library of Congress Cataloging-in-Publication Data

Fenner, Robert M.

The conscientious marine aquarist: a commonsense handbook for successful saltwater hobbyists / Robert M. Fenner; with a foreword by Christopher Turk; principal photographers Scott W. Michael, Foster Bam, and Paul Humann.

p. cm.

Includes bibliographical references and index.

ISBN 1-890087-03-3 (hardcover). — ISBN 1-890087-02-5 (pbk.)

1. Marine aquariums—Handbooks, manuals, etc. 2. Marine aquarium fishes—Handbooks, manuals, etc. I. Title.

SF457.1.F45 1998

639.34'2—dc21 97-51993

Color separations by Horsman / Williston, Vermont
Designed by Eugenie Seidenberg Delaney
Co-published by
Microcosm Ltd.
P.O. Box 550
Charlotte, VT 05445
www.microcosm-books.com

To you, the aquarist.

May your brush with captive marine fishes and invertebrates

enhance your appreciation of the living world,

inspire you to share your experiences with others,

and foster stewardship of our planet.

Contents

Foreword

I FIND MYSELF SITTING in coach at 35,000 feet on a return trip from my first Marine Aquarium Conference of North America, sipping a drink and slipping into a state of relaxation and reflection on the events of the past few days. At this moment, I am struck with an undeniable feeling of satisfaction inspired by my participation, albeit as a mere spectator, in this stimulating meeting of intelligent, competent, and intensely enthusiastic marine aquarists. I feel incredibly blessed to have become a small but integral part of a force that brings the science of marine biology together with the hobby and business of aquarium keeping—an unlikely fraternity of the academic and the commercial, where the fortunate participants are allowed to spend their lives immersed in the fascination of the coral reef.

Ah, the coral reef—a world like no other, an ecosystem teeming with incredible richness, color, and diversity, immersed in clear, blue water. How fitting that such an environment should circle the globe at its warmest and most inhabitable latitudes.

I am one of the fortunate few who grew up by the ocean and never left it. I have been a teenage mutant marine tropical fish hobbyist, a recreational collector of fish and invertebrates, a commercial collector of same, a fisheries biology student, a grunt-worker-tank-scrubber in aquaculture (just ask Martin Moe if I can scrub a tank or overflow an aquarium), and now a fish-food manufacturer and aquatic business owner. And though it's been a convoluted journey, exhausting and full of impossible schedules, I feel the ever-increasing presence of a continuity that seems to bring it together and make it all worthwhile. This continuity consists of two parts: the reef itself and the people who make it an integral part of their lives.

Bob Fenner is one of these people. Bob grew up perhaps even more involved in the marine environment than I did, so it is only natural that our paths should cross at some point. So here I find myself, some 20 years hence, with the honor and privilege of being selected to write the Foreword for his book.

Years ago, the Bob Fenner I encountered knew more Latin names, more biology, more feeding behaviors, more spawning rituals, more authors, and more publications than all of the rest of my more normal marine science friends put together. When I learned that he was finally publishing a book, I imagined his mind racing at warp speed (mere mortals are often left mentally gasping after a session with our author), and wondered how the breadth of his experience could ever be packed into a single book.

WHAT I FIND IN THESE PAGES is a carefully condensed, readable version of the uppermost slice of the total encyclopedia of Bob Fenner's knowledge. We can read with the enjoyment and confidence that what we are learning is valuable, solidly accurate, and based on years of hands-on, sometimes painful experiences. Best of all, once we read *The Conscientious Marine Aquarist*, we will know at least a piece of what Bob Fenner knows about marine aquariums and marine organisms—and that, my friends, is a great achievement.

The word "conscientious" carries weighty and serious connotations, and I have been trying to determine the bottom line of Bob's message. What is it that he would direct us to do in order to approach the keeping of marine fishes and invertebrates in a more conscientious manner? Like a coral polyp opening to take in the benefit of light and nutrient-rich water, my mind begins to blossom with a sense of understanding. What dawns on me is that first of all, Bob Fenner is the ultimate "conscientious aquarist." He lives and breathes marine science, and he cares intensely about you and me and about the animals that we endeavor to keep alive. He is, thankfully, one of the self-appointed caretakers of this hobby, dedicating himself to reading, writing, and always learning. He sees so many things that are right and wrong, and he thinks avid aquarists should see the difference and respond accordingly.

"BEING CONSCIENTIOUS as a marine aquarist," he says in his Introduction, "means being an informed, intelligent consumer . . . and it also implies a level of faith in the hobby and a deep affection for the environments we seek to mimic in miniature. It means taking certain responsibilities seriously and doing things right, both for our own peace of mind and for the well-being of our captive charges." I like that part very much, and I urge you to read his Introduction carefully—then read it again.

When you boil it all down, being "conscientious" is really very simple. Keep your fish alive. Keep your invertebrates alive. Do whatever it takes to keep all of your captive marine creatures alive. Alive is good. Dead is bad. It's as black and white as the good guy/bad guy characters in a Disney movie. It is more attitude than hard work, more commonsense frame of mind than living by an imposed code of ethics.

Fortunately, if part of being a better aquarist is keeping our marine animals alive, we are much better off today than the marine aquarist of ten or twenty years ago. We now know enough to succeed with saltwater aquariums most of the time. We have the deeper knowledge and better equipment needed to keep a captive marine environment alive and thriving. This is much more rewarding than standing by and watching the demise, fast or slow, of the creatures and aquascape we paid so dearly for and worked so hard to create.

In the pages that follow, you will learn many secrets and special techniques. Bob Fenner openly shares with us from his decades of experience not only as a marine biology student and teacher, but also as a collector, distributor, transhipper, and retail store owner. I, myself, happen to preach the importance of nutrition and feeding the best and most natural foods possible to keep our livestock healthy, colorful, and as close to their optimum condition as we can. Bob covers this topic and many others in a complete and accurate fashion, as only he could do it. You will also find the distilled advice of many of the veterans of this hobby. In short, this book will leave you with the motivation to read enough and learn enough to do things right, and will inspire you to be careful and energetic enough to get the job done properly.

I THINK BOB WANTED this book to be better than the books we grew up with 30 years ago. For one thing, he wanted fish names, both common and scientific, to be as accurate and up-to-date as possible. He also wanted information on husbandry to be thorough and based on the lessons learned by the real experts and professionals in this hobby. He wanted us all to understand the ramifications and history of collecting fishes with cyanide, and his eye-opening chapter on this problem is in keeping with making us aware of the hidden or ignored aspects of our hobby.

This chapter will be disturbing to many, but as a former fish collector myself, I feel strongly that cyanide collecting is a destructive and poorly conceived practice made even worse by the fact that it is unnecessary, especially for a collector who is in excellent physical condition as almost all collectors in modern and Third World countries are. Hand-collecting with nets is by far the preferred method for reef and fish (and collector). With training and experience, a good net collector can catch just as many if not more fish with nets than a drug collector can catch with "anesthetics." It's a different type of collecting, and it requires a different philosophy and work ethic. The net collector may have to cover more reef for the same amount of catch, but then he will automatically leave more fish behind to maintain the reef population. Collecting without drugs requires harder physical work and more creativity, but the payoff in self-satisfaction is immense, and the benefit to fish and reef is undeniable.

ALL OF THIS IS A CRUCIAL part of the conscientious equation—remembering where all these fishes, invertebrates, plants, and live rock come from. We must never forget that the incomparable coral reef is directly connected to the marine aquarium in our living rooms. In my view, we aquarists ought to have a commitment to keeping the reefs alive, healthy, and full of their unimaginable diversity of fish, corals, critters, and hundreds of species of algae (yes, algae can be great, as you will read). Let us not do anything to waste this awesome world. Specifically, we ought not to spend money on animals that have no chance of survival. We shouldn't knowingly buy fish collected with techniques that are harmful and that wreak havoc both on what's taken and on what's left behind.

The coral reefs of the world are in many cases still extremely abundant in the species that we admire and want to keep in our own slices of the ocean. That is the good news. We can probably collect enough to keep all of us happy (certain species excepted), and

the ocean can replenish and sustain this resource on its own. But if we waste the harvest, we have to collect more and more to supply our needs, and we end up placing serious and unwarranted stress on the environment we cherish and seek to mimic.

This hobby is educational, great fun, and full of many bright and enthusiastic people, but we are far from pristine in all we do. We, and those who cater to us, have left a long trail of dead fish, damaged reefs, and disenchanted hobbyists—too many reefs overfished or killed completely, and too many aquariums stored away in the garage. It's a sad situation and altogether unnecessary.

We can fix these problems if we care enough to do it right. In fact, in my opinion, we are already making great strides, led by a growing number of aquarists who are well-informed and committed to being conscientious.

In the new attitudes that are gaining acceptance, I see the potential to reverse the high level of attrition among aquarium hobbyists. Unfortunately, I sometimes hear about people trading their aquarium systems in for computers. I love computers myself, but my opinion of this move to "virtual reality" is that we too often retreat from something real to something wholly imaginary. It may not hurt as much when a computer crashes—you just turn it off and boot it back up—but to a successful aquarium enthusiast, "virtual" experiences are never as rewarding as the real thing.

A digital ocean is not the same as a dive into warm blue water with 100 feet of visibility and a gorgeous reef below, and it's not the same as being able to have a beautiful piece of reef alive in your own home. If starting or keeping up a healthy saltwater system seems overwhelming at first, consider the sensible, carefully paced route Bob Fenner lays out so clearly in these pages.

I SUGGEST YOU JUMP into this book as if it were the ocean itself. Enjoy it and use it for what it is intended to be—a practical guide to help you in your endeavors to set up, maintain, and keep a living aquarium. This book is meant to be a tool to make your life easier and your hobby more satisfying.

Make no mistake, this hobby can give us all great moments of challenge. However, if you follow the guidelines in these pages, you will always make progress by the end of the day, and eventually you will be able to sustain the thriving little ecosystem you always dreamed of.

Finally, I think the core to all of this is the word "care." If you care about the animals you keep, and care about becoming a smarter, better informed aquarist, you will be more successful, your animals will be healthier, and the unique rewards of creating a beautiful marine aquarium will be yours. I highly recommend this book to help speed you along the way.

—*Christopher Turk*
President, Ocean Nutrition

Acknowledgments

I WOULD FIRST LIKE TO EXTEND my sincere appreciation to all who have helped instill my love of and knowledge about the world of aquatic life. I am forever indebted to all the educators who have influenced me and am constantly mindful that the word "educate" comes from the Latin *ex ducere*, to lead out. You lead us out of the darkness and into the light. I am particularly grateful to my San Diego State mentor and graduate advisor Dr. Lloyd (Lo Chai) Chen. (Yes, Dr. Chen, this is the "pet-fish" ichthyology I always vowed to write.)

For their unstinting support, I thank my cronies in the science and public presentation of aquatics: Donald Wilkie, formerly of the Stephen Birch Aquarium-Museum at the Scripps Institute of Oceanography, and Mark Ferguson of the Monterey Bay Aquarium.

Many friends and associates in the commerce and hobby of keeping aquatic life deserve recognition for their ongoing openness and willingness to share information and experiences. Among the many are Bruce Ulmer and Craig Dewalt of SeaClear; Al Abrevaya of Aquarium Pharmaceuticals; Wayne Whitney at Mardel Labs; Dr. Bob Rofen of Kordon Corp.; Andy Schmidt of San Francisco Bay Brand; Bob Holley of Dolphin International; Ted, Edwin, and Millie S. Chua of All Seas Marine; Phil Shane of Quality Marine; Ken Perry of Pacific Aquatic Imports. Also: Alan Mintz and Mark Long of Tetra/ Second Nature; Chris and Carol Turk of Ocean Nutrition; and Rick Aspray, Jake Lockwood, and Jim Dorsey of Nature Etc., Inc.

I am indebted to the editors of a number of periodicals that serve all of us with an interest in aquatics: Don Dewey of *Freshwater and Marine Aquarium*; Ray Hunziker III, long-time editor of *Tropical Fish Hobbyist*; Ed Bauman of *Aquarium Fish Magazine*; and Tom Frakes of *SeaScope*. They and their hardworking staffs all deserve praise for years of sorting through and straightening out my work. At the same time, I would note the constant source of insight and ideas provided by other aquarium writers. Rest assured, I know this is a field where one toils for something other than money and fame.

Scott Michael, Foster Bam, Paul Humann and a number of other world-class underwater photographers deserve credit for providing the brilliant images herein. Dr. Peter Rubec of the International Marinelife Alliance was an invaluable scientific resource.

This book would not be what it is without the fine book-publishing folks at Microcosm. Copy editors Alice Lawrence and Tanya Stone helped transform years of writing into one readable, useful, transportable volume, and I am further obliged to art director Eugenie S. Delaney for making these words come to life. Lastly, a note of appreciation for my editor and publisher, James Lawrence, who toiled for many months with my manuscript and, as a fellow aquarist, never lost faith in the concept of a conscientious approach to marine aquarium keeping. Thank goodness for editors.

Finally, I would like to acknowledge the encouragement and patience of my wife and diving partner, Diana, and the years of friendship and support of my colleague, dear friend, and late partner, Michael Stempleski.

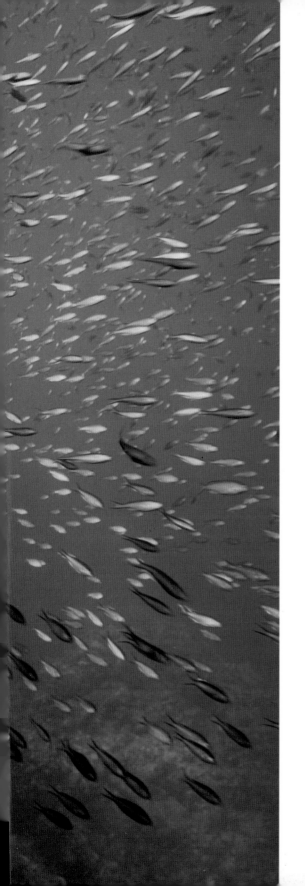

Introduction

An Argument for Marine Aquarium Keeping

ALTHOUGH MY DAYS AS A WORKADAY ACADEMIC LECTURER on the subject of marine science are long past—trying to perform as a perpetual combination of Jacques Cousteau, Charles Darwin, and Robin Williams proved too much to sustain—I'm still often reminded of a student in one of the college classes I taught. Whenever we embarked on the study of a new biological group, he would confront me with the same question: "Can we eat them?" The class would laugh while I pondered and then, in most cases, offered them a chagrined "No." We may want to dismiss this student as just a typical class clown, but I ask you, is his question really impertinent?

It seems reasonable first and foremost in any endeavor to ask ourselves whether we should do it, or, after the fact, to explain why we did it and what it was all about. In this reflective vein, perhaps we ought to ask ourselves, "If we don't intend to eat the contents of our aquariums, why are we doing this?"

Such an explanation—call it An Argu-

Profoundly beautiful and mysterious, the sea and its life forms have fascinated humans for millennia. ABOVE: Serpulid worm, Indonesia. LEFT: Sea of Cortez reef scene.

13

Exquisite Butterflyfish (*Chaetodon austriacus*): elegant but eminently unsuited to aquarium life, this species lives on coral polyps in the wild and virtually never acclimates to currently available captive diets. The conscientious marine aquarist learns to avoid organisms with specialized diets or life habits that make them poor candidates for survival in captivity.

ment for Marine Aquarium Keeping—might involve a dry essay on the benefits—psychological, social, emotional, educational, and physical—of maintaining pet-fish systems. In this age of political, ecological and even recreational correctness, such a discourse must lead to a thoughtful justification for our interest in marine aquariums.

"It's great fun," might be my own rationale for what we do, but this is a rather extraordinary hobby and it does go deeper than that.

The sheer diversity of marine life we encounter in this "hobby" is astounding. All major animal and plant groups with the exception of insects are represented and easily obtained by the aquarium enthusiast. A small piece of live rock, for example, when placed in a home aquarium may give its owner a firsthand view of a dozen phyla or more—alive and growing, perhaps reproducing, and displaying a tangle of species interactions that represents millions of years of evolution. For many of us, the beauty of these organisms catches our eye, then the mysteries and complexities of their behavior refuses to let us go.

Similarly, the background theory and gear that go with being a marine aquarist can appear daunting, complicated, and potentially very expensive. Relax; if nothing else, with this book I hope to show that pleasurable basic saltwater aquarium keeping need not be as intimidating and financially draining as you may have been led to believe.

Herein I will try to aid you in your personal adventures and endeavors by offering the tools and inspiration to help you master the basic art and science of keeping a healthy, beautiful saltwater aquarium. "Old salts" and those already initiated into the hobby are equally welcome; ours is an avocation for lifelong learners, and I hope and trust you will find new lessons and perspectives—along with a trade secret or two—on becoming a more successful, conscientious aquarist.

The word "conscientious" is derived from the Latin roots for with (*con*) and to know (*scire*). Being conscientious as a marine aquarist means being an informed, intelligent consumer. More than that, it also implies a level of faith in the hobby and a deep affection for the environments we seek to mimic in miniature. It means taking certain responsibilities seriously and doing things right, both for our own peace of mind and the well-being of our captive charges.

With this book, I would like to propose the following guiding principles for those of us who aspire to this label:

1) Be an informed aquarist; knowledge in action is indeed powerful.

2) Have the proper basic equipment to maintain healthy standards of water quality, temperature, and lighting for the animals and plants in your system.

3) Practice regular maintenance procedures to ensure adequate water-quality parameters.

4) Properly segregate and quarantine new arrivals to lessen trauma and prevent the spread of disease.

5) Know the nutritional requirements of all your specimens and feed them appropriate diets, in correct formats and intervals.

Masked Butterflyfish (*Chaetodon semilarvatus*): another exceptionally beautiful species from the genus *Chaetodon*, this one, from the Red Sea, is an infinitely better choice for the informed aquarist, with a fine history as an appropriate and long-lived aquarium species.

6) Treat diseased fish to the best of your abilities and, when necessary, dispose of dying specimens in a humane manner. Never release live aquarium specimens into local waters.

7) When acquiring specimens:
- Buy fish and invertebrates that match your abilities. As a beginner, do not purchase animals you know to be difficult or challenging to keep.
- Never take home a specimen without knowing its care requirements.
- Never buy a specimen from a source you suspect of using cyanide or other illegal capture methods.
- Never buy a specimen that is unsuited to the size of your aquarium.
- Never purchase fish, corals, or other invertebrates that are unlikely to survive in captivity or whose collection is detrimental to the health of reef environments.
- Support marine breeders in their efforts to propagate fish and invertebrates in captivity.

Underlying this list is the single biggest problem facing the marine aquarium hobby: attrition—aquarist dropout, burnout, and disillusionment. How much mysterious or "anomalous" loss of fish life, expense, and heartache can a person take before giving up? All too many aquarium handbooks ignore the issue, but herein we will face it head-on: unless you are well-informed and conscientious, your marine specimens will be dead and your aquarium will end up in a rummage sale or housing someone's Venus Fly Trap collection.

This, in my opinion, is mostly due to poor advice and a lack of accurate, honest, and meaningful information. Look at the available books on marine subjects. Aquarists want to know the basics: what gear and livestock are available, how to go about selecting and setting an aquarium up, and how to keep the system going successfully. Knowing the scientific names, the geographic ranges, and the complete natural histories of fishes, invertebrates, and algae can be fascinating, but it ought to be secondary to knowing what to look for in healthy specimens, what they eat, and whether or not the species being considered are even appropriate for a home aquarium. Therefore the purpose of this work is to give you, in an accessible format, the stimulus and commonsense information to become an accomplished marine aquarist.

Before going any further, perhaps I ought to reveal my sources of information and the experiences that have influenced my views of the aquarium world. First, Practical Experience: trial and error with hundreds of thousands of individual specimens and participation in the outright killing of more than

Emperor Angelfish (*Pomacanthus imperator*): a much-admired species with a high rate of mortality in captivity. It can do well if net-caught, carefully selected, and well-fed, but can be recommended to experienced marine aquarists only.

I care to remember. I have worked for collectors, distributors, and transshippers and was in the retail side of the pet-fish business for 17 years—including three as the livestock buyer for the largest mass merchandiser in the trade.

Second, Word of Mouth: I've spent 30 years listening to people who live by their ability to buy and sell marine livestock, to seasoned hobbyists, and to science types. Most of the wholesalers and retailers do know their business; in this information age, it's amazing what you can still learn by asking the right questions and listening carefully.

Third, The Literature: I write articles for magazines in fields that include pet fish from the hobbyist's perspective, pet fish from the trade point of view, and wild aquatics from behind the mask of a scuba diver. I also try to read everything printed in these subject areas, and I commend the practice to you. Especially useful are current magazines that you will find listed in the Sources section of this book, along with a selection of reference books that represents a wealth of information.

Fourth, Other Hobbyists: Some of the most interesting advances in keeping marine fish and invertebrates are coming not from professional public aquarists, but rather from inquisitive, intelligent amateurs. Local aquarium societies have proved a salvation for

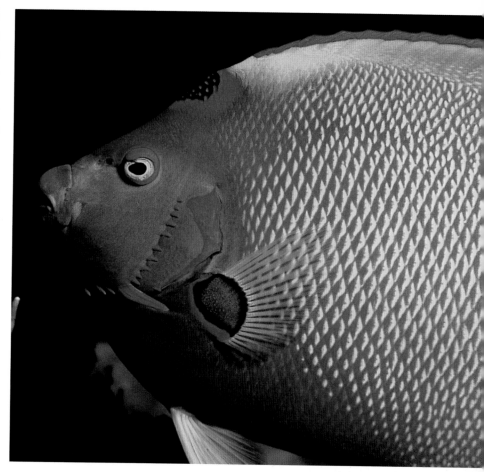

Queen Angelfish (*Holacanthus ciliaris*): regarded by many as one of the most strikingly handsome fish on the world's reefs, this species from the Florida Keys and Caribbean is relatively hardy and adapts well in properly maintained home aquarium systems. It offers a fine alternative to the more demanding large angels available in the trade.

many befuddled newcomers to the hobby. No one in your area? Get online and find other folks with similar interests and start an "interest group" in your vicinity, or a virtual one in cyberspace. There is nothing better than the open exchange of first-hand, unbiased experience to help you make decisions for yourself.

Naturally, you will learn to be open-minded and properly skeptical when taking in the advice and opinions you find here and from others. I am prepared to be frank about popular species that, in my opinion, should not be bought by the conscientious aquarist, but I am also willing to concede that there is the occasional *Pinnatus* batfish or Moorish Idol—both species whose diets challenge even the professional aquarist— that somehow thrives on simple dry food flakes.

My personal odyssey and range of experience in the aquatics industry spans most of the modern history of saltwater aquarium keeping: the last 30 years. I have been privileged to work at all levels in the field of ornamental aquatics in the United States, Japan, and the Philippines. Having been in the "nature racket" for all my adult life, I sometimes think I've heard it all before. Explanations, justifications, and rationales can be offered for gathering and distributing just about any marine organism for captive use: "The rich westerners want beautiful fishes; they don't mind that these ones are strictly coral-eaters." "Those nudibranchs will live a few weeks without food; that's long enough . . ."

To be blunt, many of these fishes, invertebrates, plants, and algae should be left alone; they just don't do well in captive environments. This situation has improved over the years, but still too many of the fishes and nonfishes currently on the market are doomed to live but a short while. If nothing else, I hope this book will help you to be smarter in selecting the best individuals of the most appropriate species, and keeping and displaying them most effectively and in robust good health.

As we will discuss in various sections of this book, you must have the discipline not to acquire specimens that are beyond your marine husbandry skills. I will argue that stony corals, for example, should be off-limits to the average fishkeeper. Before thinking yourself deprived, review the recommended species in this volume—the array of hardy, time-tested species is rich and dazzling in its variety of forms and beauty.

If caring for marine fish and invertebrates is truly within the grasp of every intelligent hobbyist, why all the problems and mortality? I think I know, and even have some notion of what we can all do to correct an unhappy situation.

Almost all of our livestock is collected from the wild, the vast majority by poor, indigenous peoples. They are "just gathering," by the least expensive means available to them, whatever the next person "up the line" will pay them to catch. This simple exchange practice, providing whatever is caught (by whatever means)

Giant Clam (*Tridacna gigas*): collected for the sushi trade and close to economic extinction in many regions, wild-caught *Tridacna* specimens are now shunned by many informed aquarists.

at a salable price, continues all the way to the end user, you and me. One of the saddest ongoing examples of how this isn't working is in the case of obligate corallivore butterflyfishes—species that must eat live coral polyps to survive. The majority of us probably know that these fishes simply cannot (yet) be made to live on artificial diets, but still they turn up in pet dealers' tanks. What's missing in the supply and demand equation? In my opinion, it's the working knowledge, among those out on the reefs and at the collection points, that we, the end consumers, will not pay for unsuitable species/individual specimens. Neither is it widely known that we do not want to encourage nonsustainable capture practices, such as the use of sodium cyanide, that harm the reefs. For the most part, the collectors have no idea that we care about the health of the livestock they bring us, the environment, or even the their own health, which can be tragically compromised by the use of chemicals like cyanide. How to make this all commonly known by all the players?

First of all, knowledge: we need to have the facts about what lives in our aquariums and why the problem species do not thrive. Is it collection methods, the aftermath of shipping stress, or are certain species unable to be kept because of dietary or other limitations? We need better methods of accumulating this data at our end of the chain.

Secondly, communication through the ranks as to what we will pay for, and, alternately, what will not be stood for: it is our dollar that must work its way back through the long trail of goods and services to pay everyone involved—from the peasant in Bali to Singapore Airlines to the neighborhood pet dealer—to get a fish from the reef into a home aquarium. Too few aquarists have come to understand that we are ultimately in control. If you don't like or agree with what you're getting or what your dealer is selling, the an-

Giant clams (*Tridacna* spp.): A profusion of captive-propagated baby clams in a Solomon Islands hatchery are destined for restocking reefs and supplying a growing market among aquarists.

Flowerpot coral (*Goniopora* sp.): widely imported and sold to unknowing aquarists, this large-polyp stony coral typically shrinks and perishes—even in the hands of expert reef aquarium keepers, who recommend that it be avoided by beginners.

swer is simple. Don't pay. Better yet, quietly let your dealer know why you won't pay. He or she may not be happy to hear what you have to say, but, believe me, the good ones listen very carefully to their customers.

When the public demands healthy specimens and viable species, the word will get back through the business hierarchy to the actual collectors and breeders. It will take some time, but they will get it. This is a campaign I've been waging my entire life, and it is a central goal in my writing this book.

Time, unfortunately, may not be on our side. Given the mortality factor inherent in any collection and distribution of nondomestic species, there are those who are ready to rally against allowing any individual to keep marine life; some of them would even shut down public aquariums and zoos. Their rationale is that all wild things belong in the wild and that the loss of life and possible habitat destruction that takes place in order to provide specimens for public displays and private collections is not worth it.

But I put it to you, what would be the real cost of our lack of exposure to marine organisms? Only in this century, with the advent of scuba, underwater photography, and viable marine aquariums has the human race had any true notion of what life is really like under the surface of the sea. By experiencing the living world of the reef firsthand, or better still, by controlling a miniature version of this world, we gain awareness of the magnificent diversity and beauty of a part of the world that was hidden from our ancestors.

Think of all you can learn about the organisms themselves, their interaction with each other and with their human keepers. Consider the water chemistry, physics, fluid mechanics, and photobiology in setting up a slice of the ocean. The nutrition, physiology and reproductive behavior—indeed the sum total biology of all living things on this planet are inextricably linked and remarkably similar. Aquariums can and do serve as paradigms of our own lives.

In the end, we "keep" aquariums because we are human. Our argument is that "it is worth it" to become much more aware of the real world. The species-centricity that denies our involvement with marine aquarium keeping would serve only to distance us emotionally and intelligently from all living things. Exposure to the living world fosters appreciation and caretaking. For those who rail against zoos and any keeping of wild species, consider these truths: Humans only love what they know; and people do not destroy what they love.

Those who discover the tremendous rewards of having a marine aquarium almost invariably develop a profound respect for the complexity and worth of marine ecosystems. Make no mistake, these are some of the most threatened environments on Earth, and a growing population of conscientious marine aquarists could be a crucial ally in finding ways to ensure their survival. Providing an economic rationale for keeping coral reefs alive, productive, and able to provide a source of livelihood for Third World families without harming the reefs themselves is no idle promise. As responsible aquarists we can do it—indeed, we are already doing it. I submit to you that we can do much to make this a truly sustainable hobby, and that we can have a great deal of fun in the process.

—*Robert M. Fenner*
San Diego, California

Star polyps (*Pachyclavularia* sp.): An excellent choice for those with reef-type marine systems, this feathery species is one of many appealing soft corals that will thrive in captivity, often reproducing even in tanks that won't support more difficult-to-keep stony corals.

Demystifying the Marine Aquarium

*Simplicity, Balance, and the Art
of Getting Off to the Right Start*

WHEN I WAS A BOY IN THE PHILIPPINES, people kept marine aquariums without electric power—there were no heaters, water-moving pumps, air bubblers, filters, protein skimmers, or ozonizers. I remember being captivated by the big cement and glass tanks with gorgeous displays of Emperor Angels, pairs of saucer-sized Collare Butterflies, and dazzling *Thalassoma* wrasses, but an observer today would probably be most impressed by the silence and absolute lack of external lifelines.

It seems impossible, but there it was. Granted, the aquarists had ready access to hardy, fresh-caught livestock, and the aquascaping materials came straight from the reef: live rock, live sand, and live corals. Even so, how could this be done? The secret is as unexciting as it is instructive: uncrowded tanks; large, stable systems; and sparse feeding.

Today, many people consider their marine aquariums as little slices of the ocean. This is what we strive to present and—when successful—what gives

ABOVE: Indo-Pacific reef aquarium aquascape. LEFT: a typical reef scene in the Red Sea. Aquariums are moving closer to replicating the appearance of authentic coral reef biotopes.

us a tremendous feeling of personal accomplishment. Behind the illusion, however, is a fact that every successful aquarist accepts as reality: a fish tank is much more like a miniature waste trap than a boxed-in piece of the open seas. You may not want to point this out as Aunt Tillie admires your sparkling version of a reef, but it helps to think pragmatically about each and every captive system first from a pollution-management point of view—it is a water-quality challenge you have created and must address.

To suit our sensibilities of what is attractive, we typically overcrowd and overfeed our livestock. What drives us to create such dense populations? In stocking aquariums, the common priority is a mix of colors, shapes, and behaviors that are visually appealing. We like our specimens fat and sassy, and we feed accordingly.

Take a look in the wild for how much life there is in an average cubic yard of reef water. While the open reef has fleeting periods of heavy population brought on by passing schools of fish, our confined tanks are densely packed by comparison. The artificial congregation of fish is always present in an aquarium, not just winging through as it would be in nature. To accommodate this constant crush of aquatic life, aquarists find themselves shoveling in copious amounts of food and then fighting the inevitable results.

We then try to cope with the consequences of crowding by turning to a modern arsenal of filters, circulating pumps, biological and chemical waste-reduction systems, constant testing, and the time-honored practice of diluting the problem with water changes. Given a nutrient overload, the natural trend in an aquarium is always toward degraded water quality, unless the aquarist intervenes.

Wouldn't it be more inspirational to dwell on the splendor of the seas and their similarities to the miniature glass or acrylic-encased "oceans" we create? I think not. The conscientious marine aquarist is faced with many challenges and opportunities—all of which are best understood if faced squarely and in the

ABOVE: the impossible illusion—a photographic prototype that too many hobbyists seek to duplicate, with a dense stocking of fishes in a modest-sized tank, artificial decor, and nothing more than undergravel filtration.
RIGHT: A sustainable version of a large, fish-only marine system, carefully populated with Red Sea fishes and maintained with a biologically active aquascape of live rock, along with brisk circulation and a powerful protein skimmer.

Focal point for a Florida home, this 230-gallon reef aquarium is carefully planned to support a profusion of colorful invertebrates and a carefully stocked population of small fishes with a minimum of maintenance.(Designed by Jeffrey Turner of Oceans, Reefs & Aquariums, Palm Beach, Florida.)

proper context. Fish tanks are artificial and only distantly related to the realities and enormity of the open seas. These are worlds of our making and manipulation, without the safety net of endless billions of gallons of water to provide dilution and stability.

Happily, much of the life we collect from the saltwater world is tough, tough, tough. The tropical storms that flatten islands and coastlines above sea level can be equally destructive below. The species we keep have evolved to survive the thundering upheaval of typhoons and hurricanes. Even in the best of weather, theirs can be an unforgiving environment, with weaker, slower individuals likely to be consumed and outcompeted on reefs and in the open sea. Millions of years of this kind of pressure have created animals that are natural survivors.

Given proper capture, handling, and adequate care up to the time of your purchase, fishes, invertebrates, algae, and live rocks are capable of weathering incredible insults. The question of balance in setting up and maintaining a living system involves two points: initial suitability and ongoing stability.

To illustrate the way we can reach these twin goals, let's start with a question that most aquarists will answer incorrectly: What is the most expensive part of our hobby? The purchase of tanks and other gear? Stocking the tank with exotic life and decor? Or could it be something else? Believe me or start tracking your own figures, it's the ongoing maintenance and service. The cost of food, water, electricity, replacement lights, and fixtures soon surpasses all other expense considerations combined. Therefore, careful planning and setup are crucial to preserving an optimized, stable environment and reducing maintenance.

It is not necessary to replicate the ocean chemically and physically to have a biologically successful marine aquarium. There have even been products that purported to allow the mixing of freshwater fishes with marine. As you can imagine, these utilized nonionic materials (sugars) to raise the specific gravity of the water without altering its electrolytic charge. This may be the bizarre extreme—and not recommended—but the fact is that marine life can be kept in water and under conditions far different from the ideal parameters of an unspoiled coral reef.

I experienced an unforgettable example of the range of tolerance marine fishes can exhibit to slow changes in water chemistry when I visited at Doc Adams's Long Beach (California) Fisheries in the 1960s. Doc, a salt wholesaler from the dark ages, utilized all manner of holding tanks for his livestock, including refrigerator liners. On one occasion, we decided to investigate one of these liners whose water level had evaporated down to the last third and whose surface sported a coating of reddish algae so thick I couldn't see the water for the scum. Whisking the muck aside, we found a tank of gorgeous black *Pterois volitans* lionfish, swimming lazily in water that was crystal clear but with an off-the-scale salinity reading. By diluting a sample of the water and checking with a hydrometer, we discovered the specific gravity was 1.055, more than twice as "salty" as natural seawater.

The lesson brought home was not that fishes ought to be kept in such conditions, but rather that marine species can be remarkably adaptable. Many saltwater organisms, contrary to widespread advice, can tolerate and even reproduce in less than perfect conditions, provided the changes do not come too abruptly.

This is not to say that sloppy husbandry should be tolerated, but rather to state plainly that marine systems are *not* difficult to create or impossible to sustain. Nor should they be shrouded in an aura of mystery and built up as delicate, magical, and beyond the means of all but the select few. Set up properly and basically left alone, other than for routine maintenance, saltwater aquariums can be simple, beautiful, and profoundly satisfying.

> *"Set up properly and basically left alone, other than for routine maintenance, saltwater aquariums can be simple, beautiful, and profoundly satisfying."*

Three Circles of Failure—or Success

I'D LIKE TO SHARE A VERY USEFUL WAY OF THINKING about the ingredients affecting the well-being of any aquarium system. I learned it from Dr. Stan Sniezsko, and practical applications of his model can be found throughout this book. There are three interlocking factors—each with many of its own components or variables—that determine your success as an aquarist:

1) The initial state of health of your livestock.
2) The starting and ongoing suitability of your (aquarium) environment.
3) The presence and degree of pathogenicity of disease-causing organisms.

Initial health includes such things as genetic heritage, developmental history, method of capture—basically the sum total of all the influences and experiences the specimen has had leading up to its arrival in your tank. How can you optimize your chances of keeping this specimen alive? Selection is critical. A large part of this book is dedicated to helping you decide which species are suitable, and determining which specimens you should buy. After more than 30 years in the aquarium trade, including 20 years servicing private marine systems and consulting with public aquariums, I can assure you that the vast majority of "anomalous" early losses of livestock are *not* due to user errors. These animals should have been left behind in the sea or in the dealers' tanks.

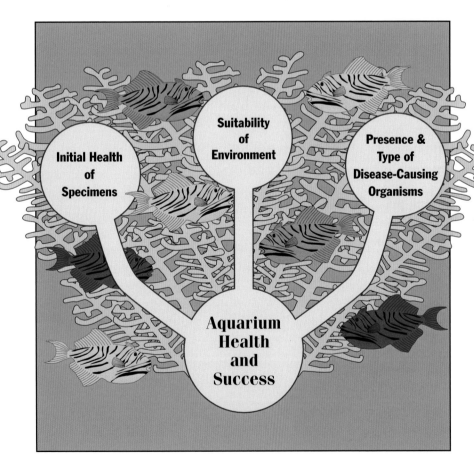

Suitability of the environment includes water chemistry, temperature, feeding, and tankmate interaction. In other words, how hospitable your system is to its inhabitants, both physically and socially. The following section of this book covers system components, the nuts and bolts, with a commonsense rationale for what should go into a working marine aquarium setup.

Disease-causing organisms do not preoccupy most successful marine aquarists, and this book does not at-

tempt to fulfill the purpose of an introductory veterinary guide. Instead, we will look at quarantine and acclimation techniques that can stop most disease problems before they gain a foothold in your system.

The strength in the interlocking factors model lies in understanding that each circle is critically important by itself. If the environment is deadly, your livestock are doomed. Similarly, if you start with diseased fishes, your chance of success is diminished. However, and this is vitally important, if you can optimize two of the three factors in the model, you will minimize the shortcomings of the third.

As an example, if your charges are healthy from the beginning and carefully placed in a suitable home, they are much more likely to recover easily from any given parasitic infestation.

In practice, you've probably already learned the validity of this model from other real-life trials. As in a three-legged stool, one weak support can throw everything off balance. My goal in writing this book is to provide you with a good practical approach to these three sets of factors along with specific suggestions—the trade secrets if you will—on the techniques and mental tools it takes to become a more knowledgeable, more successful—and a conscientious—aquarist.

Established 200-gallon home aquarium by Jeffrey Turner: secrets of long-term success start with creating a stable environment, stocking with healthy fishes and invertebrates, and preventing the introduction or proliferation of disease organisms.

CHAPTER 1

Systems

Three Approaches to Starting a Successful Marine Aquarium

I N THE 1950S AND '60S, Robert P.L. Straughan, an American marine aquarium pioneer living in Florida, discovered a "miracle" technique for success in keeping saltwater fishes alive. By setting up a new system with calcareous substrate and an undergravel filter, introducing some fishes, and waiting a few weeks, the livestock would . . . die. Most people would have drained the tank and taken up hamsters. Luckily for us, Straughan was patient and waited.

He learned that if he held off dumping and cleaning the whole tank out, the system could be restocked, and, like magic, the new specimens would survive and actually begin to thrive. We now know that Straughan had experienced the beneficial results of a process we now call "nutrient cycling."

Simple fish-only system in a 60-gallon acrylic tank with live rock, a crown of indestructible faux corals, and a young Clown Trigger as the pivotal species.

As a marine collector and experimenter, Straughan was one of the first to promote the use of undergravel filters in marine tanks as way of clarifying the water. He and others were then completely unaware of the vital role that beneficial bacteria play in breaking down toxic aquarium wastes. Straughan thought he had found a way to make water sparkle, but he had actually stumbled upon one of the complex keys to keeping marine organisms alive—by allowing natural biological filtration to make an aquarium hospitable for live specimens. By letting colonies of bacteria feed on the wastes (or even the carcasses) of the first fishes, he allowed bacterial cultures to develop in the gravel of his systems. These unseen allies were then able to break down deadly ammonia and nitrite that so often kill fishes in what we call "new tank syndrome"—a situation in which too much life is added too quickly to a freshly started system.

Today, we not only have a much better understanding of what goes on in captive systems, we have better equipment and opportunities to express our

> *"Marines are no harder or more expensive to keep than discus or other plants and fishes widely maintained in advanced freshwater systems. The 'secrets' of success are the same— proper setup and responsible maintenance."*

individual preferences as aquarists. You can scarcely count the variety of marine aquariums being kept. There are all kinds of tropical systems—from sim-

Built into a modern office setting, this reef aquarium operates in near-silence with all system equipment hidden in the cabinetry below (see facing page).

ple fish-only setups to full-blown reefs with captive invertebrates and thriving corals that absolutely defied keeping in Straughan's era. We have the emergence of biotopic marine systems that attempt to mimic microniches from the reefs and shorelines of the world. Some aquarists have begun to experiment with temperate systems or even with cold-water systems that depend on having water-chilling mechanisms. (Anyone who thinks that tropical reefs have a corner on vibrant colors hasn't seen the anemones and other inverte-

brates from the chilly upper Pacific coast of North America.) And not all systems concentrate on life below the surface. Unfettered marine aquarists are experimenting with mangrove swamp tanks—complete with emergent live trees—and even tidepool tanks that require vigorous circulation and periodic draining to simulate low-tide conditions. With the unprecedented availability of technology, livestock, and live aquascaping materials, home aquarists are now able, for the first time, to assemble many handsome and healthy

types of marine aquarium biotopes.

Unfortunately, there is an aura around the saltwater aquarium hobby that scares away many who think they'd like to give it a try. Let me state a simple truth: Marines are no harder or more expensive to keep than discus or other plants and fishes widely maintained in advanced freshwater systems. The "secrets" of success are the same— proper setup and responsible maintenance with a watchful, knowing eye on your livestock.

What type of gear does it take to

keep marines alive? At its most basic, just a chemically nonreactive container and seawater. If you pay a visit to one of the trendy natural history boutiques, you might encounter a pricey glass bubble being sold as the eternal, maintenance-free aqua system. Sealed in the globe are some algae, tiny shrimp, snails, and a bit of gravel. Given proper benign care—no extremes of temperature or lighting—these tiny ecosystems are claimed to live for years.

Of course, a real, open aquarium is both more sustainable and more interesting for most of us. Today there is a range of tanks as well as environmental-control equipment that has substantially improved and simplified the keeping of a healthy marine system. Even Straughan's approach of decades ago can still be used, but there are simple, relatively inexpensive enhancements that can make it more effective.

System Components

MOST CONTEMPORARY saltwater setups make use of the following major pieces of equipment and supplies:

An aquarium made from chemically inert materials—usually glass and silicone rubber, or acrylic—is needed. The larger, the better. (Increased volume equals more stable conditions.) Low and wide is generally a better shape than tall and narrow. (More surface area for volume of water in the tank allows for better gas diffusion, homogeneous thermal control, and generally better aquascaping possibilities.)

Seawater, either natural or synthetic,

is an obvious necessity. Most of us, including the big public aquariums, simply mix tap water with powdered salt mixes formulated for marine aquarium systems. Anyone living near an unpolluted source of ocean water may want to collect the real thing, but this is a case where man-made has certain advantages.

Adequate temperature control is needed. Water is the standard for specific heat, taking in and giving up more energy per weight than any other substance. Marine life forms have evolved in relatively stable temperature conditions of the sea and can be ill-suited to rapid fluctuations that are possible in tiny bodies of water. We need to control or mediate thermal shifts in our tanks, generally aiming for a range of 75 to 80 degrees F; most home systems

in North America and Europe will require a thermostatic aquarium heater, at least during the winter months. In some instances, a chiller will also be needed.

The right lighting, usually achieved with artificial illumination, is important in almost all cases—both for the health of your livestock and for your viewing pleasure. Natural sunlight, for various reasons, is not a desirable source of illumination for most home aquariums. Intense artificial lighting, required by many corals and other invertebrates, can be a very expensive part of your setup to purchase and operate, once you graduate beyond the basic fish-only system. Powerful lighting systems for reef tanks are not only costly but, if installed improperly, can also be the most dangerous system component.

External sumps, as in this system by Jeffrey Turner of Oceans, Reefs & Aquariums, allow the aquarist to tuck pumps, heaters, skimmer, freshwater reservoirs, and electronic controllers neatly out of sight.

Proper filtration is a necessity. For our purposes, filtration will also encompass water circulation and gas exchange (aeration). These processes ensure adequate oxygenation of the system water and the removal and/or conversion of livestock wastes and by-products. Taking a look at the hobbyist magazines, we find better filtration gadgets each and every month. There are power filters, inside filters, outside filters, undergravel, undertank, wet-dry, trickle, live sand, fluidized bed, chemical filtrants, ultraviolet sterilizers, ozonizers, protein skimmers, and foam fractionators—to name just a few. What do they do? Do you need to have them? Don't worry, as you will see in Chapter 3, there is a simple route through or around this seeming maze of equipment choices.

Substrate and aquascaping are needed. A bare tank is not an option if you care about the well-being of your specimens. Sand or gravel and rock or coral (natural or artificial) are not just for your enjoyment. Living organisms need physical cover in their environment to feel secure, to avoid bullying (including by you), and to show natural behaviors. Substrates, especially coral or other calcareous sand and gravel (dolomite, shell, marble), are important double-duty agents that serve as attachment sites for beneficial microbes and as water chemistry buffers.

Test kits and monitors will save aggravation. To manage your aquarium intelligently, you will need to test your water for its temperature, specific gravity, and for the presence or absence of pollutants. Again, the options are virtually limitless, but the beginning aquarist must have just a few basic pieces of test equipment for checking on physical and chemical parameters and keeping tabs on what changes may be taking place in the aquarium environment.

Water additives may or may not be necessary. Vitamin, mineral, and trace element additives will be required by many, but not all, systems. This is an important area of understanding with marines as, unlike their freshwater brethren, each specimen does "drink like a fish." Many invertebrates will fail to thrive, or just outright perish, without proper levels of calcium, iodine, and a balance of trace elements found in natural seawater.

Fear not. There are countless combinations of marine equipment components that can make for a healthy and beautiful aquarium. If you looked behind and under the hood of the tanks of ten of the top acknowledged expert aquarists in the world, you would likely find ten different approaches to illumination, filtration, and maintenance of water quality. The essential technology should not and (if you keep reading) will not confuse you.

Keep two things in mind:

1) Marine aquarium keeping is still part science, part craft or art, and part voodoo;

2) The real differences in filtration, lighting, and water quality standards (good, better, and best) are related to where you want to be in the spectrum, starting with a simple fish-only aquarium, moving up to a fish-and-hardy-invertebrates setup, and culminating with a full reef tank.

Before advancing in the details of equipment, filtration, water quality, and aquascaping, you may find it useful to consider the basic choices open to you as a beginning marine aquarist or one seeking to create a new or better system. Much confusion can be avoided if we think in terms of three classic types of systems: fish-only, fish with hardy invertebrates, and reef systems. Knowing the beauties—and the realities—of each can be extremely helpful as you decide what kind of aquarium is right for you at this stage in your life as a marine aquarist.

The Fish-Only System

THE VAST MAJORITY of marine aquariums are archetypal fish-only systems. They focus on the lure and color of saltwater fishes, but are usually lacking macroalgae, live rock, or invertebrates of any kind. The popularity of these simplest of salt setups is easy to understand. The fantastic beauty of coral reef fishes is what attracts most aquarists to try out the marine hobby in the first place. The majority have already kept freshwater tanks, and switching to a fish-only salt system is a relatively easy transition and extension of their aquatic-hobbyist skills.

With only fishes in a system, the worries and expenses of maintaining optimum water quality are greatly diminished. Fishes, as a rule, are far more

FISH-ONLY SYSTEM: a typical glass 55-gallon aquarium, featuring undergravel filtration, an in-tank skimmer, hardy species, cleaned shells, and artificial corals.

forgiving than nonfish livestock. For a fish, specialized, enhanced lighting is not a concern, and the most basic of biological and mechanical filtration may be employed. Further, because fish can become sick, there may be a need to manipulate your aquarium environment in ways that would be toxic to nonfish life—lowering specific gravity and treating with medications, for example. Ideally, you will have a second tank to serve as a quarantine unit, but the vast majority of beginners do not. Your main system aquarium might be called upon to serve double-duty as a treatment tank.

For a fish-only system, you will need the following essential pieces of equipment: tank, lights (simple fluorescent lighting will do), cover, heater, thermometer, basic marine test kit, and some choice of filtration components (see Chapter 3).

To start simply, I might suggest a good, simple undergravel filter, along with a decent external power filter (either a hang-on-the-tank type or a canister). Furthermore, I urge you to include a protein skimmer. Typically, these have not been recommended for fish-only systems, but they are exceptionally good at helping avert various sudden so-called "wipeout syndromes" that can suddenly decimate marine aquariums after months of seemingly healthy operation. Protein skimmers extract dissolved organic wastes, and once you've seen what they can pull out of your water, you will never want to be without one.

Nice enhancements to the fish-only system would be stronger circulation and a wet-dry filter or other large external filter to increase oxygenation and speed the breakdown of wastes. Sophisticated setups might eventually include UV sterilizers, ozonizers, digital monitoring devices, and much more. Live rock and live sand can also be added to fish-only systems for realistic aquascaping and to improve biological filtration.

There is nothing wrong with fish-only systems—despite the trend toward reef aquariums. The diversity of species you may choose for these setups is enormous. Most commonly kept marine fishes get along just fine with nonliving decor. Live rock, corals, anemones, macroalgae, and other organisms do add a great deal of beauty and potential functionality to a system, but they can also have downsides. The likelihood of overstocking, metabolite pollution, and a disastrous wipeout is increasingly greater with the addition of more species and more total bioload to a small system.

For a minimum of maintenance, lowest mandatory cost, and fewest losses, I always encourage new marine hobbyists to start first with a fish-only arrangement. Even if your budget isn't a major constraint, I would advise learning the elements of marine husbandry with easy-to-keep fishes before trying the more challenging additions of non-fish life.

The Fish-and-Hardy-Invertebrate System

IT'S HARD TO MAKE sweeping statements about fishes. Some species are timid, and some are real bruisers. There are fishes that can survive most any treatment, and others that die of fright just from having a net stuck in their tank. Pelagic triggerfishes have such indiscriminate appetites that they can be hooked by fishermen using orange peels or paper towels as "bait." At the other extreme, there are assorted butterflyfishes that have never been observed eating in captivity.

The diversity of fishes, however, pales in comparison to the invertebrates. These come as attached, swimming, burrowing, crawling, and internal and external symbionts in all marine environments, and are found from the surface to below abyssal depths. Many are incredibly beautiful. Some are incredibly tough aquarium specimens, while others will die if simply lifted from the water.

Very happily, the quality and selection of invertebrate animal life offered to marine hobbyists has vastly improved from what was available in the past. Enhanced collection, transport, and even captive culture (e.g. giant clams, macroalgae, soft and stony corals) has greatly expanded what is available and has improved the likelihood of specimen survival.

A marine system that includes invertebrates can be very similar to, or markedly different from, the typical fish-only marine setups. The same con-

FISH-ONLY SYSTEM (detail): an excellent introduction to basic marine fishkeeping, this beginner's aquarium can later be enhanced with upgraded circulation, skimming, and more intense lighting if desired.

FISH-AND-INVERTEBRATE SYSTEM: the same 55-gallon tank with live rock, an external skimmer, much stronger water circulation, and brighter fluorescent lighting.

cerns about planning, proper setup, and buying healthy, appropriate specimens apply as for fish-only systems. What is really different is a greater intolerance for poor or fluctuating water quality. People who have had good success with hardy fishes and casual maintenance habits can meet immediate failure if they try to add the more delicate invertebrates without upgrading their water quality.

Compared with fishes, invertebrates as a whole cannot stand up to metabolite poisoning from any source (including themselves), or sharp variations in specific gravity and temperature.

One useful way of reminding yourself of their vulnerability is to consider how much less mobile many invertebrates are in comparison to fishes. Most of these nonfishes can only move away from undesirable circumstances slowly in comparison to finned animals; others cannot escape under any normal circumstance. They will die if conditions in your system, or in the part of the aquarium where you place them, are adverse.

The need for diligent testing and maintenance of filtration and circulation, temperature control, overall environmental quality, and stability is greater in dealing with invertebrates. You can see the logic in practicing first with a fish-only marine setup and becoming comfortable with the basic equipment and husbandry practices before moving into keeping nonfishes.

Fortunately, there is a middle step between fish-only and full-blown reef systems. While many of the corals and coral-related organisms are far too demanding for the average beginning aquarist, there are many invertebrates that can be kept with relative ease in marine fish aquariums. For our discussion, invertebrates for a basic fish-and-invert system will include feather duster worms, peaceful starfishes, crabs, shrimps, and other crustaceans. Their inclusion, for many of us, can greatly

FISH-AND-INVERTEBRATE SYSTEM (detail): better water and lighting conditions allow the keeping of hardy invertebrates and somewhat more demanding reef fishes.

enhance the pleasure of keeping and viewing a captive marine environment.

The equipment available for invertebrate, or fish-and-invertebrate, systems is extensive—and sometimes expensive. What is actually necessary beyond the basic components and their arrangement is a matter of degree, with one important exception—lighting, which needs to be better than that found under most single-bulb "strip lights" that come with basic starter aquarium kits.

Good lighting is critical for many invertebrates. Some spineless animals contain photosynthetic algae called zooxanthellae that demand illumination approximating natural sunlight, and almost all are sensitive to irregularities in light duration, quality, and intensity. While a single fluorescent bulb might suffice for a fish-only system, we must boost the wattage of this more challenging setup. From a low of about 1 watt per gallon for the fish-only system, we must double or triple the light-

ing, allowing the introduction of green macroalgae. With a full assembly of four fluorescent tubes over the system—3 to 4 watts per gallon—we might also consider some of the beginner's soft corals, such as mushroom anemones, that do not require the intensity of full reef lighting.

In general, more light means more biological activity in a system, with new sources of algae and other natural foods for both fishes and invertebrates. Know, too, that many nonfishes appreciate full-spectrum illumination, provided on a predictable schedule, and the use of a timer on your lights should be considered mandatory.

In addition to somewhat enhanced lighting, you still need as large a system as you can get, all the elements of filtration (biological, mechanical, protein skimming), and heating and possibly chilling. Now, however, the operation must be more stringent.

You also might have left live rock and substrate out completely with your fish-only setup, but the presence of reef rock and sand can be a real ally in maintaining the stability of a reef-type aquarium, and may even be considered essential for the growth and well-being of many invertebrates. In addition to harboring beneficial bacteria, coral rock and sand will help buffer the system's pH and provide an appropriate setting for all manner of plants, moving invertebrates, such as shrimps, and sessile (stationary) specimens, such as sponges and hardy soft corals. Live rock and live sand bring with them many tiny life forms that serve as an ongoing source of living foods for browsing fishes and invertebrates. Having a live aquascape opens the doors to the keeping of a number of reef fishes that simply refuse to thrive in more barren, artificial settings.

You may have gotten away without a close-fitting tank hood with freshwater or fish-only marine systems, but you should be aware of the fact that many marine invertebrates can and will exit up and over the walls of your tank, even though they might seem incapable of doing so. In addition, you don't want to have to cope with the water loss, heat fluctuations, and salinity changes that come with having an uncovered system.

If you have been getting by with an inefficient little skimmer, this may be the time to upgrade. Many invertebrates will simply not "open up" and thrive in poorly skimmed water.

Many aquarists are content keeping fishes, but a growing number of others find their interests evolving and expanding to the world of invertebrate life. Too many hobbyists assume that such organisms are impossible to keep. This is not the case. Some are every bit as hardy, fascinating, and gorgeous as the most extravagant of fishes.

> "Having a live aquascape opens the doors to the keeping of a number of reef fishes—such as the dwarf angels—that simply refuse to thrive in more barren, artificial settings."

Creating a marine aquarium environment housing both fishes and hardy invertebrate life requires that more attention be paid to meeting the requirements of a mixed community that is less tolerant of neglect or up-and-down water quality. Repayment comes in being able to observe the beauty and sometimes bizarre behaviors of shrimps, crabs, sponges, brittlestars, macroalgae, and even members of the great Phylum Cnidaria, which includes the many and varied corals.

Reef Systems

THERE ARE FEW human-made works of art that can compare with the beauty of a full-blown tropical reef aquarium. (Actually, I can't think of any.) There are incredible shapes, colors, and patterns in the algae, fishes, and invertebrates—all mixing and moving in the currents in hypnotic undulations and rhythms. Reef tanks, however, need the most care and highest consistent water quality of all marine aquariums. In addition, these units typically demand intense lighting and heavy-duty circulation and protein skimming.

There are no secrets to keeping a reef collection, only a few steadfast rules regarding lighting, water circulation, filtration, and setup. But reef aquariums are not for everyone. In comparison to basic fish-only set-ups, they are expensive to equip, populate, and maintain. They are more time-consuming and, of the basic types of marine systems, more prone to disaster without adequate care. For these reasons and more, I implore you to practice with the easier approaches we've discussed so far and to read some of the excellent specialty books in this field before deciding to set up a reef tank.

Depending on what kinds of photosynthetic organisms you plan to keep and how hard you want to push them,

REEF SYSTEM: with intense lighting, vigorous skimming, and chaotic circulation, the same 55-gallon tank becomes a complex collection of reef organisms.

reef lighting can be simple and not too expensive, or high-powered, sophisticated, and very expensive. Starter reef aquariums can do just fine with easily obtained fluorescent lights, provided the aquarist doesn't attempt to keep reef organisms that demand intense illumination. Figuring out the amount and type of lighting can be tricky. Studying the species of reef life available to us will reveal that some organisms come from near-surface areas and demand high-intensity, full-spectrum illumination. Others come from deeper water and require less light.

Some of the hardy invertebrates we will discuss in this book can do well un-der full-spectrum, normal-output fluorescent lights, although some require the high output (HO) or very high output (VHO) versions with special ballasts. Another relatively new option are power compacts, which can brightly illuminate smaller systems with specialty bulbs that take up a fraction of the space of normal-sized fluorescents.

Metal halide bulbs, including new compact and electronic-ballast versions, produce brilliant, extremely pleasing light and greatly broaden your choices of species that can be considered. Many available photosynthetic corals and clams, in fact, require this intensity of light to grow and flourish.

Metal halides are not for beginners, however, and can easily be misused. The heat they produce can be a fire hazard (particularly in homemade lighting hoods) or can push the water temperature of your system to dangerous levels (see Chapter 2).

Filtration for a reef system can also be made extremely complex, but, happily, the clear trend among successful aquarists is to rely primarily on simplified equipment that will provide vigorous circulation and efficient skimming. Biological filtration takes place in a significant mass of live rock—typically 1 to 2 pounds of rock for each gallon of tank capacity—and a deep bed of aragonite (coral) sand, either in the aquarium or in a refugium tank or sump below or beside the display tank.

Typically, reef keepers have a main system water pump capable of turning over the entire volume of the system from five to ten times each hour. Most feed the pump from a sump below the aquarium, where protein skimming, heating, particulate filtration (if any) and other activities take place. Many now augment the main system pump with submersible powerhead pumps on random timing devices to create turbulence and the sort of chaotic currents that give some approximation of the high-energy areas of the wild reef. (Some coral enthusiasts now advocate enough total pumping capacity to circulate the system water 20 times or more per hour.) Whatever circulation gear you utilize, make your currents brisk. Many reef organisms are stimulated by strong flows, and water movement serves to distribute oxygen, remove wastes (corals will often wither if their own toxins are not whisked away), and circulate potential foods to sessile invertebrates and filter-feeding animals.

Naturally, technology buffs have many other approaches to modern-day captive reef keeping, including algal-scrubbing compartments, ozonizers, UV sterilizers, calcium reactors, limewater and trace element dosers, and much, much more. The proliferation of technology is in response to the heavy bioloading that is seen in the typical reef tank. While early saltwater aquar-

iums may have been lightly stocked, today's reef enthusiast typically populates his or her system with dozens of invertebrate specimens, pushing them to grow with intense lighting and nutrient supplements.

Current reef filter technologies include variations of wet-dry trickle units, high-tech protein skimmers, live sand beds, biological refugium tanks, and algae "scrubbers" of various types. Reef systems are crowded with life and demand effective filtration, whether it

be "natural" or highly technical.

A properly set up and stocked reef system can actually become the closest thing marine systems have to being almost maintenance-free. When the living and nonliving components of a reef setup are balanced and the population of fishes is limited, these systems become homeostatic. The average reef keeper does spend a few hours a week checking water chemistry, adjusting salinity, feeding the livestock, removing detritus, and generally fooling with

REEF SYSTEM (detail): a visual feast of lush algae, hardy corals, and eye-catching fishes and invertebrates.

the system. But performing these tasks is so enjoyable that most reef aquarists don't mind the time commitment.

I don't want to dissuade you from pursuing a reef system, but I urge you to consider what an involved, and involving, enterprise it is. Most tropical reef setups represent thousands of dollars of investment, with their keepers often spending hundreds more a month on equipment, organisms, food, and electricity. In the end, if you don't do things right, or if you choose animals that are too demanding, reef specimens can perish overnight or waste away in a matter of weeks. The challenges of keeping a fully equipped and stocked reef aquarium should never be taken lightly.

Your Species Plan

WHATEVER TYPE OF SYSTEM strikes your fancy, take the time to reflect on the fishes and other organisms you want to keep in your intended marine aquarium. Impatience is your worst foe at this point. The vast majority of new saltwater aquarists just jump right in, opting to learn the hard, expensive way. "Damn the torpedoes" may work in times of war, but in setting up a marine aquarium it almost invariably results in wasted funds and the anguish of seeing some or all of your first live specimens perish before your eyes.

A few evenings, or even just a few hours, of planning can avoid the predictable major pitfalls, and now is the time to put your ideas on paper. The stocking of a marine tank is far more involved than simply buying the first fishes that appeal to you. One of the most common serious errors the beginner is likely to make is in not stopping to consider the issues of compatibility among proposed tankmates, the types of foods they will require, and their potential growth and eventual full size. Most beginners assume that choosing the right equipment is the difficult part; in fact, more mistakes are made in selecting the first fishes than in picking appropriate hardware.

Do you, like most of us, harbor a mental image of a "must have" fish for your new system? Good—plan and build your livestock collection around that key choice. Or, are you or any family members adamant about having fishes that are red, yellow, or electric blue? Whatever your desires, there is a tried-and-true approach to picking out fishes for your system. First, write down your wish list.

I would start with a "pie-in-the-sky" inventory of what you'd really like to own if cost, compatibility, ultimate size, and difficulty in keeping were not limiting factors. Then comes what many of us find the most enlightening part of this hobby—gathering information about your chosen species. Go to your dealer with the list, call up the fellow hobbyist who got you interested in marines, and open all the books you can find—if not your own, then from the local tropical fish society or a good public library.

You want to discover everything there is to know concerning your growing roster of potential acquisitions. Are they hardy? What sort of environmental conditions do they favor? How big do they grow and how fast? Do they do best singly, in pairs, or in trios? Are they mild-mannered or aggressive? What do they eat? (If they happen to eat the smaller members on your list, this is the time to adjust the plan.) What do they cost? Are they available?

In the last 30 years, I've seen a good part of the marine hobby shift in emphasis from enjoyment and appreciation of keeping aquatic life to buying what we hear described as "pleasure from kinetic art." Too many people want the spectacle of a beautiful aquarium without knowing, or caring, about the natural histories of the creatures themselves. To my mind, this is a disturbing trend. Don't be too busy to do at least a little research before buying your livestock, and don't cheat yourself out of the rich experience of learning about your organisms.

Even more essential, if you are now contemplating setting up a new aquarium, think seriously about the type of system you want to achieve. Give some thought as to the types of organisms that really please you, and begin to plan how you can best keep them alive and healthy. Factor in the available space in your home, the available budget for this investment, and the amount of time you wish to commit. Your system is likely to evolve as your skills and confidence as an aquarist grow—remember that part of being conscientious is to make realistic decisions about the type of system you set out to create.

Small Marine Systems: Caution Advised

How SMALL IS SMALL? What volume of seawater is large and stable enough to suit you and some modicum of livestock, but not so tiny as to crash with any electrical outage, unnoticed death of a specimen, or hint of overfeeding?

To Shamu, an Olympic pool is teeny; to me, a small marine tank is 40 gallons. Anything smaller is too limiting in what you can practically keep in it, and too unstable in my opinion. Yet I've seen successful 2-, 5-, and 10-gallon setups. The inhabitants may have been only a *Condylactis* anemone, a shrimp, and a damsel, but they were alive.

Whether it's done to show off, experiment, have a portable system, or for lack of funds or space, micro saltwater systems of all types are possible. They are just not especially stable or, for many of us, practical. Aquariums with severely limited volumes—even for experts—are dangerously erratic in their temperature and many measures of water chemistry. There are advantages to larger systems, such as dilution of wastes, homeostasis of water chemistry and physics, and space for behavioral expression or retreat by the animals. If you really want to attempt a small system, there are certain things that need to be done in order to be successful.

Organisms. Of course, whatever livestock is placed in a little marine system should be, and stay, small. But there are other considerations of feeding, metab-

A 20-GALLON SYSTEM: to succeed, a small marine aquarium demands very light bioload and scrupulous avoidance of overfeeding or shifts in water conditions.

olism, and space compatibility that are not as apparent.

Due to restrictions and efficiencies of proportion, selecting organisms that can be sustained by offering little or no supplemental feeding is extremely prudent. Some folks scarcely feed their tiny reef setups, relying on the natural production of detritus, algae, and tiny invertebrate organisms to supply nutrition. The more types and volume of foods you're compelled to apply to a small marine system (because it is actually being "fed" to the whole setup, not just the intended livestock), the greater the likelihood for pollution. The great majority of aquarists overfeed their systems—in a tiny setup, this can be lethal.

Metabolism is a key element in small volumes. Animals with behavior and physiologies more akin to turtles versus hummingbirds are preferred. Consider the hawkfishes, clownfishes, gobies, blennies, small basslets, and less boisterous families, instead of the big, active triggers, angels, tangs, and butterflies.

Space compatibility refers to the minimum elbowroom requirements of and between species. Stinging-celled animals (corals, anemones, and others), sponges, and echinoderms pose possible difficulties when crowded to the point of touching. Some exude toxins to protect their territories, others even extend lethal sweeper tentacles, often at night, to sting any sessile invertebrates within reach.

Be careful about what you buy, and make sure it is fit and not bearing a latent biological disease that would cause mayhem in a small system.

Setup. Small aquariums are put together in pretty much the same way as larger systems, with special emphasis on diligent testing and patience in stocking.

Promoting nutrient cycling is best accomplished by one of two methods. For those with access to an established system (ask your dealer or a fellow hobbyist), clean, live sand may be transferred to the smaller tank. Provided your water has not just been mixed, and is not too warm or too cold, you may be able to have an almost overnight biological filter just by transferring in some good, stable, bacteria-laden substrate.

Alternatively, simply employing cured (not freshly imported or just-shipped-in) live rock is a real possibility and quite affordable for a diminutive tank. In either case, be sure to start with stable live rock and live sand that you transport home quickly and/or in clean water; any drying out, chilling, or overheating and subsequent die-off once in a small system can kill everything—including most organisms on your rock and in your sand. To be on the safe side, acquire only live rock or live sand that has

been acclimated in the dealer's system or a friend's tank for a month or more.

Lighting. While some writers have suggested that metal halide lighting ought to be employed on small systems, I urge extreme caution. The waste heat

Side view of a 20-gallon soft-coral reef tank using live rock, live sand, an external hang-on-the-tank skimmer and a small wavemaker.

and propensity to produce photo shock in the livestock in small tanks usually argues strongly for the use of fluorescent bulbs. Even the effect of fluorescents on temperature must be monitored and controlled—HO or VHO bulbs, especially in closed hoods, can easily overheat a small system.

The challenge comes when trying to supply enough light intensity to satisfy an anemone or certain corals without overheating your water. Having a fan in the light hood helps a great deal, as does using pendant lighting and having good air circulation over the top of the system. New lighting options offering greater intensity with very little waste heat are appearing and worth investigating.

Filtration. Filter types used to run the gamut from circulation-only to external sump with wet-dry filtration, bio-refugium, and more. (Some successful small-aquarium veterans actually have relatively large sumps hidden away—in cabinetry or elsewhere—to greatly increase their system volume without adding to the tank footprint.) I will go on record as sanctioning the keeping of tiny marine systems only when the aquarist uses at least some outside power filtration and a working protein skimmer. As you'll be using cured gravel and/or live rock, you can—and should—have your skimmer up and running from the very first day.

Operation and Maintenance. When all is said and done—assuming the water temperature is reasonably controlled—feeding can be the most critical factor in determining the success or failure of tiny marine aquariums. Do not overfeed, especially with foods that quickly pollute the system, such as raw squid, mussels, or bits of fish.

Frequent, regular water changes are essential, and mixing up some salt and tap water a few minutes beforehand is not acceptable. Ideally, you should be using premixed and aged or conditioned replacement water. Get a 5-gallon "aquarium-only" water bucket and keep a supply on hand, mixed up a week or more in advance. If you have a larger setup, you might use the water from it for changes in the smaller unit(s). Be religious about water changing—if you can, change 5 to 20 percent of your water volume per week. (Some who dote on small systems meticulously change a small amount daily to avoid the shock of major maneuvers.)

Altering water makeup by pouring in supplements or "adjusters" ought to be unnecessary and can easily be dangerous. Enough trace material should come from feeding, substrate interaction, and water changes to keep the system in dynamic equilibrium. Those who challenge the biological limitations of the system with dense populations of corals or clams may find the need to supplement calcium, iodine, and other trace elements. For the record, this is risky business, requiring extreme discipline not to overdose and a hawk-eyed vigilance to spot and correct problems immediately.

Final Thoughts on Small Systems. I can't for the life of me understand authors who encourage inexperienced hobbyists to attempt small marine aquariums. Maybe like adults who have forgotten how it was to first tie their shoes or ride a bike, they seem to have lost sight of how hard it was to learn what now seem like simple tasks and how agonizing it was to cope with the frustration and sense of helplessness in losing livestock.

When the same writers who advocate small marine systems as an inexpensive entryway to the hobby go on to promote halide lighting, wet-dry filters, redox testing, and high-tech paraphernalia, it becomes easy to understand why so many newcomers are confused—and unsuccessful. Given the everyday bargain prices of new glass aquariums, anyone who can't afford at least a 40- or 50-gallon tank is probably not yet ready for this hobby. In the long run, the price of the tank becomes virtually inconsequential.

Small systems—less than 40 gallons—are a bad gamble for all but the advanced aquarist. It takes real expertise and self-discipline to make a success of a micro marine aquarium, and those lovely examples that do work are almost all owned by those who will put the effort into testing and adjusting for water quality and organism interaction, and who have the facilities to move and rescue these systems if and when they start to crash.

If you are still determined to try your hand at a small marine setup as your first saltwater aquarium, be on guard for temperature fluctuations, overstocking, and overfeeding. Small can, indeed, be beautiful, but it is a real challenge in this case. The fastidious, highly disciplined aquarist (the one who *can* resist buying yet another fish once the tank reaches a good balance) can have success with a countertop or desktop system, but for the average hobbyist, bigger is better when it comes to marine aquarium size.

CHAPTER 2

Basic Equipment

Essential Gear for the Marine Aquarist: Choices and Options

"THEY DON'T MAKE THEM like they used to," is a phrase one might hear in the company of mature aquarists who remember when an aquarium was a clunky, heavy assembly with a gray slate bottom, painted steel framework, and thick glass sides. Today's fish tanks are stronger, lighter, less prone to leakage, often better for viewing, and, best of all for marine keepers, completely immune to salt corrosion and rust. Here's one piece of modern life where we can unequivocally say, "Thank goodness they aren't made the way they used to be."

Tanks

MARINE AQUARIUMS, stands, hoods, and covers share the same requirements as those for freshwater: they must be

Victorian parlor aquariums were simple delights, but lacked the water movement and stable conditions needed by tropical reef fishes and invertebrates.

strong, durable, and attractive. Due to the corrosive effects of seawater and the intolerance of marine livestock for metal and other pollution, the structural elements of marine setups must be composed of materials that are chemically unreactive to salts. Virtually all aquariums sold today meet this criterion; beware of dusting off old metal-framed models from garage sales or someone's attic. The question of tank size has been discussed in Chapter 1. Again, I caution you to avoid any system smaller than 40 gallons.

Before the hobbyist asks the next common question, glass or acrylic, the basic shape of the tank ought to be given serious thought. The physical conformation of a system is extremely important—both to the inhabitants within and to the aquarist who must maintain it.

One of the descriptions you will encounter is for aquariums called "show tanks." Some aquarium makers use the

show tank designation for all plain rectangular tanks—both tall and squat. A true show tank, however, is tall and narrow, meant to put fishes on temporary public display where they must remain

> *"Put a fat goldfish in a deep 2-liter beer stein and another in a shallow casserole dish of the same volume and see which does better. Ample surface area is very important."*

front and center. This configuration is undesirable for most livestock. Gaseous diffusion and exchange at the surface is diminished by having a system that has a poor ratio of surface to volume. Put a fat goldfish in a deep 2-liter beer stein and another in a shallow casserole

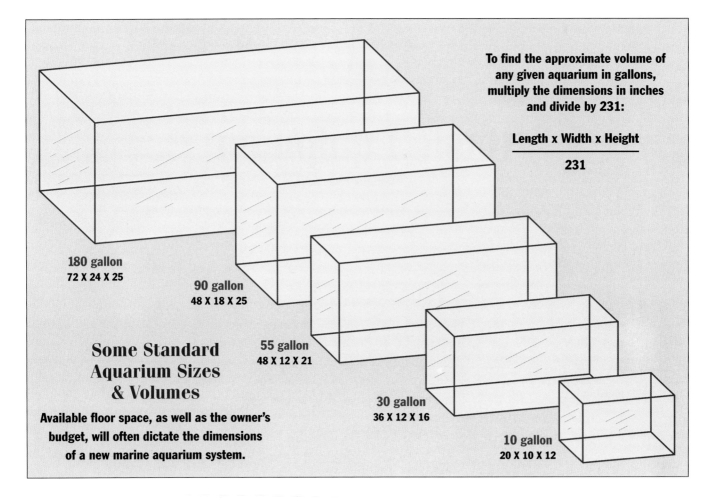

To find the approximate volume of any given aquarium in gallons, multiply the dimensions in inches and divide by 231:

$$\frac{Length \times Width \times Height}{231}$$

180 gallon
72 X 24 X 25

90 gallon
48 X 18 X 25

55 gallon
48 X 12 X 21

Some Standard Aquarium Sizes & Volumes

Available floor space, as well as the owner's budget, will often dictate the dimensions of a new marine aquarium system.

30 gallon
36 X 12 X 16

10 gallon
20 X 10 X 12

dish of the same volume and see which does better. (Save yourself and the goldfish the suffering; the broad, open-surface container is far better for pro-longed good health and survival of the fish.) Ample surface area is very impor-tant for keeping the oxygen content of an aquarium near its optimum level.

Other factors also support the low, broad designs. Though they live in a liquid world, most fishes and inverte-brates are much more two-dimensional in their activity than the average aquar-ist realizes. Consider the barrier or mist

nets used by collectors to capture wild fishes—they're not very tall. Why don't the fishes just swim over the top? Some just can't execute rapid ascents because of hydrostatic mechanism controls, but mainly it's due to the fact that many aquarium species live their entire wild lives near the safety of relatively flat bottoms and are not likely to change horizontal patterns to vertical ones.

Deep tanks are also difficult to maintain. Unless you have simian arms, any tank deeper than 24 inches is awk-ward and difficult to keep clean, even

for a 6-foot human. These aquariums need special, long-handled tools just to keep the algae off the glass or acrylic. In addition, very expensive lighting will be required if you want to keep many of the photosynthetic invertebrates prized by reef aquarists. In fact, the initial cost of a tall tank will be much more than that of a shorter one. Many people who have purchased tall "designer" tanks say they would love to go back to shallower systems—both for the increased growth of their specimens and for the ease with which they can be kept clean.

Some large tanks are constructed of concrete, fiberglass or resin, wood, or other materials with a clear viewing panel of glass or acrylic. However, most off-the-shelf, affordable systems offered in the trade are either entirely acrylic or glass and silicone rubber, usually with a plastic frame.

For most beginning aquarists, the glass aquarium has a great deal going for it—low price, good availability, and many sizes from which to choose. Glass is easy to scrape clean with a razor, and the popular brands offered everywhere these days have good records for not springing leaks unless mishandled or placed on uneven stands.

The other option is acrylic, the material of choice for many who prefer its aesthetics and many of its installation advantages. Acrylic proponents usually point out that the best that can be said of glass systems is that they are initially less expensive. But glass tanks do not retain their value. This is not the case with acrylic. I've seen many acrylic tanks sell for more than their original cost years after use.

Why do acrylic aquariums hold their value relative to glass? They are stronger, resist breaks and leakage, offer better thermal insulation (especially important with systems that are consistently kept warmer or colder than room temperature), and are clearer, lighter, and simpler to move.

No one will argue with the fact that acrylic is much easier to handle and modify for filtration and water circulation fittings by drilling or cutting. No hobbyist would attempt to drill filtration-fitting holes in a large, expensive glass tank—special tools and glass-working experience is required for that job. (Professionals usually drill the glass before assembling the tank.) On the other hand, a hobbyist and friend can easily maneuver an acrylic aquarium, and drilling is easily within the skill range of any handy person.

The biggest drawback to acrylic is that it can be scratched—a coarse scrubbing cloth can ruin an acrylic tank, and one shudders to think what a razor blade could do. Special care must be taken, using nonabrasive cleaning pads and scraping tough algae growth with a sharp-edged plastic instrument. The coralline algae that spread in a reef system are readily removed with the edge of a credit card. While both glass and acrylic can be scratched, with acrylic you can remove such scratches. The same cannot be said of glass.

Acrylic tanks are molded, cast, and fabricated into some amazingly beautiful shapes. A functional acrylic system that is a breeze to maintain and a sight to behold for 20-plus years is a better investment, to my mind, than a glass system that is much more susceptible to leakage and breakage.

There are nonassembly-line glass aquariums made—using optically superior glass, black silicon sealant, and superb craftsmanship—but for ease of setup and maintenance, prevention of evaporation, and retention of long-term value, acrylic tanks are hard to beat for marine use.

Stands

When it comes to stands, there are many materials from which to choose. But whatever the composition, an aquarium stand must be level, planar, and strong. The floor beneath it must be able to take the weight, and if it isn't level itself, the stand will have to be shimmed to compensate.

Especially with a glass system, the levelness of a tank is of great concern. Such containers are engineered to resist forces that are at right angles to their joints. Subjecting the tank to sheer forces, particularly ones that are unequal left to right or front to back, is asking for trouble.

Remember, as a rule of thumb, that aquariums filled with saltwater, sand, and rocks weigh approximately 10 pounds per gallon, not counting the stand they're sitting on. For example, a filled 50-gallon tank would be expected to weigh about 500 pounds. The tank and stand or other supporting structure must hold up this mass evenly. For a stand with individual legs—as opposed to one-piece, flat-bottomed cabinets—I strongly encourage you to provide a broad, waterproof underpinning between the legs and floor. This might be as simple as a treated piece of plywood or 1-inch planks. Whatever you use, this is meant to spread out and equalize the tank's weight over a larger area than the feet of the stand. It also enables easier leveling, an important consideration. This recommendation is not only for wooden floors; concrete floors can be surprisingly uneven.

Well-built stands and lighting hoods, as in this 150-gallon reef system by Jeffrey Turner, are highly desirable for attractive display aquariums in homes and offices.

Even if the surface of your tank stand does appear absolutely flat, it helps to place a piece of foam, styrene, felt, or other firm cushioning under the tank's bottom as an extra precaution. The malleable material will be crushed into a form-fitting underpad. Your stand or support could be generally level or planar, yet not perfectly flat and equal in supporting all the edges of your aquarium. With glass tanks, nonlevel surfaces must be avoided at all costs. Acrylic is more forgiving, but should be treated with the same respect. Stresses caused by uneven support can cause warpage and leaks.

A final critical concern is for safety against the system falling over. It is incredible how even an accidental bump can move a massive object like an aquarium. A real nightmare can be had if a small child rocks a narrow-width system back and forth. By all means, secure your system by wedging it in three dimensions in your stand design, possibly between a wall and a large piece of furniture. Better still, solidly anchor the stand to the floor and/or wall.

Covers

SOLIDS, ESPECIALLY THE SALTS in marine water, display an annoying propensity to escape from the system. Variously described as "salt creep" or "bridging," this loss of salts can become a big deal. Seawater contains about 35 parts per thousand (3.5%) salts. Salts are combinations of metals and nonmetals. Different salt constituents have a greater or lesser degree of "staying" in solution. What this means in practical terms is that the crusty white stuff you see collecting around the top of your marine tank is not of the same composition as either the original mix of salts you put in your system or what is currently in there. In the long run, this loss of salts can poison your livestock. As a responsible aquarist, you need to:

1) minimize salt loss from the system by having an adequate tank cover;

2) scrape and reintroduce the salt scum—put it back into your system, being careful that it doesn't land on any sessile invertebrates;

3) do frequent freshwater top-ups and partial water changes to average out these imbalances.

Other reasons for a good aquarium cover are that it reduces heat loss from evaporation and keeps curious hands and accidental objects from getting in.

But my primary concern about closing over the tops of systems is to prevent motile livestock from crawling, slithering, or jumping out. Noted aquatic Houdinis include eels and octopuses, but you will be amazed at what can leave your tank under its own power. A list of what cannot is extremely small—just seahorses. I've seen snails, batfishes, triggers, lions, frogfishes, and many others escape to their own doom.

As a boy working in the trade in the Philippines, one of my glorious tasks was to probe newly arrived livestock with a wooden dowel to revive them after transport. With certain fishes, this was a dangerous job. Big, active surgeonfishes that require high oxygen concentrations, like Naso and Unicorn Tangs, suffer the most from transport.

These fishes would lie gasping on the bottom, then ultimately come to, often executing one last flying leap out of the uncovered system. A launch might set a record of several feet and include a nasty cut for a hapless fish-rouser. Once you've seen fishes jumping like this, or found a valued specimen dried out and curled up on your floor, you, too, will see the value of tank covers.

You can effectively cap all those slots in glass tanks by using plastic tank cover material that can be purchased at your local fish store, or strips of glass or Plexiglas from the hardware store or window glazier.

Acrylic tanks usually have a broad lip or partial cover built on them, and the best systems come with full covering lids for all top openings. Acrylic fabricators can either custom-cut a top to accommodate your particular tank or sell you stylish acrylic slot covers.

Do not, however, become too fastidious in entombing your system. You don't want to close off the system to all air exchange. Gas diffusion occurs at the water's surface, and this area should experience a change in air every minute. If the top is tightly sealed, be sure that vigorous gas exchange is taking place in the external filtration loop, where protein skimmers, open sumps, and active trickle filters can all serve to keep your water well-oxygenated.

Lighting

Virtually all marine systems are in need of an artificial light source, both for the enjoyment of viewers and the health of the viewed. Natural sunlight provides the elusive perfect spectrum that advanced reef aquarists crave, but it has severe limitations for most of us. Aquariums placed in direct sunlight will quickly overheat unless their waters are artificially chilled. During winter months in northern latitudes, there aren't enough hours of sunlight in the day to keep marine creatures alive and thriving. Finally, the sun doesn't shine when most of us have our treasured viewing hours—in the evening.

It follows that one of the most significant investments in a marine system is the lighting. I've seen setups in which the lighting equipment cost more than the rest of the system combined.

This emphasis doesn't seem unreasonable. After all, humans are visually oriented beings; it makes little sense to have beautiful fishes in a wonderful aquascape that is poorly lit. Additionally, there are photosynthetic needs in systems that have more than fishes in them; and even piscine vertebrates require light energy (as we do) for good health.

But what an ocean of controversy and expense this can be! There is, however, really no need for confusion. Your concerns about light and lighting can be reduced to three considerations—quality, quantity, and duration.

The last is simply a matter of employing inexpensive timers. The first two measures can be satisfied by common technologies, the choice being arrived at by summing up the light range or tolerance of your desired livestock

#1. Normal "full-spectrum" 6500-degree K metal halide lighting in aquarist Michael Paletta's large stony-coral reef system.

#2. The same aquarium photographed with all-actinic fluorescent lighting, rated at 7100 degrees K, showing an overall blue cast typical of a deep reef.

#3. The Paletta reef under 20,000-degree K metal halide bulbs, displaying a slightly cool tone but better range of colors than in photographs #1 and #2.

#4. Paletta's final test, including actinics, 6500-degree K, and 20,000-degree K metal halides—perhaps the closest to true, full-spectrum reef lighting.

and what you're willing to spend on purchasing and operating the chosen lighting source.

In choosing your system's lighting, being a conscientious marine aquarist requires understanding the difference between functionality (what your organisms need) and aesthetics (what you think looks good) and making choices accordingly.

A variety of lighting regimens exist in the natural habitats of organisms that we keep in captivity, from the cold-water northern tidepool (relatively low light) to the shallow tropical fringing reef (extremely bright light). Happily, many of the specimens we keep display a wide range of adaptability to lighting conditions.

Fishes and nonphotosynthetic in-

vertebrates can get by on normal-wattage illumination provided by full-spectrum fluorescent lights. Herma-typic corals, algae, vascular plants, coralline algae-encrusted live rock, and invertebrates that harbor zooxanthel-lae all require more watts of full-spec-trum light nourishment.

Several types of lighting are inap-propriate for aquariums: incandescent, halogen, quartz, mercury, sodium vapor, and others. For the correct spectrum of light, safety, and other practical reasons, the two main forms of lighting currently available and recommended to aquarists are fluorescent and metal halide.

For most home aquarists, especially for those just starting or still finding their way along, fluorescents are by far the most appropriate, practical technology available for their aquarium. This continues to hold true for many reef tank owners, but there is a long-standing metal halide versus fluorescent debate. As it won't be solved here, my advice is that fluorescents are the easiest choice for most applications.

Fluorescent lamps of differing types abound. Be warned that the majority of lamps sold for aquarium use are not properly matched to the needs of a marine system. Plant-growing, warm, and "broad" spectrum fluorescents are a bad joke for marine livestock and plants. I want to be completely clear about this: when buying basic fluorescents, you only want full-spectrum lamps.

Although I have tried to avoid endorsing any particular brands of aquarium products, I want to make a brief exception here and specifically mention what I consider to be the benchmark standards for marine-fish, reef system, planted aquarium, and vivarium lights: Duro-Test Corporation's Vita-Lite and Vita-Lite Supreme. The original Vita-Lite hit the market in 1967 as the world's first patented, natural-daylight-stimulating fluorescent tube. For over 25 years (until the advent of their Vita-Lite Supreme), Duro's Vita-Lite was the closest simulation of natural daylight ever created by anyone, anywhere. (I'm not touting these bulbs above all others, but these are readily available from both pet, garden, and hardware shops, and anyone in doubt about a good, all-around bulb for any aquarium should know these are a fine choice.)

The standard specifications of the Vita-Lite are: 5500 degrees Kelvin (K), which is the same as the spectral rating of the noonday sun under a clear sky; a color-rendering index (CRI) of 91, which compares to the sun's CRI of 100; and 2180 lumens, which is a measure of brightness. For those looking for more luminosity, Duro-Test offers another lamp, the Vita-Lite Plus, the only specification difference being the generation of 2750 lumens. The Vita-Lite Supreme offers 5500 K, CRI 96, 2000 lumens and is the best match I am aware of to natural outdoor light.

Other manufacturers of good full-spectrum fluorescents are Phillips, General Electric, and Verilux. Full-spectrum lamps, in my opinion, are great for the marine aquarist, aquatic gardener, herptile keeper, photographer wanting to skip filters, and deskbound office human. They grow aquatic organisms better than any other basic, affordable lighting system, without specialized fixturing and at the lowest cost. What is more, your fishes and photosynthetic organisms look and live better under these lamps. In choosing among the brands, you will have to look for the CRI, temperature in Kelvin, luminosity in lumens, power curve, and average life ratings to make your own consumer judgments.

Again, be wary of lamps termed "wide" or "broad" spectrum. These are not the same as *full*-spectrum lamps that provide the total range of necessary

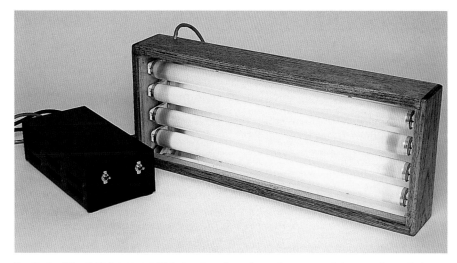

Excellent, off-the-shelf fluorescent lighting systems for reef aquariums are made by several manufacturers and typically include a remote ballast and four or more bulbs in a wooden, aluminum, or acrylic hood.

spectra, including some UV. Daylight, cool-white, and warm-white are also not full-spectrum and used by themselves will not support hermatypic (or endosymbiotic algal) life. Cool-white lamps, which are the most readily available for home and business use, are the cheapest and most efficient for those settings, but the wavelengths produced are not suitable for aquatic systems. Cool-whites have a CRI of 62, which is inadequate for our purposes.

Never place "warm" spectrum or garden-specialty bulbs over marine systems. They will not produce the wavelengths you need. Some will not support desirable life forms, and others have been reported to cause unwanted algae to spread out of control.

Full-spectrum fluorescents are available in a variety of lengths and wattages in three formats: regular, high output (HO), and very high output (VHO) formats. The HO and VHO types require special ballasts, end caps, holders, and fixture pins. Their popularity is due to greater luminosity—a regular 48-inch fluorescent bulb has 40 watts of power; HO has 60 watts; and VHO can range from 110 to 160 watts. Respective luminosities (initially) are 2000 to 3000 lumens for a regular fluorescent and up to 9000 for HO and VHO, depending on wattage and make.

Many marine aquarists have found they like the effect of adding 03 actinic, or blue actinic, fluorescent lighting to their systems. These bulbs tend to bring out the fluorescent greens and blues of fishes and corals, and they do work well as gentle lighting during dawn and dusk periods in systems that have the timers (and the number of different, separately wired bulbs) to accomplish this. Keep in mind, however, that full-spectrum lights still provide the most biologically effective lighting power, and the actinics may be doing more for your eyes than for your specimens. A generally accepted recommendation is one blue actinic bulb in combination with three full-spectrum fluorescents.

A ballast is a device used to provide the starting voltage and to stabilize the current for fluorescent and metal halide lights. For all types of fluorescents, there are now electronic ballasts on the market that aquarists all ought to use. These modern marvels run much cooler than old-style tar ballasts and extend lamp life, discount phase shift (a change in the color of light emitted over time), save electricity, and reduce waste heat production. You can also set them up on dimmer controls to simulate dawn and twilight. Electronic ballasts can also save money on high-heat end caps and lamp holders.

Bulb life for regular full-spectrum fluorescent lamps is approximately 15,000 to 20,000 hours, but due to phase shift and lumen depreciation, bulbs should be replaced every year or so. With electronic ballasts, HO and VHO bulbs can last 9 to 12 months, although some aquarists keeping stony corals advocate more frequent changes. Make notes in your aquarium logbook or label all bulbs with an indelible marker on insertion and rotate them out on a periodic basis. (As new bulbs are much stronger than old ones, it is easy to shock invertebrates by changing all the bulbs at once.)

Various writers have cited measurements of incidental insolation (sunlight) taken around the world's reefs. Often, these quanta are taken above or just below the ocean's surface on days when it is calm and clear. I have traveled and written for the sport-diving industry and consumer magazines for over 20 years and can testify that there are many days when the water where corals and giant clams are found is neither still nor very transparent; not the 100,000 lux (lumens per square meter) reported and consequently provided by some marine aquarists. I question the wisdom of attempting to duplicate these maximum lighting conditions for 12 hours a day, day in and day out. Newer switching devices for sophisticated reef tanks are beginning to make allowances for cloudy periods.

For the newcomer to marine aquariums, the general rule of thumb for lighting wattages over tanks with some macroalgae and hardy invertebrates is to provide 3 to 5 watts per gallon. Thus, a typical 50-gallon tank would need a minimum of 150 to 250 watts of lighting; this is the equivalent of four to six 48-inch fluorescent tubes of normal output. For reef aquariums with photosynthetic corals, total wattage required per gallon rises to the 7 to 10 range—or higher—and HO, VHO, compact fluorescents, or metal halide

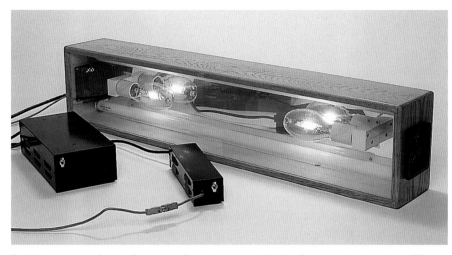

The lighting system of choice for many reef aquarists: two actinic-blue fluorescent bulbs and two 175-watt full-spectrum metal halides in a fan-cooled enclosure with an acrylic UV shield and remote ballasts.

lamps are virtually a must to deliver this amount of light in the confines of an aquarium hood.

Metal halide lamps have a mixed reputation among users, especially for reef systems. Various explanations for the poor results some people have had include improper bulb choice and poor positioning, shielding, or specimen placement. All can cause real problems.

Consider this typical scenario: a well-intentioned hobbyist removes an underpowered fluorescent light fixture, probably with fading old tubes, and installs a blazingly bright metal halide unit over the tank. Specimens that have become accustomed to relatively dim lighting may go into shock and never recover. Water temperature may soar, further complicating the problem. Others whose nitrate and dissolved organic loads are already excessive may see algae blooms beyond their wildest nightmares.

I have long cautioned people on the proper utilization of these "sun replicators." They are not cheap to acquire or energize and can be difficult for inexperienced aquarium owners to manage in terms of waste heat and ultraviolet light production.

Despite all their potential and actual pitfalls, metal halides are here to stay. They do produce great quantities of lumens and a gorgeous "shimmering" appearance underwater. Used properly by themselves, or in concert with fluorescents, they are the closest mimics of natural lighting for captive systems. Today, several well-established manufacturers offer properly designed, well-ventilated, and generally trouble-free metal halide systems. Most of these combine both metal halide and fluorescent bulbs, independently wired. By placing separate timers on the two circuits, the fluorescents can be made to come on earlier and stay on later than

the metal halides. This provides the aquarium with the simulation of a dawn and dusk period, along with a major midday lighting session with all lamps lit.

With better equipment easily available, many of the early horror stories about metal halides may fade. Newer, cooler-operating versions are also appearing, including revolutionary electronic ballast models. I expect these will prove to be a real advance for reef hobbyists, giving them safer, cooler, more efficient sources of intense lighting.

Be wary of quartz-halogen and other halides that have color temperatures of 5000 K or less. Units advertised for hydroponic growing or indoor gardening come with bulbs that are deficient in necessary blue-end spectra. The widely accepted standard for reef aquarium lighting is a Kelvin rating of 5500 to 6500 K, and even these bulbs are usually supplemented with blue actinic 03 or equivalent blue-spectrum fluorescents.

A new generation of bulbs rated at 10,000 and 20,000 K is being offered by at least one American company and by importers of European lighting systems. These have received rave reviews from some reef veterans and poor ratings from others. The light is described as either "very blue" or "brilliant white." Significant differences in performances have been noted between different brands of these newer bulbs, and I urge you to do some research before deciding on the bulbs for your system. When investing in a state-of-the-art reef

Metal halide bulbs, ranging widely in shape, size, and output, yield the most intense practical light for the home reef.

Simple and attractive with a remote ballast unit, a single-bulb metal halide offers intense lighting with good heat diffusion.

lighting system, ask people you trust, read the serious hobbyist magazines, and check the aquarium bulletin boards on the Internet for the latest favorites and current recommendations. If possible, seek out systems using the actual bulbs you are considering. If still in doubt, remember that full-spectrum lighting is the eternal standby and reliable starting point.

The most common ratings of metal halide bulbs for aquarium use are 175-watt, 250-watt and 400-watt, with some coral growers even running 1000-watt units over large home systems. Bulb life for metal halides is somewhere between 10,000 and 20,000 hours, but to replace their gradual loss of spectral integrity and brightness, they should be switched out at least once a year (or per the manufacturer's recommendations). **Placement of fixtures** is crucial and is a matter of experimentation. It is desirable to locate the lamps as close as is practical to the water's surface to max-imize light penetration and to reduce diffusion and reflection. However, depending on wattage, your water may overheat quickly, requiring countervailing equipment such as water chillers and/or fans to whisk away the heat. In most situations, the bulbs should be from 4 to 12 inches above the water's surface. Again, always check and abide by the specifications and recommendations of the manufacturers.

Shielding is important in thermal terms—not allowing the bulbs to set the hood afire. Also of concern is the production of life-damaging ultraviolet (UV) light. UV light is classified into three types on the basis of wavelength. In nanometers (nm) these are:

UV-A: 320-400 nm
UV-B: 280-320 nm
UV-C: 200-280 nm

Some UV-A is useful and is necessary for some light-using life; B and C are dangerous and/or harmful. UV-C is absorbed by the planet's ozone layer; within this band, 257 nm is the energy produced by UV sterilizers. UV-B can be screened out by glass and water; it is very destructive to life and photosynthetic activity. UV-A is effectively filtered out by special filters and bulb coatings provided by manufacturers.

I install and recommend metal halides only when they are to be used with UV filters, even though the glass sleeve of the bulbs may be coated or engineered to be used without them. Added protection against radiation poisoning may require more shielding action—usually just a thin, clear acrylic sheet—and periodic cleaning, but it is well worth the peace of mind in possibly preventing you and your livestock from damaging UV wavelengths.

These "high-pressure" light sources are also known to explode from time to time—sometimes spontaneously and sometimes after getting splashed by cool water or drenched by cumulative bubble-mist buildup. Do as the hood manufacturers recommend—keep the UV shield in place.

Specimen placement in relation to lights is a concern principally with reef-building corals. This sensitive tissue-grade life is easily overly illuminated by the "supernova" equipped aquarist. Without traveling to the specific localities to assess what sort of light conditions your aquarium specimens may have been living under in the wild, it is hard to duplicate them. Reasonable accommodation is best achieved by starting newcomers at the deepest, shaded areas of the system and slowly (over a period of days or weeks) moving them upward to a lighting level where they seem to flourish best. Check the available reference works that describe natural habitats for given genera and species to see if you can ferret out information about your specimen's preferred light levels.

Other aspects of biology are important to be aware of when using metal halides, because of their reputation for "burning" specimens. This typically occurs immediately after a change—to a new metal halide system, to fresh bulbs, or just after moving a new animal into the tank or up close to the lights. Many reef keepers have also reported sudden setbacks of corals after introducing activated carbon to their filtration system; the carbon can rapidly remove dissolved organic pigments, dramatically increasing the clarity and light transmittance of the aquarium water and shocking some specimens. It is not true "burning," but rather oxygen poisoning brought on by suddenly increased photosynthesis by the zooxanthellae found in the tissues of many corals and clams. In nature, cloudy periods, waves, and surface rippling all work to vary the intensity of sunlight blazing down on shallow-water invertebrates. But most aquariums have a steady intensity of light, and this can be too much for some animals. Always introduce new lights carefully. They can be raised up and then gradually lowered over a period of a week or more, or they can start out with shorter periods of full power. New specimens should never be placed high in the tank immediately upon arrival.

High pH is another problem that may arise in brightly lit systems, and can be countered with the use of buffers (calcareous water/Kalkwasser, et al.) and/or CO_2 infusion with a meter and doser. Efficient skimming and plentiful live rock also help. Flooding your system with intense light will do you no good, indeed very likely will work against you, if you are unwilling to balance its effects.

Be watchful with whatever new lighting array you choose—both higher output fluorescents and metal halides can quickly overheat a system. Aquariums with tight-fitting hoods and intense lighting often require chillers to prevent temperatures from vacillating wildly or exceeding 84 degrees F. In general, the closer the bulbs are to the water's surface and the poorer the air circulation is through the hood, the greater the possibility of overheating.

Hoods and Reflectors

WHETHER THEY ARE BOX, PENDANT, hanging, or side-angled, the fixture containing your lights must be shielded against the effects of heat and salt splash, have an internal reflective surface, and be composed of materials that will not rot. The external housing may be solid wood, acrylic, or aluminum—all are acceptable and the choice will come down to aesthetics and price. However, the interior lining or reflector material can make a big difference in the amount of light that actually reaches your specimens. Bright, polished aluminum and bright-white-painted sheet metal all provide enhanced reflectance. The poorest choice is a simple box with no reflective material whatsoever. To retrofit a cheap or older hood or make your own, there are stock and after-market sheets and coatings that will redirect the light energy down into the system. Even the highly reflective wide aluminum tape sold in most hardware stores has found its way into many aquarists' older lighting hoods, and it seems to work well. As well, some manufacturers now offer bulbs with built-in reflective coatings.

Light Duration and Timers

PHOTOPERIODICITY, also known as the light-dark cycle, is the amount of time each day that the aquarium lights are on and off. Most photosynthetic organisms used in marine aquariums originate in the Tropics, where day lengths don't vary much during the year. Within reason, 12 to 14 light-

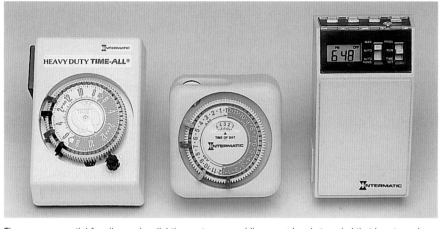

Timers are essential for all aquarium lighting systems, providing a regular photoperiod that is extremely important to the well-being of aquatic life. Simple household timing devices are sufficient for most lights.

hour days are optimum, especially if your quantity of light is on the low side. This is best determined by knowing what healthy specimens look like when provided with adequate lighting.

The regularity of the photoperiod can be very meaningful. Experiments have shown that continuous long dark or light periods (lasting 1 to 2 days) severely affect aquatic life, photosynthetic and otherwise. Unless you are always home and absolutely religious about turning your lights on and off at the same times each day, your fishes and invertebrates will be better adjusted and healthier if you have a simple timer controlling their day length. These timers can be found at any hardware store, and many reef aquarists use two or more of them to simulate pale blue dawn and dusk periods each day, with more intense, full-spectrum light during the midday. Here is one simplified schedule, adjusted for human viewing in the evening:

Lamp Type	Time On	Time Off
Actinic 03s	12 P.M.	2 A.M.
Full-Spectrum Fluorescents *or* Metal Halides	1 P.M.	1 A.M.

Some reef systems have a noon peak of bright metal halide lighting that runs for 4 hours or less; others have begun using computerized controllers to simulate the phases of the Moon and the seasons.

Even the simplest timers are great. (Just be sure you have fixtures with self-starting features.) Some scientific aquaculture laboratories even go so far as to utilize polarized light and lighting fixtures that travel overhead in an arc in an attempt to copy nature more fully. Rotating and moving metal halide light fixtures are even becoming available to well-heeled aquarium hobbyists by mail-order from some greenhouse lighting suppliers.

Electricity

WHILE ELECTRICAL DEVICES have helped revolutionize marine aquarium keeping, with greatly improved lighting, circulation, and power filtration, electricity can also be a serious hazard in this hobby. Because we are so accustomed to electricity being at our whim and will, there is a danger of complacency. Lights, heaters, pumps, meters, ozonizers, ultraviolet sterilizers, and their wiring and plug connections are all potential sources of electrical leaking, shorts, and shocks. Folk wisdom is correct on both counts: "Water and electricity do not mix," and "Water and electricity mix all too well."

Water can get around insulators through condensation and failures in the insulators themselves (wiring, plugs, fixtures). You may feel the degree of leaking as anything from "tingling" to an alarming shock. The negative effects on livestock of small stray voltages are an area of controversy, but it is certain that stray electricity is not good for you or your marine life. It has been implicated in lateral line disease, erratic livestock behavior, and death. There are devices sold that measure or effectively "drain" off errant electrons. Some of these are far better than others.

Shorts are the result of a loss of insulation. A short circuit fully electrifies some unintended part. That full potential current then may use your body to complete its circuit to the ground, resulting in severe shock or electrocution. How many ways can this happen? Abraded wiring, a light fixture falling into a tank, a cracked light socket, a split UV sterilizer lamp, broken glass on a heater, saltwater dripping onto or creating a salt bridge into an extension or multiple-outlet device—these kinds of problems result in serious accidents in our hobby several times a year.

Avoiding Electrical Hazards

Examine cords, plugs, and outlets every time you work on your system. Wearing insulating shoes and standing on a dry floor any time you have your hands in the water is a very good idea.

Create drip loops in any wiring or flexible tubing that services the system. This simple procedure will go a long way toward keeping saltwater out of appliances and outlets. Just coil and tie up (with plastic ties) a loop or more from each electrical cord and length of tubing (see illustration, page 60). Water will follow the line down to your loop and make a neat stalactite at the bottom of the coil. The drip will happen there, instead of where you don't want it (in plugs, electrical cord insertions, and pumps). This low-technology procedure really works.

Mount electrical outlet "power bars" and extension cords up off the floor, either on a vertical surface or upside down, away from places where saltwater can fall or splash into them. For 18 years, I was part owner of a company that specialized in ornamental aquatic work. Our service division designed, built, installed, and maintained liveholding systems, mainly large marine aquariums, in commercial and wealthy residential settings. We discovered not only that aquarium wiring can cause fires, but that such accidents were common enough in California that we developed a sideline business investigating and testifying about aquarium electrical failures.

Pull the plug on heaters every time you're going to do anything with the water level. The heater's glass housing can shatter in an instant if it is removed from the water while hot or plugged in while dry and then plunged into the tank.

Be aware that Styrofoam and acrylic have low flash points and are relatively flammable. Store Styrofoam boxes away from potentially overheating electrical wiring, pumps, and acrylic. Be especially wary of older, tar-type ballasts (wattage transformers) used with most fluorescent lighting and UV sterilizers. They get too hot to run in closed spaces or on acrylic surfaces.

If you can, avoid using extension cords altogether, and never plug one into another. If you are installing heavy-duty pumps, chillers, or lighting, consult an electrician or learn what the A.W.G. symbols for wire gauge really mean in terms of rating, load, and run (length).

To check for suspected gross electrical leaks, buy a cheap but useful test lamp device. It makes a good addition to any aquarist's tool box.

Install and maintain gear according to the manufacturer specifications. This may seem obvious, but it is surprising how often these specifications are ignored.

Use a ground fault interrupter (GFI). This technology is so readily available, easy-to-use, and inexpensive that I believe its use should be mandatory with every aquarium (see page 60). If you embrace nothing else from my advice, at least get and use GFIs. About 95% of all home electrical injuries, including about 1,000 electrocutions a year in the U.S., are caused by ground faults. These are avoidable with GFI-protected circuits.

Electrical Costs

EFFICIENCY IS AN IMPORTANT consideration in this world of high electrical costs. There is a huge variance in electrical consumption versus relative light produced and air and water moved. To figure out how efficient your devices are, remember:

volts x amps = watts

You pay by the kilowatt hour, the equivalent of 1000 watts used for a period of one hour's time. Therefore:

watts/1000 x number of hours on
x electrical rate = cost per day

Are you confused? Do you have concerns about the efficiency and adequacy of your aquatic electrical wiring? Good—call your local utility. Most of them will send out a service person for free to check out your arrangement, explain how to figure your costs, and give suggestions on how to reduce costs and prevent loss of life and property. This is a step well worth taking.

Ground Fault Interrupters: Please Use Them

Within the aquarium hobby, there are continual incidents of electrical shock that could have been avoided with a simple and inexpensive piece of technology. At the same time, newcomers to the hobby should know that, sooner or later, every aquarium system will have a heater, pump, or lighting fixture short or start leaking voltage. You will get shocked, perhaps severely, unless you protect yourself and everyone else who comes in contact with your aquarium.

A ground fault interrupter (GFI) is an electronic electron counter. It is a device that measures the amperes (numbers of electrons) traveling through a circuit, and quickly opens (breaks) the circuit if there is a small loss, or ground fault, such as a "brown-out" or shock to you or your livestock. These units are solid-state, rugged, and, yes, they do work. A circuit breaker alone will not necessarily "trip" open in the event of a ground fault, even in a case of gross electrocution. A ground fault interrupter will.

GFIs come in three general formats: breakers, duplex outlets, and plug-ins. All three work in the same basic way, and equally well.

Breakers mount and function in the same way as super-sensitive circuit breakers. These are useful in the panel of your house where all potentially deadly circuits (bathroom, kitchen, outdoor, pool, and aquarium) are wired. Their downsides are that they are expensive to buy and install and that hunting down the

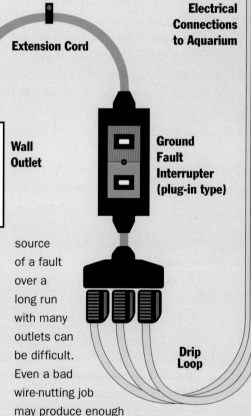

Extension Cord

Wall Outlet

Electrical Connections to Aquarium

Ground Fault Interrupter (plug-in type)

Drip Loop

source of a fault over a long run with many outlets can be difficult. Even a bad wire-nutting job may produce enough electron drift to trip a GFI.

Duplex outlets are useful for in-line protection in the same way as

circuit-breaker types, but are considerably cheaper. In addition, they offer the advantage of providing two additional protected outlets and an emergency on/off switch via the test-reset buttons.

Plug-ins come as hard-wired outlets with their own extension cords and/or as devices that push into otherwise non-GFI-protected outlets. You simply plug right into these GFI outlets—there is no wiring or installation required. These types of GFIs are worth every penny and are also very useful for plugging in power tools, such as mobile tank-cleaning systems.

By purchasing GFIs, you are purchasing peace of mind. With them, you will have virtual immunity from disastrous electrical leaks, shocks, and electrical fires. Electrical leakage can be a major stressor on tank inhabitants, and the potential for serious shock to the aquarist is a real hazard. Please don't wait. Install ground fault interrupters now.

Circulation and Filtration

WATER MOVEMENT is a crucial factor in almost every marine aquarium system as a method of removing, handling, and detoxifying wastes from fishes, invertebrates, and the remains of uneaten foods.

The next chapter covers the many circulation and filtration options, which range from the very simple and reliable to the new and experimental. At the very minimum, you will need an air or water pump, and most aquarists will want to select one or more filtration devices.

Temperature Control

CAN YOU NAME the one substance in all of the universe that can absorb or release the most thermal energy? The an-

Aquarists have many choices when selecting an external pump, which should be rated to turn over the entire water volume of the system at least five times per hour and should be quiet and energy-efficient.

swer, of course, is water, and managing its temperature is a basic part of keeping a healthy aquarium.

Most tropical marine systems and organisms do best between 74 and 80 degrees F, optimally around 75 degrees F for most. The real key to successful marine aquarium keeping in terms of temperature is stability. Ocean life enjoys a natural environment that not only varies little thermally, but if thermal gradients do occur, many organisms can change their locations. Such is not the case in our tiny captive volumes. Attached or sedentary organisms are especially vulnerable to large and/or rapid changes in temperature. In the aquarium, brief forays slightly

above 84 degrees F or below 68 degrees F are generally not disastrous if they occur gradually and all else is well—but they are to be avoided.

The expense to heat and/or cool marine systems can sometimes be substantial. Specialty lighting and fluid-moving pump costs are often large as well, and the waste heat they add to a system also figures into the temperature-control equation. A conscientious marine aquarist will take care to do all he or she can to reduce temperature fluctuation and cost of thermal maintenance. In this effort, system construction, size, shape, placement, and insulation are all key elements.

Tank (and possibly sump) construction, as well as size and shape, are all important. Acrylic is about five times better in thermal insulation property than glass. Bigger is also better; larger volumes contain more heat energy and are therefore more stable. Additionally, big tanks have thicker-walled panels that are better insulators.

Tank placement is also a factor.

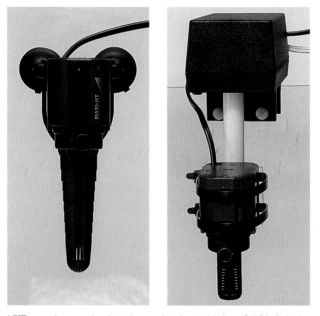

LEFT: even inexpensive, in-tank powerheads provide beneficial turbulence and circulation. RIGHT: sweeping currents are created by rotating powerheads, which direct the water flow 90 degrees back and forth.

Don't locate your tanks in direct sunlight or against outside walls. I've seen tanks significantly heated and cooled by exterior walls, as well as by the more obvious doors, windows, and heating ducts.

Heat loss by evaporation can be dramatic. The most heat leaving your system may well be from the partly or totally uncovered aquarium and/or sump surface. If you're losing water, you're losing thermal energy.

Lighting and pumps can also add enough heat to disrupt a system. Consider turning on your hottest lighting in the evenings when ambient temperatures are cooler (when you schedule day and night light cycles for your aquarium does not matter to your livestock).

Heaters

ALTHOUGH there are quartz heaters, hot air injection heaters, in/under tank-pad heaters, and many more, most hobbyists will use glass-walled electrical-resistant heaters. These popular, modern devices are comprised of a printed circuit board, heating wire, thermostat, and indicator light housed in a heat-resistant glass tube.

Never take a chance with cheap heaters. Thin-walled, reception-interfering, thermostat-sticking units have wiped out thousands of tanks, zapped millions of fishes—even killed hobbyists . . . and they're still on the market. There are some acceptable external heaters, but the safest approach is to stick to submersible heaters. These are inherently better because of their sealed components and ability to be placed low(er) in the system—warm water, like warm air, rises.

To be safe, it's always better to buy two small heaters rather than one large unit. For example, say you have a 50-gallon tank in a very cold climate and decide you want 300 watts of heating capacity; you should get two 150-watt heaters. The rationale for this is simple: it's easier to place them at opposite ends of the system and effect more uniform heating. Also, if you intend to utilize a heater chamber or a sump, put at least half of your heating capacity in the system tank. If you have two heaters and one

fails, you won't be without heat entirely until it can be replaced.

Heaters do break—I have broken many of them myself. Some were lifted out while hot, others were left exposed when I dropped the water level without unplugging them, still others were immersed in cold water when hot. Learn from my errors. Put glass heaters low (but not under gravel) where they won't be disturbed by shifting rock or damaged by big livestock. Post a reminder note above your system: "Unplug Heaters Before Working on Tank."

Chillers

A WATER-COOLING MECHANISM IS necessary for consistently cold water and for tropical systems that seasonally get to more than 84 degrees F. Most simple marine aquariums can get by without a chiller, but the addition of intense lighting in enclosed hoods will often dictate the need for a water-cooling system.

Aquarium chillers are like miniature refrigerators, capitalizing on the heat lost in the controlled phase change of a refrigerant. The water from the aquarium is typically pumped from the sump through a compact chiller unit, which can be located near the tank or placed in a remote location, such as a basement or storage room. (Like air conditioners, chillers create heat and are somewhat noisy.) With drop-in-type chiller models, an immersion coil connected by a semi-flexible pipe to the chiller is placed in the system sump or

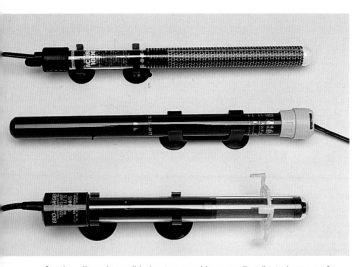

Good quality submersible heaters provide an easily adjusted source of warmth; a total of 3 watts per gallon of system water is recommended.

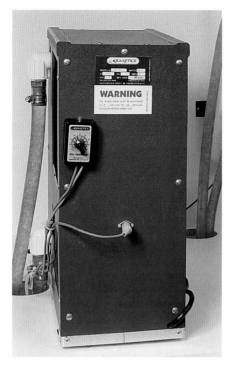

A chiller may be needed when hot lights or ambient temperatures tend to overheat a tank—with 80 to 84 degrees F often considered a safe upper limit.

in a water-filled heat exchanger tank that serves as a cold sink, through which system water is also circulated in a coiled hose or PVC piping.

A chiller is a major purchase, and you are well advised to do some research before buying. Talk to other hobbyists and/or a dealer you trust. You will have to match the capacity of the chiller to the size of your system, as well as the maximum anticipated temperature "pull down" you will need. (For example, consider a glass, uninsulated 100-gallon tank with a 25-gallon sump that could reach 95 degrees F during peak summer heating season. You don't want the temperature to exceed 80 de-grees, so a 15-degree pull down will be used to arrive at a suitable chiller model. Consulting a dealer or reference will inform you that a ⅙ hp chiller is too small and the next size, ⅕ hp, is adequate with some capacity to spare. Other factors may need to be considered, such as your system plumbing configuration, and expert advice should be sought.)

Choose carefully, and beware of low-budget chillers. In my extensive (and expensive) firsthand experience, the Teflon-coated, copper-bearing chiller units too often suffer some kind of user or manufacturer failure. The Teflon gets nicked, a weld wasn't properly done, or some unforeseen problem leads to the system getting poisoned with copper. I'll vouch for titanium heat exchangers, with water pumped through the chiller's own heat exchanger. Ask around and you will hear many, many horror stories about drop-in coils.

The range in quality, efficiency, and average useful lifespan of aquarium chillers is huge. Get literature from several companies and talk with people who are familiar with their chillers.

Thermometers

FLOATING, HANGING, STANDING, liquid-crystal stick-on types, and even electronic units with digital displays—all kinds of thermometers are available, costing from a dollar to hundreds of dollars and all fine for hobbyist use. As fancy as the digital units are, you really don't need a meter or a high-tech ther-mocouple to be a good aquarist.

The less expensive thermometers may vary by a few degrees, but it really doesn't matter in most instances. All you're really interested in is that the reading is about the same every time. There is one category of exception to this carefree attitude: every year I see livestock, and sometimes whole systems, lost from "thermometer poisoning." It's not from the red-colored alcohol or silver mercury getting into the tank, but from metal on the thermometers themselves. Never put metal thermometers into your system.

Add a column for temperature in your aquarium logbook. Get at least two thermometers, three if you have a filter sump, and place them in the water where you can read them at a glance. Check all three daily and keep a written record. When your favorite blenny dies or your giant clam spews forth eggs and milt, someone will want to know the temperature.

Because our livestock are poikilo-thermic (cool/cold-blooded), and their metabolisms are tightly bound by the temperature of their environment, it is vitally important that the temperature of their water not change much day to day. Changes of more than 1 degree F a day are rare in large bodies of water like the world's oceans. Thermal stress is all too often a starting point for the weakening of captive livestock, leading to death from other, secondary causes. Careful attention to temperature control is vital to success in maintaining a healthy marine system.

CHAPTER 3

Filtration

Through the Technology Maze to Sparkling Water and Vibrant Aquariums

I F ANY AREA OF AQUARIUM keeping can overwhelm, befuddle, perplex, and discourage a newcomer, filtration is it. One look around a pet shop or a quick flip through any of the major aquarium periodicals will make it all too obvious—here is a wonderland of competing filter products, each with bold claims telling you why it happens to be best. The choices that confront us all (even aquatic veterans continue to be amazed by the never ending output of this inventors' playground) often convince many beginners that they are sure to make an inferior, or incorrect, choice.

Happily, there are some relatively simple, time-tested solutions. People in North America and Europe have been keeping marine aquariums since the 1950s with little more than the

Huge volumes of water and complex webs of life tend to erase the problems of fish waste in nature; the aquarist must devise other filtering methods.

classic—and still worthy—undergravel filter. As we shall see, it may not be state-of-the-art, but it can still get you both simply and inexpensively into the world of marine aquariums. Please don't jump to the conclusion that you have to be an engineer or biochemist to understand aquarium filtration. You can make it as cheap and simple, or as pricey and complicated, as your heart desires.

First, a truism: In most ways, the quality of the seawater in an aquarium decreases with age. It gains biological wastes and by-products, is diminished in its buffering capacity and pH, loses its essential trace materials, and slowly degenerates in various other measures of water quality.

This is not the end of the world. Despite what you've been led to believe, the ocean's reefs are neither absolutely pristine nor immutable. Compared to most freshwater ecosystems, the normal annual range of variations in water

The trend in large reef aquariums today is toward vigorous water flow, with plumbing and pumps able to move up to 20 times the tank volume per hour.

measurements is much tighter on coral reefs, but reef inhabitants do have a tolerance for different parameters. As in freshwater systems, your first goal is to arrange for a healthy starting water chemistry and to prevent quick and drastic changes. After that, you must contend with the more subtle problems brought on by slowly declining water quality.

Removing organics in the form of nitrogenous wastes (ammonia, nitrites, nitrates), phenols, scatols, and other pollutants—both seen and unseen—is the principal goal of filtration. You might ask, "Why don't you see all this filter gear on the reefs in the wild?" Actually, you do. Next time you're underwater, take a look. There really is a lot of water per unit of livestock, and plenty of circulation and aeration coming from wave action and the tides. Notice the predominant forms of life around you—corals, sponges, and bivalves of all sorts. What mode of food gathering do they employ? They're mainly filter feeders, sieving out plankton, gametes, wastes, and suspended inorganic material. These filter feeders are one reason the water is so clear. Stuck in and among these life forms are algae—some obvious, others microscopic, still others living within the tissues of certain reef invertebrates—absorbing nutrients and making fixed carbon and oxygen through photosynthesis.

Now consider the environment in a typical marine tank setup—a small water volume with a lot of fish, happily overfed, and few, if any, plants or filter feeders. No wonder there is a continual battle to limit the buildup of their waste and a constant quest to build a better filter.

We typically think of four types of filtration as appropriate for home aquariums: mechanical, chemical, biological, and physical. Mechanical filtration removes undissolved particulate matter from the aquarium water by trapping debris in sand or polyester pads, for example. In chemical filtration, dissolved pollutants are removed from the water by absorption, adsorption, or ion exchange. The most common example is the use of activated carbon (sometimes known as aquarium charcoal) to extract molecules of dissolved organic wastes. Biological filtra-

> "Removing organics in the form of nitrogenous wastes (ammonia, nitrites, nitrates), phenols, scatols, and other pollutants—both seen and unseen—is the principal goal of filtration."

tion occurs when beneficial bacteria transform toxic nitrogenous wastes into less toxic forms. Physical filtration, for our purposes, will encompass the use of protein skimmers, ozonizers, and ultraviolet (UV) sterilization units.

As we will see, many types of commonly available aquarium filters combine mechanical, chemical and biological filtration in the same unit or assemblage of components. Protein skimming may be incorporated as well, while the use of ozone and UV sterilization are generally found only in more advanced systems. Unlike the saltwater pioneers of a generation ago, we have an unprecedented arsenal today of filtration tools that can maintain water quality—and the health of our fishes and invertebrates—as never before.

Undergravel Filters

THE ORIGINAL CAPTIVE marine systems were "semi-open" (versus closed), with their administrators constantly pouring in new water, taking out the old, and hoping and praying their thinly stocked charges would survive another day. In reality, marine livestock in those early decades was generally highly perishable, its needs poorly understood, and both fishes and corals were regularly replaced as they failed to survive.

Starting in the middle of the twentieth century, Robert P.L. Straughan and others popularized the use of undergravel plates, which allowed the water in an aquarium to be drawn constantly through a bed of calcareous gravel. The original undergravel filters did a fine job of clearing the water, and the fishes had better survival rates. The filters worked, although it wasn't really clear why they did. Now we understand that beneficial bacteria colonize and thrive in the crushed coral with a steady supply of chemical food (ammonia, nitrite, oxygen, and CO_2 as a source of carbon) flowing conveniently through their attachment sites in the porous substrate. Even today, with the advent

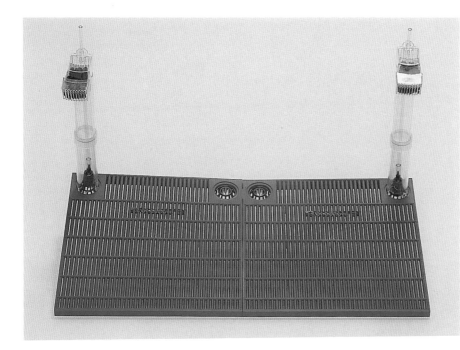

A simple, inexpensive undergravel filter is still an acceptable biological filter for many beginning marine aquarists, but its success depends on periodic maintenance and additional sources of water movement.

of many more sophisticated and costly filtration systems, undergravel filtration remains a widely used, acceptable method of boosting biological filtration, especially for fish-only aquariums. I start with this method as an approach that any beginner can understand and use—and any frustrated aquarist can come back to for a fresh start.

All closed systems need a biological filter as large and efficient as possible or practical in order to mineralize wastes into nontoxic nutrients, while providing for minimal changes in water composition—in particular, pH should remain stable. Aside from a pump or airstone to create circulation, all other filtration gear must be regarded as secondary in importance to the equipment (or natural materials) you use to encourage biological filtration. Undergravel filters are an almost surefire route to ensuring ample biological filtration in any aquarium, while the coral sand or gravel, which slowly dissolves over time, plays an important role in buffering pH shifts.

In an undergravel filter, simple plastic plates, commercial or homemade, are used to suspend a bed of calcareous gravel above the bottom of the tank and to allow a continuous, even flow of water through the whole expanse of sand. Power is provided either by air or water pumps that either push or pull the aquarium water slowly through the substrate. There is nothing wrong with old-style airstone-driven systems that are commonly sold with "starter kit" aquarium packages. These can move an acceptable volume of water, with the added benefit of increased gaseous diffusion, and they do not add waste heat. Airstones, in fact, are the lowest-cost provider of water movement—this is the inexpensive technology that has launched millions of beginning aquarium keepers.

For anyone wanting to upgrade a basic undergravel filter, I would like to recommend arranging the water flow in reverse. The most common method of accomplishing this is to employ reverse-flow powerheads to pump the system's water down under the plate, and then up through the substrate. Typically, these powerheads have foam particulate filter sponges to screen gross debris before it reaches the pump. In reverse-flow undergravel filters, the particulates end up in the easily cleanable intake screens and sponges rather than in the sand. (These must be rinsed regularly or the efficiency of the pump will be severely diminished.) This is more beneficial than the common top-down flow for most marine scenarios. The advantages include the ease of cleaning the accumulated detritus, the lack of compaction of the sand bed, and the avoidance of messy rooting problems caused by livestock digging in a debris-filled sand bed.

Standard, positive-flow undergravel filters are also fine, but they require more periodic cleaning (stirring, vacuuming of the sand) to keep them clear and unclogged. This type of undergravel filter also serves a mechanical cleaning function. Debris is quickly trapped here, provided that the depth of the sand bed, the gravel size, grating, and water-flow rate are reasonably matched. Some sort of periodic removal of this detritus is mandatory. Usually only half of the gravel bed is disturbed during a cleaning session, so as not to disrupt the beneficial bacteria colonies in the other half. Unless properly maintained, an undergravel filter will become so filled with detritus that water flow is severely impeded; oxygen content in the tank may fall, while dissolved organic compounds and phosphate will increase.

Another drawback to relying on an undergravel filter as the sole filter on a marine tank is a lack of sufficient water movement. Whether driven by air or typical powerheads, an undergravel filter simply does not create the currents needed in most marine aquariums. However, by adding a small powerhead (for circulation only), an external power filter, or additional airstones to create water currents, the aquarist can turn an undergravel system into a viable choice for simple or starter marine aquariums.

Internal Filters

LAUGH IF YOU WILL, you old-timer freshwater aquarists. The humble, air-driven sponge and internal box filters still rank high as bacterial havens for new systems and quarantine, or hospital, tanks. They are inexpensive, they endure changes (such as moving) and

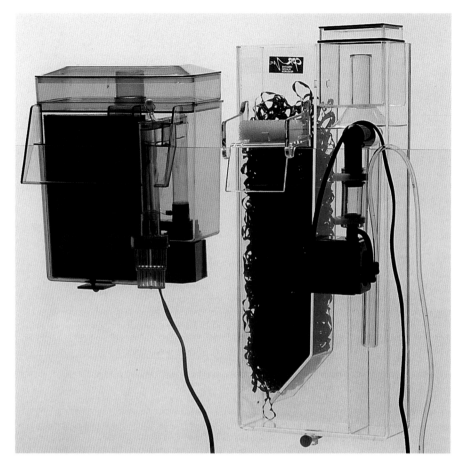

Hang-on-the-tank external power filters can provide smaller systems with physical, chemical, and limited biological filtration in a single convenient unit. These models both include integrated protein skimmers.

won't alter your water chemistry during treatments.

Newer power units meant to be submerged in the tank come in all forms and sizes—from simple and tiny to complex and bulky—and with all of the media types found in outside filters (cartridge, sponge, pad, and wet-dry). They have the obvious advantage of not leaking or fighting the effects of gravity to circulate water. Many of these internal units are well-made and do a very good job as additional or alternate fil-

ter systems. As an additional plus, an internal submersible power filter may be easily moved from an older aquarium to establish nutrient cycling in a new one, or help out in an emergency, hospital, or quarantine tank.

These submersible filters generally have very limited space for filtration media, but the major downside—and this can be a big one for many—is their obtrusive appearance. In very small systems, some submersible power units can also cause problems with waste-heat generation. As always, watch your thermometer when setting up a new system or adding new heat-generating components.

External Power Filters

BABY BOOMERS and other older aquarists may remember the bubbling air-driven outside box filters, packed with glass wool and charcoal, of decades past. These can still be found, but we must dismiss them out of hand, due to their low flow rates and other inherent maintenance demands. They are still reliable and appropriate technology for some types of small freshwater systems, but too underpowered for marine use.

The external power filter, however, is alive and well. The once-ubiquitous air pump used to run these affordable aquarium filters has largely been replaced by small, sealed, magnetic-drive motors. These units have revolutionized aquarium filtration by inexpensively providing good flow rates of system water, in some cases with substantial pressures. External power filters draw water out of the tank, run it through some sort of particulate filter medium, pass it through activated carbon (or other medium of your choice), and shoot the cleaned water back into the aquarium. Most provide beneficial circulation to the tank as well as agitating the surface. Some of the larger models can accommodate substantial systems, and there is nothing wrong with utilizing more than one or using an external power filter in combination with an undergravel unit or a small

skimmer. Some power filters, both hang-on-the-tank and canister-type, now contain porous media or special plastic plates to harbor bacteria and serve a biological filter function. In addition to speeding and stabilizing nitrogen cycling and biological filtration, these workhorses are great mechanical filters and water circulators for smaller systems. They can be easily outfitted with chemical filtrants, such as activated carbon. I strongly encourage the use of a power filter in conjunction with any undergravel filter, along with a protein skimmer, even for the simplest of marine systems. (Take care to not change all the media in power filters at once or wash any such bacterial grid plates in freshwater.)

Models that hang on the back of the tank have the advantage of being open and easily accessible, and some newer models provide impressive performance in a compact unit that easily hides behind the aquarium.

Canister filters are often sold by many dealers as the next step up and as being superior to in-tank and hang-on-the-back filters for several reasons. They can be placed below or slightly away from the aquarium itself; they typically have far more filter surface area and greater flow rates; and they are easy to set up, without the custom plumbing required by other beneath-the-tank systems.

Bigger and better canister filters continue to be invented, but be wary of simply swallowing the claims and performance of any one model or brand.

Personal endorsements by aquarist friends or store personnel you trust should be given more weight than advertising claims.

In particular, I caution you to check on the cost of media and efficiency of flow and volume of water produced per unit of energy consumed. As usual, the best and most reliable source of information is your fellow hobbyists. Ask around, and check the electronic bulletin boards on your on-line service and Internet interest groups. There is a huge disparity in terms of electrical use, pump life, ease of maintenance, and noise production.

The better canister units are silent,

Below-the-tank canister filters serve to screen out particulate matter, while serving as chemical and biological filtration units. Regular maintenance to remove accumulated detritus is mandatory.

consume only a few watts per hour, and incorporate large, three-dimensional volumes of media. These require attention only for cleaning—every few weeks to once a month or so. Cleaning should be facilitated with the use of on/off valves with or without quick disconnects. These adjuncts make the take-down and restarting process much simpler.

One warning: For some aquarists, canister filters may be an invitation to lazy housekeeping. If you do let the filter go for months between cleanings—out of sight, out of mind—you'll be circulating your entire body of system water through an accumulating mass of waste. A regular cleaning schedule is essential, and an aquarium logbook is a valuable reminder to service these filters where detritus builds up unseen. If your interest expands to the keeping of more delicate fishes or invertebrates, you may eventually want to replace the canister filter with something more open and conducive to daily observation and frequent quick cleaning.

Pressure filters are canister-type units that force water through pleated paper cartridges or other media, and they can really "polish" your water while inflating your electrical bills. Be careful to check the pump or motor rating for energy consumption and to set up and maintain your unit as recommended. For small to intermediate home systems (under a few hundred gallons), pressurized filters are best for periodic use, such as cleaning and gravel vacuuming. Remember to flush them out

when you are done, so they don't become anaerobic when idle.

Huge aquariums with heavy bioloads—usually stocked with large, big-eater livestock—may do well with a pressurized filter plumbed into the filtration loop. Some of these use cartridges, sand of different sorts, and other more novel media. They rapidly clear the water after feeding and cleaning, but be aware of their costs of operation and need for regular maintenance. (Filter cartridges do a wonderful job, but can clog rapidly and are a chore to maintain, as any swimming pool owner who uses them can attest.)

> "For some aquarists, canister filters may be an invitation to lazy housekeeping. A regular cleaning schedule is essential, and an aquarium logbook is a valuable reminder to service these filters."

Diatomaceous earth (DE) is a filter medium that can, with the right external power filter, take a murky tank and have its water crystal clear within an hour. The silky white powder is actually ultra-fine single celled (diatom) algal skeletons, which are used to screen material to less than 1 micron (about 0.00004 inch). Because they very quickly become loaded with detritus

and cause water flow to drop, these units are suitable only for periodic polishing or transferring of water. Existing models require large head pressures, use lots of energy, may produce significant heat, and clog rapidly. Diatomaceous earth does make a good quick-fix tool to have on hand for intermittent use in a conventional pressurized filter system.

Wet-dry and trickle filters: A reef-keeping friend tells me that recommending a wet-dry or trickle filter to a new aquarist is akin to telling them to buy an Edsel: it runs, it's fun to look at, and it has funky components, but it probably belongs in a museum. Unlike the Edsel, however, this type of filter had a real heyday and is still being sold as appropriate technology for home aquariums. A few years ago it was strongly suggested as the best for all serious marine aquarists with medium to larger systems and a critical piece of equipment for all wanting to try their hand at keeping corals, live rock, and other reef invertebrates.

In fact, a giant step in biologically improved water quality was taken with the popularization of the wet-dry or trickle filter beginning in the mid-1980s. At first known as the Dutch System, what it does is move filtration out of the main aquarium and into a sump, usually a tank situated below the display tank, where water drips or sprays over a mass of biomedia (coral rubble in early systems, then plastic Bio-Balls, spheres, and other shapes in an array of inert materials and colors)

A typical wet-dry filter includes a mass of biomedia—in this case blue Bio-Balls—kept constantly damp, with room above for a particulate filter pad and room below, in the sump chambers, for heaters, a block of filtration foam, and a small protein skimmer. Such units are well-suited to fish-only systems.

that are elevated above the water level of the sump. The media are kept damp by water drizzling through them 24 hours a day. Beneficial aerobic bacteria grow like crazy in this environment.

The water is often mechanically filtered before and after being run through the biomedia. Before being pumped back up to the aquarium, it is often skimmed and run through chemical media, such as activated carbon and various resins that remove nitrates, phosphates, and other materials. Compared to older systems with under-gravel and canister filters, aquariums run with wet-dry filtration often seem markedly healthier, with fishes and invertebrates living longer, healthier lives

with greatly reduced maintenance.

Properly constructed and operated, wet-dry filters perform several important functions exceedingly well. They provide enhanced circulation and exchange of water; harbor very large populations of beneficial aerobic (and often anaerobic) microbes; promote gaseous exchange; mechanically filter out large solid wastes; and their sumps allow easy inclusion of contactors, dosers, meters, and skimmers. The biomedia should never need maintenance, and the destabilizing shocks of cleaning other types of filters need never occur.

These units do have their shortcomings: improperly engineered, they can be a flood or electrical hazard, and

their pumps can be energy hogs. It is easy to fall into the trap of purchasing more and more gear with them, without really understanding how you might be (mal)affecting other aspects of the system's well-being.

The bottom line is that wet-dry filters "speed-up" the usual biological reactions, immediately improving and stabilizing water quality. They were at first considered revolutionary, because a multitude of organisms that would otherwise have died in older systems were able to be kept alive and well, even through formerly lethal nitrogen-poisoning events—the "dead anemone syndrome."

For fish-only systems, wet-dry filters continue to offer exceptionally good gas exchange and oxygenation, along with rapid biological filtration that can cope with heavy bioloads.

One further note: a good wet-dry filter should always include a mechanical screening component to keep debris out of the biomedia. Not all of them do—a surprising shortcoming. Be sure the filter you are considering has some sort of prefilter of foam sponge, spun fabric, or polyester sheet that is easy to get to and clean or replace during the weekly maintenance session. Many models have the prefilter tucked where only a contortionist can reach it. Most trickle filters also have a thick foam block to "polish" the water after it comes through the biomedia. These blocks can trap considerable amounts of matter and must be cleaned thoroughly or replaced periodically.

Good-quality live rock can be festooned with life forms, in this case snails, limpets, a sea cucumber, a small crab, a sea urchin, and other Gulf of Mexico organisms.

If it is an Edsel, the wet-dry filter continues to sell and run, but it has an important shortcoming—nitrate accumulation—that has caused most reef aquarists to move on to newer and better models.

Live Rock

AFTER THE INITIAL FASCINATION with wet-dry technology and plastic biomedia began to fade, some thoughtful aquarists noted that wet-dry filtration seemed to have the same nagging flaw as other conventional filter methods: nitrate tended to accumulate over time and build in concentration until it impacted on the health of sensitive invertebrates and fishes. In fact, the problem with all of the previous filtra-

tion methods is a "bottlenecking" of bacterial activity, in which aerobic bacterial activity produces nitrates as an end product. In the wild, anaerobic activity carries on to make use of and convert the nitrates, so they don't accumulate. In recent years, creative approaches to encouraging denitrification in the aquarium (where anaerobic conditions have traditionally been avoided) have gained much attention.

While the Dutch System was evolving, a parallel movement in Germany was experimenting with systems filled with live reef rock and employing protein skimmers or foam fractionators. This came to be called the Berlin System, and it began to show great promise for aquarists who wanted to keep soft

and stony corals. Live rock is rubble material from relatively shallow reef waters and generally represents pieces of coral broken off during crushing tropical storms. A renewable resource, this material is found in great quantities in most reef areas and is typically colonized by many marine organisms, including algae and all manner of reef invertebrates. The best quality rock, from the aquarist's point of view, is highly porous and well-colonized by both nitrifying and denitrifying bacteria. If collected and shipped properly, it arrives in the home aquarium loaded with life forms and able to assist greatly in biological filtration.

The physical and biological processes that readily occur on and within live rock expediently convert and remove the metabolites that a skimmer doesn't extract. Algae and other invertebrates use up "wastes" as chemical food; the tremendous surface area and variable circulation through the rock and life therein converts metabolites aerobically, hypoxically, and anaerobically. The latter is appreciable when you consider the vast porosity and slowed circulation through real coral rock. Breaking a piece open will reveal what I am referring to—darkened nonoxygenated zones of sulfide malodor. With a properly set up and maintained Berlin System, the health of livestock is optimized and maintenance minimized.

Word about the benefits of live rock quickly spread through the modern marine aquarium world, and many aquarists moved quickly away from the use of bleached coral skeletons to aquascapes filled with rock collected and shipped "live" from Florida and Indo-Pacific reefs.

On the theory that a new-style reef tank, full of live rock, probably has more than adequate populations of beneficial bacteria to handle nitroge-nous wastes, some hobbyists began pulling the biomedia from their trickle filters. After holding their breath, they noted two things: their systems did not crash, and nitrate control became much easier.

The accepted explanation is that the well-oxygenated, elevated mass of moist biomedia is too good at what it does, very rapidly turning ammonia to nitrite, then to nitrate. To simplify a long, complex story, the current view is that letting these processes work along at a slower pace in live rock gives anaerobic bacteria a better chance to keep up the nitrate production, turning out nitrogen gas as the end product.

Many types of live rock are available to North American aquarists, including material from various locales in the Indo-Pacific and Central and South America. Aquacultured rock from Florida-based suppliers is also an interesting and environmentally sound choice.

Whatever the origin of the rock, the aquarist should know the difference between freshly imported and "cured" live rock. Most of this material goes through a significant "die-off" period after its collection, during shipping, and for its first few weeks in a captive setting. Many types of encrusting and boring sponges do not ship well, and these signal their demise with the unmistakable odor of putrefaction. Bringing uncured rock into one's home can be a mistake you and anyone else sharing your living space will never forget.

Ideally, live rock should be cured in a setting detached from your house or office. Placed in clean, warm, circulating seawater at 70 to 80 degrees F, it will take from two to four weeks for all traces of decay and odor to disappear. A number of complete water changes may be necessary to purge the system of toxic nitrogenous wastes during the curing period.

Today, it is a fairly routine and a simple matter to insist on cured live rock. Unless you have the equipment and facilities to clean and cure your own rock, it is generally much better to let a dealer with curing tanks do this for you. The curing process, if done properly, can preserve a great deal of the original life, while sloppy or amateurish cur-

Prime Panamanian live rock, with colorful coralline algae and various macroalgae species.

Aquacultured Florida live rock with well-established sponges, algae, and other desirable species.

Branching live rock from the South Pacific is collected from reef rubble areas created by storms.

ing results in many of the desirable invertebrates that live in or on the rock dying from ammonia poisoning or lack of oxygen.

The simple route is to buy live rock from a reliable dealer who comes recommended by other aquarists. A good local retail store set to handle and store the rock is usually the best bet for most aquarists. Unfortunately, some distributors now try to sell all rock as "cured," whether it is or not. A simple sniff test will reveal the real thing: good, cured live rock has the fresh, clean smell of the sea, with good coverage by coralline algae and no traces of white, decaying material. In the original Berlin (live rock) System, there was no gravel or substrate, so Kalkwasser, or calcium hydroxide solution, was added to the aquarium to keep the pH and calcium levels high. The Berlin System today is often modified to include sand.

Live Sand

THE NEXT ADVANCE in the evolution of aquarium filtration was triggered by the work of Dr. Jean Jaubert, a French coral scientist doing research at the Monaco Aquarium. Beginning around 1990, news of a system that allowed fantastic coral growth in aquariums that had only airstone-driven circulation and no other active filtration technology began to excite North American aquarists. In brief, Jaubert had developed a method that calls for a deep bed of relatively coarse live coral sand over a buried plastic plate. Beneath the plate is a shallow (approximately 2-inch-

Live sand from the Florida Keys can harbor significant populations of beneficial bacteria as well as detritus-consuming organisms. A Blue-legged Hermit Crab and sand-sifting goby work over this sand bed.

deep) pocket of unoxygenated water that is entirely trapped under the sand. This closed-in, water-filled space is known as a plenum, or, frequently, as a Jaubert-style plenum. As water from the aquarium slowly diffuses through the sand layer, nitrogenous wastes are completely broken down, with gaseous nitrogen as a harmless end product.

With the Jaubert setup, the aquarist is actually encouraging anaerobic conditions for the benefit of microbes that aid in denitrification and that must live in low oxygen or hypoxic conditions. It is generally thought that the existence of the plenum is the key to creating the very slow movement of

water through the live sand bed and to avoid having anaerobic pockets of toxic hydrogen sulfide gas develop.

While it has helped bring live sand substrates into the home aquarium, sometimes with appreciable increases in coral growth, the Jaubert System has not met with universal success when tried outside the Monaco Aquarium. It is now generally recognized that Jaubert's own tanks using this method are thinly stocked and the sand surface is largely exposed (and cannot be buried under large areas of live rock). In addition, some of the Monaco systems have the benefit of being partially open to the Mediterranean Sea with significant water changes regularly taking place.

A good aquarium shop that caters to reef aquarists will have or can easily get live sand for you. Well-collected and properly shipped sand, like live rock, should smell relatively clean and fresh. There should be no muddiness or silt, and the presence of live worms, snails, or other invertebrates is a good sign. The smell of decay means the live sand will have to go through the same curing process as live rock.

Thanks to Jaubert and others who have modified his idea, live sand is now widely regarded as a valuable addition to virtually all marine systems. Clearly, it can provide a site for denitrification, it serves as a valuable buffer, and it is a source of soluble calcium and other minerals used by reef invertebrates. Natural sand collected from underwater near-reef areas is a varying mix of siliceous (silica-based) materials, inorganic carbonates, and "other" matter (shells, aluminas, skeletons) plus some mix of life. A number of advocates endorse the use of "sugar-fine" aragonite sand for their sand beds, others use coarse, gravelly material. Some claim the best results from using all "wild-harvested" live sand, while others believe that making your own from commercially available (mined) aragonite works just fine. This off-the-shelf material can be easily seeded with a few cups of wild-harvested live sand or sand from a well-established reef aquarium.

While some aquarists have had success with Jaubert-style plenums, others have simply added a 2-to-4-inch layer of live sand to the bottom of their reef tanks and reported improved results. Others have had problems with hydrogen sulfide and excessive hair algae growth with deep sand beds, and no single approach has yet emerged as the winner.

The Natural Method is one term for a hybrid approach now being tried by growing numbers of American reef aquarists. This method calls for ample use of live rock (1 to 2 pounds per gallon of system capacity), aggressive protein skimming (which Jaubert does not use) and a moderately deep (2-to-3-inch) layer of live sand either on the bottom of the tank or in a separate sump. A Jaubert-style plenum may or may not be used.

Refugiums

I WANT TO GO ON RECORD as encouraging a further refinement of these complete-cycling filtration methods. I suggest that a separate, tied-in sump or tank area—termed a refugium—be used. This refuge area would have a large surface area of live sand, perhaps with some live rock and emergent plants such as mangroves. The refugium would have "grow" lights on a timer, and the usual grazers and algal predators would be excluded, allowing luxuriant plant growth. Sand-shifting brittlestars and small sea cucumbers would be present to feed on detritus, and a healthy population of microflora and -fauna would be allowed to develop, out of the reach of fishes (or aquarium-cleaning brushes). Because the refugium would not be subject to physical disruption, the sudden release of hydrogen sulfide would not be a problem. The refugium would allow for complete "natural" filtration, production of food organisms, and the benefits of increased system volume; it would grant you the capacity to manipulate them all without disrupting your display aquarium. (In a pinch, you might use it as an acclimation or breeding tank as well.)

An undisturbed refugium, given a few years to develop its own populations of macroalgae, plankton, and mangroves, could become every bit as fascinating to observe as the show aquarium it serves. Julian Sprung, noted aquarium author, has published a number of photographs of just such a thriving, Jaubert-influenced refugium connected to his own reef tank.

Curiously, for those who think all of this is revolutionary and new, Robert P.L. Straughan showed photographs of a "mangrove swamp" refugium-type aquarium in his 1959 book, *The Salt-Water Aquarium in the Home*. In the same era, Lee Chin Eng's simple reef tank was considered a success partly because of the "live rock" and "live sand" he collected in local Indonesian waters.

A final word on these various reef-type systems, in which the "natural" mentality can be carried to an extreme: in my opinion, all marine systems should have at least some extra mechanical filtration in addition to the essential biological and protein-skimming systems. I know that many reef

tank owners have removed all mechanical filtration devices from their systems and still boast sparkling clear water. However, their setups are virtually all blessed with substantial filter sumps that act as settling basins for detritus, so they do have a mechanical filtration mechanism of sorts. Many advanced reef keepers still use particulate traps of one kind or another, at least on a rotating basis. In a system with excellent skimming and live rock and sand, mechanical filters may be redundant, but isn't a safety net worth the cost? It is still appropriate to screen gross particulates out of your system quickly.

Other Filtration Options

Fluidized-bed filters are more borrowed technology from the sewage treatment industry, like the Bio-Ball and "outgassing" rings. These towers or hang-on-the-tank chambers employ a fine granular material kept in constant suspension in a current-filled container designed to optimize filter surface area and nitrifying efficiency. The principle is good, and well-constructed units are especially useful in large, crowded (as in wholesale) systems with widely vacillating bioloads, but some of the new, small models for home aquariums are reported to have design problems and to "die" quickly in power outages. Get a recommendation from an aquarist you trust before committing to one of these.

A lush mangrove-swamp refugium created by author Julian Sprung to house a Jaubert-style live sand bed in an external sump next to his reef aquarium.

Algal scrubbers are filters that focus on the removal of the end-product of crowded closed marine systems—nitrates. Algal scrubbers of different sorts, with intense light, shallow running water, and specialized attachment media can eliminate amazing amounts of nitrate and other nutrients. These have typically been found in large, institutional settings, but a few companies are now offering affordable home algal scrubbers, and there are some enthusiastic reports of success with keeping corals and breeding fishes.

Dr. Walter Adey of the Smithsonian Institution has helped popularize this mode of filtration, at least in some public aquarium settings. Algae filters have been faulted for being time-consuming to maintain (keeping surge devices operating and harvesting green matter) and for the yellowing of system water caused by compounds leaching from the algae. New methods of coping with this are being proposed, but, at this point, algae-growing filters probably ought to be regarded as experimental or for more advanced and adventuresome hobbyists.

Commercial denitrators are filter module "closed box" products that claim to promote the growth of anaerobic microbes and their beneficial activities. Please be careful in making your choice. Many denitrators are high-maintenance units requiring daily adjusting and careful supplemental feeding. All have the potential problem of creating anaerobic conditions that can release hydrogen sulfide and toxify your system. In my opinion, they're not worth the hassle, cost, and possible chemical downside compared with water changes, chemical filtrants, and other "open" biological approaches.

The Nitrogen Cycle

EVERY NEW MARINE AQUARIST gets an introductory lecture on nitrogen, its cycling in the aquarium, and how to test for its presence in various forms. What makes nitrogen such a good tool for keeping an eye on water quality? Toxic wastes that can build up in your tank are largely invisible, so imagine being able to take an easy measurement of what's going on in your system metabolically. Nitrogen-compound testing makes that possible. In brief, the nitrogen cycle is explained as follows:

All living things are made up of molecular building blocks called amino acids. These are structures of carbon chains (some with sulfur), oxygen, nitrogen, and hydrogen that are linked to one another by amino bonds to form proteins. The nitrogen cycle is the sum total of processes that convert atmospheric nitrogen (N_2) into compounds useful to animals and plants that eventually "cycle" back to atmospheric nitrogen (see diagram, page 78).

For marine aquarium keeping, the picture is even simpler. Nitrogen enters the system mainly from food or from livestock that dies. Whether eaten and digested or not, most of this material is converted to (unionized) ammonia (NH_3) and (ionized) ammonium (NH_4^+)—a less toxic form. Nitrification occurs principally through bacteria metabolizing ammonia to nitrites (NO_2) followed by other groups of bacteria converting the nitrites to nitrates (NO_3).

Let's look at this in another way. The accompanying diagram shows an "idealized" time line for establishing nitrogen cycling in a new marine aquarium. At the starting point, you've just set up your system and filled it with all new, sterile, synthetic marine water. In most cases, you will shortly thereafter introduce one of these options to initiate cycling or to help "pop" the system: some hardy (nitrogenous-waste resistant) fishes, such as damsels; a chemical "feeding" system (a commercial source of ammonia, with or without a source of beneficial microbes); and some "food" as a source of decomposing ammonia to instigate bacterial mobilization, such as scraps of table fish or fish food. Live rock or live sand, providing both a source of waste and the bacteria to break it down, can also be used to start a new system.

At first, basic aquarium water test kits (ammonia, nitrite, nitrate, pH) will reveal only the presence of ammonia. Soon, however, enough ammonia is being converted by bacteria that have been intentionally or incidentally intro-

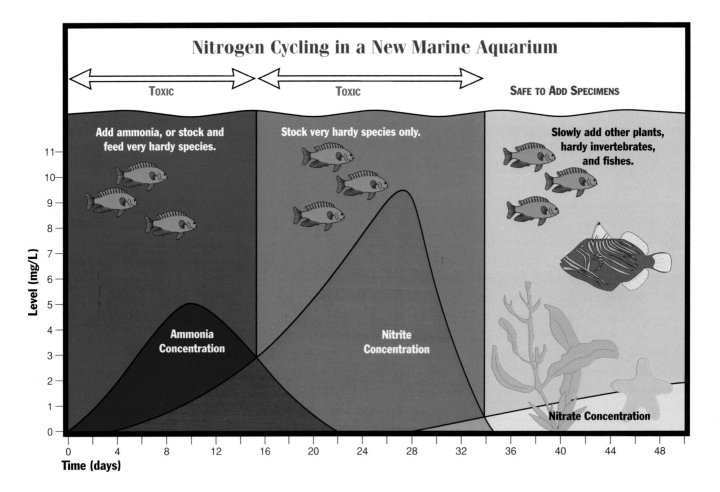

A typical scenario for nitrogen cycling in a new aquarium, starting with a few hardy damselfishes as a source of ammonia. Testing at first reveals the presence of ammonia, then nitrite, as beneficial bacteria grow. When ammonia and nitrite both measure zero, other hardy fishes and organisms may be added slowly.

Encouraging Beneficial Microbes

One measure of a system's viability and its capacity to support fish and other life is the presence, abundance, and vitality of microbes. These bacteria are to be found most everywhere; in fact, they will "fall" into your system from the air, and with anything you place in the tank. Like molds finding loaves of bread, they will get in, whether or not you purposefully introduce them. Because the job of these microscopic helpers is so critical, many contraptions and specialized media have been invented for ensuring their proliferation and survival.

Various filter materials—sponges, synthetic filter fibers, gravel substrates, ceramic and glass beads, plastic matrices and more—have been used for the primary benefit of keeping beneficial microbes healthy and metabolically active. They are housed in all types of containers—wet-dry or trickle, canister, outside/inside power filters—or left to colonize the rock, sand, and other surfaces in the tank. But what can you do to bring them on board faster? Quite a lot.

There are stock inoculations of bacteria cultures for sale for the purpose of initially establishing biological cycling. Sometimes they work, too often they don't. There are many reasons for this. Most stock cultures are feeble (too dilute) and/or made up of inappropriate species of microbes. Many times, the hobbyist is to blame. He or she puts the "bugs" in a chemically hostile, nonnutritive medium or poisons

> *"Simply transplant beneficial microbes from an established aquarium."*

the water with ammonia. If you want to use these chemical solutions to "feed" your system, read and follow their directions exactly.

A sad fact about utilizing these commercially prepared cultures is that your system would develop these same bacterial populations naturally, often in about the same amount of time (about one to two months). But the real shame is that there are other safer, faster, and less expensive methods. I would recommend simply transplanting beneficial microbes from an established marine aquarium to your new system. Pick a donor tank that has been running for a year or more and is stabilized and free of disease and medications. Take (or borrow) a few cups, pounds, or handfuls of gravel, rock, or filter media and get it quickly into your own sterile new environment—but not until your system water has aged for several days to a week and the temperature, specific gravity, and pH are all adjusted (see Water Chemistry Parameters, page 81) and the filtration is up and running. The amount of material transferred is not really important; it's just an inoculant that will quickly reproduce. Introduce the biologically active material to this warm and inviting system and you will receive instant bacterial benefits. A conditioning period with careful feeding, water testing, and sparse stocking must still be observed.

To keep bacterial populations alive and well, keep the temperature and oxygen levels of your system stable. Beware of external sources of poisoning such as fish medications. Remember, cleanliness does not mean sterility. Cleaning, vacuuming, or bleaching ornaments too much or too soon disrupts and destroys needed bacterial cultures. Don't be too eager to clean up or overhaul your system all at once; try to do major housekeeping attacks in stages. You want good, strong beneficial-microbe populations living in and on all stable surfaces in your system.

duced to the system to show the presence of the nitrification product, nitrite.

Next, the beginning of nitrite conversion activity appears, with the detectable conversion of nitrites to nitrates. As the diagram illustrates, ammonia concentration rises, quickly peaks, and generally declines rapidly. The same sort of rise, fall, and disappearance is next seen for nitrite. Both ammonia and nitrites are toxic at low levels to most fishes and invertebrates. Fortunately, generally four to eight weeks into the setup, both have fallen to acceptably low concentrations or are undetectable with simple testing methods, and the aquarist can now begin further stocking.

But the nitrates in our example continue to rise and might build to dangerous levels in a truly closed system. Intervention methods by aquarists to successfully limit the "bottleneck" accumulation of nitrates include: frequent partial water changes, chemical filtrants, macroalgae "scrubbers," and abundant live rock and live sand substrate beds, in which nitrate can be converted to harmless gaseous nitrogen.

Depending on certain factors—the amount and format of foods added, wastes produced, temperature, bacteria population dynamics, and oxygen supply—biological filtration in your system can be a breeze (virtually automatic) or, with poor aquarium management, an unending nightmare.

It's important to understand how to avoid the most common deadly pitfall of aquarium keeping—metabolite poisoning. Stock your aquarium slowly, letting the bacterial population build as needed. Never add large numbers of new fish at the same time. Don't overfeed, especially with flake foods. Why? Your livestock won't be able to find and process it all and it will simply decompose, adding to the ammonia load. In fact, the extra ammonia might overwhelm your beneficial microbes, along with your fishes and invertebrates, necessitating a minor or major reestablishment of nutrient cycling.

Test Kits

HOW CAN YOU TELL THE concentrations of ammonia, nitrite, and nitrate in your tank, and why should you care? The easy answers are A) test kits, and B) because at sufficient concentrations they're deadly to your livestock. Do you really need to be constantly aware of, and measure for, these parameters in order to be successful? No; your tank will "cycle" either way. But a conscientious aquarist wants to know what is going on in his or her system and to understand why. As time passes and the system stabilizes, the need for frequent testing will diminish. In the first weeks and months of a new aquarium, however, there is much to measure and learn.

Chemical Filters

CHEMICAL FILTRATION is the nonbiological removal of substances from seawater solution on a molecular level by adsorption, absorption, and ion exchange. Activated carbon, resins, and other types of media can be valuable adjuncts to the biological, mechanical, and physical filtration methods you choose to employ. While not absolutely necessary, they are often brought into play to remove color, odor, nutrients, and suspended solids. This enhances water quality, improves livestock health, and reduces maintenance. Even aquarists who try to live without them on a daily basis resort to chemical media periodically to restore water clarity, and, in emergencies, to rectify water problems quickly and stem crises.

Carbons come with many types of confusing labels. Strictly speaking, carbon is the "root" element of them all. Beware of "reagent, "technical," and other official-sounding grade claims in

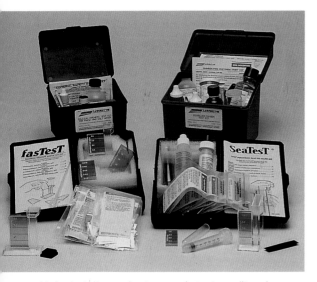

Marine test kits are a key to measuring water quality and are especially helpful in tracking the progress of a new aquarium.

commercial brands. The qualities to look for are "nitrate-free" and "phosphate-free."

Carbon, by which I mean activated carbon, has a greater adsorption rate and capacity than ordinary (shiny, irregularly shaped) charcoal from animal or wood sources. You only want activated carbon; the other stuff is a placebo, not suitable for aquarium use.

When carbon is fresh, it is at its zenith in adsorptive capacity. With use, this drops off logarithmically. As far as chemically filtering your water, the best carbons have effective lives that can run about two to three months. But carbon also acts to some degree as a biological filter bed and even as a mechanical filter. Therefore, let it be resolved that you will rotate two (or more) sets of carbon units, along with the mechanical media. (Changing everything at once can put too large a dent in your biological-filtration capacity.)

Everyone dreams of the big money they could save by somehow reversing the adsorption processes of their carbons so that they could be reused. Allow me to save you high energy bills, a stinky kitchen, and laughter from your peers. Such practices are the stuff of myth. Not near enough noxious material can be driven off by household efforts. The manufacture of useful aquarium-grade activated carbon is done under high pressure (or vacuum) and extreme heat in the presence of formulated chemicals. Mix the old, used carbon in your mulch pile and buy some new.

Ion-exchange media are electrochemically charged resin beads that remove charged particles from solution by exchanging them for others. For most systems, these materials are too expensive and limiting in their capacity for daily use. However, I am familiar with some of the research going on in developing ion-exchange technology, and there are some potentially very useful media being developed for selectively extracting aquarium pollutants.

Appropriate occasions to use chemical filtrants abound. Aquarium service companies keep these media fresh to

Chemical media that adsorb dissolved organics, pollutants and medicines from aquarium water include highly recommended activated carbon and other ion-exchange resin beads of varying types.

insure crystal clear water and optimum fish and invertebrate health. Many reef keepers employ chemical filtrants—especially activated carbon—full-time. But a significant number are sparing in their use of both carbon and aids such as nitrate and phosphate removers. (Whether or not it is true, there are suspicions that these media can strip important trace elements, such as iodine, if used on a more than limited, periodic basis.)

Other folks are more random in chemical filtering use. They'll remember to change their carbon when the water starts to yellow or the colors are fading in their most sensitive specimen.

For function and practicality, it's best to place these chemical filtration media in polyester bags and arrange their placement in a pressurized water flow (my favorite is a hang-on power or canister filter). The worst is to just throw the bag and contents into a sump or bury it in the gravel—there is not much hope of adsorption where water is not forced through the medium. (If you do add chemical media in a bag to your sump or system, be scrupulous in securing the pouch or, better yet, use a double-bag approach. Many, many pumps have been temporarily or permanently disabled by grains of carbon or other media jamming their impellers. Beware, also, of inferior bags offered on the mass market. These can disintegrate or split open within weeks of being submerged.) Lacking a pressurized filter chamber, you can place the carbon bag in an area with active water flow, perhaps in an overflow box or under the input line to your sump.

Regarding the establishment of nutrient cycling and chemical media use: most sources say to wait until full nitrification is going before adding carbon; others state that some carbon in use at all times will only slightly slow down the process of bacterial growth. I would wait until cycling is in full swing to use chemical media or, better still, utilize some carbon from an established system to get the new system started.

A pH shift, especially a shift to a much lower range—can be caused by lack of water changing, overfeeding, an undiscovered carcass, or other reasons. This may result in a release of adsorbed matter, with possible disastrous consequences. This is yet another reason for sufficient buffering, caution, use of activated-carbon and regular water changes.

There is also some real danger, especially in full-blown reef and intensive invertebrate systems, of removing too much dissolved organic carbon too quickly. Some of the adsorptive matter is biologically important, and suddenly clarifying water that has been yellowed can cause severe light shock to many delicate organisms. (The light-screening effects of dissolved organics in the water should not be underestimated.) For systems that have had no steady history of carbon filtration, Wilkens (1973) suggests building up by adding 1½ ounces of carbon per 26 gallons of water per month. Other authors' recommendations are less restrictive. The best measure of how much is right is gauged by close observation of your livestock. If you suspect that suddenly clear water is shocking your specimens, raise your lights, dim them, or cut back on your artificial day length for a while.

Some writers have voiced concerns about activated carbon removing trace elements from reef aquariums. I don't believe this to be a major concern with adequately fed and maintained systems. Some prominent small-polyp stony coral growers will disagree, believing that activated carbon can pull sufficient trace elements out of the water to cause bleaching and even death. If or when in doubt, effect a water change and/or become an additive user.

Poly Filters are another chemical filtrant that deserves mention and praise. Poly-Bio-Marine Inc.'s Poly Filter is a specially treated white fiber pad incorporating polymers for adsorbing polar organics and nitrogenous compounds. This hydrophilic polymeric material is unique, and it really works. I have used Poly Filters personally and in business for removing medications and for limiting algal growth by adsorbing phosphate, fertilizers, and other contaminants or additives that must be removed quickly. Poly Filters turn various colors as they remove certain ions (turning blue when taking copper out of a system, for example), and they will not release scavenged ions back into the system. They are especially useful with quarantine and hospital tanks, and many advanced and professional aquarists swear by them.

Physical Filtration

HERE WE WILL GROUP several filtration techniques that might also be classified as chemical, in the case of protein skimming and ozone injection, or germicidal, in the case of both ozone and ultraviolet sterilization. All will be of interest to the involved aquarist.

Protein skimming actually started back in an almost-forgotten heyday of aquarium interest in the U.S.—the 1960s to early 1970s—when skimming gained limited popularity, both with and without the use of ozone. Indeed, many European countries got out of the chlorination business for treating tap water and took up using ozone in its place. The technology spilled over into the aquarium hobby, but somehow these physical filter tools lost their popularity. I don't know why protein skimmers failed to catch the first time, but I do know that every captive marine system can benefit tremendously from their use. Protein skimmers or foam fractionators are readily available in every price range and, in my opinion, are a basic necessity for any marine system. Beyond the requisite biological filtration, nothing is better at improving water quality than a protein skimmer.

The bulk of undesirable organic wastes that we want to eliminate from our systems are "surface active," collecting near the surface of a gas-liquid interface. We can capitalize on this affinity in a column of aquarium water with air bubbles mixed in. Trapped materials, including wastes, uneaten food, and more, rise and are collected at the

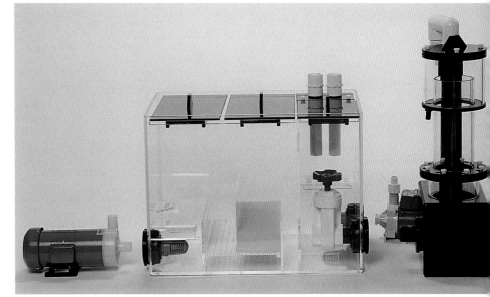

A sophisticated, compact water-handling system and protein skimmer designed to fit in a typical aquarium cabinet, including a multi-chambered sump and high-tech downdraft skimmer with its own dedicated pump.

top as foam. The tools that accomplish this are called foam separators, fractionators, air-strippers, or protein skimmers. (They actually remove much more than proteins, and purists tend to refer to them as foam fractionators, although the term protein skimmer is deeply entrenched in the aquarium lexicon.) Whatever they are called, the action is the same, with complex organic substances attaching to tiny air bubbles rising in a column or chamber. A dark, waste-laden foam concentrates at the top of the unit to be separated from the water and collected for disposal.

The efficiency of a fractionator depends on several factors, most notably air-water contact time and bubble size. The greater the contact time and the smaller the bubble size, the better. In addition, there are adjuncts, especially

ozone, that can add greatly to the efficiency of waste removal.

This is an extremely important part of successful marine aquarium keeping. Since the range of makes, models, and functionality is so huge, it is important to be familiar with the choices a salesperson will ask you to make.

There are basically three decisions to be considered in buying a skimmer:

1) Do you want the unit in or out of the tank?

2) Do you want air or venturi power?

3) Do you want counter-current or gravity flow?

The first question concerns where the unit is placed. Review the factors that determine skimmer efficiency. Most in-tank models are too short to be of much use; taller is usually better in

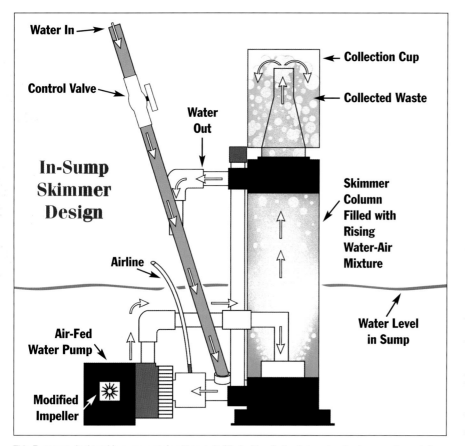

In-Sump Skimmer Design

Water In →

Control Valve →

Water Out

Collection Cup

Collected Waste

Skimmer Column Filled with Rising Water-Air Mixture

Airline →

Water Level in Sump

Air-Fed Water Pump

Modified Impeller

This European-designed in-sump protein skimmer is filled with a froth of air and water from a submerged pump with a specially modified impeller. (Based on the Turboflotor Skimmer by AquaMedic.)

this class of skimmer. Out-of-tank models provide more contact time and easier manipulation for cleaning, adjusting, and airstone changing. The potential for spillage accidents should always be considered when planning placement of a protein skimmer.

The second question concerns how air gets into the system. Venturi models suck in air through a special water nozzle and are fairly self-contained. Air models use an airstone (usually limewood) and a pump to create a profusion of fine bubbles.

Although the latter are definitely viewed as outmoded by some, there is no agreement that venturi types are better than airstone-driven models. I have seen many expensive venturi skimmers fail on one count or another. Too many of them need a far bigger pump than the maker will admit (at least before selling it to you), and many makers fail even to recommend specific pumps that will give optimum performance. Other common venturi-model faults include nonfunctioning venturis, finicky controls (too many adjustments

to make), and lack of an automatic leveling feature. Many have no waste-drain fitting and are prone to overflowing.

One salvation for these skimmers—they may be retrofitted with limewood or fine glass airstones. They will then work fine, thanks to good air pumps.

Features I'd look for in a first protein skimmer are:

1) auto leveling—a large exit fitting so that you won't have to be constantly fiddling with two or more level-control valves or variables;

2) a good venturi or other powered air-injection system or one or two wooden or fused-glass airstones, easily reachable and changeable;

3) a big, easy-to-clean waste cup, preferably with a drain fitting.

The third question regards counter-current versus gravity flow. Everything else being equal, a counter-current flow path, with the system water feeding into the skimmer in opposition to bubble flow, aids in increasing contact time and the mixing of fine air bubbles, resulting in enhanced removal.

Confused? A counter-current, air-stone-driven skimmer always works, provided you take about 3 minutes a week to clean the riser tube and another 3 minutes once a month to change or clean the airstones.

It is true that well-made venturi-type skimmers can be a joy to operate, but be sure to talk to other aquarists and seek personal recommendations before investing in an expensive unit. Also note that there are other choices.

84

A relatively new class of skimmers uses neither airstones nor conventional venturis, but rather draws air into the water intake of a dedicated pump, which uses a special impeller to create a dense froth.

For more advanced hobbyists, various high-tech skimmers are also available, including high-performance "downdraft" models, self-cleaning units, and a number of pricey European configurations. No matter what you plan to spend, always ask what pump (air or water or both) should be matched with the skimmer, and pair them properly; a mismatch can yield very unhappy results—either too little or too much foam.

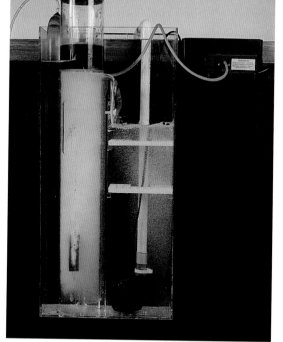

A hang-on-tank, airstone-driven, counter-current skimmer, fed by a siphon from the tank with water returned via a small powerhead.

By the way, there are chemicals that are sold from time to time that enhance "foaminess" and skimming collectant volume. I don't consider these worthwhile; a good skimmer will work without such additives. On the other hand, ozone is a tremendous boon to skimmer efficiency, and should you have the time and money for such an addition, I urge you to check into coupling an ozonizer with your foam fractionator.

With its low operating cost, high efficiency of operation in removing organics with concomitant reduction in bioload, algal growth, and enhanced water quality, a protein skimmer can effectively minimize the problems related to waste accumulation in a marine system. How much you invest is your decision, but I wouldn't have a tank without one.

Ozone (O_3) is sometimes called the "purest form of oxygen." It's the fresh smell after an electric storm, and the crispness in the air in and around large electric motors. Ozone is a highly unstable triatomic molecule. It can aid in "burning up" organics and disease-causing microbes in your system, raising pH, boosting dissolved oxygen and oxidation-reduction potential (redox), and maximizing the efficiency of your protein skimmer.

Ozone for aquariums in older, low-production units is made by a germicidal lamp, such as those in UV sterilizers. Higher-production, more modern models use a corona discharge (electrical) method of making ozone.

The optimal application of ozone is through your skimmer, with the ozone-treated water going back to a sump (usually a filter) for mixing, outgassing, and chemical filtration before returning to the main system.

Dedicated air ozonizers do not normally come with air pumps to discharge the ozone produced. The ozone-rich air in the unit must either be pushed out with pressurized air from an air pump or pulled out by the suction action of a venturi valve in your circulation system.

When using an air pump to force air through the ozonizer and into your skimmer, I recommend a strong, quiet, dedicated one—one that is only operating the skimmer. This is necessary to avoid adjustment headaches, a condition that will develop if you skimp and try to feed other outlets from your not-so-dedicated skimmer air pump.

Whether you have a pumped air or venturi delivery, you should utilize ozone-resistant tubing and a good check valve, which may come with the ozonizer. Check valves are also available from spa and pool stores and prevent back-siphoning. If you are or become a total fanatic, you can even increase your ozone production efficiency with an air dryer—a reaction chamber filled with calcium chloride or other desiccant through which air is drawn to the ozonizer. Let me hasten to add

Oxidation-Reduction Potential

Like pH, oxidation-reduction (redox) measures can give valuable insight into changes in the suitability of your water, particularly with reef setups in which organisms are more redox sensitive. Redox is a measure of a system's capacity to oxidize material. Put another way, redox is a classification category of chemical reactions.

A helpful acronym is OILRIG—Oxidation Is Losing, Reduction Is Gaining. What is being lost and gained? Electrons. You may remember from science classes that the bulk of chemical interactions around us are proton donor or acceptor (sometimes called acid/base) in nature. Redox reactions are fewer and slower by comparison. In oxidation-reduction reactions, one chemical species loses electrons, another gains them.

Redox potential is a value (number) defining how much gaining or losing a system might do. An oxidizing environment (the type we want) has a positive value.

I like John Tullock's definition of redox offered in *The Reef Tank Owner's Manual*, " . . . a measure of the ability of a system to eliminate wastes." It's not totally accurate scientifically, but it is very valuable as a subjective description.

Redox is eminently important as an indicator not only of a system's capacity for cycling waste, but of its ability to support (chemically) fish, plant, and invertebrate life. There are both oxidation (e.g. biological conversion of ammonia to nitrites to nitrates) and reduction (ridding systems of nitrate and biophosphate PO_3) that must occur readily in a truly closed system to support macrolife.

Redox is measured indirectly as the *ability* or *potential* of an aquatic system to conduct electricity—hence the term redox potential, or ORP, for Oxidation-Reduction Potential. This potential is measured in millivolts (mV). Testing can be done periodically, but ORP can change so rapidly that in order to benefit from this information, most aquarists monitor it on a continuous basis.

Any serious reef shop or marine aquarium magazine can quickly provide you with a selection of ORP monitors and controllers. These digital display units are attached to a probe that you place in your system or filter reservoir. Millivolt data may be displayed, recorded, or sent along to a fancy doser to slurp redox-enhancing fluid into your system, or sent to a switching mechanism to turn your ozonizer off or on.

"Just remember that you do want a higher, rather than a lower, ORP. . . . a daily glance at the redox meter can be a reassurance that all is well—or an electronic warning signal."

Can you have too much redox? Definitely. Redox potentials above 400 mV are dangerous to life. Ideally, you want a range of 350 to 390 mV. Most properly set up and maintained systems display an average of 300 to 340 mV, some may vary down to the 200s, but values below 300 mV should be a signal that something is wrong.

Redox fluctuates in the wild and in captive systems throughout the day. Dissolved oxygen, pH, feeding, cleaning, lighting, and more all affect ORP. When the lights switch on and photosynthesis starts, metabolites released into the system will start lowering redox after an initial small spike (due to increased oxygen from photosynthesis). When the lights go off, and macrolife "settles down," fewer metabolites are produced and ORP increases again. Redox tends to drift downward during the day, reversing the trend at night.

You can probably infer that just knowing redox values by themselves is worthless. Drain cleaner and bleach solutions have very high redox values. Would you add them to your system? To me, the real worth in redox (and actually all test gear values) is in being able to tell whether something is amiss, or about to be so.

Knowing what your system's usual ORP signature is during a given interval, and seeing a sharp loss (anything approaching 50 mV) or a steady loss (5 to 10 mV net loss per day) should lead you to further investigation—and action. Is there something dead and decomposing in the system? Did a "little helper" pour in a whole packet of food? Is your protein skimmer on the skids?

Can you, and should you, raise your redox readings? You can definitely do several things to raise and sustain high redox. Most of these are common-sense proper installation and maintenance procedures. Should you react to or alter any given value? Not really, unless your animals are not flourishing or if you see a precipitous drop within one day, or a steady loss over several days.

A great deal of measurable ORP is due to oxygen concentration. Are your oxygen levels below saturation? Change your airstones, crank up the circulation, and ORP will rise. A small ozonizer will also help boost your ORP readings. In fact, the biggest oxygen high, and the most dangerous, can be gotten from the misuse of ozone. Be careful if utilizing a high-output producer of this strong oxidizer. An oversized, incorrectly applied ozonizer is probably the biggest culprit in pushing a system over 400 mV ORP. This can kill your livestock.

This multi-purpose aquarium monitor and controller includes a probe to give ORP readings and an automatic ozonizer switch.

If you aren't ready for an ozonizer but are looking for a "natural" ORP high, try algae (like *Caulerpa*) or adequate amounts of live rock and, to some degree, live sand.

Removing organics by tuning up your skimmer, employing chemical filtrants, cleaning filter media, vacuuming substrates, or siphoning out accumulated detritus from rockwork and sumps reduces reductive influences, effectively raising ORP. If these procedures don't help, try cutting back on feeding, or reduce your bioload.

Is it absolutely critical to know what redox is and how to measure and manipulate it to be a successful marine aquarist? Do you need to understand the nature of carbon-carbon bonds and what "octane" means in order to burn gas in your car? No. But if you have the money, interest, and patience to look beyond such standard tests as pH, temperature, specific gravity, and nitrogen processing, redox is one that can grant insights into what's going on in your water and what you might do to improve conditions.

Meters, dosers, and switches cost real money and require calibration and some maintenance. This might be peanuts compared to what you've spent on livestock and the emotional investment you have in your system. You'll have to decide for yourself whether this expensive tool fits your philosophy and budget.

Just remember that you do want a higher, rather than a lower, ORP. Higher oxidation potential accelerates the oxidation of ammonia to nitrite to nitrate, and the conversion of organic PO_3 to inorganic phosphate, PO_4. For some high-tech aquarists, a daily glance at the redox meter can be a reassurance that all is well—or an electronic warning signal that something has started to go awry.

that ozonizers work fine without air dryers, and protein skimmers work fine without ozonizers.

Some authors say you must have an ORP monitor and controller attached to each ozonizer. (ORP, or Oxidation-Reduction Potential, rises with the use of ozone, and an electronic controller can be used to shut down an ozonizer unit if the readings get too high.) I am not convinced that the average hobbyist needs this level of control. Instead, I would follow the guidelines previously introduced. You should never use an ozonizer that can produce dangerous levels of ozone (most hobbyist units won't). The ozone should be drawn by a venturi or forced through wooden or glass airstones in your skimmer, and returned to a sump.

Numerous authors cite the need for carbon filtration of water and air exiting an ozone-enhanced skimmer, or even special house venting to prevent ozone poisoning of both livestock and hobbyists. These fears are unfounded—provided you are using an ozonizer intended for home aquarium use. Though I would not directly introduce ozone into an aquarium, the little that intended units produce is dissipated quickly when utilized in a skimmer or dispersed in a sump or filter box. The worst consequence of small ozone generators is the increased corrosion of rubber or silicone-tubing materials in your system. You, your fishes, and your house will not burn down, I promise.

Ozone's quick chemical degradation of large organic molecules that are responsible for off-color, turbidity, low oxygen, and some toxicities, makes its modest start-up and operational costs pale. If you're even vaguely considering an investment in any sort of meter, doser, denitrator, or ultraviolet sterilizer—*stop*. First buy and use a small aquarium ozonizer in conjunction with your skimmer. Almost all public aquariums utilize ozone with theirs—you should too.

Ultraviolet (UV) sterilizers are another commonly used form of germicidal filtration. Inquisitive aquarists sometimes become excited upon visiting a spa or swimming pool equipment shop and seeing the latest technology that might be applicable to their home fish tanks. UV sterilization is one such "miracle solution," and, in fact, UV purification is widely used in many industrial settings to kill pathogens in medical solutions, alcoholic beverages, and drinking water, among others.

Ultraviolet light is a natural part of electromagnetic radiation. In terms of frequency, it is of shorter wavelength than visible light. There are sizes, fittings, and models of UVs for virtually any aquatic application—freshwater and marine aquariums, pools, ponds, and recirculating multiple tank systems. For the indoor and backyard aquarist, UV can be very effective in reducing free-floating algae, bacteria, and other microscopic planktonic organisms.

However, a UV sterilizer should be of limited value in a properly set up and operated marine system. Too many people believe that zapping their water with a UV device greatly enhances water quality. This is not the case.

An adequately sized UV sterilizer for the volume of water in a system and rate of post-filtered flow will improve water quality nominally in terms of lowering overall free-floating microbe levels. Additionally, there is a slight improvement in dissolved oxygen, oxidation of metabolites, ozone production, and skimmer efficiency. It is up to the individual aquarist to decide whether this incremental improvement is worth the cost in procurement, electrical consumption, bulb replacement, and maintenance. UV and near-UV radiation, 295-400 nm (nanometers) have also been shown to aid in oxidation of organics, phosphate, and nitrogenous compounds through the collateral production of ozone.

Though the disease-reducing benefits above are considerable in maintaining a favorable environment, UV sterilization should not be relied on as the principal part of a filtration system. UV purification should be considered as a possible useful addition to an otherwise appropriate filtration system. Ideally, a UV sterilizer will reduce microbial levels to, or below, those in the wild. Population explosions of these organisms are most prevalent in new, disturbed systems, and ones where bioload feeding is concentrated and vacillating. This is the reason UV sterilizers are widely used in wholesale operations.

UV light is indiscriminate in the destruction of free-floating microorganisms. It kills "good guys" as well as "bad." Beneficial microbes (the "good guys") are absolutely necessary in almost all captive environments. For this reason, initial (break-in) periods of new aquatic setups should be run without UV sterilizers being turned on, and UV sterilizers should be left off in conjunction with some therapeutic treatments.

Organisms maintained in "well-filtered," strongly UV-sterilized systems seem to develop a type of immune-deficiency syndrome—they seem to lose their ability to ward off infectious diseases. This loss of apparent immunity occurs over long periods of time in a highly variable, nonselective manner. To my knowledge, this syndrome has never been scientifically documented, but I have observed it.

The water going through a UV sterilizer should first be run through biological filtration and mechanically filtered to remove particulates. Allowing air bubbles or any solid matter to pass through the UV contact chamber is contraindicated. For this reason, using an air-lift system as a means of moving water through the UV sterilizer is not a good idea. If a heat-exchanger and/or separate chemical filtration is utilized, these should be in line before the UV sterilizer. In other words, the UV unit should be the last part of the filtration system to have water passed through it before the water is returned to the live holding system. There are several reasons for this, but the two most important are: to remove as much "other stuff" from the water as possible so that the UV radiation will oper-

ate with highest efficiency, and to preserve beneficial microbes and their biological activity.

Ideal dwell time—the amount of time a given quantity of water is exposed to a given concentration of UV radiation—may be roughly gauged at about 10 gallons per hour flow per watt UV. This value, or higher, is adequate for providing a good kill rate per pass and will substantially reduce planktonic microorganisms and concentrations of organics. More vigorous flows are not necessarily to be avoided, but reducing dwell time will result in loss of efficiency per pass. Passing all the water in the system though the filter mechanisms once or more per hour is ideal.

Regular, routine upkeep is necessary to assure peak performance of a UV sterilizer. Sleeves and/or bulbs should be removed from their contact chambers and cleaned about once a month. Generally, this can be accomplished by simply wiping them with a clean, dry cloth or towel. If necessary, slime may be wiped off with rubbing alcohol.

If you decide it's worth the cost and upkeep time, here are the features to look for in buying a UV sterilizer:

1) a separate (remote) ballast unit that can be positioned in a place free of heat and water damage;

2) an indicator light to check for "on" operation;

3) an "automatic on" feature to turn the UV back on in the event of a temporary power loss;

4) couplings that are easily fitted to your system;

5) sleeving (of quartz or Teflon) at little or no additional cost;

6) guarantees and/or warranties;

7) all noncorrosive water-contact surfaces.

Ask other users about their experiences with given brand names and models, particularly in regard to leakage, ease of use, and maintenance.

ONE GOOD WORKING DEFINITION OF filtration is the sum total of all that we do to lessen the amounts of organic compounds imparted to the water by our livestock and feeding. The list of those unwanted and noxious materials is quite long. By a combination of biological, mechanical, chemical, and physical filtration, in concert with good maintenance practices, we are able to promote high water quality, preserving our aquarium inhabitants' disease resistance and overall health.

Protein skimming, ozonation, and UV sterilization, while very different, have the same goal: a reduction in the concentration of organics by removing them from the system's water. Chemical filtration provides a final polish, removing unwanted metabolites (and possibly treatment chemicals).

Each aquarist learns what combination of filtration methods is, for him or her, practical, affordable, and successful, yielding tangible results in the appearance of the water and the look and health of the fishes and invertebrates. Many combinations and configurations can be used to obtain the same excellent results. The choices are yours.

CHAPTER 4

Water

Natural Seawater, Salt Mixes, and the Pursuit of Aqueous Quality

ASKED TO NAME THE REAL secret to keeping marine aquariums successfully, to avoid serious problems and the loss of fishes, what would you say? Buying the right specimens? Disease control? Good feeding? All of these things are critical, but keeping water quality up is arguably the most important.

What is this mythical beast, this "water quality" that we are constantly reminded to track, tame, and keep under control? As you'll recall, one of the triads in our model of factors determining the well-being of any system (page 28) is "suitability of the environment." For the majority of problem situations and circumstances in a captive system, what we are talking about is water quality. Of the controllable variables of

Blue waters and Schooling Bannerfish (*Heniochus diphreutes*): marine aquarists must provide an acceptable medium for such water-bound species.

aquaculture, it is the part of the equation that most often comes apart and leads to trouble.

Everything about the health of your system is tied to water quality. If your fishes appear ill, check the quality of your water before you do anything else. More aquatic life has been saved by moving specimens to new water or executing a massive water change than by using all the available medications combined. I would say that the great majority of livestock problems in the home aquarium start and end with the water and how it is managed by the aquarist.

Let's work our way into a definition of what good water quality is and how it is best approximated. You won't have to become a chemist or physicist, I promise.

Synthetic Seawater Mixes

TWO SOURCES EXIST for the aquarist filling a marine tank: natural seawater

or synthetic salt mix added to freshwater. Real saltwater is used by very few hobbyists due to its many serious drawbacks: the cost and time involved in hauling and treating the water; the lack

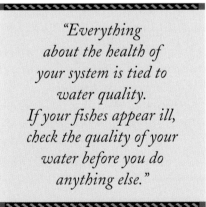

"Everything about the health of your system is tied to water quality. If your fishes appear ill, check the quality of your water before you do anything else."

of life-support or buffering; and the dangers of introducing undesirable pests and pollution.

Check the hobby magazines and you won't see many advertisements promoting gear for collecting, handling, or manipulating real seawater. Synthetic mixes are almost universally employed for captive systems, large and small. Huge public aquariums even use them, including the new National Aquarium at Baltimore. Even though it's right on the Bay, the experts who manage it mix up and recirculate hundreds of thousands of gallons of synthetic seawater—and for good biological reasons that should comfort any new aquarist who worries that he or she can't get "real seawater."

For small, closed systems, artificial seawater is highly preferred. It's convenient, cost-effective, and supports all forms of marine life. This was not, however, always the case.

One of the original questions facing the formulators of synthetic seawater was "How important is it to match the sea's chemical makeup exactly?" The first synthetic sea salt formulations met with little success biologically. These mixes were the initial attempts by chemists at a perfect duplication of nature, and they didn't work.

Starting in the 1950s in Germany, moderately successful mixes were made that focused on imitating the oceans' major constituents only, adding small amounts of trace materials as they seemed to be needed. In the United States in the early 1960s, W.E. Kelley and Richard Segedi at the Cleveland Aquarium significantly improved the German mix by lowering cost and further defining the concentration of certain trace elements. Today, this is the basic formulation used in all major, widely distributed salt mixes.

Any of the widely available synthetic salt mixes will serve the needs of most aquarium keepers; all supply the required major and minor ions and essential trace elements that occur in the world's seas.

Synthetic salt formulas have been used for decades all over the world by scientists, public aquariums, and hobbyists alike. The best available salt mixes have been demonstrated to support many invertebrates and fishes without further additives or modification. A few hundred species have been spawned and reared in this artificial medium.

Good synthetic mixes list approximately 70 trace elements in various formats in their makeup; some of these have already been deemed essential for life and the list is growing. It is a safe bet that more material will be considered necessary in synthetic mixes as time goes by.

Happily, the process of making artificial sea mix almost always involves utilizing dehydrated natural seawater that preserves some trace element material. Additional known essential trace substances are intentionally added to the rough raw mix.

The various brands differ slightly in initial pH, alkaline reserve, redox, and other measures, but with proper mixing they all seem to support most forms of captive marine life. (This is not to say that they are all the same or all created with equal care and attention to quality, but the beginning or intermediate hobbyist is hardly likely to notice the differences.)

Constituents of Natural Seawater and Salt Mixes

COMPLETE SYNTHETIC SALT MIXES contain three sets of components—major elements, minor elements, and trace elements. Major elements are defined as those occurring in concentrations of 1 part per million (ppm) or more; minor elements occur at between 1 part per billion (ppb) and 1 ppm; trace elements are present in concentrations of less than 1 ppb. (In the aquarium trade, the words "elements" and "ions" are used interchangeably.)

All commercial synthetic mixes are composed of about the same proportions of the major elements of natural seawater: chloride, sodium, sulfate, magnesium, calcium, potassium, bicarbonate, bromine, borate, strontium, and fluoride. These eleven ions make up 99.9% of the dissolved salts in natural and synthetic seawater in almost constant proportions.

Seawater also possesses smaller concentrations of all other naturally occurring elements found on Earth. Few of these have proved to be absolutely necessary to keeping marine life. Consequently, artificial saltwater is a simpler medium than natural seawater.

Some of the elements in ocean water have been found to be superfluous to successful marine aquarium keeping, while others are very important. A good example is the relative difference between the major element bromine and the minor element iodine. Bromine is present in the oceans at several thousand times the concentration of iodine, yet iodine is far more important biologically. If it becomes limited or absent, fishes exhibit goiterlike growths, soft corals can "melt down," and small-polyped stony corals can fade and die. Lack of iodine is also a common problem in keeping large sharks in captivity. Most of the trace elements in natural seawater are very minor, often transient materials of varying biological consequence. Although they are readily lost by physical, chemical, and/or biological mechanisms (including filtration) in captive systems, they are also

found in food sources, which restore much of the "trace benefit."

All major brands of salt mixes contain adequate amounts of major elements, minor elements, and essential trace elements. Standard setup and maintenance will keep you and your livestock in good stead chemically. The replacement of essential elements for almost all nonreef systems is easily made up by water changes and nutrition. Intensive aquaculture (breeding and propagation) and densely stocked reef systems may require, or benefit from, supplementation of certain major, minor, and trace elements that can become depleted in captive systems. Only in these cases will the aquarist want to consider such additives.

Using Natural Seawater

IN SOUTHERN CALIFORNIA, FREE, sand-filtered seawater is usually available 24 hours a day at the base of the pier at Scripps Institute of Oceanography, part of the University of California, San Diego, in La Jolla. This service is available at other sites in many coastal towns. It's a great spot to meet other saltwater enthusiasts, and if you are dealing with large volumes of water, the dollar savings can be considerable in using this water. It does, however, have its drawbacks.

The strongest argument against using real seawater is that it "dies," both biologically and chemically, more quickly than synthetic seawater. When using natural seawater, you *must* change part of the water more frequently. De-

pending on the size, type of setup, and filtration, 5% to 20% or more a month is often recommended. Many mixes should be changed just as frequently, but often, especially in terms of appearance (yellowing), you can "cheat" less with natural seawater.

Another factor concerning natural seawater, with both good and bad aspects, is that it contains a multitude of micro- and macroorganisms. Even if the water is sediment-filtered, diatom-filtered, ultraviolet-sterilized, and ozonized, many of these organisms will survive. There are two ways you can cope with this:

1) Place natural seawater in a dark place for a couple of weeks before using. Plankton and bacteria will die, settle to the bottom, and leave the seawater ready to filter and use.

2) Treat the water with copper salts, permanganate, formaldehyde, or chlorine, and remove the poisonous effects of the treatment with activated carbon or Poly-Bio-Marine's Poly Filter pads.

Although many dealers and hobbyists pour untreated natural seawater directly into their systems, I do not endorse this. I would treat all natural seawater as suspect and quarantine and treat it accordingly.

There are some good arguments for using real seawater containing these organisms to start up a new system. One point is that the time needed to establish bio-geo-chemical nutrient cycling is decreased greatly. Another beneficial factor is the ready seeding of the habitat for other microbial needs of the

Saltwater is best mixed in a dedicated storage vessel, but beginning aquarists may also rehydrate synthetic salt by first filling a new aquarium with tap water.

Synthetic salt mix is added at a rate of 2 cups per 5 gallons of fresh water; the water is then circulated for at least 24 hours to dissolve all solids and stabilize.

fishes, algae, and invertebrates. Some of the naturally occurring tiny creatures that come in seawater are harmful, but most are either beneficial or benign in captive applications.

Natural seawater should be monitored for pH/alkaline buffering capacity at the very least, and a supply of change water or chemical buffer preparation should be kept close at hand for adjustment. Ocean water, particularly supplies collected far from shore, can exhaust its buffering capacity very quickly (within a day).

This is not the whole story concerning natural and artificial seawater, but it illustrates the important points. In my opinion, unless you're dealing with very large volumes of water and astronomical salt-mix costs, steer clear of natural water. If you do decide to use the real thing, be prepared to devote yourself to adequate preparation and monitoring and be ready to put up with the vagaries of potential pollution, pests, and parasites. Synthetic seawater is more convenient, usually cheaper in total cost, longer lasting, safer, and—have no doubts—it works.

Salt Mix Rehydration

SYNTHETIC SALTWATER MIXES are, in a word, convenient. They serve their purpose as a viable medium for marine life and may be kept on a shelf and made ready as needed. I recommend mixing your synthetic seawater a week or more in advance of use. I also like to add a few cups of "live" system water, inoculating the mix with microbes and enzymes from an established aquarium. This will go a long way toward readying the new water biologically and chemically for use.

I highly recommend having a dedicated vessel for mixing and aging saltwater. You can use clean plastic garbage cans, 5-gallon buckets, or other containers. If recycling a storage vessel, be sure it has never been used for gasoline or other petroleum products or any sort of agricultural, industrial, or cleaning chemicals.

Source Water

THE PRINCIPAL INGREDIENT in a marine system, by weight and volume, is water. Your tap water has much more to it than just hydrogen and oxygen. Ordinary public or well water has dissolved and suspended gases, solids, other liquids, and organic life (or remnants of such). Most municipal water also comes with a sanitizer (usually chloramine). In southern California, we regularly have several hundred ppm of total dissolved solids in our tap water.

Does this pose real problems for an earnest marine aquarist? My view is that it is actually insignificant compared with all the other contributing factors affecting the makeup of your system's water. As long as you age and aerate or circulate tap water for a week, or do the same for synthetically made seawater, you should have no real worries about municipal sanitizers poisoning your livestock. When you must use tap water immediately, there are dechlorinators and dechloraminators available from your aquarium shop that will quickly remove most problem contaminants. I would urge you to buy brands from highly reputable makers such as Kordon, Tetra, and Aquarium Pharmaceuticals and follow the recommended dosages. Overdosing can cause problems. (The preparations of certain other companies contain Formalin, which irritates the fishes' skin to create a coating of protective mucous. This is *not* the way to cope with chlorine or chloramine.)

Compared with other contributing factors in marine systems, ordinary treated tap water is not typically a major source of concern in terms of added nutrients, pollutants, and/or metals. Freshwater biotopes with certain demanding fishes, such as wild discus and some killies, are a different matter. Likewise, corals and other delicate invertebrates are considered by many to demand purified source water.

Marine aquarists with reef systems and especially poor city or well water may find small home-scale reverse osmosis (RO) and deionization (DI) units of definite benefit, and more economical than the more basic cartridge-type conditioners. However, I suggest that even finicky reef types take a hard look at the quality of their skimmers and their feeding and supplementing habits before deciding that RO/DI will be their water-quality panacea. It's very often only a small part of the solution.

There is an unfortunate trend these days to blame our water source—or salt—without first considering other influences within the aquarium itself that affect water quality. Have you thought of the ongoing effects from dissolving substrates, rock, decor, feeding (1 ounce of food in 1 million ounces of water would be 1 ppm; 1 ounce of food in a 50-gallon tank is almost 160 ppm) and all the other biological processes going on in your closed sys-

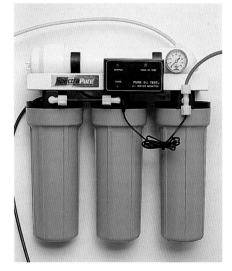

This affordable reverse osmosis/deionization unit provides 50 gallons of purified fresh water per day.

tem? Look to these first before deciding that your source water is at fault.

Water Changes

THE SINGLE MOST IMPORTANT WAY to reduce the inevitable process of captive life causing a loss of water quality is to get in the habit of doing regular water changes. This should be done on a regular, consistent time schedule. Assign yourself a day of the week or month and make it a ritual—it will become second nature after a while. Some especially fastidious aquarists prefer to do very small water changes daily—often just a gallon at a time, even for a 100-gallon tank—with excellent results. Do not be sold on any given technology that purports to make water changing unnecessary. Frequent, partial water changes are the least expensive, most effective way to ensure and sustain aquariums successfully. (See page 127, for water-changing instructions.)

Specific Gravity and Salinity

FIRST AND FOREMOST KNOW THIS: there is no one salt content, specific gravity, or salinity that is perfect for marine systems. I mention this not only so you won't agonize over constant checking and adjustment, but because it's a fact. Though below-surface values are remarkably constant in the wild, in your system, stability is far more important than actually hitting a precise salinity target. As a general rule, marine systems are best maintained between a specific gravity of 1.020 and 1.025, avoiding changes of more than a thousandth a day.

Commercial fish-only systems are frequently kept at artificially low specific gravities (1.017 to 1.020) for three principal benefits:

1) cost of salt mix is less (even aquariums that haul in natural seawater will dilute it with freshwater for a savings);

2) parasite and microbial levels are reduced (these life forms can't make the osmotic stretch as well as macrolife);

3) gas solubility or oxygen content is enhanced, increasing the carrying capacity and, possibly, the health of the system.

The margin of safety in adjusting fishes to new specific gravity is dependent on several factors, especially their adaptive state. To assist them, use a hydrometer to measure the water that your new charges come in and adjust their specific gravity toward that of your system tank over a number of days (another reason for a quarantine tank).

Fishes that originate from the Red Sea, where specific gravity is approximately 1.027, are exceptions that bear mention. These require consistent, higher specific gravity (1.023 to 1.025) to fare well. Systems with invertebrates, algae, and most types of live rock similarly appreciate upper range values and stability. While lowering the specific gravity rather dramatically can be a tool used by some to counter parasitic outbreaks in fishes, this cannot be done with sensitive invertebrates present.

An interesting aside about specific gravity: there are reports of several instances in which rapid reduction of specific gravity appeared to correlate with spawning activity. It has been suggested that lowering specific gravity might be tried as a triggering factor in captive breeding, along with light and temperature manipulation.

Measurement of Salinity

SALINITY IS A MEASURE of total salts in a given weight of seawater, generally expressed in parts per thousand. There are, as you could guess, more formal scientific definitions and many expensive ways to get precise measurements of the salt content in water. We don't need to get that involved. As aquarists, we rely on the measure of specific gravity (spg) to approximate a weight relationship between dissolved salts and salinity. The tools used for this measure are called hydrometers; they come in two basic formats, floating glass tubes and plastic-box types.

Glass hydrometers, frequently outfitted with an inner thermometer, range widely in their accuracy. Small, inexpensive models are notoriously bad, while large (12-inch-plus) ones are better, but pricey. Let me save you some money and frustration, please: whatever you pay, get and stay in the habit of using your glass

hydrometer in a separate, tall flask filled with water from your tank. I could have retired years ago on the money I've lost in broken glass hydrometers that I've left bobbing around in tanks and filter sumps. Reading your hydrometer properly is also easier in a static test chamber.

Plastic-box type hydrometers consist of a small container with an articulating pivot that floats to point to a number on an embossed scale. Get in the habit of rapping the filled box to knock off air bubbles on the pivot, and rinsing the box with freshwater after

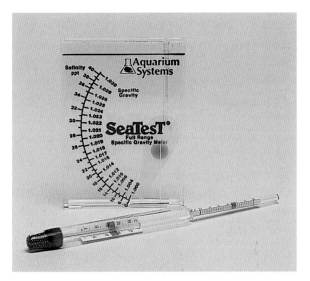

Simple hydrometers, either floating glass or plastic dip-and-read models, give sufficiently accurate readings for most aquarists.

use to attain and maintain accuracy. Although regarded by some as toylike, plastic-box hydrometers are fine for quick-and-rough measurements, and they are more accurate and precise than cheap glass hydrometers. (Electronic measuring devices are becoming more common and may appeal to those with discretionary budgets and the need or desire for more accurate readings.)

At this point you will also want to note the relationship between temperature and specific gravity readings. Cooler water is denser than warmer water. A change of 10 degrees F plus or minus is accompanied by a specific gravity reading change of about 0.001. Is this a big deal? In the grand scheme of things, no. A typical calibrated hydrometer is adjusted at 60 degrees F. Just know that if you want to keep your specific gravity at 1.025 at 80 degrees F, you will want a reading of 1.023 on the hydrometer.

Maintaining Stability

ALMOST ALL MARINE CREATURES ARE hypo-osmotic: that is, their bodies are less salty than the surrounding water. Consequently, and in contrast with freshwater organisms, they must consume seawater and eliminate the salts to fight the gradient of freshwater loss. Rapid changes (particularly increases) in salinity or specific gravity challenge their mechanisms for maintaining salt and solute balance.

Temperature can also dramatically affect the fishes and invertebrates we keep. All the marine organisms we keep are "cold-blooded"; their metabolisms are step-linked to water temperature. Both go up or down together.

How much variation in temperature and specific gravity can your specimens tolerate? If they're in good shape, quite a bit. Rapid and extreme changes are to be avoided, however; they all add up to stress. Aim for constancy in these measures.

The size of a system, believe me, can dramatically affect the stability of your specific gravity readings. Small tanks invite trouble from several steady-state points of view. Evaporation, water changes, adding food, a dying organism, temperature fluctuation from power failure, weather, or equipment failure can all conspire to raise/lower specific gravity quickly. The greater the total gallonage, the more insulated the system will be from rapid fluctuations.

Evaporation from bubblers, filtration, and the main water surface means a loss of water and an increasing concentration of the salt content. This lost water must be replaced regularly with aged, dechlorinated freshwater (purified by reverse osmosis, deionization, or other means, if you wish).

Don't believe the claims of some of the system and filter suppliers that water changes or maintenance are unnecessary. Periodically, we must remove a small percentage of the water in our systems and replace it with unpolluted seawater (natural or synthetic). Simply adding freshwater for long periods to replace what has been lost to evaporation is a very poor idea. Inevitably, the correct balance of major, minor, and trace elements will be lost. The addition of higher density matter, such as food that goes into solution, acts to raise specific gravity; many additives can also cause chemical deviations. Over time, this is not a pretty picture

if all you're doing is shoveling in more food and additives and skipping the water changes. Set up your system to reduce both salt loss and water loss. Gross as it may sound, it is good practice to scoot the crusty salt accumulation on the top and sides of your setup back into the water. This helps to retain consistency in water makeup and specific gravity. (Be careful not to let the flakes fall directly onto any invertebrates.)

When you do your religious water changes, take care to adjust the specific gravity and temperature of the replacement water toward the measurements you are aiming for. Remember also that even the best salt mixes do not dissolve instantaneously. Use a dedicated storage container (with lid, water-mixing pump or airstone, and heater) for premixing and aging synthetic saltwater for at least 24 hours and preferably for a week before adding it to a live system. (For more detailed advice on water maintenance, see pages 125-131.)

Acidity, Alkalinity, and pH

WHAT IS pH? Why are aquarists so concerned about measuring it? Do you really have to understand pH to have a beautiful marine aquarium?

Let's start by saying that pH is a "window" into water quality and a simple, powerful tool for looking at the state of our aquariums. Monitoring and controlling pH and alkalinity in your system water are crucial to your success. Although many people confuse the terms acidity and alkalinity in their relationship to pH, you'll soon understand what pH is, why it is important, and what you can and should do about it as a conscientious aquarium owner.

The symbol pH is a contraction that stands for *pondus Hydrogenii* (weight of hydrogen); pH is the relative measure of hydrogen-ion concentration. Put another way, pH is a measure of the relative presence of H^+ (hydrogen ions) versus OH^- (hydroxyl ions). Note that when these charged ions get together, they tend to form uncharged molecules of water (H_2O).

At any given moment in solutions, some hydrogen and some hydroxyl ions are getting together, falling apart, and generally floating around. The relative presence of one ion over another is what determines the pH of the solution. Since pure water, the standard reference point for the pH scale, contains 10^{-7} moles of hydrogen ions and 10^{-7} moles of hydroxyl ions per liter, it is said to have a pH of 7.0 and to be neutral. The capacity of a system to resist an upward change in pH is termed acidity. The capacity of a system to resist a downward change in pH is termed alkalinity. This is also referred to as either acidic or alkaline reserve.

In seawater, there are materials that "fight" or resist changes in pH. These include chemicals suspended, dissolved, or capable of dissolving into solution (gravel, live rock, and coral skeletons); foods; water treatments; and tap water ingredients. Using these materials in the aquarium can help or hinder efforts to change water chemistry.

Municipal water must be aged or treated with dechlorinators and dechloraminators and then tested.

The Biological Importance of pH

THERE IS AN IMPORTANT relationship between the efficiency of a physiological function (such as an enzyme system) and a range of pH. Peak efficiency of the physiologocal function is achieved only within a narrow limit of pH, with function dropping off quickly at a slightly higher or lower pH. All living things are made up of these transient collections of enzyme systems. These systems are both negatively and positively affected by suitable limits and slow changes in pH.

Let's consider the pH of human blood. The normal acceptable pH range is approximately 7.25 to 7.35—a fairly narrow margin that is slightly alkaline. If you held your breath, your blood pH would dip in sync with the buildup of carbon dioxide in your blood (actually carbonic acid). Alternatively, if

you hyperventilated, your blood pH would be driven up. Both conditions have their practical limits. Your blood has only so much buffering capacity and only so many moderating mechanisms. At some juncture in moving your blood pH too much or too fast, your body would go into shock.

The metabolisms of fishes and other aquatic life are often closely tied in with the chemistry and physics of their surrounding medium (water). This is particularly true with marine life (as opposed to freshwater species). Sea organisms have two relative strikes against them: they take in water more readily, and most have much narrower tolerances than freshwater species. For this reason, *dramatic or quick shifts in pH are very dangerous*. Even though there are buffering mechanisms to resist these changes, the fluctuations do weaken your livestock. Organisms that are not healthy may be pushed over the edge. The presence of pH shock is not always obvious at the time (if the individuals survive), but other negative influences can cause their "mysterious" demise within hours, days, or weeks. This is one reason why so much mortality occurs during shipping (pH shock from oxygen combined with the limited buffering capacity of a small volume of water) and why you should always try to wait a week or more before taking new arrivals home from the fish store (allowing time for the organisms to recover—or die—from pH shock).

What Is a "Good" pH?

THE AVERAGE PH OF OCEAN WATER IS about 7.8, ranging from 7.5 in deep areas to 8.4 in shallow reef areas (where higher temperatures and the presence of algae carrying on photosynthesis tend to use available CO_2 and make the water more basic). These measures are slightly alkaline (basic), indicating that saltwater has a natural alkaline reserve.

Logically, natural and fabricated seawater in the aquarium should be kept high (7.8 to 8.4) and, more importantly, stable. This can be done by not overcrowding and not overfeeding your livestock, setting up your system properly with adequate substrate, using proper filtration, and performing routine frequent, partial water changes. Reef aquarists generally strive to keep their pH in a tighter range, from about 8.2 at night to 8.4 or, at the maximum, 8.5, during the height of the lights-on period.

With the addition of foods, and the operation of your filters, the alkaline reserve is nicked away over time (by the accumulation of nitric acid, organic acids and phosphate) and your pH may subsequently fall (become more acidic). Your task is to guard against both slow degradation and drastic drops through monitoring and/or maintenance (typically with the use of chemical additives or buffers).

A note of caution: beware of fast changes in water chemistry. If you find yourself faced with having to adjust pH, don't change it more than 0.2 in 24 hours.

Measuring pH

THE TWO MOST POPULAR METHODS for determining pH point and alkalinity involve colorimetric and electrometric assays. The latter are the electronic pH pens, meters, and other gadgets that are the toys of chemists, advanced aquarists, and tinkerers. These electronic units give quick and convenient readings, but must be calibrated frequently for accurate results. Colorimetric (color-measure) tests are simpler, cheaper, but accurate enough for most aquarists.

Liquid, litmus paper, dry-tablet, and pillow-reagent varieties of pH colorimetric measures abound. All will do, but having the color reference standards set in permanent plastic is a bonus compared to the ultra-cheap versions printed on paper. The less expensive kits can be utilized for everyday testing, and if you have access to a bet-

ter test, you can compare and check precision and accuracy and use it for backup.

You should also buy and use an alkalinity test, especially if you are keeping or intend to acquire corals, clams, or other invertebrates. Alkalinity is a measure of the buffering capacity of water, and generally includes bicarbonates, carbonates, borates, and hydroxides. An acceptable range of alkalinity values is 2.5 to 3.5 milliequivalents per liter (meq/L).

Carbonate hardness is another measure that can be used in place of alkalinity to read the carbonate and bicarbonate content of the water; a target of 7 to 10 dKH (a German measure of hardness) is the rule for reef aquariums. The simple goal is high alkalinity (or carbonate hardness) to keep pH stable and optimize calicification by the invertebrates. Low alkalinity, carbonate hardness, or buffering capacity is a real cause for concern, as a sudden, catastrophic plummeting of pH is all the more likely.

Finally, consider that there is a hundred-fold difference in pH between readings of 7.0 and 9.0. Imagine being immersed in saltwater 24 hours a day, as your livestock are. You would become very sensitive and vulnerable to shifts in pH that are invisible to the human eye peering into a body of water. The pH affects, and in turn is affected by, many factors important to aquatic life. Keep your pH elevated and stable through correct setup, regular maintenance, and, if necessary, outside modification.

CHAPTER 5

Setup and Aquascaping

*Step-by-Step Guidelines for Planning, Equipping, Decorating,
and Stocking Simple Marine Systems*

T HERE ARE GREAT CHEFS who create whole meals without a single written recipe, relying on instinct, experience, and a keen sense of smell, taste, and timing. Most of us prefer a more orderly cookbook approach, at least in the first attempt at doing something new. For anyone starting a new saltwater aquarium, my step-by-step recipes and checklists for three basic systems follow. These are far from the only methods you might use, but they are time-tested, they will work, and they cover all of the basics. You may amend these procedures to suit your own circumstances, but remember that it helps to know, and understand, the rules before you start breaking them.

Reef tank with a bed of giant clams: creating an aquascape with species that appeal to you requires some investigation, planning, and self-discipline in not buying equipment or specimens on impulse.

Setup in 15 Steps: The Archetypal Fish-Only System

Step 1: Investigate. This step ought to be the most fun and mind-broadening step, and yet a huge percentage of newcomers to aquarium keeping breeze by it without a second thought.

How are you going to get to where you want to be if you don't know "where" it is or the best route to get you there? Knowing you want a marine aquarium is not enough. You wouldn't go into a car dealership and buy a new vehicle without first making at least a mental checklist of the features you absolutely need, the options you might like, and an idea of how much you want to spend. Too many first-time aquarium buyers acquire on impulse and later find that the tank is too small for a fish they really want or the lights too weak for an anemone or soft coral they always dreamed of having.

Resolve to visit all the good aquarium shops within easy driving distance. Ask to talk to the marine aquarium manager or a senior salesperson. Don't necessarily seek advice from the first

> *"Too many first-time aquarium buyers acquire on impulse and later find that the tank is too small for a fish they really want or the lights too weak for an anemone they always dreamed of having."*

confused teenage clerk who tries to wait on you. Let them know you are thinking about setting up a new system and that you have lots of questions. A good shop will have someone to step in and spend some time with you. Talk to other aquarists (don't be shy about talking to strangers in fish shops; most will be more than glad to share their opinions and advice with a newcomer).

Zero in on the type and size of system that appeals to you; think about the livestock that strike your fancy. In addition to chatting the subject up with other hobbyists and dealers, take the time to read books and magazines on the topic (see Bibliography, page 408). If you have computer and Internet access, check out the many sites that provide advice to aquarists. Good information is available, but it may take some searching on your part.

Step 2: Make Lists. As you will quickly appreciate, the intersecting worlds of fish species, invertebrates, and aquarium equipment hold more choices, options, and temptations than most mortal minds can sort or even begin to understand in a short time. Know that confusion is a normal state at this point; relax and look forward to years of learning and experimentation. Begin by narrowing down the scope of your system, both livestock and hardware components. My advice? Make lists; modify or copy mine (on these pages) to detail equipment you might need or want, with manufacturers, makes, models, sizes, prices, and features. (Also read the sections on Planning and Modeling, pages 115-117.)

Be bold, make copies, and take them to your dealer(s) to get more ideas and opinions of your plans. Chances are good that in your visits to local stores you will have found an owner or sales-

Marine Setup Checklist

Aquarium
- ❏ Glass or Acrylic Tank
  - Length _____
  - Width _____
  - Height _____
  - Gallonage _____

Stand
- ❏ Aquarium cabinet
- ❏ Sturdy, level shelf, counter, desk or other platform
- ❏ Custom stand or enclosure (optional)

Lighting
- ❏ Lighting hood, top, or reflector
- ❏ Glass or acrylic covering plates (with polished edges)
- ❏ Lamp(s)/bulb(s)

Circulation
- ❏ Circulation pump
- ❏ Powerhead(s))

Protein Skimmer Choices
- ❏ Internal
- ❏ External
- ❏ Hang-on-tank
- ❏ In-sump
- ❏ Air-driven
- ❏ Venturi
- ❏ Downdraft
- ❏ Other _____

Filtration Choices
- ❏ Undergravel filter
- ❏ Pump for undergravel filter (air pump or reverse-flow powerheads)
- ❏ External power filter
- ❏ Canister filter
- ❏ Wet-dry or trickle filter
- ❏ Berlin-style sump
- ❏ Other _____

Miscellaneous Filtration Items
- ❏ Necessary plumbing supplies, fittings, valves
- ❏ Airline tubing
- ❏ Check valve for airline tubing
- ❏ Filtration media (carbon, pads, foam inserts, resins)
- ❏ Other _____

System Options
- ❏ Ozonizer
- ❏ Ultraviolet sterilizer
- ❏ Other _____

Water/Water Preparation
- ❏ Seawater (natural seawater or synthetic salt mix)
- ❏ Hydrometer
- *Options*
- ❏ Storage container: to mix and age seawater (with optional heater and small circulation pump or air bubbler)

- ❏ Reverse osmosis/deionization water-purification units
- ❏ Water conditioner for treating tap water

Water-Quality Testing and Maintenance
- ❏ Saltwater test kit: tests for pH, ammonia, nitrite, nitrate.
- ❏ Dedicated-use bucket
- ❏ Siphon/gravel vacuum
- ❏ Aquarium-only cleaning pad
- ❏ Towels for tank use only

Options
- ❏ Reef test kit (low-level nitrate, phosphate, alkalinity, calcium)
- ❏ Electronic monitors (pH, temperature, ORP, etc.)
- ❏ Electronic controllers (lighting, heating, chilling, ozonizer, etc.)
- ❏ Other _____

Temperature Control
- ❏ Submersible, thermostatically controlled heater
- ❏ Thermometer(s); to check temperature.

Options
- ❏ Chiller: for hot climates and systems with high-wattage lighting

Aquascaping
- ❏ Coral rock
- ❏ Live rock

- ❏ Decorative coral (real or artificial)
- ❏ Substrate/Gravel/Sand: 1 to 1.5 pounds per gallon
- ❏ Aquarium background material (or paint)

Options
- ❏ Two-part epoxy, electrician's plastic cable ties (for creative rock assembly)

Hardware / General
- ❏ Electrical extension cords and outlets
- ❏ Ground fault interrupter
- ❏ Aquarium-only towel or paper towels
- ❏ Duct tape (attaching background to tank)
- ❏ Other _____

Maintenance
- ❏ Salt mix: for water changes
- ❏ Foods
- ❏ Net
- ❏ Supplements (calcium, buffer, magnesium, iodine/iodide, etc.)
- ❏ Other _____

Reference Materials
- ❏ Books, magazine articles
- ❏ Your own equipment list
- ❏ Your own species list
- ❏ Aquarium logbook

person who has taken the time to answer questions and who seems to offer honest advice. Ask more questions, discuss things that might be confusing to you. By the time you are done, you should have at least two lists: a species plan and a checklist of needed equipment and hardware items.

Step 3: Buy Your System Components. By this point, you will have figured out the aquarium and equipment you need and where you want to spend your money. Most aquarium stores will give substantial discounts on "starter setups." Some have very good preselected packages of equipment, but if you want to create a custom starter system, don't be afraid to ask for preferential pricing. New customers are vital to these stores, and they should be willing to work with your equipment lists. (If their starter package fails to include a protein skimmer, for example, insist that an appropriate model be included at an appropriate starter price.)

Don't even think of buying a live organism at this time. (This is not a goldfish bowl and you will not be setting up and adding livestock in the same day, or even the same weekend.)

Step 4: Preassemble Your Gear. Get everything out and check it over thoroughly. Read the boxes and inserts (I'd save all of these). Is it all there? There are few things more frustrating than discovering you don't have a part, thermometer, sufficient tubing or valves . . . after the stores are all closed.

Step 3: system components for a beginner's inexpensive 55-gallon fish-only tank, with undergravel filter, external power filter and in-tank protein skimmer.

Do a dry run trying out your equipment piece by piece with the exception of the heaters—to make sure it's all there and that you understand how it works. If seriously confused, call your contact at the shop where you bought the equipment.

Step 5: Test the Setup. Carefully rinse your aquarium with freshwater (do not use soap, Windex, or other household cleaners) and dry the outside. (Beware of using sponges, unless you are sure they do not contain antibacterial agents. Many sponges now come predosed, and the residues can kill your livestock.)

Rinse all filters, outside plumbing, and sump, if you have one. Place the dry aquarium on its stand, and be sure it is level. Connect your ground fault interrupter extension cord to the outlet you plan to use, and be sure your wiring is secure, accessible and out of the likely path of any water spills. Install all filters, pumps, and heaters, but do not plug anything in yet.

Fill the tank and filters with freshwater. Remember, no salt; this is only a test. Now, piece by piece, plug in and turn on your equipment. Start the heaters last, after they have adjusted to the temperature of the freshwater for 15 to 30 minutes. Set the thermostats for the temperature you will want, say 75 degrees F to start. Take a temperature reading. Lift the light hood into place, set your lighting timer, and test the lights. Finally, dry any wet spots on the exterior of the system.

Let it all run for at least a day to make sure everything works.

Step 6: Check for Leaks. The next day, while your system is still running freshwater, check everywhere for leaks. Chances are very good that there will be none, but if you have a problem, call the place where you bought the equipment. A good store should replace anything for free and on the spot at this early stage, unless it is apparent that you've abused it. Take another temperature reading to be sure the heater and its thermostat are working and properly set. This is the time to find out if your stand is not level, if a fitting's loose, or if your heaters are out of control. Once you've added salt, gravel, and decor, you won't want to have to empty the system to remedy these basic configurations.

Step 7: Premix the Seawater. If you're serious about this enterprise, you'll follow my advice and have one or more storage vats (clean Rubbermaid trash containers or the like are perfect) to mix and age your saltwater. These can be tucked away in a closet, the basement, garage, or a shed, but should have lids to keep out dust and debris. A small powerhead pump or air bubbler, along with a heater in cold climates, should be running in the vat when water is being prepared.

Many beginning aquarists choose to mix their saltwater in the aquarium itself, but I recommend having a supply of premixed, preaged, ready-to-use aquarium water. It will save you countless woes over the coming years, it will make routine maintenance and water changes quick and convenient, and it may even help save your system and all its contents in a water emergency.

Follow directions on the salt mix itself for rehydration; a normal ratio is 1.4 pounds of dry mix to 5 gallons of freshwater (1 kg per 30 liters). We will aim for a specific gravity of 1.023 to 1.025, but let the freshly mixed solution circulate overnight before you try to test it. If the specific gravity is too low, add more salt mix; if it's too high, add more water. Newly mixed saltwater will be cloudy, and some mixes clear more slowly than others. Measurements done before all of the salts have dissolved are worthless.

Step 8: Apply Background. The color of the back wall of your tank can make a huge difference in the overall appearance of the setup. If you've bought an acrylic aquarium with a built-in blue or black back plate, simply proceed to the next step.

For clear acrylic or glass aquariums, the simplest and quickest backdrop comes in the form of colored films, waterproof paper, foil, or other similar products available from any good pet shop. Apply it now, while you can easily get to the rear of the aquarium. Be sure all surfaces are clean and dry, and seal all four edges with duct tape or other heavy-duty, water resistant tape.

For glass aquariums, painting the outside of the back is a more permanent solution. Any latex enamel paint, applied with a brush or spray can, will work fine. (See Tank Backgrounds, page 118.)

Step 9: Fill with Saltwater. Assured that you have no leaks and all equipment has passed a freshwater test, you may now begin to fill the system for good. Unplug all electrical equipment and remove the lighting hood. If you have premixed your saltwater in separate storage containers, empty the tank and all filter chambers of the freshwater used in the test and discard the water or use it for watering the plants. Fill your aquarium with your premixed saltwater, but not all the way to the top! Leave the water level a few inches below the rim in order to accommodate displacement from your arm, other gear, and rock or other decor.

If you skipped Step 7 and have

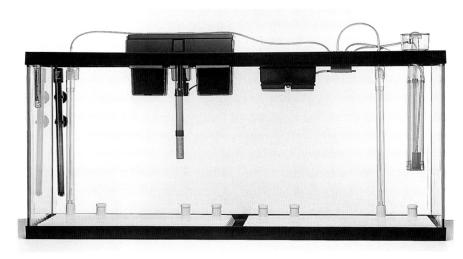

Steps 4 & 5: crucial steps too often forgotten include assembling and checking all equipment, then testing for malfunctions or leaks while the aquarium is filled with freshwater only.

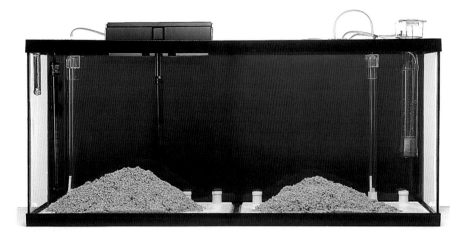

Step 10: once the tank has been checked for leaks with freshwater, the background should be applied and the aquarium situated in its permanent location. Remove heaters during aquascaping to avoid breakage.

opted to mix your saltwater directly in the display tank, add the correct amount of salt mix now, being sure not to overflow the system. Restart the pumps and heaters and allow the salts to dissolve overnight. The next day, you will likely have to adjust the specific gravity of the water (see Step 7).

At this point you may wish to sit back and let things run for a day or so to clear.

Step 10: Add Substrate. Before starting this or any other aquascaping steps, remove your heater or heaters if they are in the tank. These things are breakable! (*Always* unplug a heater before removing it.)

If you plan to use an undergravel filter or other plate system below the substrate, be sure it is in place and the air lines or powerheads are hooked up. (If the plates tend to float, release the air bubbles that have become trapped be-

neath them. It may be necessary to weigh down the undergravel plates with a piece of rock or heavy pottery until the sand is in place.)

Before adding your substrate or coral gravel, rinse it in batches in a bucket reserved for aquarium use. Put 5 to 10 pounds of sand at a time into the bucket and set it in a bathtub, shower enclosure, or outdoors. Run freshwater from a faucet or hose into the bucket while swirling the sand with your hand. As the water fills and overflows the bucket, it carries off the coral dust that you have stirred out of the substrate. At first, the rinse water will be cloudy, but will gradually clear as more dust is rinsed away. Don't worry about it being absolutely clear; this dust is harmless, but can cloud the system for a day or two if you don't rinse it away first. (If using live sand, do not rinse it. See page 74 for advice on this Jaubert-type setup.)

Gingerly pour the rinsed substrate into your tank to a depth of 1 to 2 inches. (See the section on Substrates, page 121, for additional information.)

Step 11: Do the Aquascaping. If using false corals, dry coral rock, or bleached coral skeletons, rinse each piece carefully and place in the aquarium. (See Aquascaping Materials, page 118.) Be sure to leave room—3 to 6 inches—on all sides (or at least near the front glass and two end panels) for later access with a cleaning wand or your hand. Snug the pieces of decor into the sand and ensure that everything is well-stabilized. Don't feel the need to rush. Use extreme care when placing rock or corals into the tank—these can very easily scratch acrylic or even break glass if dropped or allowed to topple over within the system. Keep your own safety in mind. A lot of corals, shells, and some types of rock are extremely sharp and pointy. Cuts, gashes, and scrapes are easy to come by, especially with large pieces. Wear long plastic gloves dedicated to your aquarium use when handling them. Step back frequently to get an overall view of how things are shaping up. The "perfect" arrangement takes time.

Step 12: Restart All Systems. Once the aquascaping is complete, re-install the heaters and start all filters and pumps, except for the protein skimmer. Hook up your lighting, timers, service switches, and other electrical items.

Step 14: when the specific gravity, pH and temperature are adjusted and stable, inoculate ("seed") the new system with beneficial bacterial cultures.

Concerned about electrical shock? Good. I strongly advise you to use a grounding probe and a ground fault interrupter. Don't handle electrical plugs or wiring with wet hands, don't stand in puddles while manipulating electrical gear, and wear rubber-soled shoes when working around water and electricity.

Step 13: Rest and Test. New setups are virtually always cloudy. Let things run for at least a day to "allow the dust to settle" and to give your system time to stabilize chemically and physically. Some folks crank up the temperature to 82 to 84 degrees F and/or extend their lights-on period to 24 hours during initial setting up, to speed up establishment of cycling and beneficial algae growth. Don't do this once any livestock are in place.

After letting some time lapse, check your water parameters. Temperature, pH, and specific gravity should all be within the recommended limits. All pumps and filters should be running (with the exception of the protein skimmer), and your system water should be circulating and well-oxygenated. If anything is amiss chemically, you must adjust and correct before moving to the next step.

Step 14: Inoculate Your System. At this point, we are ready to add the first livestock—the all-essential bacterial cultures—to the aquarium. My recommendation is to start with a cup or two (a pound or so) of gravel or live sand from a healthy, long-established marine aquarium. This will be filled with the beneficial microbes needed to "seed" your system. Other sources are filter media from another marine system, including activated charcoal that has been in place for a couple of months, biomedia, live rock, or any other material that has been colonized by the needed bacteria. (Commercially packaged cultures are available, but many aquarists have had consistently better luck launching their systems with fresh.)

You also need to add a source of nutrients to feed the bacteria and encourage them to proliferate. (Review the explanation of the nitrogen cycle starting on page 77.) Aquarium shops can sell you ammonia, which will serve the purpose (follow directions explicitly and do not overdose). A livelier alternative, and the traditional approach, is to add a few rugged appropriate damsels or blennies that can survive the initial cycling of the system. Their waste products produce the essential ammonia. Other choices are bait shrimp or bait fishes, if these are available locally. Some aquarists simply add fish food or scraps of raw fish; as they decompose, the desirable ammonia is released.

Monitor and record the nitrogen cycle until there is no measurable level of either ammonia or nitrite (see pages 77-80). This generally will take from 4 to 8 weeks, at the most; with live rock and/or live sand, the cycling process may occur much more quickly. During this period, you will likely see growths of brown or golden diatoms and the beginnings of green algal coverage. Feel free to keep up appearances by brushing these off the front and side viewing panels.

If algae seem to be overtaking your decor, you may want to add a living maintenance crew in the form of snails (*Lithopoma* [*Astraea*] species; *Turbo* species; or others) and small herbivorous hermit crabs. Reef aquarists stock as heavily as one snail or hermit crab per gallon of tank capacity. These will not keep glass surfaces perfectly clean, but will do a good job on rockwork,

substrate surfaces, and in other nooks and crannies of the aquascape.

Step 15: Begin Stocking. As soon as ammonia and nitrite readings drop to zero, you may fire up your protein skimmer, if it isn't already working, and start stocking the system—slowly. (See Stocking Techniques, page 112-114.)

Variation I: The Fish and Invertebrate System

THIS IS ESSENTIALLY A REEF SYSTEM without intensive lighting and a relatively minimal list of equipment. A nice intermediate step for the aquarist who wants to keep hardy invertebrates, it has some additional circulation, in the form of an inexpensive powerhead, and improved protein skimming from an external or hang-on-the-tank unit.

The biggest difference is the use of live rock, and possibly live sand, which gives the aquarium a much more natural appearance and provides appropriate habitat for the shrimp, sponges, starfish, and feather duster worms, snails and small hermit crabs. Because we will be using "cured" live rock that has been held in a dealer's tank for at least four weeks, we can actually expect to have effective biological filtration within days, rather than weeks. The similarities and differences in this setup are as follows:

Steps 1-9: The same procedures as described for the Fish-Only System, above.

Step 10: Add Substrate. After the system has been running for at least 24 hours with saltwater and once your test kit shows that water conditions (temperature, specific gravity, and pH) are correct and stable, you may add live sand and/or live rock.

If using dried, packaged coral gravel or sand, simply follow Step 10, as detailed in the Fish-Only System, for rinsing the sand. Place rinsed sand to a depth of 1 to 2 inches on the bottom or over an undergravel filter plate. Add a small quantity (1 to 2 cups) of live sand from another reef system and with your fingers rake it into several spots on the bed of fresh sand.

If using all live sand, add the full contents of your bucket or box to the tank. (Never rinse live sand.) Remove any obviously dead organisms, such as crabs or brittlestars, that may not have survived the trip. If the quantity of live sand does not provide enough substrate, rinse and gently mix in the amount of dried aragonite you feel is necessary.

Step 11: Add Live Rock. If the previous step has clouded the water, you may wish to wait for it to clear before attempting to arrange your live rock. This procedure assumes you are using *cured* live rock. If using fresh or uncured rock, see page 73.

The amount of rock you use may be dictated by your budget, and you may choose to include less than might be called for in a full reef system. One generally used guideline is to add 1 to 2

The gear for a Fish and Invertebrate System, which employs an upgraded hang-on-the-tank sump with biomedia and skimmer, and a circulation-boosting powerhead.

pounds of live rock per gallon of aquarium capacity, but much depends on the shape, density and porosity of the rock. For a typical reef tank, the rock will loosely fill about one-third of the display space. A Fish and Invertebrate System might very well use less to leave more swimming room for the fishes.

While waiting to add the rock, keep it moist by misting with saltwater and covering loosely with saltwater-soaked newspaper or paper towels. Do not allow the rock to become overheated or chilled; it will tolerate some abuse, but the more you treat it like a live fish, the better the organisms it carries will survive. You may also rinse it in warm, aged seawater, but never in freshwater

or just-mixed synthetic saltwater.

Add the live rock to your tank, being careful not to build tight mounds or wall-like structures. Ideally, water circulation and small fishes should be able to move easily through your rockwork. Generally speaking, the largest pieces should go in first to create a firm foundation. Your goal is to create stability without jamming the rock into a dense mass (see diagrams, pages 114-115).

Once satisfied with the aquascape, reinstall the heaters (if they are to be within the tank) and restart all equipment, including the protein skimmer. Good circulation and good skimming will help get the rock and sand through the period in which they adjust to their

new setting and water conditions.

You may find other information sources that suggest adding the live rock in stages, leaving a week or more between new additions. This is now generally frowned upon. Each new introduction can trigger a fresh wave of ammonia and nitrite production (especially if the rock is not fully cured), which can be hard on delicate organisms in the system. Plan to introduce all rock at once and *never* add uncured rock to an established display tank.

Step 12: Limit Lighting Period.
Give the system a week or more to stabilize itself before running your lights at full power for 12 hours a day. (Don't

The Fish and Invertebrate System (shown with the light hood removed) makes full use of live rock to provide biological filtration as well as a natural setting for invertebrates and realistic nooks and crannies for fishes.

Step 14: Start Stocking. Your first fishes and invertebrates should all be the most hardy, easily fed species. Many invertebrates do not react well to freshly mixed synthetic saltwater or the unsettled conditions of a new aquarium. Waiting at least three to four weeks before introducing them will reduce mortality and transplant shock. (See pages 112-114 for fish and invertebrate stocking techniques.)

Variation II: The Reef System

THE PRIMARY DIFFERENCE between the Fish and Invertebrate System and the Reef System is the intensity of the lighting and the care required in stocking the fishes. The significantly increased amount of energy being pumped into this system can quickly lead to biological chaos, wild growth of microalgae, and unsightly slime cultures.

This setup absolutely demands good-quality skimming, brisk circulation within the tank, ample quantities of live rock, and a goodly population of herbivores in the form of snails, reef hermit crabs, and grazing fishes, such as tangs. At least in the beginning months, you are well-advised to avoid the inclusion of any large, carnivorous fish specimens, as these can rapidly increase the amount of waste that the living filter must handle. (It is for this reason that most reef tanks exclude large eels, lionfishes, and groupers and tend to gravitate toward smaller species and herbivores.) Selecting fishes for a

be afraid to adjust the lighting period to allow yourself an hour or two of viewing time each day. The tank inhabitants don't care which 12 hours are the "day" period.) To feed the bacterial population, you may wish to add small amounts of fish food or other sources of ammonia. If you have a small, separate quarantine tank, this would be a good time to acquire your first few hardy fishes and begin holding them in preparation for release into your reef.

Every few days, test for ammonia, nitrite, and nitrate, and move to the next step once all traces of ammonia and nitrite have disappeared. (With well-cured live rock, you may never see the usual nitrogen cycle progression.)

Step 13: Add Herbivores. Within about two weeks, green microalgae will often begin to grow on many surfaces within the system. This is normal, and you should only be concerned about clearing away the viewing panels at the front and sides of the tank. To keep live rock looking its best, and to prevent it from being smothered with algae, herbivorous snails and small hermit crabs should now be introduced. How many to use depends on many factors, with some reef keepers employing as many as one of these herbivores per gallon. A tang or other dedicated algae grazer also makes a fine addition at this stage, if algae is proliferating.

Skipping this step will almost invariably lead to a tank full of unsightly hair algae that dominates the aquascape and chokes out most sessile invertebrates. The beauty of a properly functioning reef aquarium is that you never have to remove pieces of the aquascape for cleaning—a crew of busy snails, hermit crabs, and algae-loving fishes will do the work for you.

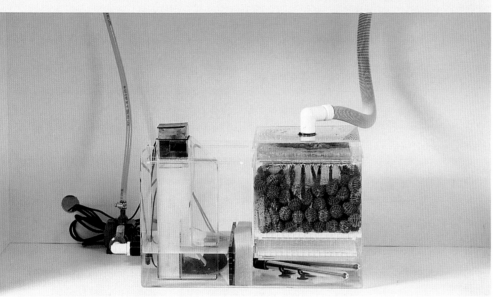

A simple reef system, using a below-the-tank sump that houses biomedia, heaters, detritus-trapping pads, and foam. A small skimmer stands in the sump, and an external pump returns water to the aquarium.

with simple hobbyist test kits.) Likewise, phosphate readings should be very low or zero.

Calcium ought to be between 400 and 500 mg/L, and the best way to start a new reef is to begin feeding calcium almost immediately. Alkalinity or carbonate hardness should also be high, above 8 dKH. This will encourage the proliferation of pink, purple, and red calcareous algae on the live rock; within a few weeks, tiny colonies of these algae should start appearing throughout the aquascape and on the sides of the tank. This is a very nice development, both for the appearance of the system and the fact that calcareous or coralline algae, once established on a surface, will usually prevent the growth of less desirable green microalgae.

Many hundreds of pages have been written in aquarium publications in many languages discussing methods of keeping calcium and alkalinity levels up in reef tanks. Your choices include the addition of Kalkwasser (a saturated solution of calcium hydroxide or calcium oxide slowly dripped into the system) or other calcium additives, including calcium chloride and two-part solutions that contain both concentrated calcium and a buffer. Newer technology involves the use of aragonite or calcium reactors, in which system water and CO_2 are circulated through a small tower of substrate. The aragonite slowly dissolves, feeding the system with calcium, magnesium, and other elements of possible use by reef organisms.

All of this need not be complicated.

typical reef aquarium requires care and experience, as many popular species relish the taste of live corals and the succulent flesh of giant clams.

Setup for the reef system is exactly the same as for the Fish and Invertebrate System, with one embellishment: you should acquire and start using a reef system test kit. The key tests will be low-level nitrate, phosphate, calcium, and alkalinity. With excellent skimming, a good bed of aragonite substrate, and a careful understocking of fishes, nitrates should remain very low, preferably lower than 10 ppm. (Many reef tanks show zero or only traces of nitrate

Beginning reef aquarists will find the addition of readily available calcium and matched buffer supplements simple and the results predictably good. (For larger systems, there are less expensive approaches.)

Other supplements that many reef aquarists use include magnesium (a key to calcification in corals), iodine or iodide, strontium, and others. Some soft corals seem prone to sudden demise (typically described as "meltdown") if iodide levels are allowed to fall. Recommendations and products are ever-changing, and you are encouraged to seek advice on this from a good reef aquarium shop or from other aquarists.

In any case, always carefully measure any supplements added to your aquarium. Heavy-handed overdoses can quickly shock or even kill delicate invertebrates.

Stocking Techniques for Fishes

WHETHER YOU ARE running a Fish-Only System or some variation of a reef aquarium, the living specimens should be purchased, quarantined if possible, acclimated, and placed into the tank in the following systematic way:

1) Introduce one species at a time, with a good two weeks between introductions. When possible, start with the less aggressive species and let them become established before the more territorial and feisty fishes arrive.

2) Feed sparsely at first.

3) In a new system, test your water for signs of elevated ammonia and/or

Marine fishes tend to acclimate better and display more natural behaviors in aquariums that provide places to hide in order to screen themselves from aggressors and carry out innate foraging and feeding activities.

nitrite after each new addition of livestock.

Species are introduced one type at a time to provide some assurance that the existing and new specimens will get along, the incidence and spread of disease will be reduced, and the newcomers will be prevented from overwhelming your biological-filtration bacteria population. A couple of weeks is adequate time for settling in and for the redistribution of territorial partitioning. It also allows for the necessary increase in natural biofilter microbe communities.

Especially with young systems, you may experience the effects of "too much, too soon" despite your best intentions. Should you register a spike in ammonia and nitrite concentrations or behavioral anomalies, there are definite things you should and should not do. Do not add any more food or specimens to the system. (Nothing in a normal marine aquarium will be harmed by several days of enforced fasting.) Partial water changes will help. If ammonia or nitrite get to dangerous levels and the stock appears distressed, you'll have to execute a massive water change, move a good part or all of the livestock, or resort to taking your chances with chemical filtrants designed to adsorb these wastes.

What if there are no chemical problems but you still observe wacky behavior after introducing new fish? Watch your tank closely for an hour. Your fishes are most likely not ill, they are probably out of balance territorially. Fishes in captivity live in communities, just as they do in the wild. There are very definite pecking orders and partitionings of resources. You will see winners, losers, and those who are ignored in any number of potential and actual interactions. The confines of a new aquarium system that must be properly conditioned to handle more livestock compel you to go slowly and steadily. Rush things and you can have an expensive, very sad crash. By pacing new additions, you allow the livestock to "rebalance" their social community.

There are a few time-tested techniques to help a new collection of fishes coexist and to prevent fatal aggression. Add more hiding places and reeflike decor—caves, nooks, crannies, and promontories or rocky walls—places where a fish can stake out a territory and disappear from time to time. You should also establish and follow a daily timetable for lighting and feeding. These routines are not very often written about, but environmental cues are crucial in the lives of coral reef organisms that follow highly ordered daily patterns dictated by the sun, moon, and the predictable availability of foods.

Disrupting their natural time frames is tremendously stressful and invites undesirable behavior. Use a timer on their lighting and try to feed at the same time or times each day. Establish a reliable routine; fishes can tell the difference.

When adding potentially aggressive new stock or when territorial problems arise, disrupt the physical environment (rock, coral, and shell skeletons). This may seem antithetical to establishing predictability—it is. In certain rare instances you want to upset the status quo in the tank in order to disorient the existing community and its territorial dynamics. Changing the landscape can give the new arrival(s) a chance to settle into a fresh milieu.

Pay attention to the biological density of your system. What if, no matter what you do, World War III is still going on in your system? Your tank may be overcrowded. It doesn't matter if your filtration can accommodate 10 more fishes; you're past the behavioral maximum for your given microenvironment. It may be time to take something out or to get a new or bigger system.

Stocking Techniques for Invertebrates

NONFISH SPECIMENS are also best introduced one at a time, with a week or two between new arrivals. Many invertebrates have chemical defense systems and can exude slime and mild toxins during and after shipping or handling.

Keepers of corals are increasingly adopting the practice of quarantining their new stock. Various infectious diseases can arrive with new specimens,

Sweeper tentacles from many scleractinians, such as this Bubble Coral (*Plerogyra sinuosa*), will sting and even kill other types of coral placed too close to it. Allow at least 6 inches of space between specimens.

and a week or two in a segregation tank is usually enough to be sure that you are not introducing a pathogen that might attack your existing corals. A rash of disease outbreaks in some of North America's best-kept stony-coral systems in recent years has been dubbed rapid tissue necrosis (RTN) and has been attributed to an unknown pathogen, perhaps a strain of *Vibrio*. It typically arrives with small colonies imported from the wild and can sweep through an entire aquarium in a matter of days, leaving many species of small-polyped stony corals dead in its wake.

Many corals, both hardy soft species and exotic stony types, produce copious quantities of slime, and their arrival can overwhelm a display system and its skimming apparatus. This overload of protein, defensive chemicals, and perhaps bacteria, can make acclimating the new corals difficult and can be a setback for existing colonies. (Old hands add a bag of fresh, activated carbon to the sump or filter during these introductions or use an ozonizer for a few days following each new arrival.)

Great care must be taken in placing any of the corals with offensive or defensive stinging capacities into your system. The tentacles of an anemone or stony coral can rapidly attack and even kill neighboring invertebrates. In general, try to leave a good 6 inches of space between specimens.

Never place a new sessile invertebrate high in the tank, close to your lights. It is best to start incoming corals

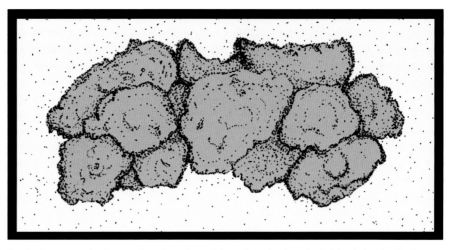
Four basic aquascaping layouts, viewed top down. This configuration is a simple island of rock, allowing swimming room all around and ample space for the aquarist to clean the sides of the tank.

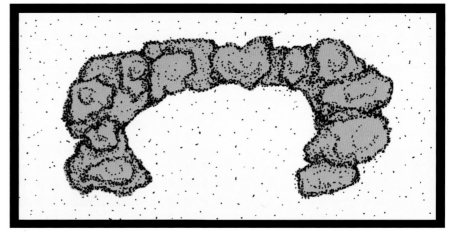
A variation of the layout at top, this arrangement of rock or other aquascaping material creates a sort of underwater lagoon or open bed of sand that particularly suits certain species of fishes and invertebrates.

lower in the tank and slowly move them upward over a period of weeks, eventually finding a combination of light intensity and water flow that seems to suit them best.

As with fishes, it pays to pace yourself and, whenever possible, to acquire new invertebrates one specimen or one species at a time.

Aquascaping

Q: "Do fish feel?"
A: "Sure, they feel slimy."

This is an old joke, but it raises a legitimate question for all of us who keep fish. How much should we take into account the emotional awareness of "simple creatures"?

There is both ample scientific and

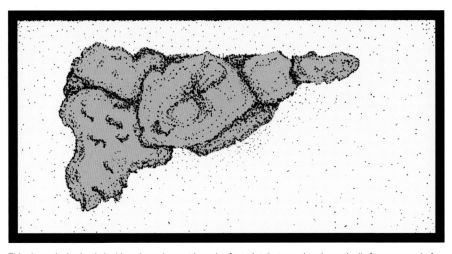

This deceptively simple-looking shape has a triangular footprint, but can rise dramatically from one end of the aquarium to the other. The large expanse of coral sand could be used for a bed of algae or baby clams.

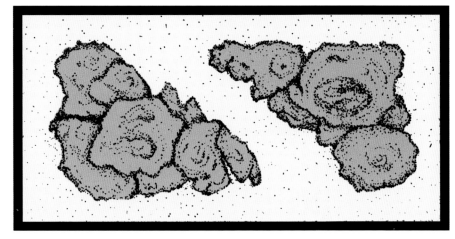

Twin peaks or a pair of triangular island shapes is simple to construct but offers many pleasing, complex viewing angles, a swimming channel for fishes, and many sites for the placement of sessile invertebrates.

anecdotal evidence that aquatic organisms (including invertebrates) are sensitive to the physical surroundings in their captive worlds.

For my senior report in ecology at San Diego State University, I did a series of experiments on "Substrate Size Preference" by the crayfish *Procambarus clarkii*, the incredible, edible crawdad from Louisiana. I set up three 10-gallon tanks, each with three sizes of gravel—alternating first, second, or third in placement. I placed a *Procambarus* in each tank, allowed it to adjust for a while and periodically looked in, recording what grade gravel it seemed to stay over. Varying light, water depth, and the size and sex of the individuals tested showed the same result. This species of crayfish displayed a clear statistical preference for finer gravel.

Would you like to spend 24 hours a day over a shiny, reflective floor in a bare room? I imagine this is how a fish must feel in a bare-bottomed tank. Every marine aquarium benefits from aquascaping—both aesthetically and functionally. A well-decorated system does much more than please the human eye—aquascaping makes the overall environment more comfortable for your livestock. Enhanced biological cycling from the increased surface area of sand and rock and added buffering capacity are just the beginning. Breaking up the physical space solves many social and psychological problems by providing hiding spaces from bullies (including you), and granting your fishes and invertebrates a sense of place. Aquascaping brings out your fishes' natural behaviors. Additionally, the aquascaping in an aquarium can play an important role in modifying the chemistry and physics of the system's water, filtration, and aeration.

Planning the Aquascape

THE AQUARIUM PLAN you started earlier to define your plans for equipment and livestock will naturally extend into the realm of aquascape preferences. Different fishes and invertebrates do best in different aquarium settings. For example, tangs like high relief and open swimming spaces; triggers need rocky spaces to hole up at night; nurse sharks require ample swimming room and large, sandy-bottom plains; and many reef species thrive only with adequate rockwork for security, foraging, and grazing.

How do you start? One avenue to take is limiting yourself to those materials you have on hand and can readily acquire from your local aquarium shops. Much more fun can be had by looking through fish and diving magazines, examining natural history picture books, watching underwater videos, or going on snorkeling trips. A visit to a good public aquarium can also spark creative ideas. Your arrangement can be biotopic (an attempt at replicating a slice of nature), political (a littered reef with a broken rum bottle and other human debris), or fanciful (a Martian landscape or a Zen garden). It's your artistic creation, and you can always add, subtract, or redo it entirely. Once the system is stocked and stabilized, however, major overhauls will be more disruptive and problematic for you and your animals.

Modeling

A USEFUL AQUASCAPE PLANNING approach is to make a full-sized grid with a cardboard bottom and background and practice stacking and arranging things before putting them in the tank. This is your chance to check aggregations of rock for stability, maybe joining them with silicone rubber, special epoxies, or reef-safe cements. Make sure the assemblies will fit through the cut-outs in your tank top if you're using an acrylic tank.

Large, gnarled pieces of live rock command premium prices but are ideal for artistic aquascaping. Many aquarists assemble the reef on a bare-bottomed tank to achieve good stability before adding substrate.

If you're using live rock, this can be a wetter, trickier, but still useful, exercise. Most aquarists simply stack their rock directly into the tank, but some exceptional effects can be had by first securing pieces of rock together to form larger assemblies—caves, bridges, ledges, and other natural-looking features. Two-part epoxies of various sorts can be used to bond rocks together permanently, and these can be had from aquarium stores, yachting hardware shops, and plumbing suppliers. Look for quick-curing epoxy without metal fillers. Plumber's Buddy is one aquarium-safe product available in small packages, while Z-Spar Splash Zone Compound is a heavy-duty two-part epoxy that comes in 2-gallon kits for large projects. For small attachment tasks, Superglue Gel from office-supply stores dries quickly and is nontoxic once dried. Portland cement may also be used to construct artificial reef structures or to join pieces of rock. The beauty of many of these materials is that they will cure underwater. Silicone rubber must be applied to dry surfaces and allowed to cure for at least 48 hours in the air before being submerged. In addition to aquatic cements, silicone, and epoxies, long plastic cable ties, found in the electrical section of hardware stores, can be very useful for securing pieces of the reefscape together. These are inert, unobtrusive, and come in all the sizes that an aquascaper might need. Have a packet or two of clear or black cable ties around at aquascaping time and you'll be amazed at how often they come in handy. Once in place in the aquarium, these are barely noticeable and, in reef tanks, will become covered by coralline algae in time.

As you assemble the rockwork, remember to consider ongoing maintenance, such as cleaning. How are you going to get around and underneath the decor to remove detritus or algae? Ideally, you should leave open space around the entire inside perimeter of the tank. If you decide to stack anything against the back or side walls, understand that it may be exceedingly difficult to remove algae from the glass or to get at detritus or other problems.

Electrician's plastic cable ties can be used to secure pieces of rock into ledges and other shapes.

Think of the water flow patterns you will create, and beware of dead spots. Also think about how to provide for total flow-through circulation by way of filter returns, a powerhead pump, or currents created by airstones.

How about concealing tubing, heaters, probes, and all the other paraphernalia? This is part of what aquascaping is all about, but be sure that rocks, coral, or other screening materials are arranged to be very stable and, in the case of hidden equipment that might fail or need servicing, removable.

Watch out for underminers among your planned tank inhabitants—blennies, gobies, eels, some crustaceans, and others seem determined to topple your aquascaping. Toppling pieces of heavy rock can severely injure or kill certain fishes—eels are common victims—so take seriously the challenge of building an aquascape that will not slide or collapse.

A new tool for creative aquascaping: two-part epoxy putty forms strong, nontoxic bonds underwater.

Tank Backgrounds

YOUR TANK MIGHT HAVE COME WITH an integral background, or you may have purchased a commercial backdrop. Most aquarists opt for something neutral—paint, paper, colored foil, felt, cork, or other creative applications. As this is all outside the system, the only real rule is not to use anything reflective. The bright mirror images drive some fishes and invertebrates crazy. At the opposite end of the spectrum is basic black. It conveys an impression of depth and becomes virtually unnoticed, letting the colors of the fishes and the beauty of your aquascaping take over. In addition, if you stick to black in selecting tubing, wiring, filtration, and other back-of-the-tank intrusions, these will tend to fade into obscurity when the background is also black. Deep blue also seems to provide a realistic backdrop and can be applied either as paint or by using an off-the-shelf aquarium backing sheet.

An old idea is to build a scene behind the back glass of the tank to give the illusion of a deep panorama. I have visited private and public aquariums all over the world, and some of the dioramas in and outside of systems I've seen are fantastic—whole caves and reefs made of fiberglass, resins, or epoxy paints. It is amazing to me how much can be done with simple tools, materials—and inspiration.

I wouldn't necessarily attempt a diorama or any elaborately engineered rockwork in a first aquascape. On the other hand, a few evenings of plotting and planning can make your aquarium easier to maintain, a better environment for your charges, and a thing of beauty that is different and distinctive.

Aquascaping Materials

THE BUILDING BLOCKS most commonly used for marine aquascaping are ancient coral rock (the off-white chalky kind), live rock, coral, and shell skeletons as well as a huge assortment of plastic, fiberglass, epoxy, and other faux material. For more advanced reef aquarists, it is now even possible to aquascape with live, reef-building corals.

Be extremely leery of putting just anything you've picked up into your system, including "treasures" from seashore excursions or freshwater decorations. Everything that goes in must either be chemically inert (nonreactive) or, if soluble, of benefit to the saltwater chemistry. Be suspicious even of things you see offered in the decor sections of pet stores. A great deal of rock offered in the pet trade is unsuitable for some or all uses because it reacts unfavorably with the water and fishes, invertebrates, plants, and macroalgae. Notable examples are geodes, some volcanic rock, and petrified woods. All "old" rock, coral, and shell material from shelves, attics, cellars, and gardens is suspect, if for no other reason than you don't know where it has been. Residue from tobacco smoke, cleaners, insecticides, or other chemicals might be on or in them. All should be thoroughly washed and adequately tested. I strongly favor a

Tank backgrounds can dramatically improve the overall impression given by an aquarium, as seen in this before and after sequence. Black suggests depth and helps bring out the colors of the live specimens.

GOOD: dry "honeycomb" coral rock from the Bahamas makes an inexpensive reef material.

BETTER: live base rock is rather uninteresting but provides a suitable foundation for aquascaping.

BEST: prime live rock, well-covered with coralline algae, is the material of choice for reef aquarists.

bioassay, using a sample of the decor and a small test tank with a few damsels. An exposure period of two weeks will generally reveal if the material is outright toxic.

A further word of caution here. Some rock, various volcanic types in particular, have been implicated in longer-term chronic poisoning of marine livestock. There are many writers, retailers, and hobbyists who will only utilize calcareous rocks (coral, limestone, or quartz) in their marine systems. Watch out for soft and granular rock or chunks of lava. Some sedimentary and metamorphic rock just dissolves away, polluting, or at least clogging up, your system. Any rock with metallic contact should be shunned.

Even considering all the problematic materials that exist, there are still many types of rock that are suitable and available to collect or buy. There are many manufacturers offering "aquar-

ium correct" decorations. Additionally, sand, gravel, and masonry-supply businesses in your area may stock rock suitable for aquarium use.

Lastly, don't underestimate your own resourcefulness. If you covet the coralline-encrusted live rock you may have seen, but refuse to pay the price, take some comfort in knowing that al-

most any appropriate rock or hard matrix will eventually become encrusted with pink and purple growths if you provide the right water conditions (proper alkalinity; high, steady pH; high calcium content) and just a few small pieces of coralline-covered live rock to seed your system.

In general, decorative corals, if you

Faux corals, modeled with inert materials in Southeast Asia from actual specimens, are appealing to some aquarists, while others prefer real coral skeletons, despite the environmental controversy involved.

Ten Classic Setup Mistakes

What Every Beginning Aquarist Should Avoid

1. Lack of planning. The success of any project depends upon the time and effort you've spent investigating the how, what, where, when, and why of everything you want to do. I've worked in stores where customers, in their haste to own a particular fish, have purchased marine livestock without even having a saltwater setup. Take some time to think, ask, read, and plan.

2. Thinking small. Imagine the smallest system you'd ever want—then double it. Or measure your available space and get the largest tank that will fit into it. Trust me, larger systems are better; they are a dream to maintain compared with smaller, less stable systems. A 40- or 50-gallon tank is the minimum size I would advise for any beginner.

3. Overstocking. Have a stocking plan and stick to it. Avoid the common impulse to buy "just one more." Formulate your plan according to how large your specimens will become. The vast majority of marine aquarium problems are caused by the aquarist and are all too often the result of trying to crowd too much life and metabolic activity into a given system.

4. Inappropriate stocking. This is not the same as overstocking. Virtually every aquarium keeper is guilty of having bought specimens that simply will not coexist with other specimens in the same tank. Life in marine environments is tough, and many species have evolved tough dispositions to survive; you need to know who the players are. Take into account the order of introduction, sex, size, and number of the different animals you select. Getting good at stocking an aquarium creatively and successfully is something that takes years of experience; avoiding the most obvious blunders isn't too difficult if you seek intelligent advice— oral or written.

5. Overfeeding. Even if you feed your livestock all the right foodstuffs, overfeeding them is deadly. Get into the habit of measuring the foods that you are offering instead of just tipping them in indiscriminately. You should also watch to see that all of it is consumed within a few minutes. Marine organisms typically survive in nutrient-limited surroundings and will grossly overeat given the opportunity. Do not kill your fishes with misguided "kindness."

6. Not quarantining. The single most effective way to prevent disease problems is to use a separate quarantine tank to segregate all incoming arrivals. It is necessary for acclimating livestock and isolating specimens that have developed symptoms. Without a quarantine tank, aquarists often poison their systems by adding medications to the main aquarium.

7. Using medications. All too many medications dosed by inexperienced hobbyists are misused or ineffective. It is unlikely that you know exactly what is wrong with your livestock. Get a few opinions from reputable sources and don't treat the affected specimens in your main system. If possible, don't use medications at all. Almost all (with the exception of internal parasites and infections) diseases can be avoided by quarantine and/or fixing poor water quality. Look to your water first as the reason for problems before dumping medicines into your tank.

8. Not premixing water. Even the best synthetic seawaters benefit from being premixed in a storage container with a heating and circulating mechanism, and being aged for a few days to a week before use. Many problems with tap water, pH, and specific gravity anomalies are solved by premixing. Never add freshly mixed synthetic seawater to a system unless it is a flat-out emergency.

9. Not keeping records. You will never learn from your mistakes and successes if you don't commit your experiences to paper. Keep track of what you bought and when, what your water tests indicate each time you do them, how your specimens are faring, and you will be miles ahead of the game.

10. Not sharing experiences. Think about what you've learned that works and what doesn't work. Ours is a social species, and marine aquarium keeping is a wonderful hobby for sharing. Talk, write, and be active with your aquatic interest. Connect with others via special-interest periodicals and the Internet. Help with a setup in a school or hospital; join your local tropical fish society; get your local library, bookstore or pet shop to carry more and better books; write an article for a hobbyist magazine. Inquiring minds want to know.

choose to include them, are a bigger challenge than rock. I would only deal with reputable sources; there is a lot to making these skeletons usable. Corals and shells need to be scrubbed clean and otherwise prepared properly. Specialty coral importers like Tideline and the Stubinger companies in Los Angeles have competent workers to do the acid washing, bleach washing, and shrink-wrapping for you. My advice is, don't try this at home. It's too much work and liability.

Substrates

THE WHOLE SUBJECT of substrates—gravel or sand covering the bottom of the aquarium—is currently the center of lively controversy. In the recent past, a number of influential writers advocated removing all sand from the aquarium and leaving a bare bottom that could be kept scrupulously clean. Whether the tank's specimens liked it or not, the traditional gravel bed was blamed for being nothing more than a detritus trap and a foe of pristine water conditions. After a period of years, arguments to the contrary are emerging and the sand-free trend is now being reversed. The average hobbyist, however, may be caught up in this debate and not know whether a gravel-covered bottom is biologically correct.

Historically, aquarium substrates have been known as filter beds. At their best, they have been counted upon to provide a system with a degree of chemical, physical, and biological stability.

Gravel or sand provides living space for beneficial microbes, worms, and other invertebrate life. It also buffers the system with a substantial alkaline reserve. Although substrate can fulfill a biological function, it is not absolutely necessary for a successful marine aquarium, but most aquarists will end up with some form of substrate anyway. There may be behavioral benefits for your livestock, and substrate is pleasing to the eye.

Your livestock can tell if there is gravel in their tanks or not. Many of the species of wrasses, eels, sea cucumbers, urchins, and others that live in or intimately close to the gravel on the reef fare poorly in bare aquariums. Conscientious wholesalers and aquarists provide at least a glass tray or other "habitat" area of sand or fine gravel for such charges. Invariably, other interesting life forms gravitate to such areas over time. The role, and sheer amount, of interstitial life in marine environments is still scarcely appreciated. Perhaps the future will find us with computerized, miniature cameras coursing through our systems, revealing what goes on at sea-floor level and even between the grains of substrate.

Soluble coral aggregates or aragonitic materials are currently in favor among reef aquarists because they slowly dissolve and release calcium and other needed elements while buffering the system. For the sake of solubility, the smaller the particle size, the better. Imagine dissolving two Alka-Seltzer tablets, one whole, one crushed up.

Which one would fizz faster? The crushed one, of course: more surface area allows faster dissolution. The ultimate in fast-dissolving, calcium-rich substrates is oolitic aragonite, so powdery that it is best mixed with a coarser coral sand to keep it in place.

The more broadly spherical the pieces of the substrate, the more consistent the water flow between them, and therefore the less channeling and packing down. The reverse is found in more flat-shaped offerings, such as silica sands, which form more compacted layers, effectively choking off water circulation and creating anaerobic conditions where hydrogen sulfide gas can collect.

Within realistic limits, the porosity of your substrate ought to be maximized to increase solubility and allow space for bacteria culture. What you want to remember is that porous material has a dull surface: choose the gravel or sand that is less reflective and less smooth.

You may opt for a mere inch of gravel to avoid having anaerobic areas, but a habitat for burrowing specimens, such as jawfishes, might call for a section of sand 4 to 6 inches deep. For most tanks, 2 inches is an acceptable average depth.

By the way, silicates (common sandbox sands) are nearly worthless as marine gravels; they do nothing to buffer pH, do not support microbial life, and get packed down too easily. In addition, excess silicates feed diatom (brown scum) algae growth—a major nuisance for many.

A marine biotope aquarium, using a mound of aquacultured live rock and naturally occurring invertebrate and plant specimens collected off the west coast of Florida in the Gulf of Mexico.

Natural coral sand, gravel, and shell substrates play an important role in the marine aquarium, providing an appropriate home for many organisms and beneficial bacteria, while serving as an effective buffer.

Choose Your Passion

EACH OF US ENDS UP with a favorite part of this hobby. For some it is reading about, searching for, and buying—even breeding—healthy specimens. Others love to tool around with the lighting, plumbing, and filtration on their systems. Some even thrive on the adrenaline of starting up new systems. For me, it is aquascaping. Amidst all your dreaming, execution, and intense contemplation, keep in mind that aquascaping is more art than science. It is not a product or destination, but a growing process—and a truly rewarding one for many aquarists.

If you don't consider yourself the artistic type, get a friend or family member involved, or just pick one of the "tried-and-true" plans shown here. If you're not completely satisfied with what you've got, recreate it.

Setting up and aquascaping a marine system is not hard when approached in a systematic way. Figure out the type of system you want for a start, determined by the livestock or biotopic presentation you're interested in; make a working checklist of all the tools and materials it's going to take to set up the system and clean it; pretest it all in a practice run; then go for it, following the cookbook approach offered above. Sounds easy when taken step by step, doesn't it? It is.

PART I

CHAPTER 6

Maintenance

Making Light Work of Marine Aquarium Upkeep

THE PERCEIVED DRUDGERY of keeping up an aquarium is the number one reason given by nonaquarists for not going into our hobby. Who can blame them? The typical stereotype of having wet sleeves, accidentally siphoning endless amounts of water onto the floor, feeding messy concoctions, removing dead and putrid livestock, having to conduct laboratory-level testing and water adjustment, and spending whole weekends doing total tear-downs and scrubbings of tanks and decor can be too much to bear.

Seasoned aquarists know that it doesn't have to be this way. Properly set up aquariums are remarkably reasonable and predictable in their maintenance demands, at least compared with

Maintenance brigade: one aquarist's color-coded system uses a blue bucket to age tap water, a gray bucket to store mixed saltwater, and a red bucket for wastewater removal during water changes.

the amount of care needed for animals like dogs and cats.

The maintenance and operation of your marine setup should follow a logical and regular pattern. There are daily, weekly, and monthly checks; regular feedings; and adjustments that can (and should) be reduced to a simple checklist of aquatic activities.

You will inevitably develop your own routines, but here is one approach to consider, with my own recommendations of what to do to keep a typical marine system up and going.

Every Time You Look at the Tank

Check Your Livestock. Are they behaving the way the way they should? Strange behavior by fishes or invertebrates is often the first clue to a mechanical failure or a degenerating water situation. This is your best chance to discover a problem in its initial stages. With a practiced eye, you will be able to

evaluate what's going on in the system at a glance and, via your fishes or invertebrates, know the general status of your water quality. If the lights are on, fishes should be lively and in good color, and sessile invertebrate specimens, if any, should be open and expanded, if that is their normal, healthy state.

Check Your Readings. This is optional, but those with clearly displayed thermometers often fall into the habit of giving them frequent glances. If you have other instruments giving readings of pH, redox, or dissolved oxygen, you'll probably make an automatic note that nothing is going astray. Again, your livestock are the best indicators, but if you like the quantitative approach, this can reassure you that nothing is wrong.

Daily

Feed Livestock. Depending on the type of system you are keeping, daily offerings of food are made once, twice, or more frequently. Turn these feeding times into observation opportunities. Feedings are the most telling chance you have of seeing whether all the stock is healthy, eating, and not being harassed by tankmates.

Take Readings. Many aquarists take the heating mechanisms of their systems for granted—don't. Though modern heaters are far superior to anything we had in the past, they do still fail. If you don't check your thermometer every time you pass the tank, get in the habit of doing it at least once a day.

Check Flow Rates. Just a quick look and listen will tell you that airstones, powerheads, and/or pumps are functional. (Complete silence is something an aquarist learns to dread—it is either from a power failure or a problem with the main pump.)

Empty the Protein Skimmer. I like

Heavily stocked fish-only tanks demand regular water changes and cleaning of skimmer collection cup and detritus-collecting media.

people to get in the habit of checking on and emptying the collection cup of their fractionator cups daily. Knowing how concentrated and disgusting the waste in the collector gets, you surely won't be surprised to find how it can interfere with the foaming action of your skimmer or how bad it can be if it spills back into the system. Dump and rinse the cup before it overfills.

The skimmer is such an important tool for preserving water quality that its functional operation should be one of your chief concerns. Are the stones bubbling optimally, or is the venturi putting out a full head of air? Is the collector doing what it should? You will become so familiar with the results of feeding and timing of the rhythms of your system that you should be able to anticipate collectant volume and know when cleaning is necessary. With well-established systems, skimmer maintenance may become a weekly chore, provided the collector cup volume is ample or has an automatic drain.

Top Up the Water Supply. In some areas with very dry conditions indoors, replacing evaporated water is a constant requirement. Some people find this needs to be done daily, but you can determine for yourself how often you'll need to replenish evaporated water. Automatic replenishment systems are available.

Weekly

Check Water-Quality Parameters. After the system has been up and running for a few months, routine checking of ammonia and nitrites is generally overlooked—unless something seems amiss. Nitrate as an end product to oxidative cycling of ammonia should be checked at the same time you perform water changes.

Alkalinity and pH of the system should be checked. If the pH is slipping or nitrates are on the rise, you should be taking corrective action to reduce or change your feeding habits, add buffering capacity, or increase water changes. Reef aquarists will also want to check the calcium level.

Check Specific Gravity. Specific gravity or salinity should be checked and adjusted at least weekly. Top up water level, if necessary, using freshwater. (Do not replace water lost to evaporation with saltwater, or your specific gravity will quickly rise out of the acceptable range.)

Some folks use only deionized, reverse osmosis (RO), or even distilled water for topping up their systems. In many areas and for many systems, aged tap water is just fine—there are more "impurities" introduced from the feeding, the fishes and invertebrates themselves, and the decor than from the usual household water supply. However, reef tank owners who find their source water contains nitrates, phosphates, or metals such as copper may be forced to use reverse osmosis and/or deionizing units. Replenish your freshwater storage supply, in preparation for use the following week.

Clean and Check Filters and Filtration Media. All sponges and wet-dry media, including trays and spray bars, should be inspected for clogging or excessive accumulation of debris and should be rinsed or replaced as necessary. Chemical filtrants, such as activated carbon, may need to be changed. I strongly encourage the use of polyester bagging of individual units of chemical filtrants, and rotating out some of the existing bags while adding some new (rather than a complete change). The usual life of carbon is highly variable, but after a few days or weeks, its ability to adsorb pollutants is near zero. It's best to rotate in newer packets, replacing older ones.

Change Water. A small weekly water change is an excellent, almost painless routine to develop. Between 5% and 10% of the total system volume is a reasonable amount to change. Siphon out a bucket of the old water and replace it with the same amount of new. (You have already topped up the system with freshwater, if needed.)

Ideally, you will be using saltwater mixed up several days to a week in advance. It should be of the same temperature and specific gravity as your system water. Once the water change is done, mix up a fresh batch of saltwater for the following week.

These water changes are a grand opportunity to vacuum part of the substrate, to clean out the sump(s), and change filter media.

Larger reef systems, such as this one by Karl Coyne, usually require vigilant attention to the skimmer, with daily or automatic additions of calcium, weekly additions of trace elements, and periodic water changes.

Clean Tank Components. While you're disrupting the system and its occupants doing a water change, this is an ideal time to wipe down the top, light fixture, and both the inside and outside of the viewing panels. I urge you to wear dedicated rubber gloves when working in your system.

Monthly

Change Water. If you haven't been changing some water weekly, now is the time to siphon out 10-20% of your old water and replace it with new. (Frankly, smaller and more frequent changes are preferable, but monthly will do.) These water changes are a good opportunity to clean out the sump(s), and change

filter media. If the rockwork or other decor needs attention, or if livestock need to be caught and moved, this is the time to do it. Replacement of water is done with premixed, stored seawater of the same temperature and specific gravity.

Clean Aquascaping. While doing a water change, it is little extra work to siphon detritus from the rockwork or other aquascaping materials. A piece of clear vinyl tubing with an inside diameter of half an inch or so makes a useful tool for drawing accumulated debris out of various nooks and crannies. Live rock, and the organisms that live on and within it, seem to generate considerable amounts of harmless detritus, and reef keepers often like to siphon it out of the system in this manner. An alternate approach for serious cleaning sessions is to take a small powerhead pump and, directing the outflow by hand, blast all loose detritus out of the rockwork. This will greatly cloud the water for a few hours, and a good particulate filter should be in place to catch and remove the waste matter while it is in suspension.

Add Supplements. This includes chemical adjuncts, such as all-in-one additives, vitamins, minerals, feeding and growth stimulants, and all other supplementary chemical additions. If you're going to use these, do so only as directed, and only on a regularly scheduled basis. The best time to do this is in concert with water changing. I am concerned with the potential poisoning effects of continually pouring these materials into a system. Add supplements if you must, but if you aren't an advanced hobbyist, I suggest doing it only immediately following a water change. (Reef aquarists typically add supplements on a weekly schedule.)

Inspect Heaters. The heaters should be carefully checked for cracks in their glass housings and for looseness, wetness, or other problems with plugs and connectors. The causes of fires from marine aquariums setups are split evenly between lighting fixtures and saltwater intrusion in heating electrics. Mount your extension plugs either vertically on the wall or inverted (with plug entry slots facing downward) to prevent saltwater entry, and check and wipe the electrical wires clean on a monthly basis.

Perform Equipment Maintenance. Change airstones in protein skimmers, if necessary. (These have a useful life of three to four weeks before becoming dark and waterlogged.) Alternately, check venturi valves and clean them if necessary. An ultraviolet sterilizer, if you have one, should be inspected and cleaned monthly.

Check Your Log. Review your written notes of when you acquired your livestock. How much have they grown? Do you have a photograph to compare against to assess growth and color changes?

Every Six to Twelve Months

Check Lighting. Lighting fluorescents, ultraviolet sterilizers, and even metal halides have effective lifetimes. But don't be fooled by the apparent luminosity (brightness) as a measure of their function. Once again, read and follow the manufacturer's recommendations for rotation or replacement of lamps and bulbs. In your log (or right on the fixtures or lamps with a grease pencil) mark the dates they were installed. Most UVs and standard output (non HO or VHO) fluorescents are good for approximately ten months, but your replacement schedule may vary depending on the fixtures and how many hours per day they're used.

Clean and Replace Substrate. It will pay to recognize the limited lifespans of certain elements of aquascaping, especially the calcareous elements of the system—substrate for gravel and filter media, coral, and shell skeletons. These, as well as the live and nonlive rock, contribute to pH buffering and biological filtration as a function of their surface area and solubility. Much of this potential is used up over time, as the tank ages and these materials exhaust themselves in maintaining chemical balance. Porous, soft, angular, and easily soluble materials diminish with a consequent loss of alkalinity and a shorter beneficial effect of any water changes.

Naturally, substantial pieces of live rock or other materials of coral origin may last for years, and disrupting them is the antithesis of maintaining a stable environment in a reef aquarium. However, it does make sense to add to or replace some of the faster-dissolving substrates, particularly coral sand or gravel, from time to time. Wholesale change is never advisable, but you may wish to remove or relocate a third of the existing material and add some new substrate—rinsed aragonite or coral gravel. (Alternatively, add a few pounds of it to your filter and sump, perhaps even keeping it in mesh bags to make replacement quick and simple.)

Most gravel substrates should be lightly vacuumed on a regular basis, although those with deep beds of live sand will want to refrain from stirring up more than the surface layer. Fish-only systems with heavy bioloads, on the other hand, usually call for aggressive substrate vacuuming and/or replacement on a periodic schedule.

Leave a third to a half of the tank untouched during such sessions to preserve the biological filter.

Check Other Nonmechanicals. Check your plumbing fittings and valves for disintegration, corrosion, and

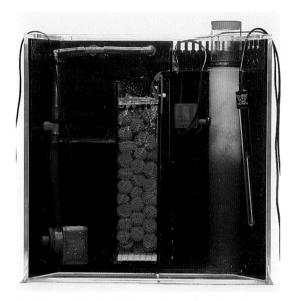

Integral sump in the back of an acrylic aquarium: biomedia should never need cleaning, but all water pumps must be checked every 6 to 12 months to ensure high performance.

salt creep. Replace drying, discolored water and air hoses as they lose elasticity. I've witnessed whole aquarium systems lost for want of a few dimes' worth of tubing.

Make sure your air valves are not leaking. Many do from time to time, but most can be repaired with a little silicon-based lubricant.

Perform Other Equipment Maintenance. Do your pump motors require periodic cleaning or lubrication? Some of the most popular fluid-moving pumps utilize a water-cooling feature, a narrow conduit that feeds a small amount of pressurized water back through the drive mechanism. Many of these pumps suffer an early death from this "tube" being ignored. You can save a lot of money and hassle by reading the materials that come with the mechanical components of your system, and adding their periodic checks and maintenance to your system-maintenance schedule.

Again, a log book or dedicated calendar for jotting these reminders, notes and "maintenance needed" dates becomes almost a necessity. A look back at your water-quality readings will often prove useful. A photographic snapshot of the system, done at least twice a year, can be a truly enlightening approach to measuring changes in the appearance of the aquarium over time.

Toxic Water Situations

THE MOST COMMON CAUSE of loss of marine life is declining water quality, mainly due to biological cycling and filtration "misunderstandings." Other toxic sources include rusting decor items or metal accidentally dropped into the system, chemical cleaners and other household poisons, and many biological sources.

Fret not; more than 99% of these problems are iatrogenic (caused by aquarists themselves), are easily avoidable, and will be made simple to understand in this section.

In order to prevent a toxic water condition, indeed to be a successful marine aquarist in general, you need to be concerned with what *not* to do. You do not need fancy instrumentation, expensive, complicated filtration, or a lot of money and time dedicated to monitoring and fooling with your system. These are more often the root of the problem rather than the salvation.

What you *do* need is a broad grasp of how your system works, a conscientious arrangement in setting it up and maintaining it properly, and the knowledge to leave it alone. Because test gear can be inaccurate, because misused water treatments can create toxic conditions, and because "quick fixes" are usually anything but, I urge you to take ten deep breaths, then consult experts and printed works before making knee-jerk decisions about your system. I realize that we are trained from early childhood to be consumers, but marine aquariums are not improved by general tampering.

Though it seems easier to point the finger at cyanide collecting practices, degradation of reef environments, or poor-quality tap water, the fact is that most marine livestock are killed by hobbyist ignorance and well-intentioned intervention. My goal is to teach you how to avoid such pitfalls.

Overstocking. If you've set up your system adequately, have patience in initially changing its bioload. Your new system needs four to eight weeks with very few organisms—fed sparingly—to establish biological nutrient cycling. Take your time. When increasing the population of fishes or invertebrates, do it slowly and in stages to allow the populations of beneficial bacteria time to adjust.

Overfeeding. Most of the foods you'll add have the same end result whether or not they're consumed. A gram of proteinaceous food is either consumed, then converted to ammonia, then nitrite, then nitrate; or *not* consumed, then converted to ammonia, then nitrite, then nitrate. In either case, the conclusion is inescapable: overfeeding will seriously impact your water quality. Don't do it.

Medications. Several common ingredients in marine aquarium remedies—antibiotics, methylene blue, potassium permanganate, and more—will kill beneficial microbes. These should never be used in your system tank. One of the recurring themes in this book is the use of a separate tank for quarantine, treatment, isolation, and backup during emergencies. Please don't waste your resources on fancy gear, test kits, and meters without first making the minor investment in at least a small treatment tank.

Nitrate Accumulation. By itself, this is not a concern for most livestock and systems. What a measure of nitrate can and should do for the conscientious aquarist is serve as a guide to the total water-quality picture. There are many other chemical and physical changes that occur in a small captive system that

are characteristic of overcrowding in an artificial environment. A high nitrate reading almost assuredly means a build-up of other dissolved organic wastes and degraded water quality. Be aware of and resist those changes by having ample filtration and circulation capacity, by removing and diluting converted wastes via regular water changes, and by using live rock and calcareous substrates.

Drop in pH. Substrates, calcareous rock, and coral skeletons alone will not maintain a pH above 8.0. Biological processes, including filtration, drive pH down, typically 0.05 to 0.1 point per week without intervention. The easiest and safest ancillary buffering method involves the simple addition of baking soda (sodium bicarbonate). Adding about 1 teaspoon (5 grams) of baking soda per 20 gallons of system water each week, in conjunction with other mandatory maintenance, will keep the pH right. Simply dissolve the baking soda in a small amount of system water and add it directly to the filter or into the flow of water returning to the aquarium from the filter.

Lack of Oxygen. This is more common and dangerous than you may believe. Tight-fitting tops and motor-driven circulation combine, often with elevated temperature, to reduce the availability of oxygen while increasing the need for it. Oxygen saturation is only about 7 ppm under normal aquarium conditions, and this can get used up quickly in the event of overfeeding, something dying unnoticed, and/or a

microbial population explosion or die-off. To avoid this problem, simply install a mechanical aerator (an air-driven airstone). Small (less than 100-gallon) systems should probably utilize these for driving their undergravel filters.

Systems with venturi-type skimmers and external wet-dry filters or open sumps won't normally have oxygen problems. Venturis boost oxygen concentration, especially when outfitted with ozonizers, and the active flow of water back and forth from a sump is a valuable contributor to oxygenation.

Pay attention to the steady-state respiratory rates of your livestock. If they are breathing hard or fast, suspect low oxygen tension and correct it by removing some livestock or increasing aeration.

Anaerobiosis. In a seriously oxygen-depleted system, the aquarium water will give off a hydrogen sulfide (rotten egg) smell, stinky bubbles will rise from stagnant areas, and dark sand will predominate. You will definitely want to avoid these possibilities. When given the right conditions, aerobic microbes will supplant anaerobes—you just need to give them the opportunity. Move and vacuum accumulating mulm (organic sediment) from in and around your decor and filter sump on your regular maintenance schedule. After any power outage, be sure to vent, clean, and/or backwash closed canister filters. They can become anaerobic in a matter of minutes and can easily flush undesirable by-products into your system when restarted.

"Bad" Foods. What are these? Foods that your livestock will not, or cannot, consume or process, and those with limited nutritional value. Gelatin-based frozen foods and air-exposed dry foods should never be used. The best foods in the trade have been extensively researched and are prepared and packaged under exacting conditions. All this effort is for naught if the manufacturer's efforts are thwarted by "repackaging" methods that expose the food to air. Use only factory-sealed foods.

Livestock Hazards. The "enemies from within" include several types of organisms—sea cucumbers, all stinging-celled animals, Spanish Dancer nudibranchs, uncured live rock and live sand—that release materials that must be dealt with through filtration/circulation provisions and maintenance. The only legitimate course of action is for the hobbyist to research the particular habits of all the life they intend to keep—both apart and together. Of course all living things are a potential problem in that when they die, their natural decay processes can quickly poison your water. The greater your system's bioload, the greater your need for diligence in maintaining water quality.

Wipe Out Syndrome. "Mysterious" total losses have been chronicled, especially in new setups and in monoculture (one species) systems. Most typical in marine setups is a sudden crash of an established population of fishes, probably brought on by a huge build-up of dissolved organic wastes. Note that protein-skimmer use and this type of Wipe Out Syndrome are almost mutually exclusive. If you use a protein skimmer (and I strongly recommend that you do), you'll avoid such a catastrophe. Always keep an eye on your livestock's behavior—if all seems to be going wrong, check your water quality and either execute a massive water change or move the livestock to your quarantine tank.

Poisoning from Decor. Metal contaminants brought in accidentally as part of your substrate and aquascaping are a slight possibility with naturally collected decor. Iron, in particular, may be a problem. Be suspicious of rust stains that appear in coral sands, gravel, and any volcanic rock. Nails, spikes, and other metal debris may be present and should be gotten out immediately; rock that shows any evidence of rust should also be removed.

Other soluble minerals (including zinc, copper, arsenic, and lead) can get into your system the same way. My experience has been that these poisonings are unusual, except in the tanks of hobbyists who use rocks from nonmarine origins. That geode, quartzite, volcanic rock, or even petrified wood may look great underwater, but is it worth the risk of poisoning your system?

Before introducing any coral skeletons or shells, ask two questions: Have they been cleaned or prepared properly? Do they allow anaerobic circulation? During routine maintenance, lift out and rinse cavernous shells occasionally—being wary not to discard or kill any fish or invertebrates hiding inside.

Cleaners and Other Household Poisons. I've seen ammoniated cleaners, especially window and counter-top types, kill whole systems. These can get into your system from your hands, cleaning tools, food, or the air supply. My advice, first and foremost, is to keep your hands out of the system as much as possible. Next, get a pair of arm-length waterproof gloves and dedicate them to aquarium use only. Likewise, be sure that the cleaning wands, sponges, and other maintenance paraphernalia that you use are restricted to aquarium use only.

Tobacco smoke is another concern. At one time, when I was involved in lake maintenance, I had to spray nicotine sulfate onto surrounding trees to reduce aphid populations on water lilies. Any overspray resulted in massive fish kill. Though there may be little documented proof of such poisoning in hobbyist tanks, I strongly recommend having an inline air filter if constant exposure to tobacco smoke is the situation in your home.

Summary. Routine operation and maintenance is the hallmark of a conscientious aquarist. There's no need to run yourself ragged; make a list and keep it with your aquarium log, noting when you added or removed livestock, any behavioral observations, and any upkeep performed. Your livestock will appreciate the stability that comes with a consistent approach to tank maintenance. Use the schedule suggested or formulate your own upkeep routine—then stick to it.

CHAPTER 7

Marine Algae

Encouraging the Desirable Forms to Combat the Nuisances

TALKING ABOUT THE ALGAE with most aquarists reminds me of the 1960s definition of weeds: "Plants for which we haven't yet found a useful purpose." Algae do have their place. They've been here for at least a billion years, and due to their ability to occupy almost all niches they are going to be here way past our time.

Given water, light, and nutrients, algae are going to invade and proliferate in your system. Rather than attacking all algae, our focus will be on preventing and controlling only the undesirable forms. As with filtration, the principal categories of algae control can be categorized as prevention, biological, mechanical, physical, and, lastly, chemical.

There are two groups of algae: those that you want and those that you don't.

Many species of macroalgae, such as this delicate and luminescent *Dictyota* sp., are attractive and useful in absorbing dissolved organic wastes.

Various types of algae serve different functions. At the simplest, they're bioindicators, giving you a good sign that your system is biologically sound (at least algae are growing in it). Some algae are incorporated in specialty filters (usually called scrubbers), and all are useful for removing nutrients from the water through bioaccumulation. Much algal matter, small and large, is used as food. And let us not forget the great stretching exercise aquarists can get by cleaning algae from tank walls, gravel, and ornaments. The algae that appear as thin films and slime coatings in the aquarium are popularly known as microalgae.

Then there are the purposely grown macroalgae. These are the forms you can reach in and remove simply by plucking them from the water. At this time, these are mainly the green algae, especially the genus *Caulerpa*. Currently the greens (*Chlorophyta*) are the only popularly exploited group, a situation that will no doubt change as people come to appreciate the brown and red algae.

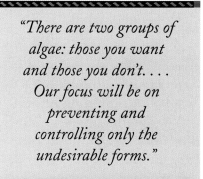

"There are two groups of algae: those you want and those you don't. . . . Our focus will be on preventing and controlling only the undesirable forms."

For now, let's clarify what the major algae groups are and how to avoid those undesirable in the aquarium, followed by how to grow the beautiful and useful macroalgae forms.

Classification

THE SIMPLEST oxygen-producing organisms on this planet are the algae. They are, for the most part, autotrophic or self-feeding, have no complex organizations and no sexual reproduction. They contain chlorophyll and other pigments, but have no true roots, stems or leaves. As a scientific assemblage, the blue-green algae are generally grouped with the bacteria; the rest of the algal "super-groups," along with the fungi, are placed in a subkingdom called Thallophyta, meaning "all about the same plant bodies" in reference to the lack of specialization of their cells.

For the most part, the botanical classification schemes separating algae into taxonomic divisions (the equivalent of animal phyla) is based on simple, observable color.

Algae occur wherever there is sufficient light for photosynthesis, water, and nutrients: in fresh- and saltwater, soil, hot springs, snow, even on and in plants and animals. They are remarkably adaptable: there are algae that live on bare rock in symbiotic union with fungi—as lichens—in the Arctic.

The algae divisions are as follows:

Blue-Green Algae. More closely related to bacteria than to other algae, they are often the scum on polluted, underaerated, stagnant, overfertilized waters. They are typically blackish and slimy to the touch. Forms include single cells, clusters, threads, and chains. The presence of this group is a danger sign in marine aquariums; usually something is seriously amiss with filtration, circulation, or water quality.

Green Algae. These are found everywhere and are the types most commonly encountered. They occur in floating, attached, and swimming forms—and in seasonal surface blooms.

Brown and Red Algae. The browns and reds are mostly marine and are most recognizable as the kelps and attached seashore forms. There are many smaller, even encrusting, species that reef aquarists cultivate, intentionally or not, on their assemblages of live rock.

Diatoms and Dinoflagellates. Here are the ubiquitous single-celled, microscopic algae, sometimes a nuisance but mostly beneficial in terms of nutrient cycling, oxygen production, and competition with less desirable forms. Though diatoms may appear as brownish or golden scums on tank walls, decor, and gravel, they rarely cause problems in marine aquariums. One exception is the genus of dinoflagellates called *Amyloodinium* (formerly *Oodinium*), a real infectious disease scourge.

Although at least five of the algal divisions are known to have symbiotic species that reside within the tissues of invertebrates, the dominant forms are dinoflagellates. These algae are known as zooxanthellae and live in a mutually beneficial relationship with their invertebrate hosts, taking up wastes and carbon dioxide and providing the host with fixed carbon (e.g. sugar) and oxygen. The predominant reef-building corals and *Tridacna* clams all bear these symbiotic zooxanthellae.

Other Algae Groups. Euglenoids, golden-brown, yellow-green algae, and others sometimes appear in aquariums but are generally not a problem in captive systems.

Sometimes aesthetically pleasing and beneficial in maintaining good water quality, but other times unwelcome guests, algae are easily controlled if understood. Most can be avoided by designing and constructing your system to limit nutrient availability, reduce excess light, or by introducing biological controls to keep the algae crop in check.

Algae Control and Prevention

Chemical Activity. Algae thrive in nutrient-rich water. If you are trying to control the growth of microalgae or hair algae, start by providing as little food or fertilizer for them as possible. I take exception with most authors on the virtues of one particular salt mix over any other, and the special treatment (reverse osmosis, deionization, distillation) of the freshwater to make it up. Unless your source water contains appreciable amounts of nitrates, phosphates, silicates, or other chemicals of use to algae, you would do well to pay attention to more likely culprits, such as detritus-loaded decor and gravel, and overfeeding. In my view, the addition of trace elements, vitamins, and other supplement mixes contributes far more to algae proliferation than does any impurity introduced by tap water or salt mix.

Circulation. Most microalgae do better under stagnant conditions. Keep your water in motion with water pumps or air pumps and airstones.

Light and Heat. This is a tricky area. If you are a fish-only or fish and non-

Green Grape Caulerpa (*Caulerpa racemosa*): good, hardy aquarium species.

Pinecone alga (*Rhipocephalus* sp.): requires good lighting and calcium

Sawblade Caulerpa (*Caulerpa serrulata*): sometimes imported on live rock

Red alga (*Halymenia* sp.) on an Indonesian reef: rarely seen in aquariums.

photosynthetic invertebrate keeper, your situation is much simpler. For the most part, the kind, amount, and light-dark cycling of your system will be a matter of personal taste; you can supply as much or as little light as you wish, dictated by what pleases you.

On the other hand, reef keepers, folks wanting to grow algae, and people with invertebrates hosting endosymbiont algae (zooxanthellae) are going to have to strike a balance of favoring desired algae over those they want to avoid.

As a practical reality, more intense light over longer photoperiods tends to favor macroalgae over micro. In some other situations, however, the opposite holds true. Most successful reef keepers are absolutely reliant on grazing animals—snails, herbivorous hermit crabs, algae-eating fishes like tangs and blennies—to keep microalgae from becoming a problem.

Similarly, and tied together with high-heat-output lighting, there is an ideal temperature range for the forms of algae you want and those you don't. Most of the desired algae species offered in the aquarium trade hail from the Caribbean, particularly Florida. They will grow best in waters in the mid-70s F. Many of the runaway algae

Calcareous alga (*Halimeda* sp.): calcium-loving choice for reef aquariums.

Feather Caulerpa (*Caulerpa sertularioides*): excellent choice when available.

problems I've seen were due to the water being too warm and fluctuating too much, negatively impacting the health of desired algae and other livestock, while promoting the growth of undesirable algae. Indo-Pacific algae, which typically arrive on pieces of live rock, can tolerate slightly higher average temperatures.

Filtration. The use of activated carbons and Poly Filters may go some distance in preventing full microalgae blooms. In my experience, most of the other products sold as nitrate and phosphate removers have limited usefulness in reducing nutrient availability.

Biological filters of several designs, if properly engineered and operated, are a key factor in keeping your system balanced in your favor. You can win by launching biological warfare with bacterial cultures—if you have these microorganisms living in your filter, they will slow nuisance algae growth by removing nutrients from the water.

Foam fractionators or protein skimmers reign supreme in preventing microalgae; they are tops in expediently removing organics that might otherwise fuel pest-algal growth.

Macroalgae. Fortunately, the attractive species of macroalgae are very useful in controlling the unsightly growth of microalgae types. They cut down on light and use some of the same nutrients otherwise available to undesirable forms. The fast-growing *Caulerpa* and encrusting corallines (a group of red algae that spread as pink, lavender, purple, and red crusts on live rock and other hard substrates) are best. There is evidence that the latter produce chemicals that preclude the growth of microalgae, especially the blue-greens (for more tips on fostering macroalgae growth, see page 137).

Pollutants. Control of these is very important. Food for algae comes from feeding your livestock and from adding vitamins and other chemical "addi-

tives." Be careful about adding anything else to your system. Wear dedicated arm-length rubber gloves to avoid introducing any pollutants from your hands and arms. Because algae are predominately composed of water, just a speck of solids from the uneaten food or other additives can result in several orders of magnitude weight in unwanted algae growth.

Frequent, partial water changes (as part of the routine maintenance discussed in Chapter 6) are the best way of diluting these algae-fostering nutrients. Advertisers who proclaim that their products "do away" with water changing should be viewed with skepticism: compare the costs of purchasing and operating their systems relative to the overall advantages of partial water changes.

There is no such thing as absolute prevention; marine systems have all the requirements (water, light, heat, dissolved gases) to grow algae. The best you can do is exercise some control over the introduction of excess nutrients.

Biological Controls. *Turbo* and *Lithopoma* (*Astraea*) snails, some blennies, some tangs, and some small herbivorous hermit crabs, among others, are good algae grazers. Snails are the most widely used herbivores and generally the best choice. Some parts of the country seem to favor the use of sea urchins or dwarf angels. The former die too easily or move the decor about; the latter can sometimes be problematic, nibbling on expensive invertebrates like giant clams and certain corals.

Mechanical Controls. The time-honored routine of brushing off the inside viewing panels of the tank and vacuuming the surface of the gravel during partial water changes quickly dislodges nuisance algae and works to disrupt its proliferation and reproduction. Some old-school aquarists still use acid and/or bleach washing of decor to remove stubborn algal growth.

Filter Controls. State-of-the-art methods include protein skimmers (to remove dissolved organics on which the algae feed), ozonizers, and ultraviolet sterilizers. The latter two remove and destroy algae on exposure and help oxidize nutrients as the water circulates.

Chemical Controls. Using any chemical to control algae is the least desirable route in terms of safety and long-term effect. There are several brands of antibiotics (usually Erythromycin or its generic equivalent) on the market; all should be avoided. The problem is that they will disrupt the beneficial bacteria in the system, treating the symptoms without dealing with the cause(s) of the algae problem. There are also the obvious downsides of altering the chemical "evolution" of your system. Antibiotics will kill much more than algae, often weakening the complex bacterial defenses of an entire aquarium setup.

In commercial and public aquarium settings, copper, usually in some kind of copper sulfate solution, is employed as an algicide, as well as a general epizootic parasite preventive. If you have or ever intend to keep invertebrates, macroalgae, or live rock in the system, do not introduce copper. This metal is superb in treatment and quarantine tanks, dips, and fish-only arrangements. The trade uses it extensively, but you must always keep in mind that it is persistent and toxic to all life, especially nonfish.

If you do use a chemical algicide, keep a close eye on the dosage and be on the lookout for toxic side effects. Several products state that under "bad conditions" the dosage may be doubled or tripled. If your water starts foaming and your fish start gasping heavily at the surface, remove the fish and change a large part of the water immediately.

Let It Be. After all this talk of controlling algae, it ought to be pointed out that sometimes it's better to let it be. Green micro- and macroalgae growth are indications of a normal, healthy state. Within moderation, algae help keep the system balanced and stable. The trick lies in the word "moderate." If you can keep the algae groomed, con-fined to the desired areas, or cropped to a short length on the back walls of your system, this will be to your advantage. By purposely having desirable forms, you can reduce the incidence of unattractive algae blooms. Should you experience a bloom, search for the root causes and try to correct them.

Growing Macroalgae

COULD GROWING ALGAE be a benefit in the aquarium? Decidedly yes, when it comes to macroalgae. They aid in biofiltering, in removing nutrients from the water and concentrating them, making these pollutants unavailable for undesirable forms of life; macroalgae can also serve as food and shelter, and, as a final bonus, they look good. Some aquarists even become hooked on the beauty and diversity of macroalgae, building lush collections of greenery.

Contrary to some advice, macroalgae are not difficult to keep or culture. You don't need a tremendously sophisticated filtration system and a Ph.D. in chemistry. Most of the live macroalgae you can buy are greens (Division Chlorophyta), though most of the advice that follows can apply to all macroalgae species. Live macroalgae can easily be brought into a system by simply adding live rock, and some suppliers routinely offer "plant rock" collected in shallow zones and having various macroalgae species attached and ready to spread. The benefits of macroalgae in your system include:

Biofiltering. Macroalgae can aid considerably in establishing and stabiliz-

Lavender coralline algae nicely protects live rock from unwanted microalgae.

Bubble alga (*Valonia* sp.): interesting but occasionally a nuisance.

ing new or "out-of-whack" systems. They bring in and help institute microorganism communities, and they absorb nutrients introduced by food, decor, and tap water. For systems with invertebrates, particularly anemones and live corals, live plant material can be especially helpful in improving water quality. In sufficient growing strength, macroalgae will remove nitrates, assist in buffering pH, take in carbon dioxide, produce oxygen, and assist in balancing trace elements (e.g. magnesium, phosphate, iron).

To some extent, macroalgae are useful bioindicators, real-time monitors of your system's viability. If your macroalgae won't live and grow, or if they start dying back, it is often a warning that something is out of kilter chemically, physically and/or biologically.

Control of Nuisance Algae. Having a batch of macroalgae intentionally growing in the system will go a long way in limiting the growth of unwanted forms (slime, string algae, fungus and bacteria) by competing for light, space, and nutrients. Reef keepers, however, should be aware that rampant macroalgae growth may affect coral health through nutrient competition, smothering, and possibly metabolite poisoning. (In the wild, herbivores keep algal growth constantly cropped and under control.) If macroalgae and live corals are kept in the same system, the reef keeper must keep them separated or regularly trim back the algae, which virtually always wins in the battle for space and available light. For this reason, most reef aquarists now keep grazing snails, small herbivorous hermit crabs, and at least one tang in their systems. To reap the benefits of having macroalgae, an increasing number of aquarists are moving it to a lighted sump or refugium tank connected to the display tank. Here it can grow, help extract nutrients from the water and not encroach on other sessile reef specimens.

Food. Many of the marine fishes and invertebrates we keep will augment their diets with algae. What better arrangement than to have some continuously available for casual munching? Similar to the importance of vegetable matter in our own diets, this home-grown algae provides many trace nutrients to your aquarium inhabitants.

Shelter/Ornament. Macroalgae serve to break up the physical environment, affording hiding spaces from tank bullies and aquarists, and peace of mind to the inhabitants. Beyond this, they are aesthetically attractive; when growing well, they add sheer beauty in terms of color, shape, size and motion.

Macroalgae Habitat

MACROALGAE ARE NEITHER difficult to keep and grow, nor are they so simple as to be automatic survivors for a beginning aquarist. To succeed, you will need to have:

1) An established, cycled, stable environment with the same healthy water parameter for most fishes. With a new setup, how can you tell when to add macroalgae? A good indicator is the presence of some of those nuisance microalgae on the scene—most obviously on the walls of your aquarium.

2) Adequate nutrient levels, which are present in most established systems. Normal maintenance, including feeding fishes or invertebrates, should provide enough in the way of chemical nutrients. There are various supplements marketed to boost macroalgae growth, but in most systems it's hard to demonstrate a need to replenish major and minor trace materials. Adding more in the presence of high-intensity lighting and, perhaps, carbon dioxide infusion, might boost the growth of both macro- and microalgae, along with other, unwanted consequences.

Without booster supplements, your macroalgae won't die, they just will not grow as fast. Several authors caution against too large a macroalgae population and of "pushing" them with additives. I concur. Algal metabolism can sway pH and other parameters and even result in livestock loss. Moderation is key.

If you succeed in having a healthy macroalgae population, remember the warning about putting any medications in your system. Macroalgae do not tolerate many of the common fish-malady drugs. Any treatments for fishes should happen in a separate tank.

3) Enough light—of the right quality, quantity, and duration. Specifically, macroalgae need balanced, full-spectrum lighting for at least 12 hours per day, at an intensity of 2 to 4 watts per gallon (see Chapter 2).

4) No voracious algae eaters. If you are serious about growing lush macroalgae, be careful to exclude or limit species of tangs, angelfishes, crabs, snails, and others that love devouring macroalgae.

5) Moderate, continuous water flow, which stimulates macroalgae growth and keeps debris off its surface.

Macroalgae Selection

For saltwater plant material, the best choices are the green algae species in the genus *Caulerpa*. These multishaped macroalgae deserve their title as "most popular." It might sound bizarre, but these are the largest single-celled organisms in the world; they're so good-looking, they often appear artificial. *Caulerpa* species grow prolifically in established aquariums, often to the point where they have to be routinely thinned to prevent their overcoming other tank inhabitants.

Most *Caulerpa* look like creeping vines with alternating leaflike projections emanating from their two-dimensional profiles. Their holdfast organs provide anchorage in the gravel and on solid decor. (They look like roots, but holdfasts do not take up nutrients or water as the root systems of terrestrial plants do.) As all the elements of the *Caulerpa* are part of the same cell, take care not to break off their interconnecting strands. This can result in the severed section disintegrating. (Trim *Caulerpa* back by crushing the thallus—the green upright stem—with your thumb and finger.)

Several of the 70 or so species of *Caulerpa* are available through retail, mail order and culture facilities. The most popular are the changeable, grapelike *C. racemosa*, the feathery *C. sertularioides* and *C. mexicana*, and the solid-bladed *C. prolifera*.

In the trade, there are a few other notable macroalgae species that have been harvested from Florida waters since the 1950s:

Penicillus sp., the Merman's Shaving Brush, is a tuft of bristles rising out of a vertical stalk. Take care to place it gently in fine sand.

Halimeda sp. is a crusty, calcified alga that looks like a bunch of small platelets strung together in a chain. This is a good choice if you have a lot of grazers, as it is tough to chew.

Udotea sp. looks like a soft green fan; some have more than one.

Of the types of macroalgae that we can easily grow for marine systems, those listed above will take undesirable nutrients out of the water, make oxygen, and produce prime food for our fishes. To my eye, they also provide beauty. A properly maintained marine aquarium will always have the predisposing conditions to grow algae. Given that reality, why not grow some that you prefer?

CHAPTER 8

Foods and Feeding

Simple Rules, Common Sense, and Hold the Goldfish

I F I HAVE AN ATTITUDE ABOUT feeding fishes, and I probably do, it must come from too much experience with the results of well-meaning hobbyists who have killed their fishes with kindness or pure ignorance.

The clearest example of the investigator finding a smoking gun often appeared when we were presented with a large, dead lionfish. The "disease" culprit in many of these cases was environmental—specifically, the feeding of live goldfish. I've seen it time and time again: death from "feeder blockage syndrome." In lionfishes and other species that gobble down feeder goldfish as fast as they can inhale them, there is a tendency for the victims' skulls to block the opening from the stomach to the intestine. From necropsying enough lion-

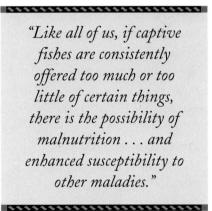

Volitans Lionfish (*Pterois volitans*): too often a victim of misguided feeding by aquarists who provide a regimen of live feeder goldfish.

fishes to fill a fish store, I would guess that feeder blockage syndrome is the lionfishes' single largest source of mortality in captivity.

Captive fishes and most invertebrates have remarkably similar nutritional requirements to our own. They need the same few fats and carbohydrates, 10 or 11 amino acids (the building blocks of proteins), vitamins, minerals, trace elements, and water. Just as with humans, most can make some of the materials necessary for good health (notably amino acids) but must derive others (such as vitamin C) from outside sources. Also, like all of us, if they are consistently offered too much or too little of certain things, there is the possibility of malnutrition, poor development, nutritional disease, and enhanced susceptibility to other maladies.

Basically, our job as aquarists is to present a palatable, nutritious mix of food items in the right quantity and at

the right times to do what it takes biochemically to make our stock stay alive, maintain its colors, grow, and perhaps even reproduce. Just as with our own diet, serious deviation from the basic

> "*Like all of us, if captive fishes are consistently offered too much or too little of certain things, there is the possibility of malnutrition . . . and enhanced susceptibility to other maladies.*"

rules of good nutrition will quickly—or over time—result in loss of vigor, poor appearance, irritability, declining health, sterility, and/or death. Happily, all of this is avoidable with most aquarium species, provided we select and portion out their foods intelligently.

Saltwater aquarists today have an unprecedented selection of prepared foods of all types in a variety of formats: flake, frozen, gelatinized, irradiated, pelletized, and dried by different methods. Within this readily available aquatic smorgasbord are all the ingredients for a completely nutritious captive diet for many, many fishes and invertebrates. The real trick is in making sure that each specimen gets what it needs.

Dry Foods

THESE ARE AMONG the most popular formats for beginning aquarists. Convenient to handle and feed, high-quality flakes, pellets, and granules are readily accepted by most common species. They are easy to store and use, less fouling than fresh or frozen foods, somewhat less likely to be too heavily dosed, and can do the job nutritionally in every way. They come in a multitude of textures (soft to crusty), sizes (powder to jumbo bites), shapes (pellets to flakes), and colors (a marketers' kaleidoscope). The range of quality in the dry foods section of many pet stores is likewise broad—from excellent to almost worthless.

One of the first considerations is freshness, which is a major factor in a fish food's palatability and nutritiousness. The leading, conscientious manufacturers (Tetra, Sera, Aquarian, O.S.I., et al.) go to amazing lengths to compose, prepare, package, and in other ways assure the quality of their products. Do not thwart their efforts. Buy what you can use in a few weeks to a few months—at most—and store it in a cool, dry spot with the lids or seals kept well-tightened.

I have strong reservations about bulk or "pack-your-own" fish food. Such serve-yourself rations may seem like a good deal, but don't waste your time, money, and your fishes' health. Consider dry fish foods as similar to freshly baked bread or corn flakes. Would you eat rolls or breakfast cereals that had been sitting around, exposed to air, light, mold spores, and insects for who knows how long?

Well-made commercially prepared foods are often packed in a high-nitrogen environment to prevent the oxidation of nutrients (mainly fats and proteins) through exposure to the air. The packaging is actually rather amazing: spill out the contents of a new canister, take a sniff, then try to get it all to fit back in the can. You can't.

Frozen Foods

THESE ARE THE REAL MAINSTAY OF most serious aquarium-fish feeding regimens. Though perhaps not as convenient as dried types, frozen foods are now available in myriad types, sizes, and formats. They are highly palatable to most stock, and are bargains compared to many strictly "fresh" or live foods. If processed properly, frozen foods can be just as nutritious as fresh.

Cubes or packs of single-species foods (e.g. brine shrimp, krill, silversides) or blended rations are the present epitome of complete nutrition in a format that appeals both to aquatic organisms and their owners.

Some writers advocate defrosting frozen foods before introducing them into the system; some even espouse rinsing. I have yet to observe any ill effects from using them in a still semi-icy form. For ease of dissemination—and to avoid having large frozen cubes end up in the filter system—many aquarists like to defrost chunks or cubes of frozen food in a cup or small dish of water from the fishes' system (not chlorinated tap water) before pouring or squirting it into the tank.

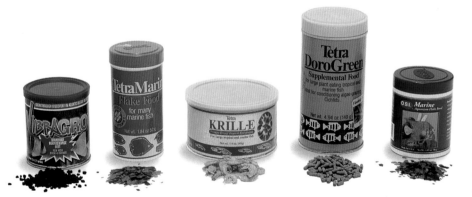

Available in myriad textures and formulations, dried and freeze-dried foods offer the aquarist many convenient and nutritionally useful options that can be a part of a varied, balanced diet.

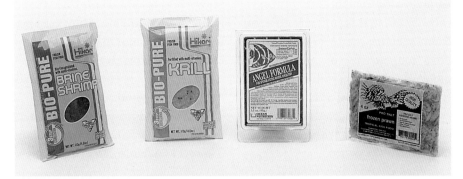

Frozen foods are the mainstay of most serious marine aquarium feeding routines, providing excellent choices of high-protein items, marine algae, plankton, and even specialty foods such as edible sponges.

Freeze-Dried Foods

THESE ARE FOOD ORGANISMS, such as krill, preserved whole through drying by air, sun, or lyophilization (freeze-drying). They are nutritionally fine and come in a rather clever and convenient format, but there is one notable drawback: they can be inordinately expensive for what you're getting. Carefully check out the equivalent price per ounce for the same food as it comes either frozen or fresh. If you have a freezer handy near your aquarium, you may very well be better off financially using frozen, although freeze-dried foods have loyal followers who believe they offer nutritional superiority. For those without a freezer handy to the aquarium, freeze-dried items can be used to enhance a diet of other dried foods.

Green Foods

HERBIVOROUS FISHES (such as the tangs) and other heavy grazers (such as many of the angels) seem to thrive only with a good complement of green foods in their diet. Fresh, dried, flake, pelletized, and frozen greens are available and commonly recommended for certain species. Some of these, in fact, have little nutritional value (other than vitamin and mineral content), but even the worst terrestrial greens sources at least provide some roughage and give the animals something to do.

Canned or cooked okra, zucchini, and spinach are fine except for the build up of oxalic acid (over time). Lettuce of different types and other green, leafy garden foods are probably best considered filler—if you choose to feed lettuce, opt for the leafy types, such as romaine. Avoid iceberg lettuce, which is largely water and very low in vitamins. "Fortified" prepared green fish foods are good, and many aquarists swear by *Spirulina* flakes as a staple for their herbivorous stock.

I strongly prefer greens of marine origin, and my optimal sources include the dried algae—noritake (Sushi Nori), kombu, and others—available in Asian food shops, health-food stores, and the exotic food sections of supermarkets. Another option is the growing selection of frozen rations for marine herbivores, some of which combine excellent palatability and a healthful list of ingredients.

Vastly superior to lettuce, dried marine seaweeds (algae) are relished by many herbivorous fish species.

Perhaps the best, or most economical, route is to grow your own. Live, plant-covered rock is a wonderful occasional feast for your foraging stock. Live rock in the system itself fulfills this role, but tends to be grazed over too quickly to grow luxuriant crops of greens. Having a lighted refugium where algae can flourish on rocks between feedings is a neat technique that yields many benefits: amelioration of the environment, reduction of metabolites in the system water, and a regular supply of green growth that your fishes will relish. If the refugium can't be part of your system, an old aquarium placed on a sunny windowsill or under a grow-light and filled with old, nitrate-rich saltwater will fulfill the same purpose. Rotate "feeder stones" in and out as the algae crop matures and is eaten.

Vitamins, Additives, and Trace Materials

THESE SUPPLEMENTS FOR FISH AND invertebrates are just as controversial as similar diet enhancers for humans. If our everyday food intake is fresh, varied, and complete, we probably don't need extra vitamins and minerals. Not sure you're offering your fishes an adequate mix of foods? Vitamin and mineral additives—soaked into the foods offered, not just added to the water where they will simply feed algal blooms—may benefit your livestock.

Natural and Live Foods

"NATURAL" IS ONE OF MY FAVORITE examples of a misused word. What is natural versus unnatural? Is vitamin C extracted from rose hips any different from or better than vitamin C from other sources? Not in my view. The molecule is the same, with the same activity, essence, aura, and biochemical consequence. My advice is to buy the quantity you need at the best price and forget about the source.

When talking about foods for marine organisms, the real discussion should be live versus frozen (or otherwise preserved) items. There is a long tradition in freshwater aquarium keeping of setting up live foods as the ideal, and there may have been more merit to this several decades ago before the vast improvements in frozen and prepared foods. I have several arguments against the use of live foods:

1) Live foods are relatively more expensive per unit of nutrition, due to the vagaries and costs associated with capture or culture, transport, maintenance, and handling. Is a freshly killed, uncooked chicken more nutritious than one that has been commercially dressed, chilled, grilled, and served on a piping hot platter?

2) Live foods pose more of the possibility of introducing pests, parasites, infectious disease, and pollutants to your aquarium. Obviously, there are techniques for minimizing these risks—using marine foodstuffs for freshwater and vice versa, rinsing before use, quarantining the food—but once again, these add directly to cost and time investment.

3) Live foods are inconvenient.

How many marriages have been rocked by one spouse harboring cultures of live worms, feeder goldfish, crickets, or homebrewed swamps of mosquito larvae and brine shrimp? More than I would care to admit.

4) Live foods may incite and intensify predaceous behavior in a system. Though I am not readily able to cite a published source of data for this, my personal theory is that feeding live foods makes animals more aggressive and "meaner."

In fact, I have a hard time making any case at all for live marine foods, unless we want to consider it more "natural" for aquatic life to be infected, for systems to be infested, and for fishes and invertebrates to be aggressive. Perhaps the only valid argument for live foods is that some species of livestock do poorly initially (or don't survive at all) in captivity without their meals live and kicking. Most of these species can be trained to accept prepared foods, and the others should not be kept. Your conscience will be your guide, along with your pocketbook.

The big exception to all this is if you are someone who has been bitten by the breeding or captive-propagation bug. You will quickly learn that you must become a live-food expert for the young you will indirectly produce. If you enjoy the involvement and challenge of culturing your own rotifers, brine shrimp, and other planktonic organisms and small crustaceans, more power to you.

However, the truth of the matter for everyday aquarists is that the livestock we keep in artificial marine systems can mostly be trained to accept nonlive foods and would do better nutritionally if fed a frozen or dried prepared diet. It's often cheaper, safer, more nutritious, and more convenient and consistent—for the same reasons we feed ourselves and our companion dogs and cats prepared and not live or freshly killed foods.

Homemade Foods

IF YOU HAVE THE TIME, creating your own rations can be an economical route to feeding your livestock. All you need is a blending tool (blender, chopper, grinder), the raw ingredients (shrimp, squid, seaweed), a binding agent (gelatin or alginate), and possible enhancers (vitamins and minerals).

Buy cheap but wholesome seafood of marine origin (not catfish or other freshwater species), rinse, and process or blend into an appropriate size. Mix with the binding agent (premixed with water), and additions (crumbled seaweed, *Spirulina* flakes, vitamins). The resulting mash can be refrigerated and used as is or frozen. Some hobbyists simply make balls of the ration, freeze them, then shave off the portions needed with a cheese grater. You can even make your own cubed foods by squeezing the fresh mash into a plastic eggcrate louver that is placed on a sheet of glass or a cookie tray. Once frozen, the cubes can be popped out and stored.

Other options include spreading and drying the mix on feeding stones, or making it into ingenious "berries."

Basic Fish-Ration Recipe

Make your own? Some serious aquarists do. Paste foods can be fed immediately, frozen, or air-dried on pieces of rock as an economical, homemade ration for your livestock. Here's my own recipe for:

Fenner's Wonderful Marine Mash

- 4 ounces peeled shrimp (any size; fresh, frozen, or canned)
- 2 ounces any kind of mollusk (clams, mussels, oysters)
- 2 ounces fresh or frozen seaweed/algae (or, if necessary, frozen or canned spinach)
- 1 packet of gelatin (food-store bought or pet-fish commercial) dissolved in 2 ounces warm tap water
- 1 ounce liquid multivitamin preparation (or specialty aquarium supplement)

Economical aquacultured shrimp are one choice as the basis for a simple bulk homemade ration for marine fishes.

Thaw any frozen ingredients. Chop the shrimp into half-inch pieces and combine all ingredients in a blender. Pulse until the solids have been chopped to the size appropriate for your fishes—very coarse for bigger eaters, fine for very small species or filter-feeding invertebrates.

The finished melange can now be frozen, either in sheets on waxed paper or as one lump formed into a ball. (The latter is then scrubbed across a cheese grater each time a portion of food is needed.) By all means, feel free to improvise and improve on this simple recipe. The only hard-and-fast rules are to avoid spoiled or contaminated ingredients and to stick with protein sources of saltwater origin.

The latter is done by diluting the mix with hot water, drawing it up into a turkey baster, and squirting it into a basin of ice water, which causes it to gel into convenient berry-sized pellets. These can be fed immediately, refrigerated for a day or two, or frozen for longer storage. This is how we used to make "lobster chow" back in college and is standard operating procedure for public aquariums and aquaculture facilities worldwide.

Feeder Goldfish

THE RITUAL OF FEEDING many varieties of larger marine and freshwater livestock with "feeders"—members of the minnow family, usually Comet Goldfish—has always struck me as questionable. Goldfish are not convenient or practical. They are neither nutritious nor inexpensive. And though they don't directly introduce infectious and parasitic disease into marine systems, they do seem to contribute negatively to both health and behavior.

In my view, there is less vitality, fecundity, and survivability of young (if breeding stock is being fed) with the use of feeder goldfish, and seemingly a greater incidence of necrotic wasting diseases like hole in the head, lateral line disease, fatty degenerative liver disorders, and lowered resistance to infectious and parasitic diseases.

The out-of-pocket costs, too, are staggering. Calculate how much these things cost per pound—more than you'd pay for prime steak for yourself. Over the lifetime of the livestock being fed, what is the total cost?

Does feeding live foods like goldfish make fish more aggressive? Many aquarists I've talked with over the years think it does. I've known tanks where a population of community fishes coexisted peacefully until the larger ones "learned"—through the eating of feeder goldfish—that they could eat their smaller tankmates.

"But my fishes won't accept their food unless it's moving," is the common excuse of feeder-goldfish addicts.

Malarkey. I've never yet come across a case where feeders had to be used. Once livestock have become accustomed to their use, it may take some effort and patience to wean them off—but it can be done. At first this may involve an intermittent offering of feeders and nonfeeders, some lengthy fasting (they won't die from it), and possibly the use of a feeding rod to mimic live food movements by moving around a piece of frozen or dried ration. Have patience; your charges won't perish for lack of feeders and they will eventually eat other prepared or frozen fare.

The alternatives are cheaper, easier to buy, keep, and use, and are more nutritionally sound. They include fresh or frozen fish, crustaceans, mollusks, and more from the seafood counter. (There are also dried alternatives: Tetra's Jumbo Min and Hikari's Floating Food Sticks are two examples of excellent foods offered as feeder replacements.)

Finally, consider the feeders themselves. Oh, what an ignominious end for the only variety of goldfish to have originated in the U.S.—it appeared as a "sport" or mutation. Do yourself, your livestock, and all those hapless Comets a favor and use a better food.

Feeding Guidelines

CONSIDERING THE RANGE OF SPECIES, sizes, and even individual specimens in such massive groups of organisms as marine fishes and invertebrates, it is not easy to make useful generalizations about feeding them well in captivity. Here, nonetheless, are a few broad suggestions, along with the acknowledgment that each aquarist must learn what works with his or her particular system and collection of organisms. Feeding is at least as much art as science—being able to gauge how much and how often to feed, how to vary your fishes' diet, and how to avoid relying too heavily on a single food.

1) Know your livestock and system. What and when do they eat in the wild? What have they been eating in captivity? What are the consequences of varying temperature, lighting, or other aspects of water quality on their appetite and energy demands?

2) Feed more frequently with smaller amounts. Never feed to excess—to the point where food goes uneaten and rots. Underfeeding is not a problem for most fishes. This is probably a situation they and their ancestors have lived with for millions of years in the wild.

3) Know how your specimens should look: robust, full-bodied, never shrunken-looking or hollow-bellied (nor should they be fat, lethargic, and constantly stuffed). Offering foods in small quantities twice a day and ensuring that everything is consumed within minutes is a good general rule.

Species that are continual grazers in the wild do best with more frequent feedings. Beware of situations where your livestock eat but still waste away. (This is too often misdiagnosed as "internal parasites.") Tangs, anthias, and others are notorious for this. Either more frequent (perhaps continuous, us-

Red-breasted Wrasse (*Cheilinus fasciatus*) swallowing a bivalve: know who will eat whom in your tank.

ing a full aquascape of live rock, or several times per day, using an automated feeder) or more nutritious food offerings are necessary.

4) For most aquarium fishes, however, when you have a choice between over- and underfeeding, underfeed. When you go on vacation, hide your foods. Taking them with you or throwing them away would be better, all incidents considered, than entrusting unpredictable youths or well-meaning neighbors. Unless you're gone for weeks (and in some cases, even if you are gone for weeks), your livestock would be better off nibbling on the rocks, gravel, and even each other than you counting on others not to overfeed or misfeed. Ask any group of experienced aquarists; vacation helpers can, and often do, kill your fishes. If you can't be otherwise dissuaded, at the very least premeasure

and date-label the amounts of foods that you want fed . . . and leave the phone number of a competent aquarist or your friendly local pet shop.

Some electrical or battery-powered automatic feeders are a big help, but beware of the various "in-the-tank feeding blocks." Most are at best a feeding placebo and at worst a melting chalk-binder gravel clogger.

Growth Factors

THINK TWICE before trying to achieve the fastest growth rate possible—a carry-over habit from the freshwater crowd and all the people force-feeding their pets to get the biggest specimens in as short a time as possible. It is possible to push the growth of fishes quite easily, by raising the temperature in their system and offering richer foods. This, naturally, means a much bigger

chore in keeping the system's water and filtration up to snuff. More importantly, it isn't necessarily the best course for the health of your charges.

For instance, it turns out that more-frequent feedings of higher protein foods in greater total quantity does shorten the lifespan of cultured marine organisms. Is enhanced growth worth this trade-off? Young fishes, of course, should be kept sufficiently fed to ensure their development into adults, but "optimum growth" for most mature and maturing marines in our care is probably very slow.

Like ourselves, your marines "are what they eat." Without you providing appropriate foods that are accepted and assimilated, the best specimens, the finest equipment, and the most scrupulous maintenance are a waste of time. Without proper nutrition, your livestock cannot resist disease, realize their potential growth, show their true colors, or reach a condition allowing reproduction.

There is no strict formula as to how much or how often to feed, only an ongoing need to use your powers of observation and good judgment. You must be the ultimate controller of the feeding schedule and of course what is offered. Only through conscientious scrutiny will you know that your livestock are all receiving adequate nutrition. Besides being a responsibility, feeding is also a source of unending fascination for you and all who take pleasure in watching the captive world you've created.

CHAPTER 9

Disease

A Brief Introduction to Marine Maladies—and How to Keep Them at Bay

IF YOU NEVER BELIEVED YOUR grandmother's old chestnut about prevention being the best medicine, you're almost guaranteed to appreciate its truth as you gain experience with marine fishes. The best home aquarists do not spend a great deal of time or energy fretting about or coping with disease, for the simple reason that they have cut most problems off at the pass. Lackadaisical hobbyists, on the other hand, will find themselves coping with a constellation of symptoms, maladies, and plagues, ending up with a medicine chest of remedies and a sad tally of lost specimens. In short, disease is relatively rare in a well-kept marine tank, but it can be a never-ending problem for the uninformed or uncaring hobbyist.

Let's start with a simple definition of disease as "any deviation from a nor-

Miniatus Grouper (*Cephalopholis miniata*) with an attached isopod, an easily removed parasite.

mal or healthy state due to infection, weakness, or environmental stress." There are many ways to describe and classify types of diseases—genetic, nutritional, developmental, viral, bacterial, parasitological, environmental, and others, depending on their perceived causative factors. By definition, infectious organisms are viruses, funguses, bacteria, and algae. Parasitic organisms are the protozoans, worms of all sorts, crustaceans, and more.

You need not be a tropical aquatic marine veterinarian to keep healthy fishes, but a minimal knowledge of disease prevention, recognition, and treatment is an essential part of your tool kit of skills.

In an aquarium, there are three areas of concern: infectious disease agents, parasites, and environmental or physical problems that develop. Avoiding and reducing the effects of these stressors involves paying attention to both transit and environmental conditions.

It cannot be stressed too emphatically that all disease in fishes is strongly affected by the aquarium environment and, especially, by water quality.

Expediently acquiring, acclimating, and placing livestock in your system with a minimum of shock and man-handling is the first opportunity the aquarist has to interact conscientiously with new specimens. This transitional period is the time of greatest losses in captive marine life.

Correctly netting, bagging, and transporting new purchases, cleansing them with dips and baths, and properly acclimating and quarantining them are the hallmarks of a responsible aquarist. These are the principal means of avoiding infectious and parasitic diseases.

Acclimating Livestock

SOME ESTIMATES OF THE LOSS OF marine life collected for the aquarium trade exceed 90% between the reef and the home aquarium. The magnitude of this loss comes as a shock to many, but fishes undergo tremendous trials in collection and distribution.

For example, a typical damselfish may pass through as many as seven sets of hands between Fiji and your home aquarium—collector, buyer, exporter, importer, jobber, retailer, and consumer. Each handles the fish as little as possible, but you can imagine the stress related to netting, shipping, and changes in water quality—typically compounded by no feeding for days or even weeks.

Healthy marine organisms are a lot tougher than many writers and hobbyists give them credit for. The oceans are vast and are slow to change in their chemical and physical makeup, but the life there is often full of drastic challenges. Reef fishes must contend with thermoclines, waves, food shortages, tidepool strandings, and ever-present predation. But as aquarists, we need to know how to best reduce and mediate the additional stressful effects put on marine life during transit.

By the time a Pacific damselfish lands in your home, it has traveled thousands of miles and been through more turbulence, delays, and changes of climate than the most grizzled travel veteran would care to endure. What you do next can make a major difference in whether it perishes or settles in for a long and vigorous life in captivity.

Acclimation and quarantine techniques could fill a book of their own, but many are appropriate primarily for commercial facilities and those with access to, and competence to handle, specialized medications and chemicals. Here we will narrow the field to a basic approach that will stand any serious hobbyist in good stead without demanding expensive or hard-to-get supplies and equipment.

The Basics

NEW FISHES AND INVERTEBRATES can be mildly to severely shocked by changes in water temperature, chemistry, and lighting. Not bothering to minimize these stresses can leave the incoming specimens in terminal shock, or weakened and vulnerable to attack by disease organisms or their own tankmates.

Water Temperature and Chemistry. To many fishes, even a small change in temperature over a short time is detrimental. Be aware that thermally stressed fishes may appear normal on arrival and placement, only to die mysteriously within a few days. The biochemical and physical damage resulting from thermal shock often takes a few days to occur. Thus it is extremely important to attempt to equilibrate the temperature in both the new and old environments. This is done by slowly blending water from your system into the shipping bag of a new specimen.

After short trips from the dealer of an hour or less, take the following steps to blend water from your system into the shipping bag. This will acclimate new stock to the water temperature and chemistry they are about to enter.

1) Place the shipping bag upright in a tub or bucket and cut open the top. Be sure the bag can't topple over.

2) Carefully dip out and discard approximately a third of the shipping water. Replace it with water from your aquarium or quarantine tank.

3) Wait 15 minutes and repeat Step #2. (Repeat again if you wish.)

4) Pour the contents of the shipping bag through a soft net into the bucket, catching the specimen in the net and then releasing it into your aquarium or quarantine tank. (Place by hand if appropriate.)

5) Discard the shipping water.

There are numerous variations on this technique, including floating acclimation cages and drip systems (a siphon is created using airline tubing knotted or clamped down to allow a very slow drip of system water into the shipping bag). All work toward the same end—a slow acclimation of the animal to a new set of water conditions.

Some techniques, however, lack the important ability to keep all the shipping water out of your system or quarantine tank. In almost all cases, you should avoid putting any transport water into your established system. The risk of introducing chemical pollutants and undesirable organisms is not worth it. However, there are two exceptional scenarios in which adding shipping water may be beneficial:

1) when the receiving setup has not been properly conditioned;

2) when the water conditions from which the livestock is coming are so

different from the new environment that the shipping water must be added to make the transition easier.

In the opposite instance, if new specimens are under duress—arriving in polluted, oxygen-depleted shipping water—they are often better off being introduced to their new water immediately, rather than allowing a gradual acclimation. The water they are being moved into should be approximately the same temperature or slightly warmer than the transporting water. In general, cold-water shock causes a great deal more harm than warm-water shock.

Lighting. Changes in lighting also can have a dramatic negative impact on new arrivals. It is important that the aquarium lights be dimmed during acclimation—especially bright sources like metal halides. This is crucial if you happen to be floating shipping bags in the display tank (to equalize water temperatures). Hot bulbs will quickly elevate the temperature of the water in the bags. This results in decreasing gas solubility in the bag, increasing metabolic rate, frightening of the livestock, not to mention the stress of being virtually "poached."

Preventive Dips and Baths

DIPS AND EXTENDED BATHS ARE techniques used to exclude undesirable organisms (and possibly chemicals) and to administer therapeutic agents or drugs via a temporary immersion of livestock in a specially prepared solution. Dips work because the fishes, and some of the invertebrates, we want to keep have higher tolerances to immersion in freshwater or exposure to certain semitoxic chemicals than do the organisms we want to exclude. Bacteria, protozoans, worms, necrotic tissue, crustaceans, and much more can be killed, or at least reduced in number and virulence, by immersing the animal in a preventive bath.

Dips and baths can also remove certain pollutants, such as transport chemicals (used by some shippers) or "fright" toxins. In the case of puffers and boxfishes, for example, the exudates they release when stressed can be poisonous to other livestock in your system.

Are dip or bath routines really worthwhile for all the added stress, time, and cost involved? Well, they are Standard Operating Procedures in all professional aquatic livestock collection, distribution, and rearing facilities—places that cannot afford to let new diseases and parasites into their systems. Especially for aquarists who have no ability to quarantine new arrivals in a separate tank, preventive dips are essential.

Hobbyists who get into the habit of dipping their incoming livestock in freshwater or a medicated solution typically have far fewer problems with diseases and parasites than those who count on good luck or the perfect health of all specimens coming from

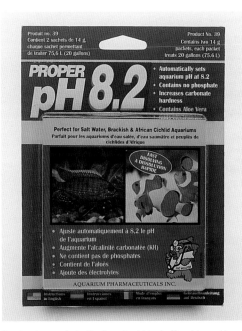

Freshwater prophylactic dips should be buffered to a pH of 8.0 to 8.3, with baking soda or a commercial buffer.

their trustworthy dealer. The best dealers don't trust anyone else's ability to ship only 100% healthy fishes, and you should be equally skeptical. A quick dip is cheap and easy insurance against some of the most expensive disasters that can befall a home system.

Dip Mixtures. Commercially available dip or bath regimens will give specifics on how to make up the actual dip liquid, but in general:

1) The water for dipping should be about the same temperature as the transport water, but if different, slightly warmer.

2) When in doubt, use actual water from your system or quarantine tank as a starting fluid and add the active ingredient(s) of the dip. Remember that you will need to have adequate oxygen

and no measurable ammonia or nitrite in the dip mix.

3) A 5-gallon plastic bucket, recycled from transporting salt mix or other harmless products, makes an excellent dipping container. The dip itself can be nothing more than freshwater, adjusted for temperature and pH by adding sodium bicarbonate (baking soda). Dissolve ¼ teaspoon of baking soda in each gallon of dip, and test the pH. It should be about 8.0. Adjust if necessary. (If you find that pH manipulating is too time-consuming, a quicker route involves the use of a buffering product such as "Proper pH" that automatically sets the pH at 8.2.) For home aquarists, other good, practical additions to the dip mix include copper sulfate, Formalin, Maracide, or Saltwater Maracyn—all easily available from any aquarium supplier.

For corals, which can carry a number of known and still unidentified infectious problems, there are proprietary dips available. Ask at a retail shop that is up-to-date on reef aquarium management. The standby dip of choice for many is strong iodine, such as Lugol's solution, or the surgical disinfectant Povidine. Using saltwater from the system in which the corals will be placed, add 5 to 10 drops of the iodine solution per liter of dip water.

For corals, it is extremely important that the dip have some form of circulation, at minimum an airstone or, preferably, a small powerhead. Most aquarium corals will tolerate 10 minutes of this treatment, and some reef

To counteract the natural tendency of aquarium pH to fall or become more acidic over time, a weekly dose of a buffering agent—either baking soda or an aquarium product—can be a simple, beneficial measure.

keepers stretch the dip out to as long as 20 minutes.

4) Watch your livestock during the dipping procedure. Unless you've done this many times, stay right there during the process. Your new acquisition might start to keel over or, alternately, fly out onto the floor. A freshwater dip typically lasts from 2 to 10 minutes, but it must be cut short if the animal shows extreme stress. The only reasonable way to gauge how much time may be too much to spend in the dip is to examine the dipped livestock's behavior. If it becomes erratic, with thrashing about, inversion, or wild attempts at missile impersonation, it's time to take it out.

5) For long-duration dips, or use of the same bath for several specimens in succession, it may be necessary to add

some aeration. Some aquarists like to have an airstone bubbling in the dip, others use a small powerhead to keep the water well-oxygenated.

6) When the animal is ready to be moved, either rinse it in an intermediate system-water-only dip, or net the stock and place into quarantine or your permanent system.

7) Keep shipping and "mixed" water out of the main system. And remember to exclude contaminated transport water from the dip, quarantine, and/or main display tank.

A Simple Dip Recipe. To make a freshwater dip, the simple method I have used countless times is to place freshwater from a reverse osmosis system or dechloraminated tap water in a bucket, adjust the temperature to about

75 degrees F, and buffer the pH upward to about 8.0 with baking soda. Next, add an ounce of 37% food-grade formaldehyde per 5 gallons of buffered water. Lower a net with the fishes in it into the bath. Depending on the type of species, size, and condition, the immersion time ranges from a few seconds to a few minutes for saltwater fishes not exhibiting discomfort (use short dips for clownfishes and other livestock that naturally live in close association with invertebrates).

For those who are leery of formaldehyde, you can make a kinder, gentler dip with methylene blue, a common aquarium medication, mixed with buffered freshwater. Add a few drops of methylene blue per liter of dip. This stuff works and is very safe. A methylene blue-freshwater dip is useful for both marine fishes and many invertebrates against ich, skin and gill flukes, funguses, *Amyloodinium*, and most other external parasitic and infectious diseases. It has several other added benefits. It's a good oxygenating dye—analogous to our blood's hemoglobin—aiding in keeping oxygen concentration high. It is also helpful in reducing light penetration and soothing frightened livestock.

The dose for these dips or baths can be more generous than the given manufacturers' specification—you want the water to be a deep royal blue.

A methylene blue dip made with freshwater is virtually nontoxic even to scaleless fishes and other sensitive groups. Add to this its low cost, ready availability, and the fact that it is hard to overdose, and we have an ideal treatment bath.

The Quarantine Tank

FIRST THE BAD NEWS: you *need* a second aquarium if you want to keep your first one healthy. Next the good news: having a simple quarantine system tucked away in a basement, garage, or spare room can be your best defense against the heartbreaking plagues that cause most people to leave the hobby of marine fishkeeping. Quarantine may seem like more of a nuisance than it really is—most aquarists soon find that having a backup tank provides more flexibility and control than they ever imagined.

A separate system for observation, treatment, and "hardening" of new livestock via quarantine is not a luxury for the privileged. It is a serious working tool of all earnest marine hobbyists. Don't wait until you have a dire need for a "hospital" system. Buy and operate a basic backup or quarantine tank in tandem with your main display setup. The advantages are numerous:

1) The principal scourges of marine reef fishes are virtually eliminated. Parasites (like *Cryptocaryon*, *Amyloodinium*, *Glugea*, and *Brooklynella*), bacteria, and most crustacean and worm problems are solved by this procedure.

2) Transit "disease" is alleviated. The jet lag some livestock goes through is greater than most people have ever endured. Given a brief respite to rest and reconstitute, new specimens are far more likely to adjust rapidly and not be bullied by existing tankmates in the main system. Very often, the animals, algae, and rock at your dealer's were on the reef just days before. Give them a break.

3) Your principal system is not disrupted every time you purchase a new specimen. Think of all the time and money you have, or will have, invested in the display unit. How would you like to tear it down completely, possibly toss the gravel, scrub, and sterilize everything because of "trouble" that could have been avoided by quarantine?

4) There are many other things you can do with an extra tank. Think of the peace of mind of knowing that you have somewhere to put your livestock should a fish need rescuing or if the main system goes down.

Components. Typically, the quarantine system is a smaller, stripped-down version of a total marine setup. A perfect choice is the cheap starter-kit aquariums sold by all pet shops as "loss leaders" to get people into the aquarium hobby. The individual components won't necessarily be of the highest quality, but will easily suffice for a quarantine system. You will need:

1) A 10-to-50-gallon tank of glass, acrylic, or other chemically inert material with a complete cover—possibly, but not necessarily, with a light fixture. Darkening the sides is a good idea.

2) Synthetic or real seawater. Some folks utilize their "spare" system to house, mix, and age new water. I suggest you go the other direction and

siphon water changes from the system tank into the quarantine tank, and use a dedicated plastic trash can for handling new water. You want the water quality in quarantine to approximate your main system—what better way than to start with water from that source?

3) Some source of biological filtration. This need not be expensive or sophisticated. A sponge filter, inside box filter, cartridge-type outside power filter, or canister filter is better than an undergravel, wet-dry, or other arrangement with a large volume of biomedia of any kind. You want to control the water chemistry in this system with a minimum of co-interaction with decor, gravel, or mass populations of microorganisms.

4) Test kits for pH, ammonia, nitrite, and any therapeutic agent you might be employing (e.g. copper).

5) Chemically unreactive hiding places. Sections of PVC pipe, ceramic flower pots, or other devices that will grant your livestock some sense of physical refuge, but won't change your water chemistry.

6) Temperature control and monitoring capabilities—a heater and thermometer.

7) Treatment chemicals, nets, and a diary. Have a small calendar and notebook handy to keep track of what you're doing and what you have observed.

Procedure. The objective of a quarantine system is to treat incoming livestock in ways that reduce the likelihood of introducing disease or a weakened specimen to the display aquarium. The

step-by-step procedure should be as follows:

1) A dip or bath in freshwater, with or without chemical additives, is executed and the new stock placed in the quarantine tank. Any chemical medications (typically copper-based) have been added to the quarantine tank and their concentration checked (and recorded) twice.

2) The livestock is closely observed daily, along with testing and adjusting for treatment concentration (if any). Unusual appearances and behavior are recorded. Feeding is light, with any uneaten excess promptly vacuumed out. (If you need to use the same isolation system at a subsequent time for nonfishes—invertebrates, rock, algae—you must dump and clean the tank out if the water has been treated with any medications for fishes.

3) A proper interval (generally a minimum of two weeks) must go by in which the specimen in the quarantine tank shows no ill effects of transport or disease. Some public aquariums wait four weeks for additional security.

Generally, we are watching for the emergence of white spots, patches of fungus, or any other appearance of parasites. The quarantined fishes should exhibit good color and healthy appetites, once settled into the quarantine tank. If any evidence of disease appears (see pages 156-159), it will be necessary to add the appropriate medications or carry out a treatment dip. If this is required, the quarantine clock must start over, with an additional two

to four weeks in isolation. (If the disease is parasitic, you must be certain that the life cycle of the parasite is broken and that no immature forms are still present.)

Keep nets, buckets, dipping containers, or any other equipment that may be contaminated reserved for your quarantine system and well away from the display aquarium. (These pieces of equipment can be disinfected with bleach, iodine solution, or methylene blue and rinsed in freshwater.)

4) After the waiting period is over, the specimen is put through the usual acclimation technique, as if it were coming in from an outside source. Catch the fish, place it in a small transfer container and slowly mix in water from your main system to adjust the temperature and acclimate the animal to a different pH, if necessary. (Ideally, your quarantine tank and display tank will have similar temperature and pH readings.)

While a number of sources say that quarantining invertebrates is unnecessary, I feel they should be segregated and watched for two weeks for the same reasons as fishes. Most should be "rinsed" in aged saltwater from the quarantine tank (many produce copious amounts of slime during shipping) immediately after being removed from the shipping bag.

To the new aquarist, the blanket recommendation that all aquarists should make it a rule to use dips, baths, and quarantine must seem like this writer's pipe-dream. Indeed, many

The Floating Bag Trick

If, for some reason, you cannot carry out the steps for basic acclimation, you should at least use the old freshwater technique of floating the animal in its shipping bag in the receiving aquarium—preferably the quarantine tank. This process should continue for a minimum of 15 to 30 minutes so that the temperature of the water in the bag can adjust to the temperature of the water in the tank. The amount of time to leave the bag in the tank will depend on the amount of water shipped, the temperature difference, and the apparent strain the stock is undergoing. It's often a good idea to monitor the temperature in both environments.

Do not open the floating bag, as the concentration gradient of oxygen may be higher if it is left sealed, and an open bag usually flops over, reducing the surface area and therefore gas exchange. Alternatively, you could open the bag and add a mechanical aerator (such as an airstone). Once the water temperature has equilibrated, pour the water from the shipping bag through a soft net into a bucket (not into the tank), catching the specimen and releasing it into the quarantine aquarium. Discard the shipping water down the drain.

hobbyists skip these steps, but all advanced aquarists, public aquariums, and breeders of marine livestock—small and large—do employ quarantine to limit their losses. You should too.

Stresses in the Aquarium

ANY TANK CONDITION that is not good for the livestock may cause excess stress, which usually leads to disease. The most common sources of stress are:

1) Improper pH or drastic and/or sudden changes in pH.

2) Improper temperature or sudden changes in temperature.

3) Improper salinity for short or extended periods.

4) Physical trauma such as pounding on the tank or sudden movements that scare the tank's inhabitants.

5) Aggressive tankmates. These can cause a fish to withdraw in hiding and miss out on feedings. Harassment or physical attack by tankmates leads to wounds, abrasions and further stress.

6) Poor diet. Deficiencies and dietary degenerative diseases are often the cause of loss of older captives.

7) High ammonia, nitrite, nitrate, or other metabolite levels. A high nitrite level prevents oxygen from reaching the cells and may cause suffocation or brain damage. Any detectable ammonia or nitrite is undesirable. For nitrates, there

are many factors affecting toxicity and differences among species susceptibility. Keeping nitrate at less than 30 ppm for fish-only systems and less than 10 ppm in aquariums with invertebrates are appropriate goals.

8) Other toxins—chlorine, copper, detergents, iron, lead, zinc, commercial ammonia, nicotine, perfume/cologne, oil, paint fumes, and insecticides, including contaminants from dog and cat flea collars.

9) Too little or too much carbon dioxide, especially prevalent in systems that are either overcrowded with life or whose owners mismanage a CO_2 infusion system.

10) Too much, too little, or irregular periods of light. Too much light (intensity, duration), affects the metabolism of all the livestock; too little light is problematic for photosynthetic invertebrates and algae. All benefit from a standard light interval of about 12 hours.

11) Dirty or cloudy water. Cloudy water is usually caused by bacteria. The bacteria in the water may use up all the available oxygen or poison your stock with their metabolites.

12) No hiding places in which the livestock can retreat to feel safe.

13) Infectious and/or parasitic disease-causing organisms.

14) Any other sudden changes in the environment.

15) Overcrowding.

Overly stressed livestock are, by definition, what we consider "sick." Stressors trigger the release of hormones that prompt the livestock to fight or flee, and they increase heart rate, blood circulation, and respiration. At worst, continual stress will cause livestock to die of exhaustion. They may become so weak that their immune systems no longer function, and they will succumb to diseases or conditions that would not otherwise affect them.

Most aquarium systems have a constant supply of funguses, bacteria, and protozoans that have little or no effect on healthy stock. Sufficiently stressed, however, livestock may fall prey to otherwise nonpathogenic organisms. Marine fishes and invertebrates are more dependent on their environment than the terrestrial examples we are more familiar with. They are totally at the mercy of their owners to provide them with proper living conditions.

Noninfectious Diseases

THE FOLLOWING "AILMENTS" are noninfectious. However, they are conditions that you should recognize. Although these "diseases" will not spread to other livestock or to you, they definitely compromise the health of the affected organism.

Popeye. This is a symptom, not an actual disease. The scientific name, exophthalmia, refers to swelling behind or in the eye. The swelling may be brought on by many factors but is most commonly caused by bacteria or, rarely, by parasites. If unilateral (only one eye involved), the cause may be mechanical injury, such as the fish bumping into something or getting thwacked by a net. Popeye is difficult to treat, but the most effective procedure seems to be the passing of time in a good environment, and receiving medicated food. Prepared mixes are available or you may make your own. Popeye may signal the need for a massive water change and better attention to water quality.

Head and Lateral Line Erosion (HLLE). This common complaint is manifested in enlarged pores and disfiguring scarring along the heads and body lateralis systems of fishes. This syndrome has been linked to poor water quality, nutritive deficiencies, and the protozoan *Octamita* (*Hexamita*) *necatrix*. Tangs and angels are especially susceptible. Definite improvement is achieved with the administration of stabilized vitamin C and vitamin D. Fresh and prepared foods should provide these, but making sure they are there by including a vitamin supplement is recommended. Lightly steamed or microwaved broccoli has also been used successfully to treat the condition.

Anecdotally, "stray voltage" has also been implicated as a causative agent for HLLE. If in doubt as to whether your

HLLE (head and lateral line erosion): typical pattern of degeneration seen in some species.

setup is grounded adequately, do test it and correct any problems.

Deformities. There are naturally occurring incidences of notched or missing fins, tweaked gill covers, weird or absent eyes, and tumorous growths of different sorts. They are neither catching nor treatable.

Swim Bladder Disease. The swim bladder is a gas-filled organ that allows a fish to stay at a certain depth in the aquarium without sinking or floating. This hydrostatic mechanism may fail when damaged by bacteria, parasites, genetic faults, or trauma.

When the swim bladder fails to function, the fish loses its ability to swim normally and may move sideways or upside-down or stay on the bottom. Once damaged, the bladder does not usually return to normal functioning, but if the fish can eat and swim without too much strain, it may live for years with the condition.

Without knowing the exact cause of the malfunction, treatment is difficult. Since internal bacteria, funguses, or parasites are the only treatable causes, medicated food, injection and/or treatment in a quarantine tank with antibiotics could be tried.

Dropsy. Dropsy or "bloat" is a name given to any disease that causes a fish to swell so much that the scales no longer lie flat against the body of the fish. By looking down on a fish you can easily spot a case of dropsy. Dropsical conditions are especially associated with the dwarf angels in the genus *Centropyge*. This is a very difficult condition to treat successfully. Daily doses of foods laced with antibiotics and optimized water quality are some of the few treatments that have proved effective.

Suffocation. Rapid breathing or gulping near the top of the tank may mean a fish is not getting enough oxygen. This may be caused by:

1) Lack of air circulation. Circulation pump, filtration, air pump, or airstones may be malfunctioning or clogged and in need of service.

2) Temperature too high. The warmer the water, the less oxygen it can absorb and hold. Watch crowded systems during heat spells.

3) Gas solubility being interrupted. Water cannot absorb oxygen or give off carbon dioxide if the surface is covered with scum or an oily film. Often you can wick this away with a plain paper towel. Another possible cause is the loss of surface area because the water level is so high that it touches the top of the tank. Occasionally, an overly zealous aquarist will seal a system shut with a cover that is too airtight.

4) Parasites. Gills attacked by parasites cannot do their job and may "leak" osmotically. This is mainly a problem with newly captured fishes bearing high fluke or crustacean parasite loads.

5) Overmedication. This can burn gills, rupture blood cells, and cause too much mucus production.

Brain Damage. A fish may show unusual behavioral symptoms. This should be offered as a diagnosis only after all other possibilities have been ruled out. Erratic, jerky swimming or spinning are common signs of brain damage. Brain damage can be caused by parasites, bruising (concussion), high or low temperatures, or toxins.

Toxic Poisoning. The symptoms look the same as brain damage, but all or most of the organisms in the system are affected at once. Spinning behavior is the most frequent sign of a toxin. Common toxins are ammoniated cleaners, paint fumes, bug sprays, copper, colognes or perfumes, and chlorine.

Prevention through education and by using dedicated gear (buckets, towels, gloves) is the only real solution to this pollution. Chemical filtrants such as activated carbon and Poly Filters, biological activity, and water changes are the most effective methods of removing poisons expediently.

Open Sores. These can be caused by medication burns, pH that is too high or too low, shipping damage, scraping on rocks or corals, bites, parasites, internal infections, and net damage during catching.

Treatment consists of eliminating the source of the problem, the use of artificial coating medication (such as Amquel or Stresscoat), and orally administered antibiotics. Be sure to watch for signs of secondary bacterial infection and treat accordingly. Lowering the specific gravity of the water can be a very effective prevention of infectious disease. Clean water will also retard the growth of infection—this is the principal benefit of filter adjuncts such as ultraviolet sterilization and ozone.

Poly Filters: highly useful in removing spent medications (and other chemicals) from tank water.

Infectious Diseases

IN THE PAST, with unsophisticated capture, holding, and transport techniques, infectious disease microorganisms were the real scourge of marine aquarium keeping. Whole tanks and even entire stores would be devastated by the sudden appearance and spread of "velvet" and/or "ich" with huge losses—sometimes within days.

It would be great to say that times have changed completely, but they haven't. Though aquatic livestock may be more vigorous and disease-free on arrival, these same problems are still very much with us. All the fancy gear, decent foods, and maintenance will do you no good should these microorganisms be allowed to enter and reproduce in your system. The three main causes of infectious disease are viruses, bacteria, and funguses.

Viruses. Viral infections are caused by particles that by some definitions are nonliving. Virus organisms are only able to function metabolically and reproduce as parasites, using the cellular machinery of their hosts. *Lymphocystis* is a commonly seen viral disease in aquatic life. It looks like white-to-grayish cauliflower-like clumps, typically at the base of the fish's fins. Its origins, cures, and spontaneous remission are somewhat mysterious. The condition may even show up in meticulously clean systems. By itself, *Lymphocystis* is rarely a damaging or fatal problem. In most cases, it cures itself by simply disappearing within a month or two.

Some authors suggest chemical treatments, biological cleaners, removing the clumpish growths from the fish by scraping with your fingers, and even the use of the antiviral compound acyclovir. I would suggest isolating afflicted specimens and letting them heal on their own.

Bacteria. These are microscopic single-celled organisms that can be found in every living environment. There are thousands of species, classified on the basis of structure, nutrition, locomotion, and more. Most bacteria are noninfectious to livestock and humans; in fact, a few are absolutely necessary.

Problems with bacteria are more often a matter of biological pollution than outright infection. In an artificial environment like a captive marine system, there are few natural checks and balances. In the wild, filter feeders, predators, dilution by currents, and other factors generally preclude the bacterial population explosions that occur in aquariums. Often the concentration of these microbes in an aquarium is several orders of magnitude greater than it is in the oceans.

The serious difficulties come about in aquariums because of nutrient robbing (oxygen, minerals) and metabolic poisoning by these quickly reproducing organisms. This in turn results in diminished resistance, weakened livestock, and disease—either by bacteria or other opportunists. From this comes the dictum that undercrowding, proper feeding, and maintenance will prevent bacterial problems.

A bacterial infection may be localized or be evident on several areas of an organism. These infections are likely to be found in or around open sores or any area where stock has lost its protective coating. Internal bacterial infections are often identified by symptoms: swelling, trouble staying on the bottom, whitish feces that float or trail off behind the fish, or lack of feces entirely (blockage). Virtually all bacterial infections of captive marine life are secondary. This means that they are the result of poor water quality, physical injury, or are from some parasitic organism. Always look first to poor water quality as the real cause.

Antibiotics added to food, or a manufactured line of medicated food, should be used to treat bacterial infections along with frequent water changes. A dirty aquarium can prevent successful treatment.

Because there are so many different types of bacteria, you may have to try several types of antibiotics before finding one that works. Be sure to do large water changes between treatments of different medications. Good quality carbon or charcoal, Poly Filter, and Chemi-Pure, among other chemical filtrants, will remove medications from the water and should not be used during any treatment with antimicrobials.

Funguses. These simple, plantlike organisms have only started to gain notice for the roles they play in marine environments. Like bacteria, they are mostly benign and of utmost importance in the wild for their roles in aiding decomposition. But they too can be infectious agents in aquariums.

Fungal diseases are rare. Most are misidentified bacterial problems or, if truly fungal, the result of a postmortem event; the specimen is long-since dead. Most fungus difficulties are easily avoided by the prophylaxis and non-contamination methods that we've covered. If you do see a real fungus, it will appear to spread evenly, starting from a central point and growing in an outward pattern. Several areas may grow outward until they overlap and give the appearance of a bacterial infection. Fungus is white with a velvety, even hairy, appearance. It is most likely to be found on the mouth, eyes, or tips of the fins.

Treatment consists of water changes, medicated food, and sulfonamides. You may find other authors suggesting the use of topical treatments (malachite, dyes, mercuricals), but I feel that these are nearly worthless. Once you've detected a true fungus on the surface of an organism, it has already penetrated below where these treatments will do any good.

Parasitic Diseases

THERE ARE MANY TYPES of parasitic organisms that can cause our marine livestock woe; almost every animal phylum (and one of the algae) contain members that parasitize fishes and invertebrates. The principal groups for us are the single-celled animals called protozoans, the dinoflagellate alga *Amyloodinium*, and various crustaceans and worms.

Due to complex life histories involving more than just one definitive host, many parasitic forms can be easily eliminated by routine quarantine that excludes the parasite's vector(s) and intermediate hosts. If you are careful in selecting and acclimating your livestock, you may never know the thrill of treating for parasitic infestations.

A parasitic infection-infestation may be pathogenic (disease-producing), latent (only mildly infectious; the livestock has more or less reached an equilibrium with its parasites due to natural or acquired immunities), or almost benign (such as "space parasites" that do little harm to their hosts).

It's important to remember that many parasites are often present in wild-caught specimens. If a healthy, stable environment deteriorates, dissolution of immunity follows, and a latent infection may become pathogenic. Diseases in wild and cultured populations of organisms may be caused by pathogenic organisms, toxic materials, or general environmental deterioration. All three factors operate together to cause parasitic-disease outbreaks.

General signs of a parasite infestation include:

1) Visible spots or threads, usually whitish, that make the fish appear as if it has been salted or covered with powdered sugar.

2) Rapid or heavy breathing. Some parasites will attack the gills before any can be seen on the fins or body, and the fish may die from suffocation.

3) Scratching. If a fish constantly rubs against objects in the tank and looks like it is trying to dislodge something, it may have parasites.

Control of parasites by the aquarist again comes down to quarantining incoming livestock and maintaining a healthy aquarium environment with high standards of cleanliness and water quality. Good nutrition, as always, is also a factor in limiting the effects of parasites.

Be aware that there is always a risk with live foods, even if they are tank-raised, of introducing parasitic organisms. In general, it is safe to feed freshwater foods to marine fishes and vice versa. Live brine shrimp, however, are still slightly suspect as carriers for *Cryptocaryon* and *Amyloodinium* even after being thoroughly rinsed in freshwater. Most commercially prepared frozen and dry foods are preferable to live foods from the standpoint of disease transfer.

Treatment of Parasites

PREVENTIVE MEASURES are preferable to treatment and are often adequate. Much care must be exercised when treating to get rid of parasites; often the cure is worse than the disease, especially if stable environmental conditions can't be maintained (i.e. you don't have a separate treatment aquarium).

In general, it is best not to treat animals infected by bacteria or funguses, as these losses can often be traced to improper environment. The most infected stocks should be removed and the problem(s) corrected.

Protozoan, helminth (worm) and arthropod (crustacean) parasites have greater resistance to immune responses of the host and must be treated differently. Often a chemical must be applied and the system later sterilized by cleaning, drying, chlorine, etc. These infections are rare if water quality and quarantine procedures are followed.

Parasite controls may be divided into biological, physical, and chemical in order of preference by most aquarists. Biocontrols include the use of the known mutualistically symbiotic cleaner fishes and shrimps that can be called into play to remove external parasites and necrotic tissue. Physical or mechanical controls include increasing circulation and filtration, altering photoperiod and strength, decreasing specific gravity, using UV sterilization, and manipulating temperature. As a last line of defense, use of chemicals is often important in situations when parasitism is highest, resistance low, and loss of livestock imminent.

When selecting a medication, several factors should be kept in mind:

1) The medication should be quickly degradable (many have residual effects).

2) The compound should be as specific as possible (few are).

3) The medication should cause as little stress to the livestock as possible. (Several compounds, e.g. metals, cause fishes to shed copious amounts of mucus; these medications must be used with a test kit and within set concentrations as the mucus serves several vital functions: defense against invasion by ectoparasites, involvement in gas exchange, and osmotic balance.)

Most metal and dye medications are deadly toxic to invertebrates, algae and live rock and sand in low concentrations (another good reason to treat infected fishes in a separate tank).

The following list of medications is far from complete, but they are the most common generic ingredients (read the labels of the packages at the store) available to amateur fishkeepers. Some estimates put the sale of "medicines" in the pet-fish industry at 10% of the gross of all goods sold; in my opinion, this is far too high. Conscientious aquarists should never use medicines as a substitute for good care. I do not encourage the use of chemical controls, except when absolutely required.

Formalin continues to be a mainstay for the prevention and treatment of external protozoans and monogenetic trematodes (flukes). It comes with an array of warnings regarding temperature, oxygen levels, and other factors to be considered during its use. I would recommend using Formalin only as a disinfectant or dip—not as an ongoing treatment, and never in a main/display system.

Malachite green is a common chemical used widely in the U. S. for the treatment of fish parasites. It is effective when used as directed, by itself or in concert with other ingredients. Be aware of its staining properties.

Organophosphate insecticides (Dylox, Dipterex, Neguvon, DTHP) for the treatment of parasitic copepods are recommended by some aquarists, but I would avoid any involvement with these poisons.

Quinines are used by some hobbyists with good results.

Potassium permanganate is a strong oxidizer and highly toxic to some species. Use carefully only as a dip (it stains everything) or disinfectant.

Methylene blue is a great and safe oxygen-carrying dye; it is useful as a dip and preventive in quarantine and is generally nontoxic to all fishes.

Copper sulfate ($CuSO_4$) is very effective when used in a citrated form (mixed with citric acid) or chelated with a stabilizing molecule to keep it in solution. Free copper ion is and has been a powerful tool in the handling of marine fishes. The general (though not only) action of copper is as a "proteinaceous precipitant," causing the production of mucus, which covers external parasites and causes them to be sloughed off.

Copper in its various formulations is a useful adjunct to dips/baths and quarantine treatment of fishes. It is used in every wholesale and public aquarium

Several commonly available aquarium remedies, from left to right: SeaCure (copper sulfate in citrated form) and Formalin, two recommended allies in fighting parasites; SPS dip and Lugol's solution (a strong iodine), two treatments for stony coral infections.

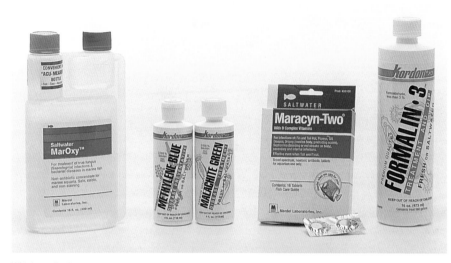

Widely available and recommended broad-spectrum treatments for dip solutions or quarantine tank water. Drugs should never be added to reef aquariums and only as a last resort to display aquarium systems.

facility I've ever been to. Nevertheless, copper, especially raw copper sulfate or homemade concoctions, should not be continuously applied to a home aquarium system, as it has been found to have cumulative deleterious effects. Be sure to adhere to the dosage requirements, test the level of copper in your quarantine tank water (it gets "used up" quickly in some circumstances), and remember that it is absolutely deadly to algae and invertebrates (some of whose members are the disease agents you're trying to kill). Copper can be an aquarist's ally, but must be used prudently.

Flagyl (metronidazole) is an antiprotozoal. I do not generally support its use or that of any antiprotozoal by inexperienced hobbyists. They are toxic to the livestock and system and can be woefully misapplied. Stay away from them.

Vermifuges or anthelminthics, such as di-N-butyl tin oxide, are deworming compounds, generally administered orally through foods. When to utilize these agents? My advice is, not at all.

Antimicrobials, such as antibiotics, "furan" compounds, and sulfonamides, are not used against parasites directly but more to ward off secondary infections from bacteria and funguses that may follow parasitic problems. Most antimicrobials are worthless when added directly to the water. Some are used in concentrated dips, others administered through feeding, and others (infrequently) injected.

Diseased animals should never be treated directly in the main system with chemicals. Many substances, such as some antibiotics and Formalin, interrupt nitrification, so treatment tanks often use physical and chemical methods of filtration, such as passing the water through carbon and using an ozonizer for ammonia conversion.

Parasites: A Rogue's Gallery

HERE'S MY PARADE OF STARS—THE most commonly encountered and written about captive marine parasitic fauna, with a few notes on treatment and eradication.

Protozoans and dinoflagellates are single-celled organisms that include two of the most deadly parasites known to marine aquarists: *Amyloodinium* (marine velvet) and *Cryptocaryon* (marine ich or white spot disease). These diseases can be responsible for large and fast losses of fish livestock.

Amyloodinium ocellatum is a dinoflagellate alga (or a flagellate protozoan, depending on whether you're a zoologist- or botanist-leaning classifier). In older texts it's called *Oodinium*. This parasite infests the gills and body surface of fish hosts, appearing as a velvety sprinkling. Behavior of afflicted fishes includes dashing, scratching, and rapid breathing, until the gills are so damaged that the fishes become lethargic and die.

Cryptocaryon irritans is the causative agent for marine ich, or white spot disease. It is a ciliated protozoan, named for its many small cilia that are utilized for locomotion. We'll include in its discussion two other ciliate protozoans, *Brooklynella hostilis*, also called anemonefish disease (though it infects all marine bony fishes), and *Uronema marinum*. All three of these organisms produce recognizable signs, are highly contagious, and can be deadly.

The rapid production of mucus

Cryptocaryon irritans (marine ich or white spot disease): easily treatable with copper formulations.

Amyloodinium (*Oodinium*) *ocellatum*: an often deadly parasitic infection; must be treated early.

Brooklynella hostilis (anemonefish disease): also deadly; demands quick diagnosis and treatment.

showing up as clumps is close to the last clue you'll get before your fishes break down with rapid to lethargic breathing. *Uronema* may reveal itself in ulcerations that look like lesions.

General treatment against protozoans and dinoflagellates calls for the affected individuals to be isolated in a separate tank and treated as soon as possible. General procedure involves dipping or baths, possibly lowering specific gravity (some aggressive treatments recommend dropping it to 1.015 over a period of 24 hours in the treatment tank). For *Amyloodinium* and *Cryptocaryon*, continuous exposure to citrated copper sulfate is prescribed. For *Brooklynella* and *Uronema*, the standard remedies are Formalin and malachite green. Antibiotic feeding can prevent secondary infections.

And you're not done yet. If any of these parasites show themselves in your main system, it is very likely that they have reproduced and left resting, nonfeeding stages of progeny in the water and on the substrate. Getting rid of these can be an ordeal. At the very least, allow the system to "go fallow" without

hosts for a month or more. This has proved to reduce numbers and virulence sufficiently. At the worst, you're looking at tearing down, sterilizing and reassembling the entire system. Coming face to face with these facts is how most of us have learned, the hard way, the value of quarantine and prevention.

Other Protozoans. Let's not leave out mention of the protozoan groups *Microsporea* and *Myxosporea*. These are all obligate parasites, many of which infest (externally) and infect (internally) fishes and invertebrates. Of the microsporeans, *Glugea* is notable as the gunky cystlike disease of seahorses, pipefishes, and their relatives. *Myxosporea* protozoans are found either living within host tissues or in the body cavity. There is no known cure for these protozoans.

Parasitic crustaceans (copepods) look nothing like the crabs or shrimp we keep or love to eat. Isopods, the "pillbugs" or roly-polies of your childhood, are not so funny when they show up in your marine system. These grayish crustaceans are big enough to see and remove from the fish's mouth or

body with forceps or tweezers. Copepods appear rather wormlike, and there are more than a thousand species of parasitic copepod crustaceans known. Some of them are very common and can be debilitating or lethal in large numbers. These copepods are specialized in their structure and feeding; some are internal with bizarre saclike and tree-branching body shapes. External species range from forms with holdfasts that permanently wedge into their host's outer covering to ones that range over the body surface with specialized cutting, puncturing, and sucking mouth parts.

The copepods that can be dealt with chemically (those on the outside of their hosts) are best eliminated through freshwater dips and copper treatment as the fishes pass through quarantine. Biological cleaning by certain shrimp, gobies, and wrasses presumably aids in restricting copepod parasitism in the wild.

Worms that can cause problems in home aquariums include flatworms, flukes, and tapeworms. Turbellarians, a group in the Phylum Platyhelminthes (flatworms) are mostly free-living, non-parasitic species. One notable exception is *Paravortex*, the causative agent of black spot disease, notably of Yellow Tangs. This is easily eliminated by freshwater dipping, though other authors suggest Formalin baths and organophosphate remedies.

Trematodes, the flukes, are divided into ectoparasitic (external) monogenes and endoparasitic (internal) digenes on the basis of their life histories. Monogeneans have a direct life cycle, and digeneans an indirect one with the use of one or more intermediary species. The monogenes are important as gill and body parasites of marine fishes.

There are many species of flukes that are common on imported livestock and may significantly reduce their health if not eliminated through acclimation techniques. Hiding, rapid breathing, discoloration, and more are symptomatic of infection/infestation, though microscopic examination of skin scrapings and gill clippings are required for positive diagnosis.

Several chemicals, including organophosphates, copper, and dips of freshwater with or without malachite or Formalin, have been described in the literature as being efficacious. Recent authors tout the use of Praziquantel (Droncit) at 1 ppm administered in a treatment tank. Digeneans rarely spread due to the absence of intermediate hosts, and many of the monogenes are species/group specific.

Tapeworms called cestodes live in digestive systems; yes, just as dogs and cats and humans can carry these parasites, so can fishes. Typically an aquarist will only become aware of their presence when a section of a worm is expelled from the fish's vent, or from postmortem dissection. Fishes are either imported with the tapeworms or pick them up from ingesting their intermediate hosts in their food. Once more, here is a good reason to be wary of live marine foods.

There are antiworm medications that work to rid fishes of intestinal parasites; you can check with local sources as to which is the "latest and greatest" available; but I wouldn't use them. The vast majority of incidents show that the cure is too late or is more deadly than the problem. Well-maintained specimens have successful relationships with their internal parasites; they're not killed by them.

Roundworms (Phylum Nematoda), like tapeworms, are rarely encountered unless seen protruding from a fish's vent or discovered upon autopsying a specimen after it has died. Many are microscopic, some are macroscale and obvious as parasites. Among all worm and wormlike groups, a nematode is recognized microscopically by its triradiate esophagus (in cross section).

With this group, the best treatment is none at all; simply optimizing the environment reduces the likelihood of loss or debilitation from roundworms. If you have an aquaculture facility or many members of the same species that you know are dying from nematodes, anthelminthics may be required.

Summary. There are no health standards imposed by law on the collection, holding, wholesale, retail, end-user treatment of marine livestock. It is up to each individual handling this aquatic life to do his or her own bit in terms of sanitation and quarantine procedures.

The only way to "get value"—as with everything else in life—is to know it and demand it or provide it yourself. You will find that in keeping a healthy marine system, this comes down to study, earnest involvement with good livestock dealers, and your own conscientious care.

It helps to know that many fish diseases are not treatable—either there is no known cure or the cure kills the fish. Some fish die from internal parasites that are not able to be diagnosed and therefore go untreated.

Aquarists can actually do much to take control of these organisms, and there is no doubt that the diagnosis and treatment of marine diseases will continue to improve. In the meantime, do your best to help your livestock stay healthy by using preventive means: providing an optimized environment and proper feeding.

Of treatable ailments—those that we can diagnose as being truly "caused" by infectious or parasitic organisms—the best plan of attack is to have a good defense. Dips, acclimation, and quarantine of newly acquired livestock, together with an optimized environment in your main system, will virtually preclude any messy involvement with biological diseases.

Cyanide Collection

Deadly Truths for Reefs, Fishermen, and Aquarists

ONCE KNOWN AS the richest concentration of marine reef fish diversity in the world, with more than 2,100 known species, the Philippine Islands was the world's principal source of marine livestock for aquariums for decades. An archipelago of some 7,000 islands and 33,000 square kilometers of reefs, the Philippines in 1950 was a paradise of corals and the fishes and invertebrates that live on, in, and among them. Today this once-bountiful profusion of fringing reefs, coral banks, and shoals stands as one of the saddest examples of resource destruction in our lifetime.

Many reefs there are dead, dying, and no longer productive, either for food fish or organisms for the aquarium trade. Fishes and invertebrates that do

Diver illegally spraying sodium cyanide or "cuscous" on an already degraded Philippine reef to stun fishes that have sought shelter in the coral.

come out of the Philippines are either viewed with suspicion or boycotted by many in the wholesale business. The reason? The Philippines has become known for the poor, inconsistent quality of its fishes due to the use of the poison sodium cyanide (NaCN) in collecting them.

Coupled with coastal developments, the dynamiting of reefs by fishermen, the extraction of coral for construction projects, and the large-scale collection of corals for ornamental markets, the use of cyanide for the taking of food fishes and aquarium specimens has contributed to the worst large-scale example of coral reef destruction in human history. As aquarists, we can either be a continuing part of this problem—or perhaps a piece of the solution.

From Nets to "Cuscous"

IN DECADES PAST, the majority of marine aquarium fishes from these islands

were gathered by Filipinos using simple, sustainable methods: hand nets, cotton gill nets, traps, barbless hooks and lines, and night diving with or without lights. In the span of just a few

T-shirt found during a diving tour of Indonesia, where the use of deadly cyanide is now spreading.

decades, all of that changed. The rapid adoption of cyanide for collecting fishes reads like a typical story of economic expediency without moral awareness. It is one of immediate short-term monetary gain at a tremendous cost to reef productivity, fishing efficiency, and indigenous human malnutrition.

Sodium cyanide, known as "cuscous" in the Philippines, was originally used as a fungicide in the palm tree industry, and to a lesser degree in other applications. Its botanical use has been supplanted, but there are some legitimate industrial uses of cyanides—in electroplating, electronics, and other operations.

Preparing a lethal cocktail of sodium or potassium cyanide and seawater, sometimes mixed with kerosene or gasoline.

The fish-stunning properties of sodium cyanide were first publicized in 1958 by a fisheries researcher in Illinois, whose work reported that the chemical could be used to produce temporary and reversible paralysis of fishes. He foresaw a useful application in the harvesting of fishes from aquaculture ponds. This research was noted and promptly put to use in the Philip-

pines, perhaps first in milkfish ponds. In the mid 1960s when I lived near Manila, cuscous was sometimes used in poison baits to catch seagulls, which were considered a delicacy. (Cooking cyanide-poisoned prey is believed to render the poison harmless to ingestion by humans, although medical research is lacking.) From there, its use rapidly expanded to the catching of live fishes for the aquarium trade from coral reefs and finally to the taking alive of large food-fish species such as groupers and wrasses.

With easy availability of cyanide from industrial sources and demand for cheap marine aquarium fishes, poison-collecting rose from casual use in the late 1950s to commonplace use in the 1970s and 1980s. Earl Kennedy, a pioneer marine exporter in the Philippines, observed a sudden increase in the supply of fishes from certain localities in 1962. A simultaneous decline in the quality of the catch led him to become suspicious that the fishes were being collected with sodium cyanide. In the early 1980s, an American fish collector named Steve Robinson and a German scuba diver/writer named Helmut Debelius attempted to warn the aquarium community about the severity of the problem. In 1979, *Freshwater and Marine Aquarium Magazine* Editor Don Dewey took a strong stand against cyanide usage—and reported receiving death threats.

In spite of these early alarms, the practice of using cyanide became ingrained in the aquarium-fish collection business in the Philippines. Worse, it spread to heavy use in the taking of food fish, both for local consumption and for the export of prime live fishes to Hong Kong, Taiwan, and other epicurean centers.

In 1985, fisheries scientist and aquarist Dr. Peter J. Rubec, wildlife veterinarian Dr. Vaughan Pratt, and Steve Robinson met and formed the International Marinelife Alliance (IMA). A Canadian ichthyologist, Dr. Don McAllister, joined the group soon after. Together they mounted a sustained effort to combat cyanide use in fish capture, gradually gaining the support of other international organizations and branches of the Philippine government.

Cyanide kills a large percentage of the animals it reaches either immediately or shortly after collection. Those that do survive may be shipped for sale at premium prices either to fish markets, fish restaurants, or aquarium shops. The fishes may appear normal to the untrained eye, and persons eating them generally suffer no ill effects. While well-heeled diners may never witness the longer-term effects of cyanide collection, aquarists have become all too familiar with the true nature of this poison. The IMA's Rubec estimates that cyanide kills an average of 50% of fishes exposed at the point of collection and about 30% of the survivors in each link of the commercial chain (from collector to buyer to exporter to importer to wholesaler to the retail store). By his calculation, more than 90% of cyanided fishes die before they reach the home aquarium—and an unknown percentage thereafter.

The Effects of Cyanide Use

How important is cyanide in causing the death of pet fish? Some observers believe it to be a leading cause of mortality, while others in the trade point to a variety of stressors that, alone or in combination, can be responsible for losses. A surprisingly large percentage of captured marine organisms die enroute through collection, transport, and distribution from wholesalers to retailers to hobbyists. Cyanide, weeks of starvation, parasite loads, metabolite "burn" from holding and transporting fishes in polluted water, shipping stress, and lack of oxygen have all been implicated. The relative importance of these factors in causing mortality among aquarium fishes, during shipment and after being sold to the hobbyist, is still largely unknown, but this does not dilute the negative impacts of cyanide.

Many fish die shortly after exposure to too much cyanide. (The application is crude and nearly impossible to control.) Those "lucky" fish that survive long enough to be picked up and moved to clean seawater must wait to be transported through middlemen, and then to wholesale shippers in major towns that are set up for international air export. These fishes are not fed for days or weeks in the process of making their way to their country of destina-

tion. Fishes being exported are intentionally starved for three reasons:

1) It costs money to feed them;

2) The animals will defecate more if they are fed, polluting their water;

3) Many fishes cannot digest their food. In scientific studies, fishes were observed to die shortly after eating their first meal, while others refused to eat and slowly starved to death. Several prominent aquarists believe that these observations are symptoms of the Cyanide Syndrome.

Rubec recalls, "In the mid 1960s, Dempster and Donaldson at the Steinhart Aquarium conducted histological studies of fishes from California waters experimentally exposed to sodium cyanide. They found damage to the liver, kidney, spleen, and brain. The cell damage observed was identical to that found with fishes imported from the Philippines.

"D.R. Bellwood wrote an article in *Freshwater and Marine Aquarium Magazine* in 1981 describing the destruction of the anterior intestine and mucosal lining of the stomach of the Three-spot Domino Damselfish (*Dascyllus trimaculatus*) from Kenya that were exposed to 1 ppm or 5 ppm of sodium cyanide in aquaria for two to three minutes. Cyanide in the stomach was found to result in the sloughing of

Tragic harvest of fishes for the aquarium trade: roughly half of all cyanided fishes die immediately on the reef, while whose those that seem to recover long enough to reach the market may never regain full health.

the gastric mucosa, followed by cell degeneration. A recent study by Hall and Bellwood indicated that degeneration of the lining of the anterior intestine was primarily the result of starvation, rather than exposure to cyanide alone or from stress alone."

Death from cyanide can be quick or prolonged. "I have personally observed marine fish drop dead for no apparent reason in dealer's tanks," says Rubec. "I have also watched marine fishes that refused to eat and took more than two months to die. Straughan in 1967 noted that shipments of fishes from the Far East were observed to 'die like flies' in importers tanks.

"The internal damage to the fish caused by cyanide can lead to longer-term delayed mortalities. There is such a thing as the Sudden Death Syndrome (SDS) in fishes, which has been described in about six scientific papers. Cyanide can cause delayed (chronic) deaths through internal damage to the fish and disruption of enzyme systems. Hall and Bellwood found that exposure to cyanide alone (10 ppm for 85 seconds) caused higher delayed mortalities (37.5%) over a 13-day period than stress alone (25%) or starvation alone (0%). Cyanide may also lead to delayed deaths by weakening the fish and reducing their resistance to other factors such as ammonia and disease."

What happens to the rest of the environment that comes in contact with this poison and its poisoned life? The effects on fisherfolk and others who handle the extremely toxic material,

immerse themselves in waters laced with cyanide, and feed poisoned fishes to their families have not yet been adequately studied. "There are up to 50% mortalities of children in coastal villages in the Philippines," says Rubec, "but it is not clear whether the children die of malnutrition, disease, or from consumption of cyanide-poisoned fish." (Rubec speculates that cases of the "bends" among poorly trained cyanide-using collectors may be a bigger human health problem than cyanide itself.)

Documentation of reefs subjected to heavy cyanide application shows that corals can bleach and die, fish and invertebrate populations can be decimated and move away, and, in the absence of active herbivores, algal growth eventually takes over.

Beyond the Philippines

OVER THE LAST DECADE, Indonesian sources and exporters in other areas have supplanted a significant part of the Philippine marine fish market. Collectors commonly refer to the Philippines as being "fished out." Aquarium-fish exports from the Philippines to the U.S. dropped to $3.2 million U.S. in 1991, from $6.5 million in 1990, and $7.2 million in 1989. From an estimated high of 85% of all marine livestock hailing from the Philippines in the 1960s, this country's export share has dropped to 55% or 60%, according to informal assessments made by the IMA and major fish exporters.

In contrast to the tainted stock from

the Philippines, animals of so-called "Indo" origins (from the Indo-Pacific) are touted by many as being entirely hand-caught. There has been increasing suspicion, however, that more and more aquarium fishes imported from that region (which has some 13,600 islands and 81,000 kilometers of coastline) are also being collected with cyanide.

In my past role as an aquatics buyer, I saw hundreds of boxes of these organisms from the Indo-Pacific. Here is what I witnessed: an abundance of "anomalous" losses (incoming animals dying for no apparent reason) and too many fishes with overly bright coloring (a side-effect of cyanide) that at first refused all foods, then quickly died when they did accept feed. I became increasingly suspicious of the possibility of cyanide use in their capture.

Traveling through Indonesia in October 1994 on the islands of Java, Bali, Lombok, and Irian Jaya, my suspicions were confirmed. I witnessed firsthand the widespread use of cyanide outside the Philippines. In fact, the poisoning of reefs was the *only* method I observed being employed for capturing "show specimen" ornamental fishes. What I saw was skin and scuba divers deployed from skiffs with float-supported keeper nets and opaque "squirt bottles" that had been loaded with tablets of cyanide

Healthy, hand-caught Clown Triggerfish (*Balistoides conspicillum*): informed aquarists who seek out net-caught specimens can help send a strong anti-cyanide message back to the collecting nations.

Net-caught fishes have been reported to show a better than 90% survival rate from reef to retail store, compared to the 10% survival rate of cyanided fishes.

dissolved in seawater or organic solvents (kerosene or gasoline). I watched them spraying their poison mix liberally over and through productive coral and rock aggregations where specimens had taken refuge. Their targets were prized show species of angelfishes, butterflyfishes, basses, and others that would scoot under a coral or rock ledge when approached or pursued. Once their hiding places in the reef were sprayed with the cyanide cocktail, they invariably either swam out as if on fire or were narcotized and retrieved with a net.

The practice is also reported by others to be migrating well beyond the Philippines. The Coral Reef Alliance (CORAL) says that, "Food-fishing operations, often using cyanide, are moving from the overharvested and devastated reefs of the Philippines to destroy remote and pristine coral reefs in eastern Indonesia, Papua New Guinea, Palau, Tuvalu, the Federated States of Micronesia, and other nations of the Western Pacific. Why do they do it? Fishermen can sell live fish, such as grouper, wrasses, rock cod, and snapper, to exporters for many times the price of dead fish. The exporters then turn around and demand five times the price they paid for the fish by selling them to foreign luxury live fish markets in Asia."

"Sullied Seas," a recent report by the World Resources Institute and IMA, cites the kind of prices that motivate this trade: "In 1996, several particularly large Giant Groupers (*Epinephelus lan-*

THE CONSCIENTIOUS MARINE AQUARIST

ceolatus) sold in Hong Kong for nearly $11,000 each. Live Napoleon Wrasse and Highfin Grouper—the most-favored species—command wholesale prices of $60 to more than $90 per kilogram. . . . One 40 kg Napoleon Wrasse may sell for as much as $5,000, $425 for the lips—considered a particular delicacy—alone."

While the push of grouper and wrasse-hunting ships into new areas is primarily driven by the prices of premium food fishes, an estimated 30% of these fishing vessels may also be supplying livestock to the aquarium trade.

Speaking Out

As early as it was known that cyanide was being used in collecting, there have been voices of reason calling for effective controls on its sale, application, and any commerce involving cyanide-poisoned fishes. In the Philippines, these efforts have been concentrated in recent years in a mix of net-training, education, enforcement, and alternative-livelihood programs.

Thankfully, there are salient definitive assays that have been developed for testing whether or not a fish has encountered cyanide. Since the early 1990s, with the assistance of the IMA-Philippines, the Philippine government has had the Cyanide Detection Test (CDT) available at various exportation sites for spot-checking shipments of fishes.

The Philippine Bureau of Fisheries and Aquatic Resources (BFAR) has promised to employ the CDT as a tool to curb the widespread use of cyanide in aquarium and food-fish collecting. A number of prosecutions have been started and some violators jailed, but progress has been slow. The IMA has assisted the Philippine government in planning a "total reform package," including enhanced enforcement, the teaching of net-catching techniques to cyanide-using fishermen, training villagers for other sources of income, and a public-awareness program.

"The presence of the CDT laboratories in the Philippines has been acting as a deterrent," says the IMA's Rubec. "The incidence of fishes found with traces of cyanide has gone from over 80% in 1993 to 47% in 1996. Filipino exporters are now cooperating with the CDT laboratories and can obtain test results to determine which collectors or middlemen sell cyanide-free fishes. The situation has been improving to the point where about six of the main exporters have almost completely cyanide-free marine aquarium fishes."

Rubec is optimistic about plans for the Bureau of Fisheries to require all fish exporters to be registered, inspected, and to cooperate with random testing. Shipments found to contain cyanided fishes would be subject to confiscation, and repeat offenders would risk losing their licenses or being prosecuted. Shipments of exported fishes from the Philippines would be accompanied by a Clearance Certificate, which would be used by the U.S. Fish and Wildlife Service and by U.S. based importers, wholesalers, and re-

tailers to ensure that the livestock came from inspected sources.

To replace the use of cyanide, fishermen are being retrained and equipped with barrier nets. The IMA estimates that net capture as an alternate method of collection can result in fish survival rates roughly 300% better than those of cyanided specimens. However, local fishermen need to be equipped with nets, taught to use them effectively, and be connected to buyers who do not want cyanide-collected animals. (Unfortunately, the wholesale middlemen are often the pushers/sellers of sodium cyanide.) Using nets can ultimately produce a better financial return for the fishermen, but reform has proved both costly and slow to take hold.

In the meantime, with cyanide collection an ongoing source of mortalities, the pet trade has continued to shift away from the Philippine Islands. (Buying and selling animals that die is, if nothing else, bad business.)

Estimates of the amount of cyanide sprayed on Philippine reefs over the past 20 years vary greatly, but recent calculations suggest an ongoing infusion as great as 1 million kilograms per year, including collections of both food fishes and aquarium fishes. Even a small fraction of this amount in air would be enough material to kill several million people.

Informed keepers of marine livestock and conscientious trade people are critical of cyanide collecting, knowing it usually kills both the fish and the coral head it came from. However, the

Collecting tangs in Hawaii: nondestructive fisheries here and in the Caribbean, Red Sea, and elsewhere are proof that reef fishes can be sustainably harvested.

majority of marine fishkeepers in the world are probably oblivious to the problem. This lack of public concern or indifference allows importers and dealers to ignore the issue. Recently, the American Marinelife Dealers Association (AMDA) was formed to educate both the pet-fish trade and hobbyists about issues such as cyanide collection.

This is a serious issue for anyone interested in aquarium fishes, but there is much that the hobbyist, retailer, and distributor can do—both individually and collectively—to end this practice.

Simply put, there is no excuse for the continuing crime of cyanide being used for food and pet-fish collecting in the Philippines and Indonesia. Sodium cyanide is a poison, producing short term foreign exchange at the cost of the resource's productivity, and enslaving local peoples in a cycle of habitat destruction, poor health, and poverty. The fact that cyanide-collecting practices among pet-fish collectors are not tolerated in the Red Sea, the Indian Ocean, the Caribbean, Hawaii, and elsewhere is proof that this practice can be prevented where responsible governments, fishermen, and livestock buyers refuse to tolerate it.

The most important task for the conscientious aquarist, in my view, is to become a better consumer. As a hobbyist, you should question outlets about their sources of fish and their cyanide philosophy. (If they seem unaware, talk to them. After reading this brief introduction to the problem, you are probably better informed on the subject than the average pet-store clerk.)

Request that prospective purchases be fed as you watch, and ask the dealer to hold them there with a deposit for a week or two. (Beware of any specimen that shows no interest in food or its surroundings. To expert eyes, many cyanided fishes appear to have undergone shock treatment. Evidence of starvation or wasting can also be a telltale sign.) Most cyanide-doomed livestock will not eat or will perish within this period once they do start to eat. If any "on hold" specimen dies in a retailer's care, you should get your deposit back. Retailers, in turn, should demand credit or replacement for these "anomalous" losses. (On the other hand, do not expect refunds for fishes that die in your care—even if shortly after purchase. A retailer loses control over the livestock the moment it leaves the shop, and it is unreasonable to count on protection for any of the myriad possible causes of death of a marine fish. If you buy from a conscientious dealer and select only specimens that are alert, responsive to external stimuli, interested in food, eating, and not emaciated, your chances of avoiding cyanided fishes are greatly improved.)

Retailers and importers with buying clout ought to demand certifiably clean shipments. Since cyanide is rapidly excreted from fish, cyanide testing in the importing country is not feasible. Here, the industry should support the efforts of IMA and other organizations to implement cyanide testing in the export-ing countries. These methods may very well save the industry from being shut down outright. While the Philippines (as the best-documented example) deserve everyone's attention, the very real spread of this practice into Indonesia and other areas must also be watched.

Poverty, greed, perceived necessity, and the expediency of fast money dictate that this system will persist, and even grow, unless the demand for poisoned livestock is extinguished. Starting with you, the informed aquarist, the word must be sent back through the long chain of buyers and sellers and collectors that we do not want cyanided fishes. These animals represent the worst of all possible choices for the marine hobbyist: they are unhealthy—damaged for whatever life they have left—and, far worse, the reefs, and, perhaps, the fishermen that provided them, have been similarly poisoned. If you don't want your dollars paying for all of this, let the system know.

Finally, if you care, stay informed. Check out what the following organizations are doing to control cyanide use, protect coral reefs, and assist Third World fisherfolk. Join them, consider making at least a small donation, and write letters of protest to the parties involved. This is the dark, dark side of aquarium keeping for all of us who want nothing to do with harming the reefs.

For every informed marine aquarist, there is a simple choice: would you rather be part of the problem or part of the solution?

FOR MORE INFORMATION, CONTACT:
Dr. Peter J. Rubec
International Marinelife
    Alliance-USA
2800 4th Street North, Suite 123
St. Petersburg, FL 33704
Phone (813) 896-8626
Fax (813) 321-9031
e-mail: prubec@compuserve.com

Dr. Don E. McAllister
Ocean Voice International
P.O. Box 37026
3332 McCarthy Road
Ottawa, ON
Canada K1V 0W0
Phone (613) 521-4205
Web site: www.conveyor.com/
    oceanvoice.html

Dr. Vaughan Pratt
IMA-Philippines
P.O. Box 12648
Ortigas Center Post Office
Pasig City, Metro Manila
Philippines 1600
Phone (632) 631-5687
Fax (632) 631-9251
e-mail: imaphil@mnl.sequel.net
IMA Web site: www.actwin.com/
    fish/ima/html

John H. Tullock
American Marinelife Dealers
    Association (AMDA)
P.O. Box 9118
Knoxville, TN 37940-0118
Phone (423) 573-0373
Web site: www.execpc.com/
    ~jkos/amda

Fishes for the Marine Aquarium

*Diversity's Wonders:
Selection and Classification*

FROM BLACK, ABYSSAL OCEAN DEPTHS to ethereal mountain springs high above the world's timberlines, in waters that range from below freezing to 109 degrees F, in sizes from ⅓ inch to 45 feet in length, and from a fraction of a gram to 20 tons in weight, there is a fathomless diversity of fishes. They appear in hues from mud-drab to hot luminescent. They can be observed swimming, walking, fly-ing, gliding—and even breathing—in and out of water. They are hawk-eyed, bifocaled, and blind; planktivorous, vegetarian, scale-eating, eye-biting, and cannibalistic; free-living, com-mensal, mutualistic, and parasitic; tasty, edi-ble, toxic, and venomous. They are the fishes.

By some measures, fishes possess the most acute vision, the best olfactory senses, and the most highly evolved sensitivity to vibrations and electrical impulses in the world. Their ability to maneuver and position themselves in their own environment is unparalleled. Imagine: there are more differences in the skulls of labrid fishes (the wrasses) than in the rest of the vertebrates (amphibians, rep-

ABOVE: Juvenile Pinnate Batfish (*Platax pinnatus*). LEFT: Black-spotted Sting Ray (*Taeniura meyeni*) with profusion of Indian Ocean reef fishes.

175

tiles, birds, and mammals) combined. There are fishes without hemoglobin that live in water lower than the freezing point. Then there is sex: some of the basses, wrasses, clownfishes, and others are first males (or females) and then switch, sometimes very rapidly, when given the needed behavioral cues.

The answer to the question "What is a fish?" is unendingly complex. Consider some of the more common, **incorrect** statements that attempt a definition:

• **Fishes respire by gills.** Not all fishes do. Labyrinth fishes (anabantoids, gouramis, etc.), lungfishes, callichthyid catfishes, and many others have to come to the surface to breathe. Many of these fishes have only vestigial gills and would actually "drown" if kept underwater.

• **Fishes live in water.** Oh really? What about the comical periophthalmids, the mudskippers, or the climbing "perch" anabas that spend more time out of the water than in it? Several fish species aestivate or otherwise "wait out" a portion of their lives virtually without water. Lungfishes and many of the egg-laying toothed carps, Cyprinodontidae (killifishes), are notable examples.

• **Fishes have scales.** Better look around. All true eels, Order Anquilliformes, are scaleless, as are catfishes—both "naked" and "armored." All the jawless fishes, Class Agnatha, the lamprey and hagfish species, are as well.

• **Fishes have fins.** Although the "typical" fish has two sets of paired fins—pectorals and pelvics—and three unpaired—dorsal (back), caudal (tail) and anal (vent), there are fishes that lack some or all of these.

• **Fishes are cold-blooded.** Not exactly. Mackerel sharks, Family Isuridae (e.g. Makos), and several tunas, Family Scombridae, are at least partially homeothermic.

• **Fishes utilize a gas bladder for buoyancy control.** Not true for the darters (Family Etheostomidae), several of the flatfishes (Order Plectognathiformes), the hawkfishes (Family Cirrhitidae), and others.

• **Fishes are slimy.** This statement comes close to meeting the criterion of

The Seven Living Classes of Vertebrates

Living fishes comprise three of the seven classes of the Subphylum Vertebrata. The other four classes—the amphibians, reptiles, birds, and mammals—number fewer in total than the approximately 25,000 scientifically described fish species.

Class Agnatha ("lacking jaws")
> The jawless fishes, lampreys, and hagfishes

Class Chondrichthyes ("cartilaginous fishes")
> Sharks, rays, skates, and chimaeras

Class Osteichthyes ("bony fishes")
> All of the other species of fishes not belonging to the first two classes

Class Amphibia ("both types of life")
> Frogs, toads, salamanders, newts, and caecilians

Class Reptilia ("the crawlers")
> Lizards, snakes, crocodilians, turtles, tortoises, terrapins, and tuatara

Class Aves ("the birds")
> All birds

Class Mammalia ("having mammary glands")
> All mammals, including humans

being a defining characteristic of fishes, but doesn't work for sharks and rays.

But the characteristics that more accurately distinguish fishes are internal rather than external. Like all vertebrates, they have a dorsal stiffening rod (a cartilaginous notochord in primitive forms and a backbone in advanced species), and other morphological (structural), embryological, and physiological characteristics. Fishes are more easily defined for what they are not than for what they are.

Organisms for Marine Systems

IF THE DIVERSITY OF AQUATIC LIFE IS ASTOUNDING, the range of species available for purchase by marine aquarists can be every bit as mind-boggling. As an aquarist living in a modern exchange-economy world, if you have the resources, you can buy most anything. Let me suggest that, as we marvel at the ever-growing selection of fishes and invertebrates we can place in captive systems, there is more involved than simply commerce, supply and demand, and the "gotta have that fish" instinct most aquarists have felt at one time or another.

The Blue-girdled Angelfish (*Pomacanthus* [*Euxiphipops*] *navarchus*) is part of a small subgenus of strikingly beautiful Pacific angels that has proved problematic for aquarists This species and its close relatives often ship and adapt poorly to captivity and may perish because of poorly understood dietary requirements. A familiarity with the taxonomic groupings of fishes and invertebrates is an important tool in everyday marine aquarium planning and husbandry.

Taxonomy for Aquarists

Making sense of the huge assemblage of animals we call fishes is no easy matter, but using a systematic method of naming and organizing them is absolutely essential in avoiding chaos. There was a time in the history of the world when we had no common language to describe the different animals or plants that people observed. In a desire to communicate with others about the scientific world, new words needed to be created. The ancient Greeks and Romans were the founders of taxonomy, the systematic naming and ordering of living things—they began the process of giving descriptive names to the plants and animals around them and classifying them into groups.

Aristotle (384-322 B.C.) is credited with the beginnings of scientific classification. He was aware of the differences between fishes and aquatic mammals (such as dolphins and whales) and accurately described some 118 species of fishes from the Aegean Sea.

In the sixth century B.C., Archelaus of Miletus developed some fundamental concepts such as "species" and the need for using one "good" name for each type. A few others who came later, including Pliny, Aelianus, and Authinecus, made further recordings of what they recounted as types of organisms. In the sixteenth and seventeenth centuries, Pierre Belon, Guillaume Rondelet, John Ray, and Francis Willughby were noted early taxonomists. Economic prosperity and enlightened interest in the living world during this time sparked exploration and collection of species, as well as an awareness that different nations did not agree on the names of living things.

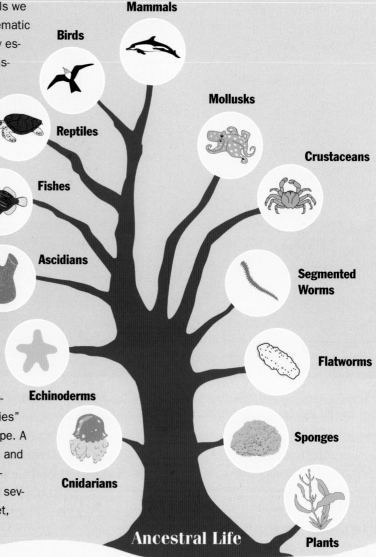

AN EVOLUTIONARY TREE: Understanding the classification of plants and animals can assist even casual aquarists in successfully choosing and keeping captive specimens. (After Allen and Steene, 1994)

The Father of Taxonomy

Although the task of classifying living things had begun, the real birth of modern taxonomy occurred with the publications of *Systema Naturae* (1735) and *Species Plantarum* (1753) by the Swedish botanist Carolus Linnaeus (Karl von Linné). His system of classification forms the basis of modern taxonomy. Linnaeus is credited with two main innovations: the arrangement of categories such as classes, orders, and families, using Latin; and binomial nomenclature ("two-word naming") of species. His method revolutionized biological labeling and set up an internationally acceptable set of rules for categorizing living things.

Linnaeus chose to use Latin because most scientists were familiar with it and many of the names that already existed were derived from Latin. In addition, Latin was considered a "dead" language (no longer subject to change) and did not favor any particular nation (it was politically neutral). To this day, we continue to expand this framework by adding Latinized Greek and modern language "borrowings" as more than a million species of living things have been described.

After studying the features that life forms have in common, taxonomists place them into more and more definitive groupings—kingdoms break down into phyla, phyla into classes, classes into orders, orders into families, families into genera, and then finally species (and to make things even more specific, all of the taxonomic categories can have sub- and super- variations). In Linnaeus's system, the last two categories constitute the accepted scientific two-part name: the genus (always capitalized and in italics) and the species (always lower case and in italics).

Of course the taxonomic system of classification is artificial, man-made, and subject to change, but it still serves as the great common communication tool for the worldwide scientific community.

Taxonomy in Action

So how can taxonomy help you in becoming a better and more conscientious aquarist? First, it is essential in talking intelligently about different forms of life; second, it helps you make decisions about an organism's habitat, behavior, and aquarium care.

As a communication tool, the scientific name ensures that you, an aquarist in Germany, one in France, and another in Japan, can all be talking about exactly the same fish, invertebrate, or plant even though the common name would be different in each country. The Latin binomial name accepted worldwide puts everyone on the same "page," so to speak. Even within the same language, there may be varying common names for a fish or invertebrate and/or several species may have the same common name. With the scientific name, these confusions are dispelled.

For making care decisions, consider the following example of how taxonomic naming can help: You might know that the Ocellaris Clownfish (*Amphiprion ocellaris*) is sensitive to certain types of medication. If you then knew that the Maroon Clownfish (*Premnas biaculeatus*) was a member of the same subfamily (Amphiprionae), you might conclude that these two different species would share similar tolerances, foods, and diseases—and they do! As a matter of fact, there are 2 genera with about 28 described species of clownfishes so far. And all of them are obligate symbionts with certain species of anemones, protandric hermaphrodites (with males transforming into females as a result of age and need), and susceptible to the same types of infections and maladies. If you know one clownfish species, you have clues to the others.

For most of us, it is infinitely easier to remember that all of the related species in one family share habits and conditions, instead of trying to memorize the natural history

(continued on following page)

(continued from previous page)

details of thousands of possible aquarium species separately. In fact, the related families of fishes in the same order (Perciformes, the perchlike fishes), with such notable aquarium species as marine angels, butterflyfishes, basses, hawkfishes, and many others all have structural and useful life-history characteristics in common.

The very word taxonomy tends to scare some people into using common names only. It shouldn't. Understanding how fishes are classified and named can make you a much better aquarist. Mispronouncing scientific names is not a mortal sin—most of us would rather hear a mangled Latin name than an imprecise common label that may apply to any of several species.

The diversity of marine fishes becomes much more comprehensible when you visualize how they are grouped. Knowing how different aquarium species are related can easily spell the difference between success and failure, life or death, with a fish that you are encountering for the first time.

After more than 20 years, thousands of hours under the seas, and writing several hundred articles about underwater natural history, I'm still overwhelmed when I encounter something new and different. Taxonomy is the tool of choice for mentally organizing these discoveries as well as communicating about them with other divers, marine scientists, fish dealers, and aquarists.

As we select and acquire organisms, the overall harmony among our livestock and their compatibility with the marine system and the physical surroundings we place them in ought to be the ultimate goals. All too often, it seems, we lose sight of this prize. Somewhere near the top of the list of reasons for aquarium specimens failing to thrive, causing their owners to become discouraged and lose interest, is the basic problem of too-hasty purchases. We buy animals that get too big, that demand water that is too pure, that attack and kill their tankmates, that require nearly full-time care and feeding, or that simply cannot be kept alive (or "happy") in aquarium conditions.

If you agree with me on this point, the next logical question should be, "How can I go about achieving this balance?"

You're doing it. The first step in accomplishing something is to define what it is. Next comes gathering facts, ideas, methods, and the means to effect the ends you have in sight. By reading and communicating with others having similar goals and objectives, we learn best how to get to what we want.

Then, and not before, we should act.

Stewardship

THE FOLLOWING SECTIONS PRESENT A BRIEF INTRODUCTION to the major groups of marine aquarium fishes and some species that are widely offered to the trade. I have chosen many that are superb choices, along with a number of commonly seen groups and species that should be avoided by most aquarists. They are to be shunned for a variety of commonsense reasons: weak disease resistance, specialized diets, demonstrated poor adaptability to aquarium conditions, quick growth and large size, or a need for exceptional conditions.

We can bring so much of the incredible universe of marine life into our homes and offices today. Some of their life-support systems may be little more than water-filled boxes, others have become quite involved. There is a wide breadth in livestock suitability and a subjective element that must be weighed in considering each organism's origin, its abundance in the wild, its ability to withstand the rigors of collection and shipment, and its adaptability to captive life. The conscientious aquarist is obviously a steward of his or her own aquarium, but we also play a subtle but direct role affecting the world's coral reefs and oceanic shallows where these fishes are collected. My overriding philosophy is to encourage people to keep only those species that can be harvested in a sustainable way and that have excellent prospects for thriving in captivity.

When buying a given marine species, you are, whether you are aware of it or not, casting your vote for its collection. Together, we aquarium keepers are perpetuating its harvesting (or, in some cases, its breeding and rearing)

and thus are having a say about the use of its native environment and even the lifestyles of people involved in supplying it to the aquarium trade. Once you know the links between the fishes you buy—or reject—and the reefs of the world, the stewardship inherent in your choices as a consumer becomes more apparent and interesting. Vote well.

Giant Moray Eel (*Gymnothorax javanicus*): a potential behemoth well known to divers and snorkelers, this is a species that grows much too large, aggressive, and hard-to-handle for most home aquarium systems.

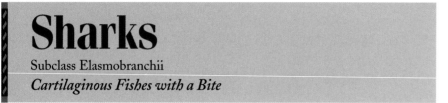

Sharks

Subclass Elasmobranchii

Cartilaginous Fishes with a Bite

WE MAY BE APPROACHING the point where we've all seen too many sharks on television, with familiarity breeding a false sense of camaraderie. A few years ago, I was a scuba diving instructor, and on a dive at San Diego's La Jolla Cove, my co-instructor came upon a 5-foot-long Pacific Angel Shark lying semi-buried on the bottom. Wanting to bring the shark's presence to his students' attention, he grabbed the shark by its tail. The shark promptly spun around more than 180 degrees and bit off the end of the man's flipper. It could just as easily have been his hand or part of his foot.

Here are animals with big mouths and sharp teeth and fascinating natural behaviors. Interest in these cartilaginous wonders has never been higher, and a sizable number of aquarists seems to dream of someday having a shark tank. Unfortunately, for a host of reasons, many shark species are either inappropriate or extremely challenging aquarium specimens. (Consider one family member, the Basking Shark, which grows to lengths of 40 feet and is one of the two largest species of fish.)

While nine out of ten of us are probably unsuited to keeping a captive shark, for lack of room, financial re-sources, or the dedication required, there is no doubt that these animals capture our attention and are well-worth learning about. I will offer advice on how certain species can best be kept alive and well, but I generally urge people to admire these fishes in the wild, on film, or in a public aquarium and to respect their size, temperament, and formidable strength.

Classification. There are certain species in the freshwater minnow family (Cyprinidae) such as the Bala, Tricolor, Red-tail, Red-fin, and others that are sometimes called sharks, but here we will cover the marine cartilaginous sharks.

The cartilaginous fishes (Class Chondrichthyes), in reference to their lack of skeletal bone, are subdivided into subclasses. Sharks belong to Subclass Elasmobranchii, with five to seven sets of lateral gill openings extending higher than the pectoral fins. There are some 8 living orders, 29 families, and 359 described species.

Range. Sharks are found worldwide in all seas, and far upstream in several rivers (such as the Mississippi and Amazon). The Bull Shark (*Carcharhinus leucas*) ascends from the sea into Lake Nicaragua.

Size. Adult sizes range from less than 7 inches (Perry's Lantern Shark) to 50 feet (Whale Shark). When choosing a shark for an aquarium, select the smallest specimen practical, and strive to keep it small through proper feeding, much as a gardener would care for a bonsai tree.

Blacktip Reef Shark (*Carcharhinus melanopterus*): one of the requiem sharks, the Blacktip is available to aquarists in small sizes but will outgrow even the largest home system and should be shunned.

Whitetip Reef Shark (*Triaenodon obesus*) swims through a school of anthias: one of many shark species best viewed in the wild, on video, or in a pubic aquarium.

Selection. Except for the smallest species with sedentary, bottom-sitting behavior, the majority of sharks are poor candidates for aquarium specimens. They are simply too big, active, and messy for all but the largest of systems. Commonly seen but not recommended sharks include:

Family Orectolobidae—the carpet sharks or wobbegongs. These are bizarre dorso-ventrally flattened specimens with camouflaged markings and flaps of skin. Species in the trade include the Ornate Wobbegong (*Orectolobus ornatus*) and the Spotted Wobbegong (*O. maculatus*). Unfortunately, these sharks reach over 7 feet in length and outgrow most home aquariums.

Family Ginglymostomatidae—the Nurse Shark (*Ginglymostoma cirratum*). This is probably the most popular, frequently offered shark in the U.S., as it occurs commonly along the eastern seaboard from Rhode Island to Brazil. They commonly attain a length of 8 feet and can reach 13 feet. They cannot be recommended to most aquarists.

If you are not yet dissuaded from selecting a shark for your aquarium, please consider only one of the tropical species suggested below or a developing embryo within an egg case. The best solution, however, is to go see sharks at a public aquarium, on a CD-ROM or video, or even in the sea.

Epaulette Shark (*Hemiscyllium ocellatum*): one of the smaller reef sharks that can be recommended to the home aquarist, this species still requires a spacious tank equipped with a high-flow-rate filtration system.

Nontropical sharks should be avoided altogether. This refers to sharks that are collected in below-room-temperature water. Many other shark-aquarium writers disagree with this, but unless you're committed to providing a very large system with adequate cooling, the animals generally fare poorly.

Be aware of the following cool-water sharks, which are often offered for sale: horn sharks (with two dorsal spines), in the Family Heterodontidae, (also sometimes called Pig, Bullhead, or Port Jacksons). The most frequently offered is the Horn Shark (*Heterodontus francisci*) from California. Also avoid the Family Squalidae (dogfishes), and Family Triakidae (smoothhounds and leopard sharks) and the Pacific Angel Shark (*Squatina californica*).

Every now and then, dealers pick up requiem sharks, such as the Lemon Shark (*Negaprion brevirostris*) and the Blacktip Reef Shark (*Carcharhinus melanopterus*). These should be left in the sea. They require enormous facilities and a tremendous amount of care.

Collecting your own specimens, except for the small hemiscyllids, is not recommended, as it is dangerous to both shark and collector.

If you are handling sharks, be extremely careful. They are faster than you are. Most of them bite. And some sharks have venomous spines.

The mishandling of sharks can cause damage to their internal organs and is a major cause of shark death. Sharks lose attachment, or herniate, easily by being struck. If or when you have to handle one: 1) wear gloves; 2) "scoop" the specimen into a suitably large and strong plastic bag(s); and 3) get help lifting and placing the specimen into a Styrofoam or other soft-sided carrier.

If, after reading these warnings, you still want to have a shark specimen in your aquarium, there are some sharks (as juveniles) and some shark eggs that have been successfully kept. They are:

Family Hemiscyllidae—the Bamboo and Epaulette Sharks, with 13 total species for the family, as well as the often misnamed "catsharks" of the genus *Chiloscyllium*. Included in this group of aquarium-appropriate species are the Brown-banded Bamboo Shark (*Chiloscyllium punctatum*), the White-spotted Bamboo Shark (*C. plagiosum*), and the Epaulette Shark (*Hemiscyllium ocellatum*).

Family Scyliorhinidae—the true catsharks and swell sharks. Most are cool-water species, but members of the genus *Atelomycterus*, such as the Coral Catshark (*A. marmoratus*), are good aquarium choices.

When choosing any shark specimen, watch for blood streaking, primarily along the underside. This may be symptomatic of physical injury or the result of a bacterial infection. Besides metabolite poisoning and psychological upset—which can both occur in a system that is too small—secondary infection is a common source of captive shark mortality.

Habitat. The bigger the tank, the better. It should have a high-flow-rate filtration system, with its full volume turning over at least two times per hour.

The tank shape should be flat and shallow, ideally with rounded corners. Minimize the physical barriers to swimming (but allow hiding places for small reef sharks, such as the hemiscyllids). Optimize surface area. Conceal tubes, heaters, airlifts, and filters; sharks are strong and they can and will bump into, tunnel under, and yank at equipment, causing potentially serious problems. At the minimum, the size of the system should be 1.5 times by 4 times the length of your specimen. (For an 18-inch bamboo shark, this would equate to a tank at least 24 inches front to back and 72 inches long, or approximately 150 to 200 gallons, depending on depth. An 8-foot long, 240-gallon tank would be even more appropriate.)

Finer, less angular gravels are preferred, to avoid scraping. Crushed coral sand is ideal.

Sharks have some special needs. Salinity should be kept constant and high, near worldwide sea readings—approximately 1.025 specific gravity. Unlike bony fishes, sharks (actually all chondrichthian fishes), are semi-isotonic (equal in concentration) with the percentage of certain charged materials (like salts) in their general environment. To some degree, they manipulate nitrogenous waste metabolism and excretion with the makeup of the surrounding water. Large, regular water changes using replacement water of the same specific gravity are important.

Monitoring and avoiding the buildup of metabolic waste is paramount. Sharks are large, metabolically active animals. One of the smallest sharks available probably weighs in at more than all the fishes you've ever kept. The need for good circulation, regular maintenance, and excellent filtration ought to be clear.

Metal of any sort is to be avoided at all costs in a shark system; ferrous (iron-bearing) matter is especially problematic. Sharks possess an acute electromagnetic sense associated with pit organs (the ampullae of Lorenzini) located beneath their heads. Other metals in solution will cause sharks to go anosmotically off-feed. Remove all metal, even plastic- or glass-encased metal, from the system. (Metal rebar or reinforcing-steel rods cast into concrete walls in public aquariums has been indicted as "driving these fishes crazy" and causing their deaths.)

Do not have a marine system without a functioning protein skimmer. With such large animals processing so much proteinaceous material (food), a good foam fractionator is an absolute necessity in a closed system.

For efficient metabolite conversion, I would consider wet-dry filters or fluidized bed systems, with conventional canister filtration being just barely adequate. Undergravel filtering is not enough; the metabolically active surface area is too small to be practical and too easily disrupted.

Spotted Wobbegong (*Orectolobus maculatus*): bizarre in appearance and sometimes imported, the carpet sharks or wobbegongs are attractive when small but typically become unmanageably large for captivity.

Finally, restrict aquascaping to the central area and keep the swimming perimeter clear. Be aware that sharks are diggers and will undermine your artistic edifices. Avoid sharp edges in your rock and coral arrangements as sharks can break into swimming frenzies and cut themselves badly.

Behavior. All sharks are talented jumpers, aquatic Houdinis at escaping through the smallest of openings, and skilled at knocking off the heftiest of covers. You must have a tight-fitting and heavy top to keep your shark in.

Though selachian brains are tiny, sharks are amazingly well-wired to do what they do, and are capable of substantial learning. Though known to chomp on their own or other shark species in feeding melees, captive sharks are usually content with the daily fare they have been trained to eat.

On the other hand, some sharks will try to eat any invertebrate, fish, or alluring object if hungry—or even just curious. I have dissected dozens of large wild-caught sharks, finding cans, rocks, jewelry, and even bicycle parts.

Introducing a specimen to the tank is simple enough. Place your shark in a "seasoned" system—one that has been established for a number of months, stable, and already supporting a healthy bioload. Ideally, a shark system ought to have been time-tested with a demonstrated ability to support a similar bioload.

Most sharks are fine with other species, providing they are not mouth-sized or slow-moving. Surprisingly, rather than being the perpetrator, your shark may be the victim of harassment by its tankmates. Large angelfishes, triggers, puffers, and others have been recorded as opportunistic shark pickers.

Sharks move about and aid their blood circulations by throwing their bodies into sinusoidal curves. They lack swim bladders, but to some degree compensate for the lack of a gaseous hydrostatic mechanism by their possession of relatively large, fatty livers, which float. Most sharks also utilize hydrostatic lift, capitalizing on having more surface area on their upper bodies than lower and by staying in constant motion. The induced drag results in lift. The shape of the tail (heterocercal, with a larger upper lobe) and pectoral fins also adds lift.

The practical implications of the sharks' mode of transport are that they need a lot of room, they can't change direction or level easily, and they "hate" square-system corners.

Reproduction. Sharks have an astounding reproductive biology. Different species lay eggs, give birth live with and without umbilical-like attachments, and have surprisingly long gestation periods and low birth rates. All utilize internal fertilization, granting an easy manner of determining whether you are looking at a male or female. Males possess claspers, specialized tube-shaped pelvic fins for genetic transmission. The pelvic fins of females lack these extensions.

Feeding. The species of sharks that are suitable for aquarium keeping are typically hearty eaters, once adjusted to their quarters. Food strikes, however, are not uncommon, especially for newly imported sharks. Try feeding at night or using live food if one of these bouts stretches on; a few weeks for a juvenile to fast is not a huge problem as long as the individual is well-fleshed. This convenient index of fitness is best assessed by examining the animal head on. The area behind the eyes should appear convex, not concave.

Frozen foods are preferred as being less expensive, easily stored, and capable of being removed if uneaten. My favorites are silversides, krill, and cleaned shellfish. Squid is widely accepted, but can be messy. Vitamin supplements are endorsed by all experienced shark people and administered by every public aquarium. You can soak the food in liquid vitamins or "sneak" vitamin capsules into whole food fishes.

Don't overfeed. Offering food two or three times per week is adequate. Sharks are known to eat infrequently in the wild. This warning against overfeeding can't be stated strongly enough. Too much too often leads directly to a double-headed problem—poor water quality and a large specimen that produces large amounts of waste.

Don't hand-feed. Besides the obvious and very real danger of a nasty laceration from biting, there is an increased risk of introducing pollution to the tank. Instead, train your shark to "stick" feed with the food skewered on a plastic rod.

To emphasize safety and demonstrate the tremendous suction power of Atlantic Nurse Sharks, I'll share an anecdote. Several years ago at Point Loma in San Diego, we had some trained *Ginglymostoma* that had grown to about 5 feet. These were routinely "click-trained" (with a metal hand device that made a cricketlike sound) to "station" for a food reward. One day a trainer thought she would help feed by placing her hand in the water near the tapioca-colored shark's subterminal mouth. Bad mistake. When these animals suck in near the surface, the force of air and water entrainment is huge. The trainer's hand suffered massive blood vessel breakage.

Disease. Sharks do very poorly when treated with many standard remedies. Copper compounds are deadly, as are many dye solution treatments. Reddening due to irritation and possible *Vibrio* bacteria may be treated with chloramphenicol (veterinary prescription needed) or tetracycline administered internally via a food bolus.

For blatant external parasite extermination, freshwater and Formalin baths can be used, but extreme caution should be taken. Often the damage to the shark (and you) from its thrashing is greater than any good the dip might do. Be careful, and follow the handling recommendations.

Sharks and their relatives are host to many worm, crustacean, and protozoan parasites. The best way to avoid problems with them is to do your best to purchase a clean, healthy specimen, give it good care, and prevent the in-troduction of these parasites. The latter is best accomplished by not using live or fresh seafoods—use frozen or freshwater instead.

Summary. Difficulties with the captive care of sharks are myriad, including the need for huge, highly filtered systems, poor adaptability in terms of behavior for most open-water species, and often neglected chemical and physical environmental insults. It is particularly important to never keep cold-to-cool-water species in warm-to-tropical temperatures, to maintain a high, stable salinity, and to avoid treating sharks with metal-based remedies. A consistent light regimen and the absence of metal in the system are absolute requirements for successful shark keeping.

A poorly chosen shark species may last less than a month in the home aquarium. Most succumb to the effects of being housed in too small a space, mishandling, or misguided treatment for disease.

There are, however, over a dozen species that are known to tolerate the vagaries and limitations of home aquarium systems. The others should be left in the seas of their origins, except those specimens afforded professional care in research and public aquariums. Far from "voracious killing-machine" top-predator status, sharks occupy many important niches—from the truly giant plankton siever to the ever-needed clean-up volunteer that ensures ecosystem fitness by eating the weak and diseased. Of the few varieties that have been studied thoroughly, they are known to have low birth rates, relatively long generation times, and modest population densities. They are far from deserving our unrestrained enmity, wanton destruction from fear of attack, fin collection, or even the minimal ca-

Nurse Shark (*Ginglymostoma cirratum*): easily obtained and often seen by hobbyists, this species can grow to a length of 13 feet and cannot be recommended for home aquariums.

sual loss due to inadequate aquarist husbandry.

If the cartilaginous species have captured your imagination and determination, please read more before you buy, be sure you have a system with the footprint and filtration needed, and always select sharks (or rays) that have a good history of survival with other serious home aquarists.

Moray Eels

Family Muraenidae
The Good, the Bad, and the Ugly

AS WITH SHARKS, most moray eels are best left in the seas from which they came. Many of them get far too big and become too ornery —even dangerous—for aquarists, occasionally inflicting bacteria-infested bites on the unwary. Of the many varieties that turn up in retailers' tanks, some refuse food or readily break out of the confines of small, inadequately secured aquariums.

Still, few aquarists can resist the spell of marine eels, and there are dozens of morays that make endearing and long-lived aquarium specimens. I will describe the whole spectrum of this group's characteristics—both appealing and undesirable. You will only be encouraged to keep the more adaptable species.

Classification. Morays are true eels (Order Anquilliformes), one of 20 some families, with a total of more than 600 species. Although some eels look snakelike, they are not snakes. Eels are fishes and snakes are reptiles.

Morays lack scales and caudal, pelvic, and pectoral fins; instead, they locomote with long, continuous dorsal and anal fins. Their scary-looking open-mouthed habit is related to their posses-

Honeycomb Moray Eels (*Gymnothorax favagineus*): pair being serviced by cleaner shrimp.

sion of small, restricted gill openings without covers—the eels are usually just breathing, not sending you a warning, although jaw-gaping can be an agonistic display. Morays are not to be confused with all the other so-called "eel-like" groups of fishes such as Wolf Eels, Spiny Eels, and many other elongated eel-like creatures.

The Muraenidae sport lateral line pores on their protruding heads, but not on their bodies—a characteristic that makes sense for animals that spend most of their time with just their heads sticking out of cover.

There are 15 genera with about 200 described species of morays. There are about a dozen species that are regularly accessible to the hobby, with half of those being suitable.

Range. Muraenids are found worldwide in tropical to subtropical seas in shallow to moderate depths and are common in many areas. In Hawaii, they are the next most numerous reef animals after the wrasses, Family Labridae.

Size. The smaller morays grow from 7 inches to 3 feet in overall length; the largest are close to 10 feet. I photographed one Giant Moray (*Gymnothorax javanicus*) that was 7 feet long,

had a girth greater than an adult male's thigh, and probably weighed more than 60 pounds.

Selection. Be sure the prospective specimen is eating and has been been well-handled. Check the entire body for sores, scrapes, and torn or infected fins. If any of these are evident, do not purchase the eel, or ask the dealer to hold it until it heals.

Anticipate erratic activity when first introducing a new moray. Often it will swim about, head out of water, maybe searching for an escape route. If things are to its liking, your eel will settle within provided cover, keeping fellow

Snowflake Moray (*Echidna nebulosa*): handsome, mild-mannered, and an excellent eel for the home aquarium.

fishes at bay. I'd leave some of the lights on low in the room or system for a day or two. Escape attempts often occur in the first few days; if you find your eel on the floor, try to reconstitute it by rinsing it off and placing it in a quarantine tank, giving it the same treatment as when it was first introduced into the

Zebra Moray (*Gymnomuraena zebra*): eye-catching and long-lived.

Chain Moray (*Echidna catenata*): peaceful and appealing Caribbean species.

Gray Moray (*Siderea grisea*): rare but commendable Red Sea species.

Honeycomb Moray (*Gymnothorax favagineus*): large and aggressive.

tank. I've seen eels that that had started to look like marine jerky recover completely.

If moving is necessary, transport maneuvers should be carefully planned and executed. Though morays are tough, they have soft and slimy skin that is easily abraded by rough handling. Netting them almost invariably results in a thrashing specimen on the floor, frazzled hobbyist nerves, and unsanctioned use of bath towels. Do this instead: pro-

cure a thick (or doubled semi-thick) fish bag, roll the edge up, place it in a scooped-up fashion in the tank, and scoot the moray into the bag underwater. Then carefully lift the eel with a minimum of tank water in the bag.

The Snowflake Moray (*Echidna nebulosa*) is, in my estimation, a fabulous aquarium species. Small by moray standards, it is compatible with other fish species and adaptable to captivity. It is certainly the most peaceful, out-

going, and desirable moray. It grows to about 30 inches in length and has a base color of silver gray with black and yellow "snowflakes" randomly sprinkled over the lower body.

Gymnomuraena zebra, the aptly named Zebra Moray, is a slow-moving beauty that is chocolate-black with vertical white stripes. Its suitability for aquariums is reflected in longevity records. People have cited captive survival histories of more than 20 years.

More subtly colored, the Atlantic Chain Moray (*Echidna catenata*) grows up to about 2 feet and is likewise peaceful and easy to maintain.

Dragon Morays (*Enchelycore pardalis*) from the Pacific, are striking, with white bodies and variegated black, yellow, and red markings. Their name is derived from the presence of elongated, pointed jaws and long posterior nostril tubes. They command a high price for their beauty and adaptability—and are worth it.

The Gray Moray (*Siderea grisea*), is a small (26-inch maximum) compatible species. It hails from the Red Sea and west Indian Ocean and usually commands a high price.

While some members of the genus *Gymnothorax* get too big and mean, about 10 of the 23 commonly seen species grow to less than 30 inches maximum length. Among the agreeable choices are the White-lipped Moray (*G. chylospilus*), the Stout Moray (*G. eurostus*), the Yellowhead Moray (*G. fimbriatus*), and the Whitemouth, Comet or Guinea Fowl Moray (*G. meleagris*).

There are certain species that should be avoided, although some may feel I am unnecessarily scaring people away. For most of us, however, the following does hold true:

Rhinomuraena quaesita, the Ribbon Eel, is among those with a low survival rate. In my estimation, 99% of these delicate beauties do not live a month in captivity. Most starve, refusing all food. Others escape through the smallest of top openings or through plumb-ing. Finally, there is that perplexing but real cause of death—simple stress.

Some *Gymnothorax* species get too big and are too aggressive and strong for all but the largest systems. If you're going to try these, watch your fingers and tankmates and secure your cover with a lock. Too often offered to the hobbyist is the Atlantic Green Moray (*G. funebris*), which grows to 8 feet. Among the other inappropriate species available to aquarists are the Leopard Moray (*G. undulatus*), the Giant Moray (*G. javanicus*), and the Honeycomb Moray (*G. favagineus*), all stretching into the 6-foot range.

Some dealers have tanks with "mixed" or "unidentified" eels; try to know what you are buying—an eel that grows too big and mean in your system will not be readily adopted by anyone else.

Habitat. There is a sharp dividing line between the species that are suitable for aquariums and the ones that are not. A suitable moray is extremely interesting behaviorally, adaptable to aquarium conditions, very disease-resistant, and readily accepts offered foodstuffs.

While it is true that they grow slowly, some having been kept in captivity for decades, some of these animals require large living quarters. They are not easily stunted to the size of their aquariums. Many morays get to be big animals, requiring large tanks and efficient filtration systems. Public aquariums, for example, typically dedicate thousands of gallons for a display of *G. javanicus*. Crowding a big eel into a small system can lead to maladjustment problems, determined escape behavior, and wildly fluctuating water quality. I would advise a minimum of 40 gallons for the smallest of morays. Tank shape should feature length and width versus "show" tank height.

Try to arrange a minimum of two

Dragon Moray (*Enchelycore pardalis*): this Pacific species commands a high price but makes a flamboyant, hardy specimen for the large system.

pleasing hiding places that are large and dark enough to allow the eel to get entirely out of view. If you have heavy pieces of rock in the system, be sure they can't be jostled loose by the moray—it's common for aquarists to find their eels crushed or injured by falling or settling rockwork.

Subdued lighting and darkened sides and backing are a bonus. Morays enjoy a high degree of routine in their environment and will appreciate a regular, timed light regimen.

Vying with starvation for the number one cause of moray death is their tendency to slither out of the tank and dry up. Look at your system from a wily escapee's point of view. Are there any openings large enough for the animal to squeeze its head through? If so, it will. Even with the water level lowered, morays can and will liberate themselves.

Eels are born hunters, and all tankmates that are small enough to swallow are potential meals, even seemingly tough fare like puffers and triggers. Otherwise smart, fast-moving basses may also be sucked in, especially at night. Keep to a systematic feeding schedule. Morays will even eat cleaner wrasses, but seem to leave symbiotic shrimps (*Lysmata* and *Periclimenes*) alone.

Different species of morays will co-exist in the aquarium, but extreme care must be taken with known predatory eels, such as the Honeycomb Moray (*G. favagineus*). Territoriality within a species can also be a problem. Provide lots of space and nooks and crannies, and carefully observe your charges.

Temperature tolerance is wide, 72 to 82 degrees F for tropical species. Specific gravity is better a little high: 1.022 to 1.025. For a useful indicator, keep your eye on pH: 8.0 or higher is a good value. As with large, heavy fishes that generate lots of waste, morays can play havoc with metabolite buildup and related degrading water quality. Morays have a highly developed sense of smell; if there is too much organic or metallic matter, they will show it by behavioral and color changes.

Due to the large amounts of proteinaceous food being digested, any tank housing an eel ought to have an efficient protein skimmer and vigorous filtration. Good circulation and aeration are paramount. The eel's open mouth does not indicate vicious demeanor, but a need for a lot of oxygen.

Frequent 10 to 20% water changes are recommended. Weekly is ideal; maybe a day or two after feeding. It is also prudent to keep the heater out of harm's way, where the moray will not smack it or get burned.

Behavior. As predators, morays are opportunistic omnivores, eating most any fish and/or invertebrate slow enough to grab. Their great sense of olfaction is coupled with bad vision. While individuals in the wild and captivity can be docile, even playful, some species and individuals are highly dangerous if provoked by the scent of food.

Not all types of morays are nocturnal, shy, and retiring—the Panamic Green Moray (*Gymnothorax castenatus*) has been known to chase divers. These morays are unpredictable, at times not distinguishing where food stops and your fingers start. Do not attempt to hand-feed them.

A few notes here regarding moray

Giant Morays (*Gymnothorax javanicus*): sometimes diver-tame, but best left on the reef.

Ribbon Eel (*Rhinomuraena quaesita*): imported in quantity but a poor survivor demanding expert care.

bites. Unless morays feel threatened, most will leave you alone. If a moray happens to grasp your hand out of fear while looking for food or just as part of an accidental encounter, it will let you go. The worst reaction to being bitten is the most common and dangerous—to jerk your hand back, cutting yourself further on the moray's recurved teeth and on the landscape. The problem with these bites is secondary infection. Microbes in the water, whether associated with the moray's mouth or not, may infect you through any break in your skin. Treat all bite, scratch, or puncture injuries seriously in a four-step approach: 1) clean; 2) disinfect; 3) cover; 4) periodically inspect. If inflammation and/or pain persists, a medical visit is advised. Using long plastic gloves dedicated to aquarium use will prevent most scrapes at home and keep hand-borne pollution down.

If you find moray eel on a restaurant menu someday, you may want to know that some morays have been involved in ciguatera (fish toxin) poisoning. If in doubt, don't order it. I have, and it wasn't memorable. Morays apparently become toxic by bioaccumulation, because they reside near the top of the food chain and ingest benthic algae-eating herbivores.

Reproduction. Spawning has been observed in the wild, with pairs swimming a sort of dance and releasing gametes into prevailing currents. Like all true eels, morays have a bizarre larval stage (leptocephalus) with ribbonlike, transparent young living as plankton for a while before metamorphosing and settling.

Feeding. All morays are carnivorous, some preferring fishes or invertebrates of different types. Are you looking at a piscivore (e.g. *Gymnothorax*) or invertebrate-eater (e.g. *Echidna*)? Check their teeth. Crushing molars are for foods such as crabs; sharp pointy types are for fish eaters.

New arrivals will most likely have to be trained on and then weaned off live foods. The few species endorsed here almost always quickly adjust to a feeding-stick routine. I advise building and using one made from rigid plastic doweling or tubing. Keep your hands out of the system for pollution and safety's sake.

Regularity of feeding is very important to these eels; smaller specimens may be fed twice a week, larger ones do very well with once a week. Try to schedule frequent water changes the day after these feedings. Provide food of appropriate size as morays don't chew. Cut-up clams, shrimp, krill, and squid will be much less messy than whole ones.

Disease. Medical measures should never be necessary if you select a healthy, clean specimen and provide a suitable habitat. The usual two-to-three-week quarantine for newcomers is recommended. Stay away from nonchelated copper and remedies containing the organophosphate DTHP (Masoten, Dylox, Dipterex, Neguvon, etc.)—these can be deadly to true eels. If your specimen seems to be developing a bacterial and/or fungal infection, check water quality, do a massive water change, or remove it to a treatment tank and treat with erythromycin to reduce overall bacterial levels.

Don't worry too much if your eel goes on a hunger strike. Morays collected in the wild often have empty stomachs, showing that eels can go for long periods (months) without eating.

Summary. The favored species mentioned above make excellent aquarium specimens, with a majority of individuals adapting to aquarium care easily, readily accepting prepared foods, and neither breaking through your system cover nor sampling their tankmates or your hand. Once acclimated to a tank, they prove to be durable and disease-resistant pets.

Other moray species are problematic, growing too large and escaping even the most heavily covered tank. Many starve outright, refusing all food, and others consider all that fit within their capacious jaws fair game.

Forewarned is forearmed. The big muraenids, as well as the delicate Ribbon Eels, are suitable only for public aquariums or for being visited in their native domains by snorkelers and scuba divers.

It is my opinion that morays provide predatory pressure in a role similar to several sharks, cleaning up the reefs by eating weakened and damaged prey. Choose from the selection of moray eels that can be housed comfortably in captivity. The conscientious aquarist should leave all other eels in the wild to prosper.

Marine Catfishes

Family Plotosidae
The Coral Cats—Full of Character, As Well As Venom

CATFISHES HAVE OFTEN been thought of as "bottom-sucking scavengers." But many aquarists are now aware that the Order Siluriformes is brimming with fantastic species that engage in all manner of spellbinding behavior and lifestyles. From tiny half-inchers to monstrous Amazonians tipping the scales at several hundred pounds, some catfishes are comical scavengers, while others are top-of-the-chain predators. There are even parasitic catfishes.

Catfishes have long been a craze in the freshwater aquarium hobby, inspiring legions of keepers who treat them not as "gravel cleaners" but as showcase species. Many of these specimens pose husbandry challenges that seem only to endear them to catfish fanatics.

Catfishes are mainly freshwater animals, but there are saltwater catfishes too. These saltwater species are few, and some are sold as brackish-to-tolerant-of-hard-alkaline-freshwater specimens. With many of the unusual behaviors and mannerisms of their inland cousins, saltwater catfishes can make for out-of-the-ordinary aquarium displays. There are two important rules to remember, however: 1) Don't put these animals on clean-up detail—they are not scavengers and will do poorly if left to survive on leftovers or recyclables.

2) These fishes are extremely venomous and will render a nasty, painful, and potentially dangerous puncture if handled carelessly.

Classification. There are several freshwater catfish families with members possessing venom-bearing spines in their dorsal and pectoral fins. Having been punctured by the worst of them, I would rate the plotosids number one in the pain department. They look beautiful and unassuming, but they are to be reckoned with. Several authorities state that their stings might be fatal.

The Eel-tail, Coral, Stinging, or Tandan Catfishes, in the Family Plotosidae, are aptly named (*plotos* in Greek means swimmers). Their tapered bodies with pointed or bluntly rounded tails are in almost constant undulating motion. There are some 40 species in 8 genera—about half fresh, half marine. Freshwater species hail from Australia and New Guinea only.

Range. Catfishes are found worldwide in tropical to temperate freshwaters— from muddy farm ponds to the broad Amazon. They are found in the Indian Ocean and the western Pacific Ocean from California to Australia, New Guinea, and the Philippines.

Size. Most individuals offered are 4 to 6 inches long. The marine species brought into the retail trade, all called "coral cats," rarely exceed a foot in captivity, although they can be longer than a yard in the wild.

Selection. This is actually a relatively easy group to sort through for viable specimens. Being naked (as opposed to armored, with all catfishes lacking scales), the plotosids take a real beating if handled and shipped without care. Take a close look at potential buys. Are their whiskers intact and all about the same length? Are the eyes clear and bright? Are there any puncture, scrape, or red marks on the body? If even one specimen in a tank has any of these symptoms, it is cause for concern.

The smaller species offered are only happy in a small group. Pick three or more youngsters—they are inexpensive in the small sizes—and introduce them to your tank all at once.

Habitat. Coral cats do well on broken to mixed bottoms, sand/gravel, and coral/rock rubble. They are often seen gathered in flanks or balls on sandy bottoms; and spawners lay eggs among rocks. They are not picky animals as far as water makeup goes, but coral cats prosper where there is a strong current and plenty of hiding spaces. As they get larger, their waste can put a heavy strain on smaller systems or ones with inadequate filtration.

Behavior. Do not take the possibility of envenomization lightly. Speaking from experience, I can tell you that you do not want to suffer the excruciating stings these fishes can inflict. My last bout occurred while putting away a large incoming Philippine shipment. A carelessly dropped cat poked me under the fingernail when I tried to scoop it up with a net. Knowing what would ensue, I told my cohorts to keep an eye on me, wrote down the name of the fish (*Plotosus lineatus*) in case I lost con-

sciousness, and rushed off to the bathroom to soak the wound site in the hottest water I could stand. Quickly heating the proteinaceous poison goes a long way to denaturing it, changing its structure and lessening the pain. (If you get jabbed, I strongly suggest you do all of the above and be ready to make a trip for professional attention.) Obviously I survived, with localized pain, swelling, and a great deal of angst.

On a less intimidating note, these catfishes have one other unusual behavior—their sound production. Marine cats hum or buzz loud enough to be heard outside the aquarium. Listen closely when feeding.

The larger members of the family may be testy toward members of their own kind as they grow. All will gladly swallow other organisms small enough to fit in their mouths, and smaller fish give them a wide berth. Other large fish-eating predators also leave these catfishes alone—even when or where the species' natural ranges don't overlap. Perhaps they recognize the folly of swallowing something with three stout venomous spines sticking out at oblique angles. However, I have seen more than one lionfish die from sucking up a plotosid cat, its spines sticking right through the lion's abdomen.

Coral cats themselves are nonspecific invertebrate predators. Marine forms focus on interstitial (between substrate) fauna, such as various worm groups, crustacea, mollusks, and others. Reef keepers take note.

Reproduction. Spawning observa-

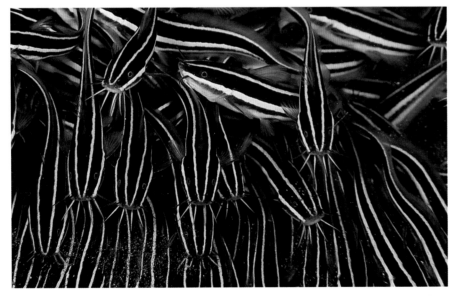

Coral Catfish (*Plotosus lineatus*): the young form balls or schools, with bold stripes and venomous barbs.

tions for *P. lineatus* are much like those of their common freshwater kin. This species spawns during the summer, with males constructing nests in shallow, rocky areas. The eggs are small (3 to 3.5 mm in diameter) and are guarded by the male for about 10 days. Some Japanese public aquariums report captive-spawning success for this species, feeding the newly yolk-absorbed young on freshly hatched brine shrimp.

Feeding. All foods—pellet, frozen, fresh, or flake—are accepted greedily by healthy specimens. I suggest twice-daily feedings, at least once with defrosted frozen food that easily can be placed in an open area on the bottom. They grow quickly when well fed, but fade away fast if starved.

Disease. Plotosid catfishes are quite susceptible to the common parasitic scourges of marine aquariums, and doubly unfortunate in their intolerance to common aquarium therapeutics. Look to them first for signs of fish disease and treat them carefully. Avoid malachite- and copper-containing treatments in favor of freshwater dips, quarantine in lowered salinities, and newer treatments like quinacrine and other quinone compounds.

Summary. Provided you start with a clean, parasite-free grouping of smaller *Plotosus* or a good individual of a larger species, coral cats are a breeze to keep. Just keep metal and dye medications, and your hands, away from them. They're wonderful to watch, but they demand cautious handling and are not for children's tanks.

Squirrelfishes

Family Holocentridae
Quiet Species for the Aquarium with a Ledge or Cave

THE SUBHABITAT of the coral reef, with its shallow caves and crannies beneath ledges, is a rich biotope—one that can be replicated for a very different type of aquarium display and that ought to appeal to those who like the unusual and the lure of an underwater netherworld.

This is the domain of the squirrelfishes—a family with a reasonably descriptive name. With their quick, jerky motions, large, bright eyes, and chattering noises, these secretive fishes have much in common with their terrestrial rodent namesakes.

It's a shame that squirrelfishes are so often passed over as marine aquarium specimens. My guess is that their bold color, perky but retiring conduct, and all-seeing eyes must lead aquarists to consider this group as being touchy to difficult. Actually, the opposite is the case. Securing a decent specimen and granting it a few provisions will reward you with a hardy, interesting, and long-term pet. Beyond that, the fact that squirrelfishes are plentiful in the wild, easily captured, and transport well makes them relatively inexpensive to acquire and assemble into a natural grouping of several specimens.

Classification. Squirrelfishes, Family Holocentridae, are members of Order Beryciformes. This order is not very familiar to many aquarists. This ordinal category includes the hard-to-keep flashlight or lanterneye fishes (Family Anomalopidae) and the bizarre deep-water pineconefishes (Family Monocentrididae). You probably know these related families from their possession of bacteria-source light organs beneath their eyes.

Some fish taxonomists separate the Family Holocentridae into the "true" squirrelfishes (Subfamily Holocentrinae) and the soldierfishes (Subfamily Myripristinae). We won't, as they are often sold interchangeably and are approximately the same in their care and selection.

The Family Holocentridae itself is represented by about 65 species in 8 genera. If one word can describe the group, it is spiny. They have a stout pelvic fin spine with 5 to 8 (usually 7) soft rays, a long dorsal fin with a sharp spiny portion (10 to 13 spines) and soft-rayed section (11 to 17 rays) deeply divided by a notch, and an anal fin with 4 spines and 7 to 16 soft rays. Their tail fins are sharply forked, with 18 or 19 principal rays. And their spininess doesn't end there—squirrelfishes have

Blackbar Soldierfish (*Myripristis jacobus*): a nocturnal Atlantic-Caribbean squirrelfish species that does best in a tank with a protective cave.

large, sharp, extremely rough scales. Lastly, take a closer look at their heads. What do these fishes have in common with marine angelfishes? That's right, spines (or small spinules) on their gill covers. All of these spines have functional, protective significance in the wild, but can cause problems in nets and in aquarists' hands.

Most squirrelfishes are reddish in color mixed with silver and white. They all have large eyes and are nocturnal, hiding in crevices or beneath ledges by day (typically with cardinalfishes, bigeyes, and sweepers). Most are shallow-water fishes, found from the surface to about 100 meters.

In some areas of the world, such as the Philippines and parts of Indonesia, squirrelfishes are important as food fishes.

Range. Squirrelfishes are found in tropical Atlantic, Indian, and Pacific reefs.

Size. Most grow to about 6 inches in captivity; some grow 12 to 18 inches in the wild.

Selection. The following is a list of some of the more frequently offered species that I've found to be better suited for captive conditions on the basis of temperament, size, and food acceptance:

• From the Atlantic is *Sargocentron coruscum*, the Reef Squirrelfish, and *S. vexillarium*, the Dusky Squirrelfish;

• From Hawaii, *S. diadema*, the Barred Squirrelfish;

• The better Indo-Pacific species include *S. punctatissimum*, the Speckled Squirrelfish; *Neoniphon opercularis*, the Clearfin Squirrelfish; and *Myripristis pralinia*, the Scarlet Soldierfish.

In terms of picking out a healthy specimen, be wary of any squirrelfish in a group

with others that display: 1) reddening in patches, especially around fins and under the body. This is often a sign of rough handling and bacterial (*Aeromonas* or *Vibrio*) infection and is usually fatal; 2) torn fins, cheekspines, scales; and/or 3) evidence of external parasite or removal damage.

Compared to other marines, collecting your own squirrelfishes is a breeze. They are easily spooked out of hiding into a carefully placed barrier or mist net and hand-netted from there. Care must be taken not to damage the catch by tangling and pulling on it in the netting, or the captor by getting poked by the squirrelfish's spines and sharp scales.

Habitat. An authentic sheltering cave for squirrelfishes might be a ledge constructed of large pieces of coral rubble or live rock for a daytime retreat, with nearby open space for food searching and nocturnal swimming room by night. A cave should have a large, dark hovering area with two openings—a perfect setting for one or more of these fishes and perhaps others they are found with in the wild. For a special effect, set one or more actinic lights on your system to cycle on and off before or after your other illumination, or leave them on all night to observe your nocturnal squirrels.

These fishes are found in areas where the water really whips at times, and brisk filtration will be appreciated, but squirrelfishes are not demanding as far as water quality is concerned. They do prefer lower water temperatures (in

Long-jawed Squirrelfish (*Sargocentron spiniferum*): displaying spiny gill covers and prominent scales typical of this family.

Crown Squirrelfish (*Sargocentron diadema*): a natural predator on shrimps, crabs, and other reef invertebrates.

Blackbar Soldierfish (*Myripristis jacobus*)

Dusky Squirrelfish (*Sargocentron vexillarium*)

Reef Squirrelfish (*Sargocentron coruscum*)

White-tipped Soldierfish (*Myripristis vittata*)

the 72 to 78 degrees F range); higher temperatures may bring on feeding strikes and odd behavior. Higher, steady specific gravity is appreciated, closer to 1.025.

Behavior. Lest you happen to have acute hearing and think something is awry in your aquarium, it helps to know that holocentrids produce audible sounds, both above and below water. They grind their pharyngeal teeth and stretch muscles against their long gas bladders, much like rubbing your fingers along a balloon.

Territoriality is generally not a problem. Squirrelfishes in the wild mostly live in aggregations when young and comfortably alone when adults. Most get along with their own kind, other species of squirrelfishes, and other tankmates. Potential predators typically give them a wide berth after looking at their overall spininess.

Think twice about using squirrels as reef-tank organisms. They are supreme choices for being hardy and interesting, but will greedily swallow any and all crustaceans that can fit into their expansive mouths. However, if you lack and/or do not intend to have shrimp(s) or crab(s) and would like to minimize bristle and other worm activity, consider a squirrelfish. Provide a good 30 gallons each for small-to-medium species and 50 for larger ones.

Reproduction. What little is known

of holocentrid reproduction suggests that they spawn in pairs, cued by lunar light cycles. They produce pelagic eggs and young. Squirrelfishes are indistinguishable externally as male or female.

Feeding. They are predators on very small fishes and mobile invertebrates, principally crustaceans in the wild. Livebearers, shrimp, and other fresh and frozen meaty foods are acceptable. Avoid pellets, flakes, and other dry prepared foods—these will not sustain them.

If your specimen(s) is new, refusing food, or goes on a feeding strike, execute a large water change and try a live shrimp or small fish from a bait shop with the lights of the system turned off. Generally, squirrelfishes can be trained to take "wiggled" krill or other shrimp.

Disease. These fishes are generally acquired free of external parasites and clean up easily with routine freshwater dips and quarantine. The usual parasitic scourges of tropical marine fishes can be handily defeated if detected early enough with standard copper remedies.

Summary. To those in Spanish-speaking countries, they're *saldados* or *matajuelo*; to the French, *malais*; in Hawaii, *alaihi*. To those in English-speaking countries, they are the aptly named squirrelfishes and soldierfishes—the Holocentridae. No matter their name, they are good aquarium specimens, whose only demands are meaty foods and a good place to hide.

Lionfishes

Family Scorpaenidae
Long-Lived and Majestic—and Venomously Worthy of Respect

THE LIONFISH is the quintessential marine aquarium specimen, with its dramatic flowing pectoral and dorsal fin rays and its uncanny ability to rivet the attention of anyone even casually passing by an aquarium. Lionfishes are the archetypal "stock" pet fishes: hardy, readily available, and second only to damsels in tolerating disastrous water conditions. Able to be trained to accept almost all types of foods and among the most disease-resistant of specimens, lions would seem to be the best of captive aquatic life. And they are—with two important caveats: there is the very real probability of getting stung by their venom-bearing fins if you are careless; and it is not difficult to kill them with misguided kindness.

Classification. Lionfishes are members of the scorpion, or rockfish, Family Scorpaenidae. This is a group of fishes important to humans both as food and as a dangerous source of envenomization (the Subfamilies Synanceinae, the stonefishes, and Pteroinae, the lionfishes, among others). The nontoxic, but still very spiny rockfishes, in the genera *Sebastes* and *Sebastolobus*, are prominent table fare, sold as Pacific snapper in the U.S.—although they are not actually in the snapper family, Lutjanidae.

The family's widespread importance as both pets and food fishes is reflected in its many colorful common names: Upside-down Flying Cod, Butterfly Cod, Turkeyfish, Firefish, Scorpionfish, Zebrafish, Stonefish, and Rockfish, among many others.

Lionfish species of interest to the aquarium hobbyist include those of the genera *Pterois* and *Dendrochirus*. The common and popular *Pterois* lions are considered the "true" full-sized lions. They have huge pectoral fins, featuring unbranched rays with degrees of connecting membranes extending beyond the body at their insertion.

Members of the other genus, *Dendrochirus* are more often sold as dwarf lions. They display smaller, branched-ray pectoral fins with the rays sporting almost continuous membranes.

There are several other genera in the scorpaenid family offered from time to time as lionfishes, but for the most part, these miscellaneous fishes are not as desirable as the species we will discuss here. In addition, the "freshwater lionfishes" sold in the trade are actually toadfishes, Family Batrachoididae. For

Zebra Lionfish (*Dendrochirus zebra*): a dwarf species suitable in size for some reef aquariums but a predator on smaller fishes and motile invertebrates such as cleaner shrimp.

Volitans Lionfish (*Pterois volitans*): sometimes called the Turkeyfish for its plumagelike display of fins, this species will do well for most aquarists, but deserves careful respect for its many venomous spines.

the record, they are neither lionfishes nor venomous.

Pterois volitans is the lionfish most commonly displayed and sold, capable of unforgettable displays of fins and sinister spines. Volitans Lions span the color range of banded red to black against alternating creamy white. Black and red volitans lions are the same species.

P. russelli, Russell's Lionfish, is too often offered in stores mistakenly as the "Luna Lion" or "Red Volitans." Russell's Lions lack the beautiful head flaps on the supraorbital bones and have more rounded, less angular heads than Volitans Lions. Most Russell's pectoral rays are connected by a web of tissue about two-thirds of their length; Volitans almost totally lack this webbing. *P. russelli* are typically rusty red-brown against a creamy background; occasionally specimens are offered that bear gorgeous bluish green color at the tips of their unpaired fins.

P. antennata is the third lion confused with the Volitans and Russell's species. Antennata Lions have strikingly different pectoral fin rays. These are long, the thickness of pencil lead, and bright white. A good way to remember the name is the connection of the word *antennata* to the lion's black and white antennae (supraorbital flaps).

P. sphex, the endemic Hawaiian Lionfish, is often mistakenly sold as the Antennata Lion, which it closely resembles in terms of its pectoral fins. Hawaiian Lion fins are shorter, less colorful, and more clubbed in appearance. Though more costly than the majority of lions that are imported from the Philippines and Indonesia, Hawaiian Lions are my favorites for hardiness.

The Clearfin or Radiata Lion (*P. radiata*) is the most chameleonic of lions, showing overtones of green, black, and various shades of red over shocking white. The salient identifying characteristic of this species is the two white horizontal bars on the caudal peduncle—the part of the body right before the tail.

"Dwarf" lionfishes in the genus *Dendrochirus* are labeled as such for their smaller size and more sedentary, bottom-dwelling habits.

The Zebra Lionfish (*Dendrochirus zebra*), the most common dwarf lion, is similar in many ways to *P. antennata* and *P. sphex*. The sure distinguishing marks of *D. zebra* are the presence of a membrane between the pectoral fin rays that extends almost to the outer end of the ray, and a black spot on the lower part of the operculum (gill cover).

The Shortfin Lionfish (*D. brachypterus*) is a commonly seen heavy-bodied dwarf, often showing up with a good deal of yellow, brown, and green mixed with red markings. These dwarf lions also have fanlike pectoral fins with almost no emerging ray tips. This is one of the most personable marine species, quickly recognizing and responding to its owner's presence.

The Twinspot or Fu Manchu Lion (*D. biocellatus*) is unmistakable with its two eye spots on the rear dorsal fin area and two whiskerlike appendages extending from the lower jaw.

Range. Lionfishes are found in tropical Pacific Ocean and Red Sea rocky reefs at a depth of anywhere from 10 to 200 feet.

Size. *Pterois* can grow to about a foot and a half; *Dendrochirus* species are approximately 6 inches in total length when full grown.

Selection. When picking a lionfish for your aquarium, there is a sharp line of distinction between good, clean specimens that are going to thrive and those that are on the brink of doom. Any specimens you are considering should not be exhibiting hard, labored, or accelerated breathing, off-color or red patches, or torn fin membranes.

Choice specimens are bright, alert, interested in their environment, and will probably be keeping a watch on you.

Lionfishes can be easily caught in the wild if you're in the right area and have all the necessary permits and capture and transport paraphernalia. Lionfishes evidently consider themselves top reef dogs and show little concern for approaching humans. The best time to net them, right out of the open water, is during the twilight times of sunup and sundown. This is when they're most active and hunting. During the day, look in nooks and crannies for *Pterois* and under rock and rubble for dwarf species.

Habitat. Other than overfeeding and relying on live goldfish rations, habitat is an area in which aquarists fail with their lions. Lionfishes, for all their apparent slow-moving, calm-breathing, seemingly low-metabolic lifestyles, need space. They will not thrive without room to move, sites where they can feel protected, and large volumes of water to provide adequate oxygen and dilution of their copious waste. (Although they will ignore sessile inverte-

Shortfin Lionfish (*Dendrochirus brachypterus*): a personable, prized dwarf species with impressive, fanlike pectoral fins.

Russell's Lionfish (*Pterois russelli*): commonly sold as the "Red Volitans."

Clearfin Lionfish (*Pterois radiata*): two white horizontal bars in front of the tail.

Twinspot Lionfish (*Dendrochirus biocellatus*): known as the Fu Manchu Lion.

Antennata Lionfish (*Pterois antennata*): note bright white pectoral fin spines.

brates, the larger lions are usually excluded from reef tank collections because of their gluttony and the resulting nitrogenous wastes they produce.)

The bigger the tank, the better; I recommend a good 30 to 40 gallons per adult *Pterois*, and half that for other species. These fish live long and grow large, and a single specimen can easily dominate a 100-gallon tank.

Though lions don't appreciate fast swings in temperature or water conditions, they have enormous range tolerance. I have "found" them in forgotten tanks at wholesalers in incredibly saline water, so high that the lions should have been floating at the top.

A common problem in lion tanks is the loss of alkaline reserve with overfeeding, inadequate filtration, or infre-

quent water changes. The scenario goes like this: The owner or keeper wants to impress most anyone and allows lionfishes to gorge at every opportunity. Water quality drops, with pH diving dangerously below 7.6. Lions go into hiding, breathing heavily. The owner calls the pet store or aquarium service company to complain. The service personnel either: 1) get there quickly and make a massive water change and/or add a buffering agent to the system; or 2) get there too late, while the tank is turning to bouillabaisse. The lesson to be learned here is: *do not overfeed*, keep a guard on water quality by at least measuring pH, and do frequent large percentage water changes for heavy feeders like big lionfish.

Filtration is extremely important. You need to be capable of handling occasional large amounts of solid waste and efficient enough to keep ammonia and nitrites low. In the ancient days of marine aquarium keeping, some writers advocated using lions instead of damsels for establishing nutrient cycling. Due to their size and cost, the damsels have won this race.

Your display should provide open and protective spaces, similar to those lions utilize in the wild. They hide during the brightest hours of the day; yours will too. (Give a lionfish a cave, and it will often rest upside-down at the ceiling, which makes for a curious downtime display.) This leads us to ideal, subdued lighting, which is best supplied by low illumination fluorescents. If you use metal halides, at least offer a dark corner. Glaring lights have been implicated in lion "blindness," a so-called environmental disease.

Behavior. Lionfishes generally don't exhibit territoriality and are very willing to share living space with their own and other lionfish species. They are known to cooperate in feeding and herding behavior in the wild.

These can be the first fishes in a new setup and are very easy to acclimate in the usual manner. The typical "wise guys"—triggers, puffers, large angels—may have to be watched as potential lionfish harassers.

Lionfishes are easygoing with anything they can't inhale, but they do have remarkably large, distensible mouths. Damsels, cardinals, clownfishes, shrimps, and other nonattached invertebrates are all so much aqua-popcorn, and should be considered certain of being sucked in sooner or later. Don't underestimate the ability of a big lionfish to swallow substantial prey; more than one naive aquarist has watched in horror as a pricey new anthias or young angel—that was thought surely too big to be eaten— became instant lion fodder.

Lionfishes are venomous, they are not poisonous. This means that they are toxic to the touch; poisoning generally comes about from ingestion.

Lionfishes are decidedly dangerous to handle, alive or not. I speak from painful first- and secondhand experience, having been stung myself a few times and present when others learned their lessons. Many people have been stuck when not exhibiting care while netting or moving a lion, either dead or alive. Statistically though, more folks get poked while performing tank maintenance. Whether lions are truly aggressive toward humans appears to be a matter of debate among recent authors. It is not to me. I have been "challenged" by head-down, spine-out lions—both while diving and as an aquarist. Whether it is out of curiosity, food-response conditioning, territorial-

Hawaiian Lionfish (*Pterois sphex*): similar to the Antennata Lionfish and a fine, hardy species, but not always available.

ity reactions, or other motives, some lionfishes will approach your arm when it's in the tank. Their motives are unpredictable. You want to have one eye on your lion(s) and one on the task at hand anytime you're in the system.

Venom passes through by mechanical means, unlike the pumping action of the stonefishes, with you and the lion jamming against each other. There is no shortage of venomous tips on a single lion: 12 to 13 dorsal spines, 3 anal spines, and 2 pelvic fin spines sheathe a glandular complex some two-thirds along the length of the anterolateral grooves.

Though not as toxic as their notorious stonefish cousins, lion stings must be taken seriously. Swelling, soreness, localized pain, respiratory and cardiac distress, and other collateral shock manifestations go with these events. Ringing your local poison center and immersing the site with water as hot as you can tolerate are immediate emergency actions to take. Most sting victims recover quickly without treatment but have to suffer hours of pain that typically leave a lifelong impression—and respect—for natural venoms.

Reproduction. There are a few European accounts of captive spawnings in public aquariums. Some scorpaenids are known to be ovoviviparous, a form of live-bearing, but *Pterois* are surface egg scatterers. Near dusk, a male and

Antennata Lionfish (*Pterois antennata*): venomous spines are a defensive weapon. Most hobbyist stings result from mishandling or carelessness.

female engage in a simple prespawning dance culminating in upward swimming and a simultaneous release of gametes while upside down beneath the surface. At this writing, there is no record of captive eggs hatched and reared to adults.

Feeding. If food is love, most lions are loved to death. Postmortem exams I've done invariably show fatty liver degeneration (yellow, floating blobs), frequently with accessory gut impaction from Excessive Feeder-Goldfish Gobbling Syndrome. Here's how it works: "Check it out, Uncle Al, this lion can swallow a dozen of these golden beauties at a throw . . ."

Don't do it to yourself, your lion, or the feeders. Goldfish are not a good steady diet for several reasons. They're nutritionally deficient, inconvenient, expensive, and may make your lion aggressive. Furthermore, they're unnecessary. Lionfishes can and should be trained to accept better foods; it is a myth that they will only eat live fare. Once acclimated, they will greedily take frozen, fresh, freeze-dried, and prepared rations of all kinds—silversides, krill, shrimp, crabs, and even crickets. Avoid oily, greasy foods.

When feeding, use a feeding stick or acrylic rod and move the offered food in front of the lion. If it is not ac-

cepted, remove the food for another day. Do not worry if your charge goes on a food strike of a few days or longer. If the fish is in good health, this pre-

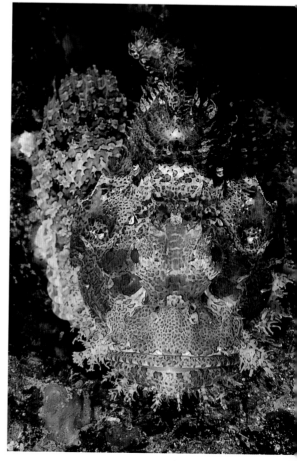

Tasseled Scorpionfish (*Scorpaenopsis oxycephala*): a bottom-hugging, ambush-hunting species related to lionfishes.

sents no problem, and is a useful technique for limiting growth. A new specimen that continues to refuse dead food may need to be weaned with live first. Try guppies or a live bait shrimp placed in front of the lion. Once eating, it should easily graduate to non-live foods.

Depending on livestock, food size, and desired growth rate, lions need be fed only once, twice, or three times a week—maximum. Keep them hungry . . . and healthy.

Disease. For lionfish acquisition, introduction, and preventive treatment, follow the suggested path as for most marines: 1) quarantine for two weeks or 2) run through a freshwater and/or a dilute Formalin bath to reduce external parasite introduction. The second step should be done at the very least.

Fin rot due to mishandling or overhandling in shipment is easily cured with furan compounds carried in the trade. The common parasitic scourges *Amyloodinium*, *Brooklynella*, and *Cryptocaryon* clear up easily with copper sulfate treatment, if observed and treated in time.

Shedding of skin is something you will experience with lionfishes. Related coughing, shaking, and other symptoms may accompany it. In related species, this activity is thought to aid in getting rid of parasites and algae growth on camouflaging skin flaps.

Summary. Lionfishes make great petfishes even for beginning aquarists if you remember three points:

1) they are venomous—respect their spines and keep your distance;

2) they are practically indestructible, except for being victims of the aquarist's tendency to overfeed them, particularly with feeder goldfish;

3) their water quality quickly degrades with overcrowding and/or inadequate filtration.

Basses

Family Serranidae
The Hardy and Sometimes Dazzling Groupers and Their Kin

WELCOME TO THE WORLD OF the basses—and one of the most confusing tangles of common names and misnomers in the entire universe of fishes.

Here in sunny southern California, we have such notables as the Large Mouth Bass (*Micropterus salmoides*, sometimes called the Florida Large Mouth), which is almost everyone's idea of what a real bass should be. (In reality, the Large Mouth is a member of the sunfish family, Centrarchidae—but who wants to announce they've caught a 10-pound sunfish?)

Next, we also have the oh-so-delicious White Sea Bass, *Cynoscion nobilis*. (However unpalatable it may sound, this fish is actually a croaker, Family Sciaenidae.) Then, there is an east coast import, the Striped Bass (*Morone saxatilis*) and the Giant, or Black Sea Bass (*Stereolepis gigas*). Neither of these are true basses; they're percichthyids, or temperate perches, whose gill covers (opercles) only have two spines—unlike the real basses, which have three.

Other regions also suffer a surplus of so-called "basses," but the knowledgeable aquarist will come to know the real thing. As a group, the true basses have the width and breadth, both literally and figuratively, to stand or swim on their own. While some are quite small, the large groupers can grow to more than 1,000 pounds. Many have drab or cryptic markings, an aid to ambushing prey; others are among the flashiest of marine fishes, gaudy to absolutely surreal.

Many of the smaller species make fine aquarium fishes—provided the aquarist knows where in the wide gamut from hardy to delicate the chosen species happens to fall.

Classification. The salient characteristics of the true bass and grouper family, Serranidae, include:

1) Opercles with three spines—one main spine, with a lesser spine above and below (in most species).

2) A lateral line that is complete and continuous.

3) A pelvic fin with one stout spine and five soft rays.

4) Three anal-fin spines (in most cases).

5) Seven branchiostegal rays (the cartilaginous gill supports).

6) Projecting lower jaw.

Depending on whose taxonomic scheme you use, there are 3 to 15 subfamilies recognized with approximately 64 genera and 449 species. Some notable members of this group? True basses and groupers, hamlets, fancy basses, coneys, anthias (see page 212), and the soapfishes. (Soapfishes are not

Miniatus Grouper (*Cephalopholis miniata*): also known as the Coral Trout, this flamboyant species should be recognized as a large predator and waste generator.

considered suitable aquarium species because they exude a toxic slime).

Range. True basses are mostly marine, with a few freshwater species. They are found worldwide in tropical to temperate seas and in shallows to more than 1,000 feet.

Size. Some groupers grow to almost 10 feet in length and can weigh almost half a ton. Many anthias, Subfamily Anthiinae (see page 212), grow to no more than a few inches and tickle the scale in mere ounces.

Selection. Look for newer arrivals with good color and outgoing or at least "curious" personalities. Most members are best purchased as subadults and allowed to grow in your system. Their adaptability declines with increasing size and the number of captive moves.

Habitat. Though identified as bullies, the groupers spend most of their time hiding and skulking. Provide plenty of caves and other dark spots for cover. Do not alter your fish's favorite hiding space unless you have to.

As far as captive marines go, most basses are very tolerant of imperfect water quality. I would suggest artificially supplementing the buffering capacity of the system with baking soda (sodium bicarbonate) or a commercial buffer. The introduction and processing of so much proteinaceous food tends to drive down alkalinity. A pinch of bicarbonate every week or so will go a long way to maintaining a pH above 8.0, with no deleterious effect. If you have a large or growing grouper, filtra-

Shy Hamlet (*Hypoplectrus guttavarius*): small member of the grouper family of Caribbean origin.

Indigo Hamlet (*Hypoplectrus indigo*): another eye-catching Caribbean hamlet uncommon in aquariums

sedate members are close to ideal.)

Behavior. As a generalization, the grouper family is "one to a tank," with individuals intolerant of the same species or others of similar size and type. Most species gather together in pairs or aggregations only for spawning or group predation. The notable exceptions are the anthias, which live in great aggregations.

Antagonistic displays against new tank members and potential challengers to their dominant position are not uncommon. Such charging and wide-mouthing generally passes without serious incident. Turning the tank lights off and darkening the room for a day or two usually cools things down.

Though most basses as species and individuals are not overtly "mean," they are still predacious and will swallow any tankmate smaller than their mouth opening. Groupers are capable of great speed, making them both efficient predators and swift escape artists.

Reproduction. The basses are simultaneous or synchronous hermaphrodites, being male and/or female at the same time, or first one then the other. Within the simultaneous species, one individual can take turns during courtship being female or male. Their pelagic young hatch out in a day or two.

Feeding. Along with water quality, diet is of primary importance in determining serranid health and color. Their sheen and intensity change from bright and shiny to washed-out and nonreflective with mood and physical well-being.

In the past, some authors have

tion must be rigorous to handle the correspondingly large waste output. (As serious waste generators and gobblers of smaller fishes and invertebrates, the large groupers do not fit well in typical reef aquariums, but some of the smaller,

210

Swissguard Basslet (*Liopropoma rubre*): small, prized Caribbean serranid.

Panther or Polkadot Grouper (*Cromileptes altivelis*): a prized Pacific food fish.

Six-lined Soapfish (*Grammistes sexlineatus*): exudes a toxic slime.

Coney (*Cephalopholis fulva*): widespread Caribbean bass; note cleaner goby.

plugged the use of live freshwater organisms as suitable food for basses. I still don't. Live goldfish are nutritionally inferior to foods of saltwater origin, and the behavioral consequences of your basses dashing about your tank, expecting to hunt and dine on moving fish may be a bad idea for the long-term safety of any tankmates. I encourage the use of dried or frozen marine foods.

Even the fussiest eater can be trained to accept these. If your bass doesn't eat for a while, for no apparent reason, don't panic. They have been known to go off-feed for days, weeks, even months.

Disease. Except for hamlets and anthias, basses are relatively disease-resistant and hardy.

Summary. If you're wondering why I haven't covered the fairy basslets (Grammidae) or dottybacks (Pseudochromidae), you've fallen prey to the pseudo-bass trap. The Grammidae and Pseudochromidae belong to separate families and are not true basses.

The true basses are generally easy to keep, long-lived, often boldly colored, and, if not always in motion, interesting in their activities and dash-and-grab feeding behavior.

Fancy Sea Basses

Subfamily Anthiinae

Vibrant Colors for Reef Aquariums—and Experienced Aquarists

SMALL, REEF-COLONIZING, so-cial, often whimsically colored and exorbitantly priced, fancy sea basses (popularly known as anthias) are the least-hardy members of their parent family. Most are unsuitable for the conditions provided by their captors. I do, however, have suggestions to offer for keeping these often delicate fishes.

Classification. Part of the true bass Family Serranidae, the Subfamily Anthiinae are the sometimes breathtakingly beautiful little basses found in brilliant swarms over Indo-Pacific reefs.

Common genera and subgenera include the popular *Anthias, Pseudanthias, Mirolabrichthys, Callanthias, Franzia,* *Nemanthias, Serranocirrhitus,* and others. The systematics of this group have yet to be adequately explained and many new species are expected to be discovered.

Range. Fancy sea basses are found in tropical reefs in the Red Sea and the Atlantic, Pacific, and Indian Oceans. Most are found in shallow waters to a few hundred feet, while some occur at extreme depths.

Size. The anthias types generally reach 3 to 6 inches in total length.

Selection. Due to cost and variability of temperament within the group, the different species available should be investigated thoroughly before purchasing. Some individuals, populations, shipments, and even species are touchy and almost impossible to keep, while others are reasonably hardy and easy going. All of them are challenging to keep and demand the skills of an experienced aquarist.

Many authors have suggested that the anthias need to be kept in schools, but I happen to agree with reef fish authority Scott Michael in feeling that it is neither necessary nor al-ways the best idea to purchase and house them as a group. The various anthiines do live in large aggregations with a definite pecking order, but this is not replicable or desirable in captive care in other than exceptionally large systems. If you want to buy a colorful male, buy only one. Similarly, unless you have a very large tank, more than one (or two) females is unnecessary and may well lead to endless fighting and loss of life. If you lose your only alpha (dominant) male, the next most dominant specimen will, in time, change sex to take its place.

To avoid fighting, house only one species to a system. If at all possible, acquire all individuals at the same time from the same batch. I have seen the species commonly offered in the trade maintained solitarily for extended periods of time. Solitude is not deadly to them.

Within a group, choose the most outgoing individual(s). Leave skulkers behind. Avoid specimens that have a poor index of fitness; that is, shun the skinny ones, particularly those that are thin behind the head. As always, confirm that the specimen is feeding.

New introductions may hide for days to weeks. Try coaxing them out with live brine shrimp and be patient.

Habitat. It is extremely important to have ample rockwork and hiding spaces

Female Lyretail Anthias (*Pseudanthias squamipinnis*): good choice among a demanding group best avoided by beginning aquarists.

Schooling Lyretail Anthias (*Pseudanthias squamipinnis*) with soft corals (*Dendronephthya* spp.) in the Red Sea. Solitary anthias specimens often do better than groups in smaller aquariums.

Pseudanthias sheni: an unusual Western Australian species.

Lyretail Anthias (*Pseudanthias squamipinnis*): male specimen.

Fathead Anthias (*Serranocirrhitus latus*): hardy species from deep water.

Dispar Anthias (*Pseudanthias dispar*): also known as the Redfin Anthias.

to reduce stress and provide escape from aggression. Exaggerate the physical features of the environment. If you're attempting to house more than one specimen per system, constant vigilance is demanded. Using biological cleaners is strongly suggested. Many anthias keepers have found cleaner shrimps in the genus *Lysmata* to be valuable in parasite control.

The group enjoys clean, consistent water quality in all areas where they are collected. They will not tolerate anything less in captivity. Most of the shallow-water species live in areas of tremendous wave action. They appreciate vigorous currents in your care—the stronger, the better. Take a look at any posters or photographs of schools of fancy bass in the wild and note the

explosive surge of water. Some species are even found at the fringe of "breaking" reefs, experiencing the full force of open ocean currents and waves. Optimal reef-tank conditions are required. The absence of aggressive fellow tankmates is very important, and some species are notorious jumpers. Keep all tank openings carefully covered.

Behavior. Anthias are very easily

spooked when being introduced to a new tank. Keep lights low and leave an outside light on for a good day or two. Keep your hands out of the system entirely at the onset and as much as possible from then on. Watch other fishes for aggressive behavior toward your fancy bass. If practical, introduce the anthias before any other species that might harass them.

Fancy bass are a standard food item for almost all predatory reef organisms big enough to stalk and catch them. The large predators, such as lionfishes, groupers, and eels, will devour them like gumdrops.

Healthy anthias can always put on a fascinating display—they are active and quick to respond to any stimuli. Males challenge all apparent challengers, and wrap themselves in a U-shape around females.

Reproduction. Among basses, the anthias are notable for being sexually dichromic and dimorphic, having color and structural differences between males and females. The more mature individual males are larger, more colorful, and, in many species, sport a few elongate dorsal spines.

Feeding. Fancy sea basses feed aggressively on any fine, meaty foods. In the wild, they eat crustaceans, fish eggs, and larvae. The more frequent and smaller the feedings, the better. Naturally this group is constantly on the prowl—mind that they do not get thin.

Live foods, such as adult brine shrimp (*Artemia*), may have to be offered at first. Food supplements are well

Bartlett's Anthias (*Pseudanthias bartlettorum*): excellent water conditions and frequent feedings required.

worth the effort. They will accept dry-prepared foods, but cannot be sustained on them or brine shrimp alone.

Disease. Unfortunately, this group as a whole is very susceptible to bacterial and protozoan infections. Any amount of stress seems to trigger problems. My experiences with fancy basses differ from those of some other authors; I've found some of them to be sensitive to poisoning by the most common cura-

tives: copper compounds, malachite, and Formalin. I encourage prevention and the use of biological cleaners.

Summary. Although challenging, anthias can make a striking addition to your tank or a nice display on their own. Read what is available, provide them with an adequate, peaceful environment and frequent, appropriate feeding, and you will be successful in keeping these colorful reef fishes.

Dottybacks

Family Pseudochromidae
Beauty to Spare—and Pugnaciousness to Match

ELECTRIFYING COLORS and personalities to match are traits of the dottybacks, usually seen darting, diving, and slinking in and out of coral and rock crevices, eliciting oohs and ahhs from observant aquarists and the occasional awed, "What was that?" Diminutive in size but not in temperament, dottybacks command your attention.

Darkstriped Dottyback (*Labracinus melanotaenia*): as feisty as it is colorful and one of the larger dottybacks that can terrorize a tank.

Very basslike, with their pear-shaped eyes, canine teeth, and—in many species—aggressive manners, these small slender fishes make great aquarium specimens—if the rest of your fishes are up to the challenge.

With very few exceptions, the pseudochromids have it in their nature to terrorize other fishes—including scrappy damsels—and may even go after motile invertebrates, like cleaner shrimp, that everything else ignores.

Classification. Known to some as pygmy basslets, dottybacks do look like miniature basses in appearance and are very grouperlike in their bravado. The dottybacks, however, are a family distinct from Family Serranidae, the true basses. (They may be readily discerned from smaller serranids on the basis of one characteristic—dorsal fin spine counts. Dottybacks, Family Pseudochromidae, have 1 to 3 spines each in the hard portion of their top fins, while true basses have 7 to 13 spiny rays.)

Although this family is divided into three subfamilies—Pseudochrominae, Anisochrominae, and Congrogadinae—only the Pseudochrominae are commonly offered in the trade. Eelblennies (Subfamily Congrogadinae) are occasionally seen. These are similar to blennies in shape, but are highly predaceous. Care requirements for eelblennies are the same as for dottybacks. For our purposes, the dottybacks will refer only to the Subfamily Pseudochrominae. The dottybacks comprise 5 genera and more than 70 species. Most often seen are the *Pseudochromis* and a few *Labracinus* "groupers" (the latter's old genus name was *Dampieria*, now it is *Labracinus*). Less familiar to marine aquarists are members of the genera *Cypho*, *Ogilbyina*, and *Assiculus*.

Noteworthy Species. The genus *Pseudochromis* consistently has some of the most beautiful and bold species offered in the trade. Don't let their size ever fool you, these small marines are tough customers that can dominate everything else in their size class on the reefs. You are well advised to have a separate system or other way of dividing your dottybacks from other fish livestock in the event of a piscine war.

Owing to their beauty and demand in the hobby, a few new species make it into the marketplace every couple of years. Around the world, the Purple, Magenta, or Strawberry Dottyback (*P. porphyreus*), the Bicolor (*P. paccagnellae*), and the Diadem (*P. diadema*), have all become standard offerings. The Red Sea endemics include the Orchid (*P. fridmani*), Springer's (*P. springeri*) and the Striped (*P. sankeyi*).

One of the nicest exceptions to the typical aggressiveness of the group, the Orchid Dottyback is held in high esteem by some reef-tank keepers for its almost fluorescent violet coloration, lack of shyness, elegant swimming style, and a "minding my own business" attitude. The *P. fridmani* can be displayed in groups in larger aquariums, although it's best to select a pair or one male and several females. (Females are smaller, with tail pigmentation that appears rounded, not sloping.) Do not confuse this species with the similar *P. porphyreus*, which is many times cheaper and nastier—not nearly as desirable in either looks, personality, or deportment. The Orchid Dottyback has purple finnage and a black slash through its eye, while *P. porphyreus* has an unadorned eye and clear fins.

The beautiful Neon Dottyback (*P. aldabraensis*) is a traditionally expensive species that is now being captive-bred and becoming readily available.

Size. Though most attain only a few inches in length, some get considerably larger. The giant of the subfamily, the Australian *Ogilbyina novaehollandiae*, grows to 6 inches. The dottybacks of the genus *Labracinus* get up to 8 inches long and fit the care and personality profile of the pseudochromids.

Selection. If ever there was a group that is both a dream and nightmare for collectors, distributors, and retailers, it is the dottybacks. The dream aspect is that these fishes do not suffer from shipping mortalities. The nightmare aspect is that one must find enough cubicles and containers to cordon them off individually. They are extremely territorial among themselves and can be living terrors if mixed with fishes they don't care for. Their interaction with each other reminds me of freshwater

male bettas (*Betta splendens*). The big difference is that dottybacks have large canine teeth and no long flowing fins to slow them down. A large proportion of these fishes are lost from jumping out of the system entirely or into compartments with each other.

Good specimens are about all that is ever offered. I wouldn't be concerned about chewed fins on a prospective purchase, as long as the fin base or body is not bloodied. They are ready healers.

Habitat. The dottybacks are found all over the Indo-Pacific and Red Sea on exposed reef flats, lagoons, and seaward reefs. The common element in their environment is the presence of hiding spaces—coral and rock crevices and caves that they can and will duck into in a flash. (When moving live rock out of a *Pseudochromis* tank, use care as these fishes will often hide in the holes and come along for the ride.)

Normal aquarium conditions suit these fishes well; many are found in shallow, changeable circumstances in the wild and are accepting of the same in confinement.

Behavior. The dottybacks define the word territorial; they're small but should be kept one to a tank. They are relentless scrappers with their own kind and other members of the genus. On

the reef, they are often found within an arm's reach of each other, and there are a few accounts of aquarists keeping two or more together in less than a 50-gallon system. But there are far more recordings of pseudochromid war losses among their own genus, and among

Purple Dottyback (*Pseudochromis porphyreus*): bright but scrappy.

gobies, wrasses, grammas, anthias, and more. Wholesalers keep pseudochromids strictly apart, and you should too. Ideally, these fishes should be placed in the system last, after the other less territorial types have secured their claim. A good method for adding a dottyback to your tank is to use a clear plastic jar with a screw or snap-on lid that has holes melted or drilled into it. The dottyback is secured in the container and then floated in the tank for a few days before release. This seems to ease tension and give all parties a chance to get acquainted without being able to get at each other. (Adopting this handy hint

Magenta Dottyback (*Pseudochromis porphyreus*)

Orchid Dottyback (*Pseudochromis fridmani*)

Diadema Dottyback (*Pseudochromis diadema*)

Neon Dottyback (*Pseudochromis aldabraensis*)

Bicolor Dottyback (*Pseudochromis paccagnellae*)

Sunrise Dottyback (*Pseudochromis flavivertex*)

for risky acclimations—either with very aggressive or very timid fishes—can save you the cost of this book many times over.) Larger, more aggressive species or individuals are best kept with triggers, large angels, tangs, and other similar fishes.

Though they can be bullies, dottybacks are often kept in all types of marine systems, from fish-only to stony coral systems. Due to their nature and eating habits, dottybacks generally leave invertebrates alone and are considered "reef safe."

Reproduction. For advanced aquarists seeking a prized species with the potential to reproduce, the pseudochromids present many new but potentially reasonable challenges. Spawning in aquariums and in the wild has been

observed (see Debelius and Baensch for the best coverage), and captive-bred pseudochromids are beginning to turn up in the trade. Breeding and rearing in aquariums is made much more feasible by the fact that these are demersal spawners, with temporary pairs producing a spherical egg mass in a protected spot (a hole in the rock or artificial cave) that is guarded by the male on the bottom. Breeders do not have to contend with the problematic pelagic or floating larval stages of so many other marine fishes. Hatching is reported to occur in 6 days. Species spawn every 2 to 3 weeks over a period of a year. Questions still remain on how hobbyists can feed the young through their early stages. Martin Moe has reported using wild plankton from the

Florida Keys in his successful experiments with the Orchid Dottyback.

Some dottybacks also show color and structural differences between the sexes, making it easier to arrange pairing. Males are typically larger, more rich in intensity and color, and, in some species, have longer unpaired fins.

Feeding. In the wild, pseudochromids are carnivores, feeding on small crustaceans, worms, and zooplankton. In captivity, they are ravenous feeders on all foodstuffs, especially frozen and fresh meaty foods. Some reef-tank owners recommend them for control of bristleworms (Class Polychaeta) that can emerge from live rock to prey on choice invertebrates. Particularly noted are the Red Sea species— *P. fridmani*, *P. aldabraensis*, and *P. springeri*—which some authors have found to be more effective at polychaete harvesting than the Pacific pseudochromids (Delbeek and Sprung, 1994).

Diseases. Dottybacks are moderately susceptible to *Amyloodinium*, but this can easily be cured with copper, Formalin, or specific gravity manipulation.

Two other "diseases" of note are color loss and the aforementioned jumping problem. On capture, they're fabulously marked and colored, but some species are notorious for fading from flashy to dull and drab. Vigorous filtration and varied diet are most often cited as slowing the loss of color. I have seen many pseudochromids lost because they catapult themselves right out of their tank. Far more are lost this way than from infectious disease. Cover all top openings big enough to allow them any launch window.

Summary. Even though, ounce for ounce, these are often more expensive than gold, as you evolve and gain confidence as a marine aquarist, you'll be tempted to try the dottybacks. Actually, the appearance of captive-bred fishes and increased collection from the Red Sea is bringing the price of some species tumbling from the prices paid in years past.

Take care to introduce your specimen carefully and only do so when you have the ability to recapture it and keep it separated if it proves to be a terror. Better yet, avoid adding a known troublemaking species to a small tank or one in which there are mild-mannered fishes it might antagonize.

Grammas

Family Grammatidae
Wonderful "Basslets" for All Types of Marine Systems

HANGING UPSIDE DOWN inside an aquarium cave or swimming at a 45-degree angle when they're out, here is a small group that can alarm the unknowing who assume they are seeing sick fish. As a pet-fish retailer years ago, I would repeatedly explain their quirky swimming habits to people who immediately jumped to the conclusion that we were selling unhealthy stock.

At any angle, the members of the Family Grammatidae make delightfully peaceful and beautiful marine aquarium additions. The Royal Gramma (*Gramma loreto*) is a real standard in the U. S., and one of the earliest commercially tank-bred and -reared marines. Every bit as appealing as the sometime fearsome Pseudochromidae (dottybacks), the Royal Gramma is less expensive and much more a species that can be recommended for all sorts of aquariums and aquarists.

Classification. The Grammatidae (formerly Grammidae) are all marine and commonly called basslets, a confusing appellation also used for Pseudochromidae and Serranidae. I prefer to call them grammas.

The 2 genera and 11 species (3 for *Gramma* and 8 for *Lipogramma*) are closely related to dottybacks, Family Pseudochromidae, and marine bettas, Family Plesiopsidae, as well as the true

Royal Gramma (*Gramma loreto*): a near-perfect fish for all marine systems, native to Florida, the Bahamas and the Caribbean.

basses, Family Serranidae. The grammas have the beauty and grace of all three, but the generally peaceful nature of the plesiopsids.

Anatomically, the small grammatid family differs from the true basses in having an interrupted or missing lateral line and a continuous dorsal fin without prominent notches in the

membranes between the spines.

Range. The Grammatidae are confined to the tropical western Atlantic from the Bahamas to Venezuela.

Size. There are accounts of some "breeder" grammas approaching a gargantuan 6 inches. The biggest I've encountered on or off the reef was 4 inches.

Selection. Only two or three species are routinely seen in the aquarium trade, including *Gramma loreto*, the Royal Gramma, which has a slightly larger variant sometimes sold as the Brazilian Gramma, and *G. melacara*, the Blackcap Gramma, with a brilliant purple body, jet black diagonal cap, and frosty white forked tail. The Blackcap Gramma usually comes from deep water and commands a premium price.

The single most important tip on picking grammas I can give you is to be patient. Wait a good week or two after your supplier receives new specimens before you take them home. For tank-raised individuals, this brief period will allow acclimation to aquarium conditions and virtually eliminate incidental losses.

Freshly imported specimens can suffer from post-decompression stress and the ill effects of chemical tranquilizing. Florida outlaws the use of quinaldine and MS-222 (tricaine), but their

Blackcap Gramma (*Gramma melacara*): a fine but somewhat uncommon aquarium fish, found on deep walls but also in shallower areas in the southern Caribbean. Note the Royal Gramma (*Gramma loreto*) in background of this reef scene.

use in other capture areas of the Caribbean is pervasive. Though not the same scourge as cyanide, quinaldine and tricaine produce decidedly higher mortalities than pure hand-netting. (These are anesthetics and do not cause the permanent damage that poisonous cyanide does.) Since it's not possible to tell which type of capture technique has been used, the best solution is simply to reserve your fish and wait a week or two.

Habitat. Grammas live close by their nooks and crannies, upside down, right side up—at all angles. These fishes are easily overlooked in the wild, being small and secretive. Having frequented their environments for more than 25 years, I can assure you that their numbers are many. A small, bright flashlight reveals them hiding up close and at angles along cave walls and ledges.

In the aquarium, they prefer as much decor and irregular environment as possible, although they are not secretive if they have hiding places nearby. These fishes make great additions to reef tanks. They stay small, do not bother invertebrates, and, as zooplanktivores, are easily fed with a variety of frozen foods. (On the other hand, the grammas themselves can easily be picked off by the usual list of aquarium predators, such as lionfishes and groupers.)

Grammatids make great bioassay organisms for an individual system or store on mixed-tank recirculation. You can think of a gramma as "the canary in the coal mine"—its color and behav-

ior will fade with diminishing water quality. Keep your water standards up and grammas will repay you with glowing coloration and obvious good health.

Behavior. Territoriality in these species dictates that they be safely kept one to a tank—unless you can buy known pairs or have a system at least 4 to 6 feet long. Although grammas will live in trios and larger groups, this doesn't necessary work in smaller aquariums without sufficient cover. If you intend to try your luck with more than one to a tank, introduce them all at once.

Reproduction. Males build nests from algae and plant scraps and guard the gray eggs, which number up to 100. The Royal Gramma was one of the earliest marine species to be tank-raised (back in the 1960s), but most specimens are still caught in the wild.

Feeding. Grammas are very fond of brine shrimp, particularly live, but readily accept all foods once they are adjusted to them.

Disease. The only cause of illness or death worth noting is environmental—from jumping out of their tanks. The grammas are aquatic rockets. Take care to keep their aquarium tops completely covered.

Summary. Outside of the possible damage from anesthetic use in collection, the grammas are exemplary marine aquarium fishes for newcomers and experts alike. Just be ready to explain their spatial orientations to visitors who fear that you have a fish that is "acting weird."

Jawfishes

Family Opistognathidae
Fascinating Tunnelers for a Quiet Environment

FAR FROM THE FLASHIEST fishes in the pet store, jawfishes are often buried in the back corners of their display tanks and commonly disappear from sight when first added to the home aquarium. Spouses of aquarists have been known to ask, "You actually paid for something that hides in the sand all the time?"

For those who know them, the jawfishes may be somewhat cryptic, but they are also exceptionally attractive, intelligent and fascinating aquarium fishes. When provided with adequate sand and rubble to produce their famous tunnel works, they provide a natural history show that provide years of observation pleasure for the aquarium keeper.

The "jaws", as many in the fish business know them, are hardy, blazingly fast, and fantastically interactive with each other. They are ideal tankmates for other peaceful fish and invertebrates and are well-suited to reef systems.

These fishes are mouthbreeders, with the males practicing oral incubation. Most of the time they hover or "tail stand" above their mouth-dug burrows. Reproductive behavior has been seen by many who keep these fishes.

Classification. A literature search of the jawfishes shows that they have moved around through different orders more than a floating thermometer in a tank. There are 3 genera (*Opistognathus, Lonchopisthus, Stalix*) with about 60 described species and another 30 under study.

In appearance, they have similarities to both the blennies and gobies, but are more similar to the grammas (Family Grammatidae) and dottybacks (Subfamily Pseudochrominae) in their evolution and behavior. Grammas, dottybacks, and jaws all have an interrupted lateral line high on the flank, terminating mid-dorsal, and an arrangement of paired fins with the pectorals located behind the pelvics.

The jawfishes' oblong body shape, long continuous dorsal and anal fins, big mouths, and enormous eyes make them unmistakable. Another more defining, distinguishing characteristic is that their bodies are covered with cycloid scales, even though their heads are "naked" of scales, spines, and other processes. This feature aids them in their continuous burrowing.

The one trait that separates the opistognathids from all other perciform fishes is the arrangement of fin supports in their pelvics. They have one spine and five soft rays (the inner three are weak and branched and the outer two are stout and unbranched).

Range. Opistognathids are all marine.

They are found in the western and central Atlantic, the Indian Ocean, and both sides of the Pacific.

Size. Most are under 4 inches, but a few attain 18 inches or more in length.

Noteworthy Species. *O. aurifrons*, the Yellow-headed or Pearly Jawfish, is one of the most popular aquarium fishes collected in the west Atlantic. It deserves its status, having a light blue anterior, grading to creamy white and yellow toward the rear half, and spending more time outside its tunnels than other jaws, once established.

The Blue-spotted (*O. rosenblatti*) of Mexico's Sea of Cortez is striking, with brilliant blue dots over its dark brownish body. The males become bright white in the front half of their bodies during spawning and courtship.

The Dusky Jawfish (*O. whitehursti*) is a camouflaged beauty that deserves more attention. Their brown mottled bodies are accentuated with glowing red to aqua eyes.

Also from the Atlantic and increasingly collected for the hobby are the Long Jaw (*O. macrognathus*) and Mottled (*O. maxillosus*). There are other species that are generally offered as "miscellaneous" jawfish. I have yet to find any that do not do well in captivity.

Selection. Most jawfishes are collected simply and by hand. A poker is dug in near the tunnel hole and positioned at an angle that drives out the occupant, and a fine mesh quickly blocks reentry. Due to their small gasbladder size, the captured specimens can be raised quickly to the surface.

Some Caribbean collectors still utilize chemical tranquilizers and these shipments often have high losses. Heed my usual advice about waiting and watching the livestock before taking it home. If a week or two goes by and the western Atlantic jaws are still frisky, I'd buy them.

Habitat. Unlike the related dottybacks and grammas, the jawfishes live on sandy reef flats in vertical burrows.

Yellow-headed Jawfish (*Opistognathus aurifrons*): burrowing mouthbrooder that requires a deep sand bed.

They fully utilize and constantly rearrange sand and rubble, shells, and small stones in making their burrows and entrances. They definitely need to do the same in captivity. A good mix of substrates for them is about three-quarters fine material (1/16 to 1/4 inch), and one-quarter coarse material (1/4 to 3/4 inch, coin-sized pieces), of a 2 to 3-inch depth minimum.

One problem that can be kept in check by habitat modification is jumping. Keep your tank covered or screened completely.

You might assume that because of their size and sedentary lifestyle, the jawfishes wouldn't require much in the way of circulation or filtration. But due to their digging and production of cave-stabilizing slime, it's better to have more water agitation than less—four or more turnovers per hour—with a skimmer in place.

Also, if you're using an undergravel filter, it will be necessary to increase the depth of gravel in at least a portion of the tank where the jaws can tunnel without disrupting things. Consider installing a fiberglass or plastic mesh barrier beneath the deep sand area, leaving an inch of gravel between the screening and the plastic undergravel plate. Secondly, be wary of utilizing air-driven lifts with these fishes as they do not appreciate the bubbling, gurgling sounds they produce. (This may be a good time to dispense with the undergravel entirely if you're ready to add some good live rock or other biological filtration.)

Behavior. These are the species to keep if you want to study interactive behavior within a single species of reef fishes. They can be very territorial, so don't try to put more than one jawfish species in the same system.

In the wild, Pearly Jaws live about 12 inches apart, and the Blue-spots often keep 3 feet separating their tunnels. Crowd your jawfishes beyond these parameters in captivity and you can expect

Dusky Jawfish (*Opistognathus whitehursti*): underappreciated, despite glowing red- to aqua-colored eyes.

perpetual war. Bruisers like the 18-inch *O. rhomaleus* should definitely be kept one to a tank.

The jawfishes ought be some of the first species introduced to your tank, and introduce them all at once if you are putting more than one in the system. These fishes are naturally timid and should not have aggressive or fast-swimming tankmates. There are a large number of predatory fishes known to elicit a strong fright reaction in jaw-fishes, including reef groupers, large tilefishes and wrasses, jacks, snappers, and triggerfishes. Keep your jawfishes with small peaceful fishes (like the small gobies or porkfishes), or easygo-ing invertebrates or lagoon macroalgae.

Reproduction. In *O. aurifrons*, males incubate the eggs in their mouths for about one week. Off the coast of Florida, this species breeds from spring to fall. Females are quickly courted by males, who spread their mouth and fins wide apart. Courting and spawning generally occur at dusk or dawn. The young are pelagic and feed principally on small crustaceans for 2 to 3 weeks before settling and digging their first tiny burrows.

The Pearly Jawfish is hard to dis-tinguish as male or female, but other species males, such as the Blue-spotted (*O. rosenblatti*) and the Atlantic Yellow (*O. gilberti*), show significant color changes at breeding times. Some

species of opistognathids have been bred and reared in captivity, but most are still wild-caught.

Feeding. These fishes are carnivores—feeding by hovering and dashing back and forth from their burrows to grab floating zooplankters.

In captivity, they are best hand-fed by the "turkey baster blast method." A crustacean food (defrosted krill, frozen brine shrimp) or minced shellfish is sucked up and discharged near the mouth of the fish's burrow. Of course, occasional live foods are highly appreci-ated.

Feeding strikes of a week for new arrivals are not unusual; try a little live food (adult brine shrimp works very well) to coerce them out of fasting.

Disease. Perhaps owing to their slim-iness, burrowing habits, and predatory pressures (the weak ones get eaten quickly), the jawfishes are remarkably free of disease and are infection-resis-tant. Professional collectors administer freshwater dips of 3 to 5 minutes dura-tion as a preventive measure.

If copper is necessary for treating tankmates, this does not seem to bother the opistognathids. These species get a very hardy rating overall.

Summary. Although your friends and family may laugh when first hearing that you spent good money on bug-eyed fishes that hide themselves away, be patient. The jawfishes will eventually come out and amaze all observers with their shimmering colors, speed, and in-dustriousness. They may even put on a reproductive show.

Cardinalfishes

Family Apogonidae
Invertebrate-safe Mouthbrooders from the Nether Reef

IT'S A SHAME that cardinalfishes are so often passed over as marine aquarium specimens. No doubt their odd shapes, quirky motions and large, wide-eyed looks must lead aquarists to consider this group as being too meek, slow, or delicate for captive use. Admittedly, the success rate in keeping these fishes *is* dismal—but for causes we can easily correct.

Cardinalfishes occupy some of the same niches on the reef and in aquariums as the damsels (Family Pomacentridae). They're plentiful, easily captured, and transport well. This results in their being relatively inexpensive to acquire and readily available.

Securing decent specimens, maintaining them in a small school, and granting them a few provisions will reward you with hardy, interesting, and long-lived specimens that are guaranteed safe in tanks with choice invertebrate life.

Classification. Cardinalfishes, Family Apogonidae, are members of the largest order of fishes, the Perciformes, and are one of the largest families, with about 22 genera and 250 species. Hobbyists are generally offered a half dozen members of the largest genus *Apogon* and the Pajama (*Sphaeramia nematoptera*) and Orbiculate (*S. orbicularis*) Cardinals. Following Dr. Gerald

Allen's mid-1990s photographic expedition to the Banggai Islands of Sulawesi in Indonesia, a beautiful black and silver species, *Pterapogon kauderni*, has become widely available as the Banggai, Borneo, or High-fin Cardinal. It has a bold personality and seems to breed readily in the aquarium.

Many cardinalfishes are reddish in color (hence their common name) mixed with silver and white. However, some species are yellow, silvery, or black, with nary a trace of red. All have large eyes—an indication that they are nocturnal, hiding in crevices or beneath ledges by day (typically with squirrelfishes, bigeyes, and sweepers). These are mostly shallow-water fishes, found from the surface to about 300 feet.

Range. Cardinalfishes are found on tropical Atlantic, Indian, and Pacific Ocean reefs. There are some estuarine

Ringtailed Cardinalfish (*Apogon aureus*): mild-mannered and especially interesting if kept in schools.

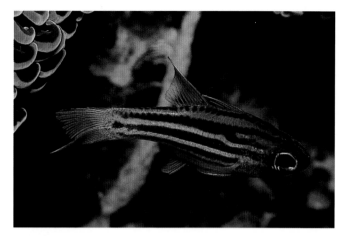

Ochre-striped Cardinalfish (*Apogon compressus*)

Flamefish (*Apogon maculatus*)

Pajama Cardinalfish (*Sphaeramia nematoptera*)

Blackstripe Cardinalfish (*Apogon nigrofasciatus*)

and freshwater members in Papua New Guinea (Allen).

Size. Most cardinalfishes grow to a few inches in the aquarium, with some species reaching 6 to 8 inches in the wild.

Selection. On arrival, cardinals display little middle-ground in their quality—they are either hardy and sure to make it, or weak and doomed to die. They share many of the same selection criteria as damselfishes.

When choosing specimens, look closely at the group on display. They should be clustered somewhat, with none trying to hide off in the corners. They should be aware of your presence. Examine each specimen carefully, especially the insertions of unpaired fins. If you see evidence of infection on any individual, pass the entire group by.

Habitat. Cardinals hide in the netherworld of ledges and corals by day and search the bottom for food by night.

They are about as undemanding and tolerant as damselfishes. Some temperate species prefer lower temperatures, but 72 to 78 degrees F is fine for the group as a whole. Elevated temperatures may bring on a feeding strike.

Cardinals will tolerate some nitrate, but little or no ammonia or nitrite. Keep the filtration brisk. These fishes are found in areas where the water is often whipped up. For an outstanding home arrangement, provide a large, dark shelter in the tank with one opening and place a group of these fishes with others they would associate with in the wild.

Behavior. Generally, cardinalfishes are not very territorial. On the reef, most live in aggregations as young and adults. In captivity, they fare well singly or in groups. As individuals, most cardinalfishes get along with their own kind, other species of apogonids, and other peaceful tankmates. Large predatory fishes will inhale them if they're small enough.

When introducing cardinals to your tank, it is best to put them in established systems, keeping some illumination on, but subdued, for a couple of days. The smaller species are strongly promoted for use in fish-only and reef-tank setups. They are supreme choices, being hardy and interesting. Their only shortcoming is that they can be shy and reclusive, but many aquarists report that their cardinals remain in the open during the day, provided that more aggressive fishes don't drive them into cover. Apogonids as a rule do not "sample" more than mouth-sized invertebrates. Many form close associations with invertebrates, living within the spiny shelter of urchins, sea stars, and more.

Reproduction. The spawning habits of several species of cardinalfishes are known. The sexes are not much differentiated but may be distinguished by the male's slightly larger size and the girth of gravid females. They are among the few marine mouthbreeders, with the males generally doing the incubating. Young are released after about a week and develop as plankton for a couple of months in the upper water column. A number of hobbyists have successfully reared the newly available Banggai Cardinal, feeding freshly hatched brine shrimp to the fry within 24 hours of their emergence from the male's mouth. While Banggai parents can be feisty with members of their own species, the young are reported to be no more difficult to raise than baby guppies. (As with freshwater livebearers, the young will be eaten by the adults unless physically separated.) Other anecdotal evidence suggests that Pajama Cardinals may also reproduce regularly in well-kept aquariums, with the only sign being the sudden complete loss of appetite of one adult, whose jaw ends up bulging as the fry develop. The young are gobbled up by the tank's inhabitants, often without the aquarist ever having noticed their arrival.

Feeding. Apogonids prey on very small fishes and mobile invertebrates, principally crustaceans. Brine shrimp and other fresh and frozen meaty foods are normally eaten with relish. Avoid pellets, flake, and other dry-prepared foods as these will not sustain them.

If your cardinals are new and refusing food, or if established specimens go on a feeding strike, execute a large water change and try some live adult brine shrimp with the lights turned off in the system.

Disease. These fishes are generally received free of external parasites and

Banggai Cardinalfish (*Pterapogon kauderni*): recently rediscovered by Dr. Gerald Allen and an overnight sensation among aquarists.

clean up easily with routine welcoming dips and quarantine. The usual protozoan scourges of tropical marine fishes can be handily defeated with standard copper remedies if detected early enough.

Summary. Don't let the apogonids' secretive nocturnal behavior or odd appearance dissuade you from trying them. They are good aquarium specimens whose only demands are a dark shelter, meaty foods, and the society of other members of their species.

Butterflyfishes

Family Chaetodontidae
Critical Choices in a Large and Alluring Group

FLITTING AROUND and through their coral haunts, always exhibiting tremendous grace and beauty, the butterflyfishes are one of the most accurately named groups—nicely likened to the Order Lepidoptera, the insects we call butterflies. These are some of the most elegant and best-loved species in the marine aquarium world.

Where would the hobby be without the Long-noses, Raccoon, Threadfin, Teardrop, and the several "Poor Man's Moorish Idols" or *Heniochus* species? Impoverished for sure. These and several other butterflyfishes are well-suited for captive systems—shipping and adjusting well, eating all types of foods, resisting disease, and adapting to a wide range of water conditions.

However, of the some 120 described species, the majority of butterflyfishes are best avoided by hobbyists. These types adapt poorly to aquarium environments for differing reasons, often because they require obscure foodstuffs to thrive. Unknown to many aquarists, the hardy species and those that are obligate corallivores and must eat live coral polyps to survive are offered to the consumer, often out of the same retail tank. How can you tell which varieties to avoid? Herein is a collection of first- and secondhand observations on what

the butterflies are, where the species lie left or right of being generally hardy, and notes on how to pick out healthy specimens and maintain them.

Classification. Butterflyfishes make up the Family Chaetodontidae, meaning "bristle tooth," a telling allusion to feeding problems with many of these fishes. Their bodies are typically palm-shaped with a protruding snout of varying length tipped with a small mouth. This pancake body plan and apical mouth arrangement are ideal for zooming in and out of the shallow coral reef habitats where most species reside.

Range. Butterflyfishes live in tropical to cooler seas—Atlantic, Indian and Pacific (principally Indo-West Pacific) waters along rocky and coral reef shores. Most live in depths of less than 20 meters, though a few have been recorded to ten times deeper.

Size. Adults span 3 to 12 inches in total length, depending on species.

Selection. When you purchase a butterflyfish, your success in keeping it alive depends on at least two considerations: the species and the individual(s) you choose.

Unless you've spent the years necessary to become an advanced aquarist, please stick to the varieties of butterflyfishes that are known survivors; never buy one of these fishes without

first looking up its eating habits—many that are virtually guaranteed to die are (it's sad to say) routinely available for sale.

Observe butterfly offerings closely. Do not buy small (less than 2-to-3-inch) or large (more than 6-inch) individuals. Leave thin ones alone. All of these adapt poorly.

Avoid fishes showing any reddening at the mouth, body, or fin origins. I am a strong believer in boycotting the whole tank if even one butterfly is off-color. Experience has taught me that once one butterfly specimen in a shipment shows signs of "breaking down," the rest generally follow. Butterflies need adequate room in shipping bags. Make sure yours can turn around completely; I believe that most are lost (prematurely) due to shipping and handling damage. Their mouths get damaged from rough net handling or thrashed by smacking against a bag that is too small. Subsequent infection and refusal to eat spirals into a dead specimen. By the way, most butterflies are caught in barrier nets, not with cyanide.

Skip buying pairs, trios, or groups of a given species unless they appear closely associated in the dealer's tank. (A few notably good schooling species are identified below.) I strongly suggest wholesale routine freshwater dipping; copper and antibiotic treatment of all new arrivals at the wholesale, importer,

Masked Butterflyfish (*Chaetodon semilarvatus*): common in the Red Sea and a spectacular, relatively hardy species for larger aquariums.

Ranking the Butterflyfishes

Everyone who has ever bought or sold marine species has his own mental list of best- and least-liked organisms, the ones that generally make it, those that don't, and those that fall somewhere in between.

Here are my opinions about the chaetodonts after handling tens of thousands over the last 30 years. No apology or vain attempt at completeness is offered. I know there is going to be no absolute agreement on my assessments, but I stand by them—they are borne out of my own observations of many individuals of all sizes from many points of origin.

I define "good" species as those found to have a survival rate of more than 70% for three or more months (decent specimens, shipped properly). "Bad" butterflyfishes have less than a 20% survival rate within the same parameters. The "questionable" ones fall in between.

"Good" Butterflyfishes

Chaetodon aculeatus, **Atlantic Long-nosed**
C. argentatus, **Black and White**
C. auriga, **Threadfin**
C. aya, **Doubleband or Bank**
C. burgessi, **Burgess's**
C. collare, **Collare, Red-tail, or Pakistani**
C. daedalma, **Wrought-iron**
C. decussatus, **Indian Ocean Vagabond**
C. ephippium, **Saddled**
C. falcifer, **Scythe**
C. falcula, **Sickle**
C. fasciatus, **Red Sea Raccoon**
C. lunula, **Raccoon**
C. melannotus, **Black-band**
C. mertensii, **Merten's or Chevron**
C. mesoleucos, **White-face**
C. miliaris, **Lemon or Millet-seed**
C. paucifasciatus, **Red-back**
C. punctatofasciatus, **Dot-dash**
C. rafflesi, **Latticed or Raffle's**
C. sedentarius, **Reef**
C. semilarvatus, **Masked or Golden**
C. tinkeri, **Tinker's**
C. ulietensis, **Pacific Double-saddle**
C. unimaculatus, **Teardrop**
C. xanthurus, **Pearlscale**
Forcipiger longirostris, **Big Long-nosed**
F. flavissimus, **Long-nosed or Yellow Long-nosed**
Heniochus **spp., Bannerfishes**
Johnrandallia (*Pseudochaetodon*) *nigrirostris,* **El Barbero, Barberfish**
Parachaetodon ocellatus, **Eye-spot**

"Questionable" Butterflyfishes

C. kleini, **Klein's**
C. multicinctus, **Pebbled or Multi-banded**
Chelmon rostratus, **Copperband**
Hemitaurichthys polylepis (often sold as *H. zoster*), **Pyramid**
Hemitaurichthys thompsoni, **Thompson's**

"Bad" Butterflyfishes

Chaetodon adiergastos, **Philippine**
C. aureofasciatus, **Golden-striped**
C. austriacus, **Exquisite or Red Sea Melon**
C. baronessa, **Baroness or Eastern Triangular**
C. bennetti, **Bennett's**
C. capistratus, **Four-eyed**
C. flavirostris, **Yellow-face or Dusky**
C. fremblii, **Bluestripe**
C. humeralis, **Cortez or East Pacific**
C. larvatus, **Orange-face**
C. lineolatus, **Lined**
C. lunulatus, **Pacific Red-fin or Oval**
C. melapterus, **Arabian or Black-fin Melon**
C. meyeri, **Meyer's**
C. ocellatus, **Spotfin**
C. octofasciatus, **Eight-banded**
C. ornatissimus, **Ornate**
C. pelewensis, **Dot-dash or Sunset**
C. plebeius, **Blue-spot**
C. quadrimaculatus, **Four-spot**
C. rainfordi, **Rainford's**
C. reticulatus, **Reticulated**
C. semeion, **Decorated or Dotted**
C. speculum, **Oval-spot or Mirror**
C. striatus, **Banded**
C. triangulum, **Rummynose or Triangular**
C. trifascialis, **Chevron or V-lined**
C. trifasciatus, **Indian Red-fin or Melon**
C. vagabundus, **Vagabond or Crisscross**
Coradion **spp., Coralfish**

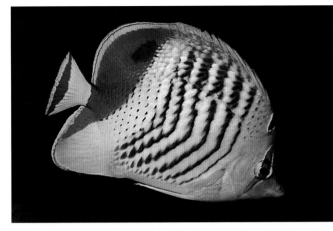

Red-back Butterflyfish (*Chaetodon paucifasciatus*): Red Sea endemic.

Merten's Butterflyfish (*Chaetodon mertensii*): hardy in captivity.

Teardrop Butterflyfish (*Chaetodon unimaculatus*): great aquarium species.

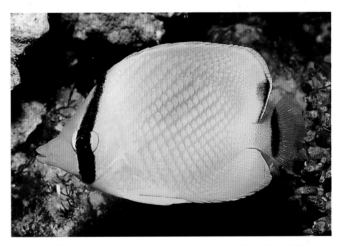

Latticed Butterflyfish (*Chaetodon rafflesi*): also called Raffle's Butterflyfish.

and/or retail level; and at least a week of quarantine for end-users.

You can collect your own if you're in the area and have the proper permits. Do it like the pros. Place a barrier/mist net in a prospective channel and "drive" the butterflies against it. Hand-net them off, decompress, and ship back home. Seriously, once you see how complicated the process is, you'll never again complain about the high cost of livestock.

Habitat. A system for butterflyfishes should be as large as possible, at least 50 gallons. They are free-ranging fishes, with large feeding and cruising territories. Just as important as enough space, they need physical cover to feel secure; one or more caves, canyons, or slots will give the butterfly a sense that it can find protective shelter.

These fishes are the aquarium equivalent of warning lights. They will show signs first whenever water qual-

ity is on a slide. Good water is a must, with high, consistent pH (8.2 to 8.3), and little to no detectable organics. Toward these ends, an efficient skimmer is of extreme importance; I wouldn't put a butterfly into a closed marine system without one. Also, the use of a coarser coral sand for substrate is recommended for higher pH buffering capacity and ease of cleaning up meaty leftovers. The use of external pH "raisers" is encouraged.

Bluestripe Butterflyfish (*Chaetodon fremblii*)

Reticulated Butterflyfish (*Chaetodon reticulatus*)

Bennett's Butterflyfish (*Chaetodon bennetti*)

Oval-spot Butterflyfish (*Chaetodon speculum*)

Vagabond Butterflyfish (*Chaetodon vagabundus*)

Baroness Butterflyfish (*C. baronessa*): juvenile

For the bulk of species, temperatures of 75 to 85 degrees F are recommended, with no worries if summer temporarily pushes this a bit higher. There are cooler and deeper-water types of butterflyfishes, so you'll want to investigate prospects before purchasing.

An important comment regarding "aged systems." Many authors cite lack of success with newly set-up systems and butterflyfishes. We don't yet know why this is so, but the possibilities include lack of algae growth and accumulated detritus and/or some chemical anomaly. Whatever the reason, tanks that are six months old and older enjoy greater butterfly survivability.

A vigorous, efficient filtration mode is needed, whatever format is em-ployed, with lots of current producing high dissolved oxygen concentration.

Overall, when it comes to your display, think of the circumstances where most of the "good" butterflyfishes are collected—in the rough-and-tumble coral shallows. In this bright nook-and-cranny world, the pH is high, the water clean, the current brisk, and the temperature constant.

Behavior. Most of the "good" butterflyfishes make fine tankmates. The same cannot be said for the "bad" ones; they hide and are easy prey for tank bullies. Some, such as the *Heniochus* species, are tolerant to appreciative of members of their own species. The vast majority, however, fight with their own or similar kind unless crowded or put in huge systems with lots of cover. Some

butterflies as juveniles are celebrated "cleaners," picking parasites and dead tissues off other species.

Handling is a very important matter that doesn't get enough coverage. It may not be as sensational as "cyanide poisoning" and the advertising and enmity that goes with that topic, but people who know the aquarium business will assure you that improper handling is, without doubt, the number one factor in the life/death of livestock.

In particular, the butterflyfishes are doomed if thrashed either by netting or by being placed in a bag that is too small. Once their mouths, fins, and bodies are damaged, they often refuse food and quickly expire.

Chaetodonts bear strong dorsal and anal spines at the anterior of these fins, giving would-be predators a potentially prickly mouthful. These stout spines are important to aquarists as well—they get caught in nets and puncture unwary hands. Knowledgeable aquarists develop a sense of how and when to lift butterflyfishes (if need be) from the water when moving them. It is best to cradle the fish, with supple hand support behind the netting, and gently restrain the fish from flopping about. Tearing of flesh and fin bases is often fatal.

Small butterflyfishes are readily eaten by larger predatory fishes. On some island groups I've visited, the locals use small butterflyfishes as bait. Do not mix and match with triggers, large basses, lionfishes, or other predators.

Almost all chaetodonts are fish-tank-system-only members. They will pick apart nearly every invertebrate in time, perhaps with the exception of hermit crabs. Most of them are definitely not for reef systems.

Reproduction. Some butterflyfish species are known to form monogamous pairs, others travel solitarily or in groups and either pair up or form loose temporary associations at spawning times. Gametes are released near nightfall at the apex of a quick swim toward the surface. There is little or no observable physical difference between the sexes.

Butterflyfishes have a peculiar bony-armored larval "tholichthys" developmental stage. These little butterfly larvae float about in currents for months before metamorphosing into minuscule adult versions and settling down, hopefully at a fortuitous location. Some species have spawned in captivity, but I don't know of any recording of a successful rearing from captive spawnings.

Feeding. Even the best species of butterflyfishes can be finicky eaters, especially on first introduction. It cannot be stressed enough that an adequate, sustainable food mix be found as soon as possible and offered often. Live brine shrimp is a good starter for newcomers, as are various types of worms and crustaceans available in the trade—live and frozen. Other meaty foods such as squid, minced clam, and prepared blends should be offered in small quantities and removed if uneaten as they will quickly foul your water.

Eight-banded Butterfly (*Chaetodon octofasciatus*)

Blue-spot Butterflyfish (*Chaetodon plebeius*)

Ornate Butterflyfish (*Chaetodon ornatissimus*)

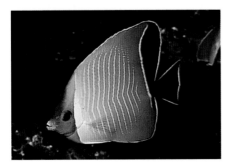
Orange-face Butterflyfish (*Chaetodon larvatus*)

Meyer's Butterflyfish (*Chaetodon meyeri*)

Banded Butterflyfish (*Chaetodon striatus*)

Exquisite Butterflyfish (*Chaetodon austriacus*)

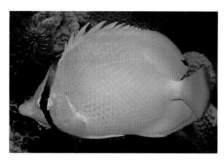
Spotfin Butterflyfish (*Chaetodon ocellatus*)

Rainford's Butterflyfish (*Chaetodon rainfordi*)

Obligate coral eaters exist in this family. Some folks have kept these going by providing scleractinian (stony) corals, live rocks, and anemones (prolific and cheap *Condylactis*) as food sources. I implore you, read up on and avoid these species unless you are really ready for the challenge. Instead, focus on the more generalized feeders.

The secret to maintaining these fishes is to offer a varied diet and to provide it often. Get your marines to eat quickly and offer algae and other foods in small amounts as frequently as practical.

Should you have a fish go on a feeding strike while others in the system are fine (indicating something other than water quality as the cause), try one or more of the following:

1) offer a fresh clam opened up and placed on the bottom;

2) offer live white, tubificid, or grindal worms set down in a small dish to prevent escape;

3) temporarily lower the specific gravity for a few days to stimulate appetite (1.025 down to 1.018);

4) apply vitamins directly to the water (and/or food); some are known to enhance feeding. (Although adding vitamin solutions directly to tank water often fuels unwanted microalgae growth in reef tanks.)

Finally, be sure your butterflies are getting their fair share of foods. By and large they are not as aggressive as many fishes kept and may need to be catered to separately while the pushier types gather elsewhere in the tank. Simultaneously offering food in two locations in your tank may help to get nutrition to your butterflies.

Disease. Butterflyfishes unfortunately are very susceptible to *Cryptocaryon*, *Amyloodinium*, and other common protozoal complaints (e.g. *Glugea*); bacterial infections; and gill fluke problems. Often they are the first fishes to show signs of such problems in a tank.

Thankfully, if caught in time, these are also quickly cured by way of traditional remedies (copper or malachite green treatments). Some species are copper-sensitive, so be sure to use a test kit to avoid overtreatment.

Summary. There are many varieties of sea life offered to the pet hobbyist. How great is the range of average survivability among all this livestock?

Huge. As a conscientious marine aquarist, you should at least be aware of the odds you are facing in attempting difficult organisms—as well as what has and has not worked for others.

If you're going to try the historically less hardy species, select good specimens, provide absolutely clean water, and be prepared to pamper them with food. Should you be unwilling or unable to provide this level of care, please do not encourage the further collection of delicate butterflies by buying them.

Bannerfish Butterflies
Heniochus spp.

"SALTWATER FISHES are so hard to keep; they have narrow chemical and physical water-quality tolerances, are finicky eaters, and die for mysterious reasons . . ."

You will hear this statement around certain pet shops, and it may be true for some species, especially some of the coral-feeders. It's hard to imagine anyone, even the most diehard goldfish lover, wanting to disparage the butterflyfishes in the genus *Heniochus* in this way. These are superbly adaptable aquarium specimens that acclimate quickly, thrive under a variety of conditions, are not quarrelsome, and readily accept all foods.

Classification. All eight species of this genus are similarly shaped with laterally compressed sides, a pointed rostrum, and a lengthened fourth dorsal ray. Their German common name is "Wimplefish." (A wimple is a type of hat with feathers, of which the heightened dorsal is reminiscent.)

For various structural similarities, *Heniochus* species are considered derived from, and closely related to, another butterfly genus *Hemitaurichthys*, which in turn is from the mega-genus *Chaetodon*.

Some brief notes on the various species:

Heniochus acuminatus: The Long-fin Bannerfish, also called "Poor Man's Moorish Idol," is the most common, readily available *Heniochus*—a species that is the exact opposite of the Moorish Idol in terms of aquarium viability. This is the best of the genus in the way of food training and overall aquarium adaptability. This beautiful bannerfish's elongated dorsal fin may exceed its body length. The best specimens are often imported from Hawaii.

H. diphreutes: Remarkably similar to *H. acuminatus* (Burgess, 1978, considers these the same species), *H. diphreutes*, the Schooling Bannerfish, may be distinguished by the possession of an additional dorsal ray, a shorter snout, and a more pointed, shorter anal fin.

H. chrysostomus: This Three-banded Bannerfish is easily separable from the other species in the genus by the presence of the first band passing through the eyes and paired fins.

H. singularius: The Philippine Bannerfish is similar to *H. monoceros*, but rare in captivity and within its range.

H. intermedius: The Red Sea Bannerfish is endemic to the Red Sea and is much less available and prohibitively expensive for Westerners. This species has a prominent skeletal lump below each eye, larger in adult males.

H. monoceros: The Unicorn Bannerfish, as the name implies, has a decided "horn" on the forehead, as well as a bony cone-shaped projection beside the eyes.

H. pleurotaenia: Bears bony ridges similar to *H. monoceros* and has the least prominent dorsal fin.

H. varius: The Brown Bannerfish is attractively colored and similar to *H. pleurotaenia*. Both have short dorsals and duplicate morphology. This species is commonly available as it is widespread over much of the tropical Western Pacific.

Selection. When acquiring a group of bannerfish, your purchasing is best done from one dealer's tank—buying all the desired individuals of the genus that you intend to keep and introducing them all at once. Though most *Heniochus* are not quarrelsome, they can become territorial in small systems. Fifteen to 20 gallons of space per specimen is a suggested minimum. Many species can attain a length of 10 inches.

Long-fin Bannerfish (*Heniochus acuminatus*): a superb aquarium fish that may be kept in pairs or schools.

Buy smaller *Heniochus* (3 to 4 inches in total length) if possible, as these adapt best. Be wary of slightly smaller ones; particularly if they are thin of musculature between the eyes in the head region. These may eat, but do not always recover to full health.

Habitat. The several species of *Heniochus* live in shallow water near the

Schooling Bannerfish (*Heniochus diphreutes*): similar to *H. acuminatus*, but with a stubbier snout and shorter anal fin.

sea bed, typically near broken shorelines. Their slim bodies make them well disposed to quick passage and safety between the rocks and corals of their wild environs.

Chemical parameters are not a major problem with *Heniochus*. Higher pHs, 8.2 to 8.4, are recommended, but these fishes are more tolerant of endogenous pollution than most commonly kept aquarium species. Your charges will be healthier and live better, longer lives if you maintain better water quality. Use of a skimmer and the

presence of healthy macroalgae, like *Caulerpa*, go a long way toward ensuring suitable water.

Behavior. *Heniochus* are social animals, being found in groups of a pair or more to veritable shoals of a few hundred individuals. It makes sense that they should not be kept solitarily if possible. Try to observe them in your dealer's tank and choose two or more that appear to associate readily. If room and/or finances restrict your selection, *H. acuminatus* seems to adjust best at being "the only heni in the tank."

Heniochus, as with butterflyfishes in general, are not aggressive; they have neither the teeth nor the body armament for it. If enough habitat is provided, they will gladly choose "flight over fight." *Heniochus*, between and among species, may "butt" with their head projections, but this is generally not dangerous.

Another bonus: Some species have been observed to be facultative cleaners, especially when young. This is yet another example of a "can-do" parasite remover, an occasional volunteer cleaner, unlike the more obligate "must-do" cleaner wrasses or gobies.

Heniochus may be eaten by typical large predatory fishes in whose mouths they can fit. Be wary of basses, lionfishes, morays, and the like. Though they are quick enough on their fins during the day, butterflyfishes "sleep"

peacefully on the bottom in the evenings and may become midnight snacks for predators.

Reproduction. Pair spawning has been observed in the wild. It is postulated that 3,000 to 4,000 eggs are released in a spawning and scattered by currents in the upper water column—they are pelagic.

Feeding. *Heniochus* are largely plankton eaters in the wild. In captivity, they readily consume frozen, flake, freeze-dried, or fresh foods—seemingly whatever is offered, even if it is hand-held at the surface. They should be given a variety of foods frequently and in small amounts, at least two or three times daily. Clean, pollution-free tubificid worms are relished, after the fish have been trained on them. Use live freshwater foods as an occasional high-protein treat. Some vegetable matter, such as *Spirulina* or any of the dried marine algae, should be offered in the diet. *Heniochus* will readily graze on any algae that appears in the system itself.

Vitamin supplements are useful applied to the food or water directly. Fructose sugar may even be applied to bolster an ailing specimen (Baensch in Allen & Steene, 1979) as marine fishes "drink" environmental water.

Disease. This genus is relatively disease-free. They are susceptible, as are most tropical marine fishes, to the two most common coral-reef parasitic "plagues"—*Amyloodinium* and *Cryptocaryon*—displaying their typical symptomology (rapid breathing, listlessness, clamped fins). Most reports show bannerfishes to be easily treated with manipulation of temperature and specific gravity, and they have no great sensitivity to common therapeutics like copper compounds.

Various external parasites may be present and become problematic in recently captured wild specimens, if overstressed. Gill flukes and parasitic copepod crustaceans may be reduced or alleviated through quarantine, dips, or other chemical treatment. More appropriately, they might be biologically controlled through the use of a cleaner relationship—utilizing an appropriate species of *Gobiosoma* gobies. *Heniochus* are prone to lateral-line disease, with both the cause and cure still under dispute. (See Chapter 9.)

Summary. By any and all means try this genus. *Heniochus* look delicate, but they are not. They are hardy, undemanding, eminently likable, peaceful enough to be kept in pairs or shoals, and are well-suited to aquarium life.

Pacific Double-saddle Butterflyfish
Chaetodon ulietensis

Looking for an exotic butterfly with beauty, brains, and staying power? Here is a species with all that and more, including the personality to coexist in a group—a truly spectacular group—of their own kind.

Although hardly commonplace in retail stores, the Pacific Double-saddle Butterflyfish is an exemplary aquarium choice for several good reasons. It is a voracious feeder on all foods, attains a reasonable maximum length of about 6 inches, ships well, adapts readily to captivity, and is very resistant to disease.

The Pacific Double-saddle is common in the western Indo-Pacific. This butterfly is found in shallow coral reefs, at the surface to more than 30 feet, especially in channels with brisk currents.

The bigger the system you keep this fish in the better, with live rock or some other three-dimensional structure to provide a sense of security and sleeping space. Only aquarists with good water quality should try (pH 8.0 to 8.3 and no measurable nitrogenous metabolic wastes). Never put one of these butterflies into a new tank.

As butterflyfishes go, *C. ulietensis* is

A Tale of Two Butterflies

The Pacific Double-saddle (*Chaetodon ulietensis*) is often called, and sold as, the "Falcula" Butterflyfish, but *Chaetodon falcula* is a separate species. Also an admirable aquarium choice, *C. falcula* is the "true" Falcula, and is also called the Sickle or the Indian Ocean Double-saddle Butterflyfish. But the two species are easily distinguished on the basis of color and markings:

Pacific Double-saddle Butterfly (*C. ulietensis*)   Falcula or Sickle Butterfly (*C. falcula*)

	C. ulietensis	C. falcula
SHAPE AND EXTENT OF SADDLE MARKINGS:	Barlike, more than half the girth	Wedge-shaped, less than half the girth
MARKINGS ON CAUDAL PEDUNCLE:	Black dot with yellow above and below	Completely black band with no yellow
EXTENT OF YELLOW BODY COLOR:	Color starts abruptly behind rear saddle	Bright yellow on dorsal surface as well as rear

Pacific Double-saddle Butterflyfish (*Chaetodon ulietensis*): commonly observed in large schools in the wild, this hardy species has a robust appetite.

exceptionally peaceful among its own kind and other fishes, and acclimation of the Double-saddle is no real problem. Butterflyfishes are very infrequently harassed as newcomers. Provide low illumination the first couple of nights and be sure that the specimen starts feeding. As with all butterflyfishes, *C. ulietensis* is not a predator on other aquarium fishes, nor prey to any but the most belligerent bully (often a trigger, puffer, or angel). Their overall philosophy may be summed up as "live and let live."

If you have a big system, do consider a trio of the Pacific Double-saddles. They are gorgeous and tough, nonfussy eaters, and, if your water quality is up to snuff, will provide you with many years of happy husbandry. All in all, an excellent aquarium choice.

El Barbero (Barberfish)
Johnrandallia nigrirostris

HERE IS ONE OF THE REAL STALWARTS among the butterflyfishes, a species that hails from Mexico's Pacific coast, the beautiful and hardy Barberfish, *Johnrandallia nigrirostris*, sometimes called the Black-nosed Butterflyfish.

Formerly classed with the banner or wimplefish genus of butterflyfishes, *Heniochus*, El Barbero was given the genus name *Johnrandallia* in honor of the esteemed ichthyologist Dr. John E. Randall of Hawaii's Bishop Museum. (Although most ichthyologists place the fish in the genus *Johnrandallia*, some sources list its genus as *Pseudochaetodon*.) The Barberfish attains an overall length of about 6 inches. It is restricted in range to the coastal Eastern Pacific from Baja, California, southward to Panama and the Galapagos.

This is one of the toughest species of its family, but an improperly captured, held, transported, or handled specimen is surely doomed. What to look for: bright, consistent color and scale pattern; good feeding behavior (they're eager eaters of all foodstuffs); and a size of 3 to 5 inches. What to avoid: red, obviously damaged mouth and fin-ray spines; any sores or ulcerations; rapid, shallow breathing; hiding in corners; and blood or other obscurity in the eyes.

The Barberfish is an undemanding species that prefers larger quarters with as much rock and coral rubble cover as you can provide. Natural habitat is rocky reefs 10 to 80 feet deep by day and night. I have never observed them in open, sandy, or other environs.

They are very tolerant of less-than-pristine water conditions, relative to other butterflies. Otherwise, El Barbero should be treated like the other hardy butterflies, and can be counted upon not to bully or be bullied by any but the biggest or meanest of tankmates. They are tolerant of their own kind in any size or number and can be kept in a small school or shoal.

The origin of the common name Barberfish (or its Spanish equivalent, El Barbero), can be traced to the fact that this is a facultative cleaner, removing parasites and dead tissue from other species and setting up temporary and

Barberfish (*Johnrandallia nigrirostris*): an unusual symbiotic cleaner of the tropical eastern Pacific.

permanent cleaning stations for grooming reef and pelagic fishes. They otherwise consume benthic crustaceans, snails, other small invertebrates, and algae in the wild. In captivity, Barberfish accept all manner of food types and in good quantity: frozen, flake, pellet, live, fresh—you name it.

This is a superb species for the marine aquarist with adequate space (at least 20 gallons per specimen). It is inexpensive and is becoming more available through growing collection sites in Mexico, Costa Rica, and elsewhere.

Looking for an unusual butterflyfish that is rugged, long-lived, and that can be kept in schools or shoals? Watch or ask for the Barberfish, *Johnrandallia nigrirostris*.

The Long-nosed Butterflyfishes
Forcipiger spp.

APPEARANCES OF FISHES can indeed be deceiving. To take one look at the long-nosed butterflyfishes, you'd expect them to be in the same category as the Pinnate Batfish: lovely but fragile, and not the least bit hardy. You'd think anything with a long, delicate beak and tiny mouth must be difficult to keep.

This is definitely not the case. If you are careful to select an individual that has not been beaten up physically and/or emotionally through collection and transport, these yellow beauties can do exceptionally well in marine sys-

tems. As an added bonus, these yellow long-noses attract attention and spark brief tankside biology lessons, with the disruptive black bar over the eyes and prominent "eye-spot" at the tail. These are fishes that have evolved to fool prospective predators at both ends, tempting attackers to focus on and strike at the less-vulnerable tail section, thus allowing them to make an escape without a mortal wound.

The two species, *Forcipiger flavissimus* and *F. longirostris*, are often sold under the same common name, although well-informed dealers will know and label them by their proper scientific names. Some sources distinguish the two by labeling *F. flavissimus* the Long-nosed (or Yellow Long-nosed) Butterflyfish and *F. longirostris* the Big Long-nosed Butterflyfish. The two species are easily distinguished from each other on the basis of relative snout length. *F. longirostris* is the "winner by a nose," as its Latin name implies. If you cruise the literature, you may find other long-nosed species in this genus, but these are invalid junior synonyms and some sources list black and brown color variants. I do not recommend the Copperband Butterfly (*Chelmon rostratus*), which is another commonly seen butterflyfish with a long snout. It is not nearly as hardy

as its yellow brethren, doing best when pampered in well-established reef aquariums.

F. flavissimus is found in most of the Pacific, Indo-Pacific, and the Red Sea; *F. longirostris* sympatrically overlaps the shorter nose over much of its range. Most specimens offered are 4 to 6 inches in overall length—tail to rostrum. A truly gargantuan long-nose will be about 8.5 inches in length.

These fishes are readily available, and at moderate prices. Though imported from the Philippines and Indonesian areas, my favorite specimens hail from the Christmas or Marshall Is-

Big Long-nosed Butterflyfish (*Forcipiger longirostris*): distinguished from the similar Long-nosed (*F. flavissimus*) by its longer nose and a mask that more fully camouflages the eyes.

lands, or Hawaii. Sporadically, good specimens are also collected from Mexico's Pacific coast.

Long-noses, like most butterflyfishes, inhabit broken reef areas where food and hiding spaces are plentiful and circulation is brisk. Your success with them will be commensurate with providing similar conditions. These are stout fishes but do require clean, well-filtered water. Although circulation should be brisk, it should not be too strong; simply keep the water moving.

Giving these marine organisms open areas as well as substantial rocks or corals where they can seek refuge results in better adjusted, longer-lived specimens. The system should be no smaller than 40 gallons, ideally with 20 or more gallons set aside per butterfly.

It should be mentioned that these fishes display some unusual behavior. Don't be unduly surprised should you catch yours swimming or hanging upside down or "spitting" water in your direction at the surface. Also, they may have a blanched whitish appearance on being exposed to light after being in dark conditions, as when emerging from sleep or a shipping box. This is normal. A loss of yellow when the lights are on and the fishes are active, however, is a sign that you need to be looking for a cause—usually diminished water quality or fright from bullying.

Outside of quarreling with other long-noses, these fishes are peaceable. Be wary of placing them with larger predatory fishes, however. I have seen them used as bait by island fisherfolk,

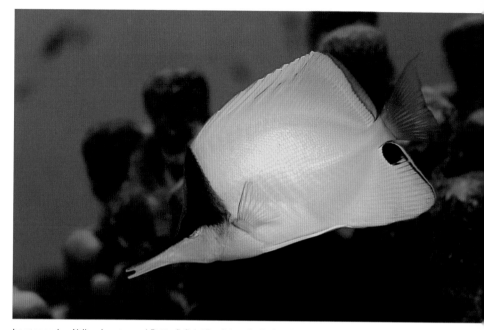

Long-nosed or Yellow Long-nosed Butterflyfish (*Forcipiger flavissimus*): elegant and fragile in appearance, this is actually one of the easiest butterflyfishes to keep and is readily available at moderate prices.

and can recount more than one tearful aquarium gulp-loss. Territoriality between long-noses can be a problem, and these fishes are best kept one to a system. One suggestion: If you are planning to have a long-nose in a new system, put it in as one of the first fishes, perhaps right after the damsels. They need to feel at home so as to get their share of offered foods.

Despite their looks, these fishes accept all types of foods—frozen, fresh, and prepared—with gusto. You'd think that their long "beaks" and tiny teeth would be only suited for snipping out invertebrates from tiny crevices, but these fishes will try almost any size and shape of foods offered.

Please do include some meaty foods daily: bloodworms, shrimps, or clams.

These fishes are active, seeking food all day on the reef and in aquariums, and do well only when offered sufficient nutrition. Be wary of relying solely on one type of dry or frozen prepared food type, and do defrost frozen items.

These fishes tend to be disease-resistant, but are more susceptible than average to marine "ich" (*Cryptocaryon*). This is easily cured with copper remedies and specific gravity manipulation (see Chapter 9).

There is a reason why these butterflies are extremely popular: They're gorgeous and they live in captivity. But don't let their frilly looks throw you. Learn what a good specimen looks like and you will be successful. If ever there were two "first-timer's" butterflyfishes, these would be the ones.

Hawaiian Butterflyfishes: Conscientious Choices

More than a few observers blame much butterflyfish mortality on poor collection, handling, and shipping practices in the Philippines and Indonesia. Fortunately, of the "good" butterflies (see my list on page 230), we are blessed with having some of the best available collected in Hawaii, where the laws and ethics favor sustainable harvesting. When we buy Hawaiian species, we can be reasonably certain that neither the reef nor the natural populations of the collected fishes are being diminished.

About a third of all the native animals and plants in Hawaii are endemic; that is, they're found only there. Hawaii has the world's highest percentage of unique flora and fauna. Of the 20 or so butterflyfishes from Hawaii, three are endemic—the Bluestripe, Lemon, and Multi-banded.

Raccoon Butterflyfish (*Chaetodon lunula*): A robust species that can reach 8 inches in length, it ranges widely in the Indo-Pacific, but the author recommends specimens from the Hawaiian Islands.

The Best from Hawaii

Wonderful aquarium species from Hawaiian waters.

***Chaetodon auriga,* Threadfin Butterflyfish.** Blessed with a robust appetite, this is a reliably hardy species; adults grow a trailing filament from the posterior dorsal fin.

***C. ephippium,* Saddled Butterflyfish.** One of the largest butterflyfishes, reaching 12 inches in length.

***C. lunula,* Raccoon Butterflyfish.** Well named for its nighttime feeding activity. Like its terrestrial mammalian namesake, in nature it is most active at night.

***C. miliaris,* Lemon or Millet-seed Butterflyfish.** Light yellow overall with pinhead black spots over the entire body.

***C. tinkeri,* Tinker's Butterflyfish.** An expensive but hardy beauty from deep waters.

***C. unimaculatus,* Teardrop Butterflyfish.** An ideal aquarium fish. Accepts all types of food readily, adapts well, and is moderate in cost.

***Forcipiger longirostris,* Big Long-nosed Butterflyfish, and *F. flavissimus,* Long-nosed Butterflyfish.**

These species look dainty but they are not. Be sure to check them for damage to their elongated snouts.

***Heniochus diphreutes,* Schooling Bannerfish.** Also called the "Poor Man's Moorish Idol," this is a hardy and sure winner that is peaceful and can be kept in schools.

Questionable Choices

Though better than most Western Pacific butterflyfishes, the following are my less-favored Hawaiian choices.

***Chaetodon citrinellus*, the Citron Butterflyfish or Lemon-colored Butterflyfish.** Similar in appearance to the "true" Lemon Butterflyfish (*C. miliaris*), but not as hardy.

***C. multicinctus*, Pebbled or Multi-banded Butterflyfish.** Some other writers give the Pebbled high marks in terms of beauty and hardiness. I cannot.

***C. kleini*, Klein's Butterflyfish.** (*C. corallicola*, the Coral Butterflyfish, was at one time considered a separate species but is now a junior synonym of *C. kleini*.) This species lives very well for Hawaiian hobbyists, but often seems to suffer from the trials of being shipped elsewhere. Good specimens are reported to be extremely hardy.

***Hemitaurichthys polylepis* (often sold as *H. zoster*) and *H. thompsoni*, Pyramid and Thompson's Butterflyfishes.** Unusual-looking, these can make good specimens with better-than-average handling, acclimation, and care.

Lemon or Millet-seed Butterflyfish (*Chaetodon miliaris*): not overly flashy, but a wonderfully hardy Hawaiian choice and a good beginner's butterflyfish.

Hawaiian Butterflyfishes To Avoid

Historically, these species from Hawaii do poorly, with the vast majority rarely living more than a month.

***Chaetodon fremblii*, Bluestripe Butterflyfish.** A lovely relic species; light yellow with blue lateral bands.

***C. lineolatus*, Lined Butterflyfish,** a deep-water form in Hawaii.

***C. ornatissimus*, Ornate Butterflyfish.** A strict coral eater that is gorgeous. Best to visit it in its habitat. Almost always starves to death within weeks in captivity.

***C. lunulatus*, the Pacific Red-fin or Oval Butterflyfish and *C. trifascialis*, the Chevron or V-lined Butterflyfish.** Impossible aquarium species, most refusing all food in captivity.

It just makes better dollars and sense for wholesalers, retailers, hobbyists, and aquarium service companies to buy from U.S.-controlled areas if the livestock they want can be obtained there. Here is the perfect opportunity to cast your votes for sustainable fish-collection practices: Buy Hawaiian.

Saddled Butterflyfish (*Chaetodon ephippium*): a strikingly beautiful species that has a greedy appetite and can fare extremely well in captivity.

The Threadfin Butterflyfish
Chaetodon auriga

HERE IS AN ELEGANT BUTTERFLY that epitomizes what's best in captive specimens, being readily available, elegantly beautiful, and the easiest of marine fishes to keep. They will feed on the widest variety of prepared and fresh foodstuffs, and are near the top of the butterflyfish list in disease resistance.

Chaetodon auriga is found widely throughout the tropical Indo-Pacific, eastward to my favorite source, Hawaii, westward to the Indian Ocean including the Red Sea. Specimens from the last are especially gorgeous and hardy. Collection and shipment from the Red Sea has become reasonable in terms of available specimens and lowered cost.

In color and pattern, Threadfins bear perpendicular bands of black lines on bright white bodies with or without a black spot on the dorsal fin. A dark eye-band obscures that sensitive area from attack and the upper rear portion of the fish is painted a golden yellow. This species' common name stems from the appearance of a long pennant-type extension of the fifth and sixth filament of the soft dorsal; this "thread" grows with increasing fish size.

In the wild, Threadfins may tip 9 inches total length, but they rarely reach such magnificent proportions in captivity. The Threadfin is quite variable in coloration and body shape over its wide range, and a number of "accidental" hybrids have been reported.

Threadfin Butterflyfish (*Chaetodon auriga*): a classic butterfly beauty that is easily fed and often long-lived.

These butterflies are most often seen in pairs or singly, only occasionally in small groups. However, unless you purchase a pair or capture them together yourself, they are best kept one to a tank. Note that other butterflyfish family members may fight if closely matched in size or shape—or if the system is overcrowded. I suggest keeping an inch or so difference in your new chaetodonts and introducing the smaller first, allowing a few weeks' gap between additions of new specimens.

Due to their spininess, these butterflies are generally left alone, except by the usual aggressive bullies, which sometimes key on the trailing dorsal filament. Reciprocally, Threadfins generally abide by a "live and let live" philosophy, with the exception of edible invertebrates; these fish are definitely not for reef setups. Stomach-content analyses of wild Threadfins reveal a mix of invertebrates (worms, snails, crustaceans), algae, and coral polyps. In captivity, they are nonfinicky eaters of freeze-dried, fresh, and frozen meaty foods (plankton, shrimp, shellfish, bits of fish fillet). Live brine shrimp or tubifex worms will encourage feeding in new specimens, and there is nothing like a freshly opened clam to "bulk up" a thin individual. As with other all-day browsing species, this butterfly is best fed small amounts at least twice daily.

In sum, the Threadfin is definitely one of the best of this family; it gets my vote as a great beginner's marine fish—for being a ready feeder on all types of foods; for easily adapting to aquarium conditions; for disease-resistance; and, of course, for sheer beauty.

244

Angelfishes

Family Pomacanthidae

The Centerpiece Species for Many Marine Aquariums

D O YOU THINK fishes are intelligent? To be sure, many species seem to be programmed as single-minded survival machines: eating, breathing, and reproducing predictably. Still, some fishes that are obviously capable of learning and remembering—fishes that seem exceptionally bright, curious about their surroundings, and aware of the hand that feeds them. The highest order of fishes—Tetraodontiformes—including the triggerfishes, filefishes, and puffer groups, is very smart indeed, using visual and auditory communication and possessing a rich repertoire of social behaviors.

The case for piscine intelligence could be made for the marine angelfishes as well. An angel will almost always become the "boss" of a captive system, establishing graceful control of the domain and recognizing its aquarist master (feeder). As an added bonus to fishkeepers, many angelfishes are strikingly beautiful.

Classification. The Family Pomacanthidae is large—9 genera with 74 species—and growing. These fishes all bear a stout spine on the gill cover that is a distinguishing feature and that is liable to get tangled in nets and poke both you and other livestock. This is an easy-to-spot anatomical marker that allows us to differentiate between them and the closely related butterflyfishes.

Range. The angelfishes are circum-tropical; prominent species are found in shallows to more than 400 feet on rocky and coral reefs worldwide. Most are found in the Western Pacific, with only nine species in the Atlantic and four in the Eastern Pacific.

Size. The angelfishes range in size from a few inches to a couple of feet. I have seen piles of fabulous 18-inch-long *Pomacanthus* angels on docks in Singapore and Thailand, on their way to someone's dinner table.

Selection. Aquarists who purchase large, showy angels are all too often devastated when the fishes fail to survive. Buying younger specimens and watching them grow is smarter—and much more satisfying in the long run. In general, for small species look for one that is 2 to 3 inches in length; for larger angels 3 to 5 inches is a good size. Tiny individuals tend to be too beaten up in the processes of collection and transport and specimens that are too big adapt poorly, refusing food and displaying unwanted behaviors.

Look for reddening—bloody color around the mouth, fins, or body flanks is definitely a bad sign and a warning not to purchase the specimen. The scales should be flat, smooth, and clean and the eyes should be clear.

Coral Beauty (*Centropyge bispinosus*): a dwarf species that sometimes suffers from shipping but will often settle down to be hardy and easy to keep, especially in well-established systems with abundant foraging.

Bicolor Angelfish (*Centropyge bicolor*): a notoriously short-lived Indo-Pacific dwarf angel that fails to adapt or wastes away in most aquariums.

Cherub or Pygmy Angelfish (*Centropyge argi*): a tiny but appealing Caribbean choice that may display courtship and spawning behavior in the aquarium.

Check the specimen for emotional problems and the possibility of poisoning. Look at the prospective purchase. Is it looking back at you? It should be. Psychologically damaged or "drugged" (poisoned is a more accurate term) specimens may look perfect in color and conformation, but they are generally lethargic. You can often even touch them without their moving. Don't even think about buying such a fish. Healthy angels are vigorous, aware animals that require skilled two-net capturing techniques. The chances of nursing a cyanide victim back to health are virtually nil.

Is the specimen eating? Ask to see it feed—more than once if it is a major investment. Poisoned fishes generally

Queen Angelfish (*Holacanthus ciliaris*): an intelligent, majestic species suitable for the larger aquarium. As with all full-size angels, it is best acquired as a healthy juvenile or young adult.

will not eat; if they do, they almost invariably expire within days thereafter.

Habitat. Because they are socially aggressive and interactive with their tankmates, the full-sized angels demand as large a system as possible with as much cover and decor as practical. Be aware that angels will be extremely aggressive toward other livestock if they are too cramped or not provided with plenty of cover.

Angelfishes, especially the larger species, should only be put into a seasoned, previously stocked system. The reasons for this are twofold. One, they prefer those water conditions, and two, it precludes the angel from developing a "this whole tank is mine" attitude.

A constant temperature in the mid 70s to low 80s is acceptable for angelfish species. Nitrates aren't critical, but pH is a good indication of overall water quality; 8.0 to 8.4 is ideal.

Make the filtration vigorous and

heavy on skimming and with good circulation. Systems with angels benefit in many ways by having high flow rates—angelfish seem to relish playing in the flow and bubbles, thereby cutting back on a lot of other "anomalous misbehavior" they could get into (like chasing and bothering other livestock). Also, these fishes are active and need the oxygen and sped-up filtration.

Behavior. In the wild, angels are either found individually or in pairs and very rarely in continuous close group associations (except during spawning times for some species). Such behavior is likely a manifestation of resource partitioning. Most species will fight with members of their own species, likely with others of the same genus, and quite possibly with other fishes similar in appearance and about the same size. The only safe approach to mixing angelfish species is to provide plenty of space and cover and to observe them

Potter's Angelfish (*Centropyge potteri*): a Hawaiian endemic species, best left to advanced fishkeepers.

carefully. In general, it is best to have only one member of an angelfish genus per system. (Ideally, it is best to have only one angel—period.) Most disputes with nonangel species are nominal, as long as the angel(s) are left at the top of the hierarchy.

Introduction is a critical moment in the life of your angel. Usually you can tell right away whether a specimen will fit into its new surroundings or whether you'll have to net it back out to stop one fish from killing another. Lightly feed the tank and turn the lighting down. Ideally, especially if you anticipate a problem, carefully place the new specimen (once it has been dipped or quarantined) floating in a transparent container into the system. This allows the angel and existing occupants to get a look at each other without being able to do anything else. Add an airstone, if necessary, and allow the individual to

visually acclimate for 30 minutes or longer. Only then should you release it, and then be prepared to spend a good hour watching the angel.

Large predators—like sharks, sea lions, and humans—eat adult-sized angels in the wild. Juveniles are relished by everything that can fit them into their mouths; do not place a small angelfish in a tank with a large lionfish, grouper, or moray eel.

Reproduction. Angels have separate sexes, though some (*Centropyge, Genicanthus*) are protogynous synchronous hermaphrodites (start as undifferentiated, then all develop into females, and later some become males). Spawning, either in pairs or in "harems," is environmentally cued by light, temperature, and other organism activities. Gametes released into the water column result in some planktonic larvae, developing and settling at the whim of currents.

Some species have been tank-bred utilizing hormonal manipulation. Young angelfish have been successfully tank-reared for *Pomacanthus*, *Centropyge*, and *Genicanthus* species.

The smaller hermaphroditic species display varying degrees of sexual difference in color and structure. Males are typically slightly larger and more colorful with longer, more trailing unpaired fins.

Feeding. Nutrition and feeding techniques are the keys to keeping angels successfully. Many are largely coral, sponge, and/or algal grazers that will fare poorly unless these foods or their substitutes are provided. Feeding strikes with these animals should not be ignored for even short periods of time. An open fresh or live clam, mussel, or shrimp may tempt your angel back from the threshold of starvation.

Angels should be fed a minimum of once daily, preferably twice. I prefer to offer meaty foods (chopped shrimp, crab, clam, squid, or other marine protein) in the morning so I can remove any leftovers at the end of the day; the afternoon meal is a vegetable-based prepared mix.

One nutritional disease—Vitamin A blindness—is problematic in angels that do not receive enough green material in their diets. Some writers suggest that at least 50% of the angel diet should be comprised of greenery. The feeding of natural algae, herbivore rations, spinach, and homemade preparations is encouraged.

Disease. Angelfishes are frequently

imported with gill and body parasites; particularly flukes, dinoflagellates, and protozoans. If the angelfish have been properly cared for before you receive them, there is little you have to do other than the standard prophylaxis (quarantine and dipping) to prevent the spread or intensification of any infection.

If you find that your angel is breathing hard, unable to close its gill covers, I would immediately check water chemistry and adjust that first. If the system water is fine, move the individual to a treatment tank for copper and possibly antibiotic treatment.

Angelfish are more susceptible to head and lateral line erosion (HLLE) than most fishes. Good water quality and adequate feeding with vitamin C-enriched foods tend to keep this in check. Another malady of angels is the viral disease *Lymphocystis*—clumps of lumpy white or gray matter at the base of fins. This is best ignored as it is usu-ally self-curing. Some writers endorse the use of biological cleaners and/or physical removal of the clumps. I would wait a month or two before attempting radical treatment and possibly doing damage.

Summary. If you read other accounts—and you should—rating the marine angel species for their aquarium suitability, you'll quickly find there are plenty of opinions. Be aware that I have had to make generalizations about animals that are profoundly individualistic. You may get a specimen from an "impossible" species to eat out of your hand; or one from a hardy variety might succumb from no apparent cause on the way home from the shop.

Bear in mind, however, that many articles and books in this field are authored and edited by those who have limited exposure to the real world of home-scale aquarium keeping. Many of them have large, complicated facili-ties that are beyond the budgets, or even the dreams, of most hobbyists. Some writers are successful collectors and intermediary dealers who don't know much about maintaining an end-user system or holding livestock for more than a week. Other writers can be hobbyists, divers, and retail workers who think that they've seen it all after having a brush with a few specimens.

Their opinions, as well as my own, should be taken with a bag of salt—not a grain. Before plunking down your hard-earned cash, try to investigate through reading and talking with people who have years of firsthand experience.

There is no other family of fishes with as much intelligence, beauty and character as the marine angels. By choosing a healthy specimen of the right species and feeding it properly, you will have a centerpiece individual for years to come.

Yellow-faced Angel (*Pomacanthus* [*Euxiphipops*] *xanthometopon*): like the adjoining species, a lovely but problematic and not-for-beginners fish.

Blue-girdled Angelfish (*Pomacanthus* [*Euxiphipops*] *navarchus*): another species that historically fails to acclimate and thrive, even for many expert aquarists.

Gray Angelfish (*Pomacanthus arcuatus*): a potentially large, hardy species closely related to the French Angel (*P. paru*) but somewhat less colorful.

Three-spot Angelfish (*Apolemichthys trimaculatus*): not a common offering in the aquarium trade, but a desirable, smaller species for reef-type systems.

The Principal Aquarium Species of Angelfishes

Genus *Centropyge*: These are the smaller species, often labeled as "dwarf" or "pygmy" angels in reference to the 2 to 4-inch maximum size for most species. They offer the aquarist some wonderful choices in terms of color, behavior, and ease of care, with several notable exceptions.

Nearly all of the 33 or more species of this genus hail from the Indo-Pacific, with *C. argi* and *C. aurantonotus* found in the Caribbean, and *C. resplendens* around Ascension Island.

The *Centropyge* angels are generally peaceful, typically only "mock fighting" to demonstrate that they are in control of a situation. Following is my version of the best, mediocre, and to-be-avoided members in this genus that are typically available.

Best *Centropyge* for aquariums: The Flame Angel (*C. loriculus*) is a fabulous beauty, and a winning species for captivity (see page 252). *C. argi*, the Cherub Angel, is tiny (up to 3 inches) and shy, but it does do well in captivity. The same can be said for the similar African Pygmy (*C. acanthops*) and Fisher's Angel (*C. fisheri*).

Mediocre *Centropyge* choices: Be cautious about purchasing *C. bispinosus* (the Coral Beauty) and *C. aurantonotus* (the Dusky Angelfish or Caribbean Flameback). Most imported batches of these species don't make it in captivity for long, but every now and then, you'll get a group or individual that is super-tough. I would put the (true) Lemon Peel, *C. flavissimus* and Golden Dwarf, *C. heraldi*, in this same category. The Keyhole Angel, *C. tibicen*, is one of my personal favorites, but it does not typically do well for aquarists. This is more of a failing of the latter than of the fish

itself. This small black angelfish is so shy it gets bullied and succumbs to the effects of starvation. *C. vroliki*, the Pearl-scaled Angel, and *C. eibli*, Eibl's Angel, are available in the trade off and on. These are a lot like certain models of automobiles, some people swear *by* them, others swear *at* them.

***Centropyge* species to avoid:** *C. bicolor* (the Bicolor, Blue and Gold, or Oriole Angelfish) used to be "good as gold" in the 1960s, coming out of the Philippines. This is definitely no longer the case; most specimens die on arrival, with the remainder rarely lasting a month. It's not much easier to keep those coming from other countries. *C. potteri* (Potter's Angel, also called the Russet Dwarf) is an endemic Hawaiian. I am generally very pro-Hawaiian, but this species doesn't adapt well to being caught and kept in the average aquarium. In my experience, many don't live beyond a few weeks. I would

250

only attempt keeping a Potter's Angel in a very large, well-conditioned reef system with a profusion of live rock and populations of amphipods, worms, and other edibles that the fish will hunt with delight. (This is generally the case with all of the *Centropyge* species; they do well in thriving reef aquariums well-stocked with live rock where they can forage continuously. New, sterile, or barren tanks are not to their liking.)

Genus *Chaetodontoplus*: These angels are so gaudily colored and marked, they look hand-painted. Though bizarre-appearing, this genus has many good species for aquarists with large systems. My favorites are *C. duboulayi* (the Scribbled Angelfish), *C. melanosoma* (the Brown Angelfish), and *C. meridithi* (the Queensland Yellowtail). The latter is sometimes wrongly identified as *C. personifer* (the Yellowtail), which is from northwest Australia and virtually unavailable in the trade.

C. mesoleucus, the Vermiculated Angel, looks a lot like a butterflyfish and has a reputation for perishing rapidly in captivity.

Genus *Genicanthus*: Here is a genus of pomacanthids notable in the contrasting color and body shapes of males and females. Most of the 10 *Genicanthus* species grow to maximum lengths of 5 to 14 inches.

These fishes are sex-reversers, being females that turn into males. Most often they are offered only as males.

G. lamarck (Lamarck's Angel) and *G. melanospilos* (the Blackspot Angel) are wonderful aquarium species.

Genus *Holacanthus*: This is an uneven genus, with some definite problem species and others that are among the most eminently suitable of angels for aquariums. On the one hand you have the obligate sponge-eating Atlantic Rock Beauty, *H. tricolor*, which does poorly in captivity. I also place the gorgeous Venustus Angel, *H. venustus*, on the sad end of the survivability scale with the Rock Beauty.

On the other hand, there's the magnificent Clarion Angel, *H. clarionensis* that you have to beat with a stick to kill. Other good, fairly rugged choices include the Queen Angel (*H. ciliaris*), the Blue Angel (*H. bermudensis*), the Passer or King Angel (*H. passer*)—showstoppers all in their adult coloration.

Genus *Pomacanthus*: The largest, showiest angels are in this and the subgenus *Euxiphipops* (see below). Unlike the latter group, *Pomacanthus* species have little going against their members other than attaining grand physical proportions.

Pomacanthus are notable for having striking color transformations going from juvenile to subadult to adult size. Haremic spawning is suspected, although pairs are seen in some areas.

P. semicirculatus, the Koran, is the quintessential starter angelfish. The French Angel, *P. paru*, is a close second. Other good choices include the Gray, *P. arcuatus*; the Cortez, *P. zonipectus*; and the Blue-ringed Angel, *P. annularis*. Should your rich uncle die and leave you a bundle, two exemplary Red Sea candidates are the Half Moon, *P. mac-*ulosus and the Asfur Angel, *P. asfur*.

The "bad apples" of the genus include *P. chrysurus*, the Ear-spot Angel, and the seldom-seen *P. striatus*, the Old Woman Angel. I've seen many die "mysteriously" within the first month. Other sources regard *P. chrysurus* as relatively hardy and I do know of a few specimens that have lived for years.

A large part of the mystery is the well-known fact that the diet of adult *Pomacanthus* fishes consists principally of sponges. This is another reason to get a small individual and train it to accept nutritious aquarium fare before it learns to love only sponges.

Subgenus *Euxiphipops*: Here, sadly, is the heartbreak group (once a genus, now a subgenus) of the angelfish family. Of the Six-barred Angel (*Pomacanthus* [*Euxiphipops*] *sexstriatus*), or Yellow-faced (*P.* [*E.*] *xanthometopon*), and Blue-girdled (*P.* [*E.*] *navarchus*), only the last has historically had more than a small success rate in aquariums. The reasons aren't entirely clear. Poor adjustment to captive conditions, inability to recover from rough collection practices, and specialized diets are all possible causes.

If you insist on throwing your money away by trying this subgenus, I strongly suggest demanding that the specimen be fed in your presence. Put down a deposit on the animal and leave it for two weeks with the dealer to see if it will survive. They are expensive, generally don't adapt at all, and usually refuse all foods.

Even experienced aquarists are very

wary of this group, which all too often proves to be a costly purchase, both in terms of money lost and the anguish of seeing a lovely fish die for no readily understandable reason.

Genus *Pygoplites*: With only one species, the Regal Angel, *P. diacanthus*, and that one rarely living out a full life in the hands of an aquarist, why even mention it? In part because it is so often offered in the trade, in part because this fish is so gorgeous it may sorely tempt you, but mainly so you will know why to avoid it (see page 256).

Genus *Apolemichthys* and *Desmoholacanthus*: I have mixed reports about these genera, but their species are only rarely offered in the trade. Two of the best are *Apolemichthys xanthurus*, the Indian Yellowtail, and *A. xanthopunctatus*, the Gold-flake Angel. The last is striking, but somewhat pricey.

The Hawaiian Bandit or Black-banded Angel, *Desmoholacanthus arcuatus* (formerly classified in the genus *Holocanthus*, then in the genus *Apolemichthys*) is an obligate sponge eater. Although attractive and sometimes collected, it usually starves to death in the aquarium. Whatever it's called, I would avoid it.

Flame Angelfish
Centropyge loriculus

THE FLAME ANGEL, one of the dwarf angelfishes, is a truly eye-catching aquarium species and one that seems to appeal to all manner of knowledge-able aquarists and casual observers. Happily, it is one of the hardiest species among the 33 in the genus *Centropyge*. The Flame Angel is readily available, adapts well to aquarium life, and has actually become reasonably inexpensive in the last few years.

The Flame Angel is found in scattered reef areas in the tropical Central to Western Pacific, including Hawaii, the Society Islands, Australia, New Guinea, and Guam. It reaches a maximum of 4 inches in length.

Some species of *Centropyge* are incredibly hardy as a rule, others are not so, and in the Flame we have a species with a high degree of variability in terms of aquarium suitability and toughness. Hardiness is positively correlated with capture, holding, and transport technique and practices—all factors that are more or less associated with country and source of origin. I would decide on the purchase of a Flame Angel specimen according to the following criteria (in this order):

1) Physical appearance: under stress, these angel species are highly susceptible to *Brooklynella* and *Amyloodinium* infections. Torn fins, bulbous eyes, and genetic deformities should rule out an individual as well.

2) Behavior: I strongly urge you to observe carefully before buying. Healthy animals are alert and aware of their environment—which includes you. Avoid individuals that show pale coloration, erratic swimming, rapid, shallow breathing, or clamped fins. You should not be able to "reach out and touch one" without it seeking shelter.

3) Origin: the Flame Angel is collected and imported from several areas. Hawaii has a limited population in deep water, yielding beautiful but relatively expensive specimens. Exporters seem to deliver a mixed lot, with some shipments being exemplary and others terrible. The best, most consistent orders I've seen have hailed from collectors in the Christmas and Marshall Islands. There are many new people in the collection world, some more conscientious than others. Ask your dealer, who should know the source, and keep your eyes open.

This species is often touted as desirable for being able to be crammed into small quarters (30 gallons and less). I advise against this. Individuals vary tremendously in their tolerance of tankmates. Close observation and quick reaction to overt aggressive behavior is the rule, even in very large aquariums.

Chasing and nipping—especially other dwarf angels—particularly of the same size and/or species, is to be expected. Don't allow your specimens to be torn and cowed. Provide lots of caves, hiding places, and escape sites. If you have more than one individual or dwarf angel species, separate the physical sites into at least two independent reef areas.

Territoriality problems with introducing a new Flame or placing new Flame specimens into established tanks can be extensive and severe; the initial minutes to hours of introduction are

Flame Angelfish (*Centropyge loriculus*): show-stoppingly colorful and an excellent choice among the smaller angels. As with all of the angelfishes, it should never be introduced into a newly set up aquarium.

and social stimuli develop into males with one or more females in the territorial harem. Males are typically larger and more colorful.

They spawn in pairs at dusk in the wild. Actual spawning behavior has sometimes been described and illustrated as a short "dance." In the dwarf angel species *C. tibicen*, the male rises first and then the female, and gametes are shed into the environment where they float off to develop or disappear into oblivion.

This is a species many hobbyists would love to have reproduce, and the Flame has been bred in captivity with some young being raised to small size. For the majority of keepers who are not interested in breeding challenges, the Flame Angel is fine as a solitary specimen.

Dwarf angels, unlike their larger brethren, are not as dependent on sponge materials for nutrition. Algae are very important, comprising upwards of half their total intake by volume. If you don't provide algae by growing it in situ, offering dry, prepared, frozen, and fresh green foods has proved efficacious. As your pocketbook and skills permit, you should consider some purchased or cultured live rock which allows self-feeding on demand with low risk of pollution. If your dwarf angels lose color, weight, or apparent interest in feeding, buy or grow them a piece of algae-covered rock or move them to a reef tank for temporary rehabilitation. Rinsed spinach is acceptable if that is all that is available, but

critical. The same tricks apply as those used for generic territoriality: move decor about to disorient the resident organisms, feed small amounts of foods frequently, and dim the aquarium lights for a day.

Dwarf angels are known prey items for many larger reef fishes, hence their inquisitive, alert, darting, secretive behavior. Be wary of placing them with large predacious species like big triggers, groupers, lionfishes, and the like.

By the same token, timid species and eminently chewable ones (like anemones, feather dusters) should not be placed with them as they will become fodder for chase and taste. Flame and other dwarf angels are best introduced into communities last or close to it. Debates still rage among reef tank aquarists about the advisability of adding them to collections of delicate invertebrates. Some individuals will definitely nibble at coral polyps and *Tridacna* clam mantles to the extent that these specimens will stay retracted and eventually wither away.

This species, and most other dwarf angels investigated, are synchronous protogynous hermaphrodites. They start out sexually undifferentiated, develop into females, and under growth greens should be offered every day.

Rarely does a healthy specimen refuse food. Make sure there is not a titanic struggle going on between tankmates. An opened fresh or frozen shellfish placed near the fish's home turf sometimes does wonders.

Health problems with this species are almost always imported, with specimens often having at least the beginnings of a protozoan infestation. Irrespective of what prevention and treatment regimen has been exercised before, you should at least run your new arrivals through a prophylactic dip (see page 151) for a good 10 minutes to knock off, or at least down, *Brooklynella* and other protozoans.

The Flame Angel is one of the hardiest, most beautiful, and longest-lived of dwarf angels—indeed of captive marine species. Coupled with its small size, reduced cost because of in-creased collection activity, and ease of solitary captivity, the Flame is an excellent prospective aquarium species.

The Cortez, Passer, and Clarion Angelfishes
Pomacanthus zonipectus,
Holacanthus passer,
and *H. clarionensis*

I CALL THESE THE THREE AMIGOS from Baja, a trio of striking angelfishes—two of moderate cost, one very expensive—that hail from the Sea of Cortez and further south. These compadre species are spunky, extroverted, and hardy, easily becoming the center of attention in larger aquariums. One of them, the Clarion Angel, is perhaps the hardiest, most undemanding species of all available marine angelfishes. Their habitats, behavior, and nutrition are similar enough to allow us to discuss all three together; all are relatively uncommon in the everyday fish trade.

The angelfishes and closely related butterflyfishes are not as well represented on the west or Pacific side of Mexico, with just these 3 species, while there are 6 species from the Gulf of Mexico to the Bahamas on the east or Atlantic side.

However, if we look at the juvenile forms of the angels found on either side of Mexico and Central America, it becomes clear that these species have ancient ties to each other. The explanation for the uncanny similarities can be traced back to a warm time one million years ago when the isthmus that is Central America was below sea level. With the reaccumulation of water as ice at the poles, the Atlantic and Pacific Oceans lost a connection. Today, these

Cortez Angelfish (*Pomacanthus zonipectus*): a large adult, obviously unsuited to a small aquarium but otherwise a hardy, extroverted, and long-lived fish.

Passer or King Angelfish (*Holacanthus passer*): an uncommon and prized species from the west coast of tropical and subtropical America.

Juvenile Clarion Angelfish (*Holacanthus clarionensis*): note the similarity of this young specimen to that of the Blue and Queen Angels, its counterparts.

Subadult Clarion Angelfish: a significant transition occurs as the juveniles assume their distinctive adult coloration—glowing orange and electric blue.

semi-matching East-West lookalikes are termed sibling species.

The three interesting species from the Pacific side of the land mass are:

1) The Cortez Angelfish, *Pomacanthus zonipectus*: compare it with the sympatric Caribbean species, the French Angel, *P. paru*, and Gray Angel, *P. arcuatus*. The Cortez undergoes a striking color transformation going from juvenile to adult: the young have alternating yellow and iridescent blue curved bars; in the adult this is replaced with a brownish gray background with broad yellow and black bars.

2) The Passer Angelfish, *Holacanthus passer* (also called the King Angelfish): the young have a series of alternating light and bright blue bars with a broad band of orange-red behind the eyes. Compare this species with the juveniles of the Queen Angelfish, *H. ciliaris*, and Blue Angelfish, *H. bermudensis*, of the Caribbean.

3) The Clarion Angelfish, *Holacanthus clarionensis*: as juveniles, they are almost identical to Passers in color and markings, with one notable exception. The head of the Passer Angelfish is yellow and the head and tail of the Clarion is bright orange. Adult Clarions live up to their name—they are brilliant to glowing orange trimmed with bright blue. Their brassy coloration comes with matching behavior—bold and behaviorally comical.

The Passer and Cortez Angelfishes are found in the Sea of Cortez—from the Upper Gulf of Baja on down the coast of the tropical Eastern Pacific. (The Sea of Cortez is the southerly extension of the San Andreas Fault.) The Clarion Angel is more restricted—and hence very expensive when it makes its way into the aquarium trade—observed occasionally near the southern apex of Baja and off Clipperton Island (west of Costa Rica), but most often collected

from the Islas Revillagigedos, approximately 250 miles southwest of Baja.

Most individuals offered are in an appropriate range of 2 to 6 inches, and all three of these angels achieve about 12 inches in total length. They need room to grow—a minimum tank size of 60 gallons to start and 150 gallons and up for full adults.

These are rocky shore reef fishes, so provide as many nooks and crannies as possible. All your specimens will be happier and healthier. The larger the system the better; I've kept tiny to medium-sized species in smallish aquariums, but the larger systems are much easier to keep stable and maintain. A good rule of thumb is 20 gallons per 1 inch of angel.

The alkaline reserve and pH of the system is a good indicator of overall water quality. Keep the latter above 8.0 by frequent, partial water changes and you will not go wrong. Temperature and specific gravity are not critical issues with the amigo angels; these are variable and range widely in their wild environs. These fishes are large, active, messy eaters and defecators. More water motion than less is advised, with suitable filtration and skimming.

Like most of their family, these fishes are grazers and pickers. In the wild they consume small organisms; sponges make up the largest part of their diet, with worms, sea squirts, corals, and coral relatives making up the bulk of the rest.

Smaller individuals eat a considerable amount of algae and are known to be facultative ("take it or leave it") cleaners, removing parasites and necrotic tissue from other fish species.

Most individuals of these three angel species can be successfully trained to feed on easy-to-procure foods. Frozen pet-fish mixes; fresh aquarium and "human"-grade seafoods such as shrimps, clams, mussels, or squid; vegetable material from the Oriental food section of the supermarket; and frozen peas (without additives) can all be used. Having growing material in the system itself is ideal, but these angels will munch most everything in a reef setup. Some writers suggest less-frequent feeding intervals, but I'd offer food twice a day for all sizes of angels.

With the North American Free Trade Agreement in place, and with the desire of the Mexicans to develop their natural resources in a conscientious, sustainable way, these three angels may someday become much better known and available to fish-loving gringos. (At the time of this writing, collection is banned in Mexico, with some specimens coming into the trade from other points in Central America.)

Give these angelfishes serious consideration when you want a hardy character for a large marine setup.

Regal Angelfish
Pygoplites diacanthus

OF THE MANY SPECIES of marine angelfishes offered to the hobby, some groups are sure winners. Most dwarf angels readily accept aquarium conditions, and many of the larger Pacific and Atlantic angels do very well for good aquarists. The Regal Angel, *Pygoplites diacanthus*, is a notable exception.

This is a beautifully colored fish that can't help but draw the attention of aquarists, but it has one of the worst survival records imaginable. Only advanced fishkeepers with large (150 gallon minimum) tanks and a proficiency with the fussier angels should even attempt to keep *P. diacanthus*. With ownership comes the responsibility to provide adequate habitat and daily animal and plant food matter of the highest quality. Even dedicated experts

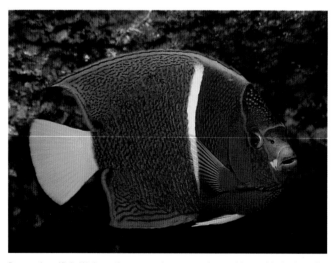

Passer Angelfish (*Holacanthus passer*): compare its markings with the juvenile Blue Angel, right, its counterpart from the eastern side of Central America.

Juvenile Blue Angelfish (*Holacanthus bermudensis*): a Caribbean species similar to the Passer Angel juvenile, left, and young Clarion Angel, page 255.

Regal Angelfish (*Pygoplites diacanthus*): a beautifully patterned and esteemed species that has one of the worst survival records of all marine angels imported.

report very poor luck trying to keep this species eating and alive.

When enough dealers lose money for lack of demand for this angelfish species, perhaps the Regal will be left in the oceans where it belongs. Some very promising marine foods are being developed, so it's possible that the secret to maintaining this, and other delicate species, will eventually be found. Until then, with so many other attractive, hardy marine angels available, the Regal should be avoided. Look at them in a book or on a video or take up diving and view Regal Angels in their natural surroundings. Watching one die in your aquarium is not a pleasant experience. Please don't buy this fish.

Emperor Angelfish
Pomacanthus imperator

CERTAINLY ONE OF THE MOST beautiful marine angelfishes, but with only a mediocre record of longevity, is the Emperor Angelfish, *Pomacanthus imperator*. Still, there is no doubt that it lives up to its majestic name, and it can be successfully kept if the aquarist understands that most losses are due to poor capture technique, transport, acclimation, and lack of nutrition. I consider the species not as easy to maintain as the Koran, *P. semicirculatus*, but certainly hardier than those in the genus *Pygoplites* and subgenus *Euxiphipops*.

As with many pomacanthids, juveniles and adults of this species are very

Adult Emperor Angelfish (*Pomacanthus imperator*): expert care recommended.

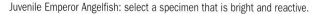
Juvenile Emperor Angelfish: select a specimen that is bright and reactive.

different in appearance. Prior to 1933, young Emperors were considered a separate species, *P. nicobariensis*. There is a wide variation in the range of natural colors and patterns in small to large specimens.

The Emperor is found exclusively associated with coral reefs in the wild, in shallow to 100-foot depths, and is widespread in the Indo-Pacific from East Africa to Hawaii (one specimen collected).

Juveniles bear markings similar to the young of the Koran (*P. semicirculatus*) and several other large related angels, with a series of concentric dark blue, black, and white rings. An individual being considered for purchase should be well colored and marked with no apparent traumas.

The primary selection criterion I would look for is "brightness"—meaning an active interest in its immediate environment. Prospective specimens should be curious and reactive to your presence. They should be aware, following motion and light and searching around anything near them.

For most hobbyists, I strongly encourage choosing individuals between 3 and 6 inches long rather than full adults. These seem best suited for beginning life in captive conditions. Larger Emperors seem to have more difficulty adapting to aquariums and smaller ones don't accept prepared foods very well. There are, of course, exceptions, but this is a good guideline.

Roger Steene, coauthor of a number of highly recommended marine texts with Gerald Allen, offers his opinion that *P. imperator* "is a sturdy aquarium species." Allen and Steene are based in Australia; unfortunately, I have not observed the same hardiness for specimens here in the West. Only individuals that appear full-bodied, alert, and that heartily accept several types of food should be considered. This demonstrated willingness will ensure your specimen receives adequate nutrition.

Be wary of too-colorful, disoriented specimens. Many of these have been collected with cyanide and are doomed see page 165). Similarly, avoid rapid breathers. More than 80 gill movements per minute is too many.

Take care in capturing and transporting members. Their gill cover (opercular) spines are often easily fouled or torn by nets, which leads to subsequent infection. I advise netless lifting, directing the intended specimen into a double or otherwise puncture-insulated bag or, as a last resort, lifting by hand. Be careful! The genus name is partly derived from the Greek word *acanthus*, meaning thorn, for good reason.

Good water quality must be optimized and constant. Use a high quality salt mix, at a 1.022 to 1.025 specific gravity, and maintain pH in the higher range—8.0 to 8.4. A protein skimmer is a must. Angels are sensitive to "new tank syndrome" and should never be the first species put into a new system. Only place them in aquariums that have been seasoned and have housed other species in good health for a few months.

Even in captivity, Emperors prefer the comfort of shelter offered by boulders, caves, and coral niches. They will do well only where offered the possibility of retreat.

Size of the aquarium? The bigger the better. I would not even start an Emperor in a system of less than 70 gallons. Ultimately, you will need one in the 180-to-200-gallon range.

Emperor Angels are among the largest members of their family, able to reach some 15 inches in length. Like most in their genera, they do best kept singly as a species and not with other angel species of a similar size.

Similar to members of the genus *Holacanthus*, Emperors and other pomacanthids are known consumers of a large amount of sponge (Phylum Porifera) material. Second to that, they will eat algae and other animal material. Will you go broke buying live sponges or specialty frozen foods made of the same? No. In captivity they can, and usually will, adapt to prepared frozen, fresh, and dry foods.

I agree with author Hans Baensch's advice regarding this and other angels: try other, easier marines first and learn the value of culturing the algae genus *Caulerpa* or other suitable bioassay species as viable indicators of water quality before making the big investment in an Emperor Angel.

Half Moon Angelfish
Pomacanthus maculosus

WHAT COMES TO MIND when you hear about livestock from the Red Sea? Golden Butterflies (*Chaetodon semilarvatus*)? Giant wrasses? More colorful and hardier versions of some of the same species found in the Indo-Pacific, like some of the lionfishes? Big, bad sharks?

Well, probably all this and more; but invariably we all have one image come to mind: the deep pockets it takes to acquire these specimens. Unfortunately, fishes hailing only from this region have traditionally been very expensive. And what a shame. Many are supremely well-suited for captive containment. With increased collection—and by some excellent outfits—the prices and availability are improving, but are unlikely ever to be considered "cheap."

The Half Moon, Yellow-band, or Maculosus Angel is an exemplary species that has now dropped into the more-affordable range; it is outstanding in many regards, being very disease-resistant, accepting all types of fresh and prepared foods greedily and behaving well with almost all other species.

The Half Moon is a typical member of the marine angelfish family, Pomacanthidae, and it fits the general description and recommendations for the genus *Pomacanthus* in overall morphology, development, size, nutrition, disease control, and water-quality

Half Moon Angelfish (*Pomacanthus maculosus*): an extremely hardy and desirable Red Sea species, also sold as the Yellow-band Angelfish. It is a bold and curious favorite of both divers and marine aquarists.

demands. The species is distributed throughout the Persian Gulf, the northwestern Indian Ocean, and the Red Sea.

It is considered sympatric with the equally desirable Arabian Angelfish (*P. asfur*) to which it is akin in shape and coloration as a subadult as well as a transformed adult (beyond 4 to 6 inches). A salient color difference is the Arabian's bright yellow tail, along with its darker camouflaging around the eyes. Both species are found in overlapping habitats in the Persian Gulf and Red Sea, and are comparably pricey and hardy. *P. maculosus*, however, is my favorite for being more outgoing.

Whatever size is available and that you can afford will probably do very well. I have rarely encountered a specimen that appeared seriously impaired by its travels or not likely to thrive in good conditions. These fish are consistently strong.

Juveniles and subadults bear different markings and colors than the adults. Comparable to younger *Euxiphipops*, *P. annularis*, *P. asfur*, *P. chrysurus*, *P. semicirculatus*, and *P. striatus*, small Half Moons are alternately bluewhite and black-banded.

Other common and scientific names allied with the species are: Blue Moon Angelfish, *Holacanthus coeruleus*, *H. lineatus* and *H. haddaja*.

Ichthyologist Gerald Allen found the species mainly in coral and rocky areas, in shallow to moderate depths (40 feet), consistent with other member-species in the genus. Considering the ultimate size of the specimen is important. Half Moons can reach 12 inches long in captivity and need at least 100 gallons of uncrowded habitat to themselves in order to fare well.

Keep your water clean and constant in its chemistry and physics. A higher density is appreciated, at least close to a specific gravity of 1.025. Be diligent in your frequent partial water changes and skimmer maintenance. If you are going to be spending a lot of money for livestock, do not scrimp on filter gear.

Like other large angels, Half Moons would enjoy a thoroughly stocked reef tank full of delectable invertebrate life. They do and will sample everything: anemones, algae, tubeworms, corals. Not much attacks them once they establish their alpha dominance. They are also very hardy. If there is an infectious, parasitic, nutritional, environmental, or other hobbyist-contrived problem, this fish will be among the last infected.

If you have the disposable income, the space, and the desire for a large, beautiful, hardy marine specimen, there are few choices that can match *P. maculosus*. Save up and invest.

French Angelfish
Pomacanthus paru

THIS BEAUTIFUL disc-shaped black, gray, and gold angel has brilliant yellow bars and blue highlights as a juvenile, fading to an elegant, lustrous gray as an adult. The French Angel is a readily available, inexpensive, and adaptable large marine specimen. It is long-lived, disease-resistant, and, with care, can become hand-tamed.

A testament to the French Angel's hardiness is its widespread use in professionally serviced aquariums, where trouble-free, visually appealing fishes are a must. Providing you allow your French Angel plenty of space, acceptable water quality, and foods with enough green and sponge material, this is a specimen that will stick with you for years.

French Angels hail from both sides of the Atlantic, from Africa to the west, mainly between Florida and the Bahamas to southeastern Brazil. Occasionally, currents carry specimens farther up the eastern seaboard, where they are occasionally snagged by aquarists who can't believe their luck. The species has been spawned in captivity, albeit with hormone treatments, and the young have been successfully raised to selling size.

Like the other Caribbean angelfish species, the French has a very similar sibling species in the Gray Angelfish, *Pomacanthus arcuatus*. French and Gray Angels are easily confused as young, being very similar in appearance and having about the same range of habitat and collection. They can be distinguished on the basis of the shape and color of the margin of their tail fins. In the French, there is a bold yellow edge around the more or less rounded caudal. The Gray's tail is more squared and more translucent, with less color. The adult Gray has a plain uniform gray

French Angelfish (*Pomacanthus paru*): stately, with lustrous trim colors and one of the most reliably hardy of all angels, this Caribbean mainstay species is best kept one to a tank. Note its typical cheek spines.

color, compared with the darker metallic gold fleckings of the French. (Just to confuse things, the Gray Angel is sometimes sold as the Black Angel.)

People who have had both in their systems usually will tell you that French Angels cost a few dollars more than Grays but are worth it in terms of their better color and more interesting behavior.

Juveniles of 3 to 4 inches in total length are best for most aquarists. They are extremely hardy at this size, adaptive behaviorally and easy to train on nonnatural foods. Most specimens offered have been collected by nondamaging means and adapt well to captivity. Disqualifying criteria are labored, rapid breathing—indicative of probable handling damage—and possible gill-parasite infestation. If the individual eats readily and seems interested in its environment, I would easily overlook a torn fin.

French Angels are extremely tolerant of less-than-perfect water conditions. They have even been used to institute nutrient cycling in place of the "indestructible" damsels. Physically, they do well under a broad range of conditions. Temperatures in the low to upper 70s are within their natural range. French Angels are euryhaline, that is, not sensitive to a wide span of salinity.

In terms of habitat, the French Angels offered in North American fish stores are found associated with rocky, broken bottoms and grassy flats from Florida to Brazil, in the Bahamas to the Gulf of Mexico. Provide numerous rock, coral, and other nooks, crannies, and comfort spaces for this angel and its tankmates.

French Angels are best kept one to a tank. If they are to be mixed with angels of other genera, it is best to introduce them as juveniles to as large a system as possible (at least 50 gallons) at the same time. Often, a new, slightly larger individual may be added in an established angel system. Moving some of the habitat around, feeding at the time of introduction, and keeping a sharp eye on the specimen are all requisite. Pay careful attention if mixing angels within this genus, as one will grow more quickly and eventually do harm to its fellows in all but the largest of systems. Occasionally, pairs that have been captured together in the wild are available from large wholesalers and collectors.

Larger to full-sized individuals, up to 16 inches, should only be tried in huge capacity systems, several hundred gallons and up. Over 6 inches or so, specimens have a greater propensity to go on food strikes and develop other poor adaptive activities. If you want a big French, either grow one yourself or purchase a trade-in; large wild-caught angels frequently fare poorly. My recommendation of an appropriate aquarium size for an adult French Angel is a minimum of 150 gallons, but 180 to 240 gallons would be even better.

Small French Angels display a fluttery motion, as if wagging their bodies when they swim. The sibling Gray Angel species does not "wag." Juvenile French Angels are renowned facultative cleaners. They may be used in place of *Labroides* wrasses, cleaner gobies, or shrimp as biological controls of parasites. In the wild, they set up formal cleaning stations. Beyond 3 to 4 inches in length, their cleaning activity drops off rapidly.

Author and marine biologist Martin Moe (1976) has described natural and captive spawning for those with gigantic systems and big dreams.

Feeding is a very critical and frequently weak area in keeping marine angelfishes. French juveniles accept live, frozen, and dry-prepared foods readily. Adults can be kept in good health by feeding cut squid, crustaceans, nutritious frozen foods, and daily helpings of green materials. *Caulerpa* and *Ulva* algae, dried marine algae, and *Spirulina* flakes are best. For optimal health and color, either a prepared sponge-containing food or live rock with sponge growth can be provided. Stomach content analyses of wild French Angels suggest the importance of sponge matter to these and other angels.

P. paru is typically disease-resistant and long-lived, providing you start with a clean specimen and keep it under proper conditions. One common problem is a type of blindness that seems to be a result of dietary deficiency. Again, using a substantial amount of plant material—frozen, fresh, or flake—with vitamin supplements avoids this problem. Check your prepared-food labels for stabilized vitamin C, or add it to the food on a regular basis.

These fish are not easily susceptible to disease; they should be among the last to show evidence of problems. The usual parasitic diseases can be quickly cured with copper medications and/or manipulation of specific gravity.

Along with the Queen, Blue, and Gray, the French Angel is a classy Caribbean species well-suited as an aquarium specimen. It is a good marine angelfish for both the serious beginning hobbyist and the professional looking for a showpiece that is hardy, elegant, and amenable to captivity.

Queen Angelfish
Holacanthus ciliaris

TRULY A MONARCH among the many beautiful marine angelfishes, the Queen Angelfish is especially colorful as a juvenile, growing into one of the most majestic of reef fishes. It is proud, stately, and a classic favorite with aquarists and divers alike. Should you ever have the opportunity to travel in the Caribbean, do take the time to snorkel in the Queen's realm. You'll find it is smart, elegant, and as likable in the wild as it is in the aquarium.

Given a healthy individual of not too small or large a size to start with, conditioned to aquarium foods, this

Juvenile French Angelfish (*Pomacanthus paru*): strikingly colored, the French juvenile closely resembles the juvenile Gray Angel (*P. arcuatus*), which has a broad, clear margin at the rear of its tail fin.

species adapts very well to captivity.

One of the 74 described species in the marine angelfish family, the Queen Angelfish is a sibling species to the Blue Angelfish (*Holacanthus bermudensis*); the juveniles of the two species are difficult to tell apart. The Queen can be distinguished from the Blue by closely observing the lines on the middle of the body. These bars are curved over the entire length of the Queen and they are straight on the Blue, except near the dorsal and anal fins. The Queen Angelfish is "crowned" with a black spot ringed in blue, which *H. bermudensis* lacks.

There is some considerable confusion in the trade and hobby regarding hybrids that occur between Queen and Blue Angels. The so-called Townsend Angelfish (*Holacanthus townsendi*) is a naturally occurring cross between these two; it is not a true species. Though all three make fine aquatic pets, of the trio, I would always choose the Queen.

Size is an important consideration in selection. Very small individuals (less than 2 inches) should be avoided as they usually adapt poorly. Perhaps they're too shaken up by capture to regain their strength. Purchase at least a 3-inch specimen but, unless you have

Queen Angelfish (*Holacanthus ciliaris*): larger specimens are often too wild to tame and acclimate to captive conditions and foods, and marine biologists advise that the collection of juveniles puts much less pressure on reef ecosystems.

the time and money to spend, not one over 6 inches. Larger specimens are often too wild to tame in terms of feeding and behavior, and it is now generally thought that the capture of younger specimens, rather than breeders, is much less of a burden on wild reef ecosystems. The largest specimens require 180-to-500 gallon systems and display best when given room to roam.

Given a choice of specimens, pick the one with full finnage and a body without blemishes, and the one most interested in its environment. Another consideration should be the intensity of coloration. Ask to see your selection eat

Juvenile Queen Angel (*Holacanthus ciliaris*): note curved blue striping pattern

Juvenile Blue Angelfish (*H. bermudensis*): note characteristic vertical stripes.

what you intend to feed. You need not be concerned about whether this species has been cyanided or not; the Queen is collected in Florida and the Caribbean with hand and barrier nets. Occasionally, the drug quinaldine is used, which doesn't seem to reduce vitality for this species.

Queens are found in the Gulf of Mexico to southern Florida and south to Brazil in shallow to about 200-foot depths. The species is found foraging and hiding around rocky reefs—not in open, upper waters or over sandy bottoms. Provide some similar habitat.

Queens are not very sensitive to water quality as saltwater aquarium species go. Some authors cite them as damsel stand-ins for initially breaking in a new system. Temperatures in the low to mid 70s, lower to "normal" specific gravity (1.018 to 1.025), and natural or synthetic saltwater are fine.

All members of the genus *Holacan-*

thus are aggressive and should be kept one specimen to a tank. Sometimes these angels can be successfully mixed by adding them at the same time, moving around parts of the habitat, disrupting their territories, or bringing in ever-larger specimens. This practice is not encouraged unless you have other facilities for sanctuary should the relationships in your main tank begin to go sour.

More than one adult female may be kept in a tank, but only in very large systems as they attain some 18 inches in length. Other non-*Holacanthus* species are generally ignored; occasionally a Queen Angel will become a bully and require "rehabilitation" or removal. Provide adequate escape spaces for tankmates and observe your charges daily.

Feeding is the most critical area in keeping most marine angels. A Queen must be weaned from natural foodstuffs in order to survive and thrive. In the

wild, juvenile Queens 3 inches and smaller reputedly feed on algae primarily—this may be the answer to the too-small-to-adapt question. They supplement this diet well in captivity with crustacean and other fresh and frozen animal foods. Postmortem analyses of wild adults typically show more than 90% sponge content in their diets.

Opened, whole shellfish, squid, and frozen and fresh crustaceans should be offered occasionally. Plant or algae materials should be fed daily. Algae and plant matter should make up at least 50% of their diet. Feed frequently and in small amounts.

The Queen Angelfish makes an excellent first or beginner angel. It's easy to find, simple to maintain when purchased at the right size and fed properly, and disease-resistant. Its beauty, intelligence, and character make it a fish that few hobbyists will ever outgrow.

Hawkfishes

Family Cirrhitidae
Curious and Colorful Raptors of the Reef

CUSTOMER: "Excuse me, but I think you have a dead fish." Shop owner: "Oh, really—where?" (Not that hawkfish again.) Customer: "There." Owner: "Well, if you look closely, you'll see it's fine. It likes to hang out on a rock, coral, or the bottom. It doesn't have a swim bladder, so it tends to perch while it waits for something to eat."

The conscientious store owner would then go on to explain that, to observe real "hawklike" behavior all you need to do is watch for a while or add some tempting food. When something of interest catches the hawkfish's eye, it will be quick to swoop in to investigate—or grab in a predatory rush.

Hawkfishes are peculiar species that fill a unique niche. Their curious swimming habits—dictated by the absence of swim bladders and unique coloring—and their tendency to live long, healthy lives in captivity, make them favorites of many aquarists. They can go from the reef tank, with certain cautions, to the community marine fish tank with a wide range of compatible tankmates.

Their patient, vigilant "perching" is about the only negative thing that can be said about the hawkfishes. They are not constantly in motion, if that happens to be what you are looking for, but before calling them sedentary, take a look at their eyes—always on full alert. These colorful, interesting fishes are undemanding in terms of water quality and foods; they get along well with other species and are generally fast enough and smart enough to avoid being harassed by tankmates. But remember, their mouths are quite large, so watch out when adding shrimps and small, slender fishes because your hawkfish is also watching out for them.

Classification. Hawkfishes comprise about 9 genera and 35 species. They bear a close resemblance to rockfishes, scorpionfishes, and lionfishes (Family Scorpaenidae), but they lack their prominent head spines. Hawkfishes have a continuous hard and soft dorsal fin of ten spines, often with cirri that resemble small pom-poms at their tips. The pectoral fins are distinctive in having elongated, unbranched lower rays. The tail fin is squared off. As already noted, the cirrhitid family lacks swim bladders, allowing them to be rapidly decompressed after capture.

Commonly available species are the

Longnose Hawkfish (*Oxycirrhites typus*): appealing and undemanding, but with an appetite for smaller prey.

Red-eyed or Arc-eye Hawkfish, *Paracirrhites arcatus*; Forster's or the Freckled Hawkfish, *Paracirrhites forsteri*; the Longnose Hawkfish, *Oxycirrhites typus*; the Red-spotted Hawkfish, *Amblycirrhitus pinos*; and the Falco Hawkfish, *Cirrhitichthys falco*.

The Longnose is the hawkfish most hobbyists want. It has a long, pointed snout, and a white body with maroon cross-hatching. Its price is high, in large part due to deep water (100 feet plus) collection. It is often caught around black corals. When you find a good specimen, don't miss out. You will enjoy the new life this character brings to your aquarium. This superlatively suitable aquarium species reaches approximately 5 inches in total length.

Range. Their distribution range is mainly Indo-Pacific with some species in the tropical West and East Atlantic. The lone example from Florida and the Caribbean is the Red-spotted Hawkfish, *Amblycirrhitus pinos*. Most species are found in shallow water with some up to a few hundred feet.

Selection. A good hawkfish is easy to find; all species and most individual specimens are suitable for captivity. They ship well and are relatively parasite-free from the wild. Standard operating procedure for all marine purchases, however, should be followed: 1) ascertain that the prospective purchase has been in the store for at least

Arc-eye Hawkfish (*Paracirrhites arcatus*): typical of the genus, with no swim bladder and a habit of perching vigilantly, awaiting a feeding opportunity.

a few days; 2) ask about its existing habitat conditions (temperature, specific gravity, pH); 3) ask to see the fish eat what you intend to feed it; and 4) if in doubt, leave a deposit for the specimen or give yourself time for further consideration.

Torn fins and suspicious blemishes are to be avoided. Shredded fins may be from bad handling or poor water quality; blemishes could be from parasitic or bacterial infection. In either case, these specimens should be passed by. Also, a hawkfish is always hungry. If it won't eat, don't buy it. Curiosity and activity are requisite behavior for any new purchase.

Habitat. No special consideration is required, just prudent maintenance. Hawkfishes are not notably demanding in terms of temperature; 75 to 80 degrees F is suggested for the entire group.

Behavior. Hawkfishes are compatible with other species as long as their tankmates are the right size: too large to eat but too small to prey on the hawkfishes. Sometimes they can become territorial after being in the same system a long time. Occasional rearrangement of part of the aquascape alleviates this problem. They may chase other fishes, but rarely do any damage. In general, it is not a good idea to mix hawkfish species for this reason.

In considering hawkfishes for reef

Redbar Hawkfish (*Cirrhitops fasciatus*): as with many of this genus, a threat to cleaner shrimp and other invertebrate life.

systems, be forewarned that a hawkfish's large jaws and sharp teeth are ideal devices for capturing crustaceans. One reef-keeping acquaintance reports an expensive lesson learned after adding 25 tiny herbivorous Blue-legged Crabs to a large reef with an Arc-eye Hawkfish. All of the crabs were gone within 24 hours, methodically picked off by the grateful hawkfish. Some small species are ideal reef additions, but they will eat crustaceans and worms. The Longnose Hawkfish has a much bigger mouth and appetite than most people suspect; it will readily display its capacious jaws and raptorlike behavior with large freeze-dried krill or frozen silversides. Cleaner shrimp are a favored prey item, at least in the aquarium. Think twice about putting one of these fish with small gobies, blennies, or dottybacks and the like.

These fishes respond to human be-

Giant Hawkfish (*Cirrhitus rivulatus*)

Freckled Hawkfish (*Paracirrhites forsteri*)

Falco Hawkfish (*Cirrhitichthys falco*)

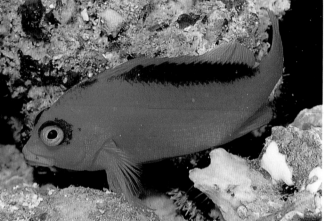

Flame Hawkfish (*Neocirrhites armatus*)

havior very quickly. They imprint easily and will "beg" at the surface and feed out of your hand.

Reproduction. One species, the Longnose, has been reported to lay patches of adhesive eggs in the aquarium, but this account is generally discounted by biologists. Observations of wild pairs of hawkfishes suggest that they spawn in male-dominated harems at dusk and that both eggs and larvae are pelagic.

Feeding. A hawkfish spends most of its time perched on a rock or piece of coral, waiting to make a sudden, fast rush at a food item. Their short, conical teeth are modified for grasping fish and other moving prey, but they accept all frozen and flake foods readily.

Disease. Hawkfishes are typically "clean" of pathogenic disease and have low parasite loads. They are not particularly sensitive to therapeutic agents or treatment regimens. Quarantine and a

prophylactic dip are suggested as always. Other fishes in the system will typically show symptoms of disease before your hawkfishes do.

Summary. The members of Family Cirrhitidae have everything going for them in terms of suitability for captive conditions—they are eye-catching, readily available, moderately priced in most cases, hardy, interesting, and accept all foods and a wide range of water conditions.

Damselfishes

Family Pomacentridae

The Quintessential Beginner's Fishes—and Much More

W HAT ARE THE TOUGHEST, scrappiest organisms on the reef? Triggers? Basses? Octopuses? These are all keen predators, but I have seen them beaten by lowly damselfishes. When diving, I've even been driven away from the nests, feeding sites, and symbiotic anemone homes of these feisty fishes.

In nature, damselfishes are an extremely important group of ubiquitous, circumtropical coral reef fishes. Along with the clown or anemonefishes, damselfishes make up the Family Pomacentridae, with some 28 genera and approximately 321 species.

Damselfishes (Subfamily Chrominae) provide a vital link both as reef-feeding and feeder fishes and are excellent beginner marine aquarium specimens. Their popularity is well-warranted, considering their diversity, beauty, tolerance of chemical and physical conditions, gregariousness when crowded, and general compatibility with fishes and invertebrates. Most species accept all types of food eagerly and are very disease-resistant.

Classification. The family's taxonomy is currently poorly known, and there are a wide number of species "groups" blending or grading between different island groups. On the higher taxonomic plane, pomacentrids are closely related to the freshwater cichlids—which they resemble in structure, form, and behavior. Both families are in the same suborder of the largest order of fishes, the Perciformes. The pomacentrids and cichlids are notable within the group for being the only two families with one pair of nostrils (nares) in most species.

Many damselfishes are brilliantly hued in blues, greens, violets, reds, and browns; several appear metallic. Quite a few damsels are, or become, drab brown or olive in later life, and there are sometimes striking color and structural differences between the sexes.

Most damsels reproduce like many substrate spawners. Their behavior is similar to typical Central American neotropical cichlids. Other similarities include an incomplete lateral line; a toothless palate; single, continuous dorsal fins; and territorial behavior.

Size. Damselfishes are generally small. Some species, such as the California Garibaldi (*Hypsypops rubicundus*) and the Giant (Mexican) Damsel (*Microspathodon dorsalis*) reach about 12 inches in length.

Selection. On any given day, a few damselfish species should be readily available from any store selling marine fishes. These generally include Three-spot Dominoes or Dascyllus (*Dascyllus*

Golden Damselfish (*Amblyglyphidodon aureus*) with Bluestreak Cleaner Wrasse (*Labroides dimidiatus*)

Indo-Pacific Sergeants (*Abudefduf vaigiensis*): as with many damsels, cute little juveniles can grow into territorial and formidable adults.

trimaculatus); Three- and Four-stripes (called "humbugs") (*Dascyllus aruanus* and *D. melanurus*); Blue Devil Damsels (*Chrysiptera cyanea*), various *Chromis* species; beau gregorys (*Stegastes* spp.); the sergeants (*Abudefduf* spp.); and perhaps the so-called "deep water" damsels (*Neoglyphidodontops* and *Plectroglyphidodontops* spp.), among others.

Despite their reputation for hardiness, many damsels are in precarious shape when sold to beginning hobbyists. The following buying advice will help in purchasing new specimens:

1) Buy from reputable dealers, ones who feed and care for their stock and your business.

2) Buy from systems with no dead or dying specimens. Look for signs of gill burn or ammonia poisoning from recent shipping or cut marks from mishandling and aggression—avoid that tank. Whole batches of damsels may be doomed by shipping traumas, and if they have started to die in your dealer's tank, don't buy any. Busy retail stores have tremendous turnover of damsels, so beware of buying from shipments

that have just arrived. Buy stock that has acclimated and stabilized. Damsels that have recovered and settled in, even if just for a few days, are a much better bet than fresh arrivals. Beware of tanks of damsels with lethargic individuals isolating themselves from the group.

3) Don't buy the tiny (smaller than ¾ inch) or jumbo (larger than 2 inches) individuals. Small ones die easily and large ones generally don't adapt well to captive conditions.

4) Purchase social damsels in small, odd-numbered lots (such as 3, 5, or 7).

270

Select individuals that are all about the same size. This reduces inter- and intraspecies aggression. The reef *Chromis* species make ideal shoaling or schooling fishes, and if you have room for a dozen or more, they make an impressive sight. (Their droppings have been shown to increase the rate of growth of wild stony corals in which they hide, and some advanced reef aquarists are using them as a natural complement to stands of captive *Acropora*.)

Habitat. Damselfishes are easy to keep in aquariums; they are not fussy in terms of water chemistry and physics. Temperatures in the low to upper 70s are ideal. Most tolerate a wide range of salinities, although some in the fish industry keep their damsels in a specific gravity of about 1.017 to 1.018 to decrease salt mix costs, increase gas solubility, reduce algae growth, and curtail epizootic outbreaks. You are encouraged to maintain yours at normal readings of 1.022 to 1.025.

Any amount of light, dim to bright, seems to be fine. Natural or synthetic water makes no difference in terms of vitality or reproduction in captivity. A pH of 7.9 to 8.3 is favored; no ammonia, nitrite, and as low a concentration of nitrates as practical is the rule (as with most marines).

Behavior. Many people take the risk of introducing pests, parasites, and pollution by using the old "floating and mixing" technique, pouring new damsels, along with their shipping water, into their system. Don't do it. At the very least, appropriate introduction procedure should include gradually making the temperature of the shipping water about equal to the system water, a freshwater dip with or without Formalin and/or copper (see Chapter 9), and, if possible, a two-week quarantine. Damselfishes as a group do better if you start feeding them as soon as possible. Frequent, small feedings of a variety of foods (dry, frozen, fresh, and live—both vegetable and animal) will help settle in the stock and reduce aggressive turmoil.

Territoriality can be a type of social disease. Keep your stock undercrowded, and observe them daily for extreme interactions. Remove all bullies. Aggression is probably the single largest source of damselfish mortality after incidental losses in collection and shipping. The trademark feistiness and territoriality of damsels may be alleviated by undercrowding, putting one per 5 to 10 gallons, and providing plenty of cover.

If possible, introduce your (odd-numbered) batch of damsels to a new, damsel-free tank all at once. If it is not possible or practical to do this, move the tank decorations around and upset existing territories when introducing new specimens. Damselfishes like hiding spaces. Provide coral, rock, shells, or plants—any sort of natural nooks, crannies, or screens—for social and psychological shelter. Some species, especially those that get larger and more aggressive, should be displayed without any other damsels. Examples include Neon-velvets, Dominoes, Hawaiian Dascyllus, Giant (Mexican) Damsels and Garibaldis. Keep your eye on your stock and move the bullies. Keeping these characters with larger angels, tangs, and most triggerfishes will quickly tone them down a peg.

Be aware that small damsels are a dietary mainstay for most fishes whose mouths are large enough to accommodate them. Take this into account be-

Blue Devil Damselfish (*Chrysiptera cyanea*)

Blue-green Chromis (*Chromis viridis*)

Blue Chromis (*Chromis cyanea*)

Three-spot Domino (*Dascyllus trimaculatus*): juveniles of this species are known to associate with sea anemones, finding protection in much the same manner as the related damsels known as clownfishes.

Juvenile Three-spot Damselfish (*Stegastes planifrons*): this common species from Florida and the Caribbean is typical of a number of damsels in progressing from a brightly colored juvenile to a drab adult.

fore introducing any lionfishes or basses to your tank.

Feeding. Some damsels are specialized planktivores or herbivores in the wild. In captivity, damsels accept all foods greedily. In fact, Sergeant Majors (*Abudefduf saxatilis*) are legendary for their use in training other shy species to feed from the surface. Frequent small feedings two to three times per day of a mix of foods sustains them well. Nutritional diseases are all but unknown.

Disease. Damselfishes are parasitized internally and externally by several species of sporozoans, *Cryptocaryon*, *Amyloodinium*, roundworms, flukes, tapeworms, and crustaceans. The presence, abundance, and susceptibility of these pathogens to varying salinities and treatments is complex. For the most part, damsels are disease-resistant, and if preventive measures have been executed and their environment well-kept, you can expect low parasite loads.

Most treatable conditions (external) can be excluded by the incoming dip treatment and quarantine previously mentioned. Damselfishes respond well to periodic prophylactic copper treatments. Internal parasites are sometimes diagnosed in a dead specimen but difficult to cure in live ones.

Summary. The damsels are an inexpensive mainstay in our aquariums, active guardians, and aqua-popcorn on the world's reefs. The greatest testimony to their toughness is that they do "damselfish duty" in "popping" new systems—establishing bio- geo- chemical cycling while giving the untrained aquarist his or her first taste of keeping marine fishes. Miraculously, most damsels manage to live through it all and some go on to live for many years.

Jumbo Damselfishes
Microspathodon dorsalis and *Hypsypops rubicundus*

NOT ALL DAMSELS ARE CHEAP, cheerful, small, and the marine equivalent of Neon Tetras or goldfish. These two defy the rules and will appeal to the aquarist attracted to the big, uncommon, and not universally loved. These are the Giant (Mexican) Damsel (*Microspathodon dorsalis*, formerly *Damalichthys vacca*) and the equally gargantuan Garibaldi Damsel (*Hypsypops rubicundus*).

As juveniles, these species are dazzling. As adults, they may be more appropriate for the grill than the home aquarium. These two jumbo damsels grow to over 12 inches long and 2 pounds in weight. And ounce for ounce, they are among the toughest, meanest turf fighters I know.

Still thinking of buying one? Be prepared to invest in a chiller. The Garibaldi lives in water that ranges from the 50s to the 60s Fahrenheit. The Giant Damsel is accustomed to water in the mid-70s. Both these fishes will become stressed at higher temperatures, so most systems will need to be kept cool—at least during the summer months—to keep these species alive.

If you are still determined to try one

of these jumbo damsels anyway, keep in mind the following:

1) Get a small specimen (1 to 3 inches); these will adapt more easily.

2) Select for brightness of color (don't worry that cyanide may have enhanced the fish's colors; these species are collected without poisons).

3) When buying a Garibaldi, purchase a specimen that has been collected in the warmer (summer) months. (Collection is banned in California as of this writing, but is about to become legal off the coast of Mexico.)

These fishes are good bioindicators—if the environment is going downhill, they will show signs quickly. Temperature strain can be seen immediately as color loss and hiding behavior. The appropriate use of a chiller or temporary means of lowering the temperature is usually the remedy.

Mixing members of the same species is generally a disaster. Unless you have a huge system (200 or more gallons), only place one jumbo damselfish to a tank.

If you still want a colorful, outgoing—to the point of being obnoxious—rough-and-tumble specimen, you have a cooler-temperature tank with a chiller and good thermal insulation, you're looking for a fish to outlive the family dog, and you don't mind it getting BIG and eating you into poverty, one of the jumbo damsels is for you.

Garibaldi Damselfish (*Hypsypops rubicundus*): Perhaps more coveted by aquarists outside its own American-Mexican waters, the Garibaldi requires a chilled system kept between 50 and 60 degrees F.

Clownfishes

Subfamily Pomacentrinae
A Natural Choice for the Less-Boisterous Aquarium

"OH MY GOSH! That plant is eating that fish!" Hearing this in the vicinity of a marine aquarium, you can almost be certain it's a true neophyte observing his or her first clownfish cavorting among the tentacles of its host sea anemone. This spectacle is so hypnotic that it has single-handedly seduced many, many hobbyists from freshwater into the marine side of the aquarium world.

Pink Skunk Clownfish (*Amphiprion perideraion*) in its host, the Magnificent Sea Anemone (*Heteractis magnifica*).

Prized for their bold and bright color patterns, comical behavior, and ability to thrive in captivity, clownfishes (also called anemonefishes) almost inevitably find their way quickly into the tanks of beginners. At the same time, even the most advanced reef-aquarium owners often include them in their rarified collections—this is a tribute to the enduring affection this group creates among its keepers.

Their undulating swimming habits can mesmerize observers, and they will often race to the front of the aquarium to greet passersby. There is also their one other salient characteristic: lifelong mutualistic symbiotic relations with certain species of anemones. This is an absolutely necessary arrangement in the wild; they are never found without their host anemones, for without the protection and shelter of the anemone, the slow-swimming clownfish would be quickly consumed. There is much known about the fascinating clownfishes, but there is also a great deal of wrong information about their selection and care.

Classification. The Subfamily Amphiprioninae, in the damselfishes family (Pomacentridae), are the damsels we call clowns. There are 28 valid species, all but one in the genus *Amphiprion*, with one member in the genus *Premnas*. These are further separated into four "complexes." Clownfishes are frequently misidentified in our hobby, and many species are wrongly given the same four or five common names.

Notable species, grouped by similarity in appearance, include:

1) Multiple-striped orange-to-tan-or-brown clowns: *Amphiprion ocellaris*, the Ocellaris Clown, often erroneously called the "Percula" Clown. The true Perculas, *A. percula*, are often distinguished by the presence of black borders of varying width along the white bands. Other similarly marked species include *A. clarkii* (Clark's Clown), *A. bicinctus* (Two-band Clown), *A. chrysopterus* (Orange-fin Clown), and the rare *A. sebae* (Sebae Clown, more often than not a misidentified *A. clarkii*). This category also includes the tear-shaped Saddleback Clown, *A. polymnus*. Other brown-to-cinnamon sebaelike clown species are not as widely available but are also suitable as aquarium additions.

2) Skunk Clowns, aptly named for their striped markings: *A. perideraion* (Pink Skunk Clown), *A. akallopisos* (Skunk Clown), *A. sandaracinos* (Orange Skunk Clown), and *A. nigripes* (Maldives Clown).

3) Tomato Clowns: *A. frenatus* (the Tomato Clown), *A. melanopus* (Red and Black Clown), *A. rubrocinctus* (Australian Clown), *A. ephippium* (Red Saddleback Clown), and *A. mccullochi* (McCulloch's Clown).

A pair of Percula Clownfish (*Amphiprion percula*) protected by a Magnificent Sea Anemone (*Heteractis magnifica*): inseparable in the wild, but not necessarily kept together in captive systems.

Clark's Clownfish (*Amphiprion clarkii*): a large anemone many host a number of clownfishes, usually of the same species, and virtually always with the dominant fish being a large female that rules the social unit.

4) The rich-reddish-colored Maroon Clown, *Premnas biaculeatus*.

For a workable key to species, see Dr. Gerald Allen's definitive guides. I bear full responsibility for the above version of unnatural Western grouping of these fishes. Clownfishes differ from the damsels in having fewer dorsal spines and structural markings on the margins of some of the head bones and other more obscure minor differences.

Range. They are found throughout the Western Indo-Pacific. Most are collected from the Philippines.

Size. Younger individuals (juveniles to young adults), adapt much better to captive conditions than larger individuals. Some clowns, such as *A. clarkii*, may reach up to 6 inches in the wild. When you are shopping, remember that optimum minimum small sizes for all species are about 1 inch for wild and ¾ inch for tank-reared.

Selection. One would think that picking a healthy clownfish would be a breeze and a pleasure. In the wild, they are abundant and easy to capture. All are found in intimate contact with certain species of sea anemones and are easily netted off their "homes" using hand nets, a cup, or just your hand. Sadly, many clownfishes meet an early end through rough handling, transport, and difficulties in acclimation. There have been estimates of some 90% mortality en route from capture to distributors. Of those surviving, another 90% may perish before even reaching the retailer's tanks.

Why? Is this another example of the toxic effects of cyanide? Actually, none are cyanided; poison costs money, and is unnecessary for clownfishes. The cause of all this mortality is stress. Being rudely pulled from the caressing, grooming, and protective arms of their anemone host, and losing the close interaction with members of their species and possibly family—all of this takes its toll. Add to this the chemical and physical insults of polluted holding water, gill and body "burn" from ammonia buildup in a tiny shipping bag, and the trauma of co-mingling with strange and exotic species in a distant clear-sided container, and it's surprising that any survive. So, what can you do as an informed and conscientious consumer?

First of all, buy tank-bred (captive-bred) stock if possible. So-called "Percula" Clowns (usually *Amphiprion ocellaris*), Clark's Clowns (*A. clarkii*), Tomato Clowns (*A. frenatus*), Maroon Clowns (*Premnas biaculeatus*), and a growing list of others are being produced in commercial numbers. In the early days of captive breeding, many of these were smaller and less-colorful than wild-caught specimens, but they did live and grow. Today, the quality of captive-bred fishes is clearly improving, with more and more well-grown and vividly colored specimens appearing under the tag "tank-raised."

Aquarium-conditioned specimens, tank-raised or not, should be well-fleshed—especially along the back—alert, feeding, and with no whitish marks on their bodies or fins. If the fish offered are lethargic, hanging out in the corner with drooping, clamped fins, not feeding, or showing whitish markings, do not buy them! (These whitish markings are either slime reactions from stress or a small infestation of parasites.) In fact, don't buy a fish from a tank where any other fish in it is displaying any of these symptoms.

Clowns should be very alert, colorful, and fat. They should swim with a wagging motion, and will usually dart to the back of the tank at your first approach, then come eagerly back to the front to look at you.

When you are buying for breeding, buy and raise a group of smaller-than-mature individuals and allow them to pair off. Several species can be sexed externally when large enough, as the females are much heavier-bodied and/or differently colored. Usually, when you buy two clowns, you should buy one larger than the other—the larger one will turn more aggressive and become the female. The clownfishes are sex-switchers. As young, they are undifferentiated; given certain social cues, they may change into males and then, when the opportunity arises, into females.

With or Without an Anemone? Do captive clownfishes really need a host anemone? The short answer is, No. Some wild-caught species, however, don't always fare very well in an anemone's absence. *A. melanopus*, *A. frenatus*, and *Premnas biaculeatus* are my top three choices for managing well without their invertebrate. The need to have an anemone in the system is also fading as more and more captive-reared clowns are being sold. In the past, it was generally believed that your chances of keeping and breeding clownfishes in captivity was greatly improved in the presence of host anemones. This view is becoming obsolete, with most commercial breeders having eliminated the hard-to-keep anemones without seeing any impairment in the the health or reproductive drive of their breeding pairs.

The mutually beneficial behavior of clowns and anemones on the reef has been well-documented and popularized, as have methods of selecting healthy symbiotic anemones. Many species of anemones commonly affected (such as *Condylactis*, from Florida, and Atlantic Carpets) are not natural choices for clownfishes (which hail from the Pacific), although some species will associate with them. Your clownfish may not easily be introduced to, or communicate with, its intended host. It may even be consumed by the anemone.

Still the clownfish-anemone relationship is wonderful to watch, and many aquarists attempt to keep an example of this fascinating duo in their systems. All too often, the anemones do not survive. These invertebrates are clearly a challenge, and should not be

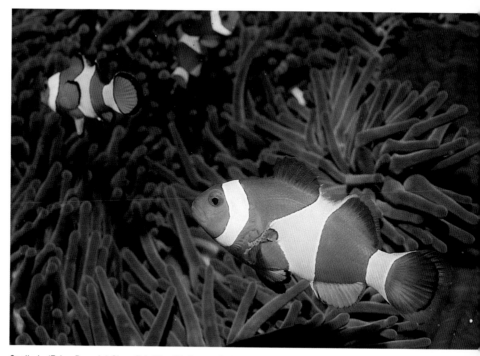

Ocellaris (False Percula) Clownfish (*Amphiprion ocellaris*): wild-caught specimens may suffer from shipping stresses, but captive-bred clowns well-acclimated to aquarium life are now widely available and affordable.

purchased unless you have intense lighting and a sure grasp of water-quality management. Anemone expert Dr. Daphne Fautin is currently urging aquarists not to buy wild-collected anemones, which she says have low reproduction rates and can easily be threatened by overexploitation.

If you do decide to acquire an anemone, buy a species of known symbiotic potential (i.e. one that is displayed with symbiotic clowns) and try to buy one as a duo, already paired with its appropriate clownfish.

Habitat. Like many organisms living in close association with invertebrates, clownfishes are sensitive to the same kinds of chemical and physical conditions and changes as the invertebrates. Short acclimating or cleansing dips should be used. Use freshwater with very little or no Formalin, copper, malachite, et al. It should be a dip, not an extended bath. System temperatures should be in the mid to high 70s, with specific gravities of about 1.023.

High water quality, especially with low levels of metabolites (proteins, albumen, phenols, and nitrogenous compounds), is advised. Suitable biofiltration, protein skimming with or without ozone, and frequent partial water changes are mandatory.

Behavior. Clownfishes can be overtly territorial, especially when any threat to their host anemone is concerned. It is suggested that they be introduced with their host anemone after other tankmates, or provided with their own system. If your clownfish are very large

and you want to try adding new specimens to their domain, try disturbing or rearranging the physical environment just before introducing the newcomers. You may also dull their aggressiveness with some temporary extra feeding and, as always, keep a watchful eye out for problems. Most other species of fishes in the tank will be left alone as long as they are previously established, larger, or more aggressive, and do not bother the clownfish's anemone or come too close while the clowns are breeding. Clownfish can and will attack you—and draw blood if so inclined.

Large, nonpaired adults generally do fight in all but the largest aquariums. Likewise, mixing species of all but juvenile sizes is chaotic. Keep them in separate systems.

There are fishes that prey on clownfishes. Allen (1974) lists the following

possible aquarium fish families as potential predators: moray eels, lizardfishes, groupers (basses), hawkfishes, snappers, scorpionfishes, and lionfishes. Actually, any tankmate with a large enough mouth may eat your clownfish, especially in the absence of a symbiotic anemone. Be forewarned: as with the rest of the damsels, clownfishes are common prey in the wild. Although a big Maroon or Tomato Clown can hold its own in an aquarium with a population of aggressive fishes, the smaller species fare best in systems with less boisterous tankmates.

Clownfishes are noisy! Clicks and grunts of various types and apparent function have been recorded, and the whole field of such communication among fishes is a rich research area. Listen carefully when they are defending their anemone or spawning—you

Two-band Clownfish (*Amphiprion bicinctus*): listen for audible underwater clicks and grunts.

Tomato Clownfish (*Amphiprion frenatus*) with Bubble Tip Sea Anemone (*Entacmaea quadricolor*): terrific beginner's fish and one of the hardier hosts.

Maroon Clownfish (*Premnas biaculeatus*), also with the Bubble Tip Anemone: another excellent species, but best kept as mated pairs or a single clownfish.

may be able to hear them through the glass if other room noise is eliminated.

Reproduction. Clownfish reproduction is a hot topic, and many hobbyists are achieving success in raising high-quality specimens in home aquariums. Briefly, clownfishes breed in much the same fashion as substrate-spawning neotropical cichlids, by cleaning a hard, smooth surface next to, or under, the base of their host anemone. They deposit eggs on the surface, then zealously guard and fan them. When the fry become free-swimming, they are dispersed like other zooplankters.

In captivity, the fry may be fed on easily cultured marine rotifers and baby brine shrimp. Clownfishes reproduce throughout the year, laying a few hundred to a few thousand eggs about once a month. Many species have been spawned and reared in captivity, and the "domesticated" second-generation clowns are reported to be easier to breed than their wild-caught brethren.

Feeding. These fishes happily and readily consume dry, prepared, freeze-dried, frozen, live, and fresh foods. In the oceans, most rely mainly on zooplankton, with some considerable algal matter found in stomach-content analyses. It is suggested that a variety of prepared fresh foods, including vegetable matter, be offered on a twice-daily basis. Watch them eat—they will share their food with their anemone.

Disease. Clownfishes are susceptible to many environmental and infectious diseases and are hosts to numerous species of ectoparasites, including isopods, monogenetic trematodes (flukes), tapeworms, and roundworms. Most fish are lost either through careless collection and transport, poor water-quality maintenance, or, regrettably, treatment with drugs.

Particularly problematic with these species are situations in which speci-

mens are extensively compromised or debilitated and rapidly "break down." Often, what is going on is a combination of bacterial, fungal, and protozoan factors. This mess is so common in newly imported clownfish that it might be termed "new clownfish syndrome."

If left unchecked and untreated, this syndrome results in mass mortalities. Among the most often identified pathogens, the algae *Amyloodinium* and the protozoans *Cryptocaryon* and *Brooklynella* are common culprits.

If you find yourself with a clownfish that has an apparent infection or infestation and if treatment seems to be necessary, first check and adjust your water quality. Most "disease" conditions of captive aquatic specimens are a result of poor water or system quality. Do not just start pouring a therapeutic treatment into your tank. Often, moving the clowns to a different system effects a fast "cure."

After quickly doing whatever you can to stabilize your system, consider further treatments in the following order of priority:

1) Biological: add a symbiotic anemone if you don't have one or move the fish(es) to a system with one. Add a cleaner—a suitable goby or shrimp.

2) Physical: lower your specific gravity. Even with most invertebrates, dropping the specific gravity a few thousandths per day to 1.018 to 1.019 will not do permanent damage and may shift the balance of favorable conditions toward your fishes.

3) Chemical: choose this option last and least. Be careful. A clownfish tends to be sensitive to the same toxins as its host anemone. Copper, other metal salts, organic or metallic dyes, furan compounds, and organophosphate pesticides can all have deleterious to disastrous effects on both clownfish and anemone. These substances in various formulations comprise most of the aquarium treatments available to hobbyists. They do have some appropriate applications in separate "hospital" tanks, but these chemical therapeutics are dangerous and unnecessary with clownfishes. Experiment with them only as a last resort.

Summary. Clownfishes have everything going for them as aquarium specimens. They're hardy, behaviorally interesting, colorful, do well on all types of foods, and—if you start with healthy specimens and meet their habitat requirements—almost certain to live long lives and become family favorites.

Wrasses

Family Labridae
Hardy, Active, and Diverse As the Reef Itself

AQUARISTS ARE OFTEN shocked to learn that many Harlequin Tuskfish (*Choerodon fasciatus*) are caught with baited barbless hooks, "jigged" by divers hovering over steep reef walls. Considered prizes by underwater photographers and aquarium keepers alike, these are wary fish, living safely out of reach within caves—but they can't resist a meaty lure.

True to their family name—Labridae, derived from the Greek *labros*, meaning greedy—the wrasses have brash appetites. Their love of eating makes many of them rugged, easy to keep, and long-lived aquarium denizens.

You are probably familiar with many of these wrasses: Bird, Dragon, Flame, Rock, Hogfish, Pudding Wife, Leopard, and various Cleaners, Flashers, and Fairies. If it had been up to me, I might have named this group the "bird fishes" in reference to their flashy colors and the smooth beat-glide-beat swimming motions they make with their pectoral fins. They utilize their tails (caudals) only for fast bursts of speed.

What a great group of fishes the wrasses are. And what a diverse and large family as well. Anatomists marvel that wrasses have more differences in the bone structures of their heads than most of the other fish families combined. Wrasses are the second-largest family of marine fishes (after the gobies) with at least 60 genera and more than 500 species.

The classification of their members is complex. It turns out that in many species, the males, females, and juveniles are markedly different—both in color and structure. Further, there are often intermediate sex change (female to male) differences and even different types of males. In harem-forming

Harlequin Tuskfish (*Choerodon fasciatus*): flamboyant wrasse from a family of startlingly beautiful and rugged species prized by aquarists.

Klunzinger's Wrasse (*Thalassoma klunzingeri*)

Cuban or Spotfin Hogfish (*Bodianus pulchellus*)

Belted Wrasse (*Stethojulis balteata*)

Spanish Hogfish (*Bodianus rufus*)

Sunset Wrasse (*Thalassoma lutescens*)

Yellowcheek Wrasse (*Halichoeres cyanocephalus*)

species, the "top-dog" alpha male is the largest, most colorful, and most aggressive individual.

Classification. Like the freshwater cichlids, a key to the wrasses' success is their protractile mouths, which allow them to sample different types of foods easily. Additionally, most wrasses have separate outwardly projecting teeth. The bird wrasse genus, *Gomphosus*, even has an elongate snout.

Wrasses are closely related (in the same suborder, Labroidei) to the parrotfishes, Family Scaridae. Both have large cycloid scales, a thick caudal peduncle (the body trunk right before the tail), and usually a broadly truncate (square) tail fin. Parrots are immediately distinguishable by their beaklike teeth. The teeth of labrids are separate,

almost fanglike; European aquarists call the wrasses "Lippfish."

Many of the wrasses are popular aquarium fishes, and rightly so. They have comical behaviors while actively swimming and searching for food, and are great at getting along with all sorts of other tankmates. On top of this, they possess some of the most brilliant colors and patterns in the animal kingdom. Occasionally, however, a wrasse may get too big (the Napoleon Wrasse exceeds 3 meters), or an individual may develop a mean streak.

Range. Labrid fishes are found worldwide in shallow waters, tropical to semi-temperate, with the exception of the Arctic and Antarctic Seas.

Size. From a few inches—perfect for even small reef aquariums—to meaty

lunkers that can provide the centerpiece dish for a banquet, wrasses come in all sizes. Research is definitely in order before acquiring an unfamiliar species, but there are desirable wrasses appropriate for virtually every size aquarium.

Selection. This should be based upon behavioral assessments more than appearances. Is the animal swimming "normally," will it take the foods you plan to offer? One important physical trait is the specimen's full-body look. Examine your prospective purchase carefully. Does it seem well-fleshed or is it emaciated? A thin specimen may also exhibit tear marks around the mouth or eyes. These are signs of previous bullying and starvation and should disqualify the fish for purchase; rarely do such specimens rally.

Cleaner Wrasses: Boycott These Fishes

There are many varieties of live-stock unsuitable for captivity. Specialized diets, adult sizes too large for home aquariums, susceptibility to disease, poor adjustment to captive conditions, being too dangerous or rare, or performing a needed function in the wild are among the traits that ought to preclude certain species from being collected and sold.

Unfortunately, this list of traits describes specimens that *are* regularly offered to the hobby. Why? The answer, not surprisingly, is that someone will buy them.

I fully suspect that most folks assume the livestock in dealers' tanks is generally suitable for aquarium care, and that someone has screened out the obvious problem species long ago. Unfortunately, this is often not the case. One genus of wrasses typically lives only a few weeks in home systems yet still can be found in the majority of pet stores in this country.

Labroides is one of the wrasse family's 60 genera, with 5 described species. The most commonly available is *L. dimidiatus*, the Bluestreak

or Common Cleaner Wrasse. The other four have other colors, and cost much more. None of these should be offered to the hobby. Hawaii banned its endemic cleaner wrasse, *L. phthirophagus*, from collection in 1996.

The main reason that these fishes should remain in the ocean is symbio-

Hawaiian Cleaner Wrasse (*Labroides phthirophagus*): illegal to collect in Hawaii and one of the obligate cleaners that ought not be removed from the reef.

sis. Cleaning symbiosis involves two different species getting together for mutual advantage—the host having parasites and necrotic tissue removed and the cleaner deriving nutrition and probably protection from the host.

Cleaners are further classified as being obligate or facultative. Facultative cleaners do their cleaning and

therefore receive nutrients more or less as a sideline, able and willing to seek other nonparasitic food sources. There are many examples of these facultative part-timers; several angelfishes and butterflyfishes as juveniles, and the Señorita Wrasse (*Oxyjulis californica*). Obligates, like the *Labroides* wrasses, get all or virtually all their nutrition from their cleaning activity—various species set up permanent cleaning stations with customer hosts coming in for regular grooming. Experimental removal of some of these cleaners in the wild has demonstrated their immense importance as parasite controls. Local and even large pelagic fish populations are quickly and negatively impacted by their removal. Fish populations drop or migrate, and remaining fishes lose fitness as measured by increased external parasite loads, sores, and torn fins.

By reviewing the literature and traveling to the areas supporting all of these *Labroides* species, I can attest that they are of limited numbers and closely defined distribution. When they are removed, the whole reef population suffers.

Further, these species have not been kept successfully for any length of time in captivity, most dying within a few days to weeks due to a lack of nutritive interaction with host fishes. I have heard stories and seen the endemic Hawaiian Cleaner, *L. phthirophagus* accepting dry-prepared, freeze-dried, fresh, and live foods, still wasting away and dying.

If you're just looking for a biological cleaner for their services or novel behavior, consider obtaining shrimps in the genera *Lysmata* or *Periclimenes*, or try cleaner gobies. They do the job, they thrive in captivity, they are prolific breeders in the wild, and their collection has much less of a deleterious effect on reef ecosystems. In fact they are increasingly available as tank-raised specimens.

Think about this every time you cast your vote by buying livestock intelligently at the fish store. The obligate cleaner *Labroides* wrasses should remain in the ocean, and you should knowingly spend your money on hardier species.

Do the planet a favor by politely talking this over with your livestock supplier if and when you see cleaner wrasses or other unkeepable species offered for sale.

Finespotted Fairy Wrasse (*Cirrhilabrus punctatus*): peaceful and luminescent species for the reef system.

Probably most wrasse deaths are attributable to the stress of their journey from reef to dealer. On the reef, most species are secretive and either live solitary lives or are social only with specific members of a group. On capture, different wrasse species are generally thrown together hodgepodge along with others they would not closely associate with on the reef. Everyone involved in the industry should copy the great deal of good that some collectors do by separating their specimens.

Even though the wrasses you purchase may have been already stressed, there is one way you can help as the end user. Get them into a healthier setting as soon as possible. I advocate not leaving them at the dealer's any longer than

necessary. Take specimens home and, after quarantining quickly, adapt them to their new homes.

Habitat. Though wrasses are a widely adaptable group, almost all of them bear the hallmarks of a secretive reef existence—cryptic coloration and patterns, and tube shapes for slipping into cracks or below the sand. Your wrasse species will do better if provided with a broken rock or coral area and at least some territory with fine sand.

A wrasse for your reef tank? Some of the peaceful species—the fairy and flasher wrasses in particular—are ideal. Keepers of *Tridacna* clams have a particular fondness for certain smaller wrasses, particularly the Six-line Wrasse (*Pseudocheilinus hexataenia*), as well as juveniles of the species *Coris gaimard*, often called the Coris Wrasse, both of which feed on tiny predatory snails that can plague their clams. Other, more rambunctious, wrasses will eat most all your invertebrates. Study before purchasing. Filtration needs to be vigorous with wrasses about; they are active, heavy meat-eating fishes that defecate a great deal and keep the bottom stirred up.

Checkerboard Wrasse (*Halichoeres centiquadrus*): large, constantly active show specimen for fish-only systems.

Juvenile Dragon Wrasse (*Novaculichthys taeniourus*): called the Rockmover for its habit of rearranging shells and stones.

Behavior. Wrasses are often harem-forming, with one supermale, other males that may become dominant, and a number of females. Otherwise, almost all wrasse species are territorial with members of their own kind. What this means for the aquarist is the need to keep just one male per species per tank.

In introducing these species to a system, aggressive, territorial types should be put in last, after all other livestock have settled in. Shy, timid species are best put in ahead of their tankmates. Being careful about who goes in, and in what order, will go a long way toward reducing fighting and hiding among your livestock. On that same note, don't fear the worst if your wrasses seem to stay under the sand or in the shadows a good deal of the time. Unless you observe evidence of bullying or starvation, this is likely their natural behavior.

Reproduction. In the different species known, courtship dancing involves elaborate swimming and interaction. This is done either as one-male pairs or multi-male group spawners, with the participants swimming towards the surface and releasing their gametes together. The young develop as plankton. Wrasse spawning events are not uncommon in the aquarium—further reason to have a good tank cover in place, as jumping can be part of the breeding frenzy.

Feeding. Wrasses consume meaty foods—shrimps of all sorts, mollusks and worms; live, frozen, or dry-prepared. Remember that their family name, Labridae, means "greedy" and this term best describes their love of eating. It's best to develop a feeding routine with these fishes and other eager eaters. (Take care if hand feeding them; they can bite.) Some food might be placed in one corner for the more aggressive feeders, while other foods are placed with a dowel or put in at the opposite end for less greedy tankmates.

The ideal wrasse setup is one that provides constant foraging opportunities—a sparsely populated system with lots of live rock, together with abundant nooks and crannies.

Disease. As a group, wrasses tend to be remarkably resistant to infectious and parasitic diseases. Be aware that this group often "scratches" by glancing off aquarium decor and the bottom. This is natural; it is probably a means for revealing food items in the wild.

Summary. Of the myriad marine fishes in the oceans, the small percentage available to the marine hobbyist includes many wrasses. The sharp-eyed aquarist will spot uncommon species from time to time in retailers' tanks and may have the vexatious pleasure of trying to identify them. With the complexity of their color patterns, wrasses are among the most interesting and unusual fishes for the aquarium.

Parrotfishes

Family Scaridae
Not Meant for the Aquarium Life

WHAT SOARS like a wild parrot, is as beautifully marked as any exotic butterfly, has a beak like a macaw, and is a major source of fine coral sand? Baffled? Meet the parrotfishes, Family Scaridae. This group would seem to have everything going for it as far as desirability to the marine aquarist. Many are spectacularly colorful with fusiform-torpedo body shapes, large, rolling eyes, and almost comical expressions. For the collectors they are numerous, and they are easy to catch at night as they lie sleeping on the reef floor. The only downside, and it's a big one, is that scarids rarely live for any length of time in captivity. They either starve to death or become terminally stressed due to the rigors of confinement. Still, these are fascinating fishes, greatly appreciated by divers and snorkelers, and mistakenly brought home by many a well-meaning aquarist. Even if they are an inappropriate choice for most captive systems, the parrotfishes are worth understanding.

Classification. Like the related wrasses, parrotfishes sport large cycloid scales, large, thick caudal peduncles, and broad, truncate caudal fins. They have nonprotractile mouths with coalesced jaw teeth that resemble a parrot's beak. According to recent surveys, there are 9 genera with approximately 83 reliably described species. Due to radical changes in color and markings related to sexual stage developments, there are many misidentified parrotfish species.

Parrotfishes are closely related to Family Labridae, the popular aquarium wrasses. They are collective members of the Suborder Labroidei in the largest living order of fishes, the Perciformes.

Range. Scarids are all marine, mainly tropical, in the Atlantic, Indian, and Pacific Oceans.

Size. Most parrots grow too large for the average home aquarium.

Selection. If you must own one, buy a species that stays small (some get to over 3 feet in length), and buy it at a small size—4 to 6 inches. Three potential choices are the Queen Parrot (*Scarus vetula*), the Stoplight Parrot (*Sparisoma viride*), and the Bicolor Parrot (*Cetoscarus bulbometopon*).

Do try to get your specimen as fresh from the sea as possible. The longer the fish stays in transit, the worse its condition. In most cases, it will get progressively more starved and stressed.

Habitat. If you're determined to try keeping a member of this family, here are my suggestions:

1) Engage as large a system as you can; consider 100 gallons the minimum.

2) The more established the tank is with mature algae growth, the better.

3) Provide vigorous circulation and filtration as scarids are avid eaters and

Stoplight Parrotfish (*Sparisoma viride*): this specimen, from the Caribbean, displays the typical Initial Phase color pattern, either a male or female. Supermale coloration can be seen on page 286.

Stoplight Parrotfish (*Sparisoma viride*): terminal phase supermale—a spectacular sight on the reef.

prodigious producers of body mucus, especially the species that spin a nightly sleep cocoon of mucus that makes them undetectable or unpalatable.

4) Prepare a suitable hiding and sleeping space—a nice coral or base rock cave with low illumination.

Behavior. Don't attempt to create a school or even a pair in your living room system. Parrotfishes don't get lonely, but they may fight (to the death), and they do get big. Because of their noncompetitive nature, don't try to mix parrots with aggressive, greedy species like large basses or damsels.

One way to observe why parrots are not suited for captivity is to observe them closely in their natural environment. Watching aquatic life in the wild yields much valuable behavioral information. Any diver or snorkeler can tell you that parrots are wide ranging, sometimes covering several hundred square yards in the course of one scuba-dive observation period. This freewheeling travel may be a matter of necessary searching through enough foraging space; it also allows living foodstuffs to recover between visits from the voracious parrots.

Obviously, such large areas are unavailable in aquarium systems and the unavoidable space restrictions apparently exert a dunning effect on parrotfish vitality. They go from being extreme extroverts to introverts, often settling lethargically on the tank bottom, whereas parrotfishes on the reef are in an almost constant search/eating mode during the day, stopping to "sleep" only at night.

Reproduction. Like the wrasses, most parrotfishes are protogynous hermaphrodites (both functional sexes, females turning into males). But it gets much more complex than this. Imagine you're looking at all the parrotfishes on Earth. You have some notion of what a "species concept" is, and structurally, genetically, and biochemically, there are distinct types of parrotfishes that are distinguishable from other types. But within these types there are some widely differing subtypes—about four or five per species.

Consider the Stoplight Parrot (*Sparisoma viride*). For this single species, there are the following subtypes: 1) undifferentiated immature individuals; 2) fish that have developed into females; 3) fish that have gone through being females and are now males; 4) fish that are/were "just" males; 5) supermales, typically the larger, most brightly colored "alpha" types.

Although, unlike some wrasse species, they don't change much morphologically (structurally) with sex switching, parrotfishes frequently have striking color differences with different age, social status, and gender. Large, colorful supermales must be seen in the wild to be fully appreciated. Now you can see why there is considerable confusion—even for professional ichthyologists—in determining who's who in the parrotfish species world.

Feeding. A common misunderstanding with this group is what, exactly, it

Queen Parrotfish (*Scarus vetula*): the beaklike mouth and fused teeth can crush hard coral skeletons.

eats. Parrotfish rarely feed on actual live coral tissue, but stomach-content analyses have shown they do derive most of their nourishment from scraping off organisms, mainly algae, that live in and among dead coral substrates. They chew off the live and dead heads of corals in gathering this material.

Some writers have listed snails, crustaceans, shellfish, and urchins as real and potential food items for captive care. Perhaps a long-term approach to feeding these species will involve algae and other mashed food being somehow applied to coral skeletons.

You can offer a variety of home-made and/or prepared food items along with sufficient fresh material and monitor their acceptance. Open—but leave in the shell—krill, shrimp, clams, mussels, and the like for calcium intake and tooth wear. Try offering these foods at the "top" of your habitat; this is where parrots feed on the reef.

Summary. Most parrotfishes are difficult, if not impossible, to keep for long under "typical" (i.e. small) aquarium conditions. In the wild, they are found continuously roving, grazing, gnawing, and scraping at dead coral substrates for their algal growth, and generating copious amounts of fine coral sand. In low volume tanks they waste away, skulking in dark corners. My advice is to seek out one of the many hardy, related wrasses. Several of these have equally vibrant colors and fare very well in captivity. Leave the parrotfishes to the sea, contentedly chewing up corals and making more sand.

Blennies and Blennylike Fishes

Family Blenniidae and others
An Endless Array of Choices—Nasty to Nice—Among the Fascinating Bottom-Dwellers

ONE OF THE MOST celebrated cases of evolutionary mimicry among the reef fishes involves the Bluestreak Cleaner Wrasse (*Labroides dimidiatus*) and an innocent-looking blenny named *Aspidontus taeniatus*. For all the world, the blenny appears to be just another slender little fish earning its way through life by picking parasites from and grooming other species that recognize the value of its curious services. The look-alike blenny has the body shape, color, and even the cleaner's trademark "dance" down perfectly. This nasty imposter isn't, however, the least bit interested in the lowly role of cleaning; its common name is the Sabretooth Blenny, and it lives by nicking pieces of flesh, usually from the faces of its victims, with a razor-sharp set of canine-type teeth.

Even among its kin, the Sabretooth is a bold rogue, and many other blennies are shy to the point of being secretive. The blennies are a huge group of sedentary fishes that are usually small, with long, continuous dorsal and anal fins and stumpy pelvic fins. But as usual, with a group this size, you must be wary of gross generalizations.

The blennies include some real nasties and a number of fishes with personality, along with many sold as tropicals that are actually cool- or cold-water organisms. The following is an introduction to sorting them out and a short listing of who's naughty and who's nice.

Classification. The name "blenny" is about as ambiguous as "bass" or "eel." All told, there are 6 families of 127 genera and 732 species of "true" blennioids (a suborder of the largest order of fishes, Perciformes). They are united for a variety of internal, structural similarities. What the average aquarist sees from external appearance is that blennioids have pelvic fins with, in most cases, one embedded spine and two to four simple soft rays—and that these fins are inserted in front of the pectoral fin bases.

Look at a "typical" blenny—they have long (rather than wide) pectorals, generally a long and continuous dorsal fin (unlike the separated ones of the gobies with whom they share the reef bottom), and various "hair," "whisker," and "eyebrow" processes called cirri that add to their comical appearance.

Red Sea Mimic Blenny (*Ecsenius gravieri*): superbly evolved to mimic predatory sabretooth or fang blennies (see page 291), this is an interesting, peaceable fish.

Blennioid Groups. If you find the gobies a complicated group, the fishes that are commonly grouped under the umbrella term "blenny" are worse, and for simplicity's sake, we will offer the briefest mention of the six legitimate blenny families—along with the bright spots and troublemakers, from the aquarist's point of view.

Triplefin blennies, Family Tripterygiidae, are the only blennies with notched dorsals; in their case, in three sections. The first two are spiny, the third composed of seven or more soft rays. The triplefins are all marine, from the Atlantic, Indian, and Pacific Oceans. They get to 10 inches in length. The genera *Enneanectes*, *Helcogramma* and *Tripterygion* are seen from time to time in the trade, with the latter having members that people find especially attractive.

The sand stargazers, Family Dactyloscopidae, have one of the most useful common names, as it describes their usual orientation (under the sand) and adaptations: extremely oblique mouths, protruded eyes on top of the head, smooth cycloid scales, and a weird branchiostegal pump for ventilating their gills while they lie in predatory wait under the sand. There are 9 genera, with about 46 species in the Atlantic and Pacific, growing to 6 inches. The Red-saddled Sand Stargazer, *Dactyloscopus pectoralis*, is occasionally collected along the North American Pacific coast.

The Family Labrisomidae, labrisomid blennies, includes some genera that are livebearing (*Xenomedea* and East Pacific species of *Starksia*). Several tiny labrisomids live in close conjunction with sea anemones and have protection from their stings. There are 16 genera with about 100 species, mostly from the tropical Atlantic and Pacific. Genera I've seen offered in the trade are *Labrisomus, Starksia, Neoclinus, Exerpes, Malacoctenus, Paraclinus, Dialommus,* the wormlike *Stathmonotus,* and *Xenomedea.*

The Family Clinidae, clinid or kelpfish blennies, includes several fishes that are dead ringers for the kelp fronds wherein they camouflage themselves. There are three tribes, about 20 genera and 73 species. All but 8 (*Ophiclinus* spp. and *Clinus* spp.) are cool-water types and need a chilled system.

The pike, tube or flag blennies, Family Chaenopsidae, have elongated scaleless bodies that are compressed somewhat side to side, and have no lateral lines; their bodies are modified for living in tubelike tunnels. There are 9 genera with at least 80 species, Atlantic and Pacific. *Acanthemblemaria, Chaenopsis, Coralliocetus, Hemiemblemaria, Emblemaria,* and *Protemblemaria* are sold, mainly to reef keepers.

The sixth legitimate blenny family, Blenniidae, needs more elaboration: **Family Blenniidae.** Commonly called the combtooth blennies, these fishes are mostly marine and tropical, from the Atlantic, Indian, and Pacific Oceans. They have scaleless bodies with large blunt heads that bear their namesake comblike teeth; the maximum size in this family is a substantial 18 inches, but most are under 6. To many aquarists, the Blenniidae are the true blennies. There are some 6 tribes, 56 genera, with about 350 species. *Parablennius, Ecsenius, Meiacanthus, Petroscirtes, Ophioblennius, Cirripectes,*

Exallias and *Istiblennius* are the genera whose members are most often available to the aquarium hobby.

Blenniids include several mimetic species that look and behave like other fishes, including other blennies, to gain advantage. Mullerian, Batesian, and aggressive mimicry are all involved, and the adventuresome hobbyist willing to invest the research time can assemble some fascinating displays of mimic blennies and the fishes they resemble.

The Caribbean Red-lipped Blenny, *Ophioblennius atlanticus,* is a ready "poster child" for the family, skittering about with its comblike dentition and prominent eyebrow cirri. A gorgeous shallow-water member from the Pacific is the Leopard Blenny, *Exallias brevis,* unfortunately an obligate coral-polypeater that should be avoided.

The genus *Ecsenius* deserves special attention: with 47 species, these are delightful, small (to 4 inches) fishes that

Diamond Blenny (*Malacoctenus boehlkei*): hides under *Condylactis* anemones.

Convict "Blenny" (*Pholidichthys leucotaenia*) juvenile: a favorite oddity.

do superbly well in reef systems and with other peaceful fish.

One of the best-known and -loved members of the *Ecsenius* genus is the Midas Blenny, *E. midas*, with changeable yellow, purple, brown, pink, and blue. The Midas is a good assay organism, as it exhibits rapid and extreme color changes when stressed. Considered to be a mimic of the Lyretail Anthias (*Pseudanthias squamipinnis*) and other basslets over its wide range, this little beauty is very unblennylike in its disposition, with a willingness to stay out from cover hiding among its adopted school of anthias. Two other favored *Ecsenius* are the orange and purple Bicolor Blenny, *E. bicolor*, and the gorgeous Red Sea Mimic Blenny, *E. gravieri*.

Cirripectes is another popular blenny genus with a handful of its 21 members sporadically offered to the trade. Their all-seeing eyes are large and protruding, even by blunt blennyhead standards. Also conspicuous are the group's fleshy lips and eyebrows (orbital cirri). *Cirripectes* are more cryptic than *Ecsenius* but just as attractive and comical.

Sabretooth Blennies. A subcategory of the Blenniidae, the sabretooth blennies, contains one genus of interest to the aquarist and two that should be avoided.

In the genus *Meiacanthus*, the beautiful, delicate-appearing blennies actually possess strong predator deterrents: enlarged canine teeth with associated venom glands. Unlike most blennioids,

Meiacanthus spp. have a fully functional swim bladder and "strut their stuff" above the bottom with impunity.

Despite the fangs, *Meiacanthus* spp. make good general aquarium and reef tank neighbors, generally being left and leaving other fishes alone. Though the genus's venomous bite does not rival a stone or lionfish sting, it is painful to humans. Avoid hand-feeding them.

The Canary Lyretail Blenny, *M. ovaluensis,* is a standard blenny offering from Fiji worthy of mention. Two of my other favorites in the genus are the Striped Lyretail Blenny, *M. grammistes,* and the Forktail Blenny, *M. atrodorsalis.*

Beware the genera *Aspidontus* and *Plagiotremus.* These should be avoided at all costs (unless you want to keep one in a tank by itself or with nonfishes). These vampires have a pair of enlarged canine teeth in their lower jaw for ripping scales and bits of flesh from other fishes. Some do this by stealth, hiding in a hole in the reef and darting out for a fast-attack chomp. Others, as we have noted, are sophisticated underwater con artists, closely mimicking benign, even beneficent fishes.

How easy is it to be fooled over which is the blenny and which is the wrasse? Even in one of the most widely circulated hobbyist books, the fish pictured is misidentified as the blenny *Aspidontus taeniatus*; it is actually the innocent wrasse, *Labroides.* The Baensch & Debelius, Axelrod/Burgess/Hunziker standard reference works cited in the Bibliography (page 408) ac-

Forktail Blenny (*Meiacanthus atrodorsalis*): protected by venom-bearing canines or "fangs."

Golden Mimic Blenny (*Plagiotremus laudandus flavus*): an imposter, mimicking the species above.

curately identify and illustrate both. The False Cleaner or Sabretooth, *A. taeniatus,* is readily differentiated by its underslung subterminal mouth.

An opposite benefit is conferred by the Forktail Blenny, *Meiacanthus atrodorsalis,* on the Golden Mimic Blenny, *Plagiotremus laudandus flavus.* As you now know, very few fishes tangle with the blennies of the genus *Meiacanthus* due to their venom-gland-bearing enlarged canines. The Golden Mimic Blenny, bold imposter that it is, uses its

Speckled Sandperch (*Parapercis hexophthalma*): blennylike predatory oddity.

Midas Blenny (*Ecsenius midas*): Indo-Pacific favorite of many fishkeepers.

Red-lipped Blenny (*Ophioblennius atlanticus*): Florida and Caribbean standby.

Yellow-mouth Pikeblenny (*Chaenopsis schmitti*): curious, eel-like species.

likeness to swagger about in the upper waters without fear.

Scooter Blennies. "Scooters" is a loose, generic term usually applied to the Families Callionymidae and Pinquipedidae, but also tagged onto a number of blennies for their manner of "scooting" or hopping along the bottom in short bursts.

Various *Ophioblennius* (e.g. *O. atlanticus*), *Petroscirtes* (e.g. *P. temmincki*), the Triplefin Blenny *Lepidoblennius* *marmoratus*, and many, many others—not to mention all the nonblennies folded into this group—are sold as "scooters" around the world. It's clearly a case of too many species and too little time or too limited experience for most in the trade to keep them straight.

Please do your best to make a sure identification with your dealer—or on your own—when considering the purchase of all such "scooter blennies". Several species sold are entirely unsuit-

able for tropical systems, hailing from consistently cool (40 to 60 degrees F) temperate surroundings, and succumbing after a few days or weeks in tropical (70 to 80 degrees F) systems.

Regrettably, many of the standard reference works in the hobby perpetrate something I call the "tropical/temperate denial game," stating that North Atlantic and Pacific fishes are fine at tropical temperatures. They are not. Don't waste your money and their lives;

Striped Lyretail Blenny (*Meiacanthus grammistes*): good choice, despite fangs.

Canary Lyretail Blenny (*Meiacanthus ovaluensis*): a suitable species from Fiji.

investigate and buy only tropical "scooters" for warm water systems.

Other "Blenny" Groups. Without the space to cover all 10 remaining families of blennioids, including the ronquils, eelpouts, quillfish, graveldivers, and others, I will exit quickly by mentioning one odd species that everyone should recognize. This blenny is in the Family Pholidichthyidae which has only one species, *Pholidichthys leucotaenia* (the Convict "Blenny" or Convict Worm "Goby") found in the southwest Philippines to Solomon Islands. Though this monotypic (one species) family is not a "true" blenny or goby family at all (it's in a different suborder, the Trachinoidei in Order Perciformes), I'll mention it here because it's one member is often commonly labeled as a blenny, and it's an outstanding aquarium species. This is one of my favorite pet-fishes.

P. leucotaenia is peaceful, hardy and easy to keep. As juveniles they look and act very much like the most common of marine catfishes, *Plotosus lineatus*, schooling together with their elongated bodies and long, continuous dorsal and anal fins coming together at a point and almost obscuring their tiny caudal fins. The small pectoral and pelvic fins add even more to their eel-like appearance.

When young, they are a handsome black with a long white dorsal stripe. As they grow, their blackish flanks break into whimsical irregular blocks separated by creamy white lines.

This striped white noneel, nongoby, nonblenny gets to about 8 inches and is great in a group or by itself. I have never known a bad specimen, or even seen one get sick. The rest of its care and demeanor fits perfectly with the blennies and gobies.

Selection. Picking out the right specimens that are clean and that have not been badly beaten by catching and transport is absolutely critical. Blennies are tough, as long as they haven't been "thermally challenged" or damaged by careless handling.

Collecting and shipping damage is difficult to assess with such small and secretive fishes, but it is necessary. Blennies are scaleless or have small embedded scales; they are otherwise protected from physical injury by their copiously slimy bodies. If they are roughly handled or scrubbed clean of mucus by physical insult or poor water quality, they can perish quickly. Look closely at their undersides and fin origins for evidence of reddening. Closely observe all the specimens offered— when one breaks down, very often the rest will as well.

A few of the blennies sold in the trade are temperate, even cold-water, organisms that won't sustain the rapid move to tropical aquariums. Don't be fooled; cool- or cold-water marines will generally live for a few days or weeks before dying "anomalously." You need to consult two or more references in order to determine which species you're looking at and its needs.

By all means, do keep the cool- or

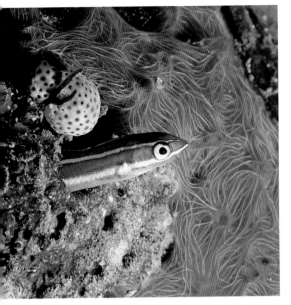
Bluestriped Fangblenny (*Plagiotremus rhinorhynchos*): a nasty little cleaner blenny mimic from the Indo-Pacific region.

Combtooth blenny (*Ecsenius* sp.): similar to the Bicolor Blenny and part of a genus that does well in reef systems.

cold-water blennies if you have a chilled tank or a cool-water reef system—they're great. I would especially recommend some of the members of the genera *Blennius* and *Parablennius*.

Being target food organisms, healthy blennioids are aware of all in their environment. Specimens offered for sale should be looking around and conscious of your presence. Don't buy dazed blennies. You should also observe their feeding habits. For their size, members of this group are gluttons. If a specimen you are considering refuses food, something is very wrong.

Habitat. Most blennies live on hard substrates and appreciate an aquarium with rocky hiding places. The blennylike members of the Family Pholidichthyidae, however, are prodigious diggers that need a bottom with mixed sizes of rubble and gravel. A pholidichthid will never be satisfied with having dug under everything just once. They literally dig until they die; arrange your decor accordingly.

With their big heads and elongate bodies, you might think that blennies are incapable of launching themselves out of your tank. Think again; they are notorious jumpers. Keep your tank covered.

Behavior. There are blenny species that are easygoing and some that are very quarrelsome. When in doubt, keep them one species and specimen to a tank.

Do not make the mistake of adding these fishes to any tank with larger piscivorous specimens. Blennies are choice food items for predatory fishes and invertebrates. As such, they need more than just being kept apart from large mouths to feel safe—provide plenty of cover, nooks, and crannies. In addition, lowered light levels will help shy blennies acclimate to their new home.

Never add shipping water that has held bagged blennies to your system. Blennies produce and release chemicals that will negatively affect their, and their tankmates', behavior.

Reproduction. Almost all blennies produce large demersal (sinking or attached) eggs that they place in sheltered holes, with the male alone tending and defending the eggs after spawning. Males tend to be larger than females and they may be differently colored during spawning.

Feeding. Blennies in the wild can be herbivores, carnivores, or omnivores, but most captive specimens can be coaxed to consume small invertebrates (such as brine shrimp, mysids, worms), dried algae, and even pellets in captivity. Their food must be small enough to swallow whole, because blennies do not chew.

Summary. Are you looking for small, intelligent—even charming—"bottom" fishes? Look no further, but do investigate the species you have in mind or in your dealer's display tank. Blennies are indeed interesting, hardy and long-lived, as long as you have the right species and the right temperature regime in your home system.

Gobies

Family Gobiidae and others

A Multitude of Species from the Floor Areas of the Reef

L IFE AT THE BOTTOM may be better than we think. Laugh, if you will, at the comical, shy gobies; with their big eyes and almost awkward movements they might seem hardly fit to survive among the sleek, fast predators of the reef, but it is they that will have the last chuckle. Gobies are the largest group of marine fishes, with more than 1,900 species. They are also the dominant element in small-fish bottom fauna on tropical reefs, which says a great deal about the strategy of staying down and near your shelter. And, yes, someday soon you will likely find a goby you can't resist and will plunk down your hard-earned cash to add one or more of them to your aquarium. The unlikely goby will have caught you.

Most species living in, on, or near the bottom are of small size, and the gobies are no exception. Among their number is the smallest fish—and the smallest vertebrate—known; females of the species *Trimmatom nanus* in the Indian Ocean reach a mere 8 to 10 mm. This is approximately the size of a grain of rice, and there are other goby species only slightly larger. One super goby species does attain a gargantuan 18 inches, but almost all his kin are less than 4 inches in total length.

Many of the gobies live in close association with invertebrates such as sponges, shrimps, and sea urchins; irregardless of goby size, they can become the center pieces of an aquarium that gives a close-up view of this symbiosis in action.

Classification. Take ten big breaths, Dear Reader; if the sheer diversity and size of such families as the butterflyfishes, cichlids, or damsels is impressive, you haven't seen anything yet.

In recent times, the Suborder Gobioidei has been divided into as many as six separate families. Clarity, it has been said, is pleasurable, and for simplicity's sake, we will treat this as a simplified introduction and cover all gobies as if they were part of one humongous Family Gobiidae.

With a bit of research, you can find numerous families and subfamilies of "true" and fancifully named gobies in the literature and real life: Family Odontobutidae; Family Eleotridae (the sleeper gobies); Family Kraemeridae (the sand fishes or sand gobies); the obscure Family Xeristhmidae; Family Microdesmidae (the fire- or dartfishes); and the Family Schindleriidae.

All told, the gobies and gobylike fishes number some 267 genera and 2,100 described species. All but about 200 are marine, mostly found on the tropical and subtropical reef.

Twinspot Gobies (*Signigobius biocellatus*): typically occur in pairs in the wild, and single individuals are reported to perish in captivity. Both the signal gobies and sleeper gobies sift substrates for food items.

Pink-spotted Shrimp Goby (*Cryptocentrus leptocephalus*): part of a large group of gobies that form symbiotic relationships with burrowing, nearly blind shrimps or prawns and are often collected together.

In the sections beginning on page 297, I will highlight the most common and available types of gobies of interest to marine aquarists, but I trust the comments above on classification allow you to see just how vast your possibilities are. (Don't be too impatient with your fish retailer for not being able to identify every goby that appears in the store; this is a group where the so-called "oddballs" or unknowns appear frequently.)

What's a Goby? The gobies are grouped together on the basis of several hard-to-discern characteristics, such as bones of the head and a family-unique sperm gland, but a few traits are of use to us as identifiers and keepers of marine life. Most gobies live in or on the bottom and are aptly adapted for a demersal existence. They are roughly torpedo- or cylindrical-shaped and have reduced lateral-line systems coupled with enhanced vision. Generally, gobies lack swim bladders and display degrees of fusion of their pelvic fins. In a few species, these are used to form a sort of suction disc to help them stay in place.

In case you're asked, gobies can be readily distinguished from the numerous fellow bottom-dwelling blennies on the basis of dorsal finnage. Most gobies have two distinct top fins; blennioids have a single long one.

Selection. Because of their diminutive stature and bottom orientation, you have to look closely at these animals before purchasing. They really come in two choices of quality: sterlingly fit or dismally doomed.

Examine the stock carefully for bloody or white markings; tanks with any bloodied or dead individuals should be shunned. Check their breathing, it should be regular and not labored; for most species kept, 60 to 90 gill beats per minute is appropriate.

Is the fish looking around, aware of it's environment and you? Gobies are heavily predated on. As a result, they are never "asleep at the wheel." If a specimen is not alert, leave it be.

Behavior. Territoriality can be a big problem with some species and certain individuals. Make and use clear, sealable containers if you don't have extra tank space to move bullies or bullied. This vigilance is not a matter of "only at introduction." When pairing, growing, and interacting with each other, gobies can and do become belligerent to the point of doing real damage. If you want a single-species group of the colonial-type gobies, I would place all individuals at one time to reduce the likelihood and intensity of aggression.

Except for the species that have natural bad-tasting slime immunity, like the coral or clown gobies, this group is like bite-sized candy bars at Halloween. Triggers, lionfishes, large angels, groupers . . . most anything with a big enough mouth and predatory instincts will suck them down.

Disease. Gobioids, for the most part, are relatively disease-resistant, with the exception of one type of plague: environmental. Though they have cycloid or ctenoid scales, they have about the same intolerance of harsh chemical treatments as "naked" fishes. I suspect that more are bumped off from misuse of copper, malachite and Formalin-containing medicants than from the infectious diseases they're used against.

Coral Gobies
Genus *Gobiodon*

THESE TINY CHUBSTERS have to be close to the best fishes for reef and mixed fish-invertebrate aquariums. Though only attaining a minuscule 2½ inches, *Gobiodon* are huge on color and spunky personality.

Due to their noxious body slime, no other fish bothers them, and they're happy as proverbial clams with some *Acropora* or coral skeletons and a little meaty food. Coral Gobies should only be housed with nonaggressive feeders such as cardinals, seahorses, and pipe-fishes, or they may be slowly starved to death.

When kept as a small group, they readily form pairs and mate. The genus is hermaphroditic, with females turning into males. The female deposits circular bands around a branch of host coral that are immediately fertilized and subsequently guarded by the male. Perhaps owing to their small size, rearing the young in captivity has not proved easy.

The lemon-drop-like Citron Goby, *Gobiodon citrinus*, is the most commonly kept. The equally adaptable Yellow Goby, *G. okinawae*, is frequently mixed-up with and sold as the Citron; it lacks the Citron's beautiful blue and white lines. Also check out the gorgeous Blue-spotted Coral Goby, *G. histrio*; often misidentified in the trade as *G. rivulatus*.

Keep your eyes open for the coral gobies of the genus *Gobiodon* and do try them if you have a mixed invertebrate/peaceful fish setup or reef system.

Firefishes, Dartfishes
Family Microdesmidae

THESE FISHES are among the most distinctive and desired gobies, with their characteristic body shape, bright colors, and flicking dorsal fins. There are two top fins—the first sporting six spines, the second with one spiny ray and four or five soft rays. There are four genera with about 30 described species.

The genus *Nemateleotris* contains the most popular species, the orange-red *N. magnifica*—*the* Firefish to many. Two other deeper-water congeners are seen occasionally: the Purple Firefish, *N. decora*, and the yellow-faced *N. helfrichi*, Helfrich's Firefish. *Nemateleotris* species are unmistakable with their elongated anterior dorsal fin spines and perpetual body-angle orientation.

Purple Firefish (*Nemateleotris decora*): relies on nearby hiding places.

Firefish (*Nemateleotris magnifica*): two may fight unless already paired.

Blue Gudgeon (*Ptereleotris heteropterus*): lovely in schools but active jumpers.

Neon Gobies (*Gobiosoma oceanops*): excellent all-around beginner's fish.

Closely related (in the same family) are the gudgeons and gobies of the genus *Ptereleotris*; the two species *P. zebra* and *P. evides* are offered worldwide.

Important habitat requirements for the fire- or dartfishes include providing sand, rocky rubble, and caves or holes where they can burrow and hide, and a decent current in which they can orient themselves. Though some folks keep them as individuals—and I have seen them as solitary specimens around the Indo-Pacific—they may be kept in a small aggregation (a few to a dozen) if put into a large enough reef-type system (20 gallons per fish) all at once, and watched.

In the wild, these fishes feed throughout the day on planktonic crustaceans, mainly copepods. In captivity, they eagerly accept all kinds of foods. Provided they aren't placed in a situation where bigger, more aggressive fishes get all the food, these pretty gobies make excellent aquarium inhabitants for reef and peaceful-fish setups.

Neon Gobies
Genus *Gobiosoma*

AH, THE GENUS *Gobiosoma* of the Western Atlantic. These sparkling black, white, and blue or gold jewels should be as common in marine aquariums as corydoras catfishes in freshwater tanks; no, more so.

These slivers of happiness are extremely hardy and of great utility: ideal first fish for the new marine hobbyist. Celebrated are the 12 or so members of the genus (often designated by the subgenus *Elacatinus*) that will pick off parasites and dead tissue from your other fishes.

Looking for a marine species to try your hand at captive breeding? Search no further. The premier Neon or Cleaner Goby, *Gobiosoma* (*Elacatinus*) *oceanops*, is a prime candidate. It has been tank-bred and reared in commercial quantities for years.

The parents are small and may be maintained easily in a 20-gallon system. They pair and spawn readily and regularly, with demersal (bottom) eggs, and parental care. Sexing is best left up to the fish by purchasing a handful and letting them sort things out. Individuals may be sexed with practice and close observation. Rather than trying to describe the relative and variable body shape and color differences between males and females, I'd rather encourage you to gauge which is which for the entire group via their genital papilla, immediately in front of their anal fins. The males' are cone-shaped and pointed at the tip; those of females are generally only visible near spawning and are short and rounded at the tip.

Commercial breeders use short sections of small-diameter plastic pipe as spawning sites and raise the eggs separate from their parents, but home aquarists may see them spawn and rear their young on most anything solid. The fry are raised on unicellular plankton (*Euplotes* and *Brachionus* are recommended). The young are fully developed in a month, which seems fast until you realize their full lifespan is but a year or two. Consult the Bibliography section (page 408) if you are intent on breeding *Gobiosoma*.

My favorite species of neon gobies are *G. oceanops* and *G. evelynae*. These two are commonly captive-bred and are widely available.

Shrimp-Goby Symbionts

GOBIES IN THE GENERA *Amblyeleotris, Ctenogobiops, Cryptocentrus, Stonogobiops,* and others form mutualistic symbiotic relationships with the pistol or snapping shrimps of the genus *Alpheus*, Family Alpheidae. The shrimp digs a burrow home that the animals share, and the goby keeps a sharp vigil for predators. Partner gobies eat microfauna they find near the bottom, the shrimps feed on what they find by burrowing. The shrimps are virtually blind and use their antennae to remain in contact with their partner gobies at all times.

These partner goby/shrimp associations make fascinating aquarium presentations. Successful habitats call for broken rubble and coarse sand 2 or more inches deep, or an artificial PVC pipe burrow, to serve a single goby or pair matched with an appropriate alpheid shrimp.

Sleeper Gobies
Genus *Valenciennea*

THE ORANGE-SPOTTED GOBY (*Valenciennea puellaris*) and Golden-headed Sleeper Goby (*V. strigata*) are standard offerings; several other congeners of this genus are at times available. They're large for gobies, at half a foot, and peaceful enough for use in all types of marine setups.

Sleeper gobies, along with the related signal gobies, prefer to sift the substrate for meaty foods. They will starve if not provided with high-protein krill and other accepted items.

Catalina or Blue-banded Goby
Lythrypnus dalli

THIS BRILLIANT RED AND BLUE beauty is from off California and Baja California's Pacific coasts. It is not tropical and will only live a short while in water in the upper 70s or 80s. It should never be sold as a warm-water organism; the Catalina Goby will not live in a tropical aquarium.

The situation is entirely opposite in a chilled system. These cool-water fishes are quite hardy when kept in the 50s and 60s F. For tropical systems, do look into the several warm-water members of this genus; *Lythrypnus zebra*, for instance, is just as gorgeous as its cold-water cousin, and is a true tropical.

Yellowheaded Sleeper Goby (*Valenciennea strigata*) juvenile

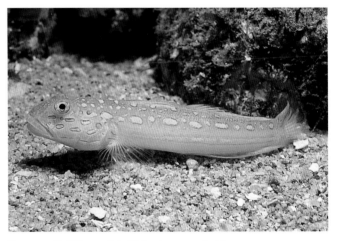

Orange-spotted Sleeper Goby (*Valenciennea puellaris*)

Catalina Goby (*Lythrypnus dalli*): eye-catching bottom-dweller for cool-water systems only.

Mandarins or Psychedelic Fishes
Dragonets

I INCLUDE the Family Callionymidae (11 genera, about 155 species) here, though they're not true gobies at all— they're members of a different order altogether. I assign them to this section for two reasons: one, because they are often erroneously called "gobies"; and two, as a convenient place to state my opinion about how unsuitable they are for most marine aquariums.

Called "psychedelic" fish, and for good reason, the mandarins make the most vivid tie-dyed shirt appear drab by comparison. Sadly, the predominantly offered genus, *Synchiropus*, particularly the members *S. splendidus*, the Mandarinfish, and *S. picturatus*, the Spotted or Psychedelic Mandarin, has had one of the most dismal survival records of captive marines.

Regardless of what others have said, it is my experience that mandarin "gobies" will almost never accept enough of anything other than live foods to sustain themselves. The root of the problem is that the live foods must be omnipresent, giving these fishes a constantly available menu for their ceaseless hunting. The only really workable captive environment is a nutrient-rich live rock reef tank; it must be very well established, that is, with substantial interstitial crustacean and worm life. It takes at least six months to even begin to meet these criteria. Depending on the density of rock and invertebrate prey, it may take 30 to 150 gallons to sustain each fish. Finally, all this assumes that no aggressive tankmates are present to interfere or compete with the mandarin's active feeding.

Don't have this sort of setup? Don't want to kill beautiful fish? Leave the dragonets to knowledgeable reef keepers or in the ocean.

Spotted or Psychedelic Mandarin (*Synchiropus picturatus*): this and the adjoining species actively forage for tiny copepods and require live foods.

Mandarinfish (*Synchiropus splendidus*): wildly patterned, but a fish that typically starves unless kept in larger, well-established, nutrient-rich systems.

Tangs, Surgeons, and Doctorfishes

Family Acanthuridae
Robust Herbivores for the Well-Kept Marine Aquarium

I SPENT MY YOUTH in the Orient as a military dependent, mainly in Japan, but for a while in the Philippine Islands—a wonderful assemblage of countries with genuinely friendly people. While there, I worked in the pet-fish industry, where my jobs mainly entailed carrying buckets of water around and cleaning.

The tedium was broken by one duty I found exciting and quite dangerous—acclimating new arrivals. On some days I watched surgeonfishes by the hundreds arriving at my employer's export facility in Manila from collectors in the out-islands. Livestock typically came to us in more or less live condition, carried in modified oil drums. Invariably, the tangs would have had the worst of the long journey, and would often be found lying on their sides on the bottom. One absolute requirement of this family is a near-saturation level of oxygen. Low gas solubility is immediately evident in their loss of color and behavior. They pant, then lie on the bottom—at first with rapid gill movements, then with diminished breathing, and finally, if you do nothing to rescue them, they exhibit no movement at all.

Clown or Blue-lined Surgeonfish (*Acanthurus lineatus*): a striking but aggressive fish that wounds other tangs with its venomous spines and needs expert care.

Common Aquarium Tangs

These species of Family Acanthuridae are the ones most readily encountered by hobbyists, followed by their usual (often confusingly similar) common names:

Genus *Acanthurus*

A. achilles (Achilles Tang)

A. coeruleus (Blue Tang)

A. japonicus (White-faced or Powder Brown Tang)

A. leucosternon (Powder Blue Tang)

A. lineatus (Clown or Blue-lined Surgeonfish)

A. nigricans (Powder Brown or Gold-rimmed Tang)

A. olivaceus (Orange-shoulder Tang)

A. sohal (Sohal Tang)

A. triostegus (Convict Surgeonfish)

Genus *Ctenochaetus*

C. hawaiiensis (Chevron Tang)

C. strigosus (Yellow-eyed or Kole Tang)

Genus *Naso*

N. brevirostris (Spotted Unicornfish)

N. lituratus (Naso or Lipstick Tang)

Genus *Paracanthurus*

P. hepatus (Hippo, Yellow-tail Blue, Regal, Blue, or Palette Tang)

Purple Tang (*Zebrasoma xanthurus*): esteemed reef aquarium herbivore from the Red Sea that constantly crops algal growth on live rock.

Genus *Zebrasoma*

Z. desjardinii (Red Sailfin or Desjardin's Sailfin Tang)

Z. flavescens (Yellow or Yellow Sailfin Tang)

Z. scopas (Brown or Scopas Tang)

Z. veliferum (Pacific Sailfin Tang)

Z. xanthurus (Purple Tang)

We were constantly driven giggly and dazed by electrical jolts. These were interspersed with having to dodge flying tangs, shooting missilelike out of the tanks. From this we learned first-hand the slashing effectiveness of the razor-sharp spines that give the surgeonfish family its name. At the same time, I came to appreciate just how important oxygen-rich water and highly aerated systems are for these fishes.

Among the most commonly collected marine specimens, the Family Acanthuridae's members—tangs, surgeons, or doctorfishes—rank near number one. Where would we be without the Yellow, Regal, Naso, and Purple Tangs?

Unfortunately, while these fishes can be robust aquarium specimens, they are too often lost prematurely due to ignorance. You do not need to resort to the wooden stick routine mentioned above, but with slightly more attention to appropriate feeding and water quality, these beautiful tangs will live longer, more vigorous, and more colorful lives in your care.

Classification. The doctor- or surgeonfish family name, Acanthuridae (from the Greek *akantho* for spine and *oura* for tail) is an allusion to the presence of one or more sharp spikes these fish sport on their caudal peduncles. These scalpel-like projections are significant for unwary aquarists and bothersome tankmates. The other common name, tang, is derived from the German word *Seetang* (seaweed) and refers to the group's feeding habits.

Our assignment was to resuscitate these fishes in the well-aerated water of our holding tanks by probing and pushing them along with wooden dowels, while trying to avoid being electrocuted by the rigged lighting system. Picture this—tanks with metal supports partially up the sides for strength, but low enough to prevent metal contamination; single incandescent lamps offering just enough light to see how dismal things were; salt crusts, water, and electrical cords everywhere. To preclude outright electrocution, we gingerly stood on Styrofoam boxes while stirring the tanks and their inhabitants.

Adult Blue Tang (*Acanthurus coeruleus*): a large Western Atlantic species.

Juvenile Blue Tang (*Acanthurus coeruleus*): destined to become a blue adult.

All surgeonfishes are herbivorous, feeding mostly on algae—sometimes in huge aggregations that can sweep over a reef. They mow down green growth and leave clouds of fertilizing waste—an important energy source for many organisms—in their wake.

There are some 6 genera and about 72 species of surgeons. Many of them are prominent reef and aquarium members. Additionally, the family includes several important human food fishes.

A related family, Siganidae, is known to aquarists as the rabbitfishes. Siganids include the familiar Foxface (*Siganus vulpinis*) and other colorful members offered at times in the trade.

Both families exhibit the following common traits: their bodies are deeply compressed laterally (side to side), their mouths are small, they have large swim bladders, and they have elongated nasal bones that give them a high-headed appearance. Tangs and rabbitfishes have a single dorsal fin with spines and soft rays, smallish gill openings, a lunate

(moon-shaped) caudal fin, and 22 or 23 vertebrae.

Another related family, Zanclidae, is made up of only one species, *Zanclus cornutus*, the Moorish Idol. These gorgeous fish are often tried but are rarely kept successfully. They differ from the acanthurines by their lack of caudal peduncle spines, by having protractile premaxillaries, the presence of a spine at the corner of the mouth of juveniles, and protuberances in front of the eyes as adults.

Range. These fishes are found in all tropical seas, mostly as reef fishes; a few are found in the open ocean.

Size. Because of the fact that there are so many more genera and species other than the familiar *Acanthurus*, *Zebrasoma*, *Naso*, and *Paracanthurus*, the maximum size of these fishes may surprise you. Some oceangoing surgeons approach 2 feet in length!

Selection. There are four major criteria to consider when judging the acquisition of members of this group:

body conformation, color, behavior, and time in captivity. To this list I will add country of origin for certain species, for reasons I will elaborate on later.

Tangs are voracious eaters, and preeminent in the checklist for examining a new specimen is noting signs of serious undernourishment that may indicate too long a period between reef and retail shop. When viewing a specimen in a display tank, note that the appearance of a pinched stomach is not always an accurate indication of starvation. Comparative values can only be ascertained on the basis of working knowledge of the color, conformation, and comportment of healthy, freshly collected specimens. In simpler terms, experience counts.

Take a look at wild surgeonfishes in coffee-table books and nature documentaries on television. Notice how robust they are. In selecting specimens, pay specific attention to the loss of flesh in the upper body, particularly the area above and behind the eyes. This region should not be shrunken or show a loss of color. Undernourished fishes should be considered diseased—they are far more susceptible to other diseases as a consequence of this stress, and nursing a starved fish back to health is not always a simple matter.

stressed or "out of phase" from being in the dark, it will be off-color. However, there should be no reddening, erosion, or blotchy discontinuities of color in healthy specimens.

The way a fish handles itself in a dealer's system is also telling. Is it ac-

specimen home sooner rather than later to prevent loss of these microfauna to prolonged drug exposure.

As to the touchiness of individual species, the two Powder Tangs—Blue and Brown—the Achilles Tang, and the Clown Surgeon often fail to survive more than three months in typical home aquariums. They look great, but may keel over under standard aquarium conditions. Most of the species here are incredibly tough, adaptable to a wide range of water quality and foods, and are disease-resistant.

Finally, please consider a gross generalization: Buy American. This is not patriotic fervor, just advice to ensure that you get the best individuals. For various reasons discussed later, the same species collected in Hawaii, Guam, and Florida are by and large in better condition than those from elsewhere.

Habitat. There are more requirements here than many suspect. First, make sure to provide plenty of aeration. Tangs are active, breathing, eating, defecating machines, accustomed to full gas saturation. Typically, they are the first to expire with rising temperatures, a power outage, and/or a mechanical air loss.

The larger open-ocean species like Naso Tangs require ample tank space to be truly happy. Yellow and Hippo (Yellow-tail Blue) Tangs can easily get along on a 10- or 15-gallon allocation when they are small; the larger species double that capacity. I would recommend at least a 50-gallon system for a growing surgeonfish. Some studies

Powder Blue Tang (*Acanthurus leucosternon*): a sometimes delicate species that is prone to parasitic infestations. Initial quarantine, a diet rich in marine algae and careful husbandry are required.

As to sizes to purchase, I do not endorse buying any tang under 3 inches in length, with the notable exception of the hardy species of the genus *Zebrasoma*. These can be remarkably robust when tiny. For other genera, when too small, most just don't have the stamina to withstand the rigors of collection and transport.

Color should be intense and uniform. True, when an individual is

tive, curious, swimming about, and "sampling" its environment? Or is it drifting and acting unaware? Ask the dealer how long they have had the surgeon. Acanthurids are subject to extensive alimentary faunas (organisms living in their "stomachs"). These populations of microorganisms appear to be beneficial to the fishes' health. If the dealer is running copper sulfate in the system, you may want to take your have measured more than 7 square yards per tang on the reef.

An important suggestion concerning the chemical, physical, and social environment of these fishes: Keep it optimized and constant. Numerous authors cite the loss of surgeon livestock by moving or changing conditions. Achilles Tangs are, in my opinion, harmed by an aquarist-induced "environmental disease." Many fish-only systems have their specific gravities manipulated to be lower than the ocean for both valid and questionable reasons: to save money on salt, to control or prevent epizootics, and to increase gas solubility. *A. achilles* does not appreciate it. Keep its salinity near that of the ocean, and homeostatic. Likewise, pH should be buffered between 8.0 and 8.4, and temperature for all but the Caribbean species kept in the upper 70 to low 80 degrees F range.

Keep organic levels low to nonexistent through vigorous filtration, undercrowding, skimming, and frequent partial water changes.

Many, if not most, surgeons are openly detritivorous, picking up important biological and mineral material from scrounging around rock and sediment. Therefore, it is important to be less than absolutely meticulous in such maintenance.

Behavior. Territoriality can be a very big problem with tangs regarding: 1) relative sizes; 2) relationships of species to each other; 3) size of the system; 4) number of fish and other livestock in the system; 5) order of introduction to the system; and 6) individual personalities.

Very rarely do Powder Brown, Blue, and Achilles Tangs mix well together, nor do the more disc-shaped species (Yellows, Convicts, Browns, and Purples). The species in the genus *Acanthurus* should be designated as the dominant fish in the system.

Except for feeding concerns, crowding surgeons is generally okay for most types available. Indeed, a small schooling group in a larger system (hundreds of gallons) makes for a spectacular showing. The use of "dither fish," typically a shoal of chromis or damsels, keeps the peace and provides constant distraction for any potential aggressors. Having a few of these quick little "aqua poodles" goes a long way toward diffusing aggression. (For smaller aquariums, the tang species encountered in schools in the wild—such as Convicts, Nasos, and Yellows—fare best singly; two may even fight to the death.)

Tangs have become almost ubiquitous in reef systems, prized for their constant nibbling of algal growth and their ability to graze emergent, unwanted greenery from between corals and in live rock nooks and crannies. The *Zebrasoma* tangs, particularly, are used to control *Valonia*, or Green Bubble Algae, which can reach plague proportions in some systems, encroaching on corals or, in extreme cases, covering everything in sight. Most tang species have a pristine reputation for ignoring

Brown or Scopas Tang (*Zebrasoma scopas*): all members of the genus *Zebrasoma* are hardy and make excellent grazers, but often engage in debilitating "turf wars" with members of their own or related species.

Red Sea Sailfin Tang (*Zebrasoma desjardinii*): from the Indian Ocean and Red Sea, closely related to the species below.

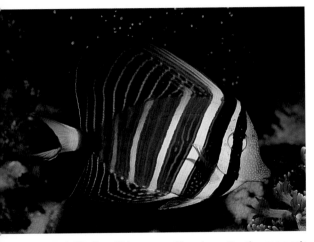
Pacific Sailfin Tang (*Zebrasoma veliferum*): an attractive, commonly available species that will constantly nibble at algae growth.

invertebrates—even to the point of starving to death. Mature, healthy reef aquariums rarely produce enough algal growth to keep even a single tang fully fed and its diet must be augmented with *Spirulina* and other rations.

Here's a little mnemonic: Tangs are easily tangled. Think and prepare before attempting to capture or net a tang.

Surgeons are powerful swimmers and those scalpel-like projections are sharp; they know how to, and will, use them to cut you. Use only fine-mesh nets or a collecting cup. Also pay attention to the stout spines in the anterior dorsal and anal fins—they are sharp and prone to tearing when a fish is not handled deftly.

Some surgeons, like the Hippo Tangs, tend to swim into and lodge themselves within coral or rock. Never attempt to pull them out. If attempting to purchase such a tang, either buy the decor, wait it out, or get another fish.

Various species at different times contain deadly amounts of ciguatoxin, and therefore are toxic for human and possibly other fish consumption.

Reproduction. Observations of surgeonfish breeding indicate that some, including a number of *Zebrasoma* species, are pair spawners. They shoot up near the surface, releasing gametes that convert to planktonic larvae and float through the open seas. Among the acanthurids, group spawning may be more prevalent, with assemblages of breeders numbering at times in the tens of thousands.

A salient characteristic of tangs is their passage through a bizarre transparent larval period termed the acronurus stage. Tangs themselves have not been successfully spawned and reared in captivity as of this writing, but there are anecdotal reports of hobby spawnings of some and of the related Moorish Idol (*Zanclus cornutus*) in large systems.

Feeding. Plump tangs in the wild are constantly foraging. On the reefs, disparate surgeons forage on different mixes of species of algae; all take vegetable material, but if you observe closely you will note that there is a great deal of "resource partitioning" with different species and sizes specializing on algal varieties. Additionally, meaty foods are needed for bulk and growth. Frozen brine shrimp is a great base; other foods should be offered, and not just dried flake foods.

I question the use of lettuce, spinach, peas, kale, okra, squashes, or any other foodstuff that pet-fish keepers have tried to use to sustain or augment the diets of tangs. Many of these contain too much oxalic acid, and all have too little nutritive value. Why would you go to all the trouble to assure decent water quality only to introduce terrestrial plants that may be carrying hundreds, even thousands, of ppm nitrates, as well as possible residual pesticides?

Either buy useful prepared frozen, pellet, flake, granular, pellet, or tablet algal foods, or go to the Asian food section of your store or other specialty outlet and buy algae processed for human

Juvenile Hippo Tangs (*Paracanthurus hepatus*) with a school of damsels.

Achilles Tang (*Acanthurus achilles*): poor survivability in average systems.

Bignose Unicornfish (*Naso vlamingi*): far too big for most aquariums.

Moorish Idol (*Zanclus cornutus*): confused with tangs, and a fish to avoid.

consumption. These are readily available and as far as fish food costs go, they are inexpensive. Dried *nori* and *kombu* are especially relished by marine fishes. (That said, I will admit to hearing many reports of tangs kept busy and happy eating romaine lettuce and other garden greens; tangs seem to relish them, but I always prefer foods of marine origin.)

If time, space, and your expense account allow, collect your own (or buy through a saltwater bait shop) green algae such as *Ulva* and *Caulerpa*, rhodophytes (red algae), and phaeophytes (brown algae) for keeping bait organisms fresh. An occasional overgrown live rock with micro and macro organisms goes a long way toward making the tank inhabitants happy.

Young surgeons are planktivorous, and most adults will consume a modicum of brine shrimp, euphausiids, and such, but will not be sustained by them.

They need their greens—daily.

Feeding strike? Don't panic. Patience will win out with an otherwise healthy specimen. There are records of hunger strikes of weeks without loss. Try offering some live brine shrimp; it is a sure winner. (Be sure to rinse or soak live brine shrimp in freshwater for a few minutes to reduce the likelihood of introducing parasites.)

Offer food often. Invest in a small automatic feeder, stock it with an appropriate mix of dry-prepared foods, and set it to the maximum number of feedings. Except when sleeping, surgeons are constantly on the prowl for edibles.

Disease. Tangs are susceptible to the scourges of tropical reef disease, *Cryptocaryon* and *Amyloodinium*. They are frequently the first in a tank to show signs of infestation, and the first to respond to a cure with copper-based medications. I do not advise continuous copper treatment of these (and all other) fishes. The tangs' digestive system microfauna have been studied quite a bit and found to be important and consistent in their makeup. Chronic copper treatment or toxicity may well account for substantial "anomalous" losses of tangs by disrupting these microfauna. Avoid these problems best by first employing a quarantine or dip, and second by treatment in a separate vessel.

In very large systems, I might suggest the use of facultative biological cleaner gobies and shrimps. Avoid all specimens with evidence of hemorrhaging, generally indicative of *Vibrio*, *Aeromonad*, or other bacterial infection. These fish are goners; only in rare cases have I seen effective cures.

Nutritional disorders of tangs are so common a cause of loss that we will mention them here as a disease that should be avoided, and that can be "cured." Much work has shown that vitamin C deficiency is a cause of color loss and lateral line erosion. This pitting may be sent into remission with the

feeding or addition of this transient vitamin in prepared or fresh foods or less effectively via vitamin supplements added directly to the water.

Summary. Proper nutrition, frequency of feeding, water quality, and behavioral mixing considerations are the key issues when and where considering tangs. Invest your time in reading and conversing with others before making a big investment in this group. The increase in longevity, vitality and your enjoyment will be worth it.

Yellow Tangs
Zebrasoma flavescens

HERE IS AN AQUARIUM surgeonfish par excellence, adapting easily to captive care, adding a bold splotch of color to any aquascape, moving constantly during daylight hours, and coming with a price tag that makes it among the most affordable marines.

Selecting healthy specimens is not particularly difficult, but here is a perfect example of a fish that is available from several geographic areas, with one clearly superior to the others. Considering their low cost, it makes it easy to recommend that you seek out Yellow Tangs from the very best source: Hawaii. They are collected from Oahu and the Big Island, where *Z. flavescens* is found all around the circumference, from the shallows to about 120 feet. At 4,038 square miles, the Big Island is about the size of Connecticut; more than twice the size of all the other

Hawaiian Islands combined. This is no tiny tropical isle, and the vast surrounding waters here produce huge numbers of Yellow Tangs. While there is controversy in the Hawaiian Islands about fish collection for the aquarium trade, the overall population of *Z. flavescens* seems undiminished after decades of collection. In my view, the population of Yellow Tangs there is healthy and most Hawaiian collectors are conscientious in their methods.

Having caught these fish myself (they're easy), I don't think they are cyanided for collection. Instead I attribute the differential mortality observed from various Pacific sources in comparison to those from Hawaii to the extended time that passes from collection, through holding, transport to a wholesale transshipper, and on to a regional distributor, and finally to the local fish shop. This can take just a few days from Hawaii, to a few weeks from other sources. If watching tangs in the wild teaches you anything, it is that they feed continuously. When deprived of grazing, Yellows fade to thinness and pale color, at some point giving up on feeding altogether. The shorter the transit time the better.

When buying these fish in a local pet store, remember that behavior is very telling with surgeons. Healthy Yellow Tangs are curious about their surroundings. Buy ones that are checking you—and their tank—out. Also keep in mind the obvious: Yellow Tangs should be yellow . . . golden, deep yellow. Every now and then you may find a brownish or yellow-white morph, which you may like, but there is a fright-and-nighttime coloration that involves a white vertical body band. You don't want these.

Be very wary of Yellow Tangs that exhibit any red markings. Look especially at the fin origins and at the acanthus (also called the spine or tang) near the tail for signs of tearing in net mishandling.

Once home, Yellow Tangs make almost ideal tankmates. Exceptions include other *flavescens* tangs of the same size and other tangs, mainly those in the genus *Zebrasoma*. The acanthus is a formidable weapon, which it can and will unsheathe and use. Yellows will not bother smaller or larger fishes unless provoked, and then mainly for show rather than for slashing. Battles between two equal-sized tangs can run for days or even months, until one succumbs, and undercrowding is always the safest bet, followed by introduction of smaller individuals first. Careful observation is a hallmark of a conscientious aquarist.

Yellow Tangs are readily susceptible to the usual parasitic infections of marine fishes, but are easily treated by common methods. Additionally, they are susceptible to a peculiar flatworm infestation, so-called black dot disease. A simple freshwater dip, without copper or other treatment, wipes them out without having to put anything into your main system.

Yellow Tangs are also notable bioassay organisms, showing the long-term effects of diminished water quality

Yellow Tang (*Zebrasoma flavescens*): a fine grazer and one of the best and brightest of beginner's species.

and/or malnutrition ahead of many other types of organisms. Erosive hole in the head, lateral line disease, and going off feed are all possibly indicative of low pH, high concentrations of dissolved organic wastes, or prolonged vitamin deficiency. Appropriate setup, water changes, and proper foods all prevent this.

In sum, this is my nomination for Best Yellow Marine Fish. It feeds well on all foods, has wide environmental tolerance, and exhibits good disease resistance. The supreme source? Hawaii. Beginning hobbyists and those who install aquariums for a living (and thus need outstanding fishes that live) have real Kona gold in the Yellow Tang. Buy them from the 50th state, where the industry and the environment are protected by U.S. law.

Powder Brown and White-faced Tangs
Acanthurus nigricans, A. japonicus

WHEN SHAKESPEARE ASKED, "What's in a name?" he could hardly have had the surgeonfishes in mind, but there is plenty of drama—both comedy and tragedy—when it comes to the common names of these species. Can you tell me which three species are called "blue" tangs? (At least the Atlantic Blue *Acanthurus coeruleus*; the fabulous Powder Blue, *A. leucosternon*; and the Indo-Pacific Blue *Paracanthurus hepatus*. The last is variously called the Hippo, Yellow-tail Blue, Regal, and Palette Tang.) How many "sailfin" tangs do you know? If there ever was an argument for using scientific names rather than common names, it's here in the tangle of

Powder Brown Tang (*Acanthurus nigricans*): historically a species that fails to feed well after capture and often perishes within weeks of being purchased.

White-faced Tang (*Acanthurus japonicus*): also sold as the Powder Brown Tang, but a significantly better candidate for a long life in the aquarium.

everyday surgeonfish nomenclature.

Consider, for example, two very similar-appearing species of surgeons whose common and scientific names are all too often interchanged in the trade. For purely intellectual reasons this misidentification might bother you, but there is more to it. The two species in question look alike, yet are very different in their likeliness to do well in captivity. Based on handling hundreds of specimens, I'd peg their relative potential at aquarium survival for more than three months at a hundred times more likely for one than for the other. Both are sold under the common name Powder Brown Tang.

Acanthurus nigricans, which we will call *the* Powder Brown Tang, is an overall varying brown with a white patch under the eye. The dorsal, anal, and ventral fins are black with blue edges. The base of the dorsal and anal fins is graced with a brilliant yellow; their tails are white with a vertical yellow bar.

Acanthurus japonicus, which we'll refer to as the White-faced Tang, is similarly marked and colored, with the following notable differences: the White-faced Tang is adorned with a red stripe on its dorsal that starts one third of the way back and extends to the end. Note the white patch under the eye; it's larger in *A. japonicus*, extending all the way to the mouth, hence the common name White-faced—sometimes White-cheeked. (To confuse the issue, some sources give *A. nigricans* the name White-cheeked Tang.)

The body shape of the White-faced is decidedly more oval than that of the Powder Brown, but, realistically, could you tell these two apart if you didn't have both on hand for comparison? And what's the big deal anyway? They're both good looking—very beautiful, in fact, when healthy and shown under proper lighting.

Ah, but one is a historically poor feeder, all too often dying within a few weeks of purchase. The other is a very hardy and desirable aquarium species. Both are often sold as Powder Browns, often for similar cost, and there indeed, is the rub. Yes, you *do* want to know how to tell one from the other, so you can purchase the White-faced *A. japonicus*, and avoid the real Powder Brown, *A. nigricans*.

The Powder Brown is widely distributed over the vast mid-Pacific area called Oceania, including Hawaii; it is also found along the East Pacific from Baja to Panama. Its range overlaps that of the White-faced Surgeon in parts of the tropical Indo-Pacific, but displaces it between New Guinea and Australia. Sources are important: for the true Powder Brown species, if you must try one, get it from Hawaii, Tonga, Christmas Island or the Marshall Islands, not the Philippines or Indonesia.

One of the most frequently encountered queries we hear in the pet-fish industry touches on the ethics of what is offered. Why do "they" offer (the organism in question) under different names, knowing that (the organism in question) doesn't do well under captive conditions?

After many years in the aquatic nature business I can assure you that:

1) No, it's not some grand conspiracy to cheat the Western consumer;

2) No, it's not a mean-spirited lesson meant to impress the diminishing value of the dollar on you;

3) Yes, it is a problem directly traceable to the state of sophistication of the collectors, shippers, wholesalers, retailers, and other go-betweens. That is, it's about as good as we all can do collectively, at this point;

4) We all, as consumers, are/have been willing to pony up our hard-earned cash for whatever is offered, without trying to become informed ahead of time.

I don't like the waste and inefficiency, and I don't think you should either. Become a more intelligent consumer and cast your votes/dollars for livestock that lives. Make a choice in favor of the White-faced Tang, *A. japonicus*. If placing a special order, be sure to use the scientific name. If you don't know how to identify the species by sight, bring along a visual reference when the fish is ready to be picked up.

Triggerfishes

Family Balistidae

Biting the Hand that Feeds and Other Endearing Behaviors

HERE IS A COMBINATION OF intelligence and fearsome teeth that neatly divides experienced aquarists into two opposing camps. Those who love triggers will tell you they've seen them trained to retrieve, swim through a hoop, ring a bell, roll over, and yes, have their bellies rubbed. Many others have physical proof of the darker side of these formidable fishes—I bear a scar on my wrist from a bite inflicted years ago by a Queen Trigger, which left me with lifelong respect for the dentition and temperament of this group.

The triggerfishes are among the best-known and most-coveted groups of marine livestock—and also the most vilified. This status is not altogether undeserved—triggers are oddly shaped, often beautifully marked, and have bizarre behavioral repertoires, including a potential for what we may see as viciousness. The group is widely, if cautiously, used for human consumption, and their rough skin is sometimes used as a biological sandpaper. They are easily acquired, acclimated, raised, and trained. Provided the keeper chooses wisely and knows what ownership may

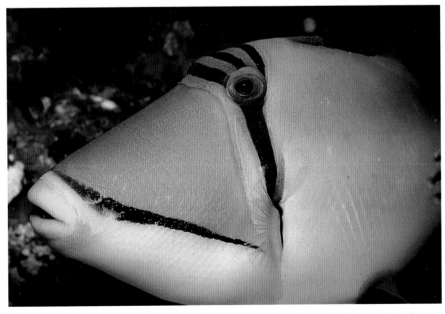

Assasi or Arabian Picasso Triggerfish (*Rhinecanthus assasi*): both loved and loathed by experienced aquarists, triggerfishes can either be well-mannered or a lethal menace to other fishes.

entail, balistids make for the best of marine keeping.

Classification. The triggerfishes, Family Balistidae, are a group of largely shallow-water marine fishes found in the Atlantic, Pacific, and Indian Oceans. There are 12 genera and 37 described species. The assemblage is characterized by laterally compressed, oblong bodies, no pelvic fins, and a "trigger"—a stout first dorsal spine locking mechanism (combined with a second smaller spine making up the actual "lock"). The upper jaw is not protractile, with two rows of protruding incisorlike teeth.

Triggers have soft dorsal and anal fins, each with 23 to 50 rays, which they use as a principal means of locomotion. Their eyes can be independently rotated—another trait that they share with the related pufferfish families. Triggerfishes have three dorsal spines, all soft fins with branched rays. Trigger scales are in regular series and are platelike, which is why they are sometimes called leatherjackets. Their upper jaws usually have eight teeth in the outer series and six in the inner series.

Systematic ichthyologists place the family in the Order Tetraodontiformes ("four teeth"), formerly called the Plectognathi, and hold this as one of the most advanced groups of fishes. They are assembled with other groups for rather technical morphological features. The fishes we are interested in here share the order with the various puffer families, the giant ocean sunfishes, the filefishes, the deepwater spikefishes, and the triplespines. The order has about 320 species in 65 genera and 8 families.

If we look carefully at these seemingly dissimilar groups, we see that externally they have little resemblance, but skeletally they are quite similar. All have reduced gill openings and elongation of pelvic bones. They also share a similar use of dorsal and anal fins for locomotion, and a reduction, specialization and loss of scales.

Range. Triggerfishes are found worldwide in tropical seas. Most species are found around reefs, but some are open-ocean pelagics.

Size. Though most species range around 6 inches, a few get over 12 inches long. The Blunt-head trigger attains 2-3 feet, but even a small Queen or Undulated Triggerfish can be a real bruiser or biter. Inch for inch, these fishes can exhibit nasty behavior, regardless of relative size.

Selection. Most triggerfishes are solitary, territorial, and with a tendency to be aggressive. Beware of most generalizations regarding these fishes, however. The group, along with its high degree of complex and learned behavior, also displays an enormous range of individuality—each specimen is different. I have seen and owned Undulated, Queen, and Clown Triggerfishes that grew up and coexisted with other very edible tankmates without incident.

That said, these can be among the most notorious of aquarium bullies. One Clown Triggerfish we had was housed with a few damselfish when it was a tiny juvenile. It grew to 6 inches in as many months, feeding on dried, frozen and live foods and coexisting with its damsel pals. One day, in a flurry of frenzied munching, the trigger bit right through a hapless damsel. It was probably an accident. All inhabitants, including the trigger, rushed for cover. But the next day, all the damsels had disappeared. Obviously, triggers can learn, and learn quickly. Although they tend to be unpredictable, they can often be trained to get along with other species.

This brings us to the number one question: Should you even acquire a trigger? If you are already saying yes, then make sure you pick one that is bright, alert, 2 to 5 inches in length, and has good coloration. Buying a small individual and watching it grow is really the best route with the triggerfishes; you won't be buying a big fish that comes with big, bad habits already in place, and you won't miss seeing it develop physically and in personality.

I would not be concerned with an individual whose fins are slightly torn or that appears thin. The family is hardy and readily repairs. It is very common for a chased trigger to wedge itself inextricably into a rock or piece of coral or other material. Please take my advice and either borrow or buy the item containing the stuck specimen—don't try to pull it out.

Queen Triggerfish (*Balistes vetula*): a magnificent fish, but one with a fierce reputation among Caribbean divers and world aquarium keepers.

If you are truly undecided about whether or not to buy a triggerfish, keep reading, especially the accompanying box that lists the predictable troublemakers. Consider the space you have and, most important, the ability of the fishes or invertebrates you already have that might become trigger fodder. **Habitat.** In their natural shallow water environment, captive species frequent coral reefs and dead reef flats with plenty of rubble, rocks, and secretive places for escape and food scavenging. You need to provide adequate sleeping, hiding, and play spaces. Your trigger will help, as it will most likely do some rearranging of your aquascape. It will move all the gravel daily, bite the heater, pull out the air lines, and swim around in circles upside down, so design and lay out its home accordingly.

Though tolerant of relatively poor conditions, triggers appreciate good and steady water quality. You will need some vigorous circulation and macro-filtration to keep up with their big and messy feedings. Temperatures should be in the high 70s or low 80s. You need to maintain a high pH value (8.2 to 8.4) and specific gravities typical for reef areas

Clown Triggerfish (*Balistoides conspicillum*): an expensive aquarium species and one that should be bought only when it is eating well and in obvious good health.

Choosing a Triggerfish for Your Aquarium

Peaceful Choices

Melichthys indicus, Blue Checkline Triggerfish

Melichthys ringens, Black-finned Triggerfish

Melichthys vidua, Pinktail Triggerfish

Rhinecanthus aculeatus, Picasso Triggerfish

Rhinecanthus assasi, Assasi Triggerfish

Rhinecanthus rectangulus, Rectangle Triggerfish

Xanthichthys auromarginatus, Blue-throat Triggerfish

Possible Troublemakers

Balistapus undulatus, Orange-lined Triggerfish

Balistes vetula, Queen Triggerfish

Balistoides conspicillum, Clown Triggerfish

Sufflamen bursa, Bursa Triggerfish

Odonus niger, Redtooth Triggerfish

Xanthichthys mento, Indian Triggerfish

(1.023 to 1.025). Frequent, partial water changes by way of gravel vacuuming are a very good idea. Watch your hands and the trigger(s) when you are working in the system—these fish do bite.

Behavior. Territoriality is a big problem with this group—triggers must not be crowded. You also have to make sure they are adequately fed. Either deficiency will result in a drab, sulking, or bullying trigger.

Initially quite shy, your new specimen will probably make a beeline for the darkest, most inaccessible cranny on first introduction. Give it a day or so, and you will soon find an almost puppylike behavior. Some species and individuals are not likely to be good tankmates for your triggerfish. Lionfishes and their relatives (such as eels) can easily become trigger chew toys unless the system is very large or filled with rocky obstructions and hiding places. Larger, more aggressive, outright distasteful fishes should be the rule for balistid companions—big

basses and groupers, beefy surgeons, and many eels and puffers of various sorts that can stand their own ground. Although triggerfishes have been found in the stomach contents of sharks, rays, morays, and more, other species are typically on the receiving end of their endless sampling—particularly crustaceans, corals, and worms—and I have yet to find an invertebrate that wasn't sampled to death. In fact, it's hard to think of a fish less suited to a reef-tank setting than a trigger.

An interesting peculiarity of this group is their ability to produce noise by grinding their teeth, vibrating their gas bladder, and articulating the pectoral girdle. In the wild, and even through the aquarium walls, you can often clearly make out their grinding, snapping, and alarm warnings as a series of rapid, audible grunts.

Triggerfishes also have a mechanism for slightly enlarging their bodies, although they can't "puff up" quite as spectacularly as their close cousins.

This is done by expanding a ventral flap supported by a large movable pelvic bone. This action is often exhibited in bullying, avoiding predation, and locking the individual into a secure position in the reef during rest or hiding.

Reproduction. At least some species display a haremic condition with one male serving several females, and with the females guarding the demersal eggs in nests for a short period. The hatched larvae then become pelagic, blown about by the currents without further parental protection.

In some species, structural or color differences between the sexes have been noted, with males usually larger. A quick note concerning interactions between humans and triggerfish in the wild: be very careful if triggers are nesting in the area you're diving. I still have a scar on my wrist from a bite inflicted by a nesting Queen Trigger. How can you tell when or where they might be spawning? Ask the local divers, or just look around underwater. You'll see no

Redtooth Triggerfish (*Odonus niger*): caution advised, but often peaceful.

Orange-lined Triggerfish (*Balistapus undulatus*): a beauty with a mean streak.

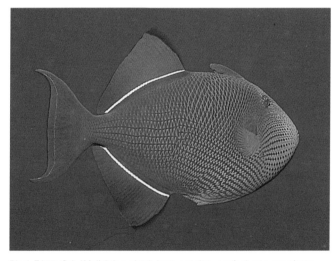

Black Triggerfish (*Melichthys niger*): large species, not for home aquariums.

Assasi Triggerfish (*Rhinecanthus assasi*): usually peaceful. Note yellow lips.

other fishes around the sites, with a "no trespass" zone that may be 30 feet in diameter.

Feeding. Triggerfish eat most anything, digestible or not. Urchins, fishes, shrimp, crabs, clams, even chunks of human fingers. Don't let their small mouths fool you, they have powerful jaws and formidable dentition.

I strongly recommend substantial, meaty, daily feedings. Your triggerfishes should not appear thin. Frequent, moderate food allowances go a long way toward reducing aggression.

Disease. Triggerfishes are subject to the usual scourges of infectious and parasitic marine infection, but happily respond to, and have a wide tolerance of, standard treatments, including copper and Formalin.

Summary. These fishes are characters! Making the trade-off of their personality and robustness for their potential aggressiveness is easy—if you have the right system and aquarium companions—but do keep in mind their imminent mood changes and potential capacity for becoming pugnacious, belligerent, or downright dangerous to your other livestock.

Filefishes

Family Monacanthidae
Trigger Types without the Temperament

IN MANY WAYS just as appealing as the triggers in color, pattern, and behavior, filefishes have better temperaments and are more suitable tankmates for many aquariums. By adhering to a few selection and maintenance criteria, even the novice can experience success in keeping many members of this unusual and likable group.

Classification. The filefish is sometimes placed in a subfamily, the Monacanthinae ("one spine") sharing the Family Balistidae with the triggerfishes, Subfamily Balistinae. (Note the convention in zoological scientific naming of designating families with an -idae ending and subfamilies with -inae.) Others, myself included, prefer to elevate the filefishes to their own family level, the Monacanthidae.

These fishes belong to the Order Tetraodontiformes. Knowing these relationships can be useful when it comes to hands-on management of these fishes. Filefishes, triggers, and puffers all get around by the same sort of undulation of their dorsal and anal fins. They all also eat many of the same meaty foods in approximately equal proportions and intervals. All of them also suffer from similar maladies and infections, and are treatable in like fashion. Their environmental demands, reproduction, intelligence, and behavior are also comparable. Remembering this information for each individual animal would be difficult, thus it is worthwhile to know it by higher category. This is part of the practical value of paying attention to taxonomic groupings.

Filefishes themselves are identified by having two dorsal spines—the second may be small or absent. Their soft dorsal, anal, and pectoral fin ray spines are unbranched. They have small scales not arranged in regular series. Their bodies are prickly to furry to the touch.

Their upper jaws usually have six teeth in the outer and four in the inner series. The filefish family includes about 31 genera, including *Aluterus*, *Amanses*, *Cantherhines*, *Chaetoderma*, *Monacanthus*, *Oxymonacanthus*, *Paraluteres*, and *Pervagor*, with about 85 species.

Range. Filefishes are found in shallow reef and rocky areas in Atlantic, Indian, and Pacific marine environments. Though often present, sometimes in large numbers, they are frequently missed by noisy, unobservant divers.

Size. Most files reach about 6 inches. One, *Aluterus scriptus*, gets to a maximum length of almost 3 feet.

Selection. Healthy specimens display good color (without blotchy or necrotic patches), good behavior (curiosity, activity), and active feeding.

Saddled Filefish or Valentini Mimic (*Paraluteres prionurus*): most filefishes are underappreciated; this small attractive species mimics the Saddled or Valentini Toby (*Canthigaster valentini*), shown on page 320.

Good Filefish Choices

Aluterus schoepfi, **Orange Filefish**

Aluterus scriptus, **Scribbled Filefish**

Aluterus monoceros, **Unicorn Leatherjacket**

Cantherhines macroceros, **Whitespotted Filefish**

Cantherhines pardalis, **Honeycomb Filefish**

Cantherhines pullus, **Orangespotted Filefish**

Cantherhines dumerili, **Vagabond Filefish**

Chaetoderma pencilligerus, **Tassel Filefish or Prickly Leatherjacket**

Monacanthus hispidus, **Planehead Filefish**

Monacanthus ciliatus, **Fringed Filefish**

Pervagor melanocephalus, **Redtail Filefish**

Pervagor spilosoma, **Fantail Filefish**

Pervagor aspricaudus, **Hawaiian Redtail Filefish**

Most species make excellent captives, with one colorful but unfortunate exception. The frequently offered Longnose Filefish (*Oxymonacanthus longirostris*), sometimes confusingly called the Orangespotted Filefish, only eats coral polyps. Leave it in the ocean unless you are farming corals. Otherwise it will starve to death in your tank.

In fact, I think the whole genus *Oxymonacanthus* is corallivorous and should be avoided. (On the other hand, *Cantherhines pullus*, also possessing the common name Orangespotted Filefish, is a suitable aquarium choice.)

A caution concerning netting filefishes: their skin and fins get stuck in most nets. It's much better to do away with nets altogether and hand-lift specimens or scoot them into a container underwater when they must be moved.

Habitat. Filefishes are not picky about water quality, but they should be given plenty of rockwork, caves, and crevices where they can hide and/or wedge themselves into secure positions when frightened or sleeping. Filefishes rely a great deal on subterfuge to avoid predation, and they seem to prosper in physical surroundings that complement their gaudy coloration. Real or faux decor including sponges, sea fans, coral skeletons, and plants that allow blending or camouflaging seem to make files feel at home.

Behavior. This whole order is best characterized as individualistic. In general, filefishes are docile toward members of the same species when they are small or when specimens are temporarily crowded, as in dealers' tanks. But don't get complacent. Filefishes can become intolerant without any apparent provocation. Most are best kept one file to the tank.

Whitespotted Filefish (*Cantherhines macroceros*): not commonly seen, but an interesting captive species.

Slender Filefish (*Monacanthus tuckeri*): appealing and pygmy-sized, but an opportunistic omnivore that may damage delicate reef tank invertebrates.

As a group, they are opportunistic omnivores. Keep your eye on things. Although they usually cause little outright damage, a file that is continually following and chewing on another fish can wear it down.

As for "turnabout is fair play," most would-be predators find filefishes too tough to bother with. In addition to having the height-increasing dorsal "trigger" mechanism, files share the triggerfishes' capacity for slightly enlarging their bodies by expanding a ventral flap supported by a large movable pelvic bone.

Reproduction. Some species of filefishes have been observed spawning in the wild. Eggs are green in color, about a millimeter in diameter, demersal (on the bottom), adhesive, hatching in a couple of days after sunset, becoming pelagic, and having planktonic larvae. In some species, the males are slightly larger and more colorful.

Feeding. Most any and all frozen and fresh foods will sustain filefishes. Meaty clams and crustacean foodstuffs will generally shake a languishing filefish out of the doldrums. Files also have a need for vegetable material. Stomach content analyses reveal a broad mix of hydrozoans, algae, sedentariate polychaetes, sponges, gastropods, amphipods, gorgonians, sea grasses, colonial anemones, and tunicates. This might be the perfect candidate for stripping an overgrown reef tank back down to bare rock.

Disease. As with virtually all others, files should go through quarantine or a quick dip in a copper or Formalin solution. The usual remedies are effective against *Amyloodinium* or *Cryptocaryon*.

Summary. Filefishes are available seasonally from different geographic areas. Check with your dealer regarding what is available now and what might be coming. You may need to place a special order if your local shop is not accustomed to ordering out-of-the-ordinary species. Don't let this or their shy, delicate appearance dissuade you. Filefishes make curious, affordable aquarium specimens that are somewhat unusual.

Puffers, Boxfishes, Cowfishes, and Porcupinefishes

Families Triodontidae, Tetraodontidae, Ostraciidae, and Diodontidae

Strong on Defense, with Intelligence to Match

WHAT WOULD YOU DO, if you were a reef fish, to lessen your chances of getting eaten? Leave a bad taste in the mouths of your foes? Cover yourself in spines and become nearly impossible to swallow? Take on cryptic colors and markings? Perhaps exude a toxic slime? Well, the fishes we call puffers beat you to it.

They do all this—and more—and it works. They are found worldwide in tropical and temperate seas and have few predators.

The various puffers, and their related families, the boxfishes, trunkfishes, cowfishes, and porcupinefishes offered to aquarists have many things going for them as good aquarium

Map Puffer (*Arothron mappa*): a large, dramatic Indo-Pacific species with great personality and capable of stopping traffic at any aquarium, but commanding lofty prices when available.

choices. They're reasonably priced, easy to feed, attractively colored, whimsically shaped, and most are hardy and long-lived. As far as intelligence, puffers go to the head of the class in the way of fishy IQs; they quickly learn who you are and that yours is the hand that feeds.

Their downsides are few but daunting if you are caught unaware: they'll eat smaller and slower fishes and most palatable nonfish; some are noted finnippers; and the cowfishes may even cause a whole system to crash in an invisible cloud of poison.

Classification. Puffer groups are part of the "last" or "highest" order of fishes, the Tetraodontiformes, along with the triggers, filefishes, and a couple of nonaquarium fish families, the spikefishes and ocean sunfishes. The various puffer groups share many characteristics with other members of their order. The prominent aquarium contenders include: Family Triodontidae: three-toothed puffers; Family Tetraodontidae: four-toothed puffers; Family Ostraciidae: boxfishes, trunkfishes, cowfishes; and Family Diodontidae: porcupinefishes.

Think of all the things you know about the filefishes and triggerfishes: their locomotion, body inflation, dentition and sound production. In their general traits and habits, this assem-

Saddled or Valentini Toby (*Canthigaster valentini*): a good aquarium choice but poisonous to its predators, this fish is closely mimicked by the Saddled Filefish (*Paraluterus prionurus*) (see page 317).

blage of families is quite similar.

Lacking typical finnage, how do puffers manage to swim? Although not at all swift, they undulate their dorsal and anal fins, using the caudal for a balancing rudder and short bursts of energy. Good defense, rather than speed, serves these fishes well.

Puffers inflate themselves to varying extents in response to threatening situations. The triggers and files also use this tactic to a lesser degree, with their distensible ventral sides aiding their elevated dorsal spines in making them harder to swallow or blow away in currents. All are missing lower ribs; the puffers forego other bony body parts and scales as well. For those who want to know the simplified mechanics of "puffing," puffers have an greatly extensible stomach that may be filled with water (or, regrettably, air) and kept there by a specialized valve. The stretched abdominal muscles expel the ingested water through the valve when danger is past.

Principal Aquarium Choices

Family Ostraciidae, from the Greek *ostracum*, meaning shell, includes the box, trunk, and cowfishes, which are found all over the tropical Atlantic, Indian, and Pacific oceans. There are 14 genera with about 33 species. These may be the most characteristic of fishes with bodies encased in a bony carapace.

The family is also notable for some members' possession of ostracitoxin, a toxic substance that is released into the water. If sufficiently disturbed, some ostraciids can can wipe out whole tanks and killing all livestock, including themselves. Though this is rare, the cautions listed later on netting, acclimation, and choice of tankmates should be heeded if you intend to try a trunkfish, boxfish, or cowfish.

Cowfishes of the genus *Lactoria*, especially the Long-horned Cowfish (*L. cornuta*) should be dealt with painstakingly; I have witnessed three episodes of whole tanks being poisoned with this species, one from a dead specimen in a filter, another from a harassed individual, the third from the careless introduction of shipping water into the display system.

Members of the genus *Lactophrys* also sport "horns," a conspicuous pair on the head and another doing rear guard near the anal fin, prompting the common name, cowfish. The Smooth Trunkfish (*L. triqueter*) is the most frequently offered member of the genus, with the Scrawled Cowfish (*L. quadricornis*) and Honeycomb Cowfish (*L. polygonia*) occasionally available. All three hail from the western tropical Atlantic and grow to at least 11 inches.

The Yellow Boxfish (*Ostracion cubicus*) is a perennial favorite of mine, especially as a bright yellow juvenile with black spots. It is a large fish in the wild, attaining some 18 inches. On a smaller scale, the Blue-spotted (male) and

Scribbled Boxfish (*Ostracion solorensis*): the ability to produce toxic slime if harassed or mishandled commands respect for the boxfishes, which should never be housed with harassing tankmates.

THE CONSCIENTIOUS MARINE AQUARIST

Black-spotted (female) Boxfish, (*O. meleagris*) is often seen as well.

The so-called "Boston beans" that turn up seasonally in the fish shops are juveniles of various species of cowfishes and boxfishes, not a single species; they grow into a variety of adult forms.

Ostraciids, unfortunately, have not had a good record of success with marine aquarists, with problems mainly related to diet or the lack of it. These fishes need food—green and meaty—on a regular basis; most are lost to outright starvation. Especially on first arrival, it is critical that the specimen begin feeding.

Family Triodontidae has only one species, *Triodon macropterus*, the Three-toothed Puffer. In addition to its trio of fused teeth, it has a strange, deep-bellied profile and is very rarely seen in the trade.

Family Tetraodontidae is the "true" puffer family to many; it contains all the nonspiny, nonarmored, non-deep-bodied puffers. These animals can really inflate their bodies, multiplying their diameter; their bodies are either naked or dotted with short prickles. The viscera, particularly the gonads, of puffers are toxic, containing the tetraodotoxin poison at times fatal to sushi-bar goers in Japan and to hapless predators on the reef.

There are two subfamilies in the Tetraodontidae. The members of the first, Subfamily Tetraodontinae, appear broadly rounded in cross section. Of the 18 genera, only *Arothron* is regularly sold in the West. This genus has noth-

Papuan Toby (*Canthigaster papuensis*): the sharpnose puffers and tobies have limited inflation abilities, but much of the personality of larger puffers. Most are hardy and peaceful, but will nibble at invertebrates.

ing but exemplary species with great personalities. Most often available are the Guinea Fowl (*A. meleagris*) and the Bulldog or Black-spotted Puffer (*A. nigropunctatus*), in black, gray, and golden forms or a splotchy mix thereof. The Indo-Pacific Stars-and-Stripes Puffer (*A. hispidus*) is found now and then and is also excellent.

The second subfamily, Canthigastrinae, includes the tobies, also called sharpnose puffers. These are laterally compressed, taller than wide in cross section, and have limited inflation capabilities. The single genus, *Canthigaster*, is readily identified by its

members' elongated, pointed snouts. The Sharpnose Puffer (*C. rostrata*) is the only Atlantic species and is common and inexpensive. The Pacific or Spotted Sharpnose (*C. punctatissimus*) and the Hawaiian or Whitespotted Toby (*C. jactator*) are almost copies of each other, with white spots against a brown background.

Other species regularly offered are the Ambon Toby (*C. amboinensis*) the Solander's or Blue-spotted Toby (*C. solandri*) and the widespread Saddled or Valentini Toby (*C. valentini*), which has a filefish (the Saddled Filefish or Valentini Mimic, *Paraluteres prionurus*)

Juvenile Yellow Boxfish (*Ostracion cubicus*): at times sold as a "Boston bean." Adult Yellow Boxfish (*Ostracion cubicus*): fully grown with typical humped nose.

that mimics it. You have to look closely to discern the filefish even when it is in the same tank with the toby; the file has a two-spine dorsal that the puffer lacks. This is a type of Batesian mimicry: the filefish suffers less predation by pretending to be an unpalatable puffer. The two species make a fascinating display when exhibited together.

Canthigaster species are hardy, small (4 inches or less), undemanding tankmates, but they will nibble at all types of invertebrate life and are not safe for reef systems. The Hawaiian Toby (*C. jactator*) is also a nasty fin nipper.

Family Diodontidae includes the porcupine or burrfishes; their inflatable bodies are covered with spines that may be either permanently erect or folded down when the animal is not inflated. There are 6 genera with 19 species in the Atlantic, Indian, and Pacific Oceans. The two genera sold, *Diodon* and *Chilomycterus*, make excellent

aquarium fishes with limitless spunk.

Selection. Picking out a good puffer is pretty simple; most are adaptable to given conditions as long as they haven't been beaten to death in transit from collection and transport.

Check the skin (particularly around the mouth and fin origins) and the eyes for sores and abrasions. These areas are tender on puffers and show white and red marks from netting and other traumas.

Never lift these fishes into the air. Their reaction is to inflate, which may look "cute," but is problematic if the inflation is with air rather than water. When resubmerged, the fish often cannot expel the trapped air and the animal suffers for it. Instead, if a puffer needs to be moved, gingerly scoot the specimen into a partially water-filled bag underwater.

Habitat. An appropriate aquarium environment for displaying puffers should

reflect their reef existence, with rock and rubble to gain comfort in cover, and sand to search and blow through looking for food.

What about puffers in other than fish-only systems? This is not advisable. They love invertebrates—all part of their natural diet. Even the smallest species will sample corals, anemones, echinoderms, crustaceans, and others to the point of terminal bedevilment. They will even eat smaller, unaware fishes.

Another caution: puffers bite, and bigger specimens have teeth that ought to command respect. They will cut into decor, including electrical cords, so be sure to make your heater connections and powerhead lines inaccessible if they're in with puffers.

Filtration. No matter what is written and offered in face-to-face advice, aquarists seem to overfeed their puffers. In the wild, a typical posture for these fishes is setting on or near the bottom, watching, resting, waiting for something of interest to investigate or eat. In captivity, they soon learn to do the dance of getting us to feed them frequently—and too much. Be aware of how much food you're throwing in, even though "poor Puffy seems so hungry." A little food daily is fine, with larger meaty meals two or three times a week.

Frequent water changes, good circulation, and protein skimming are necessary with these fishes and their indulgent owners.

Behavior. Known for their defensive habit of producing poisonous slime when stressed, these fishes should not be housed with fast-swimming or harassing tankmates. Fortunately, most captive fishes will shy away from interacting with puffers, somehow knowing their unpalatability or outright toxicity. One category of tankmates that should be avoided are the cleaners (cleaner gobies, cleaner shrimp, or *Labroides* wrasses). Incessant pecking at their sensitive hides, even by tiny *Gobiosoma*, is too much stress for puffers.

Some puffers, notably the *Canthigaster* species, are known to be haremic in the wild, but most are found singly, and, in my opinion, should be housed this way in aquariums. I know aquarists who have successfully mixed different puffer species; they give credit to having disparate sizes, adding them all at once and/or having simple good luck.

Acclimation. The careful movement of these fishes and a strict adherence to the rule of never mixing shipping water into your main or quarantine system is paramount. Much "slime-poisoning" could be alleviated by taking the time to dilute the puffer's shipping water with system water to get the specimen acclimated. A good part of the bag water should be poured off and replaced with the water the animal will be moved into; this can be done two or three times over a period of 30 minutes, effecting a serial dilution. Finally, pour the puffer and diluted water into the tank.

Reproduction. Many tropical puffers spawn year-round. *Canthigaster valentini* and *C. rostrata* release gametes on an algal nest in a side-by-side position, while others, including the boxfishes, spawn in the water column and produce pelagic eggs.

Feeding. Puffers are opportunistic omnivores; they eat most anything and everything. In the wild, they feed on all types of invertebrates, algae, and carrion. The inclusion of greenery in their diets is very important; live algae is best, but a prepared green food on the bottom will do. Especially for the boxfishes, it is imperative to get them feeding as soon as possible.

These fishes also need hard foods to wear down their ever-growing tooth plates: shrimp, crabs, and mussels in their shells are all suitable.

Feed moderate amounts and distract your greedy puffer so that other tankmates can get a share. Be leery about feeding puffers to satiation; this makes a big mess and they can quickly grow too big. Some species will get huge, longer than your arm.

Disease. Puffer species are very susceptible to *Cryptocaryon* and *Amyloodinium* (as well as to the eye, skin abrasion, and gas-from-lifting maladies already mentioned), but fortunately respond well to copper treatments.

Summary. The closest thing to pet "aqua-dogs" are the puffers. Many aquarists and puffers have formed strong attachments to each other, with the fishes occasionally squirting water into their keepers' faces for no apparent reason.

Do remember that they will bite the hand that feeds them and that they are deadly table fare. Different puffer groups are notorious not just for their poisonous slime but also for their highly poisonous internal organs. I'm an avid sushi-bar goer, but I will not eat fugu (puffer) no matter how well-trained and accredited the chef. Puffer entrails are used worldwide to kill feral animals, particularly domestic cats. Puffer or fugu toxin takes the lives of a few dozen hapless fishermen and sushi-bar patrons, mostly in Japan, every year. Puffer fishes are also implicated in another fish poison, ciguatera. The bottom line? **Don't eat them.**

Do you have a spot in a fish-only system, maybe with plenty of algae growth? Do you want to get rid of that mantis shrimp that has eaten everything else? Looking for a real "pet" for a youngster's aquarium? A puffer-type may well be the answer.

Marine Invertebrates

*Spineless but Hardy Choices
for the Diversified Aquarium*

MOMMA, DON'T LET YOUR BABIES grow up to be cowboys. Don't let them play guitars and drive pickup trucks." So twangs the old country-and-western song. Familiar to most of us whether we like it or not, this sentiment probably has an equivalent in every culture, occupation, and profession. My lyric would say, "Don't let your babies grow up to be marine scientists. Don't let them go diving or have aquariums."

As you might guess, it's too late for many of us. Before my mother could put a stop to the wet menagerie being assembled in my childhood bedroom in southern Japan, I had crossed the point of no return. It happened innocently enough when a friend and I decided to add sophistication to our game of "throw and find the Coke bottle" at Hashimi Bay— we bought masks and snorkels. Finally, we were going to get our first real look at all of the unknown underwater life forms that had been stinging, scraping, and bloodying us every time we raced into the water and reached

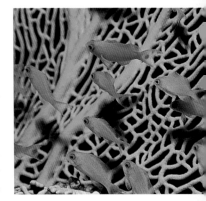

ABOVE: Lyretail Anthias (*Pseudanthias squamipinnis*) with sea fan.
LEFT: reef cuttlefish (*Sepia* sp.) over staghorn coral (*Acropora* sp.).

Diving into a realm of invertebrate diversity—Brown Tube Sponges (*Agelas conifera*) and sea fans on a Caribbean fore reef. "You can mark your own promotion from the rank of an aquarium beginner when the fishes no longer have your undivided attention and you decide to try your hand at keeping invertebrates."

down for the sinking bottle.

If you've ever snorkeled over a coral reef, you have a good idea of what happened next. We came up wide-eyed with amazement. Here was more than we could ever have concocted in our wildest imaginations—unbelievable corals, algae, octopus eggs, embryos, and so many other things that we couldn't even begin to identify. We kept shouting to each other, "What is that?" and raising our heads to exclaim "Incredible!" or "Fantastic!" I didn't really appreciate the significance at the time, but from that moment I was hooked on the wonder of aquatic environments (particularly near-shore marine), and hooked for life.

My natural history collecting suddenly blossomed from the red-bellied salamanders and fancy goldfish I'd been bringing home to simpler organisms—the marine invertebrates. This is an awakening that many saltwater aquarists also experience when they find themselves gravitating to the retail displays of anemones, mushroom corals, reef shrimps, giant clams, rock-encrusting zooanthids, or the larger soft and stony corals. Taxonomically, these organisms are ranked lower than the backboned fishes, but the marine invertebrates must rate as one of this planet's most mind-boggling displays of diversity. They encompass an entire world of almost incomprehensible shapes, forms, colors, and life histories. You can mark your own promotion from the rank of an aquarium beginner when the fishes no longer have your undivided attention and you decide to try your hand at keeping invertebrates.

The Bias of Backbones

THE LAST TIME YOU WENT TO THE ZOO, WHAT DID YOU SEE? This isn't a trick question—we all know the answer: birds and mammals. I hope that after reading this book you will be tempted to join me in urging our public zoos to take a broader view of the term "animal." Next time you're there, do what I do and cheerfully shout, "Hey, where are the fishes and invertebrates?"

The word "zoo" is from the Greek *zoion*, or animal. Of the over 1 million described animal species, only about 5% have backbones and are thus designated as vertebrates. The "other" 95% are in the invertebrate group.

This fundamental division of the Animal Kingdom is entirely artificial. A more logical separation would be "arthropods" (joint-legged animals, including vertebrates crustaceans, insects, and spiders) and "inarthropods," since the arthropods make up 85% or so of all described animal species. Or we could split the animals between tissue and nontissue-grade life—this lower group to include the stinging-celled animals, sponges, and comb jellies—a sectioning that would be more natural and useful.

The whole grouping of invertebrates, in fact, is based simply on the fact that they're just not vertebrates, instead of being based on sharing any positive characteristics. Their range in size, structure, physiology, and how they "make their lives" is enormous and disparate. Collectively, marine invertebrates are of the broadest origins, some being more closely related to vertebrates than the other invertebrate groups. From taking numerous "marine invertebrate zoology" courses in college, I can assure you there are no marine invertebrate zoologists; the groups are just too huge and diverse, with many subspecialties focusing on one aspect of their biology—morphology, embryology, and others.

Ocean Origins

THE ENTIRE ANIMAL KINGDOM arose from the ancient seas, long before the fossil record. All the major invertebrate groups have marine representatives and some (stinging-celled animals, such as the corals, anemones, and gorgonians; spiny-skinned animals, such as sea stars, cucumbers, and crinoids) are almost exclusively marine. All the animals that eventually turned to freshwater and the land originally came from the sea.

Most of the nonvertebrates of interest to marine hobbyists reside in intertidal to shallow-water habitats. There is a rich diversity of species there, some living freely in the water, others living or wandering on, in, or among the substrate, and

Tree or flower coral (*Dendronephthya* sp.) growing upside-down at the entrance to a cave in the Maldives: one of many difficult-to-keep species of *Dendronephthya* that tantalize expert aquarists.

Flame Scallop (*Lima scabra*): bizarre is the norm among the invertebrates, as in the filter-feeding appendages of this commonly collected mollusk, sometimes called the Rough Fileclam and a member of the file shell group. White tentacles, rather than reddish-orange, are typical of specimens from deeper water.

the rest attached to the substrate. All modes of nutrition are employed—there are carnivorous, filter, suspension, detritus, and deposit feeders—some relying to a degree on symbiotic relations with microscopic algae, and all ultimately dependent on algae for food and oxygen.

Brief Glimpses

EACH OF THE MARINE INVERTEBRATE GROUPS covered in this book has structural peculiarities and specialized terminology. Don't feel overwhelmed by this; skip the "classification" sections if you aren't ready for them. What is it we're really concerned about? Keeping these things alive.

Whether or not you're interested in the idiosyncrasies of their anatomy and taxonomy, bear in mind that all marine invertebrates must solve the same problems: getting enough food and oxygen, removing wastes, reproducing, and avoiding predators. How do they do it, and in what ways can you accommodate them? Are they harder to keep than fishes? The general, simple answer to the latter is, Yes. Many invertebrates are highly dependent on stable water conditions and will

TOP: Blue Starfish (*Linckia laevigata*) with various soft corals and sponge. BOTTOM: unusual color morph of a Maxima Clam (*Tridacna maxima*). All are good potential aquarium specimens.

quickly shrivel up and die in aquariums that have seemingly healthy populations of fishes. Most shouldn't even be considered if your aquarium skimming isn't first-rate, your water circulation is sluggish, or your key measures of water quality are not in order.

The following sections will introduce some of the hardiest invertebrates and provide an overview of some of the more demanding choices. The marine invertebrates that find their way into home aquariums actually range from those that are much less work than fish (requiring only good light and clean water—not even asking to be fed) to those (such as the small-polyped stony corals) that are for advanced aquarists only.

These brief glimpses represent just a few invertebrate groups and species and reflect my own biases; may they at least serve to whet your appetite. The body of knowledge on marine invertebrates is colossal and easy to find when you are ready to search further. Biological journals around the world have been published concerning these animals for more than a century. If interested, you are encouraged to look at the references listed in the Bibliography (page 408) and then make a pilgrimage to a large library's science department. Like the kid putting on a dive mask and looking down at a reef for the first time, you will be amazed at what there is to explore.

Sponges

Phylum Porifera

Natural Survivors to Brighten the Aquascape

SPONGES? Those just-barely-multicellular creatures that only a natural history fanatic could love? Animals so immobile that it's hard to tell if they're living or not? In fact, this is an amazing group of marine organisms that come in a profusion of shapes and many wonderful colors. Let's face it: any organism that can be squeezed through a cheesecloth and then rebuild itself on the other side, cell to cell, deserves our respect. And with some knowledge about their selection, care and feeding, many species of sponges offered in the aquarium trade can do well in captive marine environments.

Classification. Sponges, Phylum Porifera (meaning to bear or carry openings) are the simplest form of "tissue-grade" life, just up from protozoans (unicellular creatures) and down from cnidarians (stinging-celled organisms like corals and anemones) in many taxonomic schemes. They don't, in fact, have tissues or organs; their cells are somewhat unspecialized and quite independent; a whole sponge is more like a colony than a single animal.

There are about 150 freshwater

Yellow Tube Sponge (*Aplysina fistularis*) on a Caribbean Reef with gorgonians and a school of juvenile Bluehead Wrasses (*Thalassoma bifasciatum*) and Blue Chromis (*Chromis cyanea*).

species, but these are generally small, unremarkable, and not offered in the aquarium trade. The approximately 5,000 marine species are sessile—incapable of locomotion—and found attached to hard or soft substrates. They occur worldwide, mostly in shallow waters and come in all shapes and sizes, from a bean to a washtub. Some are cylinders, others vaselike; most are crustose and irregular.

The Porifera live up to their name by having a characteristic arrangement of specialized cells, called porocytes, that allow water into an open space in their bodies known as the atrium. The outer walls of their structure are formed of nonliving spicules. These are the skeletons we use as natural bathroom or car wash sponges.

The reason aquarists are cautioned against ever lifting a live sponge from the water is eminently clear in examining the anatomy of a sponge. Once air is trapped in the atrium, it is exceedingly difficult for the specialized cells, called choanocytes, to void it. The choanocytes, equipped with flagella, are responsible for producing the animal's internal water currents, which transport oxygen, carbon-dioxide, sex cells, and waste.

Large air bubbles are too much for them to handle and will lead to dead spots within the sponge.

Most sponges are filter feeders that subsist by sieving out very fine (submicroscopic) food particles from the water, though tiny "killer" sponges that can capture larger prey sometimes make the news.

The various sponges are broadly subdivided into the Calcarea, Hexactinellida, Sclerospongiae and Demospongiae on the basis of the chemical and physical makeup of their skeletons.

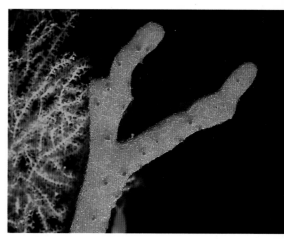

Red branching sponge (unidentified): living sponges should be kept submerged to keep air from entering the atrium.

Selection. Sponges do not enjoy a solid reputation in the aquarium hobby as hardy captive organisms. Many people consider them simply short-lived (or not living at all) ornaments. This is inaccurate, and fortunately there are some varieties that, given proper collection, transport, and intermittent care, do very well in captivity. However, before investing your hard-earned cash in

Pink tube sponge: unidentified species from Caribbean waters.

Clathria mima: encrusting sponge species from Fiji that can appear on live rock.

Red ball sponge (unidentifed species): collected along Gulf Coast of Florida.

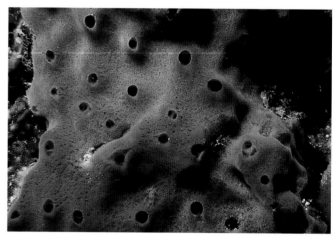
Blue encrusting sponge (*Haliclona* sp.) in the Maldives: good aquarium species.

a specimen, observe the proposed sponge in your dealer's tank carefully:

1) Is there sufficient substrate (usually a piece of live rock) attached to the sponge? The sponge may be doomed if it was removed without its substrate. There are some species that dwell in sand or mud, but most sponges are attached to hard materials that should be collected and shipped with them.

2) Ask if the specimen has ever been exposed to the air. It should not have been. Air is easily trapped inside the animal, creating dead spots. To move sponges from one place to another, they must be bagged below the surface.

3) The excurrent (outflowing) "mouth" (oscula) of the sponge should be open, indicating internal activity/water flow.

4) There should be little or no visible "dead" tissue, seen as gray or whitish patches or masses. If possible, ask the dealer to cut out any bad spots and keep the prospective purchase for you while it is regenerating.

5) Living sponges are relatively firm, evenly colored, and essentially odorless. If the tank that a sponge is in smells foul, move on.

If you purchase live rock for a reef system, you may well receive a bonus in interesting sponge material that can spread and add much interest and color to a system. Some species, such as the Chicken Liver Sponge (*Chondrilla nucula*), are notorious for dying off during live rock shipment and curing, producing a noxious odor and potent quantities of ammonia. If they survive the trip from reef to aquarium, however, they can live for years, usually hidden in the rockwork.

Among the most commonly available species are some exceptionally colorful sponges from the Gulf of Mexico and Florida Keys. Easily kept and a visual feast for the invertebrate aquarist are the Orange, Red or Blue Green Finger Sponges (*Haliclona* spp.); Red or Orange Ball Sponges (*Cinachyra* spp.); and various encrusting red, orange, and yellow sponges (*Diplasatrella*, *Monanchora*, *Phorbas*, *Spirastrella* and other genera) that must be purchased in situ on pieces of live rock. It may take a special order, but the many vase and tube sponges also make unusual aquarium specimens and come in a range of colors from lavender to pink, blue, and many shades of red. Especially prized is the magnificent Strawberry Vase Sponge (*Mycale laxissima*), available from Florida, the Bahamas, and the Caribbean.

Among the many Indo-Pacific sponges, one genus much appreciated by aquarists contains the blue sponges (*Haliclona* spp.) that form dense, firm colonies. They are often fingerlike but can assume a number of forms. Under proper conditions, they will spread nicely in the aquarium, and some reef keepers have successfully used them to cement together pieces of live rock.

Habitat. Most sponges offered have broad environmental tolerances. The shallow-water species are characteristically tougher in accommodating fluctuations in salinity, pH, and other water-quality parameters. Maintenance of sponges is simple. They do need to be vacuumed clean or lightly hosed free of detritus, gravel, and "gunk" periodically. (Many reef aquarists use a small hand-held powerhead to blow such debris off sponges and live rock.) Proper light and feeding are the most important factors for success, once a healthy specimen has been secured.

About lighting: some reef-building species (e.g. the bright purple and blue genera *Halichondria*, *Callyspongia*, and *Dysidea*) prefer bright direct red-end-shifted lighting. The majority of species offered exist in low-light habitats and should be accommodated likewise. If algae are growing on your sponges, something is wrong: photo strength, duration, quality and/or nutrient levels must be out of whack. Greenish sponges may be harboring symbiotic algae (zooxanthellae) and will require more light.

A strong water current is appreciated, from powerheads, filters, or airstones.

Predator/Prey Relations. Many opportunistic omnivores will chomp on your sponges. Most angelfishes, Family Pomacanthidae, utilize sponge material in their diets. (An exception is the dwarf angels of the genus *Centropyge*, which are generally safe with sponges.) Some species of filefishes and triggers

Extensive growth of a blue encrusting sponge (*Haliclona* sp.) on a fore reef wall in the Maldives.

are also sponge munchers. Nudibranchs, cowries, and several other mollusks are not to be trusted carte blanche with your sponges. As usual, you will have to be observant if you've acquired a prize poriferan.

Tunicates or sea squirts: often confused with sponges, these are actually more highly evolved and react to touch by quickly closing their siphons.

Some fire sponges and Red Ball Sponges are known to produce a "wipe-out syndrome" if injured or sufficiently disturbed. Especially during their introduction, care is warranted. To avoid "toxic sponge effect," be sure never to add shipping water to your aquarium or quarantine system. Fire sponges come by their name for a reason. They can sting and cause serious allergic reactions; wear rubber gloves when in doubt.

Reproduction. Sponges are known to reproduce in both sexual and asexual ways. They have several variations on splitting, and they also produce eggs and sperm that are released into the water column with environmental cues. Some develop planktonic young, others are fertilized and develop their offspring internally. Under favorable conditions, many colorful sponges will spread and produce new colonies in the aquarium. (Some amateur propagators have learned that it's possible to pulverize live sponge in a blender—always keeping the material in its seawater—then allow the tiny fragments to reattach, grow, and colonize pieces of rock or shells. Blend the sponge only briefly or the heat generated will kill its cells.)

Feeding. Sponges are largely filter-feeding organisms, constantly whipping their choanocyte flagella, which sweep in food and oxygen and create an excurrent stream that flushes out carbon dioxide, other wastes and, occasionally, sex cells for reproduction. Poor nutrition is a close runner-up to inappropriate collection as the number one source of sponge mortality.

Feeding is accomplished by temporarily turning off power filters, if any, and introducing a food broth in the area around the sponge. The actual particles ingested by sponges are tiny, and the dietary choices for captive sponges include various liquid invertebrate foods, fresh juice from mollusks (clams, oysters, or mussels for human consumption), foods for newly hatched brine shrimp, and finely divided dry-prepared foods. These foods are made into a suspension (I suggest using the blender) with tank water and squirted slowly at the sponge's surface with a baster or syringe. If you are reproducing sponges or otherwise trying to encourage maximum growth, frequent feedings are preferable, as much as several times daily. In systems with considerable sponge biomass, you may want to eliminate your particulate filter mechanism entirely. Keeping your tank clean should not mean keeping it sterile! In most aquariums, one or two feedings a week should suffice to keep sponges growing slowly, provided your fish are being fed and the water is not constantly stripped of fine particulates by aggressive filtration and skimming.

If you have a full-time power filter, I suggest rigging up an in-line timer that allows you to twist a dial, turning off your filtration during a feeding session and automatically restarting it in 15 minutes or so. Can't figure it out yourself? Go to Radio Shack or check out the pump and powerhead controller units used in reef systems. Most have a "feed" button that shuts everything off for a short period to allow fish and invertebrates to clean up the food before it is swept into the filter or sump.

Summary. Have you been told that sponges are impossible to keep? Untrue. All that's required is to know what a healthy specimen looks like, pick it out without exposing it to the air, and provide it with adequate water quality and feeding. After all, this form of life has been around since before the Cambrian Period; it's a natural survivor, given a reasonable setting.

Cnidarians

Phylum Cnidaria
The Stinging-Celled Animals

WITH THE EXPLOSION of reef aquarium keeping, there has been a simultaneous surge of interest in—and amateur experimentation with—the captive care of anemones, coral-like animals, soft and stony corals, and other members of this huge phylum.

Once called the coelenterates, the cnidarians range from bothersome hydras and jellyfish to sea anemones, tube anemones, sea pens, sea pansies, sea wasps, and Portuguese men-of-war; also included are the sea fans and all the corals—reef- and nonreef-building species, soft and hard, black, horny, and stony. Unbelievably, at least for neophytes to taxonomy, these are all stinging-celled animals.

In captivity, many species have proved hardy and practical, while others remain delicate, prone to early demise, and a challenge even to the skills of expert and professional aquarists. As in keeping other invertebrates and fishes, success rests in first selecting appropriate species, then in choosing individual specimens that have been properly collected, handled, and shipped. To avoid disappointment, the aquarist must be ready to provide appropriate habitat, suitable placement in the aquarium, and, for some species, specialized feeding.

In this section, we will take a look at what the stinging-celled animals are, how to go about identifying healthy specimens, and how to keep them alive in captivity. In addition, we'll touch on their complex and interesting biology.

Classification. The cnidarians are radially symmetrical, are made up of two basic tissue layers, and possess salient "stinging" cells. These are highly variable and are categorized as threadlike (volvent), barbed or spined with and without toxins (penetrant), and "sticky" for anchoring (glutinant).

Their body shapes come in two basic formats: sessile/polyplike, as in the anemones, or free-swimming/medusalike, as in the jellyfishes. The basic features of these body types are evident; most species are either one or the other, medusoid or polypoid, but some pass through both in their life cycle. The old phylum name, Coelenterata, refers to the singular body cavity (the *coelenteron*) formed by the tissue layers and capped by a series of tentacles around a single mouth/anus opening.

There are few freshwater members (e.g. Hydras), but most are marine and found in shallow tropical waters, though they occur worldwide at all depths. There are some 10,000 described species with a rich fossil history dating back before the Cambrian Period.

Orange polyp coral (*Tubastraea* sp.): once known as coelenterates, the cnidarians include corals, anemones, jellyfishes, and others.

The Players: Classification of the Phylum Cnidaria

Class Hydrozoa: simple, tubelike stomach; small medusa stage and a small to large polypoid stage.

  Order Hydroida: hydroids and hydromedusae.

  Order Milleporina: stinging corals; have very heavy calcareous skeletons.

  Order Stylasterina: hydrocorals; mostly deep-water.

  Order Siphonophora: typically planktonic, colonial; *Physalia*.

  Order Chondrophora: planktonic.

Class Scyphozoa: jellyfishes; have four-chambered stomachs; most have large medusa and small polyp stages.

  Order Stauromedusae: possess stalked medusae.

  Order Cubomedusae: sea wasps; medusae with four groups of tentacles.

  Order Semaeostomeae: plate-shaped medusae.

  Order Rhizostomeae: lack tentacles on the margin of the bell; *Cassiopea*.

Class Anthozoa: Polyp stage only; stomach divided into numerous compartments.

  Subclass Octocorallia: octocorals; anthozoans with eight tentacles per polyp; almost all colonial.

  Order Stolonifera: polyps arise from a creeping mat (stolon); skeleton of calcareous tubes; includes *Tubipora* (Organ Pipe Coral).

  Order Telestacea: lateral polyps on simple or branched stems; skeletons of calcareous spicules.

  Order Alcyonacea: soft corals; fleshy, rubbery; mushroomlike or variously lobate growth forms; skeleton of separate calcareous spicules.

  Order Coenothecalia: comprised of only the Indo-Pacific Blue Coral, *Heliopora*; massive calcareous skeleton.

  Order Gorgonacea: sea fans, sea whips; long, stiff, internal skeletons; horny, upright plantlike growth; colonial.

  Order Pennatulacea: sea pens; colonies as fleshy, flattened or elongate; anchored in mud or sand bottom.

  Subclass Zoantharia: solitary or colonial; eight or more tentacles, multiples of six; reef- and nonreef-building corals, anemones.

  Order Actinaria: sea anemones; solitary or clone polyps without a skeleton; two siphonoglyphs.

  Order Scleractinia: true or stony corals; solitary or colonial polyps with calcareous skeletons.

  Order Ceriantharia: tube anemones; elongate tapered bodies; live in secreted mucus tubes.

  Order Zoanthidea: colonial anemone-like polyps; one siphonoglyph, no skeleton.

  Order Antipatharia: black corals; colonial; polyps arranged around an axial skeleton.

  Order Corallimorpharia: false corals or coral anemones; solitary or colonial, flattened coral-like anemones; tentacles radially arranged; look like true corals but lack skeletons.

Selection. The rule about buying fish from people you know and trust should be doubled for the cnidarians. The cleanliness of the aquarium store and the knowledge and helpfulness of the staff or owner is a good indication of the potential chance of procuring decent stock. Do your homework and check around before making a commitment to these invertebrates; the starting health of the organism is a major factor in how well it will acclimate to your

A well-established reef aquarium with soft corals suggests the progress of aquarists both in keeping cnidarians and in replicating natural reefscapes.

Corals in the wild, on Ningaloo Reef in western Australia, with stony and soft coral species, including a large aggregation of green leathers (*Sarcophyton* sp.).

system. The odds are not in your favor in trying to nurse an anemone or any type of coral back to health, even if you've had some experience with this group.

More specific information on various cnidarian orders and species is offered later in this section. These general rules apply to most of them:

1) Purchase specimens that have been "hardened" for a week or two in your dealer's tanks. A small deposit, if necessary, should ensure timely holding. Mortality can be high in some shipments, and a good retailer will absorb this loss and return your deposit if the specimen you've picked doesn't make it. These are the dealers that deserve our support.

2) Observe the specimen closely in the retailer's display. Are all "parts" fully operational? Are its polyps extended? Are the polyps extended uniformly or are there areas with shriveled polyps?

If the specimen is an anemone, does it respond to feeding?

3) Has the specimen been "colored" artificially?

4) Smell the water and the organism itself if possible. Good ones have a clean, briny odor; those with dying tissue smell unmistakably putrid.

5) Check for necrotic, rotting "whitish" areas, evidence of regrowth or colonization. Torn or dissolving sections are indications of almost certain doom.

Habitat. Water-quality demands are highly variable in this phylum, although some groups tolerate relatively poor conditions. As an example, tube anemones (Order Ceriantharia) are found thriving in some of the muckiest conditions. However, most aquarium specimens seem very sensitive to metabolite buildup, withdrawing physically and not feeding in the presence of nitrates, low redox potential or the de-

pletion of trace elements in your water.

You'll have to (if you want to keep them alive) read up on the requirements for your new charges and meet them more than halfway.

Some organisms, such as soft corals, gorgonians, and many scleractinian corals, grow attached to rock or dead coral rubble and should come intact, naturally mounted to a piece of substrate. This substrate in turn can be wedged into an appropriate area in your reef—or cemented in place with a non-toxic underwater epoxy.

For many cnidarians, being placed at the right depth is critical. Some cnidarians demand full light and placement high in the tank, while others do best in the dim lower reaches of the aquarium. Tube anemones and other anthozoans also demonstrate preferences for certain sizes and textures of gravels.

Varieties found naturally in shallow

Gorgonians and *Dendronephthya* sp.: dazzling colors often catch the eye of aquarists, but knowing the species' care requirements is essential before purchasing.

water are more tolerant of environmental range and rapid change. Although less demanding of intense lighting, specimens from deeper waters tend not to stand up as well to the stresses of shipping and fluctuating aquarium conditions. For all cnidarians, metallic contamination and any sort of drug treatment is absolutely not recommended. Frequent partial water changes, with normal specific gravity

(1.025) and temperature (75 to 82 degrees F for tropical systems), and higher pHs (8.1 to 8.3) will support initially healthy individuals. Protein skimming (with or without ozone), better than average circulation, and the presence of live rock are also valuable in the pursuit of water quality. The undergravel filter cannot be recommended for use with cnidarian-heavy setups, and external power filtration to boost circula-

tion, oxygenation, and particulate waste removal is almost a must.

Lighting can be important in terms of strength, duration, and quality. Some stinging-celled animals are not at all desirous of being in the limelight. These are the deeper-water, shielded, colorless specimens. Alternately, algae-containing species (like reef-building corals) require strong lighting in the proper spectrum in a day-long cycle.

As for water movement, some species need it rough, some don't. Sea fans utilize currents extensively for growth, feeding, and reproduction. A few groups do fine in quiet waters, but most need at least periodic sessions of vigorous current or turbulence. Even the hardy corals from lagoon areas are subject to regular tidal flows, and most new aquarists are guilty of offering too little circulation, even for these, rather than too much. On the other hand, virtually none of this group appreciates being the constant target of a hard, direct, laminar flow of current—as found immediately in front of a stationary powerhead or water return outlet. Some experimentation is often necessary in placing these animals in your aquarium to find the best conditions, which will be evidenced by polyp extension.

Those animals with stony skeletons must also have the proper levels of buffering capacity or alkalinity and calcium to thrive or even survive. Calcareous species can absorb vast quantities of carbonates, sulfides, fluorides, and other alkaline metals. Water changes may not be enough to keep up with healthy, growing systems—and definitely won't keep up with the demands of a heavily stocked reef tank. Having and using test kits for calcium and alkalinity is well-warranted in crowded, high-calcium-using systems.

Behavior. For tissue-grade life that forever seems to live in the slow lane, cnidarians display an amazingly diversified repertoire of activity. They may move slowly, but they are decidedly aware of—and interacting with—their living and nonliving environment.

Territoriality may be extremely important—and fierce. Many corals and mobile cnidarians, anemones, tube anemones, and even sea fans can cause harm to themselves, their tankmates, and you by waging territorial "war" on each other. They can easily sting each other to death, and if different species are placed too close together in the aquarium, one will often "burn" the other back to achieve dominance and give itself room to expand. When placing any of these animals in your system, be sure to leave buffer zones between only specimens with possibly potent qualities. One generally accepted guideline is 6 inches of neutral zone between any two cnidarians. Read everything possible before purchasing, and learn from your own observations.

In very general terms, introduction of any cnidarian should follow these rules:

1) Handle specimens as little as possible. Place the animals where you want them; if they move, leave them alone.

2) Do not unnecessarily expose them to air. In the wild, some are periodically exposed at low tide, most are not. When lifted, some can tear, take in gas, or become stressed. Where possible, slip them into your transport container while they are still underwater.

3) Move them with care. They shouldn't rub themselves raw, nor roll around due to a too large or too small shipping bag or container.

4) Never allow the shipping water into your system. This water may have plummeted in quality during transport, even if there were no pests, parasites, or pollution from the source. Many cnidarians exude protective or defense slime during transport, and neither you nor your protein skimmer wants this added to your main system.

5) Don't overreact if a specimen seems flaccid at first or appears reluctant to feed. If this persists, check your system parameters, do a partial water change, change foods, temperature, or specific gravity, but mainly just be patient. Unless other tankmates seem to be bothered, leave the animal alone. Cnidarians can and do go for long periods without doing much. If the animal is photosynthetic, however, you may want to place it nearer to or further from the lights to see if this helps.

6) I do not regularly endorse prophylactic dipping of stinging-celled organisms. This practice, on average, does more harm than good with this group. Quarantine is becoming a more accepted routine with those keeping corals, but I would recommend that the conditions in such a system be appropriate for the animals in question. (More than a bare-bones fish quarantine tank is required if you intend to keep incoming cnidarians healthy for more than a day or two. Brisk circulation, efficient skimming, and the use of activated carbon to remove slime are the basics, with decent lighting if the zooxanthellae of the animal are to be kept intact.)

Gorgonian Wrapper Anemone (*Nemanthus annamensis*): these unusual small anemones from the western Pacific are often found attached to the branches of gorgonians or other sessile species with firm stalks.

Predator/Prey Relations. Cnidarians are known to be consumed to some degree by most all animal groups. Many worms, crabs, starfishes, snails, and nudibranchs should be left out of captive systems containing cnidarians or at least closely watched. Of the fishes, triggers, most large angels, most butterflies, parrotfishes, and puffers are to be avoided.

Corals and anemones are themselves known to digest other species or genotypes not to their liking.

Cnidarians are opportunistic feeders that may sting, capture, and ingest anything of an appropriate size that comes their way.

Feeding. Where in doubt, underfeed—or less. Most all members of this phylum are filter-feeders of zoo- and phytoplankton. Some get a good deal of their nutrition through photosynthetic cooperation with zooxanthellae embedded in their exposed tissues. Some species or large specimens will eat whole organisms—shrimp, fish, beef, and even poultry. Be careful here. My advice about feeding large foods to cnidarians: don't do it!

Get in the habit of preparing finely divided fresh, frozen, or prepared mashes with or without supplements and administer these while temporarily suspending particulate filtration. Remember: the protoplasm of these animals is almost entirely water; they don't need much to keep them going.

Disease. This is a real gray area at this time, with few identified maladies and even fewer known treatments.

342

Summary. Homes to frolicking clownfishes; givers of red welts and scratches to beachcombing humans; builders of monumental breakwaters; island reef makers in tropical seas—the stinging-celled animals we call cnidarians are all this and more; given the right conditions made possible by modern aquarium equipment, they can be kept in captive oceans by a conscientious marine aquarist.

Anemones
Order Actiniaria

TRY IMAGINING A COLLECTION OF reef photographs, a television show about underwater life, or a full-spectrum fish store without anemones. Hard to do, isn't it? Anemones are seemingly ubiquitous fixtures in all these. Why? They are fascinating to watch, irresistible to anyone who happens by your aquarium, and spellbinding even to old salts who can spend hours mesmerized by their undulating tentacles. Although some have proved difficult to maintain for long periods, a number of species make hardy specimens—given proper collection, treatment, and selection. They have remarkable, interesting biology.

Classification. Early classifiers termed anemones "zoophytes" or "animal plants," in reference to their flowerlike appearance. Many of us know them from their old phyletic grouping within the Coelenterata, an allusion to their gastrovascular cavity (*coel* = hollow, *enteron* = intestine). Within the Phylum Cnidaria, anemones are placed in the Class Anthozoa, which are single or colonial polyps with the medusoid stage completely missing. This group includes the bulk of cnidarian species (6,000+) encompassing corals, sea fans, and sea pansies. They are distinguished from the hydrozoans and scyphozoans by the lack of an operculum (caplike cover) on their stinging cells and several structural/embryological differences.

Sea anemones are separated from other anthozoans in the subclass Zoantharia and the Order Actiniaria. They are often called the "true anemones." They have internal separations of body parts (mesenteries) arranged in hexamerous (six) cycles, usually with two ciliated oral cavities (siphonoglyphs).

Selection. There is a well-deserved black cloud over the collection and handling of anemones. Most anemones that die quickly in hobbyists' care were doomed through miscollection or rough handling before their final purchase. I am referring to a physical tearing of the body, usually the disc or foot, through hasty separation from the wild substrate or holding aquarium. When moving anemones, care and patience are essential. Some thoughtful, conscientious wholesalers (notably Phil Shane at Quality Marine in Los Angeles) have hit upon the use of synthetic indoor/outdoor carpeting to line their

Bubble Tip Anemone (*Entacmaea quadricolor*) with Clark's Clownfish (*Amphiprion clarkii*): these fish are easy to keep, but the anemones can be a challenge unless given reef-type lighting and careful attention.

Giant Anemone (*Condylactis gigantea*): this Caribbean species is highly variable in its coloration and is relatively hardy if kept under strong lights, given vigorous water motion, and fed prudently.

Healthy specimens have long, fully expanded tentacles and a semiclean earthy/marine smell. Dead, dying specimens look shrunken or deflated, and eventually they smell putrid. An anemone that "melts down" in a smaller aquarium can send ammonia and nitrite readings skyrocketing, and may even take the rest of the tank with it.

An unhealthy specimen may be hard to discern. When acquiring anemones, avoid flaccid choices and opt instead for good turgid ones. Prime specimens should not be torn or leaking or show any grayish, whitish, necrotic, or obviously infected areas. Photosynthetic species should show evidence (color) of yellow, golden, or green symbiotic algae. Other anemones may mask their zooxanthellae with pinks, reds, or purples.

Dramatic differences exist in the survivability of different species of anemones, and I urge beginning aquarists to exercise the same caution in selection of these animals as they would in deciding on the merits of a new species of fish. A number of the reliably hardy choices come from the aquarium, and a hands-down favorite of many is the inexpensive and readily available *Condylactis gigantea*, variously known as the Florida Pink-tipped, Haitian Pink-tipped, Atlantic, or Caribbean Anemone, or simply as the "Condy." Under good conditions, these can display tentacle tips ranging in color from pink to magenta and purple, and tentacles that may be brown, cream, greenish, white, or even beaded

tanks to facilitate removal of anemones and other invertebrates that tend to attach themselves to aquarium floors and walls. Shane's holding systems, which have been adopted by many others, also manage to prevent livestock from being sucked into tank overflows.

If you must move an attached anemone, slowly slide a fingernail or credit card under the disc and around the perimeter. Go very slowly, gently and gingerly at first. Examine and bag the individual underwater. Avoid having anemones or their slime touch your wrists, eyes, or other noncalloused areas. They sting! Rinse and wipe off your hands. Most folks can tolerate occa-

sional contact with commonly offered species; should you develop a sensitivity, wear thin rubber gloves or keep your hands off.

Tinted or artificially colored specimens are still seen in the trade, albeit less often these days. In particular, Leathery and Magnificent Sea Anemones (*Heteractis crispa* and *Heteractis magnifica*, respectively) are sometimes adulterated with vegetable (and other) dyes to enhance their salability. No, the pretty color does not last and, yes, it seriously compromises the organism's vitality and chances of survival. Some do recover from a dyeing episode, but many do not.

and mottled. They can reach truly impressive sizes and can become a suitable host for large species of clownfishes, notably the Tomato Clownfish (*Amphiprion frenatus*) and Clark's Clownfish (*A. clarkii*).

The Curleycue Anemone (*Bartholomea annulata*) is another Atlantic species that survives well and makes a very interesting display when paired with the commensal shrimp that often seek shelter in or near it. Still other anemones collected in the Florida Keys and Caribbean include the highly variable and often beautiful Rock Anemone, *Epicystis crucifer*, often identified as *Phymanthus crucifer*. These may have commensal shrimps living with them, and a group of these smaller anemones can make for an eye-catching display.

Of the Indo-Pacific species, the Long Tentacle Anemone (*Macrodactyla doreensis*) is commendable, apparently prolific in the wild, and usually available at reasonable prices. It will often do well for inexpert keepers, provided the anemone is given good lighting, brisk circulation, and a deep bed of sand in which to bury its foot or column. In the Long Tentacle, this column supporting the tentacle-ringed oral disc is typically orange with pimplelike verrucae speckled around the upper portion. (Note the presence or absence of these verrucae: they are obvious in the Long Tentacle Anemone, absent in the *Condylactis* and quite inconspicuous in the Magnificent or Ritteri Anemone (*Heteractis magnifica*)—all three of which are sometimes confused or mislabeled in dealers' tanks.)

Heteractis magnifica, while one of the largest and most colorful sea anemones, has a sad record of failing to adapt to aquarium conditions. In the majority of cases, it continually repositions itself in the tank, usually in a frustrated attempt to find the right conditions of light and full exposure to active water movement. This is one of the worst anemones for ending up wounded in the filtration system or splaying itself across the front glass of the tank. Until its nutrition and care requirements are better understood, it is a species best avoided by most aquarists.

Those who do try may wish to create a high perch of live rock and allow the Magnificent Anemone to become a centerpiece; be sure the location gets vigorous surges of current, intense light, and has a pair or trio of clownfish in residence. Some 12 species of clownfish have been observed with *H. magnifica* in the wild: Percula Clowns (*Amphiprion percula*), Skunk Clowns (*A. perideraion*), and False Percula Clowns (*A. ocellaris*) would all be appropriate.

The Bubble Tip Anemone (*Entacmaea quadricolor*) is a clear favorite with many aquarists, and it is seen in a range of colors from translucent greenish blue to bright green and pale lavender, the latter being sold as the Rose or Maroon Anemone. The tentacle tips are normally red; the column has no verrucae and usually tapers down toward the base or pedal disc. The characteristic swollen tentacle tips or "bubbles" are not always present, but have been reported to appear when the anemone has sufficient light, adequate food, and/or a clownfish living

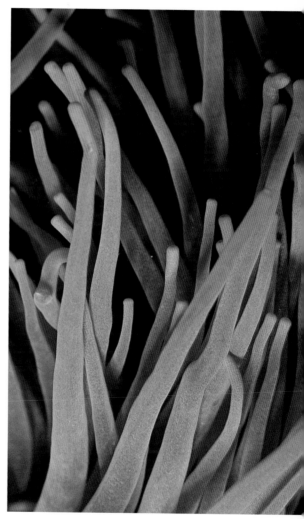

Leathery Sea Anemone (*Heteractis crispa*): one of a number of clownfish-hosting species that all too often wither in captivity.

Magnificent Anemone (*Heteractis magnifica*) with Skunk Clownfish (*Amphiprion perideraion*): the anemone is spectacular in the wild, but a very poor aquarium choice.

with it. (Some clownfish species that associate with this anemone are the Maroon (*Premnas biaculeatus*), Tomato (*Amphiprion frenatus*) and the Red and Black Clownfish (*A. melanopus*).

Somewhat similar in appearance but not nearly so hardy is the so-called Leathery Anemone (*Heteractis crispa*). Often white, pale gray, or light tan, this species has long, densely crowded, ta-pering tentacles and a leathery column with many obvious verrucae. It may be the species most often treated with ar-tificial dyes, and whether misused this way or not, it has a reputation for with-ering away in less-than-perfect aquar-ium conditions. *Heteractis malu*, known as the Delicate Anemone, has shorter, stubbier tentacles and fewer of them. The upper column is often colored to-ward the top end, with widely spaced verrucae. It needs a deep, sandy bottom and is often associated with Clark's Clownfish (*Amphiprion clarkii*).

Carpet Anemones can be attention grabbers, owing both to their size (some grow more than 3 feet across in the wild) and coloration, which can be hot pink, deep green, violet, or even blue. Unfortunately, none of these can be recommended to other than experienced aquarists. Both the Giant Carpet Anemone (*Stichodactyla gigantea*) and the Saddle (or Merten's Carpet) Anemone (*S. mertensii*) demand intense lighting and will often fail to settle down in many aquariums, moving around and stinging (or being stung by) other invertebrates.

Of the most-seen species, the one good choice is *S. haddoni*, also known as the Carpet or Saddle Anemone, but best referred to as Haddon's Anemone. It has a lush pile of tentacles, all the same height, and often displays a variegated color pattern or stripes radiating out from the mouth. (In contrast, the Giant Carpet Anemone has vibrating tentacles and a narrower column. Merten's Carpet Anemone has very noticeable orange or red verrucae on the upper column.)

The Adhesive Sea Anemone (*Cryptodendrum adhaesivum*) is uncommon—and sometimes sold as the Pizza Anemone—but a relatively small and hardy carpet. Its tentacles both cling and sting with lethal (to fishes) force.

Obviously, identifying these and many other anemones that can turn up in the aquarium trade takes some experience and a good guidebook. Once you feel comfortable with the choice of a species and your ability to care for it, specimens are best bought at local outlets where you can observe them. Inquire as to origin and how the specimen is behaving and eating. Put down a suitable deposit and retrieve the individual(s) in a week or two. This will weed out the vast majority of doomed or damaged specimens. (If the anemone is being held in a system without adequate lighting, but otherwise appears plump and with tentacles well-filled, you may be wise to get it home sooner rather than later.)

Habitat. While many popular aquarium texts advise that anemones are extremely undemanding, more recent evidence has made it clear that the survival rate of some species is very low. In addition to individuals that are hurt or terminally stressed before they arrive in the home aquarium, many anemones seem to fail in captivity because of incorrect lighting, too little circulation, accidents involving pumps and filters, or lack of proper nutrition.

In general, an ideal habitat for anemones has high-intensity fluorescent or metal halide lighting, intervals of water turbulence (which both carries suspended foods to the animal and flushes away wastes), an absence of predators (butterflyfishes, large angels, sizable crustaceans, and bristleworms) and careful screening of any pump or filter intakes where a restless anemone might become lodged and torn. A submersible heater can also burn and kill a roving anemone; move your heater to an external sump or filter compartment or carefully screen access if it must remain in the display tank. A deep bed of coral sand is needed by some species that naturally bury their feet, and others appreciate outcroppings of live rock on which to perch in the light and current.

In the past, some aquarists have described the creation of full-blown "anemonariums," and current practice seems to be moving in the direction of such specialization. We now know that most of the commonly available tropical anemones do poorly both in average fish-only systems and in crowded reef tanks, where they virtually always end up in a deadly battle with other cnidarians. Creating a biotope for one or more anemones of the same species with appropriate clownfish or damsels could be one interesting approach.

Be aware of your species' life habits, or at least be prepared to offer it a choice of light conditions, substrate types, and variable circulation.

While insufficient lighting or water motion will almost invariably cause an anemone to shrink away over time, there are few things that seem fatal to initially healthy anemones other than metal-based remedies or accidental introduction of metal ions from other sources.

For almost all species identified, absolute and varying specific gravity is not problematic. Keeping it stable at some point between 1.022 and 1.025 is recommended. Similarly, temperature should not swing wildly, but any point between 72 and 80 degrees F is fine.

I would utilize a test kit weekly and periodically "dose" the system with water changes (automatically bringing in a fresh supply of trace elements), supplemented with a pinch of sodium bicarbonate or marine aquarium buffer. Trace element additions may eventually prove to be important for captive anemones, and some aquarists report positive results from regular weekly dosing with iodine/iodide and other reef supplements. I urge caution; always start with a low dose and only increase when no ill effects have been seen.

Anemones are aerobes; they need oxygen to respire and need to shed themselves of excess carbon dioxide. Some have internal (endo)symbiotic algae (zooxanthellae) which aid in these processes, in addition to producing food sugars. Respiration is accomplished by simple osmosis and accelerated active transport. Hence the need for clean, well-aerated water around them.

There is a long list of anemone symbionts, including small shrimps, crabs, the clownfishes, other damsels, and even a Caribbean blenny. Having some of these in your system with anemones, artfully using the protective cover of the stinging tentacles, is a never-ending spectacle.

Adequate circulation is critical. I prefer a nonbubbly powerhead, canister, or inside-power filter over air-infusing mechanisms for moving the water around these animals; but whatever the means you use, do move it vigorously. One of my childhood heroes, Robert P.L. Straughan, warned against air-bubble entrapment mortality in captive anemones.

Good aquarium practices in setup and maintenance ought to preclude anemone loss. Some types of anemones have a habit of disgorging or egesting wastes in a cohesive mass. Remove this regurgitated food with a net or siphon, unless your system has a population of brittle stars or small hermit crabs, which will quickly clean it up. Foods digested by an anemone are converted almost entirely into ammonia, which should be removed by your biological filtration. Some of the filter-feeding anemones produce mucus nets, which trap particles, then pass them up to the

mouth and ingest the whole mass. Mucus strands from locomotion and filter-feeding do not appear to be toxic to anemones or other life forms, but should be filtered or otherwise removed on a regular basis.

Behavior. Beware an anemone on the loose. They can and do move and wage outright warfare with tankmates they perceive as the enemy. In particular, other stinging-celled organisms (corals, sea fans, and other anemones) may sting/digest each other to death. Suitable choice in specimens, lack of crowding, and provision of good habitat are important considerations. Some aquarists consider it folly to put two different species of anemones in the same aquarium as they seem to end up in tragic contact sooner or later.

Never introduce anemone shipping water into your "home" system (unless possibly these are the only/first live specimens). Take the anemone(s) out of the shipping water, or alternatively

Adhesive Sea Anemone (*Cryptodendrum adhaesivum*): relatively hardy species.

Beaded Sea Anemone (*Heteractis aurora*): needs deep sand, bright lights.

rinse them over with holding system water, removing wastes and excess mucus. If possible, do all this underwater, including moving them into the system via container. Place the specimens in their desired area, waiting a while for attachment. Overall circulation should be arrested to let the animal settle in. Observe the new arrivals frequently for the first day or so. Be careful about situating them near sharp corals, coral and shell skeletons, or rocks. Purposely move them if necessary, otherwise they will move themselves, and traveling anemones are prone to all sorts of mishaps, including unhappy encounters with filter intakes.

Rock anemones (*Epicystis* spp.): good beginner's anemones from shallow waters in Florida and the Caribbean.

Predator/Prey Relations. If hungry, many fishes and crustaceans will eat anemones. Triggerfishes, puffers, and many angelfishes are not to be trusted. Some butterflyfishes, such as the Raccoon, *Chaetodon lunula*, will literally gobble up anemones before your eyes. Anemones, in turn, can and do eat most anything they can snare, including seahorses, other barely mobile tankmates, and small fishes.

Reproduction. Anemone propagation in nature runs the entire gamut, both sexual and asexual. New individuals may form from a piece torn off during locomotion or trauma, or by longitudinal or transverse fission, and this sort of reproduction has been recorded in home aquariums.

Sea anemones may be of separate sexes or hermaphroditic. If they are hermaphroditic, eggs and sperm tend to be produced at different times. Fertilization and some development may occur within the body cavity. Typically, anemone larvae have a planktonic developmental phase before settling.

Locomotion. Anemone locomotion is accomplished through a muscular-ciliary-mucus gliding of the bottom (basal or pedal disc) or complete loosening and "drifting" of the animal with the current. Even mud-dwelling tube anemones are capable of moving and reinserting themselves in soft substrates. Some species are actually pelagic, swimming about by lashing their tentacles.

Feeding. Anemones possess rings of tentacles around their mouths used for prey collection and manipulation. These are arrayed with numerous stinging (cnidocyst) and sticky (spirocyst) cells below their surface. These specialized cells may be found in and on other body areas and assist in immobilizing and holding prey as well as in warding off would-be predators.

Anemone nutrition has been and will likely continue to be a contentious subject, with aquarists wrangling over the extent to which captive specimens need to be hand-fed. Here is my advice, which may be controversial: underfeed, underfeed, underfeed! Many anemone losses in captive systems are the result of overfeeding. Some anemones have been kept for years without any intentional external feeding. Know your stock. Many anemones—especially larger species—are detrivorous, filterers of small plankton, and use photosynthetic algae. Hobbyists try to overstuff them with meaty, prepared foods. Don't do this. If someone has told you to feed your anemone a jumbo cocktail shrimp every other day, find yourself another advisor. Within normal temperatures and other conditions, most anemones can and do well on once-a-week feedings. If you're going on vacation, leave them alone. They will do fine for a week or even two.

For almost all varieties, an occasional—weekly or so—perfusion or wash of live brine shrimp, a prepared mash of frozen or dried food, or a blender mix of fresh marine food meant for human consumption (shellfish, shrimp, langusto, not-so-oily fish) is adequate. Temporarily turn off your particulate filters and squirt the food onto the anemone's tentacular surface. Some of the new, frozen invertebrate rations for filter feeders are also worth a try, but do not overdo these.

Some authors suggest the use of beef and other foods unlikely to be encountered in the wild. I do not.

Disease. If a specimen shrinks down, don't automatically assume the worst and toss it. It may just be sulking over too much or too little light, poor circulation, chewing tankmates, polluted water from overfeeding, or traces of metal. Check your water quality and physical conditions (temperature, light, circulation) and come back tomorrow.

Anemones can be hardy tankmates, once they've been successfully acclimated. However, I strongly suggest attempting them only after you've had extensive experience with marine fishes and other invertebrate groups. Even then, please start with the inexpensive "beginner" types, such as the several common, plentiful, and inexpensive *Condylactis* or *Epicystis* species from Florida and the Caribbean.

These soft-bodied, stinging-celled animals do have their dark side. Too many of those collected don't live for long, being damaged by collection and transport; aquarists who bring them home to a nonsustainable environment are also guilty of adding to the waste.

(Quite a few hobbyists feel pressured to buy anemones believing that they are essential to the well-being and breeding of clownfishes. In fact, tank-raised clownfishes and most of the wild-caught varieties do fine and will reproduce without anemones.)

If you are mesmerized by the swaying tentacles and strange charm of anemones, by all means give them a try. By providing decent water and lighting conditions and avoiding the more delicate species, your chances of success will rise dramatically. With intense hues of pink, green, red, or purple and displayed with their commensal clownfish, shrimps, or crabs, they can make for some of the most arresting displays possible in the marine aquarium.

Tube Anemones
Order Ceriantharia

UNLIKE "TRUE" ANEMONES, the Order Ceriantharia, the tube anemones, are rarely colored with artificial dyes; there's no need. Those gorgeous, near-fluorescent yellows, oranges, purples, and blue-blacks are natural.

Tube anemones as a group share many of the same characteristics and general husbandry as their more commonly kept cousins in the Order Actinaria. Aspects of their selection, habitat, and maintenance warrant a separate discussion.

Classification. Within the Phylum Cnidaria and the Class Anthozoa, there are two orders that encompass anemones. The first, Order Actinaria, is detailed above. The second, Order Ceriantharia, includes the tube anemones, distinguished by having no pedal discs and only one ciliated mouth opening.

Tube anemones are found worldwide in tropical and subtropical seas, primarily in sandy or muddy bottoms. Species identifications are often impossible without dissection, but the three genera you may see in the trade include *Cerianthus*, *Arachnanthus*, and *Pachycerianthus*.

Tube anemones are characteristically slender, smooth cones topped with two sets of dissimilar tentacles. The outer fringing tentacles are particularly

Unidentified tube anemone: not true anemones, the Ceriantheria have two rings of tentacles and a leathery tube. They are notorious for snaring small fishes at night, but make a spectacular sight if properly housed.

well armed with stinging cells. The shorter (less than 2-inch) inner labial or oral tentacles assist in food gathering and manipulation.

These animals are also notable for secreting a heavy mucus tube that is continuously added to by specialized stinging cells.

Selection. Look for tears, discolored areas, flaccid, unfilled, or otherwise nondisplayed tentacles, and avoid those specimens. Additionally, healthy tube anemones exhibit a "cough" reaction when being removed from their tube or tank. If the individual in question does not forcibly eject water from its terminal vacuole on handling, leave it in the dealer's tank and move on.

Habitat. In the wild, the Ceriantharia may make dwelling tubes up to a few meters long in the soft substrate. Coating these tubes semi-continuously with layers of mucus facilitates their rapid retreat if disturbed.

In captivity, they have proved to be reasonably undemanding. However, they are too much for small tanks, and larger systems are preferable. Their burrowing behavior and expansive size, their sometimes copious waste production, and their tendency to sting tankmates dictate a minimum of 40 gallons for each specimen.

Depending on your setup, more ver-sus less substrate is preferable, the finer (4 mm or less in diameter) the better; at least 2 inches of depth is required, or enough to cover all but the tentacular crown. Tube anemones have broadly long and tapering cylindrical bodies, a few to several inches long.

Some industrious aquarists utilize a baking dish or similar container to build up enough substrate to accommodate a tube anemone in a setup without sufficient substrate overall. Others I've seen make a hollow in an elevated rock area, or place the newcomers in chemically inert bottomless cones, tubes, or pots to provide habitat where they want them. Peter Wilkens describes the building of glass and foam living spaces in his aquarium display. Once its tube is formed, the whole tube anemone and its substrate mass may be moved to a suitable location in the same system.

Temperature ranges can be very wide indeed for tube anemones. As a diver, I've recorded them in shallow, coastal areas that are subject to wide and rapid environmental changes. If you're setting the thermostat for tube anemones alone, you can keep them at temperatures as low as 70 degrees F; thermal fluctuation is not a problem.

Lighting can be as bright or subdued as you wish, but most specimens are collected from shallower areas and are accustomed to reasonably intense illumination. You'll want at least some full-spectrum fluorescent lighting to appreciate your tube anemone's color; an actinic bulb may enhance the view.

A tube anemone may or may not coexist with its own kind, but will likely sting other sessile invertebrates.

Anaerobic decomposition problems should be closely monitored with these animals due to wastes and tube slime. One simple solution is to siphon out and rinse a portion of the substrate as a part of your routine water change procedure. If you are only doing a portion every month or so, this won't interrupt bio-geo-chemical nutrient cycling.

Behavior. The tube anemone's most astounding performance is probably its initial burrowing. This is accomplished by rapidly expelling water from its oral area (vacuole) through contraction, driving the pointed end of the animal into the bottom.

Territoriality can be a big problem. Tropical and temperate tube anemones do not mix well and can and will sting each other to death if overcrowded. Some tropical species as individuals will mix. This becomes a matter of experimentation either in the dealer's tanks or your own system. I suggest a good 8-inch spacing between a tube anemone and any other sessile organism, though some writers have reported success with virtual stacking of the same tropical species, including same-species animals of different colors.

I have encountered some successful combinations of "true" (Order Actinaria) and tube (Order Ceriantharia) anemone tanks, but have heard far more sad stories about animals not surviving in such systems. If you mix these different orders, provide a very wide berth around the tubes.

Predator/Prey Relations. The same standard exceptions for tankmates

At minimum, a simple biological filtration system is all that is required, but I do suggest at least the use of an outside power filter, either a power- or canister-type. A protein skimmer will more than make up for its nominal costs of acquisition and operation by keeping the water clean and clear.

Some additional circulation is warranted, but not necessarily supervigorous. Once again, I shy away from the use of much airstone/air-powered water movement in a system with lots of fil-ter feeders. The use of a separate fluid-moving pump or a powerhead would be my choice.

When a tube anemone is procured, all mucus and tube conglomeration should be cleaned away and discarded. I advocate rinsing the new arrival with established system water and carefully discarding the shipping water to reduce the chance of introducing loose sting-ing cells. I've found that extensive acclimation and quarantine procedures are unnecessary with ceriantharians.

of other anemones apply here: triggers, puffers, large angels, large crabs, lobsters, and large snails are forbidden. Most worms, small shrimps, and small hermit crabs are fine.

Ceriantharians do not go well in small aquariums with many species or numbers of fishes. Their habit of shedding stinging cells appears to be problematic. Dwarf angels (genus *Centropyge*) and many other coral reef fishes cannot be kept with them for long; they will be stung. Slow-moving species like the tube-mouthed fishes (seahorses, pipefishes), mandarins (*Synchiropus*), et al. soon become costly food items. Keep in mind that tube anemones have caused the mysterious disappearance of countless aquarium specimens. An easy rule is simply to keep any prized or well-loved fish out of the ceriantharian tank. Finally, and emphatically, tube anemones are *not* symbiotic with clownfishes. They will eat them if given the opportunity.

There are animals that do live well with these potent cnidarians. Perhaps only the fat Innkeeper Worm (*Urechis*) comes close to rivaling tube anemones for their depth and breadth of commensal (a form of symbiosis) relations. Within their tubes can be found many numbers of individuals of crab, bristleworm, horseshoe worm (Phylum Phoronida), and other crustacean and worm species. The green algae in the genera *Caulerpa* and *Udotea* are frequently found in association with tube anemones as well.

Reproduction. Captive egg production by tube anemones has been reported. Two individuals left their tubes and were observed swollen and with tentacles intertwined, floating at the surface. Some weeks later, a large quantity of small pinkish orange eggs were observed floating at the surface. None of the larvae lasted through a developmental (planula) stage, presumably from lack of food.

Locomotion. They can move, and may, by pulling out of their tubes and allowing the current to scoot them about. This can be a dangerous time for them and for other tankmates. By exhaling strongly through its oral cavity, a tube anemone may easily tear its body or sting something else.

Feeding. Tube anemones are filter feeders; offering them large, meaty foods is definitely not advised. Twice weekly feedings of live, frozen, or macerated prepared foods circulated about and onto their tentacles while the particulate and skimmer filtration is shut off is sufficient. More frequent, smaller feedings are better than the reverse.

The intensity of color seems to be largely a function of nutrition. Vitamin supplements presoaked into their foods and mashes of high-quality prepared foods will ensure color enhancement and retention.

Disease. Tube anemones fall into the category of either altogether alive and almost impossible to kill, or outright dead. Other authors have had success in trimming away damaged or diseased tube body areas. I have never had any luck with such a procedure.

Summary. When collected and handled with care and offered a modest level of attention to food, water, and space requirements, tube anemones can make a marvelous—if slightly sinister—display.

Mushroom Anemones and Coral Anemones
Order Corallimorpharia

CORAL ANEMONES, MUSHROOM anemones, or false corals—so-called because they don't have "stony" skeletons—are perhaps the most celebratedly hardy of the soft corals, often reproducing readily in well-kept systems. They have much to their merit, being relatively inexpensive and available in striking reds, blues, greens, purples, metallic stripes, and variegated patterns. Corallimorpharians require little specialized care, as you will see.

Classification. Coral anemones are closely related to the stony or true corals, indeed they are sometimes grouped as part of the same order (Scleractinia) as a suborder. Within the Phylum Cnidaria, corallimorpharians are contained in the Subclass Zoantharia, Order Corallimorpharia. (See page 338.) Often called coral anemones, they are solitary or colonial, flattened mushroomlike anemones with short, stubby tentacles, radially arranged. They lack the skeletons of true corals. The most common genera are *Discosoma*, *Ricordea*, *Rhodactis*, and *Corynactis*.

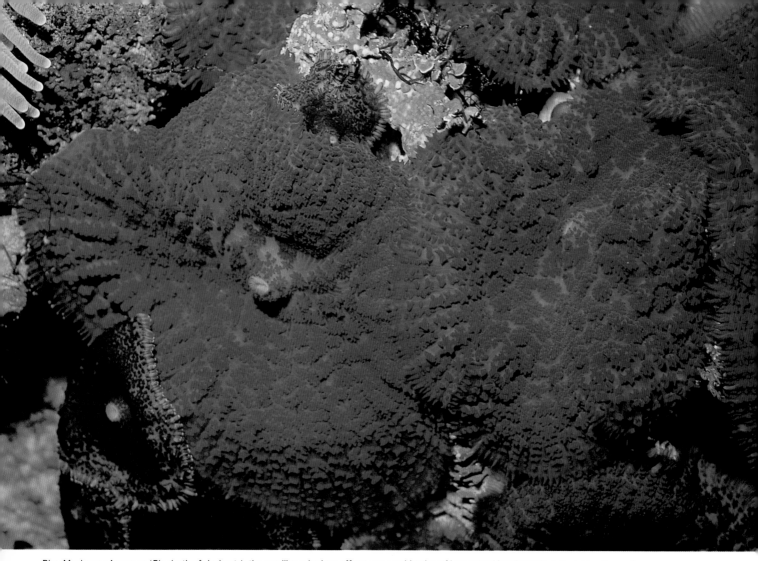

Blue Mushroom Anemone (*Rhodactis* cf. *inchoata*): the corallimorpharians offer a rare combination of beauty and hardiness in many types of aquariums.

Selection. As with their close relatives, choose specimens that are fully open with no visible dead, whitish, missing material. Coral anemones are collected along with a substantial chunk of limestone rock or coral rubble to which they are attached. If the piece was snapped off, check to see that individual polyps have not been torn asunder.

Though marketed as single- versus multiple-polyp pieces for the purpose of lowering cost per sale, an entire, unbroken group gets my strong recommendation. Do not be concerned that the individual polyps may differ markedly; this is quite normal. Similarly, be aware that they change shape cyclically, responding to light/dark, currents and nutrients in the water. Apparently healthy but pale individuals whose zooxanthellae are in decline should be avoided. The necessary endosymbionts make up the majority of the color seen in mushroom anemones, so select for well-colored specimens.

Corallimorpharia are one of the exceptions regarding whether to gamble on just-arrived shipments or exercise a wait-and-see or deposit-and-wait stance. Don't wait on them. The sooner a desired specimen is put in an appropriate environment (particularly concerning lighting), the better for its health and color. Some authors suggest isolation and antibiotic treatment regimens to reduce the possibility of fouling. In the course of handling several hundred specimens, I have found this to be unnecessary.

Habitat. Corallimorpharia are found in areas of poorer water quality than many true (hard or stony) corals. This fact has been proposed to explain their greater tolerance of hobbyist-generated pollution. They are found in shallow tropical seas in brightly lit (although sometimes shaded) and nonturbulent conditions.

There are some general water-quality control limits to be monitored: maximum nitrates 30 to 40 ppm; minimum pH 7.8; minimum-maximum temperature 72 to 85 degrees F; negligible ammonia and nitrites. Better conditions, of course, will mean better-looking specimens.

Lighting is important. For those with standard-output fluorescents only, it may be necessary to move your corallimorpharians closer to the surface. For VHO, metal halide, and other intense lighting users, deeper placement is suggested. Too much or too little light results in the specimens' polyps losing color and cupping-up in shape.

Some hobbyists swear by actinic lighting as part of the mix over mushroom anemones, and most corals do seem to thrive and look especially colorful under bluish light—particularly those with fluorescing tentacles. Under actinics, they are gorgeous.

Unlike leather and other corals, coral anemones do not do well in strong currents. Direct powerheads and water-return nozzles away from them.

Most specimens are collected from the Caribbean (*Discosoma*, *Ricordea*) and the West Pacific. Temperate or cold-water species, like my local *Corynactis californica*, must be kept in chilled systems. They will eventually dissolve in warm waters.

For filtration, common undergravel systems with outside power and an efficient skimmer have met with success.

Place new specimens, without shipping water, a good 3 to 6 inches from other sessile tankmates and allow a few to several days for the newcomer to ad-

just to system conditions. Don't be too anxious to adjust the specimen's orientation for a couple of weeks.

Predator/Prey Relations. All the typical coral-eating and -bothering organisms are to be eliminated: triggers, puffers, large angels, and urchins. Additionally, be careful in placing other stinging-celled animals nearby. The mild-mannered mushroom anemones always lose out in encounters with bubble corals and tube anemones. On the other hand, the nematocyst-bearing types such as *Rhodactis*, *Discosoma* and *Amplexidiscus* can enclose and ingest smaller, slower-moving fishes such as blennies and gobies.

Strictly speaking, corallimorphari-

Florida False Coral (*Ricordea florida*): a particularly desirable species, this mushroom-type corallimorpharian is primarily collected in the Caribbean and thrives in situations where light is neither too bright nor too dim.

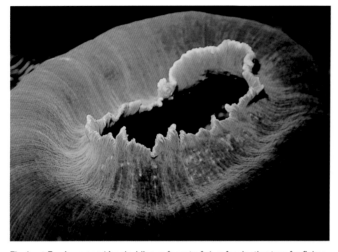

Elephant Ear Anemone (*Amplexidiscus fenestrafer*): a fascinating trap for fishes.

Discosoma sp.: easy enough for beginners, still appealing to expert aquarists.

ans do not move around—although one study of a temperate species showed it did move, but less than half a millimeter per day.

Reproduction. Reproduction is accomplished both sexually and asexually as in the true corals. The regenerative properties of this group are highly touted, with several reports of individuals torn in half both growing anew. Splitting and budding are recorded in the wild and in captivity. Once established in acceptable aquarium conditions, a colony of mushroom anemones will often spread rapidly, producing an expanding area of polyps. (Small pieces of coral rock can be placed near the base of established parent polyps to receive newcomers, which can then be moved to other parts of the aquarium or passed along to other aquarists.)

Feeding. Mushroom anemones are obligate symbionts with their zooxanthellae. That is, they must utilize zooxanthellae for food production and waste elimination. Additionally, all species filter-feed to some extent; the longer the tentacles, the more important this aspect of feeding. Their short tentacles enclose stinging cells (cnidocysts, nematocysts) and sticky spirocysts.

Once again, do not overfeed. Mushroom anemones have been kept for many months without any deliberate feeding, receiving their nutrition through photosynthetic/chemosynthetic activity. Occasionally some food may be offered by placing it on the polyps or spraying it in their general direction. Leave no excess.

Disease. These animals are either healthy or dead, and typically seem immune to disease.

Summary. Mushroom anemones, elephant ear corals, disc anemones, coral anemones—all of these members of the Order Corallimorpharia are either the hardiest group of cnidarians or close runners-up. They can be easily maintained in fish-and-hardy-invertebrate or reef-type marine aquariums; they are undemanding, often quite beautiful, and very good choices for beginning to advanced hobbyists.

Sea Fans
Order Gorgonacea

FOR MOST OF THE CIVILIZED WORLD, sea fans are those scraggly dried things you see in fish stores or hanging on the wall at your local Seafood Palace. As any diver and a growing number of reef aquarists can tell you, those are actually only the dead, brown vestiges of what once were colorful, living sea fans.

Most everyone has seen sea fans in underwater television productions, and if you've been diving in tropical seas, you've brushed members of the Order Gorgonacea "waving" in the current.

They are undeniably beautiful in the wild, but can they be kept in captivity? Yes. There is an as-yet-undeveloped place for these octocorallians in the schema of marine aquariums. Like many saltwater invertebrate groups, sea fans—especially the photosynthetic species—have been kept on the sidelines thus far for simple, correctable reasons.

Classification. Like the previous coral, tube and "true" anemone groups, the sea fans are members of the Class Anthozoa. In contrast with the other cnidarian classes (Hydrozoa, Scyphozoa) that have medusa body plans (inverted bells with either a simple body tube or one divided into four areas), the polypoid anthozoans bodies are divided into numerous chambers by septa, or partitions.

You may wish to refer back to the systematic overview of the stinging-celled animals (page 338) for a clearer picture of how this group is further placed. Sea fans, Order Gorgonacea, are colonial anthozoans that anchor on hard substrates, supported by an internal, central horny/woodlike skeleton. Their colonies are covered by a thick, rindlike skin. Unlike anemones, but like corals, sea fan polyps are interconnected by an internal germ layer (gastrodermis) and gelatinous middle layer (mesoglea.) This feature helps explain how one part can feed and sustain the rest of the colony and, unfortunately, how disease can easily spread.

Common genera include *Gorgonia*, the purple sea fans from Florida and the Caribbean, often seen as dried ornamental fan skeletons in stores; *Corallium*, the beautiful red sea fans used in jewelry; *Paragorgia*, *Pterogorgia*, *Pseudopterogorgia*, and others often encountered and available.

Gorgonians are found worldwide in tropical seas. They are prominent on most reefs, oriented to prevailing currents.

Selection. Contrary to what many aquarists think, sea fans are not delicate creatures that fall apart when touched or moved. The two most important factors that limit our success in keeping them are problems caused by collection and transportation:

1) cutting or breaking their rindlike skin by rough handling or stacking specimens on top of each other;

2) lack of continuous circulation yielding low oxygen tension.

Think about these organisms in the wild: they live firmly attached to the hard substrate, waving back and forth in the direct flow of the reef, not touching or being gouged by anything—receiving the full benefit of continuous aeration at all times. Large individuals have been carefully collected (one at a time) and kept long-term by large public and private aquariums worldwide. So what's a hobbyist to do? At the

A large sea fan (gorgonian) on a reef wall appears daunting to the aquarist's eye, but small specimens of many species often prove easy to keep and extremely attractive if given reef lighting and active water motion.

Sea Feathers (*Pseudopterogorgia bipinnata*): this and similar species will grow and spread in a healthy reef tank, and small cuttings can be made to produce captive-propagated colonies.

trid. If the skin is broken, the sea fan probably will not live long. Photosynthetic gorgonians are generally much easier to sustain, as long as your system has adequate lighting. A good dealer will be able to tell if a particular species is or is not photosynthetic. Lastly, some gorgonians filter-feed mainly at night, but most should have their polyps extended and evident during the day.

If you can get a healthy specimen, there is a very good chance of your keeping it alive. If damaged, sea fans may die easily, quickly releasing toxins into the system with disastrous results. Especially in small systems with inadequate filtration, sea fans can give off a slime when disturbed that can take them and the rest of your livestock off to Davey Jones's Locker.

Regarding your own efforts at collecting: picking up gorgonians (or any other invertebrates) is restricted in a great many places. Be careful to check with local authorities about legal permits. Where collecting is allowed, take only what you can transport and keep alive in your system. One other thing: pay attention to your surroundings while collecting. Stinging hydroids and fire corals are often found in conjunction with or even coating sea fans and will sting you painfully. Be careful.

Habitat. Making a suitable sea fan display is simple: replicate the reef. Using underwater epoxy, anchor the specimen(s) firmly on a solid rock, more or less in the direct path of moving water. Ideally, the water circulation will be switched on and off by a simple wavemaker device, or an oscillating powerhead will sweep back and forth in the area of the sea fans.

Water quality standards should be up to snuff for a basic reef tank, and lighting is important, first in terms of quality, next in quantity. The majority of species sold are shallow-water (bright) reef in origin. Many reef keepers use 5500 K to 6500 K metal halide bulbs or actinic/metal halide combinations. Other folks have had success by adding more red-end shifted and full-spectrum fluorescents. With fluorescents, you might want to employ a longer-than-usual light regimen, 14 to 16 hours per day, on a timer. Most sea fans have symbiotic algal relationships (zooxanthellae); they need the light. In a "happy" situation, with ample current and lighting, the entire colony's polyps should open up in the course of any given day, giving it a lush appearance.

Some slime production is normal, healthy, and to be anticipated. Sea fans produce and shed these coats to prevent drying when exposed and to cleanse themselves of algae, bryozoans, and other fouling organisms. Siphon or filter this material out as it occurs.

dealer's, check out the specimens that are anchored firmly upright. Examine their bases; the best are the ones with thick stems (⅜ to ½ inch wide), with large polyps, and with some part of the original substrate still attached to the holdfast. Smell the water. Bad specimens are malodorous, downright pu-

To introduce a new specimen, simply stabilize its water temperature, pull it out from its shipping bag, rinse in system water, then place appropriately. Be sure to discard the shipping water.

Behavior. Territoriality among the gorgonians doesn't seem to be a difficulty; just position your sea fans in such a way that they don't touch other living or nonliving materials. Other stinging-celled organisms will usually "win" in such scenarios, so keep them out of the reach of other corals and anemones.

Predator/Prey Relationships. This is a touchy area. How much harm and/or good is it to fret over intentional and accidental grazers? Certain polychaete worms (bristle, fire), snails (most celebratedly the Flamingo Tongue, *Cyphoma gibbosum*), even hungry/curious fishes of the usual types (angels, butterflies, triggers) may overly chew up/eat your sea fans. Keep your eye on them.

Feeding. Various authors have suggested offering live brine shrimp nauplii, rotifers, prepared mashes (macerated shrimp, clams, etc.). Feed gorgonians sparingly a few times a week. Make the feeding time and procedure routine. Turn the lights off, subdue particulate and skimmer filtration, introduce some food, wait a determinate time, and put in the rest. This will prime the sea fans' opening and feeding repertoire. Some writers encourage soaking the foodstuff with vitamin mixtures, aminoplex solution, or other additives. To each his own.

Summary. Photosynthetic sea fans and other gorgonians can and do thrive when collected, transported, and maintained with reasonable attention to good standards. They come in an amazing mix of shapes and colors and exhibit enough interesting behavior to warrant inclusion in advanced reef collections.

Stony Corals and Soft Corals
Orders Scleractinia and Alcyonacea

FOR THE TRUE, reef-building stony corals, the Scleractinia—the animals most people have in mind when they talk about corals—I would issue a few words of warning. I have two reasons for cautioning against attempting scleractinian corals; one in regards to their present incidental mortality, the second a personal opinion.

According to my associates in the marine livestock collection, wholesale and transshipping trades, a large percentage of wild-collected stony corals fail to survive from the collection point to the shipping point in their countries of origin. Of these, many more fail to live longer than three months in aquariums. I find this deplorable.

After campaigning for more than 20 years to get divers never to touch the reef, I will not encourage or sanction the wholesale breaking off of stony corals to send them as ornaments to

Indonesian sea fan (*Acabaria* sp.): with a somewhat flexible woody skeleton and a thick, rindlike skin, the gorgonians occupy a position between the soft corals and the reef-building stony or scleractinian corals.

their all-too-certain, speedy deaths. Instead, let me plead with you to try other corals and coral-like organisms that have much shorter generation times and higher growth and replacement times. If you cannot be dissuaded, please do "practice" on the soft and leather corals, coral anemones, and other stinging-celled animals first. If you aren't successful in maintaining these, you are dead-certain to fail with either wild or captive-propagated stony corals.

My earnest recommendation is to try your hand at keeping the Order Al-cyonacea, which includes a wonderful selection of soft corals that have a solid history of surviving and growing in marine aquariums. They will often expand to the point of needing to be pruned, allowing you to make cuttings and become a source of captive-propagated corals for others. Among the best choices for beginners are the finger, leather, cabbage, and colt corals (*Sinularia*, *Sarcophyton*, *Lobophytum*, and *Alcyonium* or *Cladiella*, respectively). Other attractive and hardy choices are the various star polyps (*Pachyclavularia*), tree or palm corals (*Clavularia*) and the zoanthids (*Palythoa*, *Protopalythoa*), which often come on live rock. All will do well under good fluorescent lighting (four regular-watt bulbs or the equivalent), and can make for displays that will rival any stony-coral aquarium.

Among the true stony corals, a number are solitary or free-living and abundant in nature. Among the hardy and recommended genera are *Trachyphyllia* (Open Brain Coral), *Fungia* (plate or mushroom corals), *Cynarina* (meat or button corals), and *Herpolitha* and *Polyphyllia* (tongue corals). These have the advantage of being collected without having to be broken from the reef, and they often ship and survive well, provided you give them typical reef aquarium conditions with VHO fluorescent or metal halide lights.

For the aquarist who is ready for the challenge of growing stony corals, all hope is not lost. A happier future is in store for the hobby with the increasing advent of captive "cultured" stony coral

Finger leather coral (*Sinularia* sp.)

Leather coral (*Sarcophyton* sp.)

Tree coral (*Capnella* sp.)

Green Star Polyps (*Pachyclavularia viridis*)

Daisy polyps (*Clavularia* sp.)

Pulsing Xenia (*Xenia* sp.)

stocks. Small-polyped varieties are more and more available from propagated fragments. These have proved to be consistently hardier and faster growing than stock imported from the wild.

Among the true reef-building stony corals, many desirable small-polyped genera are now being actively propagated by home aquarists and small aquaculture operations throughout North America. For very modest prices, the aspiring coral aquarist can purchase small, captive-grown colonies, started fragments, or mount-your-own fragments. Among the widely available choices are hardy species of *Pavona*, *Pocillopora*, *Montipora*, *Stylophora*, *Seriatopora*, *Porites*, and many, many species of *Acropora* (staghorn corals). All of these hail from the Indo-Pacific, but a

few tropical Atlantic/Caribbean corals are now appearing on live rock aquacultured off the coast of Florida.

Numerous amateur coral keepers have documented the exceptional growth of captive fragments, with single small branches growing more than 4 inches in a year and tiny colonies expanding to fill whole sections of moderately large reef aquariums in two to three years. Survival of these quasi-domesticated scleractinians is reported to be excellent, and under intense metal halide lighting some indescribably beautiful colors and combinations of hues can be maintained.

In short, there is no reason for the average aquarist to support the trade in wild stony-coral colonies broken or chiseled from the reef. (I am prepared

to amend my position on this in cases where the harvest is done selectively and in a sustainable rotation. This will take major educational efforts to promote in the countries where these animals are collected. I am not opposed to careful use of the planet, just ignorant, careless, and wasteful exploitation.)

Those who have mastered the keeping of soft corals and captive-grown small-polyped scleractinian corals may well want to try their hands at maintaining and propagating new colonies from the wild, but this is beyond the reach of the average aquarium hobbyist.

Though the ornamental trade for pet-fish and curios accounts for a minuscule percentage of coral reef destruction (siltation by run-off caused by deforestation, development, sewage,

Open Brain Coral (*Trachyphyllia geoffroyi*)

Plate Coral (*Heliofungia actiniformis*)

Scolymia sp.

Tongue Coral (*Polyphyllia talpina*)

Disc Coral (*Fungia fungites*)

Elegance Coral (*Catalaphyllia jardinei*)

Captive-propagated Bali Green Stony Coral (*Acropora youngei*): whether grown in aquariums or by Third World coral farmers, this is may be the future of environmentally sound stony coral culture.

boat anchoring, and dredging are far more harmful) I still will not endorse the taking of reef-building stony corals for hobby or decorative purposes. Dead coral skeletons can and should only be collected as such; I am convinced that there is less collateral harm from their collection than from the chemicals and processes used to make their artificial facsimiles.

Fanworms and Feather Duster Worms

Phylum Annelida: Family Serpulidae and Family Sabellidae
The Ideal Beginner's Invertebrates

MOST CASUAL MARINE TANK observers cannot understand why these creatures are called worms; they're simply too elegant and beautiful—coming in shades of brown, black, gray, white, blue, yellow, red, and in multicolors—to be anything as repulsive as a worm. But besides being attractive, there are so many species of marine worms occurring worldwide that environmental scientists can learn a great deal by collecting, identifying, counting, and measuring them to determine the impact of human or other activity.

Classification. All marine worms that inhabit reefs (feather dusters, duster-cluster, bristle, fire, fan, and tube worms) are placed in the Phylum Annelida, generally known as the "segmented worms," in reference to their appearance.

The group we are interested in is Class Polychaeta, Subclass Sedentaria. These are polychaetes (worms having "many bristles") that commonly are tube dwellers attached to a substrate (as opposed to the free-living Subclass Errantia, typified for the marine aquar-

ist by the notorious bristleworms). The Sedentaria display a prostomium (head) without sensory structures but with tentacles and palps or other feeding structures, and no teeth or jaws. There are several families, including the two commonly known in the aquarium trade as fanworms (Family Serpulidae, with calcareous tubes) and feather duster worms (Family Serpulidae, with parchmentlike tubes).

Social Feather Dusters (*Bispira brunna*): appearing in clusters, these common Caribbean segmented worms are filter feeders, rapidly withdrawing into their leathery tubes when startled.

Protula magnifica: this species of feather duster worm displays very attractive, spiralling twin crowns that emerge from a single hard, calcareous tube that is characteristic of the Family Serpulidae.

Selection. Do you want these spiffy worms in your marine system? Yes. They're generally hardy, easy to keep, interesting, and gorgeous. Their anatomy makes them harmless to all but tiny suspended organisms that they filter out of the water column. They don't require intense reef lighting, and they make ideal subjects for a first invertebrate aquarium. Besides, they're inexpensive (at least in relation to the prices of other marine livestock) and may even come along free with live rock. These families are worldwide in shallow tropical to temperate seas.

What to look for? First of all, vital signs. Are their crowns in evidence most of the time? Do they quickly respond to motion, shade, or touch by complete retraction? For "leather" and sandy-type tube worms, is the tube complete? That is, is the base end closed, the outer margin clean, and the body of the tube not torn? If possible, get worms with a good portion of the rock on which they arrived or were collected. Healthy specimens of both serpulids and sabellids bear a pair of large mucus-producing pads that rotate and lay down a jellylike coating on the inner surface of the tube, building and rebuilding the upper lip much like the roping technique used in pottery making. Other general questions to ask yourself: Are the "dusters" fully expanded and intact? How do specimens other than the one that catches your eye appear? Buying one nice individual from a group of worms that are beaten up or drooping can be a risky purchase. How long has the dealer had them? I err on the side of buying newer stock to avoid the detrimental effects of probable starvation since collection.

Habitat. Feather dusters and fanworms do fine in high-quality natural and synthetic water of low to medium organic load, within the usual reasonable range of temperatures. Higher specific gravities (1.023 to 1.025) are appreciated, as is the case with most invertebrates.

Vigorous water movement is helpful for aeration, excretion, and circulation of the food items they eat. Placing these worms in a couple of inches of fine coral sand, or between rock or coral rubble, is generally acceptable.

Feather duster (Family Sabellidae): a perfect choice for simple fish-and-invertebrate tanks.

Bristleworm or fireworm (Family Amphinomidae): unlike the benign feather dusters, these segmented worms bear stinging spines and will attack corals.

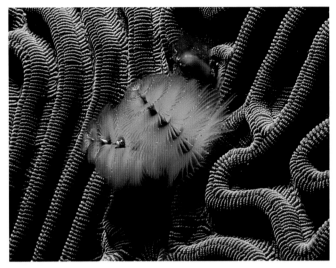

Christmas Tree Worm (*Spirobranchus giganteus*): appearing in many colors and shades, these lovely worms may be found embedded in rock or live coral.

These are benign, nonstinging animals, and territoriality is not a concern as long as sufficient food, circulation, and gaseous exchange is available. They mix well even with some of the nastier cnidarians (anemones and other stinging-celled coral animals) and are immune to the usual nettling or burning that can occur in crowded reef tanks.

Introduction and acclimation are simple. If possible, do not lift specimens from the water into the air. The water supports their bodies, and trapped gas can be a problem.

Some invertebrates and fishes can and may eat your worms. Wrasses, some basses, some butterflies, triggers, shrimps, crabs, and lobsters will try out most anything. Healthy worms will retract quickly into their tubes to avoid predation, but some of these predators are faster or more determined.

Reproduction. These worms have bizarre and varied modes of reproduction. Some sabellids replicate themselves asexually by budding or dividing the body evenly or into sections. Most reproduce sexually with the sexes being separate, although there are known hermaphrodites, with the front end of some fanworms producing eggs and the posterior making sperm. The sex products are released to the environment and develop as planktonic larvae, or may be retained and brooded within the tubes. Some of the small colonial feather dusters reproduce freely in the aquarium.

Feeding. Fanworms and feather dusters will greedily filter out any particle, plant, animal, or mineral of appropriate size. Many of these worms live for years in aquariums with no special feeding regimen, getting their sustenance from the foods offered to the fishes. To be sure they aren't starving, you can offer live foods (brine shrimp nauplii, rotifers) or prepared rations (store-bought or homemade) daily to a few times weekly. Clam juice mixed with other meaty foods can be whirred in a blender or crushed with a mortar and pestle or between spoons, then applied in the general area of the worm with a syringe or turkey baster. Switch off your particulate filtration for the duration—at least 15 minutes and up to an hour.

Summary. Tube-bearing polychaete worms are common fixtures in most shallow-water marine environments. They make for colorful, hardy aquarium additions when selected and collected appropriately. (One word of caution about collecting your own: avoid intertidal specimens from zones that are exposed to air at low tide. These generally fare poorly in constantly submerged conditions.)

Mollusks

Phylum Mollusca

From Tiny Snails to Giant Clams and Beyond

IT ISN'T EASY TO NAME another group of simple organisms that have done as much for humans as the mollusks. They've served as food, decoration, tools, even medicine and money; and nowadays, they are some of the most coveted aquarium specimens.

The diverse mix of animals we call mollusks—the clams, chitons, octopuses, snails, mussels, abalone, oysters, nudibranchs, sea hares, nautiluses, squid, tusk shells, and many more, are finally starting to get their due with marine aquarists. With improvements in water quality, foods, and lighting, as well as the quality of specimens delivered by the trade, what were once sure losers are being kept for years and even reproduced in captivity.

I am amazed at the parallel worlds of aquarium keeping and shell collecting. In late 1994, I was privileged to present my views to the Southern California Marine Aquarium Conference on the ethics and government control of marine livestock trade practices. One weekend later, I gave almost the iden-

Thorny oyster (*Spondylus* sp.): fabulous mollusk with a vibrantly pigmented mantle and a shell often encrusted with sponges and other life forms.

tical talk to the annual meeting of the Conchologists of America, a national organization of shell collectors. Our concerns are the same: no one wants to see natural resources or the environment negatively impacted by their participation.

Whether intending to keep them or not, aquarists do well to be aware of the mollusks as a group—if for no other reason than that they are likely to show up in your system sooner or later as passengers on live rock, macroalgae, other invertebrates, or foods. Some you may see are predatory on other invertebrates—anemones, sea urchins, other mollusks—and even on fishes. A few can be fatally dangerous to the aquarist.

Mollusca is Greek for "soft-bodied." As a phylum, mollusks are the second largest invertebrate group (after the arthropods); some 50,000 living species have been described, with another 35,000 known from fossil records.

This diverse group is distinguished by having a muscular foot, a calcareous shell secreted by the animal's underlying soft mantle, and a rasping feeding organ, the radula. In some subgroups, the shell and radula may be secondarily modified, sometimes radically.

Feeding behavior is of all types, from vicious suction, drilling, and poison-darting to parasitism to relatively unexciting algal scraping and filter-feeding.

Modes of reproduction vary as well. Most mollusks release their gametes into the water given environmental cues, with the young going through lar-

val stages as plankton before settling. Some have internal fertilization, releasing offspring at different degrees of development, depending on the species.

We'll discuss in some detail three of the six living classes, the Gastropoda (snails and nudibranchs), the Pelecypoda (or Bivalvia, the bivalves; clams and mussels), and the Cephalopoda (octopuses and cuttlefishes) that have members commonly kept by aquarists.

Snails
Class Gastropoda
Subclass Prosobranchia

Classification. This is the largest and, by many measures, most successful of molluscan classes, with about 75,000 existing species and another 15,000 fossil forms. Snails, often called the "stomach-footed" mollusks, are found in freshwater, and have conquered the land by converting their mantle cavity into a lung and eliminating their primitive gills. Marine species exploit all types of bottoms, while also having free-swimming forms in the pelagic environment.

The Subclass Prosobranchia has a mantle cavity and organs located anteriorly in their classically twisted (or torted) shells, which allow these animals to pull back within covered safety.

Selection. Beautifully shaped, often exquisitely colored cone snails (genus *Conus*) may be dan-

gerous to your fishes—and you. They include the poison-harpoon-equipped hunters so popular on television nature shows. In these *Conus* species, the radula is modified as a dart that can be thrust into worms or fishes, paralyzing them. The prey is then swallowed whole. There are other cone species that are not so predaceous or dangerous to their owners. Be careful around these animals; watch where you place your hands if beachcombing, diving, or snorkeling in their environments.

A few other predaceous snail groups you ought to be aware of are the murexes (Family Muricidae), snails that eat other snails; the coralliophilids (Family Coralliophilidae), that, as you might guess from their name, love to eat live coral; thiads (Family Thiadidae), olives (Family Olividae), auger shells (Family Terebridae) and turrid shells (Family Turridae). I would avoid

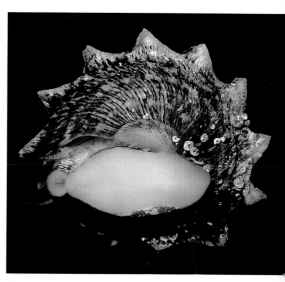

Star shell snail (*Lithopoma* [*Astraea*] sp.): active herbivores, these snails are often stocked to graze algae in reef tanks.

Cowrie (*Cyprea* sp.): known by its lustrous shell partially covered by its mantle.

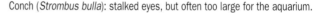

Conch (*Strombus bulla*): stalked eyes, but often too large for the aquarium.

all of these snails for the aquarium.

Limpets (Family Fissurellidae) are the Chinese-hat-looking herbivores found on rocky beaches, industriously ridding them of fine algae. Their submerged brethren are the keyhole limpets (*Diodora* spp.) with a hole on top of their shell, giving them the appearance of tiny volcanoes. Limpets are generally desirable aquarium inhabitants, staying small and busily cleaning rocky surfaces. Those keeping small-polyped corals, however, may find that limpets mow through certain species, leaving a denuded skeleton behind.

Top shells (Family Trochidae) are macroalgae eaters, often shipped from cold-water climates. A related family, the Turbinidae, or turban snails, includes the popular turbo snails (*Turbo* spp.) excellently adapted for feeding on hair algae and algal films. Another member of the family is *Trochus niloticus*, which is being propagated in Palau both as a food item and for the aquar-

ist market. Because they tend to grow large, both *Trochus* and *Turbo* snails can easily starve if competition with other snails is too keen. One *Turbo* per 5 or 10 gallons of tank capacity is a reasonable stocking rate, but be ready for them to dislodge small rocks and loose pieces of coral or decor that are not anchored in place.

Smaller than turbos and regarded by many as the best snails for reef aquariums are *Lithopoma* (*Astraea*) *americanum*, the American Star Shell, and the related West Indian Star Shell, *Lithopoma* (*Astraea*) *tectum*. They are able to get into tighter nooks, less apt to knock everything over, and reported by many aquarists to be much longer-lived than turbos in captivity. What's more, they're cheaper and readily available from Florida collectors and importers. In reef systems with huge surface areas of live rock to be kept clean, many aquarists use these snails by the dozens—as many as one per gallon.

In my opinion, tower shells (Family Turritelidae) should be employed more by marine aquarists with invertebrate systems. Their long spiral shape and burrowing behavior serves to keep the substrate loose as they feed on substrate detritus. Similarly shaped members of the Family Cerithiidae, often sold as cerith snails, are becoming known as hardy, reliable eaters of algae and diatoms.

Conchs (Family Strombidae) deserve mention because they're such an important group as human food and are increasingly available in the aquarium trade. Be aware that these are active, predaceous animals that will outgrow small systems. Besides consuming algae, they will eat other invertebrates, particularly sea stars and urchins. Another downside is their knocking over and digging up everything in the system. Aquacultured baby Queen Conchs, with attention-getting probosci and eyestalks, make curious additions to tanks with ample sandy areas.

Other gastropods that can be recommended as cleaner-uppers who leave other life alone are the whelks (Family Buccinidae) and basket whelks (Family Nassariidae) that feed on meaty leftovers and wastes. The highly prized cowries (Family Cypraeidae) have glossy shells and make gorgeous feeders on algal deposits; they do require clean, well-oxygenated water.

Summary. When using the services of marine snails as livestock and scavengers, pay attention to selection and stocking rates. Some aquarists even quarantine them to eliminate the introduction of infectious disease, but primarily dead or dying snails. Be aware of the species you are dealing with and its life habits; don't introduce more snails than your system can support—simple starvation may be the leading cause of death in the aquarium. (If the snails aren't keeping up with algal growth, you can always add more.) There are snails that can make beautiful aquarium additions, as well as the several that can be a pain, literally and figuratively.

Nudibranchs
Class Gastropoda
Subclass Opisthobranchia

CONSIDERING THEIR SMALL SIZE, often bizarre body shapes and dazzling coloration, it's no wonder nudibranchs are often unidentified by divers, aquarists, and tidepoolers who don't know them for what they are: marine snails that lack shells, just like their lowly terrestrial cousins, the slugs, found sliming around under rotting wood and vegetation. But most of us feel fascination

Nudibranchs (*Nembrotha cristata*) mating on a bed of tunicates: graphically patterned and vibrantly beautiful, most nudibranchs will starve in captivity.

rather than revulsion when we view these fantastically pigmented creatures. Unfortunately, few efforts at keeping them in captivity have been successful. Many failures are aquarist-originated: chemical poisoning, unstable conditions, and, most importantly, starvation.

Classification. Nudibranchs belong to the Class Gastropoda (with the snails) but they are in the other Subclass, the Opisthobranchia. Opisthobranchs show reduction of shell and mantle cavity, and many are detorted, that is, secondarily bilaterally symmetrical. The nudibranchs comprise four suborders, about 70 families, and more than 1,000 valid species. Two of the suborders are rarely seen in the hobby, the Dendronotacea and Arminacea, but the following information concerning the other two groups applies to them as well.

Dorids (Suborder Doridacea), dwell in rocky intertidal zones worldwide, sometimes in good numbers. Their mantles cover their entire dorsal surface and hang over their foot. Their gill plumes are arranged around a rear anal vent area and are capable of retraction into a specialized pocket. The rhinophores, or chemosensory tentacles at the head end, can likewise be retracted.

Aeolids (Suborder Aeolidacea) have clusters of elongated dorsal structures,

Nudibranch (*Chromodoris* sp.): with an anatomy stranger than fiction, this genus has evolved feathery external anal gills, paired chemosensory tentacles, and toxin-producing skin glands.

the cerata, that provide cryptic architecture and make them look like sea anemones when balled up. The cerata serve several other functions: as a respiratory surface, in some species each containing a glandular digestive lobe; and very importantly for marine aquarists, they may contain specialized cnidosomes. Take a good look at that word. It sounds a lot like the stinging cells of cnidarians (anemones, corals, jellyfish), and for good reason. To make themselves unpalatable to enemies, some of these nudibranchs eat and store undischarged nematocysts of other animals. As if these transplanted weapons on their backs weren't enough, some aeolids pack poisonous glands, spiky bundles of calcareous spicules, or noxious mucus secretions. No wonder they're not often eaten.

In addition to the pair of rhinophores that dorids possess, aeolids sport a pair of oral tentacles and parapodial tentacles. The body and foot are generally more elongated and narrower than those of the dorids.

Feeding. Unfortunately, most species of nudibranchs have proved to be very specialized feeders. Nudibranchs are carnivores that feed on attached animals: hydroids, sea anemones, soft corals, bryozoans, sponges, ascidians, barnacles, fish eggs, and others. Each family is generally restricted to one kind of prey; this is not surprising, as they are classified by their oral anatomies that have evolved to cope with different types of food. As aquarists hoping to keep an attractive nudi-

branch, how can we solve this predator-prey food problem? The best way to know that you've found a match between one of these finicky feeders and its prey is to watch it eating and then to procure (collect or buy) it together with its food source.

Unfortunately, since most nudibranchs do not come into the dealer's tanks attached to their food target, an alternate approach is to consult the pertinent literature and try to bring both together in your aquarium.

The next-to-last method is to supply a great variety of live target foods in a huge, diverse, well-established live-rock type aquarium and let your nudibranchs choose what they will.

The worst method is to buy them and hope they will accept prepared foods. The vast majority will not and will starve to death.

Behavior. Another major difficulty in keeping nudibranchs is that these snails are armed with skin glands that produce potent poisons; some species make sulfuric acid, others nonacidic noxious substances. As already mentioned, some celebrated species use the nematocysts they reprocess from eating stinging-celled animals. Others have spicules embedded in their mantle. With the sudden and mysterious death of a nudibranch in your tank, this stuff can end up in your water. To reduce the potential for toxin release and disaster, you need good chemical filtration (using activated carbon) with adequate circulation, regular partial water changes, and a watchful eye on

Dorid Nudibranch (*Phyllidia coelestis*): widespread on Indo-Pacific reefs.

Phyllidia sp.: one of many nudibranch species with unknown feeding habits.

what you have and where it is in your system.

Once at a Sears Roebuck store in the early 1970s, when they were in the live-pet business, we had a tank that was a proverbial death trap. Whenever we put a new fish in, it would become shy and perish within a few days. We tried all the usual: massive water changes, dumping the tank completely, even throwing away the gravel and the decor—all to no avail. Enough study and discussion led us finally to realize that a Spanish Dancer nudibranch (*Hexabranchus* sp.) that had been in the tank had bumped up against the tank walls, depositing a toxin it extracts from sponges. This was debilitating everything that came in contact with it. Once more, we dumped, acid-bleach-washed, and salt-scrubbed the sides of the tank. Only then were we able to keep other livestock alive.

Habitat. Water quality is the third problem in keeping nudibranchs. These snails, and more notably their live food, require optimized and stable conditions; for tropical and deeper water forms, a narrow temperature range, high (8.3) pH, no ammonia or nitrite, and minimal nitrate. Medication? Don't even think about it. Nudibranchs are very sensitive to metals and dyes; copper, for example, will kill them quickly. Treatments of fishes in the system must start with removal of either the fishes or the nudibranchs to a separate tank.

Summary. Nudibranchs are not easy by any measure. The best advice I can offer is not to buy them if you aren't serious about the challenge. If you are ready to devote the time, effort, and expense it will take, follow the biology of the snails and provide them and their food source with livable conditions and

a lack of medication. A ray of hope to those determined to keep them in captivity: *Coral Reef Animals of the Indo-Pacific*, by Gosliner, Behrens, and Williams, notes that the black-and-white dorid nudibranch *Jorunna funebris* feeds on the lovely blue sponge *Haliclona*. Both are seen in the aquarium trade, the sponge is hardy and rapidly spreads under good conditions, and the resourceful aquarist could conceivably put the two together in a sustainable display. This, obviously, will require a cooperative dealer or marine life supplier who is willing to work with you on a special order. The challenge is not impossible, but it would take patience.

Nudibranchs, with their grace and flamboyant colors, certainly rank among the oceans' most appealing creatures. (In fact, I've been waiting for someone to create a nudibranch screen saver for personal computers.) Unless or until an unexpected solution to the problem of feeding them appears, however, most of us probably ought to content ourselves to viewing them in their native habitats.

Clams, Scallops, Mussels, Oysters
Class Pelecypoda

THESE ARE THE "HATCHET-FOOTED" mollusks, familiar to most of us as delectable food items. For this group, I like the older taxonomic name, Bivalvia, which is perfectly descriptive for these creatures. Whatever we call them, most pelecypods have two shells and a fleshy foot that serves to get them around and for anchoring.

Most are found attached to or buried within the substrate. A few, notably the file shells (including the Flame Scallops), are free-roaming. Almost all are filter feeders, with some (the *Tridacna* and *Hippopus* clams) receiving considerable nutrition through photosynthetic symbiosis with zooxanthellae in their mantles.

Selection. Two factors—their mode of feeding and the keeper's difficulty in assessing whether they're alive or not—have traditionally caused the bivalves to be shunned by many aquarists. This is a real shame. For feeding, they actually require very little. In systems sparsely populated with competing filter-feeding organisms, they demand very little attention, at the most a bit of auxiliary feeding. As long as your fishes are being fed, the bivalves will simply sieve out what they need. Otherwise, a simple mash of dried, fresh, or frozen food may be periodically applied to the water while particulate and skimmer filtration is temporarily shut down.

The issue of whether they are healthy/alive/dead is a little tougher. These animals should be quarantined for a few weeks to give you confidence that they're going to make it in your main system. Sometimes when they die, they'll pollute the entire system and take everything else with them. Various mussels and oysters may be at-

Flame Scallop (*Lima scabra*): free-roaming filter feeders that grow and even spawn in some aquariums and disappear or slowly starve in others. Established, nutrient-rich systems free of harassing fishes work best.

Variable Thorny Oyster (*Spondylus varians*): common Indo-Pacific species with orange mantle and blue eyes.

tached to live rock and often perish during shipping and handling. Those that do survive, however, can live for years, unobtrusively filtering the waters of your aquarium. One spectacular aquarium species from American waters is the Atlantic Thorny Oyster (*Spondylus americanus*), which has a long-spined shell that may be orange, purple, red, or white and a lovely patterned mantle. Harvested in the Gulf of Mexico, these bivalves can reach half a foot in width and carry a profusion of encrusting sponges, macroalgae, small corals, and even other mollusks on their shells.

The swimming members of the group, variously sold as Flame or Flaming Scallops (*Lima scabra*, actually not a scallop but a file shell or file clam) I find are particularly notorious for starving or being harassed to death. Keep them only with delicate fishes, such as gobies or seahorses, and no stinging-celled animals or predatory sea stars.

Tridacnid Clams
Family Tridacnidae

A MUCH MORE SUCCESSFUL STORY is that of the tridacnid clams, Family Tridacnidae. These bivalves have become a popular item among sophisticated marine aquarists worldwide. Recent advances that allow the keeping of these animals include a ready and growing source of cultured specimens of various species, improvement in the awareness of hobbyists about lighting, and strides in maintaining stable, reeflike water conditions.

The breathtaking beauty of these bivalves comes from their brilliantly pigmented mantles (the fleshy, protruding lips) which are filled with endosymbiotic algae (zooxanthellae). This is a crucial energy source for the clam, and the zooxanthellae themselves are very demanding of intense lighting. Most clam keepers use metal halide systems to keep these clams alive, growing, and their mantles fully colored. Under average fluorescent lights, even the most gorgeous clams can lose their color and gradually shrink away.

High output (HO) or very high output (VHO) fluorescents may provide sufficient illumination, but clams should be located high in the tank to take full advantage of the available light. Actinics will accentuate the electric blue and green colors in some clams, but should always be used in conjunction with full-spectrum VHO fluorescent bulbs or metal halides. Whatever lighting mode you use, its performance will be put to the test by your tridacnid clams in color, size, and growth. Happy giant clams are fast-growing and beautiful to behold.

Though giant clams feed on nitrate and are used by some aquarists as biological filters, the chemical precursors to nitrate are toxic. Reef aquarium water conditions are called for, but some experts warn about placing clams in systems too aggressively stripped of nutrients by high-tech protein skimming or other very efficient filtration.

Selection. The aquarist buying his or her first clam is advised not to go right out and make a huge investment in a large, centerpiece-quality show specimen. The larger the tridacnid, the greater the risk it will fail to adapt to your aquarium conditions.

When buying a giant clam of any size, be sure that its mantle has no bleached areas, that it is untorn, and that it reaches out over the edges of the shell. Avoid any clam that appears pale and has a gaping opening (the inhalant siphon) that exposes its gills. The clam should react vigorously to any external stimulus, energetically closing its shell when a hand or other object approaches from above.

As might be guessed, the most spectacularly colored clams—electric blue *Tridacna crocea* and *T. maxima*—are both more expensive and a bit more challenging to keep. The brilliant colors will fade under insufficient light, and the aquarist who does not yet have a good metal halide lighting system may be better off starting with clams that have a duller brown or greenish coloration. *Tridacna derasa*, *T. gigas*, and *T. squamosa* are considered by many to be good beginner's species, somewhat more hardy and less demanding of intense lighting. All three of these clams can be extremely appealing, colorful, and long-lived.

Gemlike "baby" clams in the 1-to-2-inch range are also a good bet, being more affordable and highly resistant to the stresses of being shipped and relocated. Their primary drawback is a tendency to fall among the rockwork or become buried in the sand. A simple solution is to create a small, shallow bed of coral sand in a cleaned half shell

from another clam, oyster, or the like. Nestle your new clam gently into this substrate and it should quickly settle in, usually attaching its byssal threads to the smooth inner shell of the nest you have created. (This connection by the

byssal gland—an organ seen in many of the mussels—must never be ripped loose; if you do have to move an attached clam, cut the byssus as far from the clam shell as possible with a sharp blade. Major tears to the byssus often

Crocea (Boring) Clam (*Tridacna crocea*): intense illumination and regular calcium supplementation needed.

Maxima Clam (*Tridacna maxima*): grows to about 12 inches (30 cm).

Derasa Clam (*Tridacna derasa*): excellent choice for beginning clam keepers.

Crocea Clam (*Tridacna crocea*): more challenging than other species.

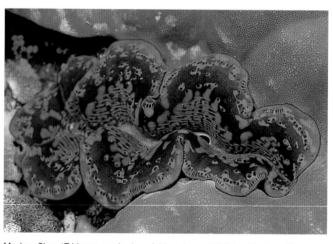

Maxima Clam (*Tridacna maxima*): variable colors, slightly hardier than *T. crocea*.

lead to death of the clam, and you should be sure that any clam purchased does not have torn byssal tissue drooping from the bottom of the animal.)

Feeding. Clams are calcium hogs, and larger specimens can cause the calcium level in aquarium water to plummet in short order. Daily or weekly supplementation with some form of calcium (see page 111) is a must in virtually all systems; aim for a constant reading of 400 to 450 mg/L. Alkalinity should also be kept high (7 to 12 dKH), pH should measure 8.0 to 8.2, and the usual reef supplements (iodine, magnesium, strontium) ought to be added, unless you have another regimen that keeps them from being depleted.

Predator/Prey Relations. Predators on giant clams are many, and the delectable mantle is irresistible to angels, butterflies, larger wrasses, triggers, puffers, and others. Even the dwarf angels will often start nibbling at the edge of the mantle, causing the clam to retract and eventually to shrivel and die. Less visible problems can come from another mollusk, snails in the Family Pyramidellidae, seen as tiny white conical shells attached to the bottom of the shell. These will multiply and attack the clam's mantle, invading the flesh within the shell where they are often undis-

376

covered until it is too late. Inspect all new clams carefully (along the shell edges, top and bottom) and brush or pick away any hangers-on; the best time to inspect is after dark, when these nocturnal pests emerge. In his handbook on clam care, German aquarist Daniel Knop recommends the use of juvenile *Coris gaimard* wrasses as a biological control of these deadly little predators. Bristleworms are another threat to tridacnid clams, and some reef aquarists rely on various members of the dottybacks (*Pseudochromis* spp.) to keep these predators at bay.

Aquacultured versus Wild-Caught.
With all the easy availability of show-quality cultivated clams, there are still some people who deal in "wild-caught" individuals. Their collection is now banned in many countries, and chances are good that the label "wild" should actually read "illegally harvested." Please don't encourage this practice by buying them. There are aquacultured specimens available of almost all giant clam species: *Tridacna gigas, T. squamosa, T. derasa, T. maxima, T. crocea, Hippopus hippopus, H. porcellanus*, in all mantle colors—blue, purple, yellow, brown, green, and even reddish

As my friends will testify, I've spent decades and thousands of dollars at the sushi bar. Never once have I ordered or eaten *mirugai*, giant clam. It saddens me to think that a human would support the killing of a huge giant clam, possibly more than a hundred years old and maybe a thousand pounds in weight, for the sake of a tasty morsel.

The hunting of giant clams as culinary delicacies had, until recently, driven them to economic extinction in broad areas of the Pacific.

Happily, the various culturing programs now underway in Palau, the Solomon Islands, the Philippines, the Cook Islands, Tonga, and elsewhere are beginning to supply farmed giant clams for restocking depleted reefs, for local sustenance, and as a new cash crop at the village level on a number of Pacific Islands. This has a nice consequence for aquarists, who can actually help in the revival of giant clams by purchasing captive-propagated stock for their reef tanks. See Coral Reef Aquaculture Sites, page 406, for sources of captive-bred giant clams if you are unable to buy them from your local retailer.

Squids, Octopuses, Cuttlefishes, and Nautiloids
Class Cephalopoda

THESE ARE THE MOST ADVANCED mollusks, and, quite possibly, the most intelligent invertebrates. They possess eyes with a focusing lens, an efficient, closed circulatory system, relatively large brains, and are capable of demonstrable learning.

Thinking of keeping an octopus? Consider their positive attributes: interesting behavior, color-changing ability, splendid appetites. But then remember the following problems: "inking," super-aggressive predation, and slippery escape potential. They eat or

Cuttlefish (*Sepia latimanus*): unusual in the aquarium trade, but keepable in larger, well-filtered systems.

Blue-ringed Octopus (*Hapalochlaena lunulata*): boycott this deadly species.

Sepia plangon: a charming little cuttlefish, rarely seen in captivity.

will try to consume most everything, will get out of any opening big enough to squeeze their beak through (or loose enough to be pushed up and out of the way), and will unknowingly commit hara-kiri if spooked into ejecting a big dose of ink. Other than that, cephalopods make good-to-suitable specialty aquarium specimens.

Chambered Nautilus (*Nautilus pompilius*): kept and bred in captivity, but for big, high-tech systems.

Squids, cuttlefishes, and chambered nautiluses have also been maintained from time to time by home aquarists. They require big systems, special care, and research on your part before attempting to keep any of them.

Special mention is due for the venomous Blue-ringed Octopus, *Hapalochlaena lunulata*. If you're bitten by this little beauty, most likely you will die. Who would be so ignorant as to collect, ship, sell, or try to keep it in captivity? Accidents happen—including a number of fatalities every year, usually to fishermen in the countries where they are collected: the Philippines and Australia. Please do not buy these animals and don't encourage anyone who trades in them.

Other mollusk classes include the limpetlike Monoplacophora (burrowing tusk or tooth shells); Scaphopoda; the strange wormlike Aplacophora; and Polyplacophora (the chitons). The first three are not of importance to the hob-

byist, as the likelihood of encountering them in the trade is extremely rare. Chitons, however, appear with some regularity stuck to shells and live rock. They are ovoid-shaped, bilaterally symmetrical, flattened top to bottom, and bear eight articulating dorsal plates. These innocuous creatures spend their days hiding from the light, adhering to solid surfaces—living-fossil algal scrapers who do no harm to anything.

Summary. With knowledge comes power; mollusks are not all bad, nor impossible to keep. Some are spectacular and among the most eye-catching reef organisms we can own. They require adequate care like any other living thing. Take some time to research the organisms you want (or that you've discovered in your system)—it will enrich your viewing and improve your chances of success. Once again, beware of metal and dye medications around all of these animals; they are among the most sensitive to such poisons.

Crustaceans

Phylum Arthropoda
Aquarium-Compatible Crabs, Lobsters, and Shrimps

WHAT WOULD THE OCEANS and our aquariums be without crustaceans—the shrimps, lobsters, crabs, and others of this armored taxonomic division? Certainly much more peaceful, but far less interesting. These joint-legged animals run the gamut from living independently, to being commensal and mutualistic with all other marine groups, all the way to being parasitic.

It is a common misconception that all the crustacean members make poor or difficult aquarium inhabitants. Several species are supreme choices—as scavengers, top predators, cleaning symbionts, and community display organisms. Which ones are they? In such a large, diverse group as the crustaceans, the best way to know is to read, then investigate and experiment for yourself.

With the insects, trilobites, spiders, scorpions, ticks, mites, sea spiders, centipedes, millipedes, and a few other various and sundry groups, the Subphylum Crustacea (from the Latin *crusta*, meaning shell) helps make up the Phylum Arthropoda, the largest taxonomic group in the Animal Kingdom, with almost two million described species. Some common characteristics of the crustaceans include:

1) Heads more or less uniform, with five pairs of appendages: two pairs of antennae, a pair of opposing, biting, grinding mandibles, and two pairs of accessory feeding appendages;

2) Bodies composed of distinct segments covered by a chitinous exoskeleton strengthened by the deposition of calcium salts;

3) Appendages typically biramous (two major elements, unlike the uniramous appendages of insects, centipedes, etc.).

Although the taxonomy of this huge phylum is of necessity complex, we will cover only the following arthropod groups that tend to interest marine aquarists:

Subphylum Chelicerata, Class Merostomata (horseshoe crabs);

Subphylum Crustacea, Class Malacostraca (almost three-fourths of all described species of crustaceans and most of the larger forms, such as crabs, lobsters, and shrimps).

Peacock Mantis Shrimp (*Odontodactylus scyallarus*): a spectacular but menacing crustacean.

Horseshoe Crabs
Class Merostomata
Subclass Xiphosura

HERE IS A TRULY ANCIENT crustacean-like organism. While actually more closely related to spiders and not technically a crustacean, the horseshoe crab is often offered as such. *Limulus polyphemus* is the most common species in the trade in the U.S., though occasionally some of the other three extant species are imported from Asian coasts.

Horseshoe crabs were once touted in hobbyist literature as all-around good marine scavengers; this is still true in some cases, but many aquarists have learned their lesson. Though an initially hardy animal that generally lives for a while in captivity, the horseshoe crab does have some disadvantages: knocking aquarium contents around by burrowing, crawling, and swimming are probably the worst, closely followed by hibernating beneath the gravel, mysteriously dying, and polluting the system.

I would keep them out of crowded tanks, especially those dominated by live rock aquascapes, and consider them appropriate only for aquariums with large open areas of deep sand. To ensure that a horseshoe crab is not slowly starving, it may occasionally be necessary to tuck pieces of food, such as a prawn, in its path with a feeding stick. They definitely get too big and destructive for most reef tanks and can become wedged or trapped in the intricate rockwork. That said, they are undeniable attention-getters and not hard to keep if given adequate room and food.

Crabs, Lobsters, and Shrimps
Class Malacostraca
Order Decapoda

THESE ANIMALS ALL have similar enough aquarium requirements and temperaments to be discussed together.

Typically, malacostracans have stalked compound eyes and 19 body segments: 5 in the head, 8 in the thorax and 6 abdominal. As the decapod order name implies (from the Greek, meaning "ten feet") these animals' chief diagnostic feature is five pairs of legs.

Brachyuran Crabs. "True" crabs (Infraorder Brachyura) have a small tail that is folded underneath their flat, broad bodies. Their eyestalks are long and fit into sockets on the carapace. Their first pair of legs is modified as a pair of pinching claws.

Some true crabs are great swimmers (Family Portunidae, like the edible Blue Crab) and are rarely found on the bottom. Others are burrowers in muddy substrates (Family Xanthidae), but most scurry along the bottom rubble (walking crabs, Family Cancridae). Aquarists often have access to a peaceful little species from Florida and the Caribbean called the Nimble Crab (*Percnon gibbesi*) (usually sold as the Sally Lightfoot Crab) that stays small

Horseshoe Crab (*Limulus polyphemus*): crawling ashore to lay its eggs.

Stareye Hermit (*Dardanus venosus*): large, omnivorous Caribbean species.

and grazes on algae. Another tropical Atlantic species is the Arrow Crab (*Stenorhynchus seticornis*), a true crab whose long legs and odd little body suggest a spider. Despite is spindly appearance, this is an aggressive beast that will attack and kill other reef crustaceans. Alone, it makes an interesting reef tank specimen.

Cruise the aquarium shops and you will be bound to encounter many new and interesting species; there are over a thousand true crabs found worldwide in terrestrial, freshwater, and marine habitats. They range from the size of a sand grain to over 15 inches across. Look for them as hitchhikers on live rock, algae, corals, sea urchins, and other livestock and incoming material.

Ever wonder why the expensive, edible, or collectible ones aren't just grown in an aquaculture facility for big money? Their larval histories are bizarre, with several molts and sometimes months going by in a planktonic existence.

Anomuran Crabs. These crabs, such as the king, porcelain, and hermit crabs, differ from brachyurans in that their fifth pair of legs is greatly reduced. The hermit crabs are of particular interest to marine aquarists; they've been put to use as scavengers since the hobby began. They are odd creatures structurally, with a typically hard anterior segment (cephalothorax) followed by a very soft, twisted abdomen that they keep hidden in a discarded shell.

There are all types of hermit crabs, frigid water to tropical, vivid scarlet and bright blue to drab, and those that decorate themselves with anemones, sponges, and more. Many are opportunistic omnivores that, given the chance and hunger, will consume other livestock. Healthy, wary fishes and mobile invertebrates have little to fear, but sessile organisms may fall prey to a hermit's picking.

Tiny (less than 1 inch) herbivorous hermit crabs make especially good maintenance helpers in any marine system that isn't subject to being dosed with medication. Some hail from intertidal zones and are very inexpensive; others are true reef creatures, collected from deeper waters, and are several times pricier. The Red Reef Hermit (*Paguristes cadenati*) comes from reef areas 25 to 100 feet down, and it makes one of the most handsome little herbivores, with brilliant crimson legs and green eyes on the tips of tan-colored eyestalks

Other good Atlantic choices include the Orangeclaw Hermit (*Calcinus tibicen*), the Polka-dotted Hermit (*Phimochirus operculatus)*, and the Redstripe Hermit (*Phimochirus holthuisi*). Highly recommended as one of the best of the lot, as far as effective grazing is concerned, is the so-called Mexican Red-legged Hermit Crab (*Clibanarius digueti*).

There are also tiny Blue-legged Hermits (*Clibanarius tricolor*) that are all the rage in reefdom. (As the name suggests, they actually have a three-part color scheme, with bands of white and red on the bright-blue legs.) They are great little herbivores, hard working and so small that they can maneuver through narrow spots in the rockwork and around corals and not dislodge anything.

Many other hermits are available, and aquarists are still discovering which make the best tank cleaners. Choose only hermits meant to stay small (some on the Pacific coast get 12 to 18 inches long) and even then, keep your eye on them. Species of bigger, destructive hermits are sometimes found mixed with their tiny, vegetarian brethren, and they can grow into problems in the reef aquarium. (Note that some fishes, including bigger wrasses and triggerfishes, will crunch tiny hermits with glee.) The rough-and-tumble larger species of hermit crabs can be quite beautiful and appropriate for aquariums without edible corals, clams, or other species of crustaceans. (Always provide a selection of empty shells so that the growing hermits can move into bigger quarters when necessary.)

Porcelain crabs (Family Porcellanidae) that make their way into the aquarium trade often arrive as hangers-on with their commensal hosts: anemones, corals, sponges, and spiny-skinned animals. Actually closer to the lobsters than to the true crabs, these are small, rather flattened anomuran crabs whose abdomens are folded close against the chest. Their pinching claws are large, broad, and flattened. If you look closely at the invertebrate stock on display at a pet shop that caters to reef keepers, you'll often spot these as

Spotted Porcelain Crab (*Neopetrolisthes maculata*): a peaceful little species that lives with anemones.

Decorator Crab (*Cyclocoeloma tuberculata*): this Indo-Pacific curiosity drapes itself with small anemones.

unpriced bonuses that should be acquired with their host species. Although small, many are gorgeous and interesting to watch.

Shrimps. Shrimps of several families are widely kept by aquarists and can make fascinating, long-lived aquarium inhabitants. Unlike crabs and lobsters, shrimps have bodies that are compressed, more or less cylindrical, and elongate. They have a long, well-developed rostrum, often longer than the thorax, with eyestalks, antennae, and legs often of extraordinary length. They also differ behaviorally—most shrimps are socially gregarious (other than some cleaners), congregating in large schools. Shrimps feed on small crustaceans, worms, fishes, algae, and more. They range in size from something akin to a mosquito to about a foot in length—the real-world jumbo shrimp.

Snapping or pistol shrimps (Family Alpheidae) appear periodically as wholesale and live rock specimens. These animals have one much-enlarged claw with a prominent "tooth" that fits like a peg into a hole. Pistol shrimps can close this claw rapidly, resulting in a cracking sound that can be heard well outside the aquarium.

Snapping shrimp species either burrow into soft and sandy substrates themselves or take up residence in a mutually satisfying (commensal) relationship with other invertebrates (such as anemones) or fishes. If you keep them, take care that they don't undermine your decor with their prodigious digging activity.

Cleaner shrimps (Families Palaemonidae, Hippolytidae, and Stenopodidae) set up "cleaning stations" on rocks and coral reef faces and use their bright bodies and antennae colors and swaying motions to call in fish host "customers." The fishes get their necrotic tissue and parasites removed, while the shrimps get a meal. Along with the cleaner gobies of the genus *Gobiosoma*, these are my favorite biological cleaners. Due to their hardiness, and the fact that they greedily eat food other than from cleaning enterprises, these shrimps make great aquarium additions.

The Banded Coral Shrimp (*Stenopus hispidus*) is an ideal choice for beginning aquarists, although it may attack soft corals in a reef aquarium. Buy the shrimp singly or in clearly bonded pairs, as unmatched individuals will often fight to the death. (They are also known as "Boxing Shrimp" for their pincers-open fighting stance and pugnacious behavior.) Take a close look

at a mated couple; they're sexually dimorphic with the female being slightly larger and broader. The bearing of bright green eggs on the underside of females is a dead give-away. Otherwise, mature females may be determined by a greenish/blue color in the ovaries that can be seen through their translucent body wall. Single animals tend to be reclusive, whereas pairs may openly parade around at all hours after becoming accustomed to their surroundings.

Do not purchase *Stenopus hispidus* specimens that have been at your dealer's store for less than 48 hours. Disease is virtually unheard of among these aquarium specimens, but losses immediately after transport are common. During this critical period, many individuals perish. Select your stock on the basis of their being active and interested in their environment and feeding. The absence of a chela (claw) or one to two legs need not remove a candidate from consideration. If the individual is otherwise healthy, these

appendages will be replaced in a succeeding molt. The Banded Coral Shrimp is a good beginner's invertebrate, but may prove to be a problem in a reef aquarium with small fishes or vulnerable corals.

Less aggressive are the Common Cleaner Shrimps, *Lysmata amboinensis* from the Indo-Pacific and *L. grabhami* from the Caribbean. With a golden body and bold red-and-white stripes along the back, they are visually appealing and will often spawn in the aquarium (although the larvae will be eaten long before they begin to resemble shrimp). Another Caribbean cleaner, the Peppermint Shrimp (*Lysmata wurdemanni*) makes a great display in clusters, and these are credited with preying on the nuisance *Aiptasia* anemones. (Don't confuse the Peppermint Shrimp with the Pacific peppermint-like shrimps, *Rhynchocinetes* spp., which have large eyes and a long, upward-pointing, beaklike rostrum. They are fine additions to many tanks, but will

Dancing Shrimp (*Rhynchocinetes durbanensis*): note long beaklike rostrum.

Peppermint Shrimp (*Lysmata wurdemanni*): *Aiptasia*-eating Caribbean species.

Common Cleaner Shrimp (*Lysmata amboinensis*): excellent aquarium species.

Banded Coral Shrimp (*Stenopus hispidus*): very hardy, and interesting in pairs.

feed on soft corals. *Lysmata wurde-manni* is much more compatible with reef tank inhabitants.)

The Scarlet or Fire Cleaner Shrimp (*Lysmata debelius*) is blood-red with white legs and spots on the carapace—a dramatic addition to the aquarium. Pederson's Cleaner Shrimp (*Periclimenes pedersoni*) and the Spotted Cleaner Shrimp (*P. yucatanicus*) live commensally in the tentacles of anemones and are exquisitely beautiful.

Saron, Marble, or Buffalo Shrimp in the genus *Saron* can be exceedingly attractive, with sometimes bizarre patterns of spots, rings, and curious blotches and bundles of hairlike cirri on the back. They are bigger, stronger, and much more destructive than the cleaner shrimp species and may seek out and eat soft corals, *Tridacna* clams, and other mollusks. These make interesting additions to more boisterous fish-and-invertebrate systems where there are no tempting corals to munch on.

None of these shrimps is immune from predation, even those that serve as community cleaners. Underfed opportunistic crustacean eaters—triggers, large angels, puffers, basses/groupers, wrasses, lionfishes, and the like—must be watched carefully and are not to be trusted. Also, unless your system is extremely large and well-equipped with numerous nooks and crannies, I would not recommend mixing other crabs, lobsters, and shrimps. They will often seek each other out, fight, and ultimately consume each other.

Lobsters. The lobsters that aquarists are likely to see belong to three families: true lobsters (Nephropsidae); spiny lobsters (Palinuridae) and slipper or Spanish lobsters (Scyllaridae). Fundamentally, lobsters are scavengers feeding on dead or decaying animal matter. My father still likes to tell me of the "poor man's bologna"—cold lobster meat—that a fellow grade-school student was harangued about bringing for

lunch years ago in Rhode Island. Seems that in those times only the poor folks had to eat such "scavengers." The North American Lobster (*Homarus americanus*), is a ferocious character that requires its own tank and chilled water, but there are more appropriate species for the marine aquarium.

Lobsters will also feed on live fish and invertebrates, even algae and vascular plants, so if you're going to try one, keep yours well fed. Clawed and spiny lobsters are notorious for eating anything and everything they can get their jointed legs on; they are always to be regarded with suspicion when any tankmate is missing. Yes, this goes not only for the dinner table-sized species, but the small tropical reef varieties as well. Keep them adequately fed, and

Painted Crayfish (*Panulirus versicolor*): undeniably beautiful but somewhat cryptic, this and other tropical lobsters make for an unusual display, but require a careful choice of settings and tankmates.

one to a tank unless they're definitely a mated pair. Know, too, that other lobsters, large crabs, and the typical bad boys—triggers, puffers, large angels, large eels, and octopuses—may all attack a lobster without provocation.

Lobsters are, obviously, not for the typical reef tank but can make beautiful but somewhat cryptic additions to an aquarium with a stony habitat. Particularly attractive are relatively small (5 to 6 inches long), soft-bodied Pacific lobsters, such as the Hawaiian Red (*Enoplometopus debelius*), the Painted Crayfish or Spiny Blue Lobster (*Panulirus versicolor*), and the Regal Slipper Lobster (*Arctides regalis*). The latter, and its slipper brethren, are unusual and likable enough to deserve more attention from aquarists.

Slipper lobsters get my nomination as the nicest of the whole lobster group. Unlike most crustaceans, slipper lobsters are not opportunistic omnivores, eating everything and not to be trusted when hungry—which is most of the time for a lobster. When occasionally available, slippers are interesting, relatively undemanding captive specimens.

The Family Scyllaridae includes the slipper, Spanish, locust, and shovel-nosed lobsters. The family has approximately 70 known species having broad and flat bodies, short and scalelike antennae, and eyes in sockets in the carapace. They range from about 6 to 14 inches in length, with weights up to 5 pounds.

Most often seen in the aquarium trade are the Spanish Slipper Lobster (*Scyllarides aequinoctialis*); the Vermilion Slipper Lobster (*S. delfosi*) from south Florida and the Caribbean Sea; *Scyllarides astori* from southern and Baja California; *S. martensi* from southern Japan; the super-flattened *Ibacus peronii* from eastern Australia; and *I. ciliatus*, a common shovel-nosed lobster imported from the Philippines.

A slipper lobster will do well in a system with a rocky aquascape; consider making a patch reef along the back or in one corner area, with an open soft-substrate pit near the front. Consistency is important in water characteristic parameters. I would opt for older, more established conditions, with an abundance of carbonaceous material (gravel, rock, coral skeletons) with an eye on higher calcium and alkalinity readings. Slipper lobsters respire by way of gills, which also serve as a primary site for the excretion of ammonia. Be aware that under certain conditions/situations this amount of ammonia can be large, change suddenly, and be toxic. Excess overfeeding and rapid lowering of specific gravity in particular bring on increased excretion. Most crustaceans produce a urine that is iso-osmotic (about equal in water pressure/concentration) with their blood, which is strongly influenced by the solute makeup and concentration of the surrounding waters. A good skim-

Hairy Lobster (*Enoplometopus occidentalis*): small but feisty predator.

Slipper Lobster (*Scyllarides haanii*): among the least aggressive of the lobsters.

mer is essential to remove dissolved wastes (which can be considerable from any larger lobster), and frequent partial water changes are important.

Among the prey groups eaten by various slipper lobsters are mollusks, actinarians, and polychaete worms. *Scyllarides squamosus* is a specialist, with mollusks comprising the most important prey group. Pieces of green or table shrimp, large krill, or other fish of marine origin will usually be eaten happily by a captive slipper. Disease is not typically a problem, and many slippers have lived long captive lives, often achieving the status of "pet lobster."

In sum, the scyllarids are oddly marked, often beautifully colored, bizarrely shaped, friendly (no big claws)—and the better lobster choice for captive marine systems.

Mantis Shrimps. The members of this group (Order Stomatopoda) deserve special attention. They are fascinating, often beautifully colored, but potentially dangerous—to livestock, to glass heater tubes, and to aquarists' hands (their nickname is "thumb splitters"). Stomatopods look like flattened lobsters with long-stalked, very mobile eyes. They have large, powerful, specialized claws. Some species are spearers with claws that have razor sharp spines that they shoot out at incredible speed, sometimes cutting their intended prey in two. Other "smashing" species utilize the heavy heel of the unfolded raptorial appendage to crush the shells of crabs and clams. There are reports of them breaking glass heaters,

Peacock Mantis Shrimp (*Odontodactylus scyallarus*): worthy of a tank of its own, but uninvited members of this group can be brought into a reef aquarium in live rock and emerge nightly to prey on fishes and inverts.

even cracking the aquarium glass.

If mantis shrimps got much larger (the biggest are about a foot in length) they would be the underwater equivalent of a *Tyrannosaurus rex.*

Know what you're getting into in putting one of the 200-some species of mantis shrimps into your system—or if one shows up from live rock, as they often do. The mantis is an active digger and hunter that can eat your expensive livestock and destroy your tank. If you can spot its lair—often a burrow in a piece of rock, it may be easiest to remove the entire rock and place it in a pail of water, then add hot water until the shrimp emerges or dies. Alterna-

tively, there are commercially available baited traps made for catching these pesky shrimp and other ne'er-do-wells like bristleworms.

Crustacean Reproduction. Most crustacean species have separate sexes and rely on the male to transfer his contribution in the context of a special dance. Eggs are fertilized as they pass over the sperm receptacle, attaching typically to the abdominal appendages of the females until they hatch. In most species, the young pass through odd molting stages as plankton; a few develop looking like miniature adults.

Reproductive activities and the production of eggs are commonly seen among the various cleaner shrimps kept by aquarists. Typical behavior consists of an elaborate dance by the male, positioning above the female, and placement of the sperm pack in a special pouch for release later by the female. Eggs are laid and fertilized shortly afterward and adhere to her underside. The young hatch out and continue to live attached to the female for some six weeks, then swim off to the upper water column as plankton, settling after a period of time and several molts. During this time period, the young make prime pickings for other tank inhabitants, and those that are not eaten are almost certain to perish in the filtration system. A number of aquarists are attempting to work out the challenges of feeding the larvae and rearing the young in captivity.

General Care. What can be stated as broadly true for the crustaceans is that they eat most anything live or dead, given the opportunity, yet there are specialty feeders, such as the Harlequin Shrimp (*Hymenocera picta*) that eat only sea stars. They are generally secretive and require cover, hiding during the light of day. Many, such as the hermit crabs, are extremely hardy and excellent for beginners. Some others, however, have an intolerance for poor water quality, low pH, deficient oxygen content, the presence of ammonia, nitrite, copper remedies, and dye medications. Fast changes in salinity can kill delicate shrimps in short order. Crustaceans of all sorts are food items for predaceous animals and are especially vulnerable during molting, when the old shell is shed and the new armor has not yet hardened.

Pest Crustaceans. Barnacles (Order Cirripedia) are crustaceans, though it's hard to believe. (I have a nightmare sometimes where I make it onto the *Jeopardy!* show, and Alex Trebek intones, "They're little crustaceans that stand on their heads in calcium houses they've made, kicking food into their mouths." In this dream, I choke—can't remember that the barnacles are actually crustaceans, not mollusks.)

Barnacles may make their way into your system on uncultured live rock or with other invertebrates. Most seen by marine aquarists are harmless, but a few have larval phases that will attack your fishes' gills and/or parasitize several groups of invertebrates. Big colonies of barnacles on rock may die off, taking everything else with them. Go see them at the seashore, or buy their cleaned and bleached shells as curious decor.

Orders Copepoda and Isopoda have members that also may be hard to recognize as crustaceans. The parasitic copepods may appear as tiny to inches-long wormlike or threadlike processes hanging off new livestock, and the isopods appear as gray or dingy white "bugs" on fishes or within their mouth or gill cavities.

Not all copepods are detrimental (of 7,500 species, about 1,000 are parasitic); often they make up the bulk of the mass in a plankton tow; I've seen published works suggesting that these tiny shrimplike animals should be harvested and pressed into "steaks of the sea" for human consumption. (I'll withhold my culinary comment.)

Avoid parasitic crustaceans if you detect them on potential livestock. Parasitic copepod and isopod adults may best be removed with forceps; chemical therapeutics such as copper might be tried, but only in treatment tanks, not in your main system.

Besides the mass of copepods that serve as food, there are, of course, the euphausiids (krill), brine shrimps, and fairy shrimps, as well as ostracods and others—more than enough to fill a lifetime of study for anyone seriously taken by the crustaceans.

Summary. Many crustaceans can—and should—be kept in marine aquariums, whether reef, invertebrate, or even fish setups. They're colorful and interesting in shape and behavior. But there are downsides to many of them; several can be mean, shy, and/or disruptive to the system's aquascape.

The key to keeping crustacean species is in knowing your animals before bringing them home, providing a nurturing, suitable habitat, and keeping your eye on them for misbehavior. In addition, you must watch for tankmates that might view the new crustaceans as too tempting to ignore.

There's no doubt that the shrimps, crabs, crayfishes, lobsters, and slipper lobsters add an element of risk to the balance of forces in a marine aquarium; for many aquarists, this both enhances the realism and the challenge of a diversified system.

Echinoderms

Phylum Echinodermata
Spiny-Skinned Animals of the Sea

CONSIDERED THE BEST characterized and distinctive phylum of the Animal Kingdom, the sea urchins, sand dollars, sea stars, basket stars, sea lilies, and sea cucumbers make up the Phylum Echinodermata. The name means "spiny-skinned," and one touch will tell you why.

A large array of these are imported and sold for marine aquariums. Sadly, many specimens do not survive very long due to poor handling, being forced into unsuitable habitats, or simply being poor candidates for captivity. Many species are an outright danger to their fellow tankmates and to you, the hobbyist. A number make useful scavengers in reef or fish-and-invertebrate systems, others are a delight to observe, and some are highly desirable aquarium specimens.

Whether you inherit echinoderms with live rock or purposefully plunk down your hard-earned cash for an individual or two, these prickly creatures are well worth knowing.

Classification. All members of the phylum are readily distinguished by: the presence of a water-vascular system (tube feet) used in locomotion and food manipulation; a subepidermal (internal) microstructured calcareous skeleton; and a pentamerous body symmetry (five parts, radiating out like spokes of a wheel from a central hub). All living species of echinoderms share these characteristics, and yet the group has considerable diversity.

Size differences between species can be dramatic. All classes have tiny representatives that grow to a maximum adult size of less than ⅜ inch. One urchin, on the other hand, has a shell (test) of over 8 inches in diameter, and there is a sea cucumber more than 6½ feet in length. Echinoderms are the only phylum with no known parasitic members, though they are often hosts themselves.

There are about 6,000 described species distributed worldwide in shallow to deepest seas. Living echinoderms are divided into five classes (some other schema lump the brittle and sea stars together, but we won't). They are:

Class Crinoidea (sea lilies and feather stars), characterized by having: 1) a stalk and being attached to the substrate (at least in the early postmetamorphic stages); 2) erect feeding structures (brachioles and/or arms) on their upper surfaces—upward and outward extending arms supported by cal-

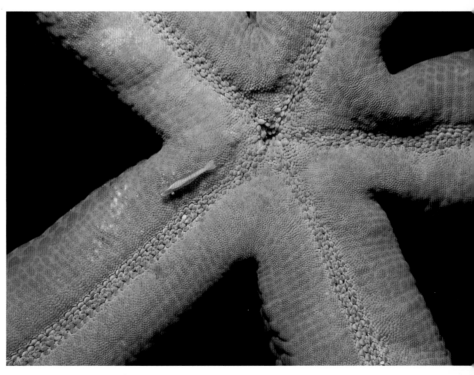

Color morph of the Blue Starfish (*Linckia laevigata*) with commensal shrimp (*Periclimenes soror*): the star's underbody shows the classic five-part echinoderm body symmetry with a central oral opening and tube feet.

careous plates; 3) mouth, water-vascular system, and anus on the body surface away from the bottom; 4) semirigid bodies restricting them to suspension feeding.

Class Asteroidea (sea stars or starfishes): arms that are supported by elements in the body wall, not separable from a central disc. They usually have five arms, though some have six or more.

Class Ophiuroidea (brittle or basket stars): slender, often branching arms capable of tremendous flexion. These arms have internal vertebrae for support and are abruptly discontinuous from the animals' central discs. Unlike the sea stars, they use their entire arms, not just tube feet, for locomotion.

Class Echinoidea (sea urchins and sand dollars): marked by having body walls composed of plates with movable spines and no arms. Their overall shape is globular to oval.

Class Holothuroidea (sea cucumbers): bearing feeding tentacles extending from their circumoral feeding ring. They show a wide range of reduction in endoskeletons.

Selection. My personal generalizations about the echinoderms are sure to please few and irritate many collectors, dealers, and their intermediaries:

• Don't buy newly arrived specimens. Leave them at least a few days

Fire Urchin (*Asthenosoma ijimai*): a common Indo-Pacific species, found in shallow reef and rock areas, well-known to divers for its venom-tipped spines, which can inflict painful stings.

at the retailer's shop if at all possible. Echinoderms can and do die quickly and mysteriously, without prior warning. Most of the massive mortality with the group occurs within a day or two of arrival. Wait.

• At all costs, avoid specimens with whitish, necrotic spots and patches. These are "challenged" specimens and are most likely infected with bacteria, fungi, and possibly debilitating parasites.

• Don't necessarily disqualify a specimen on the basis of broken spines or even chipped mouth parts. This group has a renowned regenerative capacity. If the individual is otherwise healthy and placed in a proper setting, it will repair.

• Crinoids, large or ornate sea cucumbers, and most urchin species should not be tried by any but the steady of hand and mind (and large of wallet) aquarists. Sea lilies are sometimes expensive, finicky eaters. Sea cucumbers are notorious for getting agitated and eviscerating themselves (a polite scientific term for extruding their entire digestive tract and other organs, thus dissolving themselves and killing everything in the same aquarium system). Some urchins make interesting reef aquarium specimens, but others are destructive or very dangerous to handle due to their sharp spines and stinging, venomous tube feet.

Habitat. Most starfishes and sea stars are reasonably good candidates for the aquarium, with the exception of the big, nasty Crown-of-Thorns (*Acanthaster* spp.) and a few others. The brit-

tle stars are cryptic, but excellent scavengers for reef-type systems.

For the most part, this is an assemblage that demands both high and consistent water quality. No toxic metal contamination is tolerated. Several urchins and sea stars could qualify as predictable bioassay organisms. They are among the first to show ill effects if anything is amiss in your maintenance of the system, and they let you know by dying.

Paying attention to water quality standards and stability is essential, and good filtration is critical. Though they are admittedly slow-moving, echinoderms can ingest, digest, and egest a staggering amount of material, excreting a great deal of ammonia in the process. Get and use a protein skimmer if you want to keep them alive.

As far as introduction and acclimation, I must reverse one of my most steadfast rules. This is one of those rare instances where adding shipping water (as long as it doesn't seem to be outright contaminated) into your system with the new livestock is a good idea. (The exception is sea cucumbers, whose shipping water should always be discarded.) There is a large body of evidence showing that echinoderm water has a therapeutic effect on other organisms and the system itself. I can only ask you to trust me; this isn't hocus-pocus. What occurs is a chemical balance within and without the echinoderm that has demonstrably positive effects, stabilizing the environment and making it "smell" like home.

As for other animals attacking new echinoderms in the aquarium, the exposed forms are generally too crunchy, spiky, poisonous, venomous, and odd-shaped to consume. Burrowing forms don't appear obvious to predators. Naturally, there are fishes (triggers, puffers, wrasses, and basses), crustaceans (large crabs, lobsters, some notable starfish-eating shrimp), and large marine snails that will try to consume almost anything.

Reproduction. Reproduction is almost exclusively sexual with individuals being male or female. They produce small eggs that are broadcast into the sea (external fertilization), and the zygotes turn into planktotrophic larvae; or the zygotes may be brooded (internally or externally) with direct development.

Asexual reproduction can occur either through parthenogenesis, fission, or autotomy. Parthenogenesis is a form of reproduction in which eggs develop without fertilization; that is without union with a sperm cell. This is thought to have survival value in situations of low fecundity and/or low population density. In fission, two more or less equal pieces (in the brittle stars, sea stars, sea cucumbers) can become two new individuals. In autotomy, just a fragment is able to grow into a whole new body (as in the celebrated regeneration abilities of the sea stars).

Feeding. The echinoderms are nature's surest answer to "Who's going to clean up?" Unlike groups of organisms with a rigid exoskeleton, like insects and crustaceans, the endoskeleton of echinoderms allows them to resorb calcium, getting smaller and even changing shape. If insufficient limestone (calcium carbonate) is not provided intentionally in the diet, as substrate, or dissolved in the aquarium water, your specimens will not grow and may shrink.

Feeding mechanisms vary considerably among the various groups:

Crinoids are basically passive suspension feeders, relying on water currents to bring them plankton.

Sea stars, basket stars, and urchins all have their mouths and water-vascular systems facing the bottom, allowing them to take advantage of benthic food sources.

Basket stars sweep their slender arms around and over the substrate. Some are predatory and carrion-feeding carnivores, the remainder are microphagous, feeding on small particles on the bottom or wafting about in the water column.

The sea stars are profoundly affected by the relative immobility of their more tightly secured arms. Unlike the basket stars, sea stars must move to get themselves to food, and they feed on macroprey. Their suckered feet are not necessary so much to capture or manipulate prey as they are to scale vertical impediments and resist wave/current energies. Probably the most renowned aspect of sea star biology is extra-oral feeding, with the pushing out of the "stomach" into the environment and over prey, which is then enveloped and consumed.

Urchins feed through digitating mouthparts called Aristotle's lantern. This is an arrangement of five teeth with supporting muscles and articulating structures. They feed on benthic organisms, drift food, and carrion.

Holothuroids or sea cucumbers use their feeding tentacles extending from an anterior circumoral feeding ring to capture free-living prey or to "mop-up" particulate food either in suspension or encountered in the sand. They can process impressive amounts of substrate, with some ingesting and passing through up to three times their body volume of sand daily. Aquarists with deep beds of coral sand can put this feeding behavior to good use in keeping their substrate stirred and well-cleaned.

If your spiny livestock doesn't seem to be very interested in feeding, don't be overly concerned. Feeding rate is influenced by physical factors (salinity, temperature, light) and biological variables (size, physiological state, food preferences, quality and size of food). There have been recorded instances of echinoderms going through many months of apparent nonfeeding without dying.

Summary. As anyone who has dived or snorkeled over coral reefs or really explored intertidal areas will know, the echinoderms are quite a group. These spiky creatures may never qualify as endearing aquarium pets, but they are fascinating and sometimes very attractive. Some suitable aquarium candidates (and some to avoid) are discussed on the following pages.

Sea Lilies and Feather Stars
Class Crinoidea

OFTEN MISIDENTIFIED as brittle stars or entirely overlooked as hidden or decorative ornaments due to their plantlike appearance, the immobile or anchored sea lilies and the related, mobile feather stars make up the most ancient class of the Phylum Echinodermata, the Crinoidea.

Due to easy breakage, suspension-feeding habits and shy and retiring behavior, these animals are considered challenging to keep. Most are doomed by difficulties accumulated from the time of their collection to delivery to your local dealer. Feather stars need not be impossible to keep, however.

Classification. There are about 700 living species of crinoids, 80 of the more primitive stalked sea lilies, and the bulk in the more modern branch of the class, the feather stars (Order Comatulida). They are found worldwide in marine habitats, sometimes in great numbers, from intertidal zones to abyssal depths, primarily in Indo-Pacific and polar waters.

Selection. Due to the vagaries of cost and current collection and transport techniques, the stalked, attached sea lilies are rarely offered, and when they do show up they are generally dying or already dead from being thrashed about. The free-living feather stars travel much more successfully. What you want to look for are many intact arms and an active display of them being extended for feeding. Once a specimen has been selected, it should not be touched more than necessary. Tube feet, pinnules, and whole arms snap off easily. With a shallow-depth net or spatula-shaped tool, coax/brush the animal into the shipping container underwater. Don't lift it into the air.

Habitat. Free-living crinoids need hiding spaces, out of the light, to be comfortable. Many hide during the day, coming out to feed only at night, though they may be trained to day-feed. I suggest varying the living space to allow for selection of depth and current. Most species are positively rheotactic, orienting themselves in the path of water flow to filter-feed effectively.

Feeding. Most species are nocturnal suspension feeders. Food material in the wild includes all manner of phyto- and zooplankton and general detritus. In public aquariums, cultured diets of brine shrimp nauplii, copepods, and diatoms have proved effective. Some of the newer frozen invertebrate rations might also be tried; be sure to thaw before serving. Whatever material you use, it is best to have your particulate filter shut off during feeding, perhaps continuing to use a small powerhead to direct the food into the arms of the crinoid.

Summary. Autotomy (self-breakage) of crinoid arms is a common sight when these animals fail in an aquarium.

Feather star (Class Crinoidea): as difficult to identify as they are to keep, the crinoids are like fantastic, mobile flowers, but demand excellent care and regular feedings of planktonlike foods in captivity.

High concentrations of organic wastes and sudden changes of pH, salinity, and temperature have been linked to loss of arm segments. Starvation is commonly believed to lead to many other losses. Still, the unstalked, commercially available feather stars are often brilliantly colored/marked and challenging, not impossible, to keep. They are for the most part entirely nonobnoxious, being nonpredatory and disease-free: perfect reef tank candidates for the aquarist with a well-maintained, established system who is willing to keep up with a regular feeding routine.

Sea Cucumbers
Class Holothuroidea

FROM GORGEOUS SEA APPLES TO homely Donkey Dung Sea Cucumbers, these slow-moving, brightly colored to drab and utilitarian invertebrates are well-known, at least by sight, by most aquarists. Some are wildly attractive and others hard-working scavengers, but sea cucumbers do have an unfortunate side. Like many other spiny-skinned animals, many of them should only be tried in captivity with knowledge, trepidation, and utmost vigil.

Classification. There are some 900 described species of sea cucumbers, almost exclusively marine, distributed worldwide. Most are black, brown, or olive in color, but many brilliantly colored and patterned species are encountered. They range in size from barely over an inch in length to over 6 feet.

Sea apple (*Pseudocolochirus tricolor*): bizarre and vividly colored, but they can poison whole systems.

Sea cucumbers have 10 to 30 modified podia making up the feeding tentacles that surround the mouth. They live in or on the substrate, burrow into sand and mud, "swim" or float above the bottom, or hang out in the local flora; they're everywhere in marine environments. Forms with podia creep along like sea stars. Burrowing types move by alternate contractions of longitudinal and circular muscles like earthworms. The ultrastrange deep-water Order Elaspodida "walk" on extended tube feet and constrictions of their bodies. There are even swimming sea cucumbers.

Pearlfishes, Family Carapidae (Fierasferidae) are known to live inside certain sea cucumbers, including the Leopard Sea Cucumber (*Bohadschia argus*), perhaps nibbling at the internal tissues of its host by day, emerging to feed at night. These fishes enter and exit from the cucumber's anal end.

Selection. Before even thinking about the purchase of a sea cucumber, you should understand that these animals are responsible for poisoning and wiping out countless happy aquariums. Ask any group of experienced marine hobbyists and you are sure to hear horror stories. Under the wrong conditions or in response to rough handling, objectionable water quality, pheromonal cueing, pushy tankmates, or being sucked into pump or filter intakes, sea cucumbers are known to eviscerate their internal organs in a dramatic defensive gesture. In doing so, they cast out their respiratory trees, gonads, gastrointestinal tract, and its contents through their mouth and anus. The result is poisoning/pollution/death and destruction to all other tankmates. Australasian Sea Apples (*Pseudocolochirus violaceus*)are particularly notorious for this hobby-ending activity. In the wild, this trick is usually employed to discourage an attacking predator; it works, and the cucumber is then able to recompose and regenerate itself.

Some other species have a further refinement to this anti-predation mechanism, using what are called Cuvierian organs. These sticky fibers are discharged out their ends onto threatening predators.

What to do? I am inclined to avoid these animals altogether. If you can't or won't, choose your specimens carefully and place them in suitable surroundings. The least problematic of the species usually seen by aquarists are small burrowing sea cucumbers that grow no more than 3 or 4 inches in length and usually content themselves with grinding through the sand in search of food. In reef aquariums without large fishes to harass them, they are reportedly not prone to evisceration. The greatest danger is in having them wander into powerhead intakes or other mechanical traps. (When buying sea cucumbers as sand-stirrers, be sure to avoid any that grow more than 6 inches in length; the larger species are surprisingly strong and will constantly be rearranging your rockwork or other aquascaping.) The better choices are often sold as Pygmy Sea Cucumbers or Sand Cucumbers.

Florida marine life dealers sometimes offer the Donkey Dung Sea Cucumber (*Holothuria mexicana*), a sure conversation starter. This species grows to about 16 inches in length and is a sand-swallowing dervish, putting out significant piles of cleaned and processed substrate in neat, sausagelike "castings." This is not, obviously, a creature for the fastidious reef keeper, but it might make an interesting part of a Caribbean lagoon biotope tank with deep sand, a bed of Turtle Grass, a couple of Queen Conchs, a few Sea Eggs, and perhaps a French or Queen Angel.

The Australasian Sea Apple is a bizarre sight, richly colored in deep blue, red, and white, with a bushy crown of delicate tentacles. So many of these have been responsible for the death of captive fishes and invertebrates that it should only be contemplated as part of a species tank. Never place one of them in a system with fishes, corals, or other invertebrates you would hate to lose. One more thing to worry about: sea cucumber eggs may be ingested by your fishes with fatal consequences.

When acquiring a sea cucumber, never mix or introduce the transport water into the home system. To acclimate the new arrival, add some system water to the transport bag, wait 15

Sea cucumber (Class Holothuroidea): large species do poorly in aquariums.

Pygmy Sea Cucumber (*Colochirus robustus*): small filter-feeders.

minutes, then repeat. Finally, slip the holothuroid into another container and move that into the aquarium, keeping the animal underwater at all times.

Check prospective purchases carefully for discontinuities—blemishes, tears, holes, or sores in the body wall. The cucumber should be entire, with no broken cuticular or oddly colored areas. Many species are known to adhere tenuously to objects, tank walls, rock, and even unwary human hands. Remove them carefully, with as little disturbance to the specimen as possible.

Don't discredit a specimen if its tentacles are partially to completely retracted and/or it does not seem to be interested in feeding. This happens with healthy cucumbers, which may take some time to adjust.

High and consistent water quality is a must, and many species must have fine sand in which to burrow. If you are attempting to keep one of the less common species, you'll need to research its life habits and natural habitat. There are a few species that live on algae or exposed on the surface, like our southern California *Stichopus*.

Having an arrangement of longitudinal and radial muscle bands, holothuroids are masters at squeezing in and through small openings. If yours seems stuck, do not attempt to pull it out. The animal will come out when it wants to. (Do your best to screen any in-tank heaters to avoid burns to wandering cucumbers.)

Feeding. Sea cucumbers are categorized as deposit or suspension feeders,

the former moving around and generally foraging for themselves on and in the substrate. The filter or suspension feeders are more of a challenge for the aquarist, who must arrange an infusion of fine foods (see Crinoids, above), either dried, frozen or live, on a regular basis. Many sea apples are underfed and simply waste away in captivity unless offered appropriate foods.

Summary. These echinoderms have evolved some very effective methods of repulsing predators and can fill an aquarium with lethal toxins in a matter of minutes. The offending poison, at least in some cases, is holothurin (a saponin). Few living things tend to harass them—perhaps for good reason.

Because of their beautiful colors, patterns, and alien body shapes, there will be a few hapless fools who try to maintain these animals in captivity. If

you do, dedicate a special cucumber setup to them, disconnected from any central filtration system.

Sea Urchins
Class Echinoidea

FRIENDS AND ASSOCIATES who know me to be an avid diver frequently ask whether I'm concerned with potential encounters with sharks, rays, giant squids, and the like. My standard reply is that, hour per hour spent involved in various human activities, the most dangerous thing we all engage in is driving on the freeway. As for time actually spent underwater, the most commonly harmful/hurtful organisms you need to worry about are, realistically, the sea urchins.

Still, urchins are common fare in the

Long-spined Urchin (*Diadema antillarum*): a graceful but sinister denizen of Florida and Caribbean reefs.

Sea urchin (*Mespilia globulus*): short spines divided by ten blue bands.

California Sand Dollar (*Dendraster exocentricus*): note central five-petal design.

marine aquarium trade. They can be useful and interesting scavengers and algae eaters, but just as in underwater meetings, they do present considerable risks.

Classification. Urchins and their allies, the sand dollars and heart urchins, make up the Class Echinoidea—Greek for "like a hedgehog," in reference to the spines that cover all but their bottom surface. Their mouths are directed downward, against the substrate.

Distributed between the spines are pedicellariae, specialized tube feet used for cleaning and defense. (Take a close look at a live sea urchin climbing an aquarium wall; it's an amazing show.) The globiferous feet of some species contain poison glands. Urchin body walls have a ciliated epidermis under which lies a nerve layer, then the "test"—the white, eggshell-like skeleton commonly found on the beach or in shallow water. About 800 species of sea urchins have been described.

They come in brown, black, purple, green, white, red, and multicolored. Most are 2 to 5 inches in diameter, but one giant Indo-Pacific species attains a diameter of 15 inches, and the Long-spined Urchin (*Diadema antillarum*) of the Caribbean and Florida Keys can reach almost 20 inches in diameter. The latter has needle-sharp spines that have caused agony for many swimmers, snorkelers, and divers. One species in the genus *Diadema* on tropical reefs has spines that may be more than 15 inches long.

Long or short, the spines are very sharp , hollow, and brittle, and many are accompanied by a painful irritant. Here is just one anecdote to suggest how much respect these echinoderms deserve. A number of years ago, a friend of mine had a small tip of a sea urchin spine break off in his hand. The spines have smaller recurved spines of their own like barbs on a fishhook, as well as scales and processes for working their

way—almost ratcheting themselves— into the wound. This piece got walled-off and the wound eventually healed over. Two years later, it surfaced on the other side of his hand; I was there to help him tease it out.

As if the mechanical injuries weren't bad enough, many species possess venomous poison sacs. Is this warning clear enough? Handle these animals carefully—with nets! You don't have to be punctured to be envenomized—just touched by the tip of a spine. Urchins do not attack, but if you happen to step on, kick, grab, or accidentally brush against one, you will likely carry the memory for years. (A severe incident, in which a person receives numerous spines, may require prompt medical attention. Pieces of spine should be removed with pincers, if possible, and the wound treated with antiseptic. Small fragments of spine will usually dissolve within a week or so.)

Irregularly shaped echinoids appear

bilaterally symmetrical. These include the heart and cake urchins, and the sand dollars. All are adapted for burrowing in sand and possess small, numerous spines. Irregular urchins all feed on minute organic particles in the sand in which they burrow. Our local common California Sand Dollar (*Dendraster exocentricus*) feeds almost exclusively on suspended particles, particularly diatoms. Unusual urchins are rarely offered in the trade. They have proven to be difficult to keep and likewise hard to sell.

Selection and Habitat. Sea urchins are generally adapted for living on rocks and other types of hard substrates with spines and podia for movement and secure placement to resist tidal and wave action. Most are active only at night.

They are best placed into systems that are well broken in, with some good growth of green algae. They are sensitive to very small changes in water quality. A well-functioning protein skimmer is crucial.

Urchins can be employed to graze algae from rocky aquascaping, and if you have a specific purpose in mind, you may want to isolate your specimens to that task. (Some will rasp coralline algae from live rock, and many reef keepers exclude them as being too disruptive. They can and will move to whatever area interests them and may burrow into or under things. Do not try to extricate an urchin; it can fend for itself.

For the most part, urchins are virtually predatorless under ordinary cir-

cumstances. But the aquarium can create extraordinary conditions and meetings, and certain triggers and their relatives, the puffers, will try out urchins, as will some sea stars, large butterflies, parrotfishes, surgeonfishes, and crabs. Otherwise, most organisms will leave them alone.

Reproduction. All echinoids are of separate sexes with external fertilization. There is no general structural difference between the sexes. In brooding species, the eggs are either retained in external body cavities or between spines. The feeding larvae are planktonic until the skeleton begins to form.

Feeding. Sea urchins feed on algae, sessile benthic animals, and animal remains. Deep-sea and burrowing forms "use the ooze." In captivity, they are ready eaters of most everything and anything. If your system contains sessile invertebrates, keep your eye on them! All sea urchins have a celebrated chewing apparatus, called Aristotle's lantern, composed of five large calcareous plates centered on the underside that effectively scrape algae and other organic foods from hard surfaces.

German author Peter Wilkens mentions an apparent need for supplying urchins with adequate sources of lime (calcium carbonate) for test and spine growth and for strength. Crushed shells and calcareous substrate work well. He also alludes to the unquenchable appetite his specimen showed for *Caulerpa*. I've found that Tetra Tips and other sinking pelleted marine foods are accepted by many urchins.

Sea Stars and Brittle Stars
Class Asteroidea and Class Ophiuroidea

CONSIDER THE RETICULATED SEA Star (*Oreaster reticulatus*), a large starfish common in the Turtle Grass beds of the Florida Keys, the Bahamas, and the Caribbean. Growing up to 20 inches in diameter, it consumes mollusks, even oysters, in heavily calcified, tightly shut shells, methodically and with a voracious appetite. Like others in this fascinating class, the Reticulated Sea Star possesses a cleverly evolved arsenal of hydraulic tube feet connected to an elaborate water-vascular system that encircles the animal's mouth and extends via five radial canals down the center of each arm.

Numbering in the hundreds on each arm, these tube feet can attach to a food object, such as an oyster or clam, and, with relative ease, pry open even the most defensively tightened set of bivalve shells. With even a mere crack of an opening available, the sea star can force its slippery stomach into the shell of the mollusk. There it secretes digestive enzymes that rapidly turn the animal's flesh into a puree that the sea star promptly absorbs. Momentarily satisfied, the asteroid retracts its stomach, releases its grip, and glides away, leaving an intact set of bivalve shells stripped as if an alien force had cleaned them, leaving no evidence of forced entry.

Not for nothing have the invertebrates been called "spineless wonders."

398

Orange Marble Starfish (*Fromia monilis*): boldly appealing and appropriate species for an aquarium without big predators, such as triggerfishes and lobsters.

Some species of sea stars can make fascinating and appropriate aquarium subjects, and many of the brittle stars can serve as energetic, if cryptic, scavengers in reef systems.

Classification. Sea stars and starfishes make up the Class Asteroidea. Asteroids typically have five arms radiating outward from their central disks where their mouths open toward the bottom. All have podia or tube feet projecting down along grooves on the undersides of the arms. There is no brain as such, only one or more rings of nerve tissue surrounding the esophagus to lend some coordination to the animal's movements.

Approximately 1,600 species of sea stars are known. They are found free-ranging worldwide, over and under rocky, sandy, and muddy sea bottoms. The five living asteroid orders are divided on the basis of structural differences in their water-vascular systems and ossicles (endoskeletal elements).

The brittle stars or serpent stars fall into the Class Ophiuroidea, which is characterized by having highly mobile arms that can be used to assist in (relatively) rapid locomotion. These starfishlike echinoderms are decidedly quicker and more delicate; the common names come from the sinuous, snake-

Reticulated Sea Star (*Oreaster reticulatus*): big and aggressive, but a "spineless wonder" worth knowing.

Blue Starfish (*Linckia laevigata*): a lovely, smaller species that can do very well in captive systems.

like movement of the arms and the fact that these are truly brittle and break away easily if the animal comes under attack. The podia in this class are generally used as sensory organs, rather than for active locomotion and feeding. There are over 2,000 known species worldwide, and they can be found congregating throughout shallow reef environments, hiding under rocks and within living sponges.

Although they come from two distinct classes, we will treat the sea stars and brittle stars together, as their selection and care have much in common.

Selection. Specimens of several genera are commonly offered in the trade, and more unusual species may be specially ordered through dealers. What to look for or look out for? The individual in question should be lively, moving, and turgid-bodied, with tube feet visible in the case of sea stars. A good test is to turn the animal on its back and see if it rights itself. A limp or weak individual is a poor aquarium prospect. Some may eventually recover, but many do not. Other warning signs are dark or whitish necrotic matter and vacuolations (missing areas). Lost arms are common and will usually heal over, but it is unwise to buy a specimen that is freshly wounded as infection and rapid decline may follow. (Not at all rare are detached single arms that are regenerating new bodies; this is seen as a large arm with a small body and set of small arms at one end. These are also appropriate specimens.)

Echinoderms are notable as the

only animal phylum with no known parasitic members. They are hosts to many parasites themselves, however, and you may want to check a prospective starfish for any attached parasitic problems.

The most common error in selecting sea stars is in acquiring species that grow too large or are ravenous, omnivorous eaters. Not only will they attack many reef invertebrates, they are often doomed by their own huge appetites. Unless you are willing to make a special effort to house and feed a larger sea star species, it is best to stay with the "reef safe" choices. Among the favored aquarium species are the very attractive Blue Starfish (*Linckia laevigata*), the Little Red Starfish and the Orange Marble Starfish (*Fromia elegans* and *F. monilis*, respectively).

The *Linckia* species have a relatively smooth body surface, while the various *Fromia* species are recognized by their patchworklike upper surfaces, consisting of plates of varying sizes and colors. The various *Linckia* and *Fromia* choices seem to feed on algae, detritus, and microbes on the rocks and in the sand. In reefs with delicate corals, they bear watching, but are generally regarded as mild-mannered.

Less desirable but common and attractive are the "knobbled" sea stars in the genera *Protoreaster*, *Pentaster* and *Pentaceraster*. They are distinguished by having dull spines, bumps, or knobbles on their dorsal surfaces, with these often seen in colors that contrast with the overall body pigmentation. Sold under

Sea star (*Fromia* sp.): reef aquarists with delicate sessile invertebrates should add sea stars with care.

Sea star (*Choriaster granulatus*): big, bulky Indo-Pacific echinoderm that scavenges in reef shallows.

the names Red-knobbed, Chocolate Chip, and other labels, these species are hardy but aggressive eaters, more than happy to mount and consume sessile clams, oysters, and all manner of corals, soft and stony.

Many hundreds of other possible choices could conceivably find their way into aquarium channels, but one notorious possibility deserves mention. This is the justifiably vilified Crown-of-Thorns Starfish, which manages to grab headlines from time to time as a scourge of the reefs.

Of the starfishes called Crown-of-Thorns, *Acanthaster planci* (from the Northern Australian and Philippine markets) and *A. ellisii* (from the Sea of Cortez to Peru) are the most commonly available species to the pet trade. In the wild, they have denuded large areas of coral reefs. Like most sea stars, *Acanthaster* spp. are carnivorous. Their feed-

Crown-of-Thorns (*Acanthaster planci*): a terror of the reef, with venomous spines and a voracious appetite for living corals.

ing mechanism is notorious—everting the stomach outside the body over living coral polyps, then performing extracellular digestion, leaving behind a dead, white coral skeleton. Oftentimes Crown-of-Thorns population explosions are attributed to human removal of their predators, most notably the Giant Triton (*Charonia tritornis*) and the Napoleon Wrasse (*Cheilinus undulatus*). There are stopgap measures in place in several countries to restrict the taking of these controlling species.

Crown-of-Thorns are beautiful and interesting, but dangerous. If you deal with them, exercise care. They have elongate, venomous spines and should be moved only with a net and then only cautiously. The spines are equipped with a hemolytic (blood-cell splitting) toxin. If owning one of these big, fearsome asteroids appeals to you, I would advise handling them with respect.

On the other end of the machismo scale are the brittle stars and serpent stars, which are so retiring and nocturnal that you may never see them in your system. Many reef aquarists have grown fond of them, as they diligently work the underside and unseen recesses of the captive reef, scuttling around under the ledges and rocks, eating detritus. They play an important role in keeping inaccessible areas of the tank

cleaned up, and they stir up and aerate the sand bed where the aquarist can't reach.

Selection is generally simple, allowing one of any available species per each 10 gallons of tank capacity. Many brittle stars are collected in waters off Florida, and the common choices include the Reticulated Brittle Star (*Ophionereis reticulata*), the Gaudy Brittle Star (*Ophioderma ensiferum*), and the Ruby Brittle Star (*Ophioderma rubicundum*). Tidepool explorers in the Caribbean will be familiar with the Spiny Brittle Star (*Ophiocoma paucigranulata*) and the Blunt-spined Brittle Star (*Ophiocoma echinata*), often found in masses under rocks and coral rubble. As with the sea stars, a prospective brittle star purchase should be intact, never limp, and ought to respond immediately to being touched.

Habitat. Sea stars, although they are slow, appreciate adequate open space as well as coral and rocky arrangements where they can forage, hide, and find the conditions of current, lighting, and shelter that they prefer.

Echinoderms are used as biological assay specimens for pollution, for measuring the quality of synthetic salt mixes, and for other test parameters. This gives you an indication of their sensitivity. Some of them are among the first to be malaffected by metabolite build-up in water or by the presence of metallic contaminants. Should yours start acting funny (slowing down or refusing to eat), don't hesitate—check your water quality and make necessary

Sponge Brittle Star (*Ophiothrix suensonii*): excellent aquarium scavenger.

Ruby Brittle Star (*Ophioderma rubicundum*): secretive bottom forager.

adjustments. It may be wise to move the affected specimen if your system water requires major changes.

Predators generally leave these animals alone, but I would not put it past certain triggers, large angels, puffers, large crabs, or lobsters to try out sea stars out of boredom or hunger.

Reproduction. Reproduction is by sexual means and by fragmentation. The latter capability foiled attempts in the Philippines and Australia to reduce populations of Crown-of-Thorns by having divers hack them up with machetes. This merely produced more animals and added to the reef-destruction problem. Natural predators are much more effective.

Feeding. Most of the sea stars offered in the hobby are fed bivalve mollusks (clams or mussels) or other meaty frozen foods (shrimp, krill) once every week or two. In the wild, their diets are more cosmopolitan. To keep them well-fed, the aquarist will likely need to use a feeding stick to position the target food where the star will find it immediately, before other tank inhabitants grab it or it is swept away.

Though they seem to prefer certain live coral polyps, *Acanthasters* are opportunistic omnivores, eating algae, encrusting invertebrates, dead fish, and other aquatic protein, even other starfishes. They have been trained in captivity to accept prepared and fresh foods in place of expensive stony corals.

Disease. Sea star diseases can be troublesome, especially for those with multiple specimens. Most notable are a fungus (*Branchiomycetes* sp.) and *Vibrio* bacterial infections that are primary sources of disease and mortality. Proper selection and providing an appropriate environment are not all a hobbyist can do to assure ongoing success. The use of a quarantine system for a few weeks is a good idea, possibly using special medications for fungal problems and furan compounds or antibiotics for bacterial difficulties. It bears repeating that such treatments should always be adminis-tered outside of the main system, in a tank that includes provisions for monitoring water quality.

If one or all related organisms in the phylum begin dissolving or otherwise dying in a captive system, one must act quickly—make that immediately—to arrest a total wipe-out. Changing 30% or more of the system water and/or removing affected stock to treatment quarters is strongly indicated.

Summary. Who needs science fiction when we have invertebrates like the asteroids? When chosen carefully, the sea stars can provide great interest and visual appeal in the right aquarium setting. The brittle stars are extremely reclusive, although they may occasionally scuttle out during feeding sessions, and their valuable biomaintenance services usually go unseen.

As for the Crown-of-Thorns, it is big, attention-getting, and dangerous to handle—just right for the perverse invertebrate collector with a large, specialized system.

Contacts

Marine Aquarium Societies

AQUARISTS HAVE A WEALTH OF PEOPLE and resources to turn to for information, advice, or even just moral support and special-interest camaraderie. Marine societies and clubs can be found at the local, regional, national, and international levels. Pet retailers should also know which groups in your region are involved in marine aquarium keeping, along with when and where they meet. Knowledgeable retail personnel can introduce you to other aquarists with similar interests.

Marine Aquarium Societies of North America (MASNA)
c/o Nancy Swart, President
31 Lagoon Drive
Hawthorn Woods, IL 60047
(847) 438-3917
e-mail: n_swart@msn.com
Web site: www.masna.org

Chesapeake Marine Aquaria Society (CMAS - Chesapeake)
c/o Tom Walsh, President
4220 Erdman Ave.
Baltimore, MD 21213
Web site: www.cmas-md.org/

Chicagoland Marine Aquarium Society (CMAS - Chicagoland)
c/o Dennis Gallagher, President
1455 Nottingham Lane
Hoffman Estates, IL 60195
(847) 882-8594
Web site: www.cmas.net

Cleveland Saltwater Enthusiasts Assn. (C-SEA)
c/o Peter J. Chefalo, President
3041 Lincoln Blvd.
Cleveland Heights, OH 44118-2033
(216) 371-8344
e-mail: pjc4@po.cwru.edu
Web site:
www.geocities.com/clevelandsaltwater

Dallas/Fort Worth Marine Aquarium Society (DFWMAS)
c/o Brad Ward, President
P.O. Box 1403
Bedford, TX 76095-1403
Brad Ward, President
e-mail: award@airmail.net
Web site: www.dfwmas.com

Florida Marine Aquarium Society (FMAS)
c/o Charles Keller, President

3280 S. Miami Ave.
Miami, FL 33129
e-mail: charles.keller@coulter.com
(305) 380-4804
Web site: www.gate.net/~tbc/fmas.html

Marine Aquarium Society of Los Angeles County (MASLAC)
840 N. Valley St.
Burbank, CA 91505-2736
Catherine Lee, President
e-mail: catherlee@yahoo.com
Web site: www.maslac.org

Marinelife Aquarium Society of Michigan (MASM)
1167 Tracilee Drive
Howell MI 48843
(517) 548-0164
John Dawe, President
e-mail: johndawe@umich.edu
Web site: www.masm.org

Marine Aquarium Society of Toronto (MAST)
33 Rosehill Ave.
Toronto, Canada M4T-1G4
(416) 925-1033
e-mail: flamehawk64@hotmail.com

Orlando Reef Caretakers Assn. (ORCA)
c/o John White, President
2100 Harrell Rd.
Orlando, FL 32817
(407) 482-0074
e-mail: jwhite@magicnet.net

Oklahoma Marine Aquarium Society (OMAS)
c/o Eric West, President
8044 Forest Glen Rd.
Claremore, OK 74017
(918) 266-7685
e-mail: westeric@hotmail.com
Web site: www.omas.org

Puget Sound Aquarium Society (PSAS)
c/o Bryan Petersen, President
15127 NE 24th, Suite 320
Redmond, WA 98052
e-mail: bryanp@nela.net
Web site: home.att.net/~psas.seattle/

Wasatch Marine Aquarium Society (WMAS)
537 E. 750N
Ogden, UT 84404
Mark Peterson, President
(801) 296-1563
e-mail: mrpslc@deseretonline.com
Web site: www.xmission.com/~mikeb/wmashome.html

Western Michigan Marine Aquarium Club (WMMAC)
26694 66th Ave
Lawton, MI 49065
(616) 624-6667
Web site: www.wmmac.org

Magazines

HOBBYIST MAGAZINES are another excellent way to locate groups of interest. Good aquarium shops and bookstores with magazine racks will have a range of aquarium periodicals. These vary greatly in editorial approach and scope, but most serious aquarists find at least one that suits their particular tastes. If you aren't a member of an aquarium society, a magazine is a virtually essential source for the latest information on husbandry, equipment, new species, breeding, environmental issues, and the like.

Aquarium Fish Magazine
Russ Case, Editor
Fancy Publications
P.O. Box 6050
Mission Viejo, CA 92690-6050
(949) 855-8822
Web site: www.animalnetwork.com/fish

Aquarium Frontiers On-Line
Terry Siegel, Editor
Web site: www.animalnetwork.com

Aquarium Sciences and Conservation
Chapman & Hall
400 Market Street, Suite 750
Philadelphia, PA 19106
Web site: www.thomsonscience.com
e-mail: chsub@itps.co.uk

Freshwater and Marine Aquarium
Patricia Crews, Editor
144 West Sierra Madre Boulevard
Sierra Madre, CA 91024
(818) 355-1476
Web site: www.mag-web.com/fama

Journal of MaquaCulture
Stanley Brown, Editor
P.O. Box 255373
Sacramento, CA 95865-5373
e-mail: fishxing@netcom.com

Marine Fish Monthly
Boyce Phipps, Editor
3243 Highway 61 East
Luttrell, TN 37779
e-mail: pubcon@worldnet.att.net

Ocean Realm
Charlene deJori & Cheryl Schorp, Editors
4067 Broadway
San Antonio, TX 78209
(210) 824-8099

Practical Fishkeeping
Steve Windsor, Editor
EMAP Pursuit Publishing
Bretton Court
Bretton, Peterborough
PE3 8DZ United Kingdom
011-44-1733-264666

SeaScope
Thomas A. Frakes, Editor
Aquarium Systems, Inc.
8141 Tyler Boulevard
Mentor, OH 44060
Web site: www.aquariumsystems.com

Tropical Fish Hobbyist
Mary Sweeney, Editor
One T.F.H. Plaza
Neptune, NJ 07753
(732) 988-8400
e-mail: tfhfish@tfh.com
Web site: www.tfh.com

Internet

With access to a personal computer and a modem, you can search the World Wide Web for sites of interest to saltwater aquarists. There are chat rooms, bulletin boards, databases, and electronic magazines. Look for Web site addresses in aquarist magazines and use your search engine to find new sites. (Start with key words like "aquarium," "marine," "fishes," or "reef" and you'll be off and running.) The number of aquarium-related sites and home pages increases constantly. Many of the sites listed below contain links to hundreds of other aquarium-related pages, with a wealth of information for the hobbyist.

American Marinelife Dealers Assn.
www.amdareef.com
Aqualink Aquaria Web Resources
www.aqualink.com
Breeder's Registry
www.breeders-registry.gen.ca.us
Compuserve Aquaria/Fish Forum
petsforum.com
Coral Reef Alliance
www.coral.org
Coral Reef Aquaculture Sites
farmedcoral.homestead.com
International Marinelife Alliance
www.imamarinelife.org
Marine Aquarium Council (MAC)
www.aquariumcouncil.org
#Reefs (Reef Aquarium Forum)
www.reefs.org
Reef Central
www.reefcentral.com
Reef Relief
www.reefrelief.org
U.S. Government Coral Reef Task Force
coralreef.gov

Libraries & Booksellers

While the Internet can be a godsend, there are still good old-fashioned public libraries in most communities where many titles of interest to saltwater aquarists can be found. If you can gain access to a college or university library with a good science sections, a world of applicable material awaits. In addition to references, libraries often have telephone directories from all over the world that can be a Who's Who for sources of livestock, supplies, and equipment.

Finally, there is the option of building your own personal aquatics library. Most aquarists assemble at least a small collection of reference volumes; these can serve as essential tools when problems or emergencies arise. Again, you will quickly discover which pet shops and bookstores in your area carry the best selections of special-interest books. For hard-to-find titles, good local stores will usually place special orders for you; there are also a number of reliable mail order sources.

The Aquatic Bookshop
P.O. Box 2150
Single Springs, CA
(530) 622-7157
Web site:
www.byobs.com/aquaticbookshop

Fish Books
Raymond M. Sutton, Jr.
P.O. Box 330
Williamsburg, Kentucky 40769
(606) 549-2288
Classy offerings of natural history books, with both recent works and fine antiquarian titles for serious collectors. Various catalogs available, including fishes, marine mammals, and more. Included are rarities, such as the only edition of Petri Artedi (the father of the science of fishes), Ichthyologia, *from 1738.*

Freshwater & Marine Aquarium Books
P.O. Box 487
Sierra Madre, CA 91025
(818) 355-1476
Anthologies from the pages of FAMA Magazine.

Gary Bagnall Bookseller
3100 McMillan Rd.
San Luis Obispo, CA 93041
(805) 542-9295
An amazing accumulation of old aquarium magazines, books, and other arcana—even aquatic business materials, collector fish bowls and aquariums. Write for a 20-page product listing: $3.00.

Green Turtle Publications
P.O. Box 17925
Plantation, FL 33318
Classic marine handbooks by Martin A. Moe, Jr.

Microcosm Ltd.
P.O. Box 550
Charlotte, VT 05445
(802) 425-5700
Web site: www.microcosm-books.com
Aquarium and natural history books.

Odyssey Publishing
11558 Rolling Hills Drive
El Cajon, CA 92020
(619) 579-8405
Books for aquarists and divers on Indo-Pacific natural history.

**Sea Challengers Natural
History Books**
35 Versailles Court
Danville, CA 94506
(925) 327-7750
Web site: www.seachallengers.com
*Outstanding selection of natural history
books for divers, snorkelers, and marine
hobbyists.*

T.F.H. Publications, Inc.
One T.F.H. Plaza
Neptune City, NJ 07753
(732) 988-8400
Web site: www.tfh.com
*Large offering of freshwater and marine
aquarium titles.*

Two Little Fishies
4016 El Prado Boulevard
Coconut Grove, FL 33133
(800) 969-7742
Web site:
www.petsforum.com/twolilfishies
Books and videos for marine aquarists.

Conservation
**American Marinelife Dealers
Association (AMDA)**
P.O. Box 9118
Knoxville, TN 37940-0118
Web site: www.amdareef.com
*A group of retailers and suppliers dedicated
to responsible marine aquarium keeping
and to promoting education and sustainable use of reef resources. AMDA members
avoid drug-damaged livestock and species
that are impossible to maintain, while
offering captive-propagated specimens
whenever possible.*

Breeder's Registry
P.O. Box 255373
Sacramento, CA 95865
Web site:
www.breeders-registry.gen.ca.us
*Publishes the Journal of MaquaCulture,
devoted to marine life breeding, and
maintains a database of captive-
propagation observations.*

Center for Marine Conservation
1725 De Sales Street NW
Washington, DC 20036
(202) 429-5609
Web site: www.cmc-ocean.org
*Activist organization dedicated to
protecting marine mammals, endangered
species, and environments. Quarterly
newsletter: Marine Conservation News.*

The Coral Reef Alliance
64 Shattuck Square, Suite 220
Berkeley, CA 94704
(510) 848-0110
e-mail: coralmail@aol.com
Web site: www.coral.org
*Independent, nonprofit membership
organization working to address the
problems of coral reef destruction
worldwide.*

The Cousteau Society
870 Greenbrier Circle, Suite 402
Chesapeake, VA 23320-2641
(800) 441-4395
e-mail: cousteau@infi.net
*The late Capt. Jacques-Yves Cousteau's
nonprofit educational and research
organization; publishers of Calypso Log
and, for children, Dolphin Log; bimonthly
reports on environmental topics.*

**International Marinelife
Alliance-USA**
2800 4th Street North, Suite 123
St. Petersburg, FL 33704
(813) 896-8626
e-mail: prubec@compuserve.com
Web site: www.imamarinelife.org
*Grassroots environmental group with a
history of trying to control the use of
cyanide in fish collection through
monitoring and by teaching net-catching
techniques to Third World fishermen.*

Ocean Voice International
P.O. Box 37026
3332 McCarthy Road
Ottawa, ON Canada K1V 0W0
(613) 521-4205
Web site:
www.conveyor.com/oceanvoice.html
*Canadian-based group working to end
cyanide collecting and other reef-damaging
practices.*

Author & Editor
COMMENTS ABOUT THIS BOOK
and suggestions for future editions
are invited.

Robert M. Fenner
10251 Thanksgiving Lane
San Diego, CA 92126
e-mail: fennerrobert@hotmail.com

Microcosm Ltd.
P.O. Box 550
Charlotte, VT 05445
e-mail: jml@microcosm-books.com
Web site: www.microcosm-books.com

Selected Bibliography

Adey, Walter H. & Karen Loveland. 1991. *Dynamic Aquaria: Building Living Ecosystems*. Academic Press, San Diego, CA.

Allen, Gerald R. & Roger C. Steene. 1979. *The Fishes of Christmas Island*. Indian Ocean Spec. Publ. Aust. Nat. Parks Wildlife, Canberra, Australia.

Allen, Gerald R. & Roger C. Steene. 1994. *Indo-Pacific Coral Reef Field Guide*. Tropical Reef Research, Singapore.

Allen, Gerald R. 1974. *The Anenomefishes. Their Classification and Biology*, 2nd ed. Tropical Fish Hobbyist Publications, Neptune City, NJ.

Allen, Gerald R. 1975. *Damselfishes of the South Seas*. Tropical Fish Hobbyist Publications, Neptune City, NJ.

Allen, Gerald R. 1979. *The Anenomefishes of the World: Species, Care & Breeding; Handbook for Aquarists, Divers and Scientists*. Aquarium Systems, Mentor, OH.

Allen, Gerald R. 1985. *Butterfly and Angelfishes of the World* Vol. 2, 3rd ed. Aquarium Systems, Mentor, OH.

Allen, Gerald R. 1991. *Damselfishes of the World*. Aquarium Systems, Mentor, OH.

Allen, Gerald R. 1991. *Field Guide to the Freshwater Fishes of New Guinea*. Christensen Research Institute, Madang, Papua New Guinea.

Amlacher, Erwin. 1970. *Textbook of Fish Diseases*. Translated by D.A. Conroy & R.L. Herman. Tropical Fish Hobbyist Publications, Neptune City, NJ.

Anderson, D. P. 1974. *Fish Immunology*. Tropical Fish Hobbyist Publications, Neptune City, NJ.

Andrews, Chris, Adrian Exell and Neville Carrington. 1988. *The Manual of Fish Health*. Tetra Press, Blacksburg, VA.

Axelrod, H.R. & C.W. Emmens. 1994 (9th ed., orig. 1975). *Exotic Marine Fishes*. Tropical Fish Hobbyist Publications, Neptune City, NJ.

Axelrod, H.R. & Warren E. Burgess. 1987. *Salt-Water Aquarium Fishes*. Tropical Fish Hobbyist Publications, Neptune City, NJ.

Axelrod, H.R., Warren E. Burgess & Raymond Hunziker. 1990. *Atlas of Aquarium Fishes Reference Book*. Tropical Fish Hobbyist Publications, Neptune City, NJ.

Baensch, Hans A. & Helmut Debelius. 1994. *Marine Atlas* Vol. 1. Mergus, Melle, Germany.

Baensch, Hans A. 1983. *Marine Aquarist's Manual*. Tetra Press, Blacksburg, VA.

Bannister, Keith & Andrew Campbell. 1988. *The Encyclopedia of Aquatic Life*. Facts on File, Inc., New York.

Barnes, Robert. 1987. *Invertebrate Zoology*, 5th ed. Saunders Publishing, Fort Worth, TX.

THE CONSCIENTIOUS MARINE AQUARIST

Bliss, Dorothy (ed.). 1985. *Biology of the Crustacea*. 10 volumes. Academic Press, New York.

Brusca, R.C. & G.J. Brusca. 1990. *Invertebrates*. Sinauer Associates, Inc., Sunderland, MA.

Brusca, Richard C. 1980. *Common Intertidal Invertebrates of the Gulf of California*, 2nd ed. U. of Arizona Press, Tucson, AZ.

Bullock, Graham L. 1971.*Identification of Fish Pathogenic Bacteria* in *Disease of Fishes*, Book 2B (Book series). Tropical Fish Hobbyist Publications, Neptune City, NJ.

Bullock, Graham L., David A. Conroy & S.F. Snieszko. 1971. *Bacterial Diseases of Fishes* in *Disease of Fishes,* Book 2A (Book series). Tropical Fish Hobbyist Publications, Neptune City, NJ.

Burgess, Warren A. & Herbert R. Axelrod. 1972. *Pacific Marine Fishes* Vol. 1-10. Tropical Fish Hobbyist Publications, Neptune City, NJ.

Burgess, Warren E. 1978. *Butterflyfishes of the World*. Tropical Fish Hobbyist Publications, Neptune City, NJ.

Burgess, Warren E., H.R. Axelrod & R.E. Hunziker III, 1990. *Atlas of Aquarium Fishes* Vol. 1: *Marine Fishes*. Tropical Fish Hobbyist Publications, Neptune City, NJ.

Burgess, Warren. 1987. *A Complete Introduction to Marine Aquariums*. Tropical Fish Hobbyist Publications, Neptune City, NJ.

Clark, A.M. 1977. *Starfishes and Related Echinoderms*. Tropical Fish Hobbyist Publications, Neptune City, NJ.

Clifton, Robert R. 1987. *Marine Fish—The Recognition and Treatment of Diseases*. Peregrine Publ., Wakefield, MA.

Colin, Patrick L. 1975. *The Neon Gobies; The Comparative Biology of the Genus Gobiosoma, Subgenus Elacatinus (Pisces, Gobiidae) in the Tropical Western Atlantic Ocean*. Tropical Fish Hobbyist Publications, Neptune City, NJ.

Colin, Patrick L. 1978. *Caribbean Reef Invertebrates and Plants*. Tropical Fish Hobbyist Publications, Neptune City, NJ.

Colin, Patrick L. 1988. *Marine Invertebrates and Plants of the Living Reef*. Tropical Fish Hobbyist Publications, Neptune City, NJ.

Cousteau, Jacques. 1979. *The Ocean World of Jacques Cousteau*. Harry N. Abrams Co., New York.

Crowder, William. 1959. *Seashore Life: Between the Tides*. Dover Publications, Inc., New York.

Dakin, Nick. 1992. *The Book of the Marine Aquarium*. Tetra Press, Blacksburg, VA.

Debelius, H. 1984. *Armoured Knights of the Sea*. Kernen Verlag. Essen, Germany, and Quality Marine, Los Angeles, CA.

Debelius, Helmut & Hans Baensch. 1994. *Marine Atlas* Vol. 1. Mergus, Melle, Germany, and Microcosm Ltd., Shelburne, VT.

Debelius, Helmut. 1986. *Fishes for the Invertebrate Aquarium, or Colorful Little Reef Fishes*. Meinders & Elstermann, Osnabrück, Germany.

Delbeek, J. Charles & Julian Sprung. 1994. *The Reef Aquarium* Vol. 1. Ricordea Publishing, Coconut Grove, FL.

Dogiel, V. A., G. K. Petrushevski & Yu Polyanski. 1970. *Parasitology of Fishes*. Tropical Fish Hobbyist Publications, Surrey, Great Britain.

Dulin, M.P. *Diseases of Marine Aquarium Fish*. Tropical Fish Hobbyist Publications, Neptune City, NJ.

Emmens, C.W. 1975. *The Marine Aquarium in Theory and Practice*. Tropical Fish Hobbyist Publications, Neptune City, NJ.

Emmens, Clifford. 1987. *Marine Aquariums*. Tropical Fish Hobbyist Publications, Neptune City, NJ.

Friese, U.E. 1972. *Sea Anemones*. Tropical Fish Hobbyist Publications, Neptune City, NJ.

Friese, U.E. 1973. *Marine Invertebrates in the Home Aquarium*. Tropical Fish Hobbyist Publications, Neptune City, NJ.

George, David and Jennifer. 1979. *Marine Life: An Illustrated Encyclopedia of Invertebrates in the Sea*. John Wiley & Sons, Inc., New York.

Gratzek, John B., Richard E. Wolke, Emmett B. Shotts, Jr., Donald Dawe & George C. Blasiola. 1992. *Fish Diseases and Water Chemistry*. Tetra Sales U.S.A., Morris Plains, NJ.

Halver, J.E. (ed.). 1989. *Fish Nutrition*. Academic Press, London.

Hauser, Hillary. 1992. *Skin Diver Magazine's Book of Fishes*. Gulf Publishing Co., Houston, TX.

Haywood, Martyn. 1989. *The Manual of Marine Invertebrates*. Tetra Press, Morris Plains, NJ.

Headstrom, Richard. 1979. *All About Lobsters, Crabs, Shrimps, and Their Relatives*. Dover Publ., Bloomfield, CT.

Herald, Earl S. 1967. *Living Fishes of the World*. Doubleday, New York.

Herwig, Nelson. 1979. *Handbook of Drugs and Chemicals Used in the Treatment of Fish Disease, A Manual of Fish Pharmacology and Materia Medica*. Charles C. Thomas Publisher, Springfield, IL.

Herwig, Nelson. 1980. *Starfish, Sea Urchins, and Their Kin*. RCM Publications, Sierra Madre, CA.

Howarth, Peter, 1978. *The Abalone Book*. Nature Graph., Farmington, UT.

Hyman, L.H. 1940-1967. *The Invertebrates* Vol. 1-6. McGraw-Hill Book Co., New York.

Kabata, Z. 1970, ed. by Stanislas F. Snieszko and Herbert R. Axelrod. *Crustacea and Enemies of Fishes* in *Diseases of Fishes*, Book 1. Tropical Fish Hobbyist Publications, Neptune City, NJ.

Kaplan, E.H. 1982. *A Field Guide to Coral Reefs of the Caribbean and Florida*. Peterson Field Guide Series. Houghton Mifflin Co., Boston.

Kerstitch, Alex, D.A. Thomson & L.T. Findley. 1979. *Reef Fishes of the Sea of Cortez*. Wiley Interscience, New York.

Kingsford, Edward. 1975. *Treatment of Exotic Marine Fish Diseases*. Arco Publ., New York.

Kuiter, Rudie H. & Helmut Debelius. 1994. *SouthEast Asia Tropical Fish Guide*. Tetra Press, Melle, Germany.

Lawrence, John A. 1987. *A Functional Biology of Echinoderms*. John Hopkins U. Press, Baltimore.

Marshall, N.B. 1972. *The Life of Fishes*. Universe Books, New York.

Mawdesley-Thomas, L. E., K. W. Burris, J. L. Knuckles, et al. 1974. *Diseases of Fish*. MSS Info. Co., New York.

McDaniel, David, ed. 1975 (rev. 1979). *Procedures for the Detection and Identification of Certain Fish Pathogens*. American Fisheries Society, Bethesda, MD.

McPeak, Ron, Dale Glantz & Carole Shaw. 1988. *The Amber Forest: Beauty and Biology of California's Submarine Forests*. Watersport Publishing, Inc. San Diego.

Mills, Dick. 1985. *A Fishkeeper's Guide to Marine Fishes*. Salamander Press, London, UK.

Mills, Dick. 1987. *Tetra Encyclopedia of the Marine Aquarium*. Tetra Press, Blacksburg, VA.

Moe, Martin A. 1989. *The Marine Aquarium Reference Book*. Green Turtle Publications. Plantation, FL.

Moe, Martin A. 1982. *The Marine Aquarium Handbook: Beginner to Breeder*. NORNS Publishing Co., Marathon, FL.

Neish, Gordon A. & Gilbert C. Hughes. 1980. Book 6: *Fungal Diseases of Fishes* in *Disease of Fishes* (Book series). Tropical Fish Hobbyist Publications, Neptune City, NJ.

Nelson, Joseph S. 1994. *Fishes of the World*, 3rd ed. John Wiley & Sons, Inc., New York.

Oliver, A.P.H. 1980. *The Larousse Guide to Shells of the World*. Larousse and Co., Inc., New York.

Post, George. 1987. *Textbook of Fish Health*. Tropical Fish Hobbyist Publications, Neptune City, NJ.

Randall, John E. 1968. *Caribbean Reef Fishes*. Tropical Fish Hobbyist Publications, Neptune City, NJ.

Roessler, Carl. 1986. *Coral Kingdoms*. Harry N. Abrams, New York.

Rudloe, Jack. 1984. *The Erotic Ocean*. E.P. Dutton, New York.

Schultz, Leonard P. 1948. *The Ways of Fishes*. Van Nostrand, New York.

Sinderman, C.J. 1970. *The Principal Diseases of Marine Fish and Shellfish*. Academic Press, San Diego, CA.

Smith, Ralph I. & James T. Carlton. 1975. *Light's Manual: Intertidal Invertebrates of the Central California Coast*, 3rd ed. U. of California Press, Berkeley, CA.

Spotte, Stephen. 1973. *Marine Aquarium Keeping: The Science, Animals and Art*. John Wiley & Sons, Inc., New York.

Spotte, Stephen. H. 1970. *Fish & Invertebrate Culture: Water Management in Closed Systems*. Wiley Interscience. New York.

Steene, Roger. 1985. *Butterfly and Angelfishes of the World* Volume 1, 2nd ed. Aquarium Systems, Mentor, OH.

Steffens, W. 1989. *Principles of Fish Nutrition*. Ellis Horwood, Chichester, England.

Sterba, Gunther. 1966. *Freshwater Fishes of the World*. English Translation. The Pet Library Ltd., New York.

Stoskopf, M.K. 1993. *Fish Medicine*. W.B. Saunders Co., Philadelphia.

Straughan, Robert P.L. 1976. *The Salt-Water Aquarium in the Home*, 4th ed., rev. A.S. Barnes & Co., New York.

Straughan, Robert P.L. 1971 *Keeping Live Corals and Invertebrates*. A.S. Barnes & Co., New York.

Taylor, A. E. R. and R. Muller. 1970. *Aspects of Fish Parasitology*. Blackwell Scientific, Oxford.

Thiel, Albert. 1988. *The Marine Fish and Invertebrate Aquarium*. Aardvark Press, Bridgeport, CT.

Thiel, Albert. 1990. *The Small Reef Aquarium*. Aardvark Press, Bridgeport, CT.

Thomson, Donald A., Lloyd T. Findley & Alex N. Kerstitch, 1979. *Reef Fishes of the Sea of Cortez, The Rocky-Shore Fishes of the Gulf of California*. John Wiley & Sons, Inc., New York.

Thresher, Ronald E. 1980. *Reef Fish*. Arco Publ., Palmetto, FL.

Thresher, Ronald E. 1984. *Reproduction in Reef Fishes*. Tropical Fish Hobbyist Publications, Neptune City, NJ.

Tinker, Spencer W. 1978. *Fishes of Hawaii*. Hawaiian Service, Inc., Honolulu, HI.

Vernberg, F. J., A. Calabrese, F. P. Thurberg & W. B. Vernberg. 1977. *Physiological Responses of Marine Biota to Pollutants*. Academic Press Inc., London.

Veron, J.E.N. 1986. *Corals of Australia and the Indo-Pacific*. Angus and Robertson Publishers, Sydney, Australia.

Walls, J.G. 1982. *Encyclopedia of Marine Invertebrates*. Tropical Fish Hobbyist Publications, Neptune City, NJ.

Walls, Jerry G. 1974. *Starting with Marine Invertebrates*. Tropical Fish Hobbyist Publications, Neptune City, NJ.

Wells, Jerry G. 1982. *Encyclopedia of Marine Invertebrates*. Tropical Fish Hobbyist Publications, Neptune City, NJ.

Wilkens, P. 1973. *The Saltwater Aquarium for Tropical Marine Invertebrates*. Engelbert Pfriem Verlag, Wuppertal, Germany.

Williams, Austin B. 1989. *Lobsters of the World—An Illustrated Guide*. Van Nostrand Reinhold, New York.

Wood, Elizabeth M. 1983. *Corals of the World*. Tropical Fish Hobbyist Publications, Neptune City, NJ.

Zann, Leon P. 1980. *Living Together in the Sea*. Tropical Fish Hobbyist Publications, Neptune City, NJ.

Photography & Illustration Credits

Photographers are credited by page number and by position on the page as follows:
(T)Top, (C)Center, (B)Bottom, (TL)Top left, (BL)Bottom left, etc.

Photographers

SCOTT MICHAEL: Front cover, 14, 15, 18, 113, 135(BL, BR), 136(R), 138(R), 147, 182, 184, 185, 187, 190, 191, 193, 195, 198, 199(TL, BR), 201, 203, 204(TL, TR, BL), 205, 206, 207, 211(TR, BL), 212, 214(TR, BL, BR), 216, 217, 218, 226(TL, BL), 227, 231, 232(TL, TC, TR, BL, BR), 233(TL), 234, 237, 241, 243(T), 243, 245, 248, 250(L), 253, 255(R), 256(R), 258(R), 266, 267, 268(BR), 271(L), 273, 278, 280, 281(TL, TR, BL, BR), 282, 283, 289, 290(R), 291(T), 292(TL, TR), 293, 295, 296, 299, 300, 302, 305, 306, 309, 311, 316(TL, TR, BR), 321, 333, 334(BL), 335, 339, 349, 354, 355, 356, 358, 361, 362, 363(L) 364, 367, 368(L), 370, 372, 373, 374, 375, 376, 377, 378(TR, B), 379, 384(L), 401(T)

FOSTER BAM: 12, 16, 17, 64, 140, 148, 169, 170, 172, 177, 181, 183, 189, 192, 197, 202, 204(BR), 210, 211(BR), 215, 225, 226(BR), 232(BC), 233(TC, TR, BC, BR), 235, 238, 240, 242, 243(B), 244, 246, 249, 250(R), 254, 261, 263, 268(TL,TR,BL), 269, 271(R), 272(T), 274, 277, 284, 285, 286, 287, 304, 307(TL, TR, BR), 310(L), 313, 316(BL), 317, 318, 320, 322, 323, 324, 332, 334(TL), 336, 340, 363(R), 365(R), 366, 382(T), 384(R), 390, 401(B), 402, Back cover(T,B)

PAUL HUMANN: 22, 132, 135(TR), 136(L) 138(L), 199(TR, BL), 211(TL), 213, 219, 220, 223, 224, 226(TR), 233(BL), 236, 239, 247, 257, 258(L), 259, 262, 264, 265, 270, 271(C), 272(B), 276, 279, 281(TC, BC), 290(L), 291(B), 292(BL, BR), 294, 297, 298, 301, 303, 307(BL), 310(R), 314, 319, 328, 330, 331, 344, 346, 348(L), 360, 365(L), 380(R), 383(R), 393, 395, 396, 400, 403

MARK SASAHARA: 35, 36, 37, 38, 53, 55, 56, 58, 61, 62, 67, 68, 69, 72, 73, 80, 81, 83, 87, 92, 95, 96, 98, 104, 105, 106, 107, 109, 110, 112, 116, 117, 118, 119, 123, 124, 129, 142, 143, 145, 151, 152, 157, 160, 161

JOHN GOODMAN: 25, 30, 40, 41, 43, 44, 63, 71, 85, 94, 100, 111, 122

LARRY TACKETT: 13, 90, 135(TL), 329, 342, 357, 368(R), 369, 378(TL), 382(B), 385, 387, 397(R)

JANINE CAIRNS-MICHAEL: 20, 21, 334(TR), 343, 348(R), 352, 359, 383(L), 389

DENISE NIELSEN TACKETT: 174, 175, 327, 334(BR), 337, 345, 351, 397(L), 399, Back cover(C)

STEVE LUCAS (Courtesy of Oceans, Reefs & Aquariums) 26, 29, 32, 33, 50

MICHAEL PALETTA: 52, 74

STEVEN FRINK/WATERHOUSE: 209, 229, 326

LYNN FUNKHOUSER: 164, 166, 167

JOHN RANDALL: 214(TL), 256(L), 386

DAVID BARTS (Courtesy of Robert Fenner): 24, 126

ROBERT FENNER: 165, 255(L)

Illustrations & Diagrams

Equipment

Index

Morone saxatilis (Striped Bass), 208
Mussels, 373-374
Mycale laxissima (Strawberry Vase Sponge), 335
Myripristis
  jacobus (Blackbar Soldierfish), photos, 197, 199
  pralinia (Scarlet Soldierfish), 198
  vittata (White-tipped Soldierfish), photo, 199
Myxosporea, 162

Naso
  brevirostris (Spotted Unicornfish), 302
  lituratus (Naso or Lipstick Tang), 302
  vlamingi (Bignose Unicornfish), photo, 307
Nautiloids, 377-378
Nautilus pompilius (Chambered Nautilus), photo, 378
Negaprion brevirostris (Lemon Shark), 184
Neguvon, 160
Nemanthias, 212
Nemanthus annamensis (Gorgonian Wrapper Anemone), photo, 342
Nemateleotris, 297
  decora (Purple Firefish), 297; photo, 297
  helfrichi (Helfrich's Firefish), 297
  magnifica (Firefish), 297; photo, 297
Nematodes, 163
Nembrotha cristata, photo, 369
Neocirrhites armatus (Flame Hawkfish), photo, 268
Neoclinus, 290
Neoglyphidodontops, 270
Neoniphon opercularis (Clearfin Squirrelfish), 198
Neopetrolisthes maculata (Spotted Porcelain Crab), photo, 382
Nitrate
  accumulation, 130
  optimal level, 81, 111
Nitrogen cycle, 77-80; illustration, 78
Novaculichthys taeniourus (Dragon or Rockmover Wrasse), photo, 284
Nudibranchs, 369-373; photos, 369, 370, 372
  dorid, 372; photo, 372
  Spanish Dancer, 131, 372
Nutrient cycling, 30

Octamita necatrix, 156
Octopuses, 377-378
  Blue-ringed, 378; photo, 378

Odontodactylus scyallarus (Peacock Mantis Shrimp), photos, 379, 387
Odonus niger (Redtooth Triggerfish), 315; photo, 316
Ogilbyina, 216
  novaehollandiae, 217
Oodinium. See *Amyloodinium ocellatum*
Operation of small systems, 45
Ophiclinus, 290
Ophioblennius, 290, 292
  atlanticus (Caribbean Red-lipped Blenny), 290, 292; photo, 292
Ophiocoma
  echinata (Blunt-spined Brittle Star), 402
  paucigranulata (Spiny Brittle Star), 402
Ophioderma
  ensiferum (Gaudy Brittle Star), 402
  rubicundum (Ruby Brittle Star), 402; photo, 403
Ophionereis reticulata (Reticulated Brittle Star), 402
Ophiothrix suensonii (Sponge Brittle Star), photo, 403
Opistognathus, 222
  aurifrons (Pearly or Yellow-headed Jawfish), 222, 224; photo, 223
  gilberti (Atlantic Yellow Jawfish), 224
  macrognathus (Long Jawfish), 222
  maxillosus (Mottled Jawfish), 222
  rhomaleus, 224
  rosenblatti (Blue-spotted Jawfish), 222, 224
  whitehursti (Dusky Jawfish), 222; photo, 224
Oreaster reticulatus (Reticulated Sea Star), 398; photo, 400
Orectolobus
  maculatus (Spotted Wobbegong), 183; photo, 185
  ornatus (Ornate Wobbegong), 183
Organisms. See Livestock
Organophosphate insecticides, 160
ORP (Oxidation-Reduction Potential), 86-88
Ostracion
  cubicus (Yellow Boxfish), 322; photos, 324
  meleagris (Blue-spotted or Black-spotted Boxfish), 323
  solorensis, photo, 322
Outgassing rings, 77
Overfeeding, 44, 120, 130. See also Feeding
Overstocking, 24, 120, 129-130. See also Stocking
Oxidation-Reduction Potential, 86-88

Oxycirrhites typus (Longnose Hawkfish), 267; photo, 265
Oxygen, lack of, 130
Oxyjulis californica (Señorita Wrasse), 282
Oxymonacanthus, 317-318
  longirostrus (Longnose or Orangespotted Filefish), 318
Oysters, 373-374
  thorny, photo, 366
  Thorny, Atlantic, 374
  Thorny, Variable, photo, 374
Ozone, 85-88

Pachycerianthus, 350
Pachyclavularia, 361; photo, 21
  viridis (Green Star Polyps), photo, 361
Pagurites cadenati (Red Reef Hermit Crab), 381
Paletta, Michael, aquariums designed by, photos, 52
Palythoa, 361
Panulirus versicolor (Spiny Blue Lobster or Painted Crayfish), 386; photo, 385
Parablennius, 290, 294
Paracanthurus hepatus (Hippo, Yellow-tail Blue, Regal, Indo-Pacific Blue, or Palette Tang), 302, 309; photo, 307
Parachaetodon ocellatus (Eye-spot Butterflyfish), 230
Paracirrhites
  arcatus (Red-eyed or Arc-eye Hawkfish), 267; photo, 266
  forsteri (Forster's or Freckled Hawkfish), 267; photo, 268
Paraclinus, 290
Paragorgia, 357
Paraluteres, 317
  prionurus (Saddled Filefish or Valentini Mimic), 323-324; photo, 317
Parapercis hexophthalma (Speckled Sandperch), photo, 292
Parasites, 161-163
Parasitic diseases and treatment, 159-161
Paravortex, 163
Parrotfishes, 285-288
  Bicolor, 285
  Queen, 285; photo, 287
  Stoplight, 285, 287; photos, 285, 286
Pavona, 362
Pearlfishes, 394
Penicillus (Merman's Shaving Brush), 139

Systems, aquarium, 31-45
    Berlin, 72
    components, 33-34
    Dutch, 70
    fish-and-invertebrate, 36-39, 108-110;
        photos, 37, 38, 109, 110
    fish-only, 34-36, 101-108; photos, 25, 30, 35,
        36, 104, 105, 106, 107, 126
    Jaubert, 74
    reef, 39-42; photos, 40, 41, 110-112, 127
    small, 43-45; photos, 43, 44

Taeniura meyeni (Black-spotted Sting Ray),
        photo, 174
Tangs, 137, 301-311; photo, 172
    Achilles, 302, 304, 305; photo, 307
    Blue, 302, 305; photos, 303
    Blue, Atlantic, 309
    Blue, Indo-Pacific, 309
    Blue, Yellow-tail, 302, 304, 309
    Brown, 302, 305; photo, 305
    Chevron, 302
    Convict, 305
    Gold-rimmed, 302
    Hippo, 302, 304, 306, 309; photo, 307
    Kole, 302
    Lipstick, 302
    Naso, 302, 304
    Orange-shoulder, 302
    Palette, 302, 309
    Powder Blue, 302, 304, 309; photo, 304
    Powder Brown, 302, 304, 305, 309-311;
        photo, 310
    Purple, 302, 305; photo, 302
    Regal, 302, 309
    Sailfin, Desjardin's Red, 302
    Sailfin, Pacific, 302; photo, 306
    Sailfin, Red, 302
    Sailfin, Red Sea, photo, 306
    Sailfin, Yellow, 302
    Scopas, 302; photo, 305
    White-cheeked, 310
    White-faced, 302, 309-311; photo, 310
    Yellow, 163, 302, 304, 305, 308-309; photo,
        309
    Yellow-eyed, 302
Tanks, 33, 47-49
    acrylic, 49
    backgrounds, installing, 105, 118; photos,
        118
    capacity, calculation of, 48

components, cleaning, 127
filling with seawater, 105-106
glass, 49
shape, importance of, 47-48
size, 43, 120; illustration, 48
Tapeworms, 162, 163
Taxonomy, scientific, 178-180
Temperature
    acclimation to, 150-151, 155
    and specific gravity, 97
    control, 33, 61-63
    optimal, 81
Test kits, 34, 80, 111; photo, 80
Testing new systems, 103-104, 107
Tetra, 95, 142
Thalassoma
    bifasciatum (Bluehead Wrasse), photo, 332
    klunzingeri (Klunzinger's Wrasse), photo,
        281
    lutescens (Sunset Wrasse), photo, 281
Thermometers, 63
Timers, 58; photo, 58
Toadfishes, 200
Tobies
    Ambon, 323
    Blue-spotted, 323
    Hawaiian, 323, 324
    Papuan, photo, 323
    Saddled, 323; photo, 320
    Solander's, 323
    Valentini, 323; photo, 320
    Whitespotted, 323
Trachyphyllia, 361
    geoffroyi (Open Brain Coral), photo, 362
Triaenodon obesus (Whitetip Reef Shark),
        photo, 183
Tridacna, 373; photo, 19
    crocea (Crocea or Boring Clam), 375, 377;
        photos, 375, 376
    derasa (Derasa Clam), 375, 377; photo, 376
    gigas (Giant Clam), 375, 377; photo, 18
    maxima (Maxima Clam), 375, 377; photos,
        331, 376
    squamosa, 375, 377
Triggerfishes, 311-316
    Assasi, 315; photos, 311, 316
    Black, photo, 316
    Black-finned, 315
    Blue Checkline, 315
    Blue-throat, 315
    Bursa, 315

Clown, 312, 315; photos, 30, 169, 314
Indian, 315
Orange-lined, 315; photo, 316
Picasso, 315
Picasso, Arabian, photo, 311
Pinktail, 315
Queen, 312, 315; photo, 313
Rectangle, 315
Redtooth, 315; photo, 316
Undulated, 312
Trimmatom nanus, 295
Triodon macropterus (Three-spotted Puffer),
        323
Tripterygion, 289
Trochus niloticus, 368
Trout, Coral, photo, 209
Trunkfishes, 322-323
    Smooth, 322
Tubastraea, photo, 337
Tullock, John, *The Reef Tank Owner's Manual*,
        86
Tunicates, photo, 336
Turbo, 108, 137, 368
Turner, Jeffrey, aquariums designed by, photos,
        26, 29, 32, 33, 50

Udotea, 139
Ultraviolet
    light, types, 56
    sterilizers, 88-89
Unicornfishes
    Bignose, photo, 307
    Spotted, 302
Urchins. See Sea urchins
Uronema marinum, 161, 162

Valenciennea
    puellaris (Orange-spotted Sleeper Goby),
        299; photo, 299
    strigata (Golden-headed Sleeper Goby), 299;
        photo, 299
Valentini Mimic, 323-324; photo, 317
Valonia, photo, 138
Vermifuges, 161
Vertebrates, classes, 176
VHO (very high output) fluorescent lighting,
        54
Vibrio, 114
Viral diseases, 157-158
Vita-Lite, 53
Vitamins, 144

About the Author

ROBERT M. FENNER is a marine scientist and a lifelong aquarist, with an active and continuing involvement in the academic, journalistic, trade, and hobbyist sides of aquarium keeping. He is a former marine science and aquariology instructor at the University of California and in the California State University system.

Fenner is a regular contributor to a number of aquarium publications, including *Freshwater and Marine Aquarium*, *Tropical Fish Hobbyist*, *SeaScope*, *Pet Dealer*, and several foreign hobbyist and business periodicals.

He has been a speaker and judge at many aquarium conferences and events, with subjects ranging from cyanide collection of reef fishes to koi, shell collecting, and environmental, aquarium trade, hobbyist, and scientific topics.

Fenner has worked in all phases of the aquarium business—as collector, wholesaler, jobber, retailer, hatchery worker, designer, manager, and owner. He was a founder and president of Nature Etc., an employee-owned aquatics company in San Diego, started in 1973 and encompassing Aquatic Environments (ornamental aquatics and water-feature design), Aquatic Life Services (custom aquarium system installation and maintenance), and Wet Pets (retail aquarium outlets). He continues as a consultant to a number of public aquariums and aquarium-related companies in the United States and abroad.

Robert Fenner lives in San Diego, California, and is both an active Hash House Harrier and an avid scuba diver, having completed thousands of dives throughout the Indo-Pacific region, the Red Sea, the Mediterranean, the Caribbean, Baja California, the tropical eastern Pacific, and the shorelines of his home state.